Concepts

Strategic Management
Competitiveness & Globalization

9th Edition

Michael A. Hitt
Texas A&M University

R. Duane Ireland
Texas A&M University

Robert E. Hoskisson
Rice University

SOUTH-WESTERN
CENGAGE Learning™

Australia • Brazil • Japan • Korea • Mexico • Singapore • Spain • United Kingdom • United States

SOUTH-WESTERN
CENGAGE Learning™

Strategic Management: Competitiveness and Globalization: Concepts, Ninth Edition

Michael A. Hitt, Duane Ireland, and Robert E. Hoskisson

VP/Editorial Director:
  Jack W. Calhoun

Editor-in-Chief:
  Melissa Acuna

Senior Acquisitions Editor:
  Michele Rhoades

Director of Development:
  John Abner

Senior Editorial Assistant:
  Ruth Belanger

Marketing Manager:
  Nathan Anderson

Senior Marketing Communications Manager:
  Jim Overly

Marketing Coordinator:
  Suellen Ruttkay

Content Project Manager:
  Jacquelyn K Featherly

Media Editor:
  Rob Ellington

Senior Manufacturing Coordinator:
  Sandee Milewski

Production House/Compositor:
  Cadmus Communications

Senior Art Director:
  Tippy McIntosh

Cover and Internal Designer:
  Craig Ramsdell, Ramsdell Design

Cover Image:
  ©Media Bakery

For product information and technology assistance, contact us at
Cengage Learning Customer & Sales Support, 1-800-354-9706

For permission to use material from this text or product, submit all requests online at **www.cengage.com/permissions**
Further permissions questions can be emailed to
permissionrequest@cengage.com

ExamView® and ExamView Pro® are registered trademarks of FSCreations, Inc. Windows is a registered trademark of the Microsoft Corporation used herein under license. Macintosh and Power Macintosh are registered trademarks of Apple Computer, Inc. used herein under license.

Concepts ISBN 13: 978-0-538-75309-8
Concepts ISBN 10: 0-538-75309-9

South-Western Cengage Learning
5191 Natorp Boulevard
Mason, OH 45040
USA

Cengage Learning products are represented in Canada by Nelson Education, Ltd.

For your course and learning solutions, visit **www.cengage.com**

Purchase any of our products at your local college store or at our preferred online store **www.ichapters.com**

Printed in Canada
1 2 3 4 5 6 7 13 12 11 10 09

To Ashlyn and Aubrey
Your smiles are like sunshine—they brighten my day.
—MICHAEL A. HITT

To my entire family
I love each of you dearly and remain so grateful for your incredibly strong support
and encouragement over the years. Your words and deeds have indeed showed
me how to "keep my good eye to the sun and my blind eye to the dark."
—R. DUANE IRELAND

To my wonderful grandchildren (Mara, Seth, Roselyn, Ian, Abby, Madeline,
Joseph, and Nadine), who are absolutely amazing and light up my life.
—ROBERT E. HOSKISSON

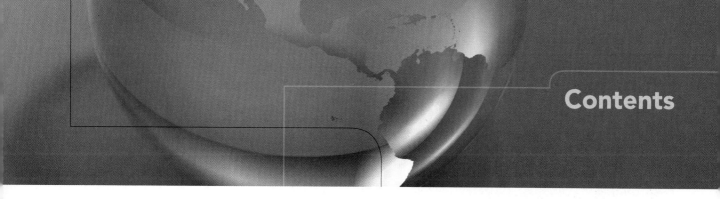

Contents

Part 2: Strategic Actions: Strategy Formulation   97

4: Business-Level Strategy   98

5: Competitive Rivalry and Competitive Dynamics   128

8: International Strategy   216

Part 3: Strategic Actions: Strategy Implementation   283

11: Organizational Structure and Controls   316

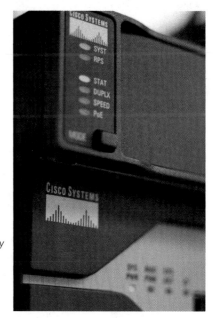

12: Strategic Leadership   350

Our goal in writing each edition of this book is to present a new, up-to-date standard for explaining the strategic management process. To reach this goal with the 9th edition of our market-leading text, we again present you with an intellectually rich yet thoroughly practical analysis of strategic management.

With each new edition, we are challenged and invigorated by the goal of establishing a new standard for presenting strategic management knowledge in a readable style. To prepare for each new edition, we carefully study the most recent academic research to ensure that the strategic management content we present to you is highly current and relevant for use in organizations. In addition, we continuously read articles appearing in many different business publications (e.g., *Wall Street Journal, BusinessWeek, Fortune, Financial Times,* and *Forbes,* to name a few); we do this to identify valuable examples of how companies are actually using the strategic management process. Though many of the hundreds of companies we discuss in the book will be quite familiar to you, some companies will likely be new to you as well. One reason for this is that we use examples of companies from around the world to demonstrate how globalized business has become. To maximize your opportunities to learn as you read and think about how actual companies use strategic management tools, techniques, and concepts (based on the most current research), we emphasize a lively and user-friendly writing style.

Several *characteristics* of this 9th edition of our book will enhance your learning opportunities:

- This book presents you with the most comprehensive and thorough coverage of strategic management that is available in the market.
- The research used in this book is drawn from the "classics" as well as the most recent contributions to the strategic management literature. The historically significant "classic" research provides the foundation for much of what is known about strategic management; the most recent contributions reveal insights about how to effectively use strategic management in the complex, global business environment in which most firms operate while trying to outperform their competitors. Our book also presents you with many up-to-date or recent examples of how firms use the strategic management tools, techniques, and concepts developed by leading researchers. Indeed, this book is strongly application oriented and presents you, our readers, with a vast number of examples and applications of strategic management concepts, techniques, and tools. In this edition, for example, we examine more than 600 companies to describe the use of strategic management. Collectively, no other strategic management book presents you with the *combination* of useful and insightful *research* and *applications* in a wide variety of organizations as does this text. Company examples range from the large U.S.-based firms such as Amazon.com, Wal-Mart, IBM, Johnson & Johnson,

Hershey, Hewlett Packard, Dell, PepsiCo, and Cisco to major foreign-based firms such as Toyota, Nokia, British Petroleum, Ryanair, Volkswagon, and Huawei. We also include examples of successful younger and newer firms such as Dylan's Candy Bar, Facebook, Honest Tea, MySpace, Yandex and Sun Tech Power and middle-sized family-owned firms such as Sargento Foods.

■ We carefully *integrate* two of the most popular and well-known theoretical concepts in the strategic management field: industrial-organization economics and the resource-based view of the firm. Other texts usually emphasize one of these two theories (at the cost of explaining the other one to describe strategic management). However, such an approach is incomplete; research and practical experience indicate that both theories play a major role in understanding the linkage between strategic management and organizational success. No other book integrates these two theoretical perspectives effectively to explain the strategic management process and its application in all types of organizations.

■ We use the ideas of prominent scholars (e.g., Raphael [Raffi] Amit, Kathy Eisenhardt, Don Hambrick, Constance [Connie] Helfat, Ming-Jer Chen, Michael Porter, C. K. Prahalad, Richard Rumelt, Ken Smith, David Teece, Michael Tushman, Oliver Williamson, and many younger, emerging scholars such as Rajshree Agarwal, Gautam Ahuja, Javier Gimeno, Amy Hillman, Michael Lennox, Yadong Luo, Jeff Reuer, Mary Tripsas, and Maurizio Zollo [along with numerous others] to shape the discussion of *what* strategic management is. We describe the practices of prominent executives and practitioners (e.g., Mike Duke, Jeffrey Immelt, Steven Jobs, Gianfranco Lanci, Indra Nooyi, and many others) to help us describe *how* strategic management is used in many types of organizations.

■ We, the authors of this book, are also active scholars. We conduct research on different strategic management topics. Our interest in doing so is to contribute to the strategic management literature and to better understand how to effectively apply strategic management tools, techniques, and concepts to increase organizational performance. Thus, our own research is integrated in the appropriate chapters along with the research of numerous other scholars, some of which are noted above.

In addition to our book's *characteristics,* there are some specific *features* of this 9th edition that we want to highlight for you:

■ **New Opening Cases and Strategic Focus Segments.** We continue our tradition of providing all-new Opening Cases and Strategic Focus segments. In addition, new company-specific examples are included in each chapter. Through all of these venues, we present you with a wealth of examples of how actual organizations, most of which compete internationally as well as in their home markets, use the strategic management process to outperform rivals and increase their performance.

■ **30 All-New Cases** with an effective mix of organizations headquartered or based in the United States and a number of other countries. Many of the cases have full financial data (the analyses of which are in the Case Notes that are available to instructors). These timely cases present active learners with opportunities to apply the strategic management process and understand organizational conditions and contexts and to make appropriate recommendations to deal with critical concerns.

■ **All New Video Case Exercises** are now included in the end-of-chapter material for each chapter and are directly connected to the textbook's Fifty Lessons video collection. These engaging exercises demonstrate for students how the concepts they are learning actually connect to the ideas and actions of the interesting individuals and companies highlighted in the videos.

■ **New and Revised Experiential Exercises** to support individuals' efforts to understand the use of the strategic management process. These exercises place active learners in a variety of situations requiring application of some part of the strategic management process.

- **Strategy Right Now** is used in each chapter to highlight companies that are effectively using a strategic management concept examined in the chapter or to provide additional coverage of a particular topic. In **Chapter 5,** for example, Wal-Mart's offering of financial services tailored to its customers' needs, such as the MoneyCard, is discussed in the context of competition among the big box retailers. In **Chapter 13,** the explosion of social media and networking, in particular Twitter, is examined in detail. This feature is a valuable tool for readers to quickly identify how a firm is effectively using a strategic management tool, technique, or concept. We follow up with the most current research and information about these firms by using Cengage Learning's Business & Company Resource Center (BCRC). Links to specific current news articles related to these companies and topics can be found on our website (www.cengage.com/management/hitt). Whenever you see the Strategy Right Now icon in the text, you will know that current research is available from the BCRC links posted to our website.

- **An Exceptional Balance** between current research and up-to-date applications of it in actual organizations. The content has not only the best research documentation but also the largest amount of effective real-world examples to help active learners understand the different types of strategies organizations use to achieve their vision and mission.

- **Access to Harvard Business School (HBS) Cases.** We have developed a set of assignment sheets and AACSB International assessment rubrics to accompany 10 of the best selling HBS cases. Instructors can use these cases and the accompanying set of teaching notes and assessment rubrics to formalize assurance of learning efforts in the capstone Strategic Management/Business Policy course.

- **Lively, Concise Writing Style** to hold readers' attention and to increase their interest in strategic management.

- **Continuing, Updated Coverage** of vital strategic management topics such as competitive rivalry and dynamics, strategic alliances, mergers and acquisitions, international strategies, corporate governance, and ethics. Also, we continue to be the only book in the market with a separate chapter devoted to strategic entrepreneurship.

- **Full four-color** format to enhance readability by attracting and maintaining readers' interests.

To maintain current and up-to-date content, new concepts are explored in the 9th edition.

In **Chapter 2,** we added the physical environment as the seventh segment of the general environment. The discussion of the physical environment emphasizes the importance of sustainability. Sustainability has become a "watchword" at many companies such as Honest Tea and Dell. For example, Dell has a goal of having a carbon neutral footprint. This discussion is integrated with the explanation in **Chapter 4** of how firms are developing a "green" strategy that is a core part of their competitive strategy. Wal-Mart is investing significant capital and effort to be a "green" firm, as are other firms such as Procter & Gamble and Target. We describe the actions a number of firms are taking regarding the physical environment in one of the Strategic Focus segments in **Chapter 2.**

In **Chapter 6,** we explore a new strategic trend also caused by the global economic crisis. While many firms downscoped in the late 1980s and 1990s because of the performance problems caused by over-diversification, the economic recession has served as a catalyst for a new trend of diversification to help firms spread their risk across several markets (to avoid bankruptcy). In **Chapter 7,** we expand our discussion of cross-border acquisitions. In fact, cross-border acquisitions remain quite popular during the global economic crisis, largely because of the number of firms in financial trouble that have undervalued assets as a result. Chinese firms have become especially active, which is discussed in detail in **Chapter 7** with special emphasis in a Strategic Focus segment. **Chapter 8** includes new content exampling emerging international firms from China (Sun Tech Power in commercial solar power and ZTE and Huawei in network equipment) and Russia (Yandex, a competitor to Google).

In **Chapter 10,** we added content related to the new actions and policies that deal with corporate governance. For example, the U.S. Securities and Exchange Commission (SEC) has implemented some new policies providing for closer oversight of companies' financial dealings. The SEC has also developed new rules to allow owners with large stakes to propose new directors. These new rules are likely to shift the balance even more in favor of outside and independent members of companies' boards of directors. We inserted a new section into this chapter to explain corporate governance in China. As a major new global economic power with several of the world's largest firms, corporate governance in China has become an important issue. Interestingly, many of the new corporate governance practices implemented in Chinese companies resemble governance practices in the United States.

In **Chapter 13**, we explain how innovation has become highly important for firms to compete effectively in global markets. As such, there have been major drives to increase the innovativeness of firms in the United States and China. The importance of innovation has been heightened by the emphasis on sustainability (developing "greener" products—see **Chapters 2 and 4**) and by the growing demand from customers that companies provide them with "excellent" value in the form of the goods or services they are making and selling (see **Chapter 2**).

Supplements

Instructors

Instructor's Resource DVD (0-538-75315-3) Key ancillaries (Instructor's Resource Manual, Instructor's Case Notes, Test Bank, ExamView™, and PowerPoint®, as well as the Fifty Lessons video collection) are provided on DVD, giving instructors the ultimate tool for customizing lectures and presentations.

New Expanded Instructor Case Notes (0-538-75461-3) To better reflect the varying approaches to teaching and learning via cases, the 9th edition offers a rich selection of case note options:

> **Basic Case Notes** – Each of the 30 cases in the 9th edition is accompanied by a succinct case note designed for ease of use while also providing the necessary background and financial data for classroom discussion.

> **Presentation Case Notes** – For a selection of 13 cases from the 9th edition, a full set of PowerPoint slides has been developed for instructors to effectively use in class, containing key illustrations and other case data.

> **Rich Assessment Case Notes** – Introduced in the 8th edition, these expanded case notes provide details about 13 additional cases from prior editions that are available on the textbook website. These expanded case notes include directed assignments, financial analysis, thorough discussion and exposition of issues in the case, and an assessment rubric tied to AACSB International assurance of learning standards that can be used for grading each case.

Available in Print, on the Instructor's Resource DVD, or Product Support Website.

Instructor's Resource Manual The Instructor's Resource Manual, organized around each chapter's knowledge objectives, includes teaching ideas for each chapter and how to reinforce essential principles with extra examples. This support product includes lecture outlines, detailed answers to end-of-chapter review questions, instructions for using each chapter's experiential exercises and video cases, and additional assignments. Available on the Instructor's Resource DVD or Product Support Website.

Certified Test Bank Thoroughly revised and enhanced, test bank questions are linked to each chapter's knowledge objectives and are ranked by difficulty and question type. We provide an ample number of application questions throughout, and we have also retained scenario-based questions as a means of adding in-depth problem-solving questions. With this edition, we introduce the concept of certification, whereby another qualified academic has proofread and verified the accuracy of the test bank questions and answers. The test bank material is also available in computerized ExamView™ format for creating custom tests in both Windows and Macintosh formats. Available on the Instructor's Resource DVD or Product Support Website.

ExamView™ Computerized testing software contains all of the questions in the certified printed test bank. This program is an easy-to-use test-creation software compatible with Microsoft Windows. Instructors can add or edit questions, instructions, and answers, and select questions by previewing them on the screen, selecting them randomly, or selecting them by number. Instructors can also create and administer quizzes online, whether over the Internet, a local area network (LAN), or a wide area network (WAN). Available on the Instructor's Resource DVD.

Video Case Program. A collection of 13 new videos from Fifty Lessons have been selected for the 9th edition, and directly connected Video Case exercises have been included in the end-of-chapter material of each chapter. These new videos are a comprehensive and compelling resource of management and leadership lessons from some of the world's most successful business leaders. In the form of short and powerful videos, these videos capture leaders' most important learning experiences. They share their real-world business acumen and outline the guiding principles behind their most important business decisions and their career progression. Available on the Instructor's Resource DVD.

PowerPoint® An all-new PowerPoint presentation, created for the 9th edition, provides support for lectures, emphasizing key concepts, key terms, and instructive graphics. Slides can also be used by students as an aid to note-taking. Available on the Instructor's Resource DVD or Product Support Website.

WebTutor™ WebTutor is used by an entire class under the direction of the instructor and is particularly convenient for distance learning courses. It provides Web-based learning resources to students as well as powerful communication and other course management tools, including course calendar, chat, and e-mail for instructors. See http://www.cengage.com/tlc/webtutor for more information.

Product Support Website (www.cengage.com/management/hitt) Our Product Support Website contains all ancillary products for instructors as well as the financial analysis exercises for both students and instructors.

The Business & Company Resource Center (BCRC) Put a complete business library at your students' fingertips! This premier online business research tool allows you and your students to search thousands of periodicals, journals, references, financial data, industry reports, and more. This powerful research tool saves time for students—whether they are preparing for a presentation or writing a reaction paper. You can use the BCRC to quickly and easily assign readings or research projects. Visit http://www.cengage.com/bcrc to learn more about this indispensable tool. For this text in particular, BCRC will be especially useful in further researching the companies featured in the text's 30 cases. We've also included BCRC links for the Strategy Right Now feature on our website, as well as in the Cengage NOW product.

Student Premium Companion Site The new optional student premium website features text-specific resources that enhance student learning by bringing concepts to life. Dynamic interactive learning tools include online quizzes, flashcards, PowerPoint slides, learning games, and more, helping to ensure your students come to class prepared! Ask your Cengage Learning sales representative for more details.

Students

Financial analyses of some of the cases are provided on our Product Support Website for both students and instructors. Researching financial data, company data, and industry data is made easy through the use of our proprietary database, the Business & Company Resource Center. Students are sent to this database to be able to quickly gather data needed for financial analysis.

Make It Yours – Custom Case Selection

Cengage Learning is dedicated to making the educational experience unique for all learners by creating custom materials that best suit your course needs. With our Make It Yours program, you can easily select a unique set of cases for your course from providers such as Harvard Business School Publishing, Darden, and Ivey. See http://www.custom.cengage.com/makeityours/hitt9e for more details.

Acknowledgments

We express our appreciation for the excellent support received from our editorial and production team at South-Western. We especially wish to thank Michele Rhoades, our Senior Acquisitions Editor; John Abner, our Development Editor; Nate Anderson, our Marketing Manager; and Jaci Featherly, our Content Project Manager. We are grateful for their dedication, commitment, and outstanding contributions to the development and publication of this book and its package of support materials.

We are highly indebted to the reviewers of the 8th edition in preparation for this current edition:

Erich Brockmann
University of New Orleans

Scott Elston
Iowa State University

Carol Jacobson
Purdue University

Consuelo M. Ramirez
University of Texas at San Antonio

Deepak Sethi
Old Dominion University

Len J. Trevino
Washington State University

Marta Szabo White
Georgia State University

Diana J. Wong-MingJi
Eastern Michigan University

Bruce H. Charnov
Hofstra University

Susan Hansen
University of Wisconsin-Platteville

Frank Novakowski
Davenport University

Manjula S. Salimath
University of North Texas

Manisha Singal
Virginia Tech

Edward Ward
Saint Cloud State University

Michael L Williams
Michigan State University

Wilson Zehr
Concordia University

Finally, we are very appreciative of the following people for the time and care that went into preparing the supplements to accompany this edition:

Charles Byles
Virginia Commonwealth University

Richard H. Lester
Texas A&M University

Paul Friga
University of North Carolina

Paul Mallette
Colorado State University

Kristi L. Marshall

Michael A. Hitt
R. Duane Ireland
Robert E. Hoskisson

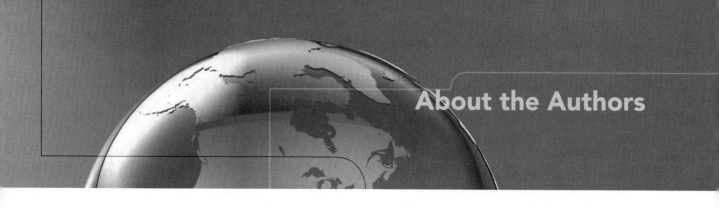

Michael A. Hitt

Michael A. Hitt is a Distinguished Professor and holds the Joe B. Foster Chair in Business Leadership at Texas A&M University. He received his Ph.D. from the University of Colorado. He has more than 260 publications including 26 co-authored or co-edited books and was cited as one of the 10 most-cited scholars in management over a 25-year period in an article published in the 2008 volume of the *Journal of Management*.

Some of his books are *Downscoping: How to Tame the Diversified Firm* (Oxford University Press, 1994); *Mergers and Acquisitions: A Guide to Creating Value for Stakeholders* (Oxford University Press, 2001); *Competing for Advantage,* 2nd edition (South-Western, 2008); and *Understanding Business Strategy,* 2nd edition (South-Western Cengage Learning, 2009). He is co-editor of several books including the following: *Managing Strategically in an Interconnected World* (1998); *New Managerial Mindsets: Organizational Transformation and Strategy Implementation* (1998); *Dynamic Strategic Resources: Development, Diffusion, and Integration* (1999); *Winning Strategies in a Deconstructing World* (John Wiley & Sons, 2000); *Handbook of Strategic Management* (2001); *Strategic Entrepreneurship: Creating a New Integrated Mindset* (2002); *Creating Value: Winners in the New Business Environment* (Blackwell Publishers, 2002); *Managing Knowledge for Sustained Competitive Advantage* (Jossey-Bass, 2003); *Great Minds in Management: The Process of Theory Development* (Oxford University Press, 2005), and *The Global Mindset* (Elsevier, 2007). He has served on the editorial review boards of multiple journals, including the *Academy of Management Journal, Academy of Management Executive, Journal of Applied Psychology, Journal of Management, Journal of World Business,* and *Journal of Applied Behavioral Sciences.* Furthermore, he has served as consulting editor and editor of the *Academy of Management Journal.* He is currently a co-editor of the *Strategic Entrepreneurship Journal.* He is the current past president of the Strategic Management Society and is a past president of the Academy of Management.

He is a Fellow in the Academy of Management and in the Strategic Management Society. He received an honorary doctorate from the Universidad Carlos III de Madrid and is an Honorary Professor and Honorary Dean at Xi'an Jiao Tong University. He has been acknowledged with several awards for his scholarly research and he received the Irwin Outstanding Educator Award and the Distinguished Service Award from the Academy of Management. He has received best paper awards for articles published in the *Academy of Management Journal, Academy of Management Executive,* and *Journal of Management.*

R. Duane Ireland

R. Duane Ireland is a Distinguished Professor and holds the Foreman R. and Ruby S. Bennett Chair in Business from the Mays Business School, Texas A&M University where he previously served as head of the management department. He teaches strategic management courses at all levels (undergraduate, masters, doctoral, and executive). He has over 175 publications including more than a dozen books. His research, which focuses on diversification, innovation, corporate entrepreneurship, and strategic entrepreneurship, has been published in a number of journals, including *Academy of Management Journal, Academy of Management Review, Academy of Management Executive, Administrative Science Quarterly, Strategic Management Journal, Journal of Management, Strategic Entrepreneurship Journal, Human Relations, Entrepreneurship Theory and Practice, Strategic Entrepreneurship Journal, Journal of Business Venturing,* and *Journal of Management Studies,* among others. His recently published books include *Understanding Business Strategy,* 2nd edition (South-Western Cengage Learning, 2009), *Entrepreneurship: Successfully Launching New Ventures,* 3rd edition (Prentice-Hall, 2010), and *Competing for Advantage,* 2nd edition (South-Western, 2008). He is serving or has served as a member of the editorial review boards for a number of journals, including *Academy of Management Journal, Academy of Management Review, Academy of Management Executive, Journal of Management, Strategic Enterprenurship Journal, Journal of Business Venturing, Entrepreneurship Theory and Practice, Journal of Business Strategy,* and *European Management Journal.* He is the current editor of the *Academy of Management Journal.* He has completed terms as an associate editor for *Academy of Management Journal,* as an associate editor for *Academy of Management Executive,* and as a consulting editor for *Entrepreneurship Theory and Practice.* He has co-edited special issues of *Academy of Management Review, Academy of Management Executive, Journal of Business Venturing, Strategic Management Journal, Journal of High Technology and Engineering Management,* and *Organizational Research Methods* (forthcoming). He received awards for the best article published in *Academy of Management Executive* (1999) and *Academy of Management Journal* (2000). In 2001, his co-authored article published in *Academy of Management Executive* won the Best Journal Article in Corporate Entrepreneurship Award from the U.S. Association for Small Business & Entrepreneurship (USASBE).

He is a Fellow of the Academy of Management and is a 21st Century Entrepreneurship Research Scholar. He served a three-year term as a Representative-at-Large member of the Academy of Management's Board of Governors. He received the 1999 Award for Outstanding Intellectual Contributions to Competitiveness Research from the American Society for Competitiveness and the USASBE Scholar in Corporate Entrepreneurship Award (2004).

Robert E. Hoskisson

Robert E. Hoskisson is the George R. Brown Chair of Strategic Management at the Jesse H. Jones Graduate School of Business, Rice University. He received his Ph.D. from the University of California-Irvine. Professor Hoskisson's research topics focus on corporate governance, acquisitions and divestitures, corporate and international diversification, corporate entrepreneurship, privatization, and cooperative strategy. He teaches courses in corporate and international strategic management, cooperative strategy, and strategy consulting, among others. Professor Hoskisson's research has appeared in over 120 publications, including articles in the *Academy of Management Journal, Academy of Management Review, Strategic Management Journal, Organization Science, Journal of Management, Journal of International Business Studies, Journal of Management Studies, Academy of Management Perspectives, Academy of Management Executive, California Management Review,* and 26 co-authored books. He is currently an associate editor of the *Strategic Management Journal* and a consulting editor for the *Journal of International Business Studies,* as well as serving on the Editorial Review board of

the *Academy of Management Journal*. Professor Hoskisson has served on several editorial boards for such publications as the *Academy of Management Journal* (including consulting editor and guest editor of a special issue), *Journal of Management* (including associate editor), *Organization Science, Journal of International Business Studies* (consulting editor), *Journal of Management Studies* (guest editor of a special issue) and *Entrepreneurship Theory and Practice.* He has co-authored several books including *Understanding Business Strategy*, 2nd Edition (South-Western Cengage Learning, 2009), *Competing for Advantage,* 2nd edition (South-Western, 2008), and *Downscoping: How to Tame the Diversified Firm* (Oxford University Press, 1994).

He has an appointment as a Special Professor at the University of Nottingham and as an Honorary Professor at Xi'an Jiao Tong University. He is a Fellow of the Academy of Management and a charter member of the Academy of Management Journals Hall of Fame. He is also a Fellow of the Strategic Management Society. In 1998, he received an award for Outstanding Academic Contributions to Competitiveness, American Society for Competitiveness. He also received the William G. Dyer Distinguished Alumni Award given at the Marriott School of Management, Brigham Young University. He completed three years of service as a representative at large on the Board of Governors of the Academy of Management and currently is on the Board of Directors of the Strategic Management Society.

CHAPTER 1

Strategic Management and Strategic Competitiveness

Studying this chapter should provide you with the strategic management knowledge needed to:

1. Define strategic competitiveness, strategy, competitive advantage, above-average returns, and the strategic management process.

2. Describe the competitive landscape and explain how globalization and technological changes shape it.

3. Use the industrial organization (I/O) model to explain how firms can earn above-average returns.

4. Use the resource-based model to explain how firms can earn above-average returns.

5. Describe vision and mission and discuss their value.

6. Define stakeholders and describe their ability to influence organizations.

7. Describe the work of strategic leaders.

8. Explain the strategic management process.

MCDONALD'S CORPORATION: FIRING ON ALL CYLINDERS WHILE PREPARING FOR THE FUTURE

Currently on a "tear," McDonald's ability to create value for its stakeholders (such as customers, shareholders, and employees) during the challenging times of the global recession that started roughly in early 2008 and continued throughout 2009 is indeed impressive. As one indicator of the quality of its performance, consider the fact that during 2008, McDonald's and Wal-Mart were the only two Dow Jones Industrial Average stocks to end the year with a gain.

With one of the world's most recognized brand names, mid-2009 found McDonald's operating roughly 32,000 restaurants in 118 countries. The largest fast-food restaurant chain in the world, McDonald's sales revenue was $70.7 billion in 2008, up from $64.1 billion the year before. The chain serves over 58 million customers daily. McDonald's dominates the quick-service restaurant industry in the United States, where its revenue is several times larger than Burger King and Wendy's, its closest competitors.

McDonald's impressive performance as the first decade of the twenty-first century came to a close suggests that the firm is effectively implementing its strategy. (We define strategy in this chapter as an integrated and coordinated set of commitments and actions designed to exploit core competencies and gain a competitive advantage.) However, the picture for McDonald's was much less positive in 2003. In that year, some analysts concluded that McDonald's "looked obsolete" as it failed to notice changes in its customers' interests and needs. The fact that the company reported its first-ever quarterly loss in

McDonalds restaurant in Berlin, Germany. McDonalds is the largest fast-food restaurant chain in the world, operating in 118 countries.

2003 and the decline in its stock price from roughly $48 per share to $13 per share suggested that McDonald's was becoming less competitive. However, by mid-2009 things had changed dramatically for McDonald's. Its "stock was trading at nearly $60, same-store sales (had) grown for the 56th straight month and the company (could) boast of having achieved double-digit operating-income growth during the onset of the financial crisis." How was this dramatic turnaround achieved?

After examining their firm's deteriorating situation in 2003, McDonald's strategic leaders decided to change its corporate-level strategy and to take different actions to implement its business-level strategy. From a business-level strategy perspective (we discuss business-level strategies in Chapter 4), McDonald's decided to focus on product innovations and upgrades of its existing properties instead of continuing to rapidly expand the number of units while relying almost exclusively on the core products it had sold for many years as the source of its sales revenue. From a corporate-level perspective (corporate-level strategies are discussed in Chapter 6), McDonald's decided to become less diversified. To reach this objective, the firm disposed of its interests in the Chipotle Mexican Grill restaurant concept and the Boston Market chain and sold its minority interest in Prêt a Manger as well. Operationally, McDonald's starting listening carefully to its customers, who were demanding value for their dollars and convenience as well as healthier products. One analyst describes McDonald's responses to what it was hearing from its customers this way: "McDonald's eliminated the super size option, offered more premium salads and chicken sandwiches and provided greater value options. It also initiated better training for employees, extended hours of service and redesigned stores to appeal to younger consumers." In part, these actions were taken to capitalize on an ever-increasing number of consumers who were becoming and remain today very conscious about their budgets.

However, as McDonald's experiences in the early 2000s indicate, corporate success is never guaranteed. The likelihood of a company being successful in the long term increases when strategic leaders continually evaluate the appropriateness of their firm's strategies as well as actions being taken to implement them. Given this, and in light of its decision in 2003 to continuously offer innovative food items to customers, McDonald's added McCafe coffee bars to all of its U.S. locations in 2009. McDonald's coffee drinks create value for customers by giving them high-quality drinks at prices that often are lower than those of competitors such as Starbucks. A Southern-style chicken sandwich was also added to the firm's line of chicken-based offerings. Allowing customers to order from in-store kiosks is an example of an action the firm recently took to create more convenience for customers. The firm continues upgrading its existing stores and in anticipation of a global economic recovery, is buying prime real estate in Europe "… on the cheap as a result of the overall downturn in construction spending." This real estate is the foundation for McDonald's commitment to add 1,000 new European locations in the near future. Thus, McDonald's strategic leaders appear to be committed to making decisions today to increase the likelihood that the firm will be as successful in the future as it was in the last years of the twenty-first century's first decade.

Sources: J. Adamy, 2009, McDonald's seeks way to keep sizzling, *Wall Street Journal*, http;://www.wsj.com, March 10; M. Arndt, 2009, McDonald's keeps gaining, *BusinessWeek*, http://www.businessweek.com, April 22; M. Cavallaro, 2009, Still lovin' the Golden Arches, *Forbes*, http://www.forbes.com, March 6; S. Dahle, 2009, McDonald's loves your recession, *Forbes*, http://www.forbes.com, February 17; D. Patnaik & P. Mortensen, 2009, The secret of McDonald's recent success, *Forbes*, http://www.forbes.com, February 4; M. Peer, 2009, Double-edge dollar at McDonald's, *Forbes*, http://www.forbes.com, January 26; A. Raghavan, 2009, McDonald's European burger binge, *Forbes*, http://www.forbes.com, January 23; P. Ziobro, 2009, McDonald's pounds out good quarter, *Wall Street Journal*, http://www.wsj.com, April 23; 2009, McDonald's Corp., Standard & Poor's Stock Report, http://www.standardandpoors.com, April 23.

As we see from the Opening Case, McDonald's was quite successful in 2008 and 2009, outperforming Burger King and Wendy's, its two main rivals. McDonald's performance during this time period suggests that it is highly competitive (something we call a condition of *strategic competitiveness*) as it earned *above-average returns*. All firms, including McDonald's, use the strategic management process (see Figure 1.1) as the foundation for the commitments, decisions, and actions they will take when pursuing strategic competitiveness and above-average terms. The strategic management process is fully explained in this book. We introduce you to this process in the next few paragraphs.

Strategic competitiveness is achieved when a firm successfully formulates and implements a value-creating strategy. A **strategy** is an integrated and coordinated set of commitments and actions designed to exploit core competencies and gain a competitive advantage. When choosing a strategy, firms make choices among competing alternatives as the pathway for deciding how they will pursue strategic competitiveness.[1] In this sense, the chosen strategy indicates what the firm *will do* as well as what the firm *will not do*.

As explained in the Opening Case, McDonald's sold its interests in other food concepts (e.g., Boston Market) in order to focus on developing new products and upgrading existing facilities in its portfolio of McDonald's restaurants around the globe.[2] Thus, McDonald's strategic leaders decided that the firm *would* pursue product innovations and that it *would not* remain involved with additional food concepts such as Boston Market and Chipotle. In-N-Out Burger, the privately held, 232-unit restaurant chain with locations in only Arizona and California, focuses on product quality and will not take any action with the potential to reduce the quality of its food items.[3] A firm's strategy also demonstrates how it differs from its competitors. Recently, Ford Motor Company devoted efforts to explain to stakeholders how the company differs from its competitors. The main idea is that Ford claims that it is "greener" and more technically advanced than its competitors, such as General Motors and Chrysler Group LLC (an alliance between Chrysler and Fiat SpA).[4]

A firm has a **competitive advantage** when it implements a strategy competitors are unable to duplicate or find too costly to try to imitate.[5] An organization can be confident

Strategic competitiveness is achieved when a firm successfully formulates and implements a value-creating strategy.

A **strategy** is an integrated and coordinated set of commitments and actions designed to exploit core competencies and gain a competitive advantage.

A firm has a **competitive advantage** when it implements a strategy competitors are unable to duplicate or find too costly to try to imitate.

Figure 1.1 The Strategic Management Process

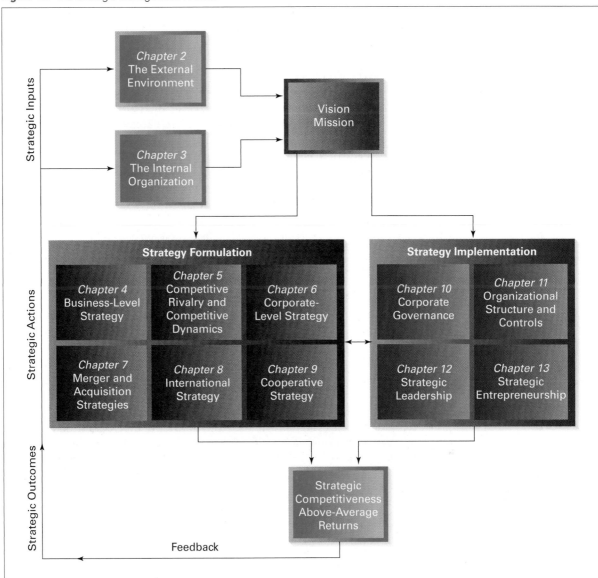

that its strategy has resulted in one or more useful competitive advantages only after competitors' efforts to duplicate its strategy have ceased or failed. In addition, firms must understand that no competitive advantage is permanent.[6] The speed with which competitors are able to acquire the skills needed to duplicate the benefits of a firm's value-creating strategy determines how long the competitive advantage will last.[7]

Above-average returns are returns in excess of what an investor expects to earn from other investments with a similar amount of risk. **Risk** is an investor's uncertainty about the economic gains or losses that will result from a particular investment.[8] The most successful companies learn how to effectively manage risk. Effectively managing risks reduces investors' uncertainty about the results of their investment.[9] Returns are often measured in terms of accounting figures, such as return on assets, return on equity, or return on sales. Alternatively, returns can be measured on the basis of stock market returns, such as monthly returns (the end-of-the-period stock price minus the beginning stock price, divided by the beginning stock price, yielding a percentage return). In smaller, new venture firms, returns are

Above-average returns are returns in excess of what an investor expects to earn from other investments with a similar amount of risk.

Risk is an investor's uncertainty about the economic gains or losses that will result from a particular investment.

sometimes measured in terms of the amount and speed of growth (e.g., in annual sales) rather than more traditional profitability measures[10] because new ventures require time to earn acceptable returns (in the form of return on assets and so forth) on investors' investments.[11]

Understanding how to exploit a competitive advantage is important for firms seeking to earn above-average returns.[12] Firms without a competitive advantage or that are not competing in an attractive industry earn, at best, average returns. **Average returns** are returns equal to those an investor expects to earn from other investments with a similar amount of risk. In the long run, an inability to earn at least average returns results first in decline and, eventually, failure. Failure occurs because investors withdraw their investments from those firms earning less-than-average returns.

After carefully evaluating its deteriorating performance and options, Circuit City decided in 2009 to liquidate its operation.[13] (Linens 'n Things, Bombay Co., Mervyn's LLC., and Sharper Image Corp. also liquidated in 2009, suggesting the difficulty of the competitive environment for consumer retailers during the economic downturn.) Prior to the liquidation decision, Circuit City filed for bankruptcy in November 2008. However, because the firm could not find a buyer and could not reach a deal with an investor as the means of gaining access to the financial capital it needed to successfully emerge from bankruptcy, it had no choice other than to liquidate. Here is how then-acting CEO James Marcum described Circuit City's situation and liquidation decision: "We are extremely disappointed by this outcome. We were unable to reach an agreement with our creditors and lenders to structure a going-concern transaction in the limited timeframe available, and so this is the only possible path for our company."[14]

As we explain in the Strategic Focus, stiff competition from Best Buy and mistakes made when implementing its strategy are the primary causes of Circuit City's failure and subsequent disappearance from the consumer electronics retail sector. Commenting about errors made at Circuit City, one analyst said, "This company made massive mistakes."[15] Additionally, Circuit City's focus on short-term profits likely was a problem as well in that such a focus tends to have a negative effect on a firm's ability to create value in the long term.[16]

Best Buy was performing well following Circuit City's demise. However, as we noted above, there are no guarantees of permanent success. This is true for McDonald's, even considering its excellent current performance, and for Best Buy. Although Best Buy clearly outperformed Circuit City, its primary direct rival for many years, the firm now faces a strong competitive challenge from Wal-Mart.[17] In order to deal with this challenge Best Buy is positioning itself as the provider of excellent customer service while selling high-end products with new interactive features. Additionally, the firm is rapidly expanding its private-label electronics business. In this business, Best Buy is using "…the mountains of customer feedback it collects from its stores to make simple innovations to established electronic gadgetry."[18] In contrast, Wal-Mart is positioning itself in the consumer electronics segment as the low-price option and seeks to sell its increasing breadth of consumer electronics products to a larger number of the more than 100 million customers who shop in its stores weekly.[19]

The **strategic management process** (see Figure 1.1) is the full set of commitments, decisions, and actions required for a firm to achieve strategic competitiveness and earn above-average returns. The firm's first step in the process is to analyze its external environment and internal organization to determine its resources, capabilities, and core competencies—the sources of its "strategic inputs." With this information, the firm develops its vision and mission and formulates one or more strategies. To implement its strategies, the firm takes actions toward achieving strategic competitiveness and above-average returns. Effective strategic actions that take place in the context of carefully integrated strategy formulation and implementation efforts result in positive outcomes. This dynamic strategic management process must be maintained as ever-changing markets

Average returns are returns equal to those an investor expects to earn from other investments with a similar amount of risk.

The **strategic management process** is the full set of commitments, decisions, and actions required for a firm to achieve strategic competitiveness and earn above-average returns.

CIRCUIT CITY: A TALE OF INEFFECTIVE STRATEGY IMPLEMENTATION AND FIRM FAILURE

When Circuit City announced on January 16, 2009, that it was out of options and that liquidation was the only viable course of action for it to take, the firm employed approximately 34,000 people to operate its 567 stores in the United States and was the second largest consumer electronics retailer in the United States. What caused Circuit City's failure? As we'll see, it appears that poor implementation of the firm's strategy was a key factor leading to the firm's demise.

Circuit City's genesis was in 1949, when Samuel S. Wurtzel opened the first Wards Company retail store in Richmond, Virginia. A television and home appliances retailer, Wards had a total of four stores in Richmond in 1959. The firm became public in 1961 and earned $246 million in revenue in 1983. Between 1969 and 1982, Wards grew by acquiring numerous electronics retailers across the United States. In 1984, the company's name was changed to Circuit City and the firm was listed on the New York Stock Exchange. Revenue growth continued, reaching $2 billion in 1990. Circuit City established CarMax, a retail venture selling used vehicles, in 1993. After some initial challenges, CarMax become quite successful. In 2002, Circuit City announced that in order to focus on its core retail consumer electronics business, it would spin off its CarMax subsidiary into a separate publicly traded company. By late 2008, the firm was in serious trouble; as a result, 155 stores were closed and 17 percent of its workforce was laid off.

With hindsight, we see that in the 1990s Circuit City was complacent and rather ineffective in its intense competition with Best Buy, its chief rival. Alan Wurtzel, the son of the firm's founder and a former Circuit City CEO, supports this position, saying that Circuit City "… didn't take the threat from Best Buy seriously enough and at some points was too focused on short-term profit rather than long-term value."

Among the actions Best Buy took during the 1990s to compete against Circuit City was to establish larger stores in superior locations. Circuit City's commitment to focus on short-term profits prevented the firm's leaders from being acutely aware of the value these new stores created for Best Buy. This short-term focus led to what turned out to be some

Ramin Talaie/CORBIS

A large "going out of business" sign hangs over a Circuit City store in Downtown Brooklyn. All of the electronics retailer's stores were closed by the end of March 2009, laying off more than 30,000 workers.

highly damaging decisions, such as the one to lay off thousands of its veteran, higher-paid employees, including sales personnel. These salespeople, who were earning attractive commissions because of their productivity, were replaced with lower-paid, less-experienced personnel. Circuit City leaders thought that sales would not suffer as a result of this decision. According to an analyst, "They (sales) did, and the damage to revenue—and Circuit City's reputation—was never undone."

In addition to concentrating on finding ways to reduce costs rather than find ways to create more value for customers, some believe that Circuit City made other mistakes while implementing its strategy. For example, the failure to effectively manage its inventory diminished the firm's ability to pay its existing debts in a timely manner and to keep its stores stocked with the latest, most innovative products. Poor customer service is another mistake. Of course, the decision to lay off the highest-paid (and most productive) employees immediately reduced the firm's ability to effectively serve customers. It is very hard for a firm to achieve strategic competitiveness and earn above-average returns when it fails to successfully implement its strategy.

Sources: E. Gruenwedel, 2009, Best Buy, Wal-Mart winners in Circuit City shuttering, *Home Media Magazine*, http://www.homemediamagazine.com, January 19; 2009, Best Buy Co. Inc., *Standard & Poor's Stock Report*, http://www.standardandpoors.com, April 18; 2009, Circuit City to liquidate U.S. stores, *MSNBC.com*, http://www.msnbc.com, January 16; S. Cranford, 2008, Circuit City: Schoonover's brand disconnect, *Seeking Alpha*, http://www.seekingalpha.com, February 17; A. Hamilton, 2008, Why Circuit City busted, while Best Buy boomed, *Time*, http://www.time.com, November 11.

and competitive structures are coordinated with a firm's continuously evolving strategic inputs.[20]

In the remaining chapters of this book, we use the strategic management process to explain what firms do to achieve strategic competitiveness and earn above-average returns. These explanations demonstrate why some firms consistently achieve competitive success while others fail to do so.[21] As you will see, the reality of global competition is a critical part of the strategic management process and significantly influences firms' performances.[22] Indeed, learning how to successfully compete in the globalized world is one of the most significant challenges for firms competing in the current century.[23]

Several topics will be discussed in this chapter. First, we describe the current competitive landscape. This challenging landscape is being created primarily by the emergence of a global economy, globalization resulting from that economy, and rapid technological changes. Next, we examine two models that firms use to gather the information and knowledge required to choose and then effectively implement their strategies. The insights gained from these models also serve as the foundation for forming the firm's vision and mission. The first model (the industrial organization or I/O model) suggests that the external environment is the primary determinant of a firm's strategic actions. Identifying and then competing successfully in an attractive (i.e., profitable) industry or segment of an industry are the keys to competitive success when using this model.[24] The second model (resource-based) suggests that a firm's unique resources and capabilities are the critical link to strategic competitiveness.[25] Thus, the first model is concerned primarily with the firm's external environment while the second model is concerned primarily with the firm's internal organization. After discussing vision and mission, direction-setting statements that influence the choice and use of strategies, we describe the stakeholders that organizations serve. The degree to which stakeholders' needs can be met increases when firms achieve strategic competitiveness and earn above-average returns. Closing the chapter are introductions to strategic leaders and the elements of the strategic management process.

The Competitive Landscape

The fundamental nature of competition in many of the world's industries is changing. The reality is that financial capital is scarce and markets are increasingly volatile.[26] Because of this, the pace of change is relentless and ever-increasing. Even determining the boundaries of an industry has become challenging. Consider, for example, how advances in interactive computer networks and telecommunications have blurred the boundaries of the entertainment industry. Today, not only do cable companies and satellite networks compete for entertainment revenue from television, but telecommunication companies are moving into the entertainment business through significant improvements in fiber-optic lines.[27] Partnerships among firms in different segments of the entertainment industry further blur industry boundaries. For example, MSNBC is co-owned by NBC Universal and Microsoft. In turn, General Electric owns 80 percent of NBC Universal while Vivendi owns the remaining 20 percent.[28]

There are other examples of fundamental changes to competition in various industries. For example, many firms are looking for the most profitable and interesting way to deliver video on demand (VOD) online besides cable and satellite companies. Raketu, a voice over the Internet protocol (VoIP) phone service in the United Kingdom, is seeking to provide customers with a social experience while watching the same entertainment on a VOD using a chat feature on its phone service.[29] Raketu's vision is to "… bring together communications, information and entertainment into one service, to remove the complexities of how people communicate with one another, make a system that is contact centric, and to make it fun and easy to use."[30] In addition, the competitive possibilities and challenges for more "traditional" communications companies that are suggested by social networking sites such as Facebook, MySpace, and Friendster appear to be endless.[31]

Other characteristics of the current competitive landscape are noteworthy. Conventional sources of competitive advantage such as economies of scale and huge advertising budgets are not as effective as they once were in terms of helping firms earn above-average returns. Moreover, the traditional managerial mind-set is unlikely to lead a firm to strategic competitiveness. Managers must adopt a new mind-set that values flexibility, speed, innovation, integration, and the challenges that evolve from constantly changing conditions.[32] The conditions of the competitive landscape result in a perilous business world, one where the investments that are required to compete on a global scale are enormous and the consequences of failure are severe.[33] Effective use of the strategic management process reduces the likelihood of failure for firms as they encounter the conditions of today's competitive landscape.

Hypercompetition is a term often used to capture the realities of the competitive landscape. Under conditions of hypercompetition, assumptions of market stability are replaced by notions of inherent instability and change.[34] Hypercompetition results from the dynamics of strategic maneuvering among global and innovative combatants.[35] It is a condition of rapidly escalating competition based on price-quality positioning, competition to create new know-how and establish first-mover advantage, and competition to protect or invade established product or geographic markets.[36] In a hypercompetitive market, firms often aggressively challenge their competitors in the hopes of improving their competitive position and ultimately their performance.[37]

Several factors create hypercompetitive environments and influence the nature of the current competitive landscape. The emergence of a global economy and technology, specifically rapid technological change, are the two primary drivers of hypercompetitive environments and the nature of today's competitive landscape.

The Global Economy

A **global economy** is one in which goods, services, people, skills, and ideas move freely across geographic borders. Relatively unfettered by artificial constraints, such as tariffs, the global economy significantly expands and complicates a firm's competitive environment.[38]

Interesting opportunities and challenges are associated with the emergence of the global economy.[39] For example, Europe, instead of the United States, is now the world's largest single market, with 700 million potential customers. The European Union and the other Western European countries also have a gross domestic product that is more than 35 percent higher than the GDP of the United States.[40] "In the past, China was generally seen as a low-competition market and a low-cost producer. Today, China is an extremely competitive market in which local market-seeking MNCs [multinational corporations] must fiercely compete against other MNCs and against those local companies that are more cost effective and faster in product development. While it

A **global economy** is one in which goods, services, people, skills, and ideas move freely across geographic borders.

Imaginechina via AP Images

General Electric received a $300 million contract from China to supply turbines and compression gear that will propel natural gas from the nation's remote north-western regions to booming eastern cities such as Shanghai.

is true that China has been viewed as a country from which to source low-cost goods, lately, many MNCs, such as P&G [Procter and Gamble], are actually net exporters of local management talent; they have been dispatching more Chinese abroad than bringing foreign expatriates to China."[41] India, the world's largest democracy, has an economy that also is growing rapidly and now ranks as the fourth largest in the world.[42] Many large multinational companies are also emerging as significant global competitors from these emerging economies.[43]

The statistics detailing the nature of the global economy reflect the realities of a hypercompetitive business environment and challenge individual firms to think seriously about the markets in which they will compete. Consider the case of General Electric (GE). Although headquartered in the United States, GE expects that as much as 60 percent of its revenue growth between 2005 and 2015 will be generated by competing in rapidly developing economies (e.g., China and India). The decision to count on revenue growth in developing countries instead of in developed countries such as the United States and European nations seems quite reasonable in the global economy. In fact, according to an analyst, what GE is doing is not by choice but by necessity: "Developing countries are where the fastest growth is occurring and more sustainable growth."[44] Based on its analyses of world markets and their potential, GE estimates that by 2024, China will be the world's largest consumer of electricity and will be the world's largest consumer and consumer-finance market (business areas in which GE competes). GE is making strategic decisions today, such as investing significantly in China and India, in order to improve its competitive position in what the firm believes are becoming vital geographic sources of revenue and profitability.

The March of Globalization

Globalization is the increasing economic interdependence among countries and their organizations as reflected in the flow of goods and services, financial capital, and knowledge across country borders.[45] Globalization is a product of a large number of firms competing against one another in an increasing number of global economies.

In globalized markets and industries, financial capital might be obtained in one national market and used to buy raw materials in another one. Manufacturing equipment bought from a third national market can then be used to produce products that are sold in yet a fourth market. Thus, globalization increases the range of opportunities for companies competing in the current competitive landscape.[46]

Wal-Mart, for instance, is trying to achieve boundary-less retailing with global pricing, sourcing, and logistics. Through boundary-less retailing, the firm seeks to make the movement of goods and the use of pricing strategies as seamless among all of its international operations as has historically been the case among its domestic stores. The firm is pursuing this type of retailing on an evolutionary basis. For example, most of Wal-Mart's original international investments were in Canada and Mexico, because it was easier for the firm to apply its global practices in countries that are geographically close to its home base, the United States. Because of the success it has had in proximate international markets, Wal-Mart is now seeking boundary-less retailing across its operations in countries such as Argentina, Brazil, Chile, China, Japan, and the United Kingdom. (The importance of Wal-Mart's international operations is indicated by the fact that the firm is divided into three divisions: Wal-Mart, Sam's Club, and International.[47])

Firms experiencing and engaging in globalization to the degree Wal-Mart is must make culturally sensitive decisions when using the strategic management process.

Additionally, highly globalized firms must anticipate ever-increasing complexity in their operations as goods, services, people, and so forth move freely across geographic borders and throughout different economic markets.

Overall, it is important for firms to understand that globalization has led to higher levels of performance standards in many competitive dimensions, including those of quality, cost, productivity, product introduction time, and operational efficiency. In addition to firms competing in the global economy, these standards affect firms competing on a domestic-only basis. The reason is that customers will purchase from a global competitor rather than a domestic firm when the global company's good or service is superior. Because workers now flow rather freely among global economies, and because employees are a key source of competitive advantage, firms must understand that increasingly, "the best people will come from … anywhere."[48] Firms must learn how to deal with the reality that in the competitive landscape of the twenty-first century, only companies capable of meeting, if not exceeding, global standards typically have the capability to earn above-average returns.

Although globalization does offer potential benefits to firms, it is not without risks. Collectively, the risks of participating outside of a firm's domestic country in the global economy are labeled a "liability of foreignness."[49]

One risk of entering the global market is the amount of time typically required for firms to learn how to compete in markets that are new to them. A firm's performance can suffer until this knowledge is either developed locally or transferred from the home market to the newly established global location.[50] Additionally, a firm's performance may suffer with substantial amounts of globalization. In this instance, firms may overdiversify internationally beyond their ability to manage these extended operations.[51] The result of overdiversification can have strong negative effects on a firm's overall performance.

Thus, entry into international markets, even for firms with substantial experience in the global economy, requires effective use of the strategic management process. It is also important to note that even though global markets are an attractive strategic option for some companies, they are not the only source of strategic competitiveness. In fact, for most companies, even for those capable of competing successfully in global markets, it is critical to remain committed to and strategically competitive in both domestic and international markets by staying attuned to technological opportunities and potential competitive disruptions that innovations create.[52]

Technology and Technological Changes

Technology-related trends and conditions can be placed into three categories: technology diffusion and disruptive technologies, the information age, and increasing knowledge intensity. Through these categories, technology is significantly altering the nature of competition and contributing to unstable competitive environments as a result of doing so.

Technology Diffusion and Disruptive Technologies

The rate of technology diffusion, which is the speed at which new technologies become available and are used, has increased substantially over the past 15 to 20 years. Consider the following rates of technology diffusion:

> It took the telephone 35 years to get into 25 percent of all homes in the United States. It took TV 26 years. It took radio 22 years. It took PCs 16 years. It took the Internet 7 years.[53]

Perpetual innovation is a term used to describe how rapidly and consistently new, information-intensive technologies replace older ones. The shorter product life cycles resulting from these rapid diffusions of new technologies place a competitive premium on being able to quickly introduce new, innovative goods and services into the marketplace.[54]

In fact, when products become somewhat indistinguishable because of the widespread and rapid diffusion of technologies, speed to market with innovative products may be the primary source of competitive advantage (see Chapter 5).[55] Indeed, some argue that the global economy is increasingly driven by or revolves around constant innovations. Not surprisingly, such innovations must be derived from an understanding of global standards and global expectations in terms of product functionality.[56]

Another indicator of rapid technology diffusion is that it now may take only 12 to 18 months for firms to gather information about their competitors' research and development and product decisions.[57] In the global economy, competitors can sometimes imitate a firm's successful competitive actions within a few days. In this sense, the rate of technological diffusion has reduced the competitive benefits of patents. Today, patents may be an effective way of protecting proprietary technology in a small number of industries such as pharmaceuticals. Indeed, many firms competing in the electronics industry often do not apply for patents to prevent competitors from gaining access to the technological knowledge included in the patent application.

Disruptive technologies—technologies that destroy the value of an existing technology and create new markets[58]—surface frequently in today's competitive markets. Think of the new markets created by the technologies underlying the development of products such as iPods, PDAs, WiFi, and the browser. These types of products are thought by some to represent radical or breakthrough innovations.[59] (We talk more about radical innovations in Chapter 13.) A disruptive or radical technology can create what is essentially a new industry or can harm industry incumbents. Some incumbents though, are able to adapt based on their superior resources, experience, and ability to gain access to the new technology through multiple sources (e.g., alliances, acquisitions, and ongoing internal research).[60]

The Information Age

Dramatic changes in information technology have occurred in recent years. Personal computers, cellular phones, artificial intelligence, virtual reality, massive databases, and multiple social networking sites are a few examples of how information is used differently as a result of technological developments. An important outcome of these changes is that the ability to effectively and efficiently access and use information has become an important source of competitive advantage in virtually all industries. Information technology advances have given small firms more flexibility in competing with large firms, if that technology can be efficiently used.[61]

Both the pace of change in information technology and its diffusion will continue to increase. For instance, the number of personal computers in use in the United States is expected to reach 278 million by 2010. The declining costs of information technologies and the increased accessibility to them are also evident in the current competitive landscape. The global proliferation of relatively inexpensive computing power and its linkage on a global scale via computer networks combine to increase the speed and diffusion of information technologies. Thus, the competitive potential of information technologies is now available to companies of all sizes throughout the world, including those in emerging economies.

The Internet is another technological innovation contributing to hypercompetition. Available to an increasing number of people throughout the world, the Internet provides an infrastructure that allows the delivery of information to computers in any location. Access to the Internet on smaller devices such as cell phones is having an ever-growing impact on competition in a number of industries. However, possible changes to Internet Service Providers' (ISPs) pricing structures could affect the rate of growth of Internet-based applications. In mid-2009, ISPs such as Time Warner Cable and Verizon were "… trying to convince their customers that they should pay for their service based on how much data they download in a month."[62] Users downloading or streamlining high-definition movies, playing video games online, and so forth would be affected the most if ISPs were to base their pricing structure around total usage.

Increasing Knowledge Intensity

Knowledge (information, intelligence, and expertise) is the basis of technology and its application. In the competitive landscape of the twenty-first century, knowledge is a critical organizational resource and an increasingly valuable source of competitive advantage.[63] Indeed, starting in the 1980s, the basis of competition shifted from hard assets to intangible resources. For example, "Wal-Mart transformed retailing through its proprietary approach to supply chain management and its information-rich relationships with customers and suppliers."[64] Relationships with customers and suppliers are an example of an intangible resource.

Knowledge is gained through experience, observation, and inference and is an intangible resource (tangible and intangible resources are fully described in Chapter 3). The value of intangible resources, including knowledge, is growing as a proportion of total shareholder value in today's competitive landscape.[65] The probability of achieving strategic competitiveness is enhanced for the firm that realizes that its survival depends on the ability to capture intelligence, transform it into usable knowledge, and diffuse it rapidly throughout the company.[66] Therefore, firms must develop (e.g., through training programs) and acquire (e.g., by hiring educated and experienced employees) knowledge, integrate it into the organization to create capabilities, and then apply it to gain a competitive advantage.[67] In addition, firms must build routines that facilitate the diffusion of local knowledge throughout the organization for use everywhere that it has value.[68] Firms are better able to do these things when they have strategic flexibility.

Strategic flexibility is a set of capabilities used to respond to various demands and opportunities existing in a dynamic and uncertain competitive environment. Thus, strategic flexibility involves coping with uncertainty and its accompanying risks.[69] Firms should try to develop strategic flexibility in all areas of their operations. However, those working within firms to develop strategic flexibility should understand that the task is not easy, largely because of inertia that can build up over time. A firm's focus and past core competencies may actually slow change and strategic flexibility.[70]

To be strategically flexible on a continuing basis and to gain the competitive benefits of such flexibility, a firm has to develop the capacity to learn. In the words of John Browne, former CEO of British Petroleum: "In order to generate extraordinary value for shareholders, a company has to learn better than its competitors and apply that knowledge throughout its businesses faster and more widely than they do."[71] Continuous learning provides the firm with new and up-to-date sets of skills, which allow it to adapt to its environment as it encounters changes.[72] Firms capable of rapidly and broadly applying what they have learned exhibit the strategic flexibility and the capacity to change in ways that will increase the probability of successfully dealing with uncertain, hypercompetitive environments.

The I/O Model of Above-Average Returns

From the 1960s through the 1980s, the external environment was thought to be the primary determinant of strategies that firms selected to be successful.[73] The industrial organization (I/O) model of above-average returns explains the external environment's dominant influence on a firm's strategic actions. The model specifies that the industry or segment of an industry in which a company chooses to compete has a stronger influence on performance than do the choices managers make inside their organizations.[74] The firm's performance is believed to be determined primarily by a range of industry properties, including economies of scale, barriers to market entry, diversification, product differentiation, and the degree of concentration of firms in the industry.[75] We examine these industry characteristics in Chapter 2.

Strategic flexibility is a set of capabilities used to respond to various demands and opportunities existing in a dynamic and uncertain competitive environment.

Grounded in economics, the I/O model has four underlying assumptions. First, the external environment is assumed to impose pressures and constraints that determine the strategies that would result in above-average returns. Second, most firms competing within an industry or within a segment of that industry are assumed to control similar strategically relevant resources and to pursue similar strategies in light of those resources. Third, resources used to implement strategies are assumed to be highly mobile across firms, so any resource differences that might develop between firms will be short-lived. Fourth, organizational decision makers are assumed to be rational and committed to acting in the firm's best interests, as shown by their profit-maximizing behaviors.[76] The I/O model challenges firms to find the most attractive industry in which to compete. Because most firms are assumed to have similar valuable resources that are mobile across companies, their performance generally can be increased only when they operate in the industry with the highest profit potential and learn how to use their resources to implement the strategy required by the industry's structural characteristics.[77]

The five forces model of competition is an analytical tool used to help firms find the industry that is the most attractive for them. The model (explained in Chapter 2) encompasses several variables and tries to capture the complexity of competition. The five forces model suggests that an industry's profitability (i.e., its rate of return on invested capital relative to its cost of capital) is a function of interactions among five forces: suppliers, buyers, competitive rivalry among firms currently in the industry, product substitutes, and potential entrants to the industry.[78]

Firms use the five forces model to identify the attractiveness of an industry (as measured by its profitability potential) as well as the most advantageous position for the firm to take in that industry, given the industry's structural characteristics.[79] Typically, the model suggests that firms can earn above-average returns by producing either standardized goods or services at costs below those of competitors (a cost leadership strategy) or by producing differentiated goods or services for which customers are willing to pay a price premium (a differentiation strategy). (The cost leadership and product differentiation strategies are discussed in Chapter 4.) The fact that "…the fast food industry is becoming a 'zero-sum industry' as companies' battle for the same pool of customers"[80] suggests that McDonald's is competing in a relatively unattractive industry. However, as described in the Opening Case, by focusing on product innovations and enhancing existing facilities while buying properties outside the United States at attractive prices as the foundation for selectively building new stores, McDonald's is positioned in the fast food (or quick-service) restaurant industry in a way that allows it to earn above-average returns.

As shown in Figure 1.2, the I/O model suggests that above-average returns are earned when firms are able to effectively study the external environment as the foundation for identifying an attractive industry and implementing the appropriate strategy. Companies that develop or acquire the internal skills needed to implement strategies required by the external environment are likely to succeed, while those that do not are likely to fail. Hence, this model suggests that returns are determined primarily by external characteristics rather than by the firm's unique internal resources and capabilities.

Research findings support the I/O model, in that approximately 20 percent of a firm's profitability is explained by the industry in which it chooses to compete. However, this research also shows that 36 percent of the variance in firm profitability can be attributed to the firm's characteristics and actions.[81] These findings suggest that the external environment and a firm's resources, capabilities, core competencies, and competitive advantages (see Chapter 3) all influence the company's ability to achieve strategic competitiveness and earn above-average returns.

As shown in Figure 1.2, the I/O model considers a firm's strategy to be a set of commitments and actions flowing from the characteristics of the industry in which the firm has decided to compete. The resource-based model, discussed next, takes a different view of the major influences on a firm's choice of strategy.

Figure 1.2 The I/O Model of Above-Average Returns

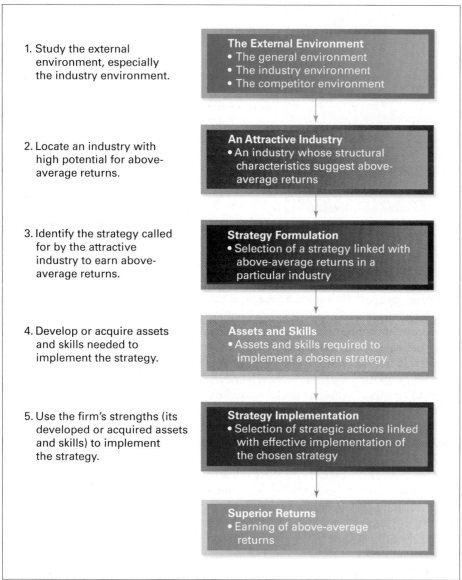

1. Study the external environment, especially the industry environment.

The External Environment
- The general environment
- The industry environment
- The competitor environment

2. Locate an industry with high potential for above-average returns.

An Attractive Industry
- An industry whose structural characteristics suggest above-average returns

3. Identify the strategy called for by the attractive industry to earn above-average returns.

Strategy Formulation
- Selection of a strategy linked with above-average returns in a particular industry

4. Develop or acquire assets and skills needed to implement the strategy.

Assets and Skills
- Assets and skills required to implement a chosen strategy

5. Use the firm's strengths (its developed or acquired assets and skills) to implement the strategy.

Strategy Implementation
- Selection of strategic actions linked with effective implementation of the chosen strategy

Superior Returns
- Earning of above-average returns

The Resource-Based Model of Above-Average Returns

The resource-based model assumes that each organization is a collection of unique resources and capabilities. The *uniqueness* of its resources and capabilities is the basis of a firm's strategy and its ability to earn above-average returns.[82]

Resources are inputs into a firm's production process, such as capital equipment, the skills of individual employees, patents, finances, and talented managers. In general, a firm's resources are classified into three categories: physical, human, and organizational capital. Described fully in Chapter 3, resources are either tangible or intangible in nature.

Individual resources alone may not yield a competitive advantage.[83] In fact, resources have a greater likelihood of being a source of competitive advantage when they are formed into a capability. A **capability** is the capacity for a set of resources to perform a task or an activity in an integrative manner. Capabilities evolve over time and must be managed

Resources are inputs into a firm's production process, such as capital equipment, the skills of individual employees, patents, finances, and talented managers.

A **capability** is the capacity for a set of resources to perform a task or an activity in an integrative manner.

Best Buy as well as many other companies collect extensive data about their customers' buying behavior and preferences to make better business decisions.

dynamically in pursuit of above-average returns.[84] **Core competencies** are resources and capabilities that serve as a source of competitive advantage for a firm over its rivals. Core competencies are often visible in the form of organizational functions. For example, we noted earlier that Best Buy is processing the extensive amount of data it has about its customers to identify private-label consumer electronic products it can produce to meet customers' needs. Best Buy relies on its strong customer service and information technology capabilities to spot ways to do this.

According to the resource-based model, differences in firms' performances across time are due primarily to their unique resources and capabilities rather than the industry's structural characteristics. This model also assumes that firms acquire different resources and develop unique capabilities based on how they combine and use the resources; that resources and certainly capabilities are not highly mobile across firms; and that the differences in resources and capabilities are the basis of competitive advantage.[85] Through continued use, capabilities become stronger and more difficult for competitors to understand and imitate. As a source of competitive advantage, a capability "should be neither so simple that it is highly imitable, nor so complex that it defies internal steering and control."[86]

The resource-based model of superior returns is shown in Figure 1.3. This model suggests that the strategy the firm chooses should allow it to use its competitive advantages in an attractive industry (the I/O model is used to identify an attractive industry).

Not all of a firm's resources and capabilities have the potential to be the foundation for a competitive advantage. This potential is realized when resources and capabilities are valuable, rare, costly to imitate, and nonsubstitutable.[87] Resources are *valuable* when they allow a firm to take advantage of opportunities or neutralize threats in its external environment. They are *rare* when possessed by few, if any, current and potential competitors. Resources are *costly to imitate* when other firms either cannot obtain them or are at a cost disadvantage in obtaining them compared with the firm that already possesses them. And they are *nonsubstitutable* when they have no structural equivalents. Many resources can either be imitated or substituted over time. Therefore, it is difficult to achieve and sustain a competitive advantage based on resources alone.[88] When these four criteria are met, however, resources and capabilities become core competencies.

As noted previously, research shows that both the industry environment and a firm's internal assets affect that firm's performance over time.[89] Thus, to form a vision and mission, and subsequently to select one or more strategies and to determine how to implement them, firms use both the I/O and the resource-based models.[90] In fact, these models complement each other in that one (I/O) focuses outside the firm while the other (resource-based) focuses inside the firm. Next, we discuss the forming of the firm's vision and mission—actions taken after the firm understands the realities of its external environment (Chapter 2) and internal organization (Chapter 3).

Vision and Mission

Core competencies are capabilities that serve as a source of competitive advantage for a firm over its rivals.

After studying the external environment and the internal organization, the firm has the information it needs to form its vision and a mission (see Figure 1.1). Stakeholders (those who affect or are affected by a firm's performance, as explained later in the chapter) learn a great deal about a firm by studying its vision and mission. Indeed, a key purpose of

Figure 1.3 The Resource-Based Model of Above-Average Returns

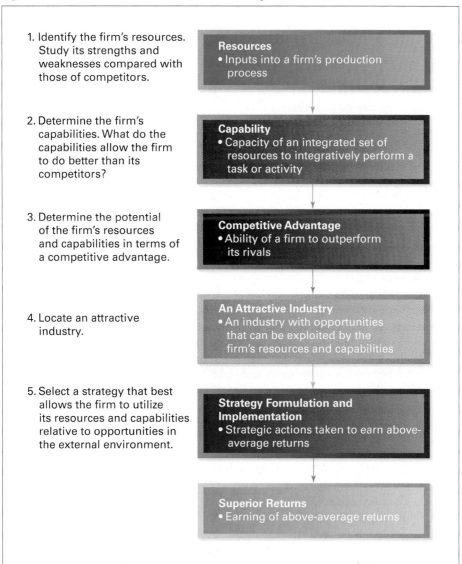

1. Identify the firm's resources. Study its strengths and weaknesses compared with those of competitors.

Resources
• Inputs into a firm's production process

2. Determine the firm's capabilities. What do the capabilities allow the firm to do better than its competitors?

Capability
• Capacity of an integrated set of resources to integratively perform a task or activity

3. Determine the potential of the firm's resources and capabilities in terms of a competitive advantage.

Competitive Advantage
• Ability of a firm to outperform its rivals

4. Locate an attractive industry.

An Attractive Industry
• An industry with opportunities that can be exploited by the firm's resources and capabilities

5. Select a strategy that best allows the firm to utilize its resources and capabilities relative to opportunities in the external environment.

Strategy Formulation and Implementation
• Strategic actions taken to earn above-average returns

Superior Returns
• Earning of above-average returns

vision and mission statements is to inform stakeholders of what the firm is, what it seeks to accomplish, and who it seeks to serve.

Vision

Vision is a picture of what the firm wants to be and, in broad terms, what it wants to ultimately achieve.[91] Thus, a vision statement articulates the ideal description of an organization and gives shape to its intended future. In other words, a vision statement points the firm in the direction of where it would eventually like to be in the years to come.[92] Vision is "big picture" thinking with passion that helps people *feel* what they are supposed to be doing in the organization.[93] People feel what they are to do when their firm's vision is simple, positive, and emotional. However, an effective vision stretches and challenges people as well.

It is also important to note that vision statements reflect a firm's values and aspirations and are intended to capture the heart and mind of each employee and, hopefully,

Vision is a picture of what the firm wants to be and, in broad terms, what it wants to ultimately achieve.

many of its other stakeholders. A firm's vision tends to be enduring while its mission can change in light of changing environmental conditions. A vision statement tends to be relatively short and concise, making it easily remembered. Examples of vision statements include the following:

> *Our vision is to be the world's best quick service restaurant. (McDonald's)*

> *To make the automobile accessible to every American. (Ford Motor Company's vision when established by Henry Ford)*

As a firm's most important and prominent strategic leader, the CEO is responsible for working with others to form the firm's vision. Experience shows that the most effective vision statement results when the CEO involves a host of stakeholders (e.g., other top-level managers, employees working in different parts of the organization, suppliers, and customers) to develop it. In addition, to help the firm reach its desired future state, a vision statement should be clearly tied to the conditions in the firm's external environment and internal organization. Moreover, the decisions and actions of those involved with developing the vision, especially the CEO and the other top-level managers, must be consistent with that vision. At McDonald's, for example, a failure to openly provide employees with what they need to quickly and effectively serve customers would be a recipe for disaster.

Mission

The vision is the foundation for the firm's mission. A **mission** specifies the business or businesses in which the firm intends to compete and the customers it intends to serve.[94] The firm's mission is more concrete than its vision. However, like the vision, a mission should establish a firm's individuality and should be inspiring and relevant to all stakeholders.[95] Together, vision and mission provide the foundation the firm needs to choose and implement one or more strategies. The probability of forming an effective mission increases when employees have a strong sense of the ethical standards that will guide their behaviors as they work to help the firm reach its vision.[96] Thus, business ethics are a vital part of the firm's discussions to decide what it wants to become (its vision) as well as who it intends to serve and how it desires to serve those individuals and groups (its mission).[97]

Even though the final responsibility for forming the firm's mission rests with the CEO, the CEO and other top-level managers tend to involve a larger number of people in forming the mission. The main reason is that the mission deals more directly with product markets and customers, and middle- and first-level managers and other employees have more direct contact with customers and the markets in which they are served. Examples of mission statements include the following:

> *Be the best employer for our people in each community around the world and deliver operational excellence to our customers in each of our restaurants. (McDonald's)*

> *Our mission is to be recognized by our customers as the leader in applications engineering. We always focus on the activities customers desire; we are highly motivated and strive to advance our technical knowledge in the areas of material, part design and fabrication technology. (LNP, a GE Plastics Company)*

Notice how the McDonald's mission statement flows from its vision of being the world's best quick-service restaurant. LNP's mission statement describes the business areas (material, part design, and fabrication technology) in which the firm intends to compete.

Some believe that vision and mission statements fail to create value for the firms forming them. One expert believes that "Most vision statements are either too vague, too broad in scope, or riddled with superlatives."[98] If this is the case, why do firms spend so much time developing these statements? As explained in the Strategic Focus, vision and mission statements that are poorly developed do not provide the direction the firm needs to take appropriate strategic actions. Still, as shown in Figure 1.1, the firm's vision and

STRATEGY
RIGHT NOW

Explore how Juniper Networks, a leader in high-performance networking, established a vision for product innovation.

www.cengage.com/ management/hitt

A **mission** specifies the business or businesses in which the firm intends to compete and the customers it intends to serve.

STRATEGIC FOCUS

EFFECTIVE VISION AND MISSION STATEMENTS: WHY FIRMS NEED THEM

Some clearly believe that working on vision and mission statements is a waste of time and energy. "We have more important things to accomplish"; "We are too busy fighting daily fires to spend time thinking about the future or dreaming about what we might want to be"; and "All vision and mission statements look alike across companies—there's just no difference among them, so why bother?" Almost everyone who has been involved with or worked for an organization either on or off campus has likely heard similar comments.

Thinking about the challenges facing firms today allows us to understand the reasons for the negative perspective some have about the benefits organizations gain by forming vision and mission statements. A difficult competitive environment and the realities of globalization are but two reasons that may cause some to react less-than-positively when asked to participate in efforts to form vision and mission statements for their organization. In addition, the difficulty and challenge associated with developing *effective* or *meaningful* vision and mission statements may be the key reasons some prefer not to bother trying to do so.

A vision is a picture of what the firm wants to be and, in broad terms, what it ultimately wants to achieve. Based on the vision, a firm's mission indicates the business or businesses in which the firm will compete and the customers it will serve. An important aspect of these statements is that deep, critical, and reflective thinking is required to form them. Moreover, forming these statements requires choices to be made—about what the firm wants to be, what it wants to achieve, and the businesses it will compete in, and the specific groups of customers it will serve.

CORBIS/Jupiter Images

Simultaneously, the firm is deciding what it won't become, won't try to achieve, where it won't compete, and who it won't serve. These are hard choices that result only from intensive thinking and analysis. Having obtained information about the firm's external environment and its internal organization, those asked to form the firm's vision and mission statements must be willing to rigorously and thoroughly debate the realities and possibilities associated with the information that has been gathered.

There are benefits for organizations willing to accept the challenge of rigorously examining and interpreting this information. Internally, the benefits include (1) providing the direction required to select the firm's strategies, (2) prioritizing how the firm's resources will be allocated, (3) providing opportunities for people to work together to deal with significant issues, (4) gaining an appreciation for the necessity of making trade-offs, and (5) learning more about the firm's culture and character. Benefits for the firm's external environment include (1) showing how the organization differs from competitors, (2) reflecting the organization's priorities, and (3) signaling aspects of the firm's culture and values. In addition, strategic leaders should be aware of research evidence suggesting that there is a positive relationship between forming vision and mission statements that is consistent with the realities of their external environment and internal organization and performance.[99] Thus, there are multiple reasons for firms to take the steps required to effectively develop a vision statement and a mission statement.

Sources: H. Ibarra & O. Obodaru, 2009, Women and the vision thing, *Harvard Business Review*, 87(1): 62–70; B. Bartkus & M. Glassman, 2008, Do firms practice what they preach? The relationship between mission statements and stakeholder management, *Journal of Business Ethics*, 83: 207–216; B. Perkins, 2008, State your purpose, *Computerworld*, May 12, 35; L. S. Williams, 2008, The mission statement, *Journal of Business Communication*, 45: 94–119; J. Davis, J. A. Ruhe, M. Lee, & U. Rajadhyaksha, 2007, Mission possible: Do school mission statements work? *Journal of Business Ethics*, 70: 99–110.

mission are critical aspects of the *strategic inputs* it requires to engage in *strategic actions* as the foundation for achieving strategic competitiveness and earning above-average returns. Therefore, as we discuss in the Strategic Focus, firms must accept the challenge of forming effective vision and mission statements.

Stakeholders

Every organization involves a system of primary stakeholder groups with whom it establishes and manages relationships.[100] **Stakeholders** are the individuals and groups who can affect the firm's vision and mission, are affected by the strategic outcomes achieved, and have enforceable claims on the firm's performance.[101] Claims on a firm's performance are enforced through the stakeholders' ability to withhold participation essential to the organization's survival, competitiveness, and profitability.[102] Stakeholders continue to support an organization when its performance meets or exceeds their expectations.[103] Also, research suggests that firms that effectively manage stakeholder relationships outperform those that do not. Stakeholder relationships can therefore be managed to be a source of competitive advantage.[104]

Although organizations have dependency relationships with their stakeholders, they are not equally dependent on all stakeholders at all times;[105] as a consequence, not every stakeholder has the same level of influence.[106] The more critical and valued a stakeholder's participation, the greater a firm's dependency on it. Greater dependence, in turn, gives the stakeholder more potential influence over a firm's commitments, decisions, and actions. Managers must find ways to either accommodate or insulate the organization from the demands of stakeholders controlling critical resources.[107]

Classifications of Stakeholders

The parties involved with a firm's operations can be separated into at least three groups.[108] As shown in Figure 1.4, these groups are the capital market stakeholders (shareholders and the major suppliers of a firm's capital), the product market stakeholders (the firm's primary customers, suppliers, host communities, and unions representing the workforce), and the organizational stakeholders (all of a firm's employees, including both nonmanagerial and managerial personnel).

Each stakeholder group expects those making strategic decisions in a firm to provide the leadership through which its valued objectives will be reached.[109] The objectives of the various stakeholder groups often differ from one another, sometimes placing those involved with a firm's strategic management process in situations where trade-offs have to be made. The most obvious stakeholders, at least in U.S. organizations, are *shareholders*—individuals and groups who have invested capital in a firm in the expectation of earning a positive return on their investments. These stakeholders' rights are grounded in laws governing private property and private enterprise.

Stakeholders are the individuals and groups who can affect the firm's vision and mission, are affected by the strategic outcomes achieved, and have enforceable claims on the firm's performance.

Figure 1.4 The Three Stakeholder Groups

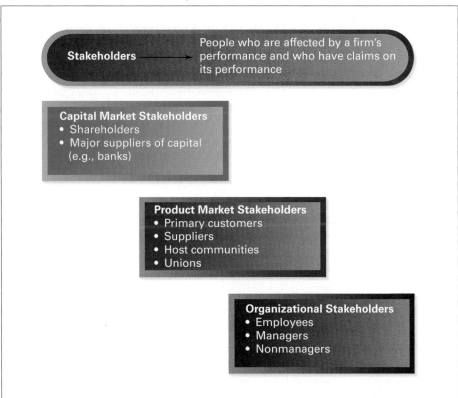

In contrast to shareholders, another group of stakeholders—the firm's customers—prefers that investors receive a minimum return on their investments. Customers could have their interests maximized when the quality and reliability of a firm's products are improved, but without a price increase. High returns to customers might come at the expense of lower returns negotiated with capital market shareholders.

Because of potential conflicts, each firm is challenged to manage its stakeholders. First, a firm must carefully identify all important stakeholders. Second, it must prioritize them, in case it cannot satisfy all of them. Power is the most critical criterion in prioritizing stakeholders. Other criteria might include the urgency of satisfying each particular stakeholder group and the degree of importance of each to the firm.[110]

When the firm earns above-average returns, the challenge of effectively managing stakeholder relationships is lessened substantially. With the capability and flexibility provided by above-average returns, a firm can more easily satisfy multiple stakeholders simultaneously. When the firm earns only average returns, it is unable to maximize the interests of all stakeholders. The objective then becomes one of at least minimally satisfying each stakeholder. Trade-off decisions are made in light of how important the support of each stakeholder group is to the firm. For example, environmental groups may be very important to firms in the energy industry but less important to professional service firms.[111] A firm earning below-average returns does not have the capacity to minimally satisfy all stakeholders. The managerial challenge in this case is to make trade-offs that minimize the amount of support lost from stakeholders. Societal values also influence the general weightings allocated among the three stakeholder groups shown in Figure 1.4. Although all three groups are served by firms in the major industrialized nations, the priorities in their service vary because of cultural differences. Next, we present additional details about each of the three major stakeholder groups.

Capital Market Stakeholders

Shareholders and lenders both expect a firm to preserve and enhance the wealth they have entrusted to it. The returns they expect are commensurate with the degree of risk accepted with those investments (i.e., lower returns are expected with low-risk investments while higher returns are expected with high-risk investments). Dissatisfied lenders may impose stricter covenants on subsequent borrowing of capital. Dissatisfied shareholders may reflect their concerns through several means, including selling their stock.

When a firm is aware of potential or actual dissatisfactions among capital market stakeholders, it may respond to their concerns. The firm's response to stakeholders who are dissatisfied is affected by the nature of its dependency relationship with them (which, as noted earlier, is also influenced by a society's values). The greater and more significant the dependency relationship is, the more direct and significant the firm's response becomes. Before liquidating, Circuit City took several actions to try to satisfy its capital market stakeholders. In part, these actions were taken because of the significance of Circuit City's dependence on its capital market stakeholders. Closing stores, changing members of the firm's top management team, and seeking potential buyers are examples of the actions Circuit City took in the final few years before liquidating.[112] However, the reality is that none of these actions resulted in outcomes that allowed Circuit City to meet the expectations of its capital market stakeholders.

Product Market Stakeholders

Some might think that product market stakeholders (customers, suppliers, host communities, and unions) share few common interests. However, all four groups can benefit as firms engage in competitive battles. For example, depending on product and industry characteristics, marketplace competition may result in lower product prices being charged to a firm's customers and higher prices being paid to its suppliers (the firm might be willing to pay higher supplier prices to ensure delivery of the types of goods and services that are linked with its competitive success).[113]

Customers, as stakeholders, demand reliable products at the lowest possible prices. Suppliers seek loyal customers who are willing to pay the highest sustainable prices for the goods and services they receive. Host communities want companies willing to be long-term employers and providers of tax revenue without placing excessive demands on public support services. Union officials are interested in secure jobs, under highly desirable working conditions, for employees they represent. Thus, product market stakeholders are generally satisfied when a firm's profit margin reflects at least a balance between the returns to capital market stakeholders (i.e., the returns lenders and shareholders will accept and still retain their interests in the firm) and the returns in which they share.

Organizational Stakeholders

Employees—the firm's organizational stakeholders—expect the firm to provide a dynamic, stimulating, and rewarding work environment. As employees, we are usually satisfied working for a company that is growing and actively developing our skills, especially those skills required to be effective team members and to meet or exceed global work standards. Workers who learn how to use new knowledge productively are critical to organizational success. In a collective sense, the education and skills of a firm's workforce are competitive weapons affecting strategy implementation and firm performance.[114] As suggested by the following statement, strategic leaders are ultimately responsible for serving the needs of organizational stakeholders on a day-to-day basis: "[T]he job of [strategic] leadership is to fully utilize human potential, to create organizations in which people can grow and learn while still achieving a common objective, to nurture the human spirit."[115] Interestingly, research suggests that outside directors are more likely to propose layoffs compared to inside strategic leaders, while such insiders are likely to use preventative cost-cutting measures and seek to protect incumbent employees.[116]

Strategic Leaders

Strategic leaders are people located in different parts of the firm using the strategic management process to help the firm reach its vision and mission. Regardless of their location in the firm, successful strategic leaders are decisive, committed to nurturing those around them[117] and are committed to helping the firm create value for all stakeholder groups.[118] In this vein, research evidence suggests that employees who perceive that their CEO emphasizes the need for the firm to operate in ways that are consistent with the values of all stakeholder groups rather than focusing only on maximizing profits for shareholders identify that CEO as a visionary leader. In turn, visionary leadership is related to extra effort by employees, with employee effort leading to enhanced firm performance. These intriguing findings suggest that decision-making values "… that are oriented toward a range of stakeholders may yield more favorable outcomes for leaders than values that focus primarily on economic-based issues."[119] These findings are consistent with the argument that "To regain society's trust … business leaders must embrace a way of looking at their role that goes beyond their responsibility to the shareholder to include a civic and personal commitment to their duty as institutional custodians."[120]

When identifying strategic leaders, most of us tend to think of chief executive officers (CEOs) and other top-level managers. Clearly, these people are strategic leaders. And, in the final analysis, CEOs are responsible for making certain their firm effectively uses the strategic management process. Indeed, the pressure on CEOs to manage strategically is stronger than ever.[121] However, many other people in today's organizations help choose a firm's strategy and then determine the actions for successfully implementing it.[122] The main reason is that the realities of twenty-first–century competition that we discussed earlier in this chapter (e.g., the global economy, globalization, rapid technological change, and the increasing importance of knowledge and people as sources of competitive advantage) are creating a need for those "closest to the action" to be the ones making decisions and determining the actions to be taken.[123] In fact, the most effective CEOs and top-level managers understand how to delegate strategic responsibilities to people throughout the firm who influence the use of organizational resources.[124]

Organizational culture also affects strategic leaders and their work. In turn, strategic leaders' decisions and actions shape a firm's culture. **Organizational culture** refers to the complex set of ideologies, symbols, and core values that are shared throughout the firm and that influence how the firm conducts business. It is the social energy that drives—or fails to drive—the organization.[125] For example, Southwest Airlines is known for having a unique and valuable culture. Its culture encourages employees to work hard but also to have fun while doing so. Moreover, its culture entails respect for others—employees and customers alike. The firm also places a premium on service, as suggested by its commitment to provide POS (Positively Outrageous Service) to each customer.

Some organizational cultures are a source of disadvantage. It is important for strategic leaders to understand, however, that whether the firm's culture is functional or dysfunctional, their work takes place within the context of that culture. The relationship between organizational culture and strategic leaders' work is reciprocal in that the culture shapes how they work while their work helps shape an ever-evolving organizational culture.

The Work of Effective Strategic Leaders

Perhaps not surprisingly, hard work, thorough analyses, a willingness to be brutally honest, a penchant for wanting the firm and its people to accomplish more, and tenacity are prerequisites to an individual's success as a strategic leader.[126] In addition, strategic leaders must be able to "think seriously and deeply … about the purposes of the organizations they head or functions they perform, about the strategies, tactics, technologies, systems,

Strategic leaders are people located in different parts of the firm using the strategic management process to help the firm reach its vision and mission.

Organizational culture refers to the complex set of ideologies, symbols, and core values that are shared throughout the firm and that influence how the firm conducts business.

IBM's organizational culture holds that there is indeed a corporate responsibility to bettering society at large.

and people necessary to attain these purposes and about the important questions that always need to be asked."[127] In addition, effective strategic leaders work to set an ethical tone in their firms. For example, Kevin Thompson, IBM's Manager of Corporate Citizenship, suggests, "We don't think you can survive without integrating business and societal values."[128]

Strategic leaders, regardless of their location in the organization, often work long hours, and their work is filled with ambiguous decision situations.[129] However, the opportunities afforded by this work are appealing and offer exciting chances to dream and to act.[130] The following words, given as advice to the late Time Warner chair and co-CEO Steven J. Ross by his father, describe the opportunities in a strategic leader's work:

There are three categories of people—the person who goes into the office, puts his feet up on his desk, and dreams for 12 hours; the person who arrives at 5 A.M. and works for 16 hours, never once stopping to dream; and the person who puts his feet up, dreams for one hour, then does something about those dreams.[131]

The organizational term used for a dream that challenges and energizes a company is vision. Strategic leaders have opportunities to dream and to act, and the most effective ones provide a vision as the foundation for the firm's mission and subsequent choice and use of one or more strategies.

Predicting Outcomes of Strategic Decisions: Profit Pools

Strategic leaders attempt to predict the outcomes of their decisions before taking efforts to implement them, which is difficult to do. Many decisions that are a part of the strategic management process are concerned with an uncertain future and the firm's place in that future.[132]

Mapping an industry's profit pool is something strategic leaders can do to anticipate the possible outcomes of different decisions and to focus on growth in profits rather than strictly growth in revenues. A **profit pool** entails the total profits earned in an industry at all points along the value chain.[133] (We explain the value chain in Chapter 3 and discuss it further in Chapter 4.) Analyzing the profit pool in the industry may help a firm see something others are unable to see by helping it understand the primary sources of profits in an industry. There are four steps to identifying profit pools: (1) define the pool's boundaries, (2) estimate the pool's overall size, (3) estimate the size of the value-chain activity in the pool, and (4) reconcile the calculations.[134]

Let's think about how McDonald's might map the quick-service restaurant industry's profit pools. First, McDonald's would need to define the industry's boundaries and, second, estimate its size. As discussed in the Opening Case, these boundaries would include markets across the globe. As noted, the size of the U.S. market is not currently expanding. The net result of this is that McDonald's is trying to increase its market share by taking market share away from competitors such as Burger King and Wendy's. Growth is more likely in international markets, which is why McDonald's is establishing more units internationally than it is domestically. Armed with information about its industry, McDonald's would then be prepared to estimate the amount of profit potential in each part of the value chain (step 3). In the quick-service restaurant industry, marketing campaigns and customer service are likely more important sources of potential profits than are inbound logistics' activities (see Chapter 3). With an understanding of where

A **profit pool** entails the total profits earned in an industry at all points along the value chain.

the greatest amount of profits are likely to be earned, McDonald's would then be ready to select the strategy to use to be successful where the largest profit pools are located in the value chain.[135] As this brief discussion shows, profit pools are a tool the firm's strategic leaders can use to help recognize the actions to take to increase the likelihood of increasing profits.

The Strategic Management Process

As suggested by Figure 1.1, the strategic management process is a rational approach firms use to achieve strategic competitiveness and earn above-average returns. Figure 1.1 also features the topics we examine in this book to present the strategic management process to you.

This book is divided into three parts. In Part 1, we describe what firms do to analyze their external environment (Chapter 2) and internal organization (Chapter 3). These analyses are completed to identify marketplace opportunities and threats in the external environment (Chapter 2) and to decide how to use the resources, capabilities, core competencies, and competitive advantages in the firm's internal organization to pursue opportunities and overcome threats (Chapter 3). With knowledge about its external environment and internal organization, the firm forms its vision and mission.

The firm's strategic inputs (see Figure 1.1) provide the foundation for choosing one or more strategies and deciding how to implement them. As suggested in Figure 1.1 by the horizontal arrow linking the two types of strategic actions, formulation and implementation must be simultaneously integrated if the firm is to successfully use the strategic management process. Integration happens as decision makers think about implementation issues when choosing strategies and as they think about possible changes to the firm's strategies while implementing a currently chosen strategy.

In Part 2 of this book, we discuss the different strategies firms may choose to use. First, we examine business-level strategies (Chapter 4). A business-level strategy describes the actions a firm decides to take in order to exploit its competitive advantage over rivals. A company competing in a single product market (e.g., a locally owned grocery store operating in only one location) has but one business-level strategy while a diversified firm competing in multiple product markets (e.g., General Electric) forms a business-level strategy for each of its businesses. In Chapter 5, we describe the actions and reactions that occur among firms while using their strategies in marketplace competitions. As we will see, competitors respond to and try to anticipate each other's actions. The dynamics of competition affect the strategies firms choose to use as well as how they try to implement the chosen strategies.[136]

For the diversified firm, corporate-level strategy (Chapter 6) is concerned with determining the businesses in which the company intends to compete as well as how to manage its different businesses. Other topics vital to strategy formulation, particularly in the diversified corporation, include acquiring other companies and, as appropriate, restructuring the firm's portfolio of businesses (Chapter 7) and selecting an international strategy (Chapter 8). With cooperative strategies (Chapter 9), firms form a partnership to share their resources and capabilities in order to develop a competitive advantage. Cooperative strategies are becoming increasingly important as firms seek ways to compete in the global economy's array of different markets.[137]

To examine actions taken to implement strategies, we consider several topics in Part 3 of the book. First, we examine the different mechanisms used to govern firms (Chapter 10). With demands for improved corporate governance being voiced today by many stakeholders, organizations are challenged to learn how to simultaneously satisfy their stakeholders' different interests.[138] Finally, the organizational structure and actions needed to control a firm's operations (Chapter 11), the patterns of strategic leadership appropriate for today's firms and competitive environments (Chapter 12), and strategic entrepreneurship (Chapter 13) as a path to continuous innovation are addressed.

Before closing this introductory chapter, it is important to emphasize that primarily because they are related to how a firm interacts with its stakeholders, almost all strategic management process decisions have ethical dimensions.[139] Organizational ethics are revealed by an organization's culture; that is to say, a firm's decisions are a product of the core values that are shared by most or all of a company's managers and employees. Especially in the turbulent and often ambiguous competitive landscape of the twenty-first century, those making decisions that are part of the strategic management process are challenged to recognize that their decisions affect capital market, product market, and organizational stakeholders differently and to evaluate the ethical implications of their decisions on a daily basis.[140] Decision makers failing to recognize these realities accept the risk of putting their firm at a competitive disadvantage when it comes to consistently engaging in ethical business practices.[141]

As you will discover, the strategic management process examined in this book calls for disciplined approaches to serve as the foundation for developing a competitive advantage. These approaches provide the pathway through which firms will be able to achieve strategic competitiveness and earn above-average returns. Mastery of this strategic management process will effectively serve you, our readers, and the organizations for which you will choose to work.

SUMMARY

- Firms use the strategic management process to achieve strategic competitiveness and earn above-average returns. Strategic competitiveness is achieved when a firm has developed and learned how to implement a value-creating strategy. Above-average returns (in excess of what investors expect to earn from other investments with similar levels of risk) provide the foundation a firm needs to simultaneously satisfy all of its stakeholders.

- The fundamental nature of competition is different in the current competitive landscape. As a result, those making strategic decisions must adopt a different mind-set, one that allows them to learn how to compete in highly turbulent and chaotic environments that are producing disorder and a great deal of uncertainty. The globalization of industries and their markets and rapid and significant technological changes are the two primary factors contributing to the turbulence of the competitive landscape.

- Firms use two major models to help them form their vision and mission and then choose one or more strategies to use in pursuit of strategic competitiveness and above-average returns. The core assumption of the I/O model is that the firm's external environment has more of an influence on the choice of strategies than do the firm's internal resources, capabilities, and core competencies. Thus, the I/O model is used to understand the effects an industry's characteristics can have on a firm when deciding what strategy or strategies to use to compete against rivals. The logic supporting the I/O model suggests that above-average returns are

earned when the firm locates an attractive industry or part of an industry and successfully implements the strategy dictated by that industry's characteristics. The core assumption of the resource-based model is that the firm's unique resources, capabilities, and core competencies have more of an influence on selecting and using strategies than does the firm's external environment. Above-average returns are earned when the firm uses its valuable, rare, costly-to-imitate, and nonsubstitutable resources and capabilities to compete against its rivals in one or more industries. Evidence indicates that both models yield insights that are linked to successfully selecting and using strategies. Thus, firms want to use their unique resources, capabilities, and core competencies as the foundation for one or more strategies that will allow them to compete in industries they understand.

- Vision and mission are formed in light of the information and insights gained from studying a firm's internal and external environments. Vision is a picture of what the firm wants to be and, in broad terms, what it wants to ultimately achieve. Flowing from the vision, the mission specifies the business or businesses in which the firm intends to compete and the customers it intends to serve. Vision and mission provide direction to the firm and signal important descriptive information to stakeholders.

- Stakeholders are those who can affect, and are affected by, a firm's strategic outcomes. Because a firm is dependent on the continuing support of stakeholders (shareholders, customers, suppliers, employees, host communities, etc.), they have enforceable claims on the company's performance. When earning above-average returns, a firm has the resources it needs to at minimum simultaneously satisfy the interests of all stakeholders. However, when earning only average returns, the firm must carefully manage its stakeholders in order to retain their support. A firm earning below-average returns must minimize the amount of support it loses from unsatisfied stakeholders.

- Strategic leaders are people located in different parts of the firm using the strategic management process to help the firm reach its vision and mission. In the final analysis, though, CEOs are responsible for making certain that their firms properly use the strategic management process. Today, the effectiveness of the strategic management process is increased when it is grounded in ethical intentions and behaviors. The strategic leader's work demands decision trade-offs, often among attractive alternatives. It is important for all strategic leaders and especially the CEO and other members of the top-management team to work hard, conduct thorough analyses of situations facing the firm, be brutally and consistently honest, and ask the right questions of the right people at the right time.

- Strategic leaders predict the potential outcomes of their strategic decisions. To do this, they must first calculate profit pools in their industry that are linked to value chain activities. Predicting the potential outcomes of their strategic decisions reduces the likelihood of the firm formulating and implementing ineffective strategies.

REVIEW QUESTIONS

1. What are strategic competitiveness, strategy, competitive advantage, above-average returns, and the strategic management process?

2. What are the characteristics of the current competitive landscape? What two factors are the primary drivers of this landscape?

3. According to the I/O model, what should a firm do to earn above-average returns?

4. What does the resource-based model suggest a firm should do to earn above-average returns?

5. What are vision and mission? What is their value for the strategic management process?

6. What are stakeholders? How do the three primary stakeholder groups influence organizations?

7. How would you describe the work of strategic leaders?

8. What are the elements of the strategic management process? How are they interrelated?

EXPERIENTIAL EXERCISES

EXERCISE 1: BUSINESS AND BLOGS

One element of industry structure analysis is the leverage that buyers can exert on firms. Is technology changing the balance of power between customers and companies? If so, how should business respond?

Blogs offer a mechanism for consumers to share their experiences—good or bad—regarding different companies. Bloggers first emerged in the late 1990s, and today the Technorati search engine currently monitors roughly 100 million blogs. With the wealth of this "citizen media" available, what are the implications for consumer power? One of the most famous cases of a blogger drawing attention to a company was Jeff Jarvis of the Web site http://www.buzzmachine.com. Jarvis, who writes on media topics, was having problems with his Dell computer and shared his experiences on the Web. Literally thousands of other people recounted similar experiences, and the phenomena became known as "Dell hell." Eventually, Dell created its own corporate blog in an effort to deflect this wave of consumer criticism. What are the implications of the rapid growth in blogs? Work in a group on the following exercise.

Part One

Visit a corporate blog. Only a small percentage of large firms maintain a blog presence on the Internet. *Hint:* Multiple wikis online provide lists of such companies. A Web search using the term *Fortune 500 blogs* will turn up several options. Review the content of the firm's blog. Was it updated regularly or not? Multiple contributors or just one? What was the writing style?

Did it read like a marketing brochure or something more informal? Did the blog allow viewer comments or post replies to consumer questions?

Part Two

Based on the information you collected in the blog review, answer the following questions:

- Have you ever used blogs to help make decisions about something that you are considering purchasing? If so, how did the blog material affect your decision? What factors would make you more (or less) likely to rely on a blog in making your decision?
- How did the content of corporate blogs affect your perception of that company and its good and services? Did it make you more or less likely to view the company favorably, or have no effect at all?
- Why do so few large companies maintain blogs?

EXERCISE 2: CREATING A SHARED VISION

Drawing on an analysis of internal and external conditions, firms create a mission and vision as a cornerstone of their strategy. This exercise examines some of the challenges associated with creating a firm's shared direction.

Part One

The instructor will break the class into a set of small teams. Half of the teams will be given an "A" designation, and the other half assigned as "B." Each individual team will need to plan a time outside class to complete Part 2; the exercise should take about half an hour.

Teams given the A designation will meet in a face-to-face setting. Each team member will need paper and a pen or pen-

cil. Your meeting location should be free from distraction. The location should have enough space so that no person can see another's notepad.

Teams given the B designation will meet electronically. You may choose to meet through text messaging or IM. Be sure to confirm everyone's contact information and meeting time beforehand.

Part Two

Each team member prepares a drawing of a real structure. It can be a famous building, a monument, museum, or even your dorm. Do not tell other team members what you drew.

Randomly select one team member. The goal is for everyone else to prepare a drawing as similar to the selected team member as possible. That person is not allowed to show his or her drawing to the rest of the team. The rest of the group can ask questions about the drawing, but only ones that can be answered "yes" or "no."

After 10 minutes, have everyone compare their drawings. If you are meeting electronically, describe your drawings, and save them for the next time your team meets face to face.

Next, select a second team member and repeat this process again.

Part Three

In class, discuss the following questions:

- How easy (or hard) was it for you to figure out the "vision" of your team members?
- Did you learn anything in the first iteration that made the second drawing more successful?
- What similarities might you find between this exercise and the challenge of sharing a vision among company employees?
- How did the communication structure affect your process and outcomes?

VIDEO CASE

THE VALUE OF SETTING A LONG-TERM STRATEGY

Anders Dahlvig/Group President and CEO/IKEA Services

IKEA is a brand famous for its focus on innovative solutions to the business of selling high-quality, low-price home furnishings. Anders Dahlvig, IKEA's Group President and CEO, argues that long-term strategic planning is a key to their success. For the financial year ending August 2008, IKEA posted a 7 percent increase in sales over the prior annual period, recording €21.1 billion in revenue. The firm has more than 128,000 employees and operates in 24 countries.

Be prepared to discuss the following concepts and questions in class:

Concepts

- Vision and mission
- Long-term strategy
- Stakeholders
- Global economy
- Strategic leaders
- Organizational culture

Questions

1. What is this firm's vision?
2. What is the firm's mission or business idea?
3. Describe its competitive advantage. Why do you think competitors have found this concept difficult to imitate?
4. What is in the news about this company?
5. Describe Anders Dahlvig as a strategic leader.
6. Do you believe Anders Dahlvig is constrained in his strategic decision making because of the unique organizational culture at IKEA, or is he free to create and implement strategic decisions as he sees best for the firm?

NOTES

1. J. McGregor, 2009, Smart management for tough times, *BusinessWeek*, http://www.businessweek.com, March 12.

2. McDonald's Corp., 2009, Standard & Poor's Stock Reports, http://www.standardandpoors.com, April 23.

3. The secret sauce at In-N-Out Burger, 2009, *BusinessWeek*, April 20, 68–69.

4. D. Kiley, 2009, Ford heats out on a road of its own, *BusinessWeek*, January 19, 47–49.

5. H. R. Greve, 2009, Bigger and safer: The diffusion of competitive advantage, *Strategic Management Journal*, 30: 1–23; D. G. Sirmon, M. A. Hitt, & R. D. Ireland, 2007, Managing firm resources in dynamic environments to create value: Looking inside the black box, *Academy of Management Review*, 32: 273–292.

6. R. D. Ireland & J. W. Webb, 2009, Crossing the great divide of strategic entrepreneurship: Transitioning between exploration and exploitation, *Business Horizons*, in press; D. Lei & J. W. Slocum, 2005, Strategic and organizational requirements for competitive advantage, *Academy of Management Executive*, 19(1): 31–45.

7. J. A. Lamberg, H. Tikkanen, T. Nokelainen, & H. Suur-Inkeroinen, 2009, Competitive dynamics, strategic consistency, and organizational survival, *Strategic Management Journal*, 30: 45–60; G. Pacheco-de-Almeida & P. Zemsky, 2007, The timing of resource development and sustainable competitive advantage, *Management Science*, 53: 651–666.

8. K. D. Miller, 2007, Risk and rationality in entrepreneurial processes, *Strategic Entrepreneurship Journal*, 1: 57–74.

9. R. M. Stulz, 2009, 6 ways companies mismanage risk, *Harvard Business Review*, 87(3): 86–94.

10. P. Steffens, P. Davidsson, & J. Fitzsimmons, 2009, Performance configurations over time: Implications for growth- and profit-oriented strategies, *Entrepreneurship Theory and Practice*, 33: 125–148.

11. J. C. Short, A. McKelvie, D. J. Ketchen, Jr., & G. N. Chandler, 2009, Firm and industry effects on firm performance: A generalization and extension for new ventures, *Strategic Entrepreneurship Journal*, 3: 47–65; T. Bates, 2005, Analysis of young, small firms that have closed: Delineating successful from unsuccessful closures, *Journal of Business Venturing*, 20: 343–358.

12. K. D. Miller, F. Fabian, & S.-J. Lin, 2009, Strategies for online communities, *Strategic Management Journal*, 30: 305–322; A. M. McGahan & M. E. Porter, 2003, The emergence and sustainability of abnormal profits, *Strategic Organization*, 1: 79–108.

13. J. Kell, 2009, Circuit City to liquidate, meaning 30,000 job losses, *Wall Street Journal*, http://www.wsj.com, January 16.

14. P. B. Kavilanz, 2009, Circuit City to shut down, *CNN Money*, http://www.cnn.money.com, January 16.

15. Ibid.

16. D. Marginson & L. McAulay, 2008, Exploring the debate on short-termism: A theoretical and empirical analysis, *Strategic Management Journal*, 29: 273–292.

17. M. Bustillo, 2009, Best Buy confronts newer nemesis, *Wall Street Journal*, http://www.wsj.com, March 16.

18. M. Bustillo & C. Lawton, 2009, Best Buy expands private-label brands, *Wall Street Journal*, http://www.wsj.com, April 27.

19. 2009, Best Buy vs. Wal-Mart: Is there room for both, and others? *Knowledge@Wharton*, http://knowledge.wharton.upenn.com, April 1.

20. T. R. Crook, D. J. Ketchen, Jr., J. G. Combs, & S. Y. Todd, 2008, Strategic resources and performance: A meta-analysis, *Strategic Management Journal*, 29: 1141–1154; J. T. Mahoney & A. M. McGahan, 2007, The field of strategic management within the evolving science of strategic organization, *Strategic Organization*, 5: 79–99.

21. J. Barthelemy, 2008, Opportunism, knowledge, and the performance of franchise chains, *Strategic Management Journal*, 29: 1451–1463.

22. J. Li, 2008, Asymmetric interactions between foreign and domestic banks: Effects on market entry, *Strategic Management Journal*, 29: 873–893.

23. P. Ghemawat & T. Hout, 2008, Tomorrow's global giants, *Harvard Business Review*, 86(11): 80–88.

24. M. A. Delmas & M. W. Toffel, 2008, Organizational responses to environmental demands: Opening the black box, *Strategic Management Journal*, 29: 1027–1055; A. M. McGahan & M. E. Porter, 1997, How much does industry matter, really? *Strategic Management Journal*, 18 (Special Issue): 15–30.

25. T. R. Holcomb, R. M. Holmes, Jr., & B. L. Connelly, 2009, Making the most of what you have: Managerial ability as a source of resource value creation, *Strategic Management Journal*, 30: 457–485; J. Acedo, C. Barroso, & J. L. Galan, 2006, The resource-based theory: Dissemination and main trends, *Strategic Management Journal*, 27: 621–636.

26. E. Thornton, 2009, The new rules, *BusinessWeek*, January 19, 30–34; T. Friedman, 2005, *The World Is Flat: A Brief History of the 21s Century*, New York: Farrar, Strauss and Giroux.

27. D. Searcey, 2006, Beyond cable. Beyond DSL. *Wall Street Journal*, July 24, R9.

28. 2009, NBC Universal company overview, http://www.nbcuniversal.com, April 23.

29. P. Taylor, 2007, Tools to bridge the divide: Raketu aims to outperform Skype in Internet telephony while throwing in a range of information and entertainment services, *Financial Times*, May 11, 16.

30. 2009, Be entertained, http://www.raketu.com, April 22.

31. 2009, Social networking websites review, http://www.social-networking-websites-review.toptenreivews.com, April 22.

32. D. F. Kuratko & D. B. Audretsch, 2009, Strategic entrepreneurship: Exploring different perspectives of an emerging concept, *Entrepreneurship Theory and Practice*, 33: 1–17.

33. J. Hagel, III, J. S. Brown, & L. Davison, 2008, Shaping strategy in a world of constant disruption, *Harvard Business Review*, 86(10): 81–89; G. Probst & S. Raisch, 2005, Organizational crisis: The logic of failure, *Academy of Management Executive*, 19(1): 90–105.

34. J. W. Selsky, J. Goes, & O. N. Babüroglu, 2007, Contrasting perspectives of strategy making: Applications in "Hyper" environments, *Organization Studies*, 28(1): 71–94; G. McNamara, P. M. Vaaler, & C. Devers, 2003, Same as it ever was: The search for evidence of increasing hypercompetition, *Strategic Management Journal*, 24: 261–278.

35. A. V. Izosimov, 2008, Managing hypergrowth, *Harvard Business Review*, 86(4): 121–127.

36. R. A. D'Aveni, 1995, Coping with hypercompetition: Utilizing the new 7S's framework, *Academy of Management Executive*, 9(3): 46.

37. D. J. Bryce & J. H. Dyer, 2007, Strategies to crack well-guarded markets, *Harvard Business Review* 85(5): 84–92; R. A. D'Aveni, 2004, Corporate spheres of influence, *MIT Sloan Management Review*, 45(4): 38–46; W. J. Ferrier, 2001, Navigating the competitive landscape: The drivers and consequences of competitive aggressiveness, *Academy of Management Journal*, 44: 858–877.

38. S. H. Lee & M. Makhija, 2009, Flexibility in internationalization: Is it valuable during an economic crisis? *Strategic Management Journal*, 30: 537–555; S. J. Chang & S. Park, 2005, Types of firms generating network externalities and

MNCs' co-location decisions, *Strategic Management Journal*, 26: 595–615.

39. S. E. Feinberg & A. K. Gupta, 2009, MNC subsidiaries and country risk: Internalization as a safeguard against weak external institutions, *Academy of Management Journal*, 52: 381–399; R. Belderbos & L. Sleuwaegen, 2005, Competitive drivers and international plant configuration strategies: A product-level test, *Strategic Management Journal*, 26: 577–593.

40. 2005, Organisation for Economic Cooperation and Development, OCED Statistical Profile of the United States—2005, http://www.oced.org; S. Koudsi & L. A. Costa, 1998, America vs. the new Europe: By the numbers, *Fortune*, December 21, 149–156.

41. Y. Luo, 2007, From foreign investors to strategic insiders: Shifting parameters, prescriptions and paradigms for MNCs in China, *Journal of World Business*, 42(1): 14–34.

42. M. A. Hitt & X. He, 2008, Firm strategies in a changing global competitive landscape, *Business Horizons*, 51: 363–369; A. Ratanpal, 2008, Indian economy and Indian private equity, *Thunderbird International Business Review*, 50: 353–358.

43. Y. Gorodnichenko, J. Svejnar, & K. Terrell, 2008, Globalization and innovation in emerging markets, NBER Working Paper No. w14481. Available at SSRN: http://ssrn.com/abstract=1301929.

44. K. Kranhold, 2005, GE pins hopes on emerging markets, *Wall Street Journal*, http://www.wsj.com, March 2.

45. C. H. Oh, 2009, The international scale and scope of European multinationals, *European Management Journal*, in press; G. D. Bruton, G. G. Dess & J. J. Janney, 2007, Knowledge management in technology-focused firms in emerging economies: Caveats on capabilities, networks, and real options, *Asia Pacific Journal of Management*, 24(2): 115–130;

46. A. Ciarione, P. Piselli, & G. Trebeschi, 2009, Emerging markets' spreads and global financial conditions, *Journal of International Financial Markets, Institutions and Money*, 19: 222–239.

47. 2009, Wal-Mart Stores Inc., *Standard & Poor's Stock Reports*, http://www.standardandpoors.com, April 18.

48. M. A. Prospero, 2005, The march of war, *Fast Company*, May, 14.

49. B. Elango, 2009, Minimizing effects of "liability of foreignness": Response strategies of foreign firms in the United States, *Journal of World Business*, 44: 51–62.

50. D. J. McCarthy & S. M. Puffer, 2008, Interpreting the ethicality of corporate governance decisions in Russia: Utilizing integrative social contracts theory to evaluate the relevance of agency theory norms, *Academy of Management Review*, 33: 11–31.

51. M. A. Hitt, R. E. Hoskisson, & H. Kim, 1997, International diversification: Effects on innovation and firm performance in product-diversified firms, *Academy of Management Journal*, 40: 767–798.

52. R. D. Ireland & J. W. Webb, 2007, Strategic entrepreneurship: Creating competitive advantage through streams of innovation, *Business Horizons*, 50(1): 49–59; G. Hamel, 2001, Revolution vs. evolution: You need both, *Harvard Business Review*, 79(5): 150–156.

53. K. H. Hammonds, 2001, What is the state of the new economy? *Fast Company*, September, 101–104.

54. B. Peters, 2009, Persistence of innovation: Stylised facts and panel data evidence, *The Journal of Technology Transfer*, 34: 226–243.

55. J. L. Boyd & R. K. F. Bresser, 2008, Performance implications of delayed competitive responses: Evidence from the U.S. retail industry, *Strategic Management Journal*, 29: 1077–1096; T. Talaulicar, J. Grundei, & A. V. Werder, 2005, Strategic decision making in startups: The effect of top management team organization and processes on speed and comprehensiveness, *Journal of Business Venturing*, 20: 519–541.

56. J. Kao, 2009, Tapping the world's innovation hot spots, *Harvard Business Review*, 87(3): 109–117.

57. C. W. L. Hill, 1997, Establishing a standard: Competitive strategy and technological standards in winner-take-all industries, *Academy of Management Executive*, 11(2): 7–25.

58. J. L. Funk, 2008, Components, systems and technological discontinuities: Lessons from the IT sector, *Long Range Planning*, 41: 555–573; C. M. Christensen, 1997, *The Innovator's Dilemma*, Boston: Harvard Business School Press.

59. C. M. Christensen, 2006, The ongoing process of building a theory of disruption, *Journal of Product Innovation Management*, 23(1): 39–55; R. Adner, 2002, When are technologies disruptive? A demand-based view of the emergence of competition, *Strategic Management Journal*, 23: 667–688; G. Ahuja & C. M. Lampert, 2001, Entrepreneurship in the large corporation: A longitudinal study of how established firms create breakthrough inventions, *Strategic Management Journal*, 22 (Special Issue): 521–543.

60. C. L. Nichols-Nixon & C. Y. Woo, 2003, Technology sourcing and output of established firms in a regime of encompassing technological change, *Strategic Management Journal*, 24: 651–666; C. W. L. Hill & F. T. Rothaermel, 2003, The performance of incumbent firms in the face of radical technological innovation, *Academy of Management Review*, 28: 257–274.

61. K. Celuch, G. B. Murphy, & S. K. Callaway, 2007, More bang for your buck: Small firms and the importance of aligned information technology capabilities and strategic flexibility, *Journal of High Technology Management Research*, 17: 187–197.

62. V. Godinez, 2009, Broadband ISPs test download caps, face resistance from more data-heavy users, *The Dallas Morning News*, http://www.dallasnews.com, April 26.

63. C. F. Fey & P. Furu, 2008, Top management incentive compensation and knowledge sharing in multinational corporations, *Strategic Management Journal*, 29: 1301–1323.

64. M. Gottfredson, R. Puryear, & S. Phillips, 2005, Strategic sourcing: From periphery to the core, *Harvard Business Review*, 83(2): 132–139.

65. L. F. Mesquita, J. Anand, & T. H. Brush 2008, Comparing the resource-based and relational views: Knowledge transfer and spillover in vertical alliances, *Strategic Management Journal*, 29: 913–941; K. G. Smith, C. J. Collins, & K. D. Clark, 2005, Existing knowledge, knowledge creation capability, and the rate of new product introduction in high-technology firms, *Academy of Management Journal*, 48: 346–357.

66. A. Capaldo, 2007, Network structure and innovation: The leveraging of a dual network as a distinctive relational capability, *Strategic Management Journal*, 28: 585–608; S. K. Ethirau, P. Kale, M. S. Krishnan, & J. V. Singh, 2005, Where do capabilities come from and how do they matter? *Strategic Management Journal*, 26: 25–45.

67. Sirmon, Hitt, & Ireland, Managing firm resources.

68. A. C. Inkpen, 2008, Knowledge transfer and international joint ventures: The case of NUMMI and General Motors, *Strategic Management Journal*, 29: 447–453; P. L. Robertson & P. R. Patel, 2007, New wine in old bottles: Technological diffusion in developed economies, *Research Policy*, 36(5): 708–721; K. Asakawa & M. Lehrer, 2003, Managing local knowledge assets globally: The role of regional innovation relays, *Journal of World Business*, 38: 31–42.

69. R. E. Hoskisson, M. A. Hitt, & R. D. Ireland, 2008, *Competing for Advantage*, 2nd ed., Cincinnati: Thomson South-Western; K. R. Harrigan, 2001, Strategic flexibility in old and new economies, in M. A. Hitt, R. E. Freeman, & J. S. Harrison (eds.), *Handbook of Strategic Management*, Oxford, UK: Blackwell Publishers, 97–123.

70. S. Nadkarni & V. K. Narayanan, 2007, Strategic schemas, strategic flexibility, and firm performance: The moderating role of industry clockspeed, *Strategic Management Journal*, 28: 243–270.

71. L. Gratton & S. Ghoshal, 2005, Beyond best practice, *MIT Sloan Management Review*, 46(3): 49–55.

72. A. C. Edmondson, 2008, The competitive imperative of learning, *Harvard Business Review*, 86(7/8): 60–67; K. Shimizu & M. A. Hitt, 2004, Strategic flexibility:

Organizational preparedness to reverse ineffective strategic decisions, *Academy of Management Executive*, 18(4): 44–59; K. Uhlenbruck, K. E. Meyer, & M. A. Hitt, 2003, Organizational transformation in transition economies: Resource-based and organizational learning perspectives, *Journal of Management Studies*, 40: 257–282.

73. R. E. Hoskisson, M. A. Hitt, W. P. Wan, & D. Yiu, 1999, Swings of a pendulum: Theory and research in strategic management, *Journal of Management*, 25: 417–456.

74. E. H. Bowman & C. E. Helfat, 2001, Does corporate strategy matter? *Strategic Management Journal*, 22: 1–23.

75. M. A. Delmas & M. W. Toffel, 2008, Organizational responses to environmental demands: Opening the black box, *Strategic Management Journal*, 29: 1027–1055; J. Shamsie, 2003, The context of dominance: An industry-driven framework for exploiting reputation, *Strategic Management Journal*, 24: 199–215.

76. J. Galbreath & P. Galvin, 2008, Firm factors, industry structure and performance variation: New empirical evidence to a classic debate, *Journal of Business Research*, 61: 109–117.

77. M. B. Lieberman & S. Asaba, 2006, Why do firms imitate each other? *Academy of Management Journal*, 31: 366–385; L. F. Feldman, C. G. Brush, & T. Manolova, 2005, Co-alignment in the resource-performance relationship: Strategy as mediator, *Journal of Business Venturing*, 20: 359–383.

78. M. E. Porter, 1985, *Competitive Advantage*, New York: Free Press; M. E. Porter, 1980, *Competitive Strategy*, New York: Free Press.

79. J. C. Short, D. J. Ketchen, Jr., T. B. Palmer, & G. T. M. Hult, 2007, Firm, strategic group, and industry influences on performance, *Strategic Management Journal*, 28: 147–167.

80. P. Ziobro, 2009, McDonald's pounds out good quarter, *Wall Street Journal*, http://www.wsj.com, April 23.

81. A. M. McGahan, 1999, Competition, strategy and business performance, *California Management Review*, 41(3): 74–101; McGahan & Porter, How much does industry matter, really?

82. S. L. Newbert, 2008, Value, rareness, competitive advantage, and performance: A conceptual-level empirical investigation of the resource-based view of the firm, *Strategic Management Journal*, 29: 745–768; F. J. Acedo, C. Barroso, & J. L. Galan, 2006, The resource-based theory: Dissemination and main trends, *Strategic Management Journal*, 27: 621–636.

83. E. Verwall, H. Commandeur, & W. Verbeke, 2009, Value creation and value claiming in strategic outsourcing decisions: A resource contingency perspective, *Journal of Management*, 35: 420–444; B.-S. Teng & J. L. Cummings, 2002, Trade-offs in managing resources and capabilities, *Academy of Management Executive*, 16(2): 81–91.

84. S. Kaplan, 2008, Cognition, capabilities, and incentives: Assessing firm response to the fiber-optic revolution, *Academy of Management Journal*, 51: 672–694; S. A. Zahra, H. Sapienza, & P. Davidsson, 2006, Entrepreneurship and dynamic capabilities: A review, model and research agenda, *Journal of Management Studies*, 43(4): 927–955; M. Blyler & R. W. Coff, 2003, Dynamic capabilities, social capital, and rent appropriation: Ties that split pies, *Strategic Management Journal*, 24: 677–686.

85. S. L. Newbert, 2007, Empirical research on the resource-based view of the firm: An assessment and suggestions for future research, *Strategic Management Journal*, 28: 121–146; P. Bansal, 2005, Evolving sustainability: A longitudinal study of corporate sustainable development, *Strategic Management Journal*, 26: 197–218.

86. P. J. H. Schoemaker & R. Amit, 1994, Investment in strategic assets: Industry and firm-level perspectives, in P. Shrivastava, A. Huff, & J. Dutton (eds.), *Advances in Strategic Management*, Greenwich, CT: JAI Press, 9.

87. A. A. Lado, N. G. Boyd, P. Wright, & M. Kroll, 2006, Paradox and theorizing within the resource-based view, *Academy of Management Review*, 31: 115–131; D. M. DeCarolis, 2003, Competencies and imitability in the pharmaceutical industry: An analysis of their relationship with firm performance, *Journal of Management*, 29: 27–50.

88. C. Zott, 2003, Dynamic capabilities and the emergence of intraindustry differential firm performance: Insights from a simulation study, *Strategic Management Journal*, 24: 97–125.

89. E. Levitas & H. A. Ndofor, 2006, What to do with the resource-based view: A few suggestions for what ails the RBV that supporters and opponents might accept, *Journal of Management Inquiry*, 15(2): 135–144; G. Hawawini, V. Subramanian, & P. Verdin, 2003, Is performance driven by industry- or firm-specific factors? A new look at the evidence, *Strategic Management Journal*, 24: 1–16.

90. M. Makhija, 2003, Comparing the resource-based and market-based views of the firm: Empirical evidence from Czech privatization, *Strategic Management Journal*, 24: 433–451; T. J. Douglas & J. A. Ryman, 2003, Understanding competitive advantage in the general hospital industry: Evaluating strategic competencies, *Strategic Management Journal*, 24: 333–347.

91. R. D. Ireland, R. E. Hoskisson, & M. A. Hitt. 2009, *Understanding Business Strategy*, 2nd Edition, Cincinnati: South-Western Cengage Learning, 6.

92. S. Ward, 2009, Vision statement, *About.com*, http://www.sbinfocanada .about.com, April 22; R. Zolli, 2006, Recognizing tomorrow's hot ideas today, *BusinessWeek*, September 25: 12.

93. 2005, The CEO's secret handbook, *Business 2.0*, July, 69–76.

94. S. Kemp & L. Dwyer, 2003, Mission statements of international airlines: A content analysis, *Tourism Management*, 24: 635–653; R. D. Ireland & M. A. Hitt, 1992, Mission statements: Importance, challenge, and recommendations for development, *Business Horizons*, 35(3): 34–42.

95. J. I. Siciliano, 2008, A comparison of CEO and director perceptions of board involvement in strategy, *Nonprofit and Voluntary Sector Quarterly*, 27: 152–162; W. J. Duncan, 1999, *Management: Ideas and Actions*, New York: Oxford University Press, 122–125.

96. J. H. Davis, J. A. Ruhe, M. Lee, & U. Rajadhyaksha, 2007, Mission possible: Do school mission statements work? *Journal of Business Ethics*, 70: 99–110.

97. L. W. Fry & J. W. Slocum, Jr., 2008, Maximizing the triple bottom line through spiritual leadership, *Organizational Dynamics*, 37: 86–96; A. J. Ward, M. J. Lankau, A. C. Amason, J. A. Sonnenfeld, & B. A. Agle, 2007, Improving the performance of top management teams, *MIT Sloan Management Review*, 48(3): 85–90.

98. M. Rahman, 2009, Why strategic vision statements *won't* measure up, *Strategic Direction*, 25: 3–4.

99. R. Kaufman, 2006, *Change, Choices, and Consequences: A Guide to Mega Thinking and Planning*, Amherst, MA: HRD Press; J. Humphreys, 2004, The vision thing, *MIT Sloan Management Review*, 45(4): 96.

100. K. Basu & G. Palazzo, 2008, Corporate social responsibility: A process model of sensemaking, *Academy of Management Review*, 33: 122–136.

101. D. A. Bosse, R. A. Phillips, & J. S. Harrison, 2009, Stakeholders, reciprocity, and firm performance, *Strategic Management Journal*, 30: 447–456; J. P. Walsh & W. R. Nord, 2005, Taking stock of stakeholder management, *Academy of Management Review*, 30: 426–438; T. M. Jones & A. C. Wicks, 1999, Convergent stakeholder theory, *Academy of Management Review*, 24: 206–221.

102. G. Donaldson & J. W. Lorsch, 1983, *Decision Making at the Top: The Shaping of Strategic Direction*, New York: Basic Books, 37–40.

103. S. Sharma & I. Henriques, 2005, Stakeholder influences on sustainability practices in the Canadian Forest products industry, *Strategic Management Journal*, 26: 159–180.

104. A. Mackey, T. B. Mackey, & J. B. Barney, 2007, Corporate social responsibility and firm performance: Investor preferences and corporate strategies, *Academy of Management Review*, 32: 817–835; A. J. Hillman & G. D. Keim, 2001, Shareholder value, stakeholder management, and

social issues: What's the bottom line? *Strategic Management Journal*, 22: 125–139.

105. G. Van der Laan, H. Van Ees, & A. Van Witteloostuijn, 2008, Corporate social and financial performance: An extended stakeholder theory, and empirical test with accounting measures, *Journal of Business Ethics*, 79: 299–310; J. M. Stevens, H. K. Steensma, D. A. Harrison, & P. L. Cochran, 2005, Symbolic or substantive document? The influence of ethics codes on financial executives' decisions, *Strategic Management Journal*, 26: 181–195.

106. M. L. Barnett & R. M. Salomon, 2006, Beyond dichotomy: The curvilinear relationship between social responsibility and financial performance, *Strategic Management Journal*, 27: 1101–1122.

107. T. Kuhn, 2008, A communicative theory of the firm: Developing an alternative perspective on intra-organizational power and stakeholder relationships, *Organization Studies*, 29: 1227–1254; L. Vilanova, 2007, Neither shareholder nor stakeholder management: What happens when firms are run for their short-term salient stakeholder? *European Management Journal*, 25(2): 146–162.

108. J. L. Murrillo-Luna, C. Garces-Ayerbe, & P. Rivera-Torres, 2008, Why do patterns of environmental response differ? A stakeholders' pressure approach, *Strategic Management Journal*, 29: 1225–1240; R. E. Freeman & J. McVea, 2001, A stakeholder approach to strategic management, in M. A. Hitt, R. E. Freeman, & J. S. Harrison (eds.), *Handbook of Strategic Management*, Oxford, UK: Blackwell Publishers, 189–207.

109. R. Boutilier, 2009, *Stakeholder Politics: Social Capital, Sustainable Development, and the Corporation*, Sheffield, United Kingdom: Greenleaf Publishing; C. Caldwell & R. Karri, 2005, Organizational governance and ethical systems: A conventional approach to building trust, *Journal of Business Ethics*, 58: 249–267.

110. F. G. A. de Bakker & F. den Hond, 2008, Introducing the politics of stakeholder influence, *Business & Society*, 47: 8–20; C. Hardy, T. B. Lawrence, & D. Grant, 2005, Discourse and collaboration: The role of conversations and collective identity, *Academy of Management Review*, 30: 58–77.

111. P. Berrone & L. R. Gomez-Meija, 2009, Environmental performance and executive compensation: An integrated agency-institutional perspective, *Academy of Management Journal*, 52: 103-126; S. Maitlis, 2005, The social process of organizational sensemaking, *Academy of Management Journal*, 48: 21–49.

112. 2009, Circuit City to liquidate U.S. stores, *MSNBC*, http://www.msnbc.com, January 16.

113. L. Pierce, 2009, Big losses in ecosystems niches: How core firm decisions drive complementary product shakeouts,

Strategic Management Journal, 30: 323-347; B. A. Neville & B. Menguc, 2006, Stakeholder multiplicity: Toward an understanding of the interactions between stakeholders, *Journal of Business Ethics*, 66: 377–391.

114. D. A. Ready, L. A. Hill, & J. A. Conger, 2008, Winning the race for talent in emerging markets, *Harvard Business Review*, 86(11): 62–70; A. M. Grant, J. E. Dutton, & B. D. Rosso, 2008, Giving commitment: Employee support programs and the prosocial sensemaking process, *Academy of Management Journal*, 51: 898–918; T. M. Gardner, 2005, Interfirm competition for human resources: Evidence from the software industry, *Academy of Management Journal*, 48: 237–256.

115. J. A. Byrne, 2005, Working for the boss from hell, *Fast Company*, July, 14.

116. N. Abe & S. Shimizutani, 2007, Employment policy and corporate governance—An empirical comparison of the stakeholder and the profit-maximization model, *Journal of Comparative Economics*, 35: 346–368.

117. J. Welch & S. Welch, 2009, An employee bill of rights, *BusinessWeek*, March 16, 72.

118. J. P. Jansen, D. Vera, & M. Crossan, 2008, Strategic leadership for exploration and exploitation: The moderating role of environmental dynamism, *The Leadership Quarterly*, 20: 5–18; E. T. Prince, 2005, The fiscal behavior of CEOs, *MIT Sloan Management Review*, 46(3): 23–26.

119. M. S. de Luque, N. T. Washburn, D. A. Waldman, & R. J. House, 2008, Unrequited profit: How stakeholder and economic values related to subordinates' perceptions of leadership and firm performance, *Administrative Science Quarterly*, 53: 626–654.

120. R. Khurana & N. Nohria, 2008, It's time to make management a true profession, *Harvard Business Review*, 86(10): 70–77.

121. N. Byrnes, 2009, Executives on a tightrope, *BusinessWeek*, January 19, 43; D. C. Hambrick, 2007, Upper echelons theory: An update, *Academy of Management Review*, 32: 334–339.

122. J. C. Camillus, 2008, Strategy as a wicked problem, *Harvard Business Review* 86(5): 99–106; A. Priestland & T. R. Hanig, 2005, Developing first-level managers, *Harvard Business Review*, 83(6): 113–120.

123. R. J. Harrington & A. K. Tjan, 2008, Transforming strategy one customer at a time, *Harvard Business Review*, 86(3): 62–72; R. T. Pascale & J. Sternin, 2005, Your company's secret change agent, *Harvard Business Review*, 83(5): 72–81.

124. Y. L. Doz & M. Kosonen, 2007, The new deal at the top, *Harvard Business Review*, 85(6): 98–104.

125. B. Stevens, 2008, Corporate ethical codes: Effective instruments for influencing behavior, *Journal of Business Ethics*, 78: 601–609; D. Lavie, 2006, The competitive advantage of interconnected firms: An extension of the resource-based view,

Academy of Management Review, 31: 638–658.

126. H. Ibarra & O. Obodru, 2009, Women and the vision thing, *Harvard Business Review*, 87(1): 62–70; M. Crossan, D. Vera, & L. Nanjad, 2008, Transcendent leadership: Strategic leadership in dynamic environments, *The Leadership Quarterly*, 19: 569–581.

127. T. Leavitt, 1991, *Thinking about Management*, New York: Free Press, 9.

128. 2007, 100 best corporate citizens for 2007, *CRO Magazine*, http://www.thecro com, June 19.

129. C. A. Montgomery, 2008, Putting leadership back into strategy, *Harvard Business Review*, 86(1): 54–60; D. C. Hambrick, S. Finkelstein, & A. C. Mooney, 2005, Executive job demands: New insights for explaining strategic decisions and leader behaviors, *Academy of Management Review*, 30: 472–491; J. Brett & L. K. Stroh, 2003, Working 61 plus hours a week: Why do managers do it? *Journal of Applied Psychology*, 88: 67–78.

130. J. A. Byrne, 2005, Great work if you can get it, *Fast Company*, April, 14.

131. M. Loeb, 1993, Steven J. Ross, 1927–1992, *Fortune*, January 25, 4.

132. K. M. Green, J. G. Covin, & D. P. Slevin, 2008, Exploring the relationship between strategic reactiveness and entrepreneurial orientation: The role of structure-style fit, *Journal of Business Venturing*, 23: 356–383.

133. O. Gadiesh & J. L. Gilbert, 1998, Profit pools: A fresh look at strategy, *Harvard Business Review*, 76(3): 139–147.

134. O. Gadiesh & J. L. Gilbert, 1998, How to map your industry's profit pool, *Harvard Business Review*, 76(3): 149–162.

135. C. Zook, 2007, Finding your next CORE business, *Harvard Business Review*, 85(4): 66–75; M. J. Epstein & R. A. Westbrook, 2001, Linking actions to profits in strategic decision making, *Sloan Management Review*, 42(3): 39–49.

136. T. Yu, M. Subramaniam, & A. A. Cannella, Jr., 2009, Rivalry deterrence in international markets: Contingencies governing the mutual forbearance hypothesis, *Academy of Management Journal*, 52: 127–147; D. J. Ketchen, C. C. Snow, & V. L. Street, 2004, Improving firm performance by matching strategic decision-making processes to competitive dynamics, *Academy of Management Executive*, 18(4): 29–43.

137. P. Ozcan & K. M. Eisenhardt, 2009, Origin of alliance portfolios: Entrepreneurs, network strategies, and firm performance, *Academy of Management Journal*, 52: 246–279.

138. S. D. Julian, J. C. Ofori-Dankwa, & R. T. Justis, 2008, Understanding strategic responses to interest group pressures, *Strategic Management Journal*, 29: 963–984; C. Eesley & M. J. Lenox, 2006, Firm responses to secondary stakeholder action, *Strategic Management Journal*, 27: 765–781.

139. Y. Luo, 2008, Procedural fairness and interfirm cooperation in strategic alliances, *Strategic Management Journal*, 29: 27–46; S. J. Reynolds, F. C. Schultz, & D. R. Hekman, 2006, Stakeholder theory and managerial decision-making: Constraints and implications of balancing stakeholder interests, *Journal of Business Ethics*, 64: 285–301; L. K. Trevino & G. R. Weaver, 2003, *Managing Ethics in Business Organizations*, Stanford, CA: Stanford University Press.

140. D. Pastoriza, M. A. Arino, & J. E. Ricart, 2008, Ethical managerial behavior as an antecedent of organizational social capital, *Journal of Business Ethics*, 78: 329–341.

141. B. W. Heineman Jr., 2007, Avoiding integrity land mines, *Harvard Business Review*, 85(4): 100–108.

CHAPTER 2

The External Environment: Opportunities, Threats, Industry Competition, and Competitor Analysis

Studying this chapter should provide you with the strategic management knowledge needed to:

1. Explain the importance of analyzing and understanding the firm's external environment.

2. Define and describe the general environment and the industry environment.

3. Discuss the four activities of the external environmental analysis process.

4. Name and describe the general environment's seven segments.

5. Identify the five competitive forces and explain how they determine an industry's profit potential.

6. Define strategic groups and describe their influence on the firm.

7. Describe what firms need to know about their competitors and different methods (including ethical standards) used to collect intelligence about them.

PHILIP MORRIS INTERNATIONAL: THE EFFECTS OF ITS EXTERNAL ENVIRONMENT

Employing over 75,000 people, Philip Morris International (PMI) is the leading international tobacco company in terms of market share. The firm's product line features seven of the world's top 15 brands, including Marlboro, which is the top-selling cigarette brand on a worldwide basis. (In 2008, PMI sold 310.7 billion Marlboro cigarettes. Altria Group, Inc., which spun-off PMI from its operations in March 2008, sells the Marlboro brand in the United States.) PMI sells products in over 160 countries, holds about a 16 percent share of the total international cigarette market outside the United States, and has the largest market share in 11 of the top 30 cigarette markets, excluding the U.S. market. PMI continues to innovate across its brand portfolio to serve different needs of various customers and as a means of stimulating sales of its products.

As is true for all firms, the strategic actions (see Figure 1.1) PMI is taking today and will take in the future are influenced by conditions in its external environment. The challenge for a firm's strategic leaders (including those at PMI) is to understand what the external environment's effects are on the firm today and to predict (with as high a degree of accuracy as possible) what those effects will be on the firm's strategic actions in the future.

The regulations that are a part of the *political/legal segment* of PMI's general environment (the general environment and all of its segments are discussed in this chapter) affect how PMI conducts its business. In general, the regulations regarding the selling of tobacco products are less restrictive in global markets than in the U.S. market. Nonetheless, PMI must be aware of how the regulations might change in the markets it does serve as well as those it may desire to serve in the future and must prepare to deal with these changes. Aware of the possible effects of the political/legal environment on its operations in the future, PMI has made the following public pronouncement: "We are proactively working with governments and other stakeholders to advocate for a comprehensive, consistent and cohesive regulatory framework that applies to all to tobacco products and is based on the principle of harm reduction." (Encouraging all companies competing in the tobacco industry to develop products with the potential to reduce the risk of tobacco-related diseases is part of the harm reduction principle.)

Catherine Karnow/CORBIS

Advertising such as this Marlboro Man billboard is more highly restricted in the United States than in many global markets.

The *global segment* of the general environment also affects PMI's strategic actions. To pursue what it believes are opportunities to sell additional quantities of its products, PMI recently acquired companies in Colombia, Indonesia, and Serbia to establish a stronger foothold in emerging markets. The facts that taxes on tobacco products are lower in many emerging markets compared to developed markets and that the consumption of tobacco products is increasing in these markets are conditions in the external environment influencing the choices PMI makes as it seeks growth. These conditions differ from those in the U.S. market where cigarette consumption is declining by approximately 3 to 4 percent annually and where in mid-2009, the U.S. Congress passed legislation (which President Obama then signed into law) that empowered the Food and Drug Administration to regulate "cigarettes and other forms of tobacco for the first time."

While cigarette consumption is increasing in some of its markets, PMI predicts that this will not always be the case. In this respect, PMI anticipates that changes will occur in the *sociocultural segment* of the general environment such that fewer people will be willing to risk disease by consuming tobacco products. Anticipating this possibility, PMI recently formed a joint venture with Swedish Match AB to market smokeless tobacco worldwide. This collaborative arrangement unites the world's largest seller of smokeless tobacco (Swedish Match) with a marketing powerhouse that has a strong global presence across multiple markets (PMI). Because it is less dangerous than cigarettes in terms of disease, smokeless tobacco is seen as a product with long-term growth potential. PMI will likely remain committed to the importance of its social performance as it pursues this joint venture. As a measure of the effects of the *physical environment segment* of the external environment, PMI says that it is strongly committed to the "promotion of sustainable tobacco farming, the efficient use of natural resources, the reduction of waste in (its) manufacturing processes, eliminating child labor and giving back to the communities in which (it) operates."

Sources: 2009, Altria Group Inc., *Standard & Poor's Stock Report*, http://standardandpoors.com, April 25; 2009, Philip Morris International home page, http://www.philipinternational.com, May 15; N. Byrnes & F. Balfour, Philip Morris' global race, *BusinessWeek Online*, http://www.businessweek.com, April 23; K. Helliker, 2009, Smokeless tobacco to get push by venture overseas, *Wall Street Journal Online*, http://www.wsj.com, February 4; A. Pressman, 2009, Philip Morris unbound, *BusinessWeek*, May 4, 66; D. Wilson, 2009, Senate votes to allow FDA to regulate tobacco, *Wall Street Journal Online*, http://www.wsj.com, June 12.

As described in the Opening Case and suggested by research, the external environment affects a firm's strategic actions.[1] For example, Philip Morris International (PMI) seeks to grow through a joint venture with Swedish Match AB to distribute smokeless tobacco in multiple global markets.[2] Because it is less dangerous than cigarettes in terms of contributing to disease, smokeless tobacco is thought to have growth potential in many markets.[3] In addition to this health-related influence that is a part of the sociocultural segment of PMI's external environment, the firm's strategic actions are affected by conditions in other segments of its general environment, such as the political/legal and the physical environment segments. As we explain in this chapter, a firm's external environment creates both opportunities (e.g., the opportunity for PMI to enter the smokeless tobacco market) and threats (e.g., the possibility that additional regulations in its markets will reduce consumption of PMI's tobacco products). Collectively, opportunities and threats affect a firm's strategic actions.[4]

Regardless of the industry in which they compete, the external environment influences firms as they seek strategic competitiveness and the earning of above-average returns. This chapter focuses on how firms analyze their external environment. The understanding about conditions in its external environment that the firm gains by analyzing that environment is matched with knowledge about its internal organization (discussed in the next chapter) as the foundation for forming the firm's vision, developing its mission, and identifying and implementing strategic actions (see Figure 1.1).

As noted in Chapter 1, the environmental conditions in the current global economy differ from historical conditions. For example, technological changes and the continuing growth of information gathering and processing capabilities increase the need for firms to develop effective competitive actions on a timely basis.[5] (In slightly different words, firms have little time to correct errors when implementing their competitive actions.) The rapid sociological changes occurring in many countries affect labor practices and the nature of products demanded by increasingly diverse consumers. Governmental policies and laws also affect where and how firms choose to compete.[6] In addition, changes to nations' financial regulatory systems that were enacted in 2009 and beyond are expected to increase the complexity of organizations' financial transactions.[7]

Viewed in their totality, the conditions that affect firms today indicate that for most organizations, their external environment is filled with uncertainty.[8] To successfully deal with this uncertainty and to achieve strategic competitiveness and thrive, firms must be aware of and fully understand the different segments of the external environment.

Firms understand the external environment by acquiring information about competitors, customers, and other stakeholders to build their own base of knowledge and capabilities.[9] On the basis of the new information, firms take actions, such as building new capabilities and core competencies, in hopes of buffering themselves from any negative environmental effects and to pursue opportunities as the basis for better serving their stakeholders' needs.[10] A firm's strategic actions are influenced by the conditions in the three parts (the general, industry, and competitor) of its external environment (see Figure 2.1).

The General, Industry, and Competitor Environments

The **general environment** is composed of dimensions in the broader society that influence an industry and the firms within it.[11] We group these dimensions into seven environmental *segments:* demographic, economic, political/legal, sociocultural, technological, global, and physical. Examples of *elements* analyzed in each of these segments are shown in Table 2.1.

Firms cannot directly control the general environment's segments. The recent bankruptcy filings by General Motors and Chrysler Corporation highlight this fact. These firms could not directly control various parts of their external environment, including the economic and political/legal segments; however, these segments are influencing the actions the firms are taking now including the forming of Chrysler's alliance with Fiat.[12] Because firms cannot directly control the segments of their external environment, successful ones learn how to gather the information needed to understand all segments and their implications for selecting and implementing the firm's strategies.

AP Photo/Seth Wenig

A woman bearing Chrysler paperwork waits to enter U.S. Bankruptcy Court for the Chrysler bankruptcy case in New York, Monday, May 4, 2009. Aspects of the external environment both contributed to Chrysler's bankruptcy filing as well as influenced the terms under which it quickly re-emerged.

Figure 2.1 The External Environment

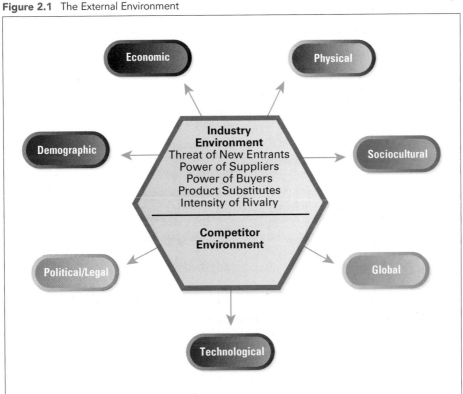

The **general environment** is composed of dimensions in the broader society that influence an industry and the firms within it.

Table 2.1 The General Environment: Segments and Elements

Demographic Segment	• Population size • Age structure • Geographic distribution	• Ethnic mix • Income distribution
Economic Segment	• Inflation rates • Interest rates • Trade deficits or surpluses • Budget deficits or surpluses	• Personal savings rate • Business savings rates • Gross domestic product
Political/Legal Segment	• Antitrust laws • Taxation laws • Deregulation philosophies	• Labor training laws • Educational philosophies and policies
Sociocultural Segment	• Women in the workforce • Workforce diversity • Attitudes about the quality of work life	• Shifts in work and career preferences • Shifts in preferences regarding product and service characteristics
Technological Segment	• Product innovations • Applications of knowledge	• Focus of private and government-supported R&D expenditures • New communication technologies
Global Segment	• Important political events • Critical global markets	• Newly industrialized countries • Different cultural and institutional attributes
Physical Environment Segment	• Energy consumption • Practices used to develop energy sources • Renewable energy efforts • Minimizing a firm's environmental footprint	• Availability of water as a resource • Producing environmentally friendly products

The **industry environment** is the set of factors that directly influences a firm and its competitive actions and responses:[13] the threat of new entrants, the power of suppliers, the power of buyers, the threat of product substitutes, and the intensity of rivalry among competitors. In total, the interactions among these five factors determine an industry's profit potential; in turn, the industry's profit potential influences the choices each firm makes about its strategic actions. The challenge for a firm is to locate a position within an industry where it can favorably influence the five factors or where it can successfully defend against their influence. The greater a firm's capacity to favorably influence its industry environment, the greater the likelihood that the firm will earn above-average returns.

How companies gather and interpret information about their competitors is called *competitor analysis*. Understanding the firm's competitor environment complements the insights provided by studying the general and industry environments.[14] This means, for example, that Philip Morris International wants to learn as much as it can about its two

The **industry environment** is the set of factors that directly influences a firm and its competitive actions and competitive responses: the threat of new entrants, the power of suppliers, the power of buyers, the threat of product substitutes, and the intensity of rivalry among competitors.

major competitors—British American Tobacco and Japan Tobacco International—while also learning about its general and industry environments.

Analysis of the general environment is focused on environmental trends while an analysis of the industry environment is focused on the factors and conditions influencing an industry's profitability potential and an analysis of competitors is focused on predicting competitors' actions, responses, and intentions. In combination, the results of these three analyses influence the firm's vision, mission, and strategic actions. Although we discuss each analysis separately, performance improves when the firm integrates the insights provided by analyses of the general environment, the industry environment, and the competitor environment.

External Environmental Analysis

Most firms face external environments that are highly turbulent, complex, and global—conditions that make interpreting those environments difficult.[15] To cope with often ambiguous and incomplete environmental data and to increase understanding of the general environment, firms engage in external environmental analysis. This analysis has four parts: scanning, monitoring, forecasting, and assessing (see Table 2.2). Analyzing the external environment is a difficult, yet significant, activity.[16]

Identifying opportunities and threats is an important objective of studying the general environment. An **opportunity** is a condition in the general environment that if exploited effectively, helps a company achieve strategic competitiveness. For example, recent market research results suggested to Procter & Gamble (P&G) that an increasing number of men across the globe are interested in fragrances and skin care products. To take advantage of this opportunity, P&G is reorienting "… its beauty business by gender, 'to better serve him and her' rather than its typical organization around product categories."[17]

A **threat** is a condition in the general environment that may hinder a company's efforts to achieve strategic competitiveness.[18] The once-revered firm Polaroid can attest to the seriousness of external threats. Polaroid was a leader in its industry and considered one of the top 50 firms in the United States. When its competitors developed photographic equipment using digital technology, Polaroid was unprepared and never responded effectively. It filed for bankruptcy in 2001. In 2002, the former Polaroid Corp. was sold to Bank One's OEP Imaging unit, which promptly changed its own name to Polaroid Corp. Jacques Nasser, a former CEO at Ford, took over as CEO at Polaroid and found that the brand had continued life. Nasser used the brand in a partnership with Petters Group to put the Polaroid name on "TVs and DVDs made in Asian factories and sell them through Wal-Mart and Target."[19] Polaroid went public again and was later

> An **opportunity** is a condition in the general environment that if exploited effectively, helps a company achieve strategic competitiveness.
>
> A **threat** is a condition in the general environment that may hinder a company's efforts to achieve strategic competitiveness.

Table 2.2 Components of the External Environmental Analysis

Scanning	• Identifying early signals of environmental changes and trends
Monitoring	• Detecting meaning through ongoing observations of environmental changes and trends
Forecasting	• Developing projections of anticipated outcomes based on monitored changes and trends
Assessing	• Determining the timing and importance of environmental changes and trends for firms' strategies and their management

sold to Petters Group in 2005. However, the firm then failed again, resulting in another bankruptcy filing in December 2008. On April 16, 2009, Polaroid was sold to a joint venture of Hilco Consumer Capital LP of Toronto and Gordon Brothers Brands LLC of Boston. At the time, the only assets remaining were the firm's name, its intellectual property, and its photography collection.[20] Thus, not responding to threats in its external environment resulted in the failure of the once highly successful Polaroid Corp.

Firms use several sources to analyze the general environment, including a wide variety of printed materials (such as trade publications, newspapers, business publications, and the results of academic research and public polls), trade shows and suppliers, customers, and employees of public-sector organizations. People in *boundary-spanning* positions can obtain a great deal of this type of information. Salespersons, purchasing managers, public relations directors, and customer service representatives, each of whom interacts with external constituents, are examples of boundary-spanning positions.

Scanning

Scanning entails the study of all segments in the general environment. Through scanning, firms identify early signals of potential changes in the general environment and detect changes that are already under way.[21] Scanning often reveals ambiguous, incomplete, or unconnected data and information. Thus, environmental scanning is challenging but critically important for firms, especially those competing in highly volatile environments.[22] In addition, scanning activities must be aligned with the organizational context; a scanning system designed for a volatile environment is inappropriate for a firm in a stable environment.[23]

Many firms use special software to help them identify events that are taking place in the environment and that are announced in public sources. For example, news event detection uses information-based systems to categorize text and reduce the trade-off between an important missed event and false alarm rates.[24] The Internet provides significant opportunities for scanning. Amazon.com, for example, records significant information about individuals visiting its Web site, particularly if a purchase is made. Amazon then welcomes these customers by name when they visit the Web site again. The firm sends messages to customers about specials and new products similar to those they purchased in previous visits. A number of other companies such as Netflix also collect demographic data about their customers in an attempt to identify their unique preferences (demographics is one of the segments in the general environment).

Philip Morris International continuously scans segments of its external environment to detect current conditions and to anticipate changes that might take place in different segments. For example, PMI always studies various nations' tax policies on cigarettes (these policies are part of the political/legal segment). The reason for this is that raising cigarette taxes might reduce sales while lowering these taxes might increase sales.

Monitoring

When *monitoring,* analysts observe environmental changes to see if an important trend is emerging from among those spotted through scanning.[25] Critical to successful monitoring is the firm's ability to detect meaning in different environmental events and trends. For example, the buying power of Hispanics is projected to increase to $1.3 trillion by 2013 (up from $984 billion in 2008). Particularly in the southwestern part of the United States, grocers believe that this growing population will increase its purchases of ethnic-oriented food products.[26] The recent financial crisis found companies carefully monitoring the emerging trend of customers deciding to "go back to basics" when purchasing products. A reduction in brand loyalty may be an outcome of this trend. Companies selling carefully branded products should monitor this trend to determine its meaning—both in the short and long term.[27]

Effective monitoring requires the firm to identify important stakeholders as the foundation for serving their unique needs.[28] (Stakeholders' unique needs are described in Chapter 1.) Scanning and monitoring are particularly important when a firm competes in an industry with high technological uncertainty.[29] Scanning and monitoring can provide the firm with information; they also serve as a means of importing knowledge about markets and about how to successfully commercialize new technologies the firm has developed.[30]

Forecasting

Scanning and monitoring are concerned with events and trends in the general environment at a point in time. When *forecasting,* analysts develop feasible projections of what might happen, and how quickly, as a result of the changes and trends detected through scanning and monitoring.[31] For example, analysts might forecast the time that will be required for a new technology to reach the marketplace, the length of time before different corporate training procedures are required to deal with anticipated changes in the composition of the workforce, or how much time will elapse before changes in governmental taxation policies affect consumers' purchasing patterns.

Forecasting events and outcomes accurately is challenging. Already in place, the trend of firms outsourcing call center work and logistics' activities to companies specializing in these activities appeared to accelerate as a result of the recent global crisis. Having noticed (through scanning) and monitoring these outsourcing trends for some time, logistics companies such as FedEx and United Parcel Service and call center provider Convergys are developing forecasts about possible increases in their business and how long the increasing trend of using their services might continue.[32] On the other hand, Procter & Gamble (P&G) and Colgate-Palmolive, two firms selling carefully branded consumer products, are now forecasting the effects of the trend for retailers to "… tout their lower-priced, private-label goods and pressure their suppliers for lower prices." Thus, P&G and Colgate are forecasting the effects of the twin issues of the decisions by the retailers to whom they sell products to manufacture and sell their own consumer products while simultaneously seeking lower prices on the products they do buy from them.[33]

Assessing

The objective of *assessing* is to determine the timing and significance of the effects of environmental changes and trends that have been identified.[34] Through scanning, monitoring, and forecasting, analysts are able to understand the general environment. Going a step further, the intent of assessment is to specify the implications of that understanding. Without assessment, the firm is left with data that may be interesting but are of unknown competitive relevance. Even if formal assessment is inadequate, the appropriate interpretation of that information is important: "Research found that how accurate senior executives are about their competitive environments is indeed less important for strategy and corresponding organizational changes than the way in which they interpret information about their environments."[35] Thus, although gathering and organizing information is important, appropriately interpreting that intelligence to determine if an identified trend in the external environment is an opportunity or threat is equally important.

As previously noted, through forecasting P&G and Colgate have identified a trend among many of the retailers to whom they sell their carefully branded products. Essentially, the trend is for these retailers to pressure firms such as P&G, Colgate, H. J. Heinz, and Kellogg's—to name a few—to reduce the prices at which they sell their products to the retailers. The ability of these retailers to produce and sell their own private-label merchandise supports their efforts to receive lower prices from branding giants such as those mentioned.

In addition, firms with well-known brands have detected a trend among consumers to receive more "value" when purchasing branded products. Having forecasted that this

STRATEGIC FOCUS

CONSUMERS' DESIRE TO RECEIVE ADDITIONAL VALUE WHEN PURCHASING BRAND-NAME PRODUCTS

In Chapter 3, we note that *value* is measured by a product's performance characteristics and by its attributes for which customers are willing to pay. A number of companies producing brand-name products believe that the recent global crisis is producing a trend in which what customers *value* is changing. In slightly different words, through monitoring and scanning, companies are forecasting that the performance characteristics and product attributes for which today's customers are willing to pay are changing as a result of the recent global crisis. In addition, through assessment, companies producing name-brand products believe that changes in how customers define value are significant and may be long-lasting. In response, some firms are changing some of the performance characteristics and attributes of their products to create more value for customers. A comment from an analyst about this trend is: "... companies are having to consider their 'value' equation to try to serve the millions of consumers who either can't afford premium experiences, or just don't want them anymore."

Let's consider some examples of "different" value that companies are now providing to customers. The desire for smaller homes is a trend spotted by builders of premium-priced homes. The fact that the average size of a new home built in the United States declined in 2008 for the first time in 35 years is an indicator of this trend. Builders of premium homes are using better designs to improve space utilization and traffic flow and increases in energy efficiency to create more value for customers. Facilitating these builders' efforts are changes appliance manufacturers are making to the performance characteristics of their products, also in attempts to create more value for their customers. General Electric, for example, is offering a hybrid electric water heater that is estimated to save consumers $250 annually. The value created by this product is twofold—reduced cost to the consumer and a reduction to energy consumption as a benefit to society as a whole. Kohler is offering energy-efficient faucets, toilets, and showerheads at virtually the same price as its less energy-efficient products. Thus, these products also create customer value in the form of reduced cost while being environmentally friendly. Other appliance firms such as Whirlpool are producing products with similar performance characteristics to create customer value.

The attributes desired by buyers of premium homes are changing, and home builders are responding by delivering value in the form of greater energy efficiency and more modern designs. Would a smaller, more environmentally efficient home be of more value to you than a larger, less efficient one?

Elmund Sumner/Photolibrary

Other types of companies are also redefining the value their products provide to customers. Believing that "... value is not just cost; it's also taste, nutrition and quality," Del Monte Foods's advertising campaigns now emphasize that compared to some frozen and even fresh items, canned foods can offer better value when the customer combines cost with nutritional benefits. Frito-Lay (a division of PepsiCo) is increasing customer value by adding 20 percent more product to selected bags of Cheetos, Fritos, and Tostitos without increasing prices. Michaels, a large chain of craft outlets, now emphasizes that when customers purchase their goods as raw materials for making various items they are becoming more sustainable in that they are "making stuff" rather than simply "buying more stuff."

As these examples suggest, all types of companies (and especially those selling brand-name products) are trying to create a different type of value for customers in response to trends they are observing in their general environment. Regardless of the good or service a firm offers, it seems that the following words from an analyst capture the challenge facing today's companies: "So here's a call to all companies: evaluate everything you are offering consumers to see how you can infuse the value of good value into your brand."

Sources: A. Athavaley, 2009, Eco-friendly—and frugal, *Wall Street Journal Online*, http://www.wsj.com, February 11; S. Elliott, 2009, Food brands compete to stretch a dollar, *New York Times Online*, http://www.nytimes.com, May 10; D. Kaplan, 2009, Value-oriented chains thrive amid recession, *Houston Chronicle Online*, http://www.chron.com, April 24; M. Penn, 2009, Value is the new green, *Wall Street Journal Online*, http://www.wsj.com, March 13; C. C. Miller, 2008, For craft sales, the recession is a help, *New York Times Online*, http://www.nytimes.com, December 23.

trend toward "wanting more value" may last beyond the current global recession, many of these firms are taking actions in response to their assessment of the significance of what may be a long-lasting trend toward value purchases. In the Strategic Focus, we describe actions some firms with well-known brands are taking in response to an assessment that this trend may have significant effects on their operations, at least in the short run if not longer term as well.

Segments of the General Environment

The general environment is composed of segments that are external to the firm (see Table 2.1). Although the degree of impact varies, these environmental segments affect all industries and the firms competing in them. The challenge to each firm is to scan, monitor, forecast, and assess the elements in each segment to determine their effects on the firm. Effective scanning, monitoring, forecasting, and assessing are vital to the firm's efforts to recognize and evaluate opportunities and threats.

The Demographic Segment

The **demographic segment** is concerned with a population's size, age structure, geographic distribution, ethnic mix, and income distribution.[36] Demographic segments are commonly analyzed on a global basis because of their potential effects across countries' borders and because many firms compete in global markets.

Population Size

The world's population doubled (from 3 billion to 6 billion) in the roughly 40-year period between 1959 and 1999. Current projects suggest that population growth will continue in the twenty-first century, but at a slower pace. The U.S. Census Bureau projects that the world's population will be 9 billion by 2040.[37] By 2050, India is expected to be the most populous nation in the world (with over 1.8 billion people). China, the United States, Indonesia, and Pakistan are predicted to be the next four largest nations by population count in 2050. Firms seeking to find growing markets in which to sell their goods and services want to recognize the market potential that may exist for them in these five nations.

While observing the population of different nations and regions of the world, firms also want to study changes occurring within different populations to assess their strategic implications. For example, in 2006, 20 percent of Japan's citizens were 65 or older, while the United States and China will not reach this level until 2036.[38] Aging populations are a significant problem for countries because of the need for workers and the burden of

The **demographic segment** is concerned with a population's size, age structure, geographic distribution, ethnic mix, and income distribution.

funding retirement programs. In Japan and other countries, employees are urged to work longer to overcome these problems. Interestingly, the United States has a higher birthrate and significant immigration, placing it in a better position than Japan and other European nations.

Age Structure

As noted earlier, in Japan and other countries, the world's population is rapidly aging. In North America and Europe, millions of baby boomers are approaching retirement. However, even in developing countries with large numbers of people under the age of 35, birth rates have been declining sharply. In China, for example, by 2040 there will be more than 400 million people over the age of 60. The more than 90 million baby boomers in North America may postpone retirement given the recent financial crisis. In fact, data now suggest that baby boomers (those born between 1946 and 1965) are struggling to meet their retirement goals and are uncertain if they will actually be able to retire as originally expected. This is partly because of declines in the value of their homes as well as declines in their other retirement investments[39]—a number of baby boomers experienced at least a 20 percent decline in their retirement assets between 2007 and 2008. The possibility of future declines is creating uncertainty for baby boomers about how to invest and when they might be able to retire.[40] On the other hand, delayed retirements by baby boomers with value-creating skills may facilitate firms' efforts to successfully implement their strategies. Moreover, delayed retirements may allow companies to think of creative ways for skilled, long-time employees to impart their accumulated knowledge to younger employees as they work a bit longer than originally anticipated.

Geographic Distribution

For decades, the U.S. population has been shifting from the north and east to the west and south. Firms should consider the effects of this shift in demographics as well. For example, Florida is the U.S. state with the largest percentage of its population (17.6 percent) 65 years or older.[41] Thus, companies providing goods and services that are targeted to senior citizens might pay close attention to this group's geographic preference for states in the south (such as Florida) and the southwest (such as Texas). Similarly, the trend of relocating from metropolitan to nonmetropolitan areas continues in the United States. These trends are changing local and state governments' tax bases. In turn, business firms' decisions regarding location are influenced by the degree of support that different taxing agencies offer as well as the rates at which these agencies tax businesses.

Geographic distribution patterns are not identical throughout the world. For example, in China, 60 percent of the population lives in rural areas; however, the growth is in urban communities such as Shanghai (with a current population in excess of 13 million) and Beijing (over 12.2 million). These data suggest that firms seeking to sell their products in China should recognize the growth in metropolitan areas rather than in rural areas.[42]

Ethnic Mix

The ethnic mix of countries' populations continues to change. For example, with a population in excess of 40 million, Hispanics are now the largest ethnic minority in the United States. In fact, the U.S. Hispanic market is the third largest "Latin American" economy behind Brazil and Mexico. Spanish is now the dominant language in parts of U.S. states such as Texas, California, Florida, and New Mexico.[43] Given these facts, some firms might want to assess the degree to which their goods or services could be adapted to serve the unique needs of Hispanic consumers. This is particularly appropriate for companies competing in consumer sectors such as grocery stores, movie studios, financial services, and clothing stores.

Changes in the ethnic mix also affect a workforce's composition.[44] In the United States, for example, the population and labor force will continue to diversify, as immigration accounts for a sizable part of growth. Projections are that the combined Latino and Asian population shares will increase to more than 20 percent of the total U.S. population by 2014.[45] Interestingly, much of this immigrant workforce is bypassing high-cost coastal cities and settling in smaller rural towns. Many of these workers are in low-wage, labor-intensive industries such as construction, food service, lodging, and landscaping.[46] For this reason, if border security is tightened, these industries will likely face labor shortages.

Income Distribution

Understanding how income is distributed within and across populations informs firms of different groups' purchasing power and discretionary income. Studies of income distributions suggest that although living standards have improved over time, variations exist within and between nations.[47] Of interest to firms are the average incomes of households and individuals. For instance, the increase in dual-career couples has had a notable effect on average incomes. Although real income has been declining in general in some nations, the household income of dual-career couples has increased, especially in the United States. These figures yield strategically relevant information for firms. For instance, research indicates that whether an employee is part of a dual-career couple can strongly influence the willingness of the employee to accept an international assignment.[48]

The assessment by some that in 2005 about 55 percent of the world's population could be defined as "middle class" generates interesting possibilities for many firms. (For the purpose of this survey, middle class was defined as people with one third of their income left for discretionary spending after providing for basic food and shelter.) The size of this market may have "… immense implications for companies selling their products and services on a global scale."[49] Of course, the recent global financial crisis may affect the size of the world's "middle class."

The Economic Segment

The **economic environment** refers to the nature and direction of the economy in which a firm competes or may compete.[50] In general, firms seek to compete in relatively stable economies with strong growth potential. Because nations are interconnected as a result of the global economy, firms must scan, monitor, forecast, and assess the health of their host nation and the health of the economies outside their host nation.

As firms prepare to compete during the second decade of the twenty-first century, the world's economic environment is quite uncertain. Some businesspeople were even beginning to question the ability of economists to provide valid and reliable predictions about trends to anticipate in the world's economic environment.[51] The lack of confidence in predictions from those specializing in providing such predictions complicates firms' efforts to understand the conditions they might face during future competitive battles.

In terms of specific economic environments, companies competing in Japan or desiring to do so might carefully evaluate the meaning of the position recently taken by some that this nation's economy has ingrained flaws such as "… unwieldy corporate structures, dogged loyalty to increasingly commoditized business lines and a history of punting problems into the future."[52] Because of its acknowledged growth potential, a number of companies are evaluating the possibility of entering Russia to compete or, for those already competing in that nation, to expand the scope of their operations. However, statements by analysts in mid-2009 that "the banking crisis in Russia is in its very beginning"[53] warrant careful attention. If this prediction comes true, the Russian economy could become destabilized. In contrast, Vietnam's economy was expanding during late 2009 and being recognized as one in which opportunities might exist for companies from across the globe to pursue.[54]

The **economic environment** refers to the nature and direction of the economy in which a firm competes or may compete.

The Political/Legal Segment

The **political/legal segment** is the arena in which organizations and interest groups compete for attention, resources, and a voice in overseeing the body of laws and regulations guiding interactions among nations as well as between firms and various local governmental agencies.[55] Essentially, this segment represents how organizations try to influence governments and how they try to understand the influences (current and projected) of those governments on their strategic actions.

When regulations are formed in response to new laws that are legislated (e.g., the Sarbanes-Oxley Act dealing with corporate governance—see Chapter 10 for more information), they often influence a firm's strategic actions. For example, less-restrictive regulations on firms' actions are a product of the recent global trend toward privatization of government-owned or government-regulated firms. Some believe that the transformation from state-owned to private firms occurring in multiple nations has substantial implications for the competitive landscapes in a number of countries and across multiple industries.[56] In the United States, the 2009 allocation by the federal government of $13 billion to high-speed train travel is expected to provide a critical boost to the nation's efforts to reduce traffic congestion and cut pollution.[57] For global firms manufacturing high-speed rail equipment, this political support in the United States of systems requiring their products is a trend to forecast and assess.

Firms must carefully analyze a new political administration's business-related policies and philosophies. Antitrust laws, taxation laws, industries chosen for deregulation, labor training laws, and the degree of commitment to educational institutions are areas in which an administration's policies can affect the operations and profitability of industries and individual firms across the globe. For example, early signals from President Obama's administration that policies might be formed with the intention of reducing the amount of work U.S. companies outsource to firms in other nations seemingly could affect information technology outsourcing firms based in countries such as India.[58] The introduction of legislation in the U.S. Congress during the early tenure of the Obama administration suggested at least some support for these stated intentions.[59] Thus, these companies might want to carefully examine the newly elected U.S. administration's intentions to understand their potential effects.

To deal with issues such as those we are describing, firms develop a political strategy to influence governmental policies that might affect them. Some argue that developing an effective political strategy is essential to the newly formed General Motors' efforts to achieve strategic competitiveness.[60] In addition, the effects of global governmental policies (e.g., those related to firms in India that are engaging in IT outsourcing work) on a firm's competitive position increase the need for firms to form an effective political strategy.[61]

Firms competing in the global economy encounter an interesting array of political/legal questions and issues. For example, in mid-2009, leaders from South Korea and the European Union remained committed to developing a free trade agreement between the relevant parties. At the time, the two parties had worked for over two years to develop an agreement that many thought would benefit both by creating a host of opportunities for firms to sell their goods and services in what would be a new market for them. The key political challenge affecting the parties' efforts was the European Union's decision not to permit "… refunds South Korea pays to local companies who import parts from third countries before exporting finished goods."[62] Both South Korea and European Union firms are monitoring the progress of these talks in order to be able to forecast the effects of a possible trade agreement on their strategic actions.

The Sociocultural Segment

The **sociocultural segment** is concerned with a society's attitudes and cultural values. Because attitudes and values form the cornerstone of a society, they often drive demographic, economic, political/legal, and technological conditions and changes.

The **political/legal segment** is the arena in which organizations and interest groups compete for attention, resources, and a voice in overseeing the body of laws and regulations guiding interactions among nations as well as between firms and various local governmental agencies.

The **sociocultural segment** is concerned with a society's attitudes and cultural values.

Societies' attitudes and cultural values appear to be undergoing possible changes at the start of the second decade of the twenty-first century. This seems to be the case in the United States and other nations as well. Attitudes and values about health care in the United States is an area where sociocultural changes might occur. Statistics are a driving force for these potential changes. For example, while the United States "… has the highest overall health care expenditure as well as the highest expenditure per capital of any country in the world,"[63] millions of the nation's citizens lack health insurance. Some feel that effective health care reform in the United States requires securing coverage for all citizens and lowering the cost of services.[64] Changes to the nature of health care policies and their delivery would likely affect business firms, meaning that they must carefully monitor this possibility and future trends regarding health care in order to anticipate the effects on their operations.

As the U.S. labor force has increased, it has also become more diverse as significantly more women and minorities from a variety of cultures entered. In 1993, the total U.S. workforce was slightly less than 130 million; in 2005, it was slightly greater than 148 million. It is predicted to grow to more than 192 million by 2050. In the same year, 2050, the U.S. workforce is forecasted to be composed of 48 percent female workers, 11 percent Asian American workers, 14 percent African American workers and 24 percent Hispanic workers.[65] The growing gender, ethnic, and cultural diversity in this workforce creates challenges and opportunities, including combining the best of both men's and women's traditional leadership styles. Although diversity in the workforce has the potential to improve performance, research indicates that management of diversity initiatives is required in order to reap these organizational benefits. Human resource practitioners are trained to successfully manage diversity issues to enhance positive outcomes.[66]

Another manifestation of changing attitudes toward work is the continuing growth of contingency workers (part-time, temporary, and contract employees) throughout the global economy. This trend is significant in several parts of the world, including Canada, Japan, Latin America, Western Europe, and the United States. In the United States, the fastest growing group of contingency workers is those with 15 to 20 years of work experience. The layoffs resulting from the recent global crisis and the loss of retirement income of many "baby boomers"—many of whom feel they must work longer to recover losses to their retirement portfolios—are a key reason for this. Companies interested in hiring on a temporary basis may benefit by gaining access to the long-term work experiences of these newly available workers.[67]

Although the lifestyle and workforce changes referenced previously reflect the values of the U.S. population, each country and culture has unique values and trends. As suggested earlier, national cultural values affect behavior in organizations and thus also influence organizational outcomes.[68] For example, the importance of collectivism and social relations in Chinese and Russian cultures lead to the open sharing of information and knowledge among members of an organization.[69] Knowledge sharing is important for defusing new knowledge in organizations and increasing the speed in implementing innovations. Personal relationships are especially important in China as *guanxi* (personal connections) has become a way of doing business within the country and for individuals to advance their careers in what is becoming a more open market society.[70] Understanding the importance of guanxi is critical for foreign firms doing business in China.

The Technological Segment

Pervasive and diversified in scope, technological changes affect many parts of societies. These effects occur primarily through new products, processes, and materials. The **technological segment** includes the institutions and activities involved with creating new knowledge and translating that knowledge into new outputs, products, processes, and materials.

Given the rapid pace of technological change, it is vital for firms to thoroughly study the technological segment.[71] The importance of these efforts is suggested by the finding that early adopters of new technology often achieve higher market shares and earn

The **technological segment** includes the institutions and activities involved with creating new knowledge and translating that knowledge into new outputs, products, processes, and materials.

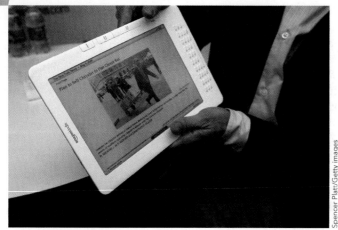

The Kindle DX, a new purpose-built reading device, features storage for up to 3,500 books. Amazon has also partnered with select major newspapers to offer readers discounts on the DX in return for long-term subscriptions.

Spencer Platt/Getty Images

higher returns. Thus, both large and small firms should continuously scan the external environment to identify potential substitutes for technologies that are in current use, as well as to identify newly emerging technologies from which their firm could derive competitive advantage.[72]

As a significant technological development, the Internet has become a remarkable capability to provide information easily, quickly, and effectively to an ever-increasing percentage of the world's population. Companies continue to study the Internet's capabilities to anticipate how it may allow them to create more value for customers in the future and to anticipate future trends.

In spite of the Internet's far-reaching effects, wireless communication technology is predicted to be the next significant technological opportunity for companies to apply when pursuing strategic competitiveness. Handheld devices and other wireless communications equipment are used to access a variety of network-based services. The use of handheld computers with wireless network connectivity, Web-enabled mobile phone handsets, and other emerging platforms (e.g., consumer Internet-access devices) is expected to increase substantially, soon becoming the dominant form of communication and commerce.[73]

Amazon.com's Kindle is an emerging wireless technology with capabilities firms should evaluate. In addition to books, customers can download an ever-increasing array of products to the Kindle. In mid-2009, over 275,000 of Amazon's books were available through the Kindle. Magazines and newspapers are available for purchase and use on the Kindle as well. The ease of reading daily newspapers on the Kindle without charge instead of waiting for hard copy to be delivered is threatening the very existence of a host of newspapers. The Kindle can also be used to surf the Web and send e-mail messages.[74]

Currently in its second generation, there is no doubt that Amazon will continue developing more advanced versions of the Kindle with each version having additional functionalities. As a service, the Kindle creates opportunities for those wanting to distribute knowledge electronically but is a threat to companies whose strategies call for the distribution of physical "hard copies" of written words. As such, many firms should study this technology to understand its competitive implications.

The Global Segment

The **global segment** includes relevant new global markets, existing markets that are changing, important international political events, and critical cultural and institutional characteristics of global markets.[75] There is little doubt that markets are becoming more global and that consumers as well as companies throughout the world accept this fact. Consider the automobile industry as an example of this. The global auto industry is one in which an increasing number of people believe that because "we live in a global community," consumers in multiple nations are willing to buy cars and trucks "from whatever area of the world."[76]

When studying the global segment, firms (including automobile manufacturers) should recognize that globalization of business markets may create *opportunities* to enter new markets as well as *threats* that new competitors from other economies may enter their market as well. This is both an opportunity and a threat for the world's automobile manufacturers—worldwide production capacity is now a potential threat to all of these global companies while entering another market to sell a company's products appears to be an opportunity. In terms of overcapacity, evidence indicated that in mid-2009, this global industry had "… the capacity to make an astounding 94 million vehicles each year (which is roughly) 34 million too many based on current sales."[77] This prediction of excess capacity suggests that most if not all automobile manufacturers may decide

The **global segment** includes relevant new global markets, existing markets that are changing, important international political events, and critical cultural and institutional characteristics of global markets.

to enter markets that are new to them in order to try to sell more of the units they are producing.

The markets from which firms generate sales and income are one indication of the degree to which they are participating in the global economy. For example, in 2008 53 percent of McDonald's operating income was accounted for by its international operations.[78] Food giant H. J. Heinz earns over 60 percent of its revenue outside the United States.[79] Consumer products giant Procter & Gamble, with operations in over 180 countries, recently generated over 56 percent of its sales revenue in markets outside the United States.[80] Thus, for these companies and so many others, understanding the conditions of today's global segment and being able to predict future conditions is critical to their success.

The global segment presents firms with both opportunities and threats or risks. Because of the threats and risks, some firms choose to take a more cautious approach to competing in international markets. These firms participate in what some refer to as *globalfocusing.* Globalfocusing often is used by firms with moderate levels of international operations who increase their internationalization by focusing on global niche markets.[81] In this way, they build on and use their special competencies and resources while limiting their risks with the niche market. Another way in which firms limit their risks in international markets is to focus their operations and sales in one region of the world.[82] In this way, they can build stronger relationships in and knowledge of their markets. As they build these strengths, rivals find it more difficult to enter their markets and compete successfully.

In all instances, firms competing in global markets should recognize the different sociocultural and institutional attributes of global markets. Earlier, we mentioned that South Korea and the European Union remain committed to developing a trade agreement that benefits both parties. If this happens, European Union companies (as well as those from other regions of the world as well) who choose to compete in South Korea must understand the value placed on hierarchical order, formality, and self-control, as well as on duty rather than rights. Furthermore, Korean ideology emphasizes communitarianism, a characteristic of many Asian countries. Korea's approach differs from those of Japan and China, however, in that it focuses on *inhwa,* or harmony. Inhwa is based on a respect of hierarchical relationships and obedience to authority. Alternatively, the approach in China stresses *guanxi*—personal relationships or good connections—while in Japan, the focus is on *wa,* or group harmony and social cohesion.[83] The institutional context of China suggests a major emphasis on centralized planning by the government. The Chinese government provides incentives to firms to develop alliances with foreign firms having sophisticated technology in hopes of building knowledge and introducing new technologies to the Chinese markets over time.[84]

The Physical Environment Segment

The **physical environment segment** refers to potential and actual changes in the physical environment and business practices that are intended to positively respond to and deal with those changes.[85] Concerned with trends oriented to sustaining the world's physical environment, firms recognize that ecological, social, and economic systems interactively influence what happens in this particular segment.[86]

There are many parts or attributes of the physical environment that firms should consider as they try to identify trends in this segment. Some argue that global warming is a trend firms and nations should carefully examine in efforts to predict any potential effects on the global society as well as on their business operations.[87] Energy consumption is another part of the physical environment that concerns both organizations and nations. Canada, for example, "… has formulated various strategic measures to accelerate the development of energy efficiency systems and renewable energy technologies and has made significant progress."[88]

Because of increasing concern about sustaining the quality of the physical environment, a number of companies are developing environmentally friendly policies.

The **physical environment segment** refers to potential and actual changes in the physical environment and business practices that are intended to positively respond to and deal with those changes.

Target Corporation operates in ways that will minimize the firm's environmental footprint. In the company's words, "Target strives to be a responsible steward of the environment. In addition to complying with all environmental legislation, we seek to understand our impact and continuously improve our business practices in many areas."[89] (Additional commentary about Target's actions toward the physical environment appears in a Strategic Focus in Chapter 4.) As noted in the Opening Case, Philip Morris International is committed to sustainable tobacco farming and the efficient use of resources in recognition of the effects of its operations on the physical environment.

We discuss other firms' efforts to "reduce their environmental footprint" and to be good stewards of the physical environment as a result of doing so in the following Strategic Focus. As we note, the number of "green" products companies are producing continues to increase.

As our discussion of the general environment shows, identifying anticipated changes and trends among external elements is a key objective of analyzing the firm's general environment. With a focus on the future, the analysis of the general environment allows firms to identify opportunities and threats. It is necessary to have a top management team with the experience, knowledge, and sensitivity required to effectively analyze this segment of the environment.[90] Also critical to a firm's choices of strategic actions to take is an understanding of its industry environment and its competitors; we consider these issues next.

Industry Environment Analysis

An **industry** is a group of firms producing products that are close substitutes. In the course of competition, these firms influence one another. Typically, industries include a rich mixture of competitive strategies that companies use in pursuing above-average returns. In part, these strategies are chosen because of the influence of an industry's characteristics.[91]

Compared with the general environment, the industry environment has a more direct effect on the firm's strategic competitiveness and ability to earn above-average returns.[92] An industry's profit potential is a function of five forces of competition: the threats posed by new entrants, the power of suppliers, the power of buyers, product substitutes, and the intensity of rivalry among competitors (see Figure 2.2, on page 52).

The five forces model of competition expands the arena for competitive analysis. Historically, when studying the competitive environment, firms concentrated on companies with which they competed directly. However, firms must search more broadly to recognize current and potential competitors by identifying potential customers as well as the firms serving them. For example, the communications industry is now broadly defined as encompassing media companies, telecoms, entertainment companies, and companies producing devices such as phones and iPods. In such an environment, firms must study many other industries to identify firms with capabilities (especially technology-based capabilities) that might be the foundation for producing a good or a service that can compete against what they are producing.[93] Using this perspective finds firms focusing on customers and their needs rather than on specific industry boundaries to define markets.

When studying the industry environment, firms must also recognize that suppliers can become a firm's competitors (by integrating forward) as can buyers (by integrating backward). For example, several firms have integrated forward in the pharmaceutical industry by acquiring distributors or wholesalers. In addition, firms choosing to enter a new market and those producing products that are adequate substitutes for existing products can become a company's competitors. Next, we examine the five forces the firm analyzes to understand the profitability potential within the industry (or a segment of an industry) in which it competes or may choose to compete.

An **industry** is a group of firms producing products that are close substitutes.

FIRMS' EFFORTS TO TAKE CARE OF THE PHYSICAL ENVIRONMENT IN WHICH THEY COMPETE

The number of companies throughout the world that recognize that they compete within the confines of the physical environment and that they are expected to reduce the negative effect of their operations on the physical environment while competing continues to increase. Those concerned about the physical environment value this trend.

Producing and selling additional "green" (i.e., environmentally friendly) products is one company response to this trend. By mid-2009, for example, firms had launched almost 460 new green products such as toilet paper, diapers, and household cleaning products in the United States alone. Analysts saw these launchings, which represented a threefold increase compared to launches in 2008, as more evidence that "green" is going mainstream.

In addition to products, companies across the globe are committing to or increasing their commitment to environmental sustainability. McDonald's, for example, "takes its responsibility to the environment seriously." Green restaurant design, sustainable packaging and waste management, and energy efficiency are areas where McDonald's acts to reduce its environmental footprint. Dell Inc. recently announced that its operations are now "carbon neutral." Dell envisions this as an important step in the firm's quest to become "the greenest technology company on the planet." Google and Yahoo! have also pledged to become carbon neutral.

Honest Tea produces "delicious, truly healthy, organic beverages." Since its founding in 1998, the firm has had a very strong commitment to environmentally friendly business practices, including the way its new corporate headquarters was designed. In the company's words, "When it came time for a new office, we did our best to walk our talk and create an office that is environmentally friendly to both the planet and our employees."

Procter & Gamble's easily shipped PUR packets have helped provide over 1 billion liters of clean drinking water since the creation of the Children's Safe Drinking Water program in 2004.

Honest Tea used reclaimed bricks, flooring, and desks when building its new facility.

Procter & Gamble (P&G) recently announced increased targets for its 2012 sustainability goals. Among the goals are those to (1) "develop and market at least $50 billion in cumulative sales of sustainable innovation products, (2) deliver a 20 percent reduction (per unit of production) in carbon dioxide emissions, energy consumption, water usage and disposed waste from P&G plants, and (3) enable 300 million children to Live, Learn and Thrive and deliver three billion liters of clean water through P&G's Children's Safe Drinking Water program." Dutch consumer products giant Unilever also has an ongoing commitment to sustainability. The firm's sustainability actions include reducing water usage in its plants, working with its suppliers to encourage sustainability practices on their parts, and improving the eco-efficiency of their manufacturing facilities.

A number of other companies mirror the commitments of these firms in response to emerging trends in the physical environment segment. In addition to positively responding to the observed trends in this segment of the general environment, there is some evidence that firms engaging in these types of behaviors outperform those failing to do so. This emerging evidence suggests that these behaviors benefit companies, their stakeholders, and the physical environment in which they operate.

Sources: 2009, Eco-friendly growth, *BusinessWeek*, May 4,5–6; 2009, Honest Tea, http://www.honesttea.com; June 12; 2009, McDonald's Corporate Responsibility, http://www.mcdonalds.com, June 12; 2009, Procter & Gamble deepens corporate commitment to sustainability, http://www.pandg.com, April 29; 2009, Introduction to Unilever, http://www .unilever.com, June 12; 2008, Procter & Gamble, Sustainability Full Report, http://www.pandg.com, May 10; J. Ball, 2008, Green goal of "carbon neutrality" has limits, *Wall Street Journal Online*, http://www.wsj.com, December 28; T. B. Porter, 2008, Managerial applications of corporate social responsibility and systems thinking for achieving sustainability outcomes, *Systems Research and Behavioral Science*, 25: 397–411.

Threat of New Entrants

Identifying new entrants is important because they can threaten the market share of existing competitors.[94] One reason new entrants pose such a threat is that they bring additional production capacity. Unless the demand for a good or service is increasing, additional capacity holds consumers' costs down, resulting in less revenue and lower returns for competing firms. Often, new entrants have a keen interest in gaining a large market share. As a result, new competitors may force existing firms to be more efficient and to learn how to compete on new dimensions (e.g., using an Internet-based distribution channel).

The likelihood that firms will enter an industry is a function of two factors: barriers to entry and the retaliation expected from current industry participants. Entry barriers make it difficult for new firms to enter an industry and often place them at a competitive disadvantage even when they are able to enter. As such, high entry barriers tend to increase

Figure 2.2 The Five Forces of Competition Model

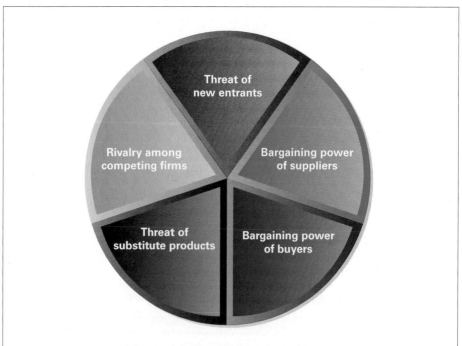

the returns for existing firms in the industry and may allow some firms to dominate the industry.[95] Thus, firms competing successfully in an industry want to maintain high entry barriers in order to discourage potential competitors from deciding to enter the industry.

Barriers to Entry

Firms competing in an industry (and especially those earning above-average returns) try to develop entry barriers to thwart potential competitors. For example, the server market is hypercompetitive and dominated by IBM, Hewlett-Packard, and Dell. Historically, the scale economies these firms have developed by operating efficiently and effectively have created significant entry barriers, causing potential competitors to think very carefully about entering the server market to compete against them. Recently though, Oracle paid $7.4 billion to acquire Sun Microsystems, which is primarily a computer hardware company. Early evidence suggests that Oracle intends to "… focus Sun's server business on a small but promising segment of the market: computer appliances preloaded with Oracle software."[96] The degree of success Oracle will achieve as a result of its decision to enter the server market via an acquisition remains uncertain.

Several kinds of potentially significant entry barriers may discourage competitors from entering a market.

Economies of Scale   *Economies of scale* are derived from incremental efficiency improvements through experience as a firm grows larger. Therefore, the cost of producing each unit declines as the quantity of a product produced during a given period increases. This is the case for IBM, Hewlett-Packard, and Dell in the server market, as previously described.

Economies of scale can be developed in most business functions, such as marketing, manufacturing, research and development, and purchasing.[97] Increasing economies of scale enhances a firm's flexibility. For example, a firm may choose to reduce its price and capture a greater share of the market. Alternatively, it may keep its price constant to increase profits. In so doing, it likely will increase its free cash flow, which is very helpful during financially challenging times.

New entrants face a dilemma when confronting current competitors' scale economies. Small-scale entry places them at a cost disadvantage. Given the size of Sun Microsystems relative to the three major competitors in the server market, Oracle may be at least initially be at a disadvantage in competing against them. Alternatively, large-scale entry, in which the new entrant manufactures large volumes of a product to gain economies of scale, risks strong competitive retaliation.

Some competitive conditions reduce the ability of economies of scale to create an entry barrier. Many companies now customize their products for large numbers of small customer groups. Customized products are not manufactured in the volumes necessary to achieve economies of scale. Customization is made possible by flexible manufacturing systems (this point is discussed further in Chapter 4). In fact, the new manufacturing technology facilitated by advanced information systems has allowed the development of mass customization in an increasing number of industries. Although it is not appropriate for all products and implementing it can be challenging, mass customization has become increasingly common in manufacturing products.[98] In fact, online ordering has enhanced the ability of customers to obtain customized products. They are often referred to as "markets of one."[99] Companies manufacturing customized products learn how to respond quickly to customers' needs in lieu of developing scale economies.

Product Differentiation   Over time, customers may come to believe that a firm's product is unique. This belief can result from the firm's service to the customer, effective advertising campaigns, or being the first to market a good or service. Currently, Ford Motor Company is seeking to differentiate its products from competitors on the basis that it is "... stronger, greener, and more technologically advanced than those other guys."[100] If successful with these efforts, Ford hopes those buying its cars today will generate the type of loyalty that results in repeat purchases.

Companies such as Procter & Gamble (P&G) and Colgate-Palmolive spend a great deal of money on advertising and product development to convince potential customers of their products' distinctiveness and of the value buying their brands provides.[101] Customers valuing a product's uniqueness tend to become loyal to both the product and the company producing it. In turn, customer loyalty is an entry barrier for firms thinking of an entering an industry and competing against the likes of P&G and Colgate. To compete against firms offering differentiated products to individuals who have become loyal customers, new entrants often allocate many resources to overcome existing customer loyalties. To combat the perception of uniqueness, new entrants frequently offer products at lower prices. This decision, however, may result in lower profits or even losses.

Capital Requirements   Competing in a new industry requires a firm to have resources to invest. In addition to physical facilities, capital is needed for inventories, marketing activities, and other critical business functions. Even when a new industry is attractive, the capital required for successful market entry may not be available to pursue the market opportunity. For example, defense industries are difficult to enter because of the substantial resource investments required to be competitive. In addition, because of the high knowledge requirements of the defense industry, a firm might acquire an existing company as a means of entering this industry. But it must have access to the capital necessary to do it. Obviously, Oracle had the capital required to acquire Sun Microsystems as a foundation for entering the server market.

Switching Costs   Switching costs are the one-time costs customers incur when they buy from a different supplier. The costs of buying new ancillary equipment and of retraining employees, and even the psychic costs of ending a relationship, may be incurred in switching to a new supplier. In some cases, switching costs are low, such as when the consumer switches to a different soft drink or when a smoker switches from a Philip Morris International cigarette to one produced by competitor Japan Tobacco International. Switching costs can vary as a function of time. For example, in terms of credit hours toward graduation, the cost to a student to transfer from one university to another as a freshman is much lower than it is when the student is entering the senior year. Occasionally, a decision made by manufacturers to produce a new, innovative product creates high switching costs for the final consumer. Customer loyalty programs, such as airlines' frequent flyer miles, are intended to increase the customer's switching costs.

If switching costs are high, a new entrant must offer either a substantially lower price or a much better product to attract buyers. Usually, the more established the relationships between parties, the greater are switching costs.

Access to Distribution Channels   Over time, industry participants typically develop effective means of distributing products. Once a relationship with its distributors has been built a firm will nurture it, thus creating switching costs for the distributors. Access to distribution channels can be a strong entry barrier for new entrants, particularly in consumer nondurable goods industries (e.g., in grocery stores where shelf space is limited) and in international markets. New entrants have to persuade distributors to carry their products, either in addition to or in place of those currently distributed. Price breaks and cooperative advertising allowances may be used for this purpose; however, those practices reduce the new entrant's profit potential.

Cost Disadvantages Independent of Scale   Sometimes, established competitors have cost advantages that new entrants cannot duplicate. Proprietary product technology, favorable access to raw materials, desirable locations, and government subsidies are examples.

Successful competition requires new entrants to reduce the strategic relevance of these factors. Delivering purchases directly to the buyer can counter the advantage of a desirable location; new food establishments in an undesirable location often follow this practice.

Government Policy   Through licensing and permit requirements, governments can also control entry into an industry. Liquor retailing, radio and TV broadcasting, banking, and trucking are examples of industries in which government decisions and actions affect entry possibilities. Also, governments often restrict entry into some industries because of the need to provide quality service or the need to protect jobs. Alternatively, deregulation of industries, exemplified by the airline industry and utilities in the United States, allows more firms to enter.[102] However, some of the most publicized government actions are those involving antitrust. In 2009, for example, the European Commission announced a fine of $1.4 billion—the largest the Commission had assessed—against Intel, the world's largest computer-chip maker. The fine was for "… breaking European antitrust rules."[103] The Commission's major conclusion was that Intel's competitive actions were blocking effective access by competitors to European markets. In response to the announcement, Intel indicated that it would appeal the fine as well as the ruling that the firm would have to change its business practices in the European Union.[104] These rulings caused other dominant firms such as Microsoft and Google to wonder about potential governmental rulings that the Commission might assess against them in the future.

Expected Retaliation

Companies seeking to enter an industry also anticipate the reactions of firms in the industry. An expectation of swift and vigorous competitive responses reduces the likelihood of entry. Vigorous retaliation can be expected when the existing firm has a major stake in the industry (e.g., it has fixed assets with few, if any, alternative uses), when it has substantial resources, and when industry growth is slow or constrained. For example, any firm attempting to enter the airline industry at the current time can expect significant retaliation from existing competitors due to overcapacity.

Locating market niches not being served by incumbents allows the new entrant to avoid entry barriers. Small entrepreneurial firms are generally best suited for identifying and serving neglected market segments. When Honda first entered the U.S. motorcycle market, it concentrated on small-engine motorcycles, a market that firms such as Harley-Davidson ignored. By targeting this neglected niche, Honda avoided competition. After consolidating its position, Honda used its strength to attack rivals by introducing larger motorcycles and competing in the broader market. Competitive actions and competitive responses between firms such as Honda and Harley-Davidson are discussed more fully in Chapter 5.

Bargaining Power of Suppliers

Increasing prices and reducing the quality of their products are potential means suppliers use to exert power over firms competing within an industry. If a firm is unable to recover cost increases by its suppliers through its own pricing structure, its profitability is reduced by its suppliers' actions. A supplier group is powerful when

- It is dominated by a few large companies and is more concentrated than the industry to which it sells.
- Satisfactory substitute products are not available to industry firms.
- Industry firms are not a significant customer for the supplier group.
- Suppliers' goods are critical to buyers' marketplace success.
- The effectiveness of suppliers' products has created high switching costs for industry firms.
- It poses a credible threat to integrate forward into the buyers' industry. Credibility is enhanced when suppliers have substantial resources and provide a highly differentiated product.

The airline industry is one in which suppliers' bargaining power is changing. Though the number of suppliers is low, the demand for major aircraft is also relatively low. Boeing and Airbus aggressively compete for orders of major aircraft, creating more power for buyers in the process. In mid-2009, United Airlines announced that it might place a "significant" order for wide-body airliners with either Airbus or Boeing in the fourth quarter of the year if the firm could earn an acceptable return on its investment. United's expectation that the winning bid from either Airbus or Boeing would include a financing arrangement that would strengthen its "… balance sheet over the long term and not impact (the firm's) cash flow position"[105] highlights the buyer's power in this proposed transaction.

Bargaining Power of Buyers

Firms seek to maximize the return on their invested capital. Alternatively, buyers (customers of an industry or a firm) want to buy products at the lowest possible price—the point at which the industry earns the lowest acceptable rate of return on its invested capital. To reduce their costs, buyers bargain for higher quality, greater levels of service, and lower prices. These outcomes are achieved by encouraging competitive battles among the industry's firms. Customers (buyer groups) are powerful when

■ They purchase a large portion of an industry's total output.
■ The sales of the product being purchased account for a significant portion of the seller's annual revenues.
■ They could switch to another product at little, if any, cost.
■ The industry's products are undifferentiated or standardized, and the buyers pose a credible threat if they were to integrate backward into the sellers' industry.

Armed with greater amounts of information about the manufacturer's costs and the power of the Internet as a shopping and distribution alternative have increased consumers' bargaining power in many industries. One reason for this shift is that individual buyers incur virtually zero switching costs when they decide to purchase from one manufacturer rather than another or from one dealer as opposed to a second or third one.

ICP-UK/Alamy

With consumer access to news at their fingertips via the iPhone and other wireless devices, newspapers and other traditional news sources face increasing competition for customers.

Threat of Substitute Products

Substitute products are goods or services from outside a given industry that perform similar or the same functions as a product that the industry produces. For example, as a sugar substitute, NutraSweet (and other sugar substitutes) places an upper limit on sugar manufacturers' prices—NutraSweet and sugar perform the same function, though with different characteristics. Other product substitutes include e-mail and fax machines instead of overnight deliveries, plastic containers rather than glass jars, and tea instead of coffee. Newspaper firms have experienced significant circulation declines over the past decade or more. The declines are due to substitute outlets for news including Internet sources, cable television news channels, and e-mail and cell phone alerts. These products are increasingly popular, especially among younger, and technologically savvy people, and as product substitutes they have significant potential to continue to reduce overall newspaper circulation sales.

In general, product substitutes present a strong threat to a firm when customers face few, if any, switching costs and when the substitute product's price is lower or its quality and performance capabilities are equal to or greater than those of the competing product. Differentiating a product along dimensions that customers value (such as quality, service after the sale, and location) reduces a substitute's attractiveness.

Intensity of Rivalry Among Competitors

Because an industry's firms are mutually dependent, actions taken by one company usually invite competitive responses. In many industries, firms actively compete against one another. Competitive rivalry intensifies when a firm is challenged by a competitor's actions or when a company recognizes an opportunity to improve its market position.

Firms within industries are rarely homogeneous; they differ in resources and capabilities and seek to differentiate themselves from competitors.[106] Typically, firms seek to differentiate their products from competitors' offerings in ways that customers value and in which the firms have a competitive advantage. Common dimensions on which rivalry is based include price, service after the sale, and innovation.

Next, we discuss the most prominent factors that experience shows to affect the intensity of firms' rivalries.

Numerous or Equally Balanced Competitors

Intense rivalries are common in industries with many companies. With multiple competitors, it is common for a few firms to believe they can act without eliciting a response. However, evidence suggests that other firms generally are aware of competitors' actions, often choosing to respond to them. At the other extreme, industries with only a few firms of equivalent size and power also tend to have strong rivalries. The large and often similar-sized resource bases of these firms permit vigorous actions and responses. The competitive battles between Airbus and Boeing exemplify intense rivalry between relatively equal competitors, and almost certainly will be so as the companies bid for the order to produce wide-body planes for United Airlines.

Slow Industry Growth

When a market is growing, firms try to effectively use resources to serve an expanding customer base. Growing markets reduce the pressure to take customers from competitors. However, rivalry in no-growth or slow-growth markets (slow change) becomes more intense as firms battle to increase their market shares by attracting competitors' customers.[107]

Typically, battles to protect market share are fierce. Certainly, this has been the case in the airline industry and in the fast-food industry as McDonald's, Wendy's, and Burger King try to win each other's customers. The instability in the market that results from these competitive engagements may reduce the profitability for all firms engaging in such competitive battles.

High Fixed Costs or High Storage Costs

When fixed costs account for a large part of total costs, companies try to maximize the use of their productive capacity. Doing so allows the firm to spread costs across a larger volume of output. However, when many firms attempt to maximize their productive capacity, excess capacity is created on an industry-wide basis. To then reduce inventories, individual companies typically cut the price of their product and offer rebates and other special discounts to customers. However, these practices, common in the automobile manufacturing industry in the recent past, often intensify competition. The pattern of excess capacity at the industry level followed by intense rivalry at the firm level is observed frequently in industries with high storage costs. Perishable products, for example, lose their value rapidly with the passage of time. As their inventories grow, producers of perishable goods often use pricing strategies to sell products quickly.

Lack of Differentiation or Low Switching Costs

When buyers find a differentiated product that satisfies their needs, they frequently purchase the product loyally over time. Industries with many companies that have successfully differentiated their products have less rivalry, resulting in lower competition for individual firms. Firms that develop and sustain a differentiated product that cannot be easily imitated by competitors often earn higher returns. However, when buyers view products as commodities (i.e., as products with few differentiated features or capabilities), rivalry intensifies. In these instances, buyers' purchasing decisions are based primarily on price and, to a lesser degree, service. Personal computers are a commodity product. Thus, the rivalry between Dell, Hewlett-Packard, and other computer manufacturers is strong and these companies are always trying to find ways to differentiate their offerings (Hewlett-Packard now pursues product design as a means of differentiation.)

High Strategic Stakes

Competitive rivalry is likely to be high when it is important for several of the competitors to perform well in the market. For example, although it is diversified and is a market leader in other businesses, Samsung has targeted market leadership in the consumer electronics market and is doing quite well. This market is quite important to Sony and other major competitors, such as Hitachi, Matsushita, NEC, and Mitsubishi, suggesting that rivalry among these competitors will remain strong.

High strategic stakes can also exist in terms of geographic locations. For example, Japanese automobile manufacturers are committed to a significant presence in the U.S. marketplace because it is the world's largest single market for automobiles and trucks. Because of the stakes involved in this country for Japanese and U.S. manufacturers, rivalry among firms in the U.S. and the global automobile industry is intense. With the excess capacity in this industry we mentioned earlier in this chapter, there is every reason to believe that the rivalry among global automobile manufacturers will become even more intense, certainly in the foreseeable future.

High Exit Barriers

Sometimes companies continue competing in an industry even though the returns on their invested capital are low or negative. Firms making this choice likely face high exit barriers, which include economic, strategic, and emotional factors causing them to remain in an industry when the profitability of doing so is questionable. Exit barriers are especially high in the airline industry. Although earning even average returns is difficult for these firms, they face substantial exit barriers, such as their ownership of specialized assets (e.g., large aircraft).[108] Common exit barriers include the following:

- Specialized assets (assets with values linked to a particular business or location)
- Fixed costs of exit (such as labor agreements)
- Strategic interrelationships (relationships of mutual dependence, such as those between one business and other parts of a company's operations, including shared facilities and access to financial markets)
- Emotional barriers (aversion to economically justified business decisions because of fear for one's own career, loyalty to employees, and so forth)
- Government and social restrictions (often based on government concerns for job losses and regional economic effects; more common outside the United States).

Interpreting Industry Analyses

Effective industry analyses are products of careful study and interpretation of data and information from multiple sources. A wealth of industry-specific data is available to be analyzed. Because of globalization, international markets and rivalries must be included in the firm's analyses. In fact, research shows that in some industries, international variables are more important than domestic ones as determinants of strategic competitiveness. Furthermore, because of the development of global markets, a country's borders no longer restrict industry structures. In fact, movement into international markets enhances the chances of success for new ventures as well as more established firms.[109]

Analysis of the five forces in the industry allows the firm to determine the industry's attractiveness in terms of the potential to earn adequate or superior returns. In general, the stronger competitive forces are, the lower the profit potential for an industry's firms. An unattractive industry has low entry barriers, suppliers and buyers with strong bargaining positions, strong competitive threats from product substitutes, and intense rivalry among competitors. These industry characteristics make it difficult for firms to achieve strategic competitiveness and earn above-average returns. Alternatively, an attractive industry has high entry barriers, suppliers and buyers with little bargaining power, few competitive threats from product substitutes, and relatively moderate rivalry.[110] Next, we explain strategic groups as an aspect of industry competition.

Strategic Groups

A set of firms that emphasize similar strategic dimensions and use a similar strategy is called a **strategic group**.[111] The competition between firms within a strategic group is greater than the competition between a member of a strategic group and companies outside that strategic group. Therefore, intrastrategic group competition is more intense than is interstrategic group competition. In fact, more heterogeneity is evident in the performance of firms within strategic groups than across the groups. The performance leaders within groups are able to follow strategies similar to those of other firms in the group and yet maintain strategic distinctiveness to gain and sustain a competitive advantage.[112]

The extent of technological leadership, product quality, pricing policies, distribution channels, and customer service are examples of strategic dimensions that firms in a strategic group may treat similarly. Thus, membership in a particular strategic group defines the essential characteristics of the firm's strategy.[113]

The notion of strategic groups can be useful for analyzing an industry's competitive structure. Such analyses can be helpful in diagnosing competition, positioning, and the profitability of firms within an industry.[114] High mobility barriers, high rivalry, and low resources among the firms within an industry limit the formation of strategic groups.[115] However, research suggests that after strategic groups are formed, their membership remains relatively stable over time, making analysis easier and more useful.[116] Using strategic groups to understand an industry's competitive structure requires the firm to plot companies' competitive actions and competitive responses along strategic dimensions such as pricing decisions, product quality, distribution channels, and so forth. This type of analysis shows the firm how certain companies are competing similarly in terms of how they use similar strategic dimensions.

Strategic groups have several implications. First, because firms within a group offer similar products to the same customers, the competitive rivalry among them can be intense. The more intense the rivalry, the greater the threat to each firm's profitability. Second, the strengths of the five industry forces differ across strategic groups. Third, the closer the strategic groups are in terms of their strategies, the greater is the likelihood of rivalry between the groups.

Competitor Analysis

The competitor environment is the final part of the external environment requiring study. Competitor analysis focuses on each company against which a firm directly competes. For example, Philip Morris International and Japan Tobacco International, Coca-Cola and PepsiCo, Home Depot and Lowe's, and Boeing and Airbus are keenly interested in understanding each other's objectives, strategies, assumptions, and capabilities. Indeed,

A **strategic group** is a set of firms emphasizing similar strategic dimensions to use a similar strategy.

intense rivalry creates a strong need to understand competitors.[117] In a competitor analysis, the firm seeks to understand the following:

- What drives the competitor, as shown by its *future objectives*
- What the competitor is doing and can do, as revealed by its *current strategy*
- What the competitor believes about the industry, as shown by its *assumptions*
- What the competitor's capabilities are, as shown by its *strengths* and *weaknesses*.[118]

Information about these four dimensions helps the firm prepare an anticipated response profile for each competitor (see Figure 2.3). The results of an effective competitor analysis help a firm understand, interpret, and predict its competitors' actions and responses. Understanding the actions of competitors clearly contributes to the firm's ability to compete successfully within the industry.[119] Interestingly, research suggests that executives often fail to analyze competitors' possible reactions to competitive actions their firm takes,[120] placing their firm at a potential competitive disadvantage as a result.

Critical to an effective competitor analysis is gathering data and information that can help the firm understand its competitors' intentions and the strategic implications resulting from them.[121] Useful data and information combine to form **competitor intelligence**: the set of data and information the firm gathers to better understand and better anticipate competitors' objectives, strategies, assumptions, and capabilities. In competitor analysis, the firm gathers intelligence not only about its competitors, but also regarding public policies in countries around the world. Such intelligence facilitates an understanding of the strategic posture of foreign competitors. Through effective competitive and public policy intelligence, the firm gains the insights needed to make effective strategic decisions about how to compete against its rivals.

Figure 2.3 Competitor Analysis Components

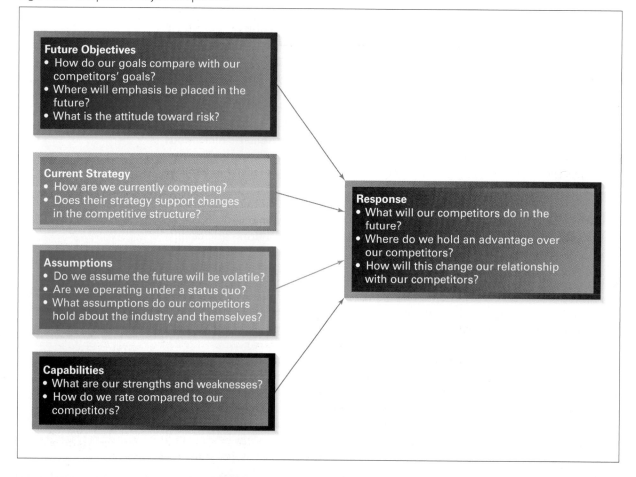

Future Objectives
- How do our goals compare with our competitors' goals?
- Where will emphasis be placed in the future?
- What is the attitude toward risk?

Current Strategy
- How are we currently competing?
- Does their strategy support changes in the competitive structure?

Assumptions
- Do we assume the future will be volatile?
- Are we operating under a status quo?
- What assumptions do our competitors hold about the industry and themselves?

Capabilities
- What are our strengths and weaknesses?
- How do we rate compared to our competitors?

Response
- What will our competitors do in the future?
- Where do we hold an advantage over our competitors?
- How will this change our relationship with our competitors?

When asked to describe competitive intelligence, it seems that a number of people respond with phrases such as "competitive spying" and "corporate espionage." These phrases denote the fact that competitive intelligence is an activity that appears to involve trade-offs.[122] According to some, the reason for this is that "what is ethical in one country is different from what is ethical in other countries." This position implies that the rules of engagement to follow when gathering competitive intelligence change in different contexts. However, firms avoid the possibility of legal entanglements and ethical quandaries only when their competitive intelligence gathering methods are governed by a strict set of legal and ethical guidelines.[123] This means that ethical behavior and actions as well as the mandates of relevant laws and regulations should be the foundation on which a firm's competitive intelligence-gathering process is formed. We address this matter in greater detail in the next section.

When gathering competitive intelligence, firms must also pay attention to the complementors of its products and strategy.[124] **Complementors** are companies or networks of companies that sell complementary goods or services that are compatible with the focal firm's good or service. When a complementor's good or service adds value to the sale of the focal firm's good or service it is likely to create value for the focal firm.

There are many examples of firms whose good or service complements other companies' offerings. For example, firms manufacturing affordable home photo printers complement other companies' efforts to sell digital cameras. Intel and Microsoft are perhaps the most widely recognized complementors. The Microsoft slogan "Intel Inside" demonstrates the relationship between two firms who do not directly buy from or sell to each other but whose products have a strong complementary relationship. Alliances among airline operations (e.g., the Star Alliance and the SkyTeam Alliance) find these companies sharing their route structures and customer loyalty programs as means of complementing each others' operations. (Each alliance is a network of complementors.) Recently, Continental Airlines announced that it was leaving the SkyTeam Alliance to join the Star Alliance. The primary reason for this change was to provide greater global coverage to Continental's customers by combining its routes with those of the other members of the Star Alliance.[125] In essence, Continental's conclusion was that the complementors of the Star Alliance created more value for its customers than did its complementors in the SkyTeam Alliance.

As our discussion shows, complementors expand the set of competitors firms must evaluate when completing a competitor analysis. For example, when Delta Airlines wants to study Continental Airlines, it must examine Continental's strategic actions as an independent company as well as its actions as a member of the Star Alliance. The same is true in reverse—Continental must study Delta's actions as an independent firm as well as its actions as a member of the SkyTeam Alliance. Similarly, Intel and Microsoft analyze each other's actions in that those actions might either help each firm gain a competitive advantage or damage each firm's ability to exploit a competitive advantage.

Ethical Considerations

Firms must follow relevant laws and regulations as well as carefully articulated ethical guidelines when gathering competitor intelligence. Industry associations often develop lists of these practices that firms can adopt. Practices considered both legal and ethical include (1) obtaining publicly available information (e.g., court records, competitors' help-wanted advertisements, annual reports, financial reports of publicly held corporations, and Uniform Commercial Code filings), and (2) attending trade fairs and shows to obtain competitors' brochures, view their exhibits, and listen to discussions about their products. In contrast, certain practices (including blackmail, trespassing, eavesdropping, and stealing drawings, samples, or documents) are widely viewed as unethical and often are illegal.

Some competitor intelligence practices may be legal, but a firm must decide whether they are also ethical, given the image it desires as a corporate citizen. Especially with electronic transmissions, the line between legal and ethical practices can be difficult to determine. For example, a firm may develop Web site addresses that are similar to those

Competitor intelligence is the set of data and information the firm gathers to better understand and better anticipate competitors' objectives, strategies, assumptions, and capabilities.

Complementors are companies or networks of companies that sell complementary goods or services that are compatible with the focal firm's good or service.

of its competitors and thus occasionally receive e-mail transmissions that were intended for those competitors. The practice is an example of the challenges companies face in deciding how to gather intelligence about competitors while simultaneously determining how to prevent competitors from learning too much about them. To deal with these challenges, firms should establish principles and take actions that are consistent with them. ING, a global financial company offering banking, investments, life insurance, and retirement services, expresses the principles guiding its actions as follows: "ING conducts business on the basis of clearly defined business principles. In all our activities, we carefully weigh the interests of our various stakeholders: customers, employees, communities and shareholders. ING strives to be a good corporate citizen."[126]

Open discussions of intelligence-gathering techniques can help a firm ensure that employees, customers, suppliers, and even potential competitors understand its convictions to follow ethical practices for gathering competitor intelligence. An appropriate guideline for competitor intelligence practices is to respect the principles of common morality and the right of competitors not to reveal certain information about their products, operations, and strategic intentions.[127]

SUMMARY

- The firm's external environment is challenging and complex. Because of the external environment's effect on performance, the firm must develop the skills required to identify opportunities and threats existing in that environment.

- The external environment has three major parts: (1) the general environment (elements in the broader society that affect industries and their firms), (2) the industry environment (factors that influence a firm, its competitive actions and responses, and the industry's profit potential), and (3) the competitor environment (in which the firm analyzes each major competitor's future objectives, current strategies, assumptions, and capabilities).

- The external environmental analysis process has four steps: scanning, monitoring, forecasting, and assessing. Through environmental analyses, the firm identifies opportunities and threats.

- The general environment has seven segments: demographic, economic, political/legal, sociocultural, technological, global, and physical. For each segment, the firm wants to determine the strategic relevance of environmental changes and trends.

- Compared with the general environment, the industry environment has a more direct effect on the firm's strategic actions. The five forces model of competition includes the threat of entry, the power of suppliers, the power of buyers, product

substitutes, and the intensity of rivalry among competitors. By studying these forces, the firm finds a position in an industry where it can influence the forces in its favor or where it can buffer itself from the power of the forces in order to achieve strategic competitiveness and earn above-average returns.

- Industries are populated with different strategic groups. A strategic group is a collection of firms following similar strategies along similar dimensions. Competitive rivalry is greater within a strategic group than between strategic groups.

- Competitor analysis informs the firm about the future objectives, current strategies, assumptions, and capabilities of the companies with which it competes directly. A thorough analysis examines complementors that sustain a competitor's strategy and major networks or alliances in which competitors participate. When analyzing competitors, the firm should also identify and carefully monitor major actions taken by firms with performance below the industry norm.

- Different techniques are used to create competitor intelligence: the set of data, information, and knowledge that allows the firm to better understand its competitors and thereby predict their likely strategic and tactical actions. Firms should use only legal and ethical practices to gather intelligence. The Internet enhances firms' capabilities to gather insights about competitors and their strategic intentions.

REVIEW QUESTIONS

1. Why is it important for a firm to study and understand the external environment?

2. What are the differences between the general environment and the industry environment? Why are these differences important?

3. What is the external environmental analysis process (four steps)? What does the firm want to learn when using this process?

4. What are the seven segments of the general environment? Explain the differences among them.

5. How do the five forces of competition in an industry affect its profit potential? Explain.

6. What is a strategic group? Of what value is knowledge of the firm's strategic group in formulating that firm's strategy?

7. What is the importance of collecting and interpreting data and information about competitors? What practices should a firm use to gather competitor intelligence and why?

EXPERIENTIAL EXERCISES

EXERCISE 1: AIRLINE COMPETITOR ANALYSIS

The International Air Transport Association (IATA) reports statistics on the number of passengers carried each year by major airlines. Passenger data for 2007 are reported for the top 10 carriers in three categories:

- International flights
- Domestic flights
- Combined traffic, domestic and international flights

The following table lists both passenger data and rankings for each category.

Airline	Intl Rank	Intl Passengers	Domestic Rank	Domestic Passengers	Combined Rank	Combined Passengers
Air France	3	31,549			8	50,465
All Nippon Airways			6	44,792		
American Airlines	7	21,479	2	76,687	2	98,166
British Airways	5	28,302				
Cathay Pacific	10	17,695				
China Southern Airlines			5	52,505	5	56,522
Continental Airlines			9	37,175	9	49,059
Delta Air Lines			3	61,651	3	73,086
Easyjet	4	30,173				
Emirates	8	20,448				
Japan Airlines International			10	35,583		
KLM	6	23,165				
Lufthansa	2	41,322			7	54,165
Northwest Airlines			7	44,337	6	54,696
Ryanair	1	49,030			10	49,030
Singapore Airlines	9	18,957				
Southwest Airlines			1	101,911	1	101,911
United Airlines			4	58,162	4	68,363
US Airways Inc.			8	37,560		

For this exercise, you will develop competitor profiles of selected air carriers.

Part One

Working in groups of five to seven people, each team member selects one airline from the table. The pool of selected airlines should contain a roughly even balance of three regions: North America, Europe/Middle East, and Asia. Answer the following questions:

1. What drives this competitor (i.e., what are its objectives)?
2. What is its current strategy?
3. What does this competitor believe about its industry?
4. What are its strengths and weaknesses?
5. Does this airline belong to an airline alliance (e.g., Oneworld, Star, SkyTeam)?

When researching your companies, you should use multiple resources. The company's Web site is a good starting point. Public firms headquartered in the United States will also have annual reports and 10-K reports filed with the Securities and Exchange Commission.

Part Two

As a group, summarize the results of each competitor profile into a single table with columns for objectives, current strategy, beliefs, strengths, weaknesses, and alliance partner(s). Then, discuss the following topics:

1. Which airlines had the most similar strategies? The most different? Would you consider any of the firms you studied to be in the same strategic group (i.e., a group of firms that follows similar strategies along similar dimensions)?
2. Create a composite five forces model based on the firms you reviewed. How might these elements of industry structure (e.g., substitutes, or bargaining power of buyers) differ from the perspective of individual airlines?
3. Which airlines appear best positioned to succeed in the future? Why?

EXERCISE 2: WHAT DOES THE FUTURE LOOK LIKE?

A critical ingredient to studying the general environment is identifying opportunities and threats. As discussed in this chapter, an opportunity is a condition in the environment that, if exploited, helps a company achieve strategic competitiveness. In order to identify opportunities, one must be aware of current and future trends affecting the world around us.

Thomas Fry, senior futurist at the DaVinci Institute, says that the chaotic nature of interconnecting trends and the vast array of possibilities that arise from them is somewhat akin to watching a spinning compass needle. From the way we use phones and e-mail, or recruit new workers to organizations, the climate for business is changing and shifting dramatically and at rapidly increasing rates. Sorting out these changes and making sense of them provides the basis for opportunity decision making. Which ones will dominate and which will fade? Understanding this is crucial for business success.

Your challenge (either individually or as a group) is to identify a trend, technology, entertainment, or design that is likely to alter the way in which business is conducted in the future. Once you have identified your topic, be prepared to discuss:

- Which of the seven segments of the general environment will this affect? (There may be more than one.)
- Describe the impact.
- List some business opportunities that will come from this.
- Identify some existing organizations that stand to benefit.
- What, if any, are the ethical implications?

You should consult a wide variety of sources. For example, the Gartner Group and McKinsey & Company produce market research and forecasts for business. There are also many Web forecasting tools and addresses such as TED (Technology, Entertainment, Design). TED hosts an annual conference for groundbreaking ideas, and you can find videos of their discussions on their Web site. Similarly the DaVinci Institute, Institute for Global Futures, and a host of others offer their own unique vision for tomorrow's environment.

VIDEO CASE

OUTWORK YOUR COMPETITION

Jerry Rice/Former Professional Football Player/NFL Hall of Famer

Jerry Rice (born October 13, 1962) is widely regarded as the greatest wide receiver ever and one of the greatest players in National Football League (NFL) history. He is the all-time leader in every major statistical category for wide receivers. In 20 NFL seasons, he was selected to the Pro Bowl 13 times (1986–1996, 1998, and 2002) and named All-Pro 10 times. He won three Super Bowl rings playing for the San Francisco 49ers and an AFC Championship with the Oakland Raiders.

Besides his exceptional ability as a receiver, Rice is remembered for his work ethic and dedication to the game. In his

20 NFL seasons, he missed only 10 regular season games. His 303 games are by far the most ever played by an NFL wide receiver. In addition to staying on the field, his work ethic showed in his dedication to conditioning and running precise routes.

Before you watch the video consider the following concepts and questions and be prepared to discuss them in class:

Concepts
- Competition
- Opportunity
- Threat
- Industry environment—five forces
- Competitor analysis

Questions

1. How competitive are you? How does this manifest itself in your everyday life?

2. What about goal setting in your life. Do you have objectives that you want to achieve five years after graduation?

3. How is your preparation and planning matched to your long-term objectives?

4. What, if any, difference is there between a company's objectives and those of its employees?

NOTES

1. D. A. Bosse, R. A. Phillips, & J. S. Harrison, 2009, Stakeholders, reciprocity, and firm performance, *Strategic Management Journal*, 30: 447–456.
2. K. Helliker, 2009, Smokeless tobacco to get push by venture overseas, *Wall Street Journal Online*, http://www.wsj.com, February 4.
3. K. Helliker, 2009, Smokeless tobacco to get push by venture overseas, *Wall Street Journal Online*, http://www.wsj.com, February 4.
4. P. Berrone & L. R. Gomez-Mejia, 2009, Environmental performance and executive compensation: An integrated agency-institutional perspective, *Academy of Management Journal*, 52: 103–126; P. Chattopadhyay, W. H. Glick, & G. P. Huber, 2001, Organizational actions in response to threats and opportunities, *Academy of Management Journal*, 44: 937–955.
5. C. Weigelt & M. B. Sarkar, 2009, Learning from supply-side agents: The impact of technology solution providers' experiential diversity on clients' innovation adoption, *Academy of Management Journal*, 52: 37–60; D. G. Sirmon, S. Gove, & M. A. Hitt, 2008, Resource management in dyadic competitive rivalry: The effects of resource bundling and deployment, *Academy of Management Journal*, 51: 919–935.
6. J. P. Bonardi, G. I. F. Holburn, & R. G. Vanden Bergh, 2006, Nonmarket strategy performance: Evidence from U.S. electric utilities, *Academy of Management Journal*, 49: 1209–1228.
7. S. Labaton, 2009, Obama plans fast action to tighten financial rules, *New York Times Online*, http://www.nytimes.com, January 25.
8. J. Welch & S. Welch, 2009, The economy: A little clarity, *BusinessWeek*, May 4, 80.
9. J. Uotila, M. Maula, T. Keil, & S. A. Zahra, 2009, Exploration, exploitation, and financial performance: Analysis of S&P 500 corporations, *Strategic Management Journal*, 30: 221–231; J. L. Murillo-Luna, C. Garces-Ayerbe, & P. Rivera-Torres, 2008, Why do patterns of environmental response differ? A stakeholder's pressure approach, *Strategic Management Journal*, 29: 1225–1240.
10. A. Kacperczyk, 2009, With greater power comes greater responsibility? Takeover protection and corporate attention to stakeholders, *Strategic Management Journal*, 30: 261–285; C. Eesley & M. J. Lenox, 2006, Firm responses to secondary stakeholder action, *Strategic Management Journal*, 27: 765–781.
11. L. Fahey, 1999, *Competitors*, New York: John Wiley & Sons; B. A. Walters & R. L. Priem, 1999, Business strategy and CEO intelligence acquisition, *Competitive Intelligence Review*, 10(2): 15–22.
12. A. P. Kellogg & J. Bennett, 2009, Chrysler' bankruptcy deals blow to affiliates, *Wall Street Journal Online*, http://www.wsj.com, May 2.
13. J. C. Short, D. J. Ketchen, Jr., T. B. Palmer, & G. T. Hult, 2007, Firm, strategic group, and industry influences on performance, *Strategic Management Journal*, 28: 147–167.
14. K. P. Coyne & J. Horn, 2009, Predicting your competitor's reaction, *Harvard Business Review*, 87(4): 90–97.
15. D. Sull, 2009, How to thrive in turbulent markets, *Harvard Business Review*, 87(2): 78–88; J. Hagel, III, J. S. Brown, & L. Davison, 2008, Shaping strategy in a world of constant disruption, *Harvard Business Review* 86(10): 80–89.
16. J. A. Lamberg, H. Tikkanen, T. Nokelainen, & H. Suur-Inkeroinen, 2009, Competitive dynamics, strategic consistency, and organizational survival, *Strategic Management Journal*, 30: 45–60.
17. E. Byron, 2009, P&G makes a bigger play for men, *Wall Street Journal Online*, http://www.wsj.com, April 29.
18. W. B. Gartner, K. G. Shaver, & J. Liao, 2008, Opportunities as attributions: Categorizing strategic issues from an attributional perspective, *Strategic Entrepreneurship Journal*, 2: 301–315.
19. P. Lattman, 2005, Rebound, *Forbes*, March 28, 58.
20. P. Lattman & J. McCracken, 2009, Vultures vie in auction for the remains of Polaroid, *Wall Street Journal*, http://www.wsj.com, April 17.
21. W. H. Stewart, R. C. May, & A. Kalla, 2008, Environmental perceptions and scanning in the United States and India: Convergence in entrepreneurial information seeking? *Entrepreneurship Theory and Practice*, 32: 83–106; K. M. Patton & T. M. McKenna, 2005, Scanning for competitive intelligence, *Competitive Intelligence Magazine*, 8(2): 24–26.
22. J. O. Schwarz, 2008, Assessing the future of futures studies in management, *Futures*, 42: 237–246; K. M. Eisenhardt, 2002, Has strategy changed? *MIT Sloan Management Review*, 43(2): 88–91.
23. J. R. Hough & M. A. White, 2004, Scanning actions and environmental dynamism: Gathering information for strategic decision making, *Management Decision*, 42: 781–793; V. K. Garg, B. A. Walters, & R. L. Priem, 2003, Chief executive scanning emphases, environmental dynamism, and manufacturing firm performance, *Strategic Management Journal*, 24: 725–744.
24. C.-P. Wei & Y.-H. Lee, 2004, Event detection from online news documents for supporting environmental scanning, *Decision Support Systems*, 36: 385–401.
25. Fahey, *Competitors*, 71–73.
26. J. Moreno, 2009, Wal-Mart gives its Supermercado concept a tryout, *Houston Chronicle Online*, http://www.chron.com, April 30.
27. S. M. Kalita, 2009, Companies world-wide rethink strategies, *Wall Street Journal Online*, http://www.wsj.com, April 29.
28. T. M. Jones, W. Felps, & G. A. Bigley, 2007, Ethical theory and stakeholder-related decisions: The role of stakeholder culture, *Academy of Management Review*, 32: 137–155.
29. M. J. Leiblein & T. L. Madsen, 2009, Unbundling competitive heterogeneity: Incentive structures and capability influences on technological innovation, *Strategic Management Journal*, 30: 711–735.
30. D. Matten & J. Moon, 2008, Implicit and explicit CSR: A conceptual framework for a comparative understanding of corporate social responsibility, *Academy of Management Review*, 33: 404–424; F. Sanna-Randaccio & R. Veugelers, 2007, Multinational knowledge spillovers with decentralized R&D: A game theoretic approach, *Journal of International Business Studies*, 38: 47–63.
31. Fahey, *Competitors*.
32. S. Lohr, 2009, How crisis shapes the corporate model, *Wall Street Journal Online*, http://www.wsj.com, March 29.

33. E. Byron, 2009, P&G investors need a little pampering, *Wall Street Journal Online*, http://www.wsj.com, April 30.

34. P. E. Bierly, III, F. Damanpour, & M. D. Santoro, 2009, The application of external knowledge: Organizational conditions for exploration and exploitation, *Journal of Management Studies*, 46: 481–509; Fahey, *Competitors*, 75–77.

35. K. M. Sutcliffe & K. Weber, 2003, The high cost of accurate knowledge, *Harvard Business Review*, 81(5): 74–82.

36. E. K. Foedermayr & A. Diamantopoulos, 2008, Market segmentation in practice: Review of empirical studies, methodological assessment, and agenda for future research, *Journal of Strategic Marketing*, 16: 223–265; L. Fahey & V. K. Narayanan, 1986, *Macroenvironmental Analysis for Strategic Management*, St. Paul, MN: West Publishing Company, 58.

37. U.S. Census Bureau, 2009, International data base, http://www.census.gov/pic/www/idb/worldpopgraph.html, May 24.

38. S. Moffett, 2005, Fast-aging Japan keeps its elders on the job longer, *Wall Street Journal*, June 15, A1, A8.

39. S. Armour, 2009, Mortgage crisis robbing seniors of golden years, *USA Today*, June 5–7, A1 & A2.

40. J. M. Nittoli, 2009, Now is no time to skimp on retirement plans, *Wall Street Journal*, http://www.wsj.com, June 5.

41. 2009, Migration and geographic distribution, http://www.medicine.jrank.org, June 5.

42. 2009, CultureGrams world edition, http://www.culturegrams.com, June 5.

43. 2009, StrictlySpanish, The growing Hispanic market in the United States, http://www.strictlyspanish.com, June 5.

44. J. A. Chatman & S. E. Spataro, 2005, Using self-categorization theory to understand relational demography-based variations in people's responsiveness to organizational culture, *Academy of Management Journal*, 48: 321–331.

45. 2006, Characteristics of the civilian labor force, 2004 and 2014, U.S. Department of Labor, Bureau of Labor Statistics data, http://www.bls.gov, May.

46. J. Millman, 2005, Low-wage U.S. jobs get "Mexicanized," but there's a price, *Wall Street Journal*, May 2, A2.

47. A. K. Fosu, 2008, Inequality and the growth-poverty nexus: Specification empirics using African data, *Applied Economics Letters*, 15: 563–566; A. McKeown, 2007, Periodizing globalization, *History Workshop Journal*, 63(1): 218–230.

48. O. Sullivan, 2008, Busyness, status distinction and consumption strategies of the income rich, time poor, *Time & Society*, 17: 5–26.

49. 2009, Half the world is middle class???, http://www.edwardsglobal.com, May 10.

50. D. Vrontis & P. Pavlou, 2008, *Journal for International Business and Entrepreneurship Development*, 3: 289–307; A. Jones & N. Ennis, 2007, Bringing the environment into economic development, *Local Economy*, 22(1): 1–5; Fahey & Narayanan, *Macroenvironmental Analysis*, 105.

51. P. Coy, 2009, What good are economists anyway? *BusinessWeek*, April 27, 26–31.

52. J. Simms, 2009, Losses at Japan's electronics companies are no shock, *Wall Street Journal Online*, http://www.wsj.com, February 4.

53. J. Bush, 2009, The worries facing Russia's banks, *Wall Street Journal Online*, http://www.wsj.com, April 13.

54. A. Peaple & N. P. Muoi, 2009, Vietnam's market—the fizz is deliberate, *Wall Street Journal Online*, http://www.wsj.com, June 11.

55. R. H. Lester, A. Hillman, A. Zardkoohi, & A. A. Cannella, Jr., 2008, Former government officials as outside directors: The role of human and social capital, *Academy of Management Journal*, 51: 999–1013; C. Oliver & I. Holzinger, 2008, The effectiveness of strategic political management: A dynamic capabilities framework, *Academy of Management Review*, 33: 496–520.

56. J. W. Spencer, 2008, The impact of multinational enterprise strategy on indigenous enterprises: Horizontal spillovers and crowding out in developing countries, *Academy of Management Review*, 33: 341–361; W. Chen, 2007, Does the colour of the cat matter? The red hat strategy in China's private enterprises, *Management and Organizational Review*, 3: 55–80.

57. P. Engardio, 2009, Clearing the track for high-speed rail, *BusinessWeek*, May 4, 29.

58. M. Srivastava, 2009, The sudden chill at an Indian hot spot, *BusinessWeek*, May 4, 59.

59. 2009, Taking aim at outsources on U.S. soil, *BusinessWeek*, June 15, 10.

60. H. W. Jenkins, Jr., 2009, GM needs a political strategy, *Wall Street Journal Online*, http://www.wsj.com, June 10.

61. G. L. F. Holburn & R. G. Vanden Bergh, 2008, The effectiveness of strategic political management: A dynamic capabilities framework, *Academy of Management Review*, 33: 521–540; M. A. Hitt, L. Bierman, K. Uhlenbruck, & K. Shimizu, 2006, The importance of resources in the internationalization of professional service firms: The good, the bad, and the ugly, *Academy of Management Journal*, 49: 1137–1157.

62. K. Olsen, 2009, S. Korea, EU call for early conclusion of trade pact, *Houston Chronicle Online*, http://www.chron.com, May 23.

63. L. Manchikanti, 2008, Health care reform in the United States: Radical surgery needed now more than ever, *Pain Physician*, 11: 13–42.

64. S. A. Burd, 2009, How Safeway is cutting health-care costs, *Wall Street Journal Online*, http://www.wsj.com, June 12.

65. 2009, Characteristics of the civilian labor force, U.S. Department of Labor, Bureau of Labor Statistics data, http://www.bls.gov, June.

66. E. S. W. Ng, 2008, Why organizations choose to manage diversity: Toward a leadership-based theoretical framework, *Human Resource Development Review*, 7: 58–78.

67. A. McConnon, 2009, For a temp giant, a boom in boomers, *BusinessWeek*, June 1, 54.

68. F. Moore & C. Rees, 2008, Culture against cohesion: Global corporate strategy and employee diversity in the UK plant of a German MNC, *Employee Relations*, 30: 176–189; B. L. Kirkman, K. B. Lowe, & C. B. Gibson, 2006, A quarter of a century of culture's consequences: A review of old empirical research incorporating Hofstede's cultural values framework, *Journal of International Business Studies*, 37: 285–320.

69. S. Michailova & K. Hutchings, 2006, National cultural influences on knowledge sharing: A comparison of China and Russia, *Journal of Management Studies*, 43: 384–405.

70. J. B. Knight & L. Yueh, 2008, The role of social capital in the labour market in China, *Economics of Transition*, 16: 389–414; P. J. Buckley, J. Clegg, & H. Tan, 2006, Cultural awareness in knowledge transfer to China—The role of guanxi and mianzi, *Journal of World Business*, 41: 275–288.

71. R. K. Sinha & C. H. Noble, 2008, The adoption of radical manufacturing technologies and firm survival, *Strategic Management Journal*, 29: 943–962.

72. K. H. Tsai & J.-C. Wang, 2008, External technology acquisition and firm performance: A longitudinal study, *Journal of Business Venturing*, 23: 91–112; D. Lavie, 2006, Capability reconfiguration: An analysis of incumbent responses to technological change, *Academy of Management Review*, 31: 153–174.

73. S. A. Brown, 2008, Household technology adoption, use, and impacts: Past, present, and future, *Information Systems Frontiers*, 10: 397–402.

74. W. S. Mossberg, 2009, The latest Kindle: Bigger, not better, than its sibling, *Wall Street Journal Online*, http://www.wsj.com, June 11.

75. L. F. Mesquita & S. G. Lazzarini, 2008, Horizontal and vertical relationships in developing economies: Implications for SMEs' access to global markets, *Academy of Management Journal*, 51: 359–380; W. P. Wan, 2005, Country resource environments, firm capabilities, and corporate diversification strategies, *Journal of Management Studies*, 42: 161–182.

76. J. R. Healey, 2009, Penske-Saturn deal could change how cars are sold, *USA Today*, June 8, B2.

77. D. Welch, 2009, A hundred factories too many, *BusinessWeek*, January 12, 42–43.

78. 2009, McDonald's Corp, *Standard & Poor's Stock Report*, http://www.standardandpoors.com, May 16.

79. G. Marcial, 2009, Heinz: The time may be ripe, *BusinessWeek*, May 11, 67.

80. 2009, Procter & Gamble Co, *Standard & Poor's Stock Report*, http://www .standardandpoors.com, May 16.

81. K. E. Meyer, 2009, Uncommon common sense, *Business Strategy Review*, 20: 38–43; K. E. Meyer, 2006, Globalfocusing: From domestic conglomerates to global specialists, *Journal of Management Studies*, 43: 1110–1144.

82. C. H. Oh & A. M. Rugman, 2007, Regional multinationals and the Korean cosmetics industry, *Asia Pacific Journal of Management*, 24: 27–42.

83. P. K. Ong & Y. Kathawala, 2009, Competitive advantage through good Guanxi in the marine industry, *International Journal of Chinese Culture and Management*, 2: 28–55; X.-P. Chen & S. Peng, 2008, Guanxi dynamics: Shifts in the closeness of ties between Chinese coworkers, *Management and Organizational Review*, 4: 63–80; M. A. Hitt, M. T. Dacin, B. B. Tyler, & D. Park, 1997, Understanding the differences in Korean and U.S. executives' strategic orientations, *Strategic Management Journal*, 18: 159–167.

84. M. A. Hitt, D. Ahlstrom, M. T. Dacin, E. Levitas, & L. Svobodina, 2004, The institutional effects on strategic alliance partner selection: China versus Russia, *Organization Science*, 15: 173–185.

85. L. Berchicci & A. King, 2008, Postcards from the edge: A review of the business and environment literature, in J. P. Walsh & A. P. Brief (eds.) *Academy of Management Annals*, New York: Lawrence Erlbaum Associates, 513–547.

86. M. J. Hutchins & J. W. Sutherland, 2008, An exploration of measures of social sustainability and their application to supply chain decisions, *Journal of Cleaner Production*, 16: 1688–1698.

87. P. K. Dutta & R. Radner, 2009, A strategic analysis of global warming: Theory and some numbers, *Journal of Economic Behavior & Organization*, in press.

88. H. Liming, E. Haque, & S. Barg, 2008, Public policy discourse, planning and measure toward sustainable energy strategies in Canada, *Renewable and Sustainable Energy Reviews*, 12: 91–115.

89. 2009, Target Corporation, Environment, http://www.target.com, June 12.

90. C. A. Bartlett & S. Ghoshal, 2003, What is a global manager? *Harvard Business Review*, 81(8): 101–108; M. A. Carpenter & J. W. Fredrickson, 2001, Top management teams, global strategic posture and the moderating role of uncertainty, *Academy of Management Journal*, 44: 533–545.

91. J. Galbreath & P. Galvin, 2008, Firm factors, industry structure and performance variation: New empirical evidence to a classic debate, *Journal of Business Research*, 61: 109–117; B. R. Koka & J. E. Prescott, 2008, Designing alliance networks: The influence of network position, environmental change, and strategy on firm performance, *Strategic Management Journal*, 29: 639–661.

92. V. F. Misangyl, H. Elms, T. Greckhamer, & J. A. Lepine, 2006, A new perspective on a fundamental debate: A multilevel approach to industry, corporate, and business unit effects, *Strategic Management Journal*, 27: 571–590; G. Hawawini, V. Subramanian, & P. Verdin, 2003, Is performance driven by industry or firm-specific factors? A new look at the evidence, *Strategic Management Journal*, 24: 1–16.

93. D. Bonnet & G. S. Yip, 2009, Strategy convergence, *Business Strategy Review*, 20: 50–55; E. Nelson, R. van den Dam, & H. Kline, 2008, A future in content(ion): Can telecom providers win a share of the digital content market? *Journal of Telecommunications Management*, 1: 125–138.

94. K. E. Kushida & J. Zysman, 2009, The services transformation and network policy: The new logic of value creation, *Review of Policy Research*, 26: 173–194; E. D. Jaffe, I. D. Nebenzahl, & I. Schorr, 2005, Strategic options of home country firms faced with MNC entry, *Long Range Planning*, 38: 183–196.

95. M. R. Peneder, 2008, Firm entry and turnover: The nexus with profitability and growth, *Small Business Economics*, 30: 327–344; A. V. Mainkar, M. Lubatkin, & W. S. Schulze, 2006, Toward a product-proliferation theory of entry barriers, *Academy of Management Review*, 31: 1062–1075; J. Shamsie, 2003, The context of dominance: An industry-driven framework for exploiting reputation, *Strategic Management Journal*, 24: 199–215.

96. S. Hamm, 2009, Oracle faces its toughest deal yet, *BusinessWeek*, May 4, 24.

97. S. K. Ethiraj & D. H. Zhu, 2008, Performance effects of imitative entry, *Strategic Management Journal*, 29: 797–817; R. Makadok, 1999, Interfirm differences in scale economies and the evolution of market shares, *Strategic Management Journal*, 20: 935–952.

98. M. J. Rungtusanatham & F. Salvador, 2008, From mass production to mass customization: Hindrance factors, structural inertia, and transition hazard, *Production and Operations Management*, 17: 385–396; F. Salvador & C. Forza, 2007, Principles for efficient and effective sales configuration design, *International Journal of Mass Customisation*, 2(1,2): 114–127.

99. F. Keenan, S. Holmes, J. Greene, & R. O. Crockett, 2002, A mass market of one, *BusinessWeek*, December 2, 68–72.

100. D. Kiley, 2009, Ford heads out on a road of its own, *BusinessWeek*, January 19, 47–49.

101. E. Byron, 2009, P&G, Colgate hit by consumer thrift, *Wall Street Journal Online*, http://www.wsj.com, May 1.

102. M. A. Hitt, R. M. Holmes, T. Miller, & M. P. Salmador, 2006, Modeling country institutional profiles: The dimensions and dynamics of institutional environments, presented at the Strategic Management Society Conference, October.

103. P. Kiviniem, 2009, Intel to get EU antitrust fine, *Wall Street Journal Online*, http://www.wsj.com, May 14.

104. C. Forelle & D. Clark, 2009, Intel fine jolts tech sector, *Wall Street Journal Online*, http://www.wsj.com, May 14.

105. L. Ranson, 2009, United confirms aircraft order talks with Airbus and Boeing, *FlightGlobal*, http://www.flightglobal.com, April 6.

106. D. G. Sirmon, S. Gove, & M. H. Hitt, 2008, Resource management in dyadic competitive rivalry: The effects of resource bundling and deployment, *Academy of Management Journal*, 51: 919–935.

107. S. Nadkarni & V. K. Narayanan, 2007, Strategic schemas, strategic flexibility, and firm performance: The moderating role of industry clockspeed, *Strategic Management Journal*, 28: 243–270.

108. P. Prada & M. Esterl, 2009, Airlines predict more trouble, broaden cuts, *Wall Street Journal Online*, http://www.wsj.com, June 12.

109. S. E. Feinberg & A. K. Gupta, 2009, MNC subsidiaries and country risk: Internalization as a safeguard against weak external institutions, *Academy of Management Journal*, 52: 381–399.

110. M. E. Porter, 1980, *Competitive Strategy*, New York: Free Press.

111. B. Kabanoff & S. Brown, 2008, Knowledge structures of prospectors, analyzers, and defenders: Content, structure, stability, and performance, *Strategic Management Journal*, 29: 149–171; M. S. Hunt, 1972, Competition in the major home appliance industry, 1960–1970 (doctoral dissertation, Harvard University); Porter, *Competitive Strategy*, 129.

112. G. McNamara, D. L. Deephouse, & R. A. Luce, 2003, Competitive positioning within and across a strategic group structure: The performance of core, secondary, and solitary firms, *Strategic Management Journal*, 24: 161–181.

113. F. Zen & C. Baldan, 2008, The strategic paths and performance of Italian mutual banks: A nonparametric analysis, *International Journal of Banking, Accounting and Finance*, 1: 189–214; M. W. Peng, J. Tan, & T. W. Tong, 2004, Ownership types and strategic groups in an emerging economy, *Journal of Management Studies*, 41: 1105–1129.

114. W. S. DeSarbo & R. Grewal, 2008. Hybrid strategic groups, *Strategic Management Journal*, 29: 293–317; M. Peteraf & M. Shanley, 1997, Getting to know you: A theory of strategic group identity, *Strategic Management Journal*, 18(Special Issue): 165–186.

115. J. Lee, K. Lee, & S. Rho, 2002, An evolutionary perspective on strategic group emergence: A genetic algorithm-based model, *Strategic Management Journal*, 23: 727–746.

116. J. A. Zuniga-Vicente, J. M. de la Fuente Sabate, & I. S. Gonzalez, 2004, Dynamics of the strategic group membership-performance linkage in rapidly changing

environments, *Journal of Business Research*, 57: 1378–1390.

117. T. Yu, M. Subramaniam, & A. A. Cannella, Jr., 2009, Rivalry deterrence in international markets: Contingencies governing the mutual forbearance hypothesis, *Academy of Management Journal*, 52: 127–147.

118. Porter, *Competitive Strategy*, 49.

119. L. Capron & O. Chatain, 2008, Competitors' resource-oriented strategies: Acting on competitors' resources through interventions in factor markets and political markets, *Academy of Management Review*, 33: 97–121; M. B. Lieberman & S. Asaba, 2006, Why do firms imitate each other? *Academy of Management Journal*, 31: 366–385.

120. D. B. Montgomery, M. C. Moore, & J. E. Urbany, 2005, Reasoning about competitive reactions: Evidence from executives, *Marketing Science*, 24: 138–149.

121. S. Jain, 2008, Digital piracy: A competitive analysis, *Marketing Science*, 27: 610–626.

122. J. G. York, 2009, Pragmatic sustainability: Translating environmental ethics into competitive advantage, *Journal of Business Ethics*, 85: 97–109.

123. K. A. Sawka, 2008, The ethics of competitive intelligence, *Kiplinger Business Resource Center Online*, http://www.kiplinger.com, March.

124. T. Mazzarol & S. Reboud, 2008, The role of complementary actors in the development of innovation in small firms, *International Journal of Innovation Management*, 12: 223–253; A. Brandenburger & B. Nalebuff, 1996, *Co-opetition*, New York: Currency Doubleday.

125. 2009, Continental to join Star alliance, *Continental Airlines Homepage*, http://www.continental.com, June 12.

126. 2009, ING Profile and fast facts, http://www.ing.com, June 12.

127. C. S. Fleisher & S. Wright, 2009, Examining differences in competitive intelligence practice: China, Japan, and the West, *Thunderbird International Business Review*, 51: 249–261; A. Crane, 2005, In the company of spies: When competitive intelligence gathering becomes industrial espionage, Business Horizons, 48(3): 233–240.

CHAPTER 3

The Internal Organization: Resources, Capabilities, Core Competencies, and Competitive Advantages

Studying this chapter should provide you with the strategic management knowledge needed to:

1. Explain why firms need to study and understand their internal organization.

2. Define value and discuss its importance.

3. Describe the differences between tangible and intangible resources.

4. Define capabilities and discuss their development.

5. Describe four criteria used to determine whether resources and capabilities are core competencies.

6. Explain how value chain analysis is used to identify and evaluate resources and capabilities.

7. Define outsourcing and discuss reasons for its use.

8. Discuss the importance of identifying internal strengths and weaknesses.

APPLE DEFIES GRAVITY WITH INNOVATIVE GENIUS

During a bad recession in 2008, Apple recorded record sales. The firm's strong performance in poor economic times is largely credited to its innovation capabilities. Apple has continued to upgrade its current products, such as its laptops, with enhancements (e.g., MacBook and MacBook Pro). Analysts believe that these innovative additions will keep Apple's "hot streak" alive and well. Furthermore, projections suggest that smartphone sales will surge over the next few years. These projections include a 200 percent increase in the sales of high-end mobile phones by 2013, to 300 million in annual sales. The growing popularity of Web 2.0 applications such as Facebook and Twitter are increasing the desire for these phones. Such demand is very positive for the future of BlackBerry and Apple's iPhone. By 2013, analysts believe that approximately 23 percent of all new mobile phone sales will be smartphones.

Apple has also continued to upgrade its innovative iPod with its second generation of iPod touch. One analyst gave it a perfect score for the significant enhancements made. And the iPod touch serves some similar functions as the iPhone such as providing an Internet connection, using the same touchscreen, and playing music and videos in the same way. An example of the continuous innovation is the 4-gigabyte iPod Shuffle introduced in 2009. It is less than two inches long (smaller than a double-A battery) and can store approximately 1,000 songs. This is the third-generation Shuffle—the first-generation Shuffle

Apple now offers more than 50,000 applications for the iPhone, enabling their customers to continually discover new uses for their smartphone.

launched in 2005 could store approximately 240 songs. In addition to increased storage, the new Shuffle can handle songs in 14 different languages. Apple has "set the standard" for design of personal computer since the mid-1990s. Since 1996, Apple product innovations include developing a tool that created a quantum increase in the sale of digital music, creating a mobile phone—a flexible computer—that is fun to use, and, in customer service, developing a chain of unique and popular retail stores. Thus, most external observers argue that Apple's innovative products have led to their becoming one of the fastest-growing companies in the United States.

Coupled with its innovation, Apple is an aggressive marketer. While most firms are paring back their costs and advertising during the recession, Apple has increased its marketing and advertising programs. It is the second most prolific technology advertiser, behind Microsoft.

While Apple is in a positive market position, it did experience potential problems in 2009. Its charismatic leader, Steve Jobs, had to take a medical leave of absence, causing uncertainty about the company's future. It also lost a few other top managers to key positions in other firms. Thus, investors became nervous and analysts questioned whether the firm could continue to be a market innovator, especially without Jobs.

Sources: C. Wildstrom, 2008, Apple laptops: The hits keep coming, *BusinessWeek*, http://businessweek.com, November 4; C. Edwards, 2008, Apple's superlative sequel: The latest iPod touch, *BusinessWeek*, http:// businessweek.com, November 20; R. Waters & C. Nutialin, 2009, Apple moves to clear up uncertainty ahead of Jobs' absence, *Financial Times*, http://www.ft.com, January 16; B. Stone, 2009, Can Apple fill the void? *The New York Times*, http://www.nytimes.com, January 16; Apple bobbing, *Financial Times*, http://www.ft.com, January 22; N. Lomas, 2009, Smartphones set to surge, *Business Week*, http://businessweek.com, February 3; B. Stone, 2009, In campaign wars, Apple still has Microsoft's number, *The New York Times*, http://www.nytimes.com, February 4; P. Elmer-Dewitt, 2009, Apple is 14th fastest-growing tech company, *Fortune*, http://www.fortune .com, February 6; Apple launches smaller, 4-gigabyte iPod shuffle, *Houston Chronicle*, http://www.chron.com, March 11.

As discussed in the first two chapters, several factors in the global economy, including the rapid development of the Internet's capabilities[1] and of globalization in general have made it increasingly difficult for firms to find ways to develop a competitive advantage that can be sustained for any period of time.[2] As is suggested by Apple's experiences, innovation may be a vital path to efforts to develop sustainable competitive advantages.[3] Sometimes, product innovation serves simultaneously as the foundation on which a firm is started as well as the source of its competitive advantages. This occurred with Apple. Steve Jobs was one of the cofounders of the company and helped to develop the personal computer that the company introduced to the market. Later, Jobs and the board of directors of Apple felt the need for more marketing expertise. So, a new CEO with a strong marketing background was brought in to the firm. Later Jobs was forced out and Apple lost its innovative approach. However, Jobs was brought back into the firm in 1997; he is commonly believed to be the savior of the company because he was able to revitalize the firm's innovation capabilities. Thus, his departure on medical leave, announced in December 2008 (see opening case), created uncertainty and concern on the part of investors.[4]

Competitive advantages and the differences they create in firm performance are often strongly related to the resources firms hold and how they are managed.[5] "Resources are the foundation for strategy, and unique bundles of resources generate competitive advantages that lead to wealth creation."[6] As Apple's experience shows, resources must be managed to simultaneously allow production efficiency and an ability to form competitive advantages such as the consistent development of innovative products.

To identify and successfully use resources over time, those leading firms need to think constantly about how to manage them to increase the value for customers who "are arbiters of value"[7] as they compare firms' goods and services against each other before making a purchase decision. As this chapter shows, firms achieve strategic competitiveness and earn above-average returns when their unique core competencies are effectively acquired, bundled, and leveraged to take advantage of opportunities in the external environment in ways that create value for customers.[8]

People are an especially critical resource for helping organizations learn how to continuously innovate as a means of achieving successful growth.[9] In other words, "smart growth" happens when the firm manages its need to grow with its ability to successfully manage growth.[10] People are a critical resource to efforts to grow successfully at 3M, where the director of global compensation says that harnessing the innovative powers of the firm's employees is the means for rekindling growth.[11] And, people at 3M as well as virtually all other firms who know how to effectively manage resources to help organizations learn how to continuously innovate are themselves a source of competitive advantage.[12] In fact, a global labor market now exists as firms seek talented individuals to add to their fold. As Richard Florida argues, "[W]herever talent goes, innovation, creativity, and economic growth are sure to follow."[13]

The fact that over time the benefits of any firm's value-creating strategy can be duplicated by its competitors is a key reason for having employees who know how to manage resources. These employees are critical to firms' efforts to perform well. Because all competitive advantages have a limited life,[14] the question of duplication is not if it will happen, but when. In general, the sustainability of a competitive advantage is a function of three factors: (1) the rate of core competence obsolescence because of environmental changes, (2) the availability of substitutes for the core competence, and (3) the imitability of the core competence.[15] The challenge for all firms, then, is to effectively manage current core competencies while simultaneously developing new ones.[16] Only when firms develop a continuous stream of capabilities that contribute to competitive advantages do they achieve strategic competitiveness, earn above-average returns, and remain ahead of competitors (see Chapter 5).

In Chapter 2, we examined general, industry, and competitor environments. Armed with this knowledge about the realities and conditions of their external environment, firms have a better understanding of marketplace opportunities and the characteristics of the competitive environment in which those opportunities exist. In this chapter, we focus on the firm itself. By analyzing its internal organization, a firm determines what it can do. Matching what a firm can do (a function of its resources, capabilities, core competencies, and competitive advantages) with what it might do (a function of opportunities and threats in the external environment) allows the firm to develop vision, pursue its mission, and select and implement its strategies.

We begin this chapter by briefly discussing conditions associated with analyzing the firm's internal organization. We then discuss the roles of resources and capabilities in developing core competencies, which are the sources of the firm's competitive advantages. Included in this discussion are the techniques firms use to identify and evaluate resources and capabilities and the criteria for selecting core competencies from among them. Resources and capabilities are not inherently valuable, but they create value when the firm can use them to perform certain activities that result in a competitive advantage. Accordingly, we also discuss the value chain concept and examine four criteria to evaluate core competencies that establish competitive advantage.[17] The chapter closes with cautionary comments about the need for firms to prevent their core competencies from becoming core rigidities. The existence of core rigidities indicates that the firm is too anchored to its past, which prevents it from continuously developing new competitive advantages.

Using a global mind-set, Volkswagen's leaders decided that the firm should open facilities in Slovakia. Opening these facilities long before their competitors has led to a distinct competitive advantage for VW in Slovakia and surrounding countries.

Analyzing the Internal Organization

The Context of Internal Analysis

In the global economy, traditional factors such as labor costs, access to financial resources and raw materials, and protected or regulated markets remain sources of competitive advantage, but to a lesser degree.[18] One important reason is that competitors can apply their resources to successfully use an international strategy (discussed in Chapter 8) as a means of overcoming the advantages created by these more traditional sources. For example, Volkswagen began establishing production facilities in Slovakia "shortly after the Russians moved out" as part of its international strategy. Volkswagen is thought to have a competitive advantage over rivals such as France's Peugeot Citroen and South Korea's Kia Motors, firms that are now investing in Slovakia in an effort to duplicate the competitive advantage that has accrued to Volkswagen. In 2008, a total of 770,000 automobiles were manufactured in Slovakia[19]

© AP Photo/CTK, Jan Koller

Increasingly, those who analyze their firm's internal organization should use a **global mind-set** to do so. A global mind-set is the ability to analyze, understand, and manage (if in a managerial position) an internal organization in ways that are not dependent on the assumptions of a single country, culture, or context.[20] Because they are able to span artificial boundaries,[21] those with a global mind-set recognize that their firms must possess resources and capabilities that allow understanding of and appropriate responses to competitive situations that are influenced by country-specific factors and unique societal cultures. Firms populated with people having a global mind-set have a "key source of long-term competitive advantage in the global marketplace."[22]

Finally, analysis of the firm's internal organization requires that evaluators examine the firm's portfolio of resources and the *bundles* of heterogeneous resources and capabilities managers have created.[23] This perspective suggests that individual firms possess at least some resources and capabilities that other companies do not—at least not in the same combination. Resources are the source of capabilities, some of which

A **global mind-set** is the ability to analyze, understand and manage an internal organization in ways that are not dependent on the assumptions of a single country, culture, or context.

lead to the development of a firm's core competencies or its competitive advantages.[24] Understanding how to *leverage* the firm's unique bundle of resources and capabilities is a key outcome decision makers seek when analyzing the internal organization.[25] Figure 3.1 illustrates the relationships among resources, capabilities, and core competencies and shows how firms use them to create strategic competitiveness. Before examining these topics in depth, we describe value and its creation.

Creating Value

By exploiting their core competencies to meet if not exceed the demanding standards of global competition, firms create value for customers.[26] **Value** is measured by a product's performance characteristics and by its attributes for which customers are willing to pay. Customers of Luby Cafeterias, for example, pay for meals that are value-priced, generally healthy, and served quickly in a casual setting.[27]

Firms with a competitive advantage offer value to customers that is superior to the value competitors provide.[28] Firms create value by innovatively bundling and leveraging their resources and capabilities.[29] Firms unable to creatively bundle and leverage their resources and capabilities in ways that create value for customers suffer performance declines. Sometimes, it seems that these declines may happen because firms fail to understand what customers value. For example, after learning that General Motors (GM) intended to focus on visual design to create value for buyers, one former GM customer said that in his view, people buying cars and trucks valued durability, reliability, good fuel economy, and a low cost of operation more than visual design.[30]

Ultimately, creating value for customers is the source of above-average returns for a firm. What the firm intends regarding value creation affects its choice of business-level strategy (see Chapter 4) and its organizational structure (see Chapter 11).[31] In Chapter 4's discussion of business-level strategies, we note that value is created by a product's low cost, by its highly differentiated features, or by a combination of low cost and high differentiation, compared with competitors' offerings. A business-level strategy

Value is measured by a product's performance characteristics and by its attributes for which customers are willing to pay.

Figure 3.1 Components of Internal Analysis Leading to Competitive Advantage and Strategic Competitiveness

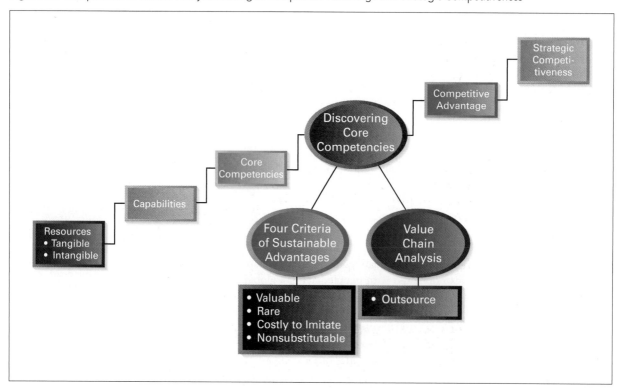

is effective only when it is grounded in exploiting the firm's core competencies and competitive advantages. Thus, successful firms continuously examine the effectiveness of current and future core competencies and advantages.[32]

At one time, the strategic management process was concerned largely with understanding the characteristics of the industry in which the firm competed and, in light of those characteristics, determining how the firm should be positioned relative to competitors. This emphasis on industry characteristics and competitive strategy underestimated the role of the firm's resources and capabilities in developing a competitive advantage. In fact, core competencies, in combination with product-market positions, are the firm's most important sources of competitive advantage.[33] The core competencies of a firm, in addition to results of analyses of its general, industry, and competitor environments, should drive its selection of strategies. The resources held by the firm and their context are important when formulating strategy.[34] As Clayton Christensen noted, "Successful strategists need to cultivate a deep understanding of the processes of competition and progress and of the factors that undergird each advantage. Only thus will they be able to see when old advantages are poised to disappear and how new advantages can be built in their stead."[35] By emphasizing core competencies when formulating strategies, companies learn to compete primarily on the basis of firm-specific differences, but they must be aware of how things are changing in the external environment as well.[36]

The Challenge of Analyzing the Internal Organization

The strategic decisions managers make about the components of their firm's internal organization are nonroutine,[37] have ethical implications,[38] and significantly influence the firm's ability to earn above-average returns.[39] These decisions involve choices about the assets the firm needs to collect and how to best use those assets. "Managers make choices precisely because they believe these contribute substantially to the performance and survival of their organizations."[40]

Making decisions involving the firm's assets—identifying, developing, deploying, and protecting resources, capabilities, and core competencies—may appear to be relatively easy. However, this task is as challenging and difficult as any other with which managers are involved; moreover, it is increasingly internationalized.[41] Some believe that the pressure on managers to pursue only decisions that help the firm meet the quarterly earnings expected by market analysts makes it difficult to accurately examine the firm's internal organization.[42]

The challenge and difficulty of making effective decisions are implied by preliminary evidence suggesting that one-half of organizational decisions fail.[43] Sometimes, mistakes are made as the firm analyzes conditions in its internal organization.[44] Managers might, for example, identify capabilities as core competencies that do not create a competitive advantage. This misidentification may have been the case at Polaroid Corporation as decision makers continued to believe that the skills it used to build its instant film cameras were highly relevant at the time its competitors were developing and using the skills required to introduce digital cameras.[45] When a mistake occurs, such as occurred at Polaroid, decision makers must have the confidence to admit it and take corrective actions.[46] A firm can still grow through well-intended errors; the learning generated by making and correcting mistakes can be important to the creation of new competitive advantages.[47] Moreover, firms and those managing them can learn from the failure resulting from a mistake—that is, what not to do when seeking competitive advantage.[48] Thus, difficult managerial decisions concerning resources, capabilities, and core competencies are characterized by three conditions: uncertainty, complexity, and intraorganizational conflicts (see Figure 3.2).[49]

Managers face *uncertainty* in terms of new proprietary technologies, rapidly changing economic and political trends, transformations in societal values, and shifts in customer demands.[50] Environmental uncertainty increases the *complexity* and range of issues to examine when studying the internal environment.[51] Consider the complexity associated with the decisions Gregory H. Boyce is encountering as CEO of Peabody Energy Corp.

Figure 3.2 Conditions Affecting Managerial Decisions about Resources, Capabilities, and Core Competencies

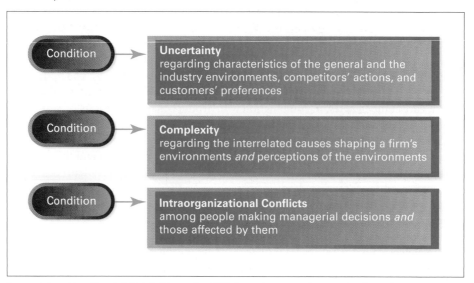

Source: Adapted from R. Amit & P. J. H. Schoemaker, 1993, Strategic assets and organizational rent, *Strategic Management Journal*, 14: 33.

Peabody is the world's largest coal company. But coal is thought of as a "dirty fuel," meaning that some think its future prospects are dim in light of global warming issues. Boyce is building a new "clean" coal-fired plant to produce energy and is a proponent of strong emissions standards. The firm argues for more use of "clean coal." Obviously, the complexity of these decisions is quite significant.[52] Biases about how to cope with uncertainty affect decisions about the resources and capabilities that will become the foundation of the firm's competitive advantage.[53] For example, Boyce strongly believes in coal's future, suggesting that automobiles capable of burning coal should be built. Finally, *intraorganizational conflict* surfaces when decisions are made about the core competencies to nurture as well as how to nurture them.

In making decisions affected by these three conditions, judgment is required. *Judgment* is the capability of making successful decisions when no obviously correct model or rule is available or when relevant data are unreliable or incomplete. In this type of situation, decision makers must be aware of possible cognitive biases. Overconfidence, for example, can often lower value when a correct decision is not obvious, such as making a judgment as to whether an internal resource is a strength or a weakness.[54]

When exercising judgment, decision makers often take intelligent risks. In the current competitive landscape, executive judgment can be a particularly important source of competitive advantage. One reason is that, over time, effective judgment allows a firm to build a strong reputation and retain the loyalty of stakeholders whose support is linked to above-average returns.[55]

As explained in the Strategic Focus, GE's managers build their capabilities in its executive leadership program. This program, which is recognized as one of the best in the world, helps GE's managers develop the capabilities to deal with uncertainty, complexity, and intraorganizational conflict. As such, they learn to use their judgment to make decisions that help GE navigate effectively in an uncertain and complex competitive landscape. The effectiveness of GE's managers and their ability to exercise good judgment in making strategic decisions is shown in the value GE has created for its shareholders and the number of former GE managers who are now CEOs of other major companies.

In the next section, we discuss how resources (such as young professionals and low-level managers) are developed and bundled to create capabilities.

GE BUILDS MANAGEMENT CAPABILITIES AND SHARES THEM WITH OTHERS

For many years, GE was considered one of the best organizations for management talent in the world. For the period, 1993–2002, GE was ranked first or second in market value added among the Stern Stewart 1,000 firms. In fact, GE was one of the top producers of shareholder value through the more than 20 years of Jack Welch's tenure as CEO. Most analysts attribute this phenomenal record to GE's exceptional leadership development program.

Approximately 9,000 managers participated in programs annually at GE's Leadership Center in Crotonville, New York. Managers received extensive leadership and team-based training in these programs. They even provided internal consulting by working on major GE projects, such as evaluating joint venture partners and analyzing opportunities for the use of artificial intelligence. Its world-class management development programs provided GE with an inventory of successors for almost any management position in the company. In fact, many analysts believe that the management development programs helped GE achieve a competitive advantage. Some argue that the management development process has the characteristics of a core competence; it is valuable, rare, difficult to imitate, and nonsubstitutable.

Jack Welch was often quoted as saying that people came first and strategy second. He actively participated in the management development program, sharing his expertise with other GE managers. Welch's successor, Jeff Immelt, does the same. Immelt believes that effective leaders learn constantly and also help others in the firm to learn as well. GE's leadership development program is so good that many companies look for talent among GE's management team because the program produces more leaders than it can usefully absorb. Thus, there are many company CEOs who are former GE managers. A study of these CEOs found they outperformed non-GE CEOs by a significant margin.

GE is experiencing problems in the economic malaise of 2008–2009. This is partly because of problems in its major financial services business (similar to the whole financial services industry). However, it is also partly due to the current CEO's emphasis on innovation for the future of the company. To innovate effectively requires that the firm invest now for returns several years later, which involves taking risks. As such, shorter-term returns are likely to suffer with high costs and lower returns awaiting the major longer-term payoffs of important innovations. Only time will tell if these investments to create innovations with long-term payoffs (as opposed to short-term returns) will work.

AP Photo/Mark Lennihan

GE CEO Jeff Immlet, like his predecessor Jack Welch, believes the development of leaders within the organization is an essential investment.

Sources: G. Spotts, 2006, GE's Immelt may have "ecomagination," but he needs project managers for jumbo-sized ideas, *FastCompany*, http://www.fastcompany.com, June 11; Things leaders do, *FastCompany*, http://www.fastcompany.com, December 19; S. Hamm, 2008, Tech innovations for tough times, ADNetAsia, http://www.zdnetasia.com, December 26; E. Smith, 2009, At GE, management development is a continuous process. Aprendia Corp, http://www.aprendiacorp.com, February 15; G. Rowe, R. E. White, D. Lehmbert, and J. R. Phillips, 2009, General Electric: An outlier in CEO talent development, *IVEY Business Journal*, http://www.iveybusinessjournal.com/article, January/February; P. Eavis & L. Denning, 2009, GE needs a circuit breaker, *Wall Street Journal*, http://www.wsj.com, March 5; P. Eaves, 2009, GE paper cut is greeted with relief, *Wall Street Journal*, http://www.wsj.com, March 13; D. Lehmberg, W. G. Rowe, R. E. White, and R. R. Phillips, 2009, The GE paradox: Competitive advantage through tangible non-firm-specific investment, *Journal of Management*, in press.

Resources, Capabilities, and Core Competencies

Resources, capabilities, and core competencies are the foundation of competitive advantage. Resources are bundled to create organizational capabilities. In turn, capabilities are the source of a firm's core competencies, which are the basis of competitive advantages.[56] Figure 3.1, on page 74, depicts these relationships. Here, we define and provide examples of these building blocks of competitive advantage.

Resources

Broad in scope, resources cover a spectrum of individual, social, and organizational phenomena.[57] Typically, resources alone do not yield a competitive advantage.[58] In fact, a competitive advantage is generally based on the unique bundling of several resources.[59] For example, Amazon.com combined service and distribution resources to develop its competitive advantages. The firm started as an online bookseller, directly shipping orders to customers. It quickly grew large and established a distribution network through which it could ship "millions of different items to millions of different customers." Lacking Amazon's combination of resources, traditional bricks-and-mortar companies, such as Borders, found it difficult to establish an effective online presence. These difficulties led some of them to develop partnerships with Amazon. Through these arrangements, Amazon now handles the online presence and the shipping of goods for several firms, including Borders—which now can focus on sales in its stores.[60] These types of arrangements are useful to the brick-and-mortar companies because they have little experience in shipping large amounts of diverse merchandise directly to individuals.

Some of a firm's resources (defined in Chapter 1 as inputs to the firm's production process) are tangible while others are intangible. **Tangible resources** are assets that can be observed and quantified. Production equipment, manufacturing facilities, distribution centers, and formal reporting structures are examples of tangible resources. Intangible resources are assets that are rooted deeply in the firm's history and have accumulated over time. Because they are embedded in unique patterns of routines, **intangible resources** are relatively difficult for competitors to analyze and imitate. Knowledge, trust between managers and employees, managerial capabilities, organizational routines (the unique ways people work together), scientific capabilities, the capacity for innovation, brand name, and the firm's reputation for its goods or services and how it interacts with people (such as employees, customers, and suppliers) are intangible resources.[61]

The four types of tangible resources are financial, organizational, physical, and technological (see Table 3.1). The three types of intangible resources are human, innovation, and reputational (see Table 3.2).

Tangible resources are assets that can be observed and quantified.

Intangible resources include assets that are rooted deeply in the firm's history, accumulate over time, and are relatively difficult for competitors to analyze and imitate.

Table 3.1 Tangible Resources

Financial Resources	• The firm's borrowing capacity • The firm's ability to generate internal funds
Organizational Resources	• The firm's formal reporting structure and its formal planning, controlling, and coordinating systems
Physical Resources	• Sophistication and location of a firm's plant and equipment • Access to raw materials
Technological Resources	• Stock of technology, such as patents, trademarks, copyrights, and trade secrets

Sources: Adapted from J. B. Barney, 1991, Firm resources and sustained competitive advantage, *Journal of Management*, 17: 101; R. M. Grant, 1991, *Contemporary Strategy Analysis*, Cambridge, U.K.: Blackwell Business, 100–102.

Table 3.2 Intangible Resources

Human Resources	• Knowledge • Trust • Managerial capabilities • Organizational routines
Innovation Resources	• Ideas • Scientific capabilities • Capacity to innovate
Reputational Resources	• Reputation with customers • Brand name • Perceptions of product quality, durability, and reliability • Reputation with suppliers • For efficient, effective, supportive, and mutually beneficial interactions and relationships

Sources: Adapted from R. Hall, 1992, The strategic analysis of intangible resources, *Strategic Management Journal*, 13: 136–139; R. M. Grant, 1991, *Contemporary Strategy Analysis*, Cambridge, U.K.: Blackwell Business, 101–104.

Tangible Resources

As tangible resources, a firm's borrowing capacity and the status of its physical facilities are visible. The value of many tangible resources can be established through financial statements, but these statements do not account for the value of all the firm's assets, because they disregard some intangible resources.[62] The value of tangible resources is also constrained because they are hard to leverage—it is difficult to derive additional business or value from a tangible resource. For example, an airplane is a tangible resource, but "You can't use the same airplane on five different routes at the same time. You can't put the same crew on five different routes at the same time. And the same goes for the financial investment you've made in the airplane."[63]

Although production assets are tangible, many of the processes necessary to use these assets are intangible. Thus, the learning and potential proprietary processes associated with a tangible resource, such as manufacturing facilities, can have unique intangible attributes, such as quality control processes, unique manufacturing processes, and technology that develop over time and create competitive advantage.[64]

Intangible Resources

Compared to tangible resources, intangible resources are a superior source of core competencies.[65] In fact, in the global economy, "the success of a corporation lies more in its intellectual and systems capabilities than in its physical assets. [Moreover], the capacity to manage human intellect—and to convert it into useful products and services—is fast becoming the critical executive skill of the age.[66]

Because intangible resources are less visible and more difficult for competitors to understand, purchase, imitate, or substitute for, firms prefer to rely on them rather than on tangible resources as the foundation for their capabilities and core competencies. In fact, the more unobservable (i.e., intangible) a resource is, the more sustainable will be the competitive advantage that is based on it.[67] Another benefit of intangible resources is that, unlike most tangible resources, their use can be leveraged. For instance, sharing knowledge among employees does not diminish its value for any one person. To the contrary, two people sharing their individualized knowledge sets often can be leveraged to create additional knowledge that, although new to each of them, contributes to performance improvements for the firm. This is especially true when members of the top management team share knowledge with each other to make more effective decisions. The new knowledge created is then often shared with managers and employees in each of the units managed by executives in the top management team.[68] With intangible resources, the larger the network of users, the greater the benefit to each party.

As shown in Table 3.2, the intangible resource of reputation is an important source of competitive advantage. Indeed, some argue that "a firm's reputation is widely considered to be a valuable resource associated with sustained competitive advantage."[69] Earned through the firm's actions as well as its words, a value-creating reputation is a product of years of superior marketplace competence as perceived by stakeholders.[70] A reputation indicates the level of awareness a firm has been able to develop among stakeholders and the degree to which they hold the firm in high esteem.[71]

A well-known and highly valued brand name is an application of reputation as a source of competitive advantage.[72] A continuing commitment to innovation and aggressive advertising facilitate firms' efforts to take advantage of the reputation associated with their brands.[73] Because of the desirability of its reputation, the Harley-Davidson brand name, for example, has such status that it adorns a limited edition Barbie doll, a popular restaurant in New York City, and a line of cologne. Additionally, the firm offers a broad range of clothing items, from black leather jackets to fashions for tots through Harley-Davidson MotorClothes.[74] Even established firms need to build their reputations in new markets that they enter. For example, Ford hired a well-respected Indian actor, Sunil Shetty, to serve as the brand ambassador for the Ford Endeavor launch in India. The Endeavor had the highest sales of SUVs in 2008.[75]

Harley Davidson's iconic reputation transcends motorcycles and for some represents an entire lifestyle.

Lon C. Diehl /PhotoEdit

Capabilities

Capabilities exist when resources have been purposely integrated to achieve a specific task or set of tasks. These tasks range from human resource selection to product marketing and research and development activities.[76] Critical to the building of competitive advantages, capabilities are often based on developing, carrying, and exchanging information and knowledge through the firm's human capital.[77] Client-specific capabilities often develop from repeated interactions with clients and the learning about their needs that occurs. As a result, capabilities often evolve and develop over time.[78] The foundation of many capabilities lies in the unique skills and knowledge of a firm's employees and, often, their functional expertise. Hence, the value of human capital in developing and using capabilities and, ultimately, core competencies cannot be overstated.[79]

While global business leaders increasingly support the view that the knowledge possessed by human capital is among the most significant of an organization's capabilities and may ultimately be at the root of all competitive advantages,[80] firms must also be able to utilize the knowledge they have and transfer it among their business units.[81] Given this reality, the firm's challenge is to create an environment that allows people to integrate their individual knowledge with that held by others in the firm so that, collectively, the firm has significant organizational knowledge.[82] As noted in the earlier Strategic Focus, GE has been effective in developing its human capital and in promoting the transfer of their knowledge throughout the company. Building important capabilities is critical to achieving high firm performance.[83]

As illustrated in Table 3.3, capabilities are often developed in specific functional areas (such as manufacturing, R&D, and marketing) or in a part of a functional area (e.g., advertising). Table 3.3 shows a grouping of organizational functions and the capabilities that some companies are thought to possess in terms of all or parts of those functions.

Core Competencies

Defined in Chapter 1, core competencies are capabilities that serve as a source of competitive advantage for a firm over its rivals. Core competencies distinguish a company competitively and reflect its personality. Core competencies emerge over time through an

Table 3.3 Examples of Firms' Capabilities

Functional Areas	Capabilities	Examples of Firms
Distribution	Effective use of logistics management techniques	Wal-Mart
Human Resources	Motivating, empowering, and retaining employees	Microsoft
Management Information Systems	Effective and efficient control of inventories through point-of-purchase data collection methods	Wal-Mart
Marketing	Effective promotion of brand-name products Effective customer service Innovative merchandising	Procter & Gamble Polo Ralph Lauren Corp. McKinsey & Co. Nordstrom Inc. Norrell Corporation Crate & Barrel
Management	Ability to envision the future of clothing Effective organizational structure	Hugo Boss PepsiCo
Manufacturing	Design and production skills yielding reliable products Product and design quality Miniaturization of components and products	Komatsu Witt Gas Technology Sony
Research & Development	Innovative technology Development of sophisticated elevator control solutions Rapid transformation of technology into new products and processes Digital technology	Caterpillar Otis Elevator Co. Chaparral Steel Thomson Consumer Electronics

organizational process of accumulating and learning how to deploy different resources and capabilities.[84] As the capacity to take action, core competencies are "crown jewels of a company," the activities the company performs especially well compared with competitors and through which the firm adds unique value to its goods or services over a long period of time.[85]

Innovation is thought to be a core competence at Xerox today. It is not surprising because this firm was built on a world-changing innovation—xerography. And even though Xerox was the first firm to integrate the mouse with the graphical user interface of a PC, it was Apple Computer that initially recognized the value of this innovation and derived value from it. In 2000, then-CEO Paul Allaire admitted that Xerox's business model no longer worked and that the firm had lost its innovative ability. Some nine-plus years later, things have changed for the better at Xerox. Using the capabilities of its scientists, engineers, and researchers, Xerox has reconstituted innovation as a core competence. For example, Xerox received more than 230 industry awards for the attributes of a range of products and services including image quality, performance, and technical innovation. One example of a recent focus of Xerox's research is on identifying products and services that help customers deal with the information explosion, according to Xerox's Chief Technology Officer, Sophie Vandebroek.[86]

How many core competencies are required for the firm to have a sustained competitive advantage? Responses to this question vary. McKinsey & Co. recommends that its clients identify no more than three or four competencies around which their strategic actions can be framed. Supporting and nurturing more than four core competencies may prevent a firm from developing the focus it needs to fully exploit its competencies in the marketplace. At Xerox, services expertise, employee talent, and technological skills are thought to be core competencies along with innovation.[87]

Building Core Competencies

Two tools help firms identify and build their core competencies. The first consists of four specific criteria of sustainable competitive advantage that firms can use to determine those capabilities that are core competencies. Because the capabilities shown in Table 3.3 have satisfied these four criteria, they are core competencies. The second tool is the value chain analysis. Firms use this tool to select the value-creating competencies that should be maintained, upgraded, or developed and those that should be outsourced.

Four Criteria of Sustainable Competitive Advantage

As shown in Table 3.4, capabilities that are valuable, rare, costly to imitate, and nonsubstitutable are core competencies. In turn, core competencies are sources of competitive advantage for the firm over its rivals. Capabilities failing to satisfy the four criteria of sustainable competitive advantage are not core competencies, meaning that although every core competence is a capability, not every capability is a core competence. In slightly different words, for a capability to be a core competence, it must be valuable and unique from a customer's point of view. For a competitive advantage to be sustainable, the core competence must be inimitable and nonsubstitutable by competitors.[88]

A sustained competitive advantage is achieved only when competitors cannot duplicate the benefits of a firm's strategy or when they lack the resources to attempt imitation. For some period of time, the firm may earn a competitive advantage by using capabilities that are, for example, valuable and rare, but imitable. For example, some firms are trying to gain an advantage by out-greening their competitors. Wal-Mart initiated a major sustainability program that helped to reduce the use of containers, saving approximately 1,000 barrels of oil and thousands of trees while simultaneously saving $2 million. GE's ecomanagement system, through which it has developed and introduced new, "greener" products to meet growing demand, is another example.[89] The length of time a firm can expect to retain its competitive advantage is a function of how quickly competitors can successfully imitate a good, service, or process. Sustainable competitive advantage results only when all four criteria are satisfied.

Valuable

Valuable capabilities allow the firm to exploit opportunities or neutralize threats in its external environment. By effectively using capabilities to exploit opportunities, a firm creates value for customers. Under former CEO Jack Welch's leadership, GE built a valuable competence in financial services. It built this powerful competence largely through acquisitions and its core competence in integrating newly acquired businesses. In addition, making such competencies as financial services highly successful required placing the right people in the right jobs. As noted in the opening case, Welch emphasized human capital because it is important in creating value for customers. That emphasis has continued in the company after Welch retired.

Table 3.4 The Four Criteria of Sustainable Competitive Advantage

Valuable Capabilities	• Help a firm neutralize threats or exploit opportunities
Rare Capabilities	• Are not possessed by many others
Costly-to-Imitate Capabilities	• Historical: A unique and a valuable organizational culture or brand name • Ambiguous cause: The causes and uses of a competence are unclear • Social complexity: Interpersonal relationships, trust, and friendship among managers, suppliers, and customers
Nonsubstitutable Capabilities	• No strategic equivalent

Valuable capabilities allow the firm to exploit opportunities or neutralize threats in its external environment.

Rare

Rare capabilities are capabilities that few, if any, competitors possess. A key question to be answered when evaluating this criterion is, "How many rival firms possess these valuable capabilities?" Capabilities possessed by many rivals are unlikely to be sources of competitive advantage for anyone of them. Instead, valuable but common (i.e., not rare) resources and capabilities are sources of competitive parity.[90] Competitive advantage results only when firms develop and exploit valuable capabilities that differ from those shared with competitors.

Costly to Imitate

Costly-to-imitate capabilities are capabilities that other firms cannot easily develop. Capabilities that are costly to imitate are created because of one reason or a combination of three reasons (see Table 3.4). First, a firm sometimes is able to develop capabilities because of *unique historical conditions*. As firms evolve, they often acquire or develop capabilities that are unique to them.[91]

A firm with a unique and valuable *organizational culture* that emerged in the early stages of the company's history "may have an imperfectly imitable advantage over firms founded in another historical period;"[92] one in which less valuable or less competitively useful values and beliefs strongly influenced the development of the firm's culture. Briefly discussed in Chapter 1, organizational culture is a set of values that are shared by members in the organization. This will be explained in more detail in Chapter 12. An organizational culture is a source of advantage when employees are held together tightly by their belief in it.[93]

For example, culture is a competitive advantage for Mustang Engineering (an engineering and project management firm based in Houston, Texas). Established as a place where people are expected to take care of people, Mustang offers "a company culture that we believe is unique in the industry. Mustang is a work place with a family feel. A client once described Mustang as a world-class company with a mom-and-pop culture."[94]

A second condition of being costly to imitate occurs when the link between the firm's capabilities and its competitive advantage is *causally ambiguous*.[95] In these instances, competitors can't clearly understand how a firm uses its capabilities as the foundation for competitive advantage. As a result, firms are uncertain about the capabilities they should develop to duplicate the benefits of a competitor's value-creating strategy. For years, firms tried to imitate Southwest Airlines' low-cost strategy but most have been unable to do so, primarily because they can't duplicate Southwest's unique culture. Of all Southwest imitators, Ryanair, an Irish airline headquartered in Dublin, is the most successful. However, Ryanair is also a controversial company, praised by some, criticized by others as described in the Strategic Focus. Ryanair's core competence is its capability to keep its costs excessively low and to generate alternative sources of revenue.

Social complexity is the third reason that capabilities can be costly to imitate. Social complexity means that at least some, and frequently many, of the firm's capabilities are the product of complex social phenomena. Interpersonal relationships, trust, friendships among managers and between managers and employees, and a firm's reputation with suppliers and customers are examples of socially complex capabilities. Southwest Airlines is careful to hire people who fit with its culture. This complex interrelationship between the culture and human capital adds value in ways that other airlines cannot, such as jokes on flights by the flight attendants or the cooperation between gate personnel and pilots.

Nonsubstitutable

Nonsubstitutable capabilities are capabilities that do not have strategic equivalents. This final criterion for a capability to be a source of competitive advantage "is that there must be no strategically equivalent valuable resources that are themselves either not rare or imitable. Two valuable firm resources (or two bundles of firm resources) are strategically equivalent when they each can be separately exploited to implement the same strategies."[96] In general, the strategic value of capabilities increases as they become more

Rare capabilities are capabilities that few, if any, competitors possess.

Costly-to-imitate capabilities are capabilities that other firms cannot easily develop.

Nonsubstitutable capabilities are capabilities that do not have strategic equivalents.

RYANAIR: THE PASSIONATE COST CUTTER THAT IS BOTH LOVED AND HATED

Ryanair is the leading low-cost airline in Europe. It has achieved a high market share by relentlessly holding down costs and thereby offering the lowest prices on its routes. To attract new customers, it once offered flights for one penny to selected destinations. It sold almost 500,000 tickets with the promotion. While Michael O'Leary, Ryanair CEO, is known to be cheap (he will not provide employees with pens; he recommends that they get them from hotels where they stay overnight), the primary reason for Ryanair's lowest cost status is that it has the fastest turnarounds in the industry (their speed resembles that of an auto racing pit crew). O'Leary is also constantly identifying new revenue streams such as charges for use of airport check-in facilities, charging for each piece of luggage, offering rental cars at the destination, charging to use the toilet on the plane, etc.

To obtain free publicity, O'Leary or other executives often make outrageous statements and roundly criticize their competitors to get Ryanair's name in the news. The firm uses multiple marketing gimmicks such as advertising that directly criticizes competitors and even some "off-color" advertising slogans. The firm's core competence is the capability to maintain the lowest costs in the industry and to generate alternative revenues. Because of its very low fares, its passenger load grew at an annual rate of approximately 25 percent until the economic crisis that began in 2008, but the company remained profitable in 2008.

Despite its success, Ryanair receives a significant amount of criticism. In 2006, for example, it was voted as the least favorite airline (despite its popularity evidenced in passenger numbers). Critics have also accused Ryanair of poor customer service, an unfriendly, uncaring staff, and hidden charges. Yet O'Leary believes that Ryanair may be one of the few airlines in Europe left standing after the latest severe economic recession. He is planning growth (although the airline announced some small reductions in service and staff in 2009) and is negotiating with Boeing and Airbus to buy as many as 400 new aircraft. With its decided strengths and acknowledged weaknesses, the future of Ryanair will be interesting to witness.

Sources: 2005, Ryanair exercises options on five Boeing 737s, Wikinews, http://en.wikinews.org, June 13; M. Scott, 2007, Ryanair flying high, *BusinessWeek*, http://www.businessweek.com, July 31; A. Davidson, 2008, Michael O'Leary: Ryanair's rebel with a cause, *The Sunday Times*, http://business.timesonline.co.uk, December 7; K. Done, 2009, Ryanair in talks to buy 400 aircraft, *Financial Times*, http://www.ft.com, February 2; K. Done, 2009, Virgin and Ryanair to cut jobs, *Financial Times*, http://www.ft.com, February 12; 2009, Ryanair Holdings PLC, http://www.answers.com, March 13; 2009, Ryanair, Wikipedia. http://www.wikipedia.org, March 13.

ULRICH PERREY/dpa/Landov

Michael O'Leary, CEO of low-cost airline Ryanair, poses with a model of an aircraft during a press conference in Hamburg, Germany. O'Leary's intense scrutiny of costs and monetizing of services may contribute to lower ticket prices but not necessarily customer satisfaction.

Table 3.5 Outcomes from Combinations of the Criteria for Sustainable Competitive Advantage

Is the Resource or Capability Valuable?	Is the Resource or Capability Rare?	Is the Resource or Capability Costly to Imitate?	Is the Resource or Capability Nonsubstitutable?	Competitive Consequences	Performance Implications
No	No	No	No	Competitive disadvantage	Below-average returns
Yes	No	No	Yes/no	Competitive parity	Average returns
Yes	Yes	No	Yes/no	Temporary competitive advantage	Average returns to above-average returns
Yes	Yes	Yes	Yes/no	Sustainable competitive advantage	Above-average returns

difficult to substitute. The more invisible capabilities are, the more difficult it is for firms to find substitutes and the greater the challenge is to competitors trying to imitate a firm's value-creating strategy. Firm-specific knowledge and trust-based working relationships between managers and nonmanagerial personnel, such as existed for years at Southwest Airlines, are examples of capabilities that are difficult to identify and for which finding a substitute is challenging. However, causal ambiguity may make it difficult for the firm to learn as well and may stifle progress, because the firm may not know how to improve processes that are not easily codified and thus are ambiguous.[97]

In summary, only using valuable, rare, costly-to-imitate, and nonsubstitutable capabilities creates sustainable competitive advantage. Table 3.5 shows the competitive consequences and performance implications resulting from combinations of the four criteria of sustainability. The analysis suggested by the table helps managers determine the strategic value of a firm's capabilities. The firm should not emphasize capabilities that fit the criteria described in the first row in the table (i.e., resources and capabilities that are neither valuable nor rare and that are imitable and for which strategic substitutes exist). Capabilities yielding competitive parity and either temporary or sustainable competitive advantage, however, will be supported. Some competitors such as Coca-Cola and PepsiCo may have capabilities that result in competitive parity. In such cases, the firms will nurture these capabilities while simultaneously trying to develop capabilities that can yield either a temporary or sustainable competitive advantage.

Value Chain Analysis

Value chain analysis allows the firm to understand the parts of its operations that create value and those that do not.[98] Understanding these issues is important because the firm earns above-average returns only when the value it creates is greater than the costs incurred to create that value.[99]

The value chain is a template that firms use to analyze their cost position and to identify the multiple means that can be used to facilitate implementation of a chosen business-level strategy.[100] Today's competitive landscape demands that firms examine their value chains in a global rather than a domestic-only context.[101] In particular, activities associated with supply chains should be studied within a global context.[102]

As shown in Figure 3.3, a firm's value chain is segmented into primary and support activities. **Primary activities** are involved with a product's physical creation, its sale and distribution to buyers, and its service after the sale. **Support activities** provide the assistance necessary for the primary activities to take place.

The value chain shows how a product moves from the raw-material stage to the final customer. For individual firms, the essential idea of the value chain is to create additional value without incurring significant costs while doing so and to capture the value that has

Primary activities are involved with a product's physical creation, its sale and distribution to buyers, and its service after the sale.

Support activities provide the assistance necessary for the primary activities to take place.

Figure 3.3 The Basic Value Chain

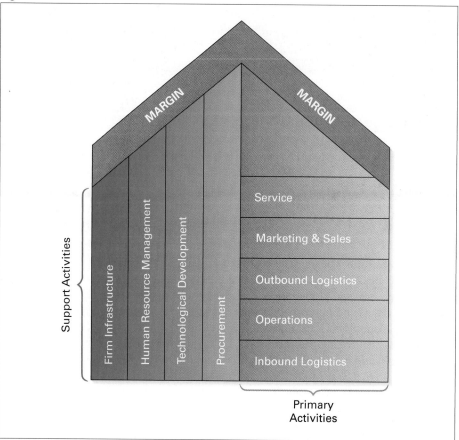

been created. In a globally competitive economy, the most valuable links on the chain are people who have knowledge about customers. This locus of value-creating possibilities applies just as strongly to retail and service firms as to manufacturers. Moreover, for organizations in all sectors, the effects of e-commerce make it increasingly necessary for companies to develop value-adding knowledge processes to compensate for the value and margin that the Internet strips from physical processes.[103]

Table 3.6 lists the items that can be evaluated to determine the value-creating potential of primary activities. In Table 3.7, the items for evaluating support activities are shown. All items in both tables should be evaluated relative to competitors' capabilities. To be a source of competitive advantage, a resource or capability must allow the firm (1) to perform an activity in a manner that provides value superior to that provided by competitors, or (2) to perform a value-creating activity that competitors cannot perform. Only under these conditions does a firm create value for customers and have opportunities to capture that value.

Creating value through value chain activities often requires building effective alliances with suppliers (and sometimes others to which the firm outsources activities, as discussed in the next section) and developing strong positive relationships with customers. When firms have such strong positive relationships with suppliers and customers, they are said to have "social capital."[104] The relationships themselves have value because they produce knowledge transfer and access to resources that a firm may not hold internally.[105] To build social capital whereby resources such as knowledge are transferred across organizations requires trust between the parties. The partners must trust each other in order to allow their resources to be used in such a way that both parties will benefit over time and neither party will take advantage of the other.[106] Trust and social capital usually evolve over time with repeated interactions but firms can also establish special means to jointly

Table 3.6 Examining the Value-Creating Potential of Primary Activities

Inbound Logistics

Activities, such as materials handling, warehousing, and inventory control, used to receive, store, and disseminate inputs to a product.

Operations

Activities necessary to convert the inputs provided by inbound logistics into final product form. Machining, packaging, assembly, and equipment maintenance are examples of operations activities.

Outbound Logistics

Activities involved with collecting, storing, and physically distributing the final product to customers. Examples of these activities include finished-goods warehousing, materials handling, and order processing.

Marketing and Sales

Activities completed to provide means through which customers can purchase products and to induce them to do so. To effectively market and sell products, firms develop advertising and promotional campaigns, select appropriate distribution channels, and select, develop, and support their sales force.

Service

Activities designed to enhance or maintain a product's value. Firms engage in a range of service-related activities, including installation, repair, training, and adjustment.

Each activity should be examined relative to competitors' abilities. Accordingly, firms rate each activity as *superior, equivalent,* or *inferior.*

Source: Adapted with the permission of The Free Press, an imprint of Simon & Schuster Adult Publishing Group, from *Competitive Advantage: Creating and Sustaining Superior Performance,* by Michael E. Porter, pp. 39–40, Copyright © 1985, 1998 by Michael E. Porter.

Table 3.7 Examining the Value-Creating Potential of Support Activities

Procurement

Activities completed to purchase the inputs needed to produce a firm's products. Purchased inputs include items fully consumed during the manufacture of products (e.g., raw materials and supplies, as well as fixed assets—machinery, laboratory equipment, office equipment, and buildings).

Technological Development

Activities completed to improve a firm's product and the processes used to manufacture it. Technological development takes many forms, such as process equipment, basic research and product design, and servicing procedures.

Human Resource Management

Activities involved with recruiting, hiring, training, developing, and compensating all personnel.

Firm Infrastructure

Firm infrastructure includes activities such as general management, planning, finance, accounting, legal support, and governmental relations that are required to support the work of the entire value chain. Through its infrastructure, the firm strives to effectively and consistently identify external opportunities and threats, identify resources and capabilities, and support core competencies.

Each activity should be examined relative to competitors' abilities. Accordingly, firms rate each activity as *superior, equivalent,* or *inferior.*

Source: Adapted with the permission of The Free Press, an imprint of Simon & Schuster Adult Publishing Group, from *Competitive Advantage: Creating and Sustaining Superior Performance,* by Michael E. Porter, pp. 40–43, Copyright © 1985, 1998 by Michael E. Porter.

manage alliances that promote greater trust with the outcome of enhanced benefits for both partners.[107]

Sometimes start-up firms create value by uniquely reconfiguring or recombining parts of the value chain. FedEx changed the nature of the delivery business by reconfiguring outbound logistics (a primary activity) and human resource management (a support activity) to provide overnight deliveries, creating value in the process. As shown in Figure 3.4, the Internet has changed many aspects of the value chain for a broad range of firms. A key reason is that the Internet affects how people communicate, locate information, and buy goods and services.

Evaluating a firm's capability to execute its primary and support activities is challenging. Earlier in the chapter, we noted that identifying and assessing the value of a firm's resources and capabilities requires judgment. Judgment is equally necessary when using value chain analysis, because no obviously correct model or rule is universally available to help in the process.

Figure 3.4 Prominent Applications of the Internet in the Value Chain

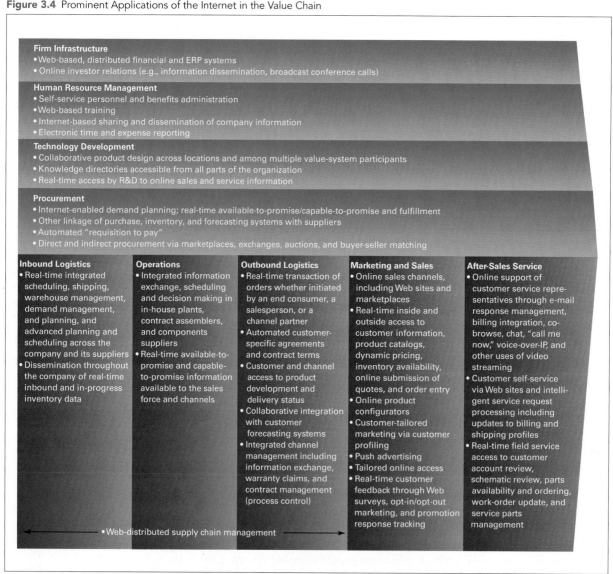

What should a firm do about primary and support activities in which its resources and capabilities are not a source of core competence and, hence, of competitive advantage? Outsourcing is one solution to consider.

Outsourcing

Concerned with how components, finished goods, or services will be obtained, **outsourcing** is the purchase of a value-creating activity from an external supplier.[108] Not-for-profit agencies as well as for-profit organizations actively engage in outsourcing.[109] Firms engaging in effective outsourcing increase their flexibility, mitigate risks, and reduce their capital investments.[110] In multiple global industries, the trend toward outsourcing continues at a rapid pace.[111] Moreover, in some industries virtually all firms seek the value that can be captured through effective outsourcing. As with other strategic management process decisions, careful analysis is required before the firm decides to engage in outsourcing.[112]

Outsourcing can be effective because few, if any, organizations possess the resources and capabilities required to achieve competitive superiority in all primary and support activities. For example, research suggests that few companies can afford to develop internally all the technologies that might lead to competitive advantage.[113] By nurturing a smaller number of capabilities, a firm increases the probability of developing a competitive advantage because it does not become overextended. In addition, by outsourcing activities in which it lacks competence, the firm can fully concentrate on those areas in which it can create value.

Firms must outsource only activities where they cannot create value or where they are at a substantial disadvantage compared to competitors.[114] To verify that the appropriate primary and support activities are outsourced, managers should have four skills: strategic thinking, deal making, partnership governance, and change management.[115] Managers need to understand whether and how outsourcing creates competitive advantage within their company—they need to think strategically. To complete effective outsourcing transactions, these managers must also be deal makers, able to secure rights from external providers that can be fully used by internal managers. They must be able to oversee[116] and govern appropriately the relationship with the company to which the services were outsourced. Because outsourcing can significantly change how an organization operates, managers administering these programs must also be able to manage that change, including resolving employee resistance that accompanies any significant change effort.[117]

The consequences of outsourcing cause additional concerns.[118] For the most part, these concerns revolve around the potential loss in firms' innovative ability and the loss of jobs within companies that decide to outsource some of their work activities to others. Thus, innovation and technological uncertainty are two important issues to consider in making outsourcing decisions. However, firms can also learn from outsource suppliers how to increase their own innovation capabilities.[119] Companies must be aware of these issues and be prepared to fully consider the concerns about opportunities from outsourcing suggested by different stakeholders (e.g., employees). The opportunities and concerns may be especially great when firms outsource activities or functions to a foreign supply source (often referred to as offshoring).[120] Bangalore and Belfast are the newest hotspots for technology outsourcing, competing with major operations in China and India.[121] Yet, IBM recently made the decision to keep outsourced activities in the United States instead of moving them to a foreign location.[122]

As is true with all strategic management tools and techniques, criteria should be established to guide outsourcing decisions. Outsourcing is big business, but not every outsourcing decision is successful. For example, amid delays and cost overruns, Electronic Data Systems abandoned a $1 billion opportunity to run Dow Chemical Co.'s phone and computer networks. These less-than-desirable outcomes indicate that firms should carefully study outsourcing opportunities to verify that they will indeed create value that exceeds the cost incurred.

STRATEGY
RIGHT NOW

Read how Boeing's experience with the 787 Dreamliner highlights many of the benefits and concerns associated with outsourcing.

www.cengage.com/
management/hitt

Outsourcing is the purchase of a value-creating activity from an external supplier.

Competencies, Strengths, Weaknesses, and Strategic Decisions

At the conclusion of the internal analysis, firms must identify their strengths and weaknesses in resources, capabilities, and core competencies. For example, if they have weak capabilities or do not have core competencies in areas required to achieve a competitive advantage, they must acquire those resources and build the capabilities and competencies needed. Alternatively, they could decide to outsource a function or activity where they are weak in order to improve the value that they provide to customers.[123]

Therefore, firms need to have the appropriate resources and capabilities to develop the desired strategy and create value for customers and other stakeholders such as shareholders.[124] Managers should understand that having a significant quantity of resources is not the same as having the "right" resources. Moreover, decision makers sometimes become more focused and productive when their organization's resources are constrained.[125] Managers must help the firm obtain and use resources, capabilities, and core competencies in ways that generate value-creating competitive advantages.

Noel Vasquez/Getty Images

Tools such as outsourcing help the firm focus on its core competencies as the source of its competitive advantages. However, evidence shows that the value-creating ability of core competencies should never be taken for granted. Moreover, the ability of a core competence to be a permanent competitive advantage can't be assumed. The reason for these cautions is that all core competencies have the potential to become *core rigidities*. Thus, a core competence is usually a strength because it is a source of competitive advantage. If emphasized when it is no longer competitively relevant, it can become a weakness, a seed of organizational inertia.

The Ford Flex, which the company launched in fall 2008, was designed to turn heads and excite consumers interested in crossover vehicles. Could the Flex represent a shift toward more customer-centered product development?

Inertia embedded in the organizational culture may be a problem at Ford Motor Company, where some argue that the firm's culture has become a core rigidity that is constraining efforts to improve performance. In one writer's words: "One way or another, the company will have to figure out how to produce more vehicles that consumers actually want. And doing that will require addressing the most fundamental problem of all: Ford's dysfunctional, often defeatist culture."[126] In contrast, Toyota constantly reexamines product planning, customer service, sales and marketing, and employee training practices to prevent "being spoiled by success."[127]

Events occurring in the firm's external environment create conditions through which core competencies can become core rigidities, generate inertia, and stifle innovation. "Often the flip side, the dark side, of core capabilities is revealed due to external events when new competitors figure out a better way to serve the firm's customers, when new technologies emerge, or when political or social events shift the ground underneath."[128] However, in the final analysis, changes in the external environment do not cause core competencies to become core rigidities; rather, strategic myopia and inflexibility on the part of managers are the causes.

After studying its external environment to determine what it might choose to do (as explained in Chapter 2) and its internal organization to understand what it can do (as explained in this chapter), the firm has the information required to select a business-level strategy that will help it reach its vision and mission. We describe different business-level strategies in the next chapter.

SUMMARY

- In the global business environment, traditional factors (e.g., labor costs and superior access to financial resources and raw materials) can still create a competitive advantage. However, these factors are less often a source of competitive advantage in the current competitive landscape. In the current landscape, the resources, capabilities, and core competencies in the firm's internal organization likely have a stronger influence on its performance than do conditions in the external environment. The most effective organizations recognize that strategic competitiveness and above-average returns result only when core competencies (identified by studying the firm's internal organization) are matched with opportunities (determined by studying the firm's external environment).

- No competitive advantage lasts forever. Over time, rivals use their own unique resources, capabilities, and core competencies to form different value-creating propositions that duplicate the value-creating ability of the firm's competitive advantages. In general, the Internet's capabilities are reducing the sustainability of many competitive advantages. Because competitive advantages are not permanently sustainable, firms must exploit their current advantages while simultaneously using their resources and capabilities to form new advantages that can lead to future competitive success.

- Effectively managing core competencies requires careful analysis of the firm's resources (inputs to the production process) and capabilities (resources that have been purposely integrated to achieve a specific task or set of tasks). The knowledge possessed by human capital is among the most significant of an organization's capabilities and ultimately provides the base for most competitive advantages. The firm must create an environment that allows people to integrate their individual knowledge with that held by others so that, collectively, the firm has significant organizational knowledge.

- Individual resources are usually not a source of competitive advantage. Capabilities are a more likely source of competitive advantages, especially more sustainable ones. The firm's nurturing and support of core competencies that are based on capabilities are less visible to rivals and, as such, they are more difficult to understand and imitate.

- Only when a capability is valuable, rare, costly to imitate, and nonsubstitutable is it a core competence and a source of competitive advantage. Over time, core competencies must be supported, but they cannot be allowed to become core rigidities. Core competencies are a source of competitive advantage only when they allow the firm to create value by exploiting opportunities in its external environment. When it can no longer do so, the company shifts its attention to selecting or forming other capabilities that satisfy the four criteria of a sustainable competitive advantage.

- Value chain analysis is used to identify and evaluate the competitive potential of resources and capabilities. By studying their skills relative to those associated with primary and support activities, firms can understand their cost structure and identify the activities through which they can create value.

- When the firm cannot create value in either an internal primary or support activity, outsourcing is considered. Used commonly in the global economy, outsourcing is the purchase of a value-creating activity from an external supplier. The firm should outsource only to companies possessing a competitive advantage in terms of the particular primary or support activity under consideration. In addition, the firm must continuously verify that it is not outsourcing activities from which it could create value.

REVIEW QUESTIONS

1. Why is it important for a firm to study and understand its internal organization?

2. What is value? Why is it critical for the firm to create value? How does it do so?

3. What are the differences between tangible and intangible resources? Why is it important for decision makers to understand these differences? Are tangible resources linked more closely to the creation of competitive advantages than are intangible resources, or is the reverse true? Why?

4. What are capabilities? How do firms create capabilities?

5. What are the four criteria used to determine which of a firm's capabilities are core competencies? Why is it important for firms to use these criteria in developing capabilities?

6. What is value chain analysis? What does the firm gain when it successfully uses this tool?

7. What is outsourcing? Why do firms outsource? Will outsourcing's importance grow as we progress in the twenty-first century? If so, why?

8. How do firms identify internal strengths and weaknesses? Why is it vital that managers have a clear understanding of their firm's strengths and weaknesses?

EXPERIENTIAL EXERCISES

EXERCISE 1: WHAT MAKES A GREAT OUTSOURCING FIRM?

The focus of this chapter is on understanding how firm resources and capabilities serve as the cornerstone for competencies, and, ultimately, a competitive advantage. However, when firms cannot create value in either a primary or support activity, outsourcing becomes a potential strategy. Yet with the recession that began in 2007 there seems to be a shift occurring. According to the International Association of Outsourcing Professionals (IAOP) at their 2008 annual conference, nearly 75 percent of organizations will do the same or more outsourcing in response to the financial crisis and that greater contract flexibility is their top need. However, 25 percent of organizations reported lower volumes and 19 percent said they have renegotiated lower prices on existing contracts. In addition, the IAOP reports more than 53 percent of respondents say they are doing more due diligence and also favor working with larger providers.

During that same 2008 conference, the IAOP announced their Global Outsourcing 100, a ranking of the world's best outsourcing service providers. The evaluation process mirrors that employed by many top customers and considers four key criteria: (1) size and growth in revenue, employees, centers, and countries served; (2) customer experience as demonstrated through the value being created for the company's top customers; (3) depth and breadth of competencies as demonstrated through industry recognition, relevant certifications, and investment in the development of people, processes, and technologies; and (4) management capabilities as reflected in the experience and accomplishments of the business's top leaders and investments in management systems that ensure outsourcing success. Below are the top 10 for 2008.

1. Accenture
2. IBM
3. Infosys Technologies
4. Sodexo
5. Capgemini
6. Tata Consultancy Services
7. Wipro Technologies
8. Hewlett-Packard
9. Genpact
10. Tech Mahindra

Split up into groups and pick one of the Global Outsourcing 100 to analyze. The complete list can be found on the IAOP website at http://www.outsourcingprofessional.org/. (A new list is published annually in *Fortune* magazine and updated on the IAOP website.) Prepare a brief presentation using your research and the contents of this chapter that addresses at a minimum the following questions:

- Why was this company chosen? What has been their history as regards outsourcing as a source of revenue?
- How does the firm describe, or imply, its value proposition?
- What unique competitive advantage does the firm exhibit?
- Do you consider this to be a sustainable competitive advantage? Utilize the four sources of sustainable competitive advantage as your guide.

EXERCISE 2: COMPETITIVE ADVANTAGE AND PRO SPORTS

What makes one team successful while another team struggles? At first glance, a National Football League franchise or Women's National Basketball Association team may not seem like a typical business. However, professional sports have been around for a long time: pro hockey in the United States emerged around World War I, and pro basketball shortly after World War II; both could be considered newcomers relative to the founding of baseball leagues. Pro sports are big business as well, as evidenced by the Boston Red Sox's 2009 opening day payroll of $121,745,999.

With this exercise, we will use tools and concepts from the chapter to analyze factors underlying the success or failure of different sports teams. Working as a group, pick two teams that play in the same league. For each team, address the following questions:

- How successful are the two teams you selected? How stable has their performance been over time?
- Make an inventory of the characteristics of the two teams. Characteristics you might choose to identify include reputation, coaching, fan base, playing style and tactics, individual players, and so on. For each characteristic you describe:
  - Decide if it is best characterized as tangible, intangible, or a capability.
  - Apply the concepts of value, rarity, imitation, and sustainability to analyze its value-creating ability.
- Is there evidence of bundling in this situation (i.e., the combination of different resources and capabilities)?
- What would it take for these two teams to substantially change their competitive position over time? For example, if a team is successful, what types of changes in resources and capabilities might affect it negatively? If a team is below average, what changes would you recommend to its portfolio of resources and capabilities?

VIDEO CASE

BRIDGING THE KNOWING–DOING GAP

Professor Jeffrey Pfeffer/Graduate School of Business, Stanford University

Professor Jeffrey Pfeffer of Stanford Business School comments on a concept he coined the knowing–doing gap in which he discusses why conventional wisdom is often the correct path but quite often not the one taken. Why is this so?

Before you watch the video consider the following concepts and questions and be prepared to discuss them in class:

Concepts

- Human capital
- Value of intangible resources
- Sustainable competitive advantage
- Internal organization
- Capabilities
- Core competence

Questions

1. Do you think common sense today is a bit uncommon? If so, why do you think that is so? For example, at times are the things we know we need to do, not something we actually do?

2. What internal factors might inhibit organizations or individuals from doing the right thing

NOTES

1. M. E. Mangelsdorf, 2007, Beyond enterprise 2.0, *MIT Sloan Management Review*, 48(3): 50–55.

2. J. G. Covin & M. P. Miles, 2007, Strategic use of corporate venturing, *Entrepreneurship Theory and Practice*, 31: 183–207; R. R. Wiggins & T. W. Ruefli, 2002, Sustained competitive advantage: Temporal dynamics and the incidence of persistence of superior economic performance, *Organization Science*, 13: 82–105.

3. W. M. Becker & V. M. Freeman, 2006, Going from global trends to corporate strategy, *McKinsey Quarterly*, Number 3:17–27; S. K. McEvily, K. M. Eisenhardt, & J. E. Prescott, 2004, The global acquisition, leverage, and protection of technological competencies, *Strategic Management Journal*, 25: 713–722.

4. J. Schenck & N. Wingfield, 2008, How Apple could survive without Steve Jobs, *Wall Street Journal*, http://www.wsj.com, December 8.

5. R. T. Crook, D. J. Ketchen, J. G. Combs, & S. Y. Todd, 2008, Strategic resources and performance: A meta-analysis, *Strategic Management Journal*, 29: 1141–1154; N. T. Sheehan & N. J. Foss, 2007, Enhancing the prescriptiveness of the resource-based view through Porterian activity analysis, *Management Decision*, 45: 450-461; S. Dutta, M. J. Zbaracki, & M. Bergen, 2003, Pricing process as a capability: A resource-based perspective, *Strategic Management Journal*, 24: 615–630.

6. C. G. Brush, P. G. Greene, & M. M. Hart, 2001, From initial idea to unique advantage: The entrepreneurial challenge of constructing a resource base, *Academy of Management Executive*, 15(1): 64–78.

7. L. Priem, 2007, A consumer perspective on value creation, *Academy of Management Review*, 32: 219–235.

8. D. G. Sirmon, M. A. Hitt, & R. D. Ireland, 2007, Managing firm resources in dynamic markets to create value: Looking inside the black box, *Academy of Management Review*, 32: 273–292.

9. A. Leiponen, 2008, Control of intellectual assets in client relationships: Implications for innovation, *Strategic Management Journal*, 29: 1371–1394; S. C. Kang, S. S. Morris, & S. A. Snell, 2007, Relational archetypes, organizational learning, and value creation: Extending the human resource architecture, *Academy of Management Review*, 32: 236–256.

10. S. Raisch & G. von Krog, 2007, Navigating a path to smart growth, MIT *Sloan Management Review*, 48(3): 65–72.

11. D. DePass, 2006, Cuts in incentives upset 3M supervisors, *Star Tribune*, December 16.

12. C. D. Zatzick & R. D. Iverson, 2007, High-involvement management and work force reduction: Competitive advantage or disadvantage? *Academy of Management Journal*, 49: 999–1015.

13. R. Florida, 2005, *The Flight of the Creative Class*, New York: HarperBusiness.

14. A. W. King, 2007, Disentangling interfirm and intrafirm causal ambiguity: A conceptual model of causal ambiguity and sustainable competitive advantage, *Academy of Management Review*, 32: 156–178; J. Shamsie, 2003, The context of dominance: An industry-driven framework for exploiting reputation, *Strategic Management Journal*, 24: 199–215.

15. U. Ljungquist, 2007, Core competency beyond identification: Presentation of a model, *Management Decision*, 45: 393–402; M. Makhija, 2003, Comparing the resource-based and market-based view of the firm: Empirical evidence from Czech privatization, *Strategic Management Journal*, 24: 433–451.

16. R. D. Ireland & J. W. Webb, 2007, Strategic entrepreneurship: Creating competitive advantage through streams of innovation, *Business Horizons*, 50: 49–59.

17. M. A. Peteraf & J. B. Barney, 2003, Unraveling the resource-based tangle, *Managerial and Decision Economics*, 24: 309–323; J. B. Barney, 2001, Is the resource-based "view" a useful perspective for strategic management research? Yes, *Academy of Management Review*, 26: 41–56.

18. D. P. Lepak, K. G. Smith, & M. Susan Taylor, 2007, Value creation and value capture: A multilevel perspective, *Academy of Management Review*, 32: 180–194.

19. T. Papot, 2009, Slovakia's headache as car sales fall, Radio Netherlands Worldwide, http://www.radionetherlands.nl, March 5; Z. Vilikovska, 2008, Slovak factories

manufactured around 770,000 cars in 2008, Flash News, http://www.spector.sk; G. Katz. 2007, Assembling a future, *Houston Chronicle*, July 5, D1, D4.

20. M. Javidan, R. M. Steers, & M. A. Hitt (eds.), 2007, *The Global Mindset*, Amsterdam: Elsevier Ltd; T. M. Begley & D. P. Boyd, 2003, The need for a corporate global mindset, MIT *Sloan Management Review*, 44(2): 25–32.

21. L. Gratton, 2007, Handling hot spots, *Business Strategy Review*, 18(2): 9–14.

22. O. Levy, S. Beechler, S. Taylor, & N. A. Boyacigiller, 2007, What we talk about when we talk about "global mindset": Managerial cognition in multinational corporations, *Journal of International Business Studies*, 38: 231–258.

23. Sirmon, Hitt, & Ireland, Managing resources in a dynamic environment.

24. E. Danneels, 2008, Organizational antecedents of second-order competences, *Strategic Management Journal*, 29: 519–543; Barney, Is the resource-based "view" a useful perspective for strategic management research? Yes.

25. S. Kaplan, 2008, Cognition, capabilities, and incentives: Assessing firm response to the fiber-optic revolution, *Academy of Management Journal*, 51: 672–695; K. J. Mayer & R. M. Salomon, 2006, Capabilities, contractual hazards, and governance: Integrating resource-based and transaction cost perspectives, *Academy of Management Journal*, 49: 942–959.

26. S. K. McEvily & B. Chakravarthy, 2002, The persistence of knowledge-based advantage: An empirical test for product performance and technological knowledge, *Strategic Management Journal*, 23: 285–305.

27. D. Kaplan, 2007, A new look for Luby's, *Houston Chronicle*, July 4, D1, D5.

28. J. Barthelemy, 2008, Opportunism, knowledge, and the performance of franchise chains, *Strategic Management Journal*, 29: 1451–1463; J. L. Morrow, Jr., D. G. Sirmon, M. A. Hitt, & T. R. Holcomb, 2007, Creating value in the face of declining performance: Firm strategies and organizational recovery, *Strategic Management Journal*, 28: 271–283.

29. D. G. Sirmon, S. Gove, & M. A. Hitt, 2008, Resource management in dyadic competitive rivalry: The effects of resource bundling and deployment, *Academy of Management Journal*, 51: 919–935; E. Danneels, 2007, The process of technological competence leveraging, *Strategic Management Journal*, 28: 511–533.

30. Putting co-creation to work for you: Build more value by co-creating with your customers, 2009, Internetviz, http://www.intemetviz-newsletters.com. J. J. Neff, 2007, What drives consumers not to buy cars, *BusinessWeek*, July 9, 16.

31. K. Chaharbaghi, 2007, The problematic of strategy: A way of seeing is also a way of not seeing, *Management Decision*, 45: 327–339.

32. V. Shankar & B. L. Bayus, 2003, Network effects and competition: An empirical analysis of the home video game industry, *Strategic Management Journal*, 24: 375–384.

33. Morrow, Sirmon, Hitt, & Holcomb, Creating value in the face of declining performance; G. Hawawini, V. Subramanian, & P. Verdin, 2003, Is performance driven by industry- or firm-specific factors? A new look at the evidence, *Strategic Management Journal*, 24: 1–16.

34. J. Woiceshyn & L. Falkenberg, 2008, Value creation in knowledge-based firms: Aligning problems and resources, *Academy of Management Perspectives*, 22 (2): 85–99; M. R. Haas & M. T. Hansen, 2005, When using knowledge can hurt performance: The value of organizational capabilities in a management consulting company, *Strategic Management Journal*, 26: 1–24.

35. C. M. Christensen, 2001, The past and future of competitive advantage, *Sloan Management Review*, 42(2): 105–109.

36. O. Gottschalg & M. Zollo, 2007, Interest alignment and competitive advantage, *Academy of Management Review*. 32: 418–437.

37. D. P. Forbes, 2007, Reconsidering the strategic implications of decision comprehensiveness, *Academy of Management Review*, 32: 361–376; J. R. Hough & M. A. White, 2003, Environmental dynamism and strategic decision-making rationality: An examination at the decision level, *Strategic Management Journal*, 24: 481–489.

38. T. M. Jones, W. Felps, & G. A. Bigley, 2007, Ethical theory and stakeholder-related decisions: The role of stakeholder culture, *Academy of Management Review*, 32: 137–155; D. C. Kayes, D. Stirling, & T. M. Nielsen, 2007, Building organizational integrity, *Business Horizons*, 50: 61–70.

39. Y. Deutsch, T. Keil, & T. Laamanen, 2007, Decision making in acquisitions: The effect of outside directors' compensation on acquisition patterns, *Journal of Management*. 33: 30–56.

40. M. De Rond & R. A. Thietart, 2007, Choice, chance, and inevitability in strategy, *Strategic Management Journal*, 28: 535–551.

41. A. Phene & P. Almieda, 2008, Innovation in multinational subsidiaries: The role of knowledge assimilation and subsidiary capabilities, *Journal of International Business Studies*, 39: 901–919; C. C. Miller & R. D. Ireland, 2005, Intuition in strategic decision making: Friend or foe in the fast-paced 21st century? *Academy of Management Executive*, 19(1): 19–30.

42. L. M. Lodish & C. F. Mela, 2007, If brands are built over years, why are they managed over quarters? *Harvard Business Review*, 85(7/8): 104–112; H. J. Smith, 2003, The shareholders vs. stakeholders debate, MIT *Sloan Management Review*, 44(4): 85–90.

43. P. C. Nutt, 2002. *Why Decisions Fail*, San Francisco: Berrett-Koehler Publishers.

44. R. Martin, 2007. How successful leaders think, *Harvard Business Review*, 85(6): 61–67.

45. Polaroid Corporation, 2007, Wikipedia, http://en.wikipedia.org/wiki/Polaroid_Corporation, July 5.

46. 46. J. M. Mezias & W. H. Starbuck, 2003, What do managers know, anyway? *Harvard Business Review*, 81 (5): 16–17.

47. I. Mitroff, 2008, Knowing: How we know is as important as what we know, *Journal of Business Strategy*, 29 (3): 13–22; P. G. Audia, E. Locke, & K. G. Smith, 2000, The paradox of success: An archival and a laboratory study of strategic persistence following radical environmental change, *Academy of Management Journal*, 43: 837–853.

48. C. O. Longenecker, M. J. Neubert, & L. S. Fink, 2007, Causes and consequences of managerial failure in rapidly changing organizations, *Business Horizons*, 50:145–155; G. P. West III & J. DeCastro, 2001, The Achilles' heel of firm strategy: Resource weaknesses and distinctive inadequacies, *Journal of Management Studies*, 38: 417–442; G. Gavetti & D. Levinthal, 2000, Looking forward and looking backward: Cognitive and experimental search, *Administrative Science Quarterly*, 45: 113–137.

49. R. Amit & P. J. H. Schoemaker, 1993, Strategic assets and organizational rent, *Strategic Management Journal*, 14: 33–46.

50. S. J. Carson, A. Madhok, & T. Wu, 2006, Uncertainty, opportunism, and governance: The effects of volatility and ambiguity on formal and relational contracting, *Academy of Management Journal*. 49: 1058–1077; R. E. Hoskisson & L. W. Busenitz, 2001, Market uncertainty and learning distance in corporate entrepreneurship entry mode choice, in M. A. Hitt, R. D. Ireland, S. M. Camp, & D. L. Sexton (eds.), *Strategic Entrepreneurship: Creating a New Integrated Mindset*, Oxford, UK: Blackwell Publishers, 151–172.

51. C. M. Fiol & E. J. O'Connor, 2003, Waking up! Mindfulness in the face of bandwagons, *Academy of Management Review*. 28: 54–70.

52. P. Davidson, Coal king Peabody cleans up, *USA Today*, http://www.usatoday.com, August 18; J. Pasternak, 2008, Global warming has a new battleground: Coal plants, *Chicago Tribune*, http://www.chicagotribune.com, April 14.

53. G. P. West, III, 2007, Collective cognition: When entrepreneurial teams, not individuals, make decisions, *Entrepreneurship Theory and Practice*, 31: 77–102.

54. N. J. Hiller & D. C. Hambrick, 2005, Conceptualizing executive hubris: The role of (hyper-) core self-evaluations

in strategic decision making, *Strategic Management Journal*, 26: 297–319.

55. C. Stadler, 2007, The four principles of enduring success, *Harvard Business Review*, 85(7/8): 62–72.

56. Mayer & Salomon, Capabilities, contractual hazards, and governance; D. M. De Carolis, 2003, Competencies and imitability in the pharmaceutical industry: An analysis of their relationship with firm performance, *Journal of Management*, 29: 27–50.

57. R. H. Lester, A. Hillman, A. Zardkoohi, & A. A. Cannella, 2008, Former government officials as outside directors: The role of human and social capital, *Academy of Management Journal*, 51: 999–1013; G. Ahuja & R. Katila, 2004, Where do resources come from? The role of idiosyncratic situations, *Strategic Management Journal*, 25: 887–907.

58. K. Meyer, S. Estrin, S. K. Bhaumik, & M. W. Peng, 2009, Institutions, resources, and entry strategies in emerging economies, *Strategic Management Journal*, 30: 61–80; J. McGee & H. Thomas, 2007, Knowledge as a lens on the jigsaw puzzle of strategy, *Management Decision*, 45: 539–563.

59. Sirmon, Hitt, & Ireland, Managing firm resources in dynamic environments; S. Berman, J. Down, & C. Hill, 2002, Tacit knowledge as a source of competitive advantage in the National Basketball Association, *Academy of Management Journal*, 45: 13–31.

60. 2007, Borders teamed with Amazon.com, http://www.amazon.com, July 7.

61. K. G. Smith, C. J. Collins, & K. D. Clark, 2005, Existing knowledge, knowledge creation capability, and the rate of new product introduction in high-technology firms, *Academy of Management Journal*, 48: 346–357; S. G. Winter, 2005, Developing evolutionary theory for economics and management, in K. G. Smith and M. A. Hitt (eds.), *Great Minds in Management: The Process of Theory Development*, Oxford, UK: Oxford University Press, 509–546.

62. J. A. Dubin, 2007, Valuing intangible assets with a nested logit market share model, *Journal of Econometrics*, 139: 285–302.

63. A. M. Webber, 2000, New math for a new economy, *Fast Company*, January/February, 214–224.

64. F. T. Rothaermel & W. Boeker, 2008, Old technology meets new technology: Complementarities, similarities, and alliance formation, *Strategic Management Journal*, 29: 47–77; M. Song, C. Droge, S. Hanvanich, & R. Calantone, 2005, Marketing and technology resource complementarity: An analysis of their interaction effect in two environmental contexts, *Strategic Management Journal*, 26: 259–276.

65. M. A. Hitt & R. D. Ireland, 2002, The essence of strategic leadership: Managing human and social capital, *Journal of Leadership and Organization Studies*, 9(1): 3–14.

66. J. B. Quinn, P. Anderson, & S. Finkelstein, 1996, Making the most of the best, *Harvard Business Review*, 74(2): 71–80.

67. N. Stieglitz & K. Heine, 2007, Innovations and the role of complementarities in a strategic theory of the firm, *Strategic Management Journal*, 28: 1–15.

68. S. A. Fernhaber, B. A. Gilbert, & P. P. McDougal, 2008, International entrepreneurship and geographic location: An empirical examination of new venture internationalization, *Journal of International Business Studies*, 39: 267–290; R. D. Ireland, M. A. Hitt, & D. Vaidyanath, 2002, Managing strategic alliances to achieve a competitive advantage, *Journal of Management*, 28: 416–446.

69. E. Fischer & R. Reuber, 2007, The good, the bad, and the unfamiliar: The challenges of reputation formation facing new firms, *Entrepreneurship Theory and Practice*, 31: 53–75.

70. D. L. Deephouse, 2000. Media reputation as a strategic resource: An integration of mass communication and resource-based theories, *Journal of Management*, 26: 1091–1112.

71. P. Engardio & M. Arndt, 2007, What price reputation? *BusinessWeek*, July 9, 70–79.

72. P. Berthon, M. B. Holbrook, & J. M. Hulbert, 2003, Understanding and managing the brand space, *MIT Sloan Management Review*, 44(2): 49–54; D. B. Holt, 2003, What becomes an icon most? *Harvard Business Review*, 81(3): 43–49.

73. J. Song & J. Shin, 2008, The paradox of technological capabilities: A study of knowledge sourcing from host countries of overseas R&D operations, *Journal of International Business Studies*, 39: 291–303; J. Blasberg & V. Vishwanath, 2003, Making cool brands hot, *Harvard Business Review*, 81(6): 20–22.

74. 2007, Harley-Davidson Motor Clothes Merchandise, July 7, http://www.harley-davidson.com.

75. S. Kalepu, 2009, Ford names Sunil Shetty as its brand ambassador, *CaretradeIndia*, http://www.cartradeindia.com, January 22.

76. T. Isobe, S. Makino, & D. B. Montgomery, 2008, Technological capabilities and firm performance: The case of small manufacturing firms in Japan, *Asia Pacific Journal of Management*, 25: 413–425; S. Dutta, O. Narasimhan, & S. Rajiv, 2005, Conceptualizing and measuring capabilities: Methodology and empirical application, *Strategic Management Journal*, 26: 277–285.

77. M. Kroll, B. A. Walters, & P. Wright, 2008, Board vigilance, director experience and corporate outcomes, *Strategic Management Journal*, 29: 363–282; J. Bitar & T. Hafsi, 2007, Strategizing through the capability lens: Sources and outcomes of integration, *Management Decision*, 45: 403–419.

78. S. K. Ethiraj, P. Kale, M. S. Krishnan, & J. V. Singh, 2005, Where do capabilities come from and do they matter? A study in the software services industry, *Strategic Management Journal*, 26: 25–45; M. G. Jacobides & S. G. Winter, 2005, The co-evolution of capabilities and transaction costs: Explaining the institutional structure of production, *Strategic Management Journal*, 26: 395–413.

79. T. A. Stewart & A. P. Raman, 2007, Lessons from Toyota's long drive, *Harvard Business Review*, 85(7/8): 74–83.

80. Y. Uu, J. G. Combs, D. J. Ketchen, Jr., & R. D. Ireland, 2007, The value of human resource management for organizational performance, *Business Horizons*, 50: 503–511.

81. B. Connelly, M. A. Hitt, A. S. DeNisi, & R. D. Ireland, 2007, Expatriates and corporate-level international strategy: Governing with the knowledge contract, *Management Decision*, 45: 564–581.

82. M. J. Tippins & R. S. Sohi, 2003, IT competency and firm performance: Is organizational learning a missing link? *Strategic Management Journal*, 24: 745–761.

83. M. B. Neeley & R. Jacobson, 2008, The recency of technological inputs and financial performance, *Strategic Management Journal*, 29: 723–744.

84. 84. Meyer, Estrin, Bhaumik, & Peng, Institutions, resources, and entry strategies in emerging markets; C. Zott, 2003, Dynamic capabilities and the emergence of intraindustry differential firm performance: Insights from a simulation study, *Strategic Management Journal*, 24:97–125.

85. H. R. Greve, 2009, Bigger and safer: The diffusion of competitive advantage, *Strategic Management Journal*, 30: 1–23; C. K. Prahalad & G. Hamel, 1990, The core competence of the corporation, *Harvard Business Review*, 68(3): 79–93.

86. D. Bidleman, 2009, Xerox innovation shines through industry recognition, *YAHOO!Finance*, http://finance.yahoo.com, January 26.

87. D. K. Taft, 2009, Microsoft, Xerox invest in innovation, *eWeek*, http://www.eweek.com, March 5; 2006, Xerox Annual Report, December, http://www.xerox.com.

88. S. Newbert, 2008, Value, rareness, competitive advantage, and performance: A conceptual-level empirical investigation of the resource-based view of the firm, *Strategic Management Journal*, 29: 745–768.

89. D. Seidman, 2008, Out-greening delivers sustainable competitive advantage, *BusinessWeek*, http://www.businessweek.com, December 5.

90. S. A. Zahra, 2008, The virtuous cycle of discovery and creation of entrepreneurial opportunities, *Strategic Entrepreneurship Journal*, 2: 243–257; J. B. Barney, 1995, Looking inside for competitive advantage,

Part 1: Strategic Management Inputs

Academy of Management Executive, 9(4): 49–60.

91. G. Pacheco-de-Almeida, J. E. Henderson, & K. O. Cool, 2008, Resolving the commitment versus flexibility trade-off: The role of resource accumulation lags, *Academy of Management Journal*, 51: 517–536.

92. J. B. Barney, 1991, Firm resources and sustained competitive advantage, *Journal of Management*, 17: 99–120.

93. L. E. Tetrick & N. Da Silva, 2003, Assessing the culture and climate for organizational learning, in S. E. Jackson, M. A. Hitt, & A. S. DeNisi (eds.), *Managing Knowledge for Sustained Competitive Advantage*, San Francisco: Jossey-Bass, 333–359.

94. K. Stinebaker, 2007, Global company puts focus on people, *Houston Chronicle Online*, http://www.chron.com, February 18.

95. A. W. King & C. P. Zeithaml, 2001, Competencies and firm performance: Examining the causal ambiguity paradox, *Strategic Management Journal*, 22: 75–99.

96. Barney, Firm resources, 111.

97. A. K. Chatterjee, 2009, Spawned with a silver spoon? Entrepreneurial performance and innovation in the medical device industry, *Strategic Management Journal*, 30: 185–206; S. K. McEvily, S. Das, & K. McCabe, 2000, Avoiding competence substitution through knowledge sharing, *Academy of Management Review*, 25: 294–311.

98. D. J. Ketchen, Jr., & G. T. M. Hult, 2007, Bridging organization theory and supply chain management: The case of best value supply chains, *Journal of Operations Management*, 25: 573–580.

99. M. E. Porter, 1985, *Competitive Advantage*, New York: Free Press, 33–61.

100. J. Alcacer, 2006, Location choices across the value chain: How activity and capability influence co-location, *Management Science*, 52: 1457–1471.

101. H. U. Lee & J.-H. Park, 2008, The influence of top management team international exposure on international alliance formation, *Journal of Management Studies*, 45: 961–981; 2007, Riding the global value chain, *Chief Executive Online*, January/February, http://www.chiefexecutive.net.

102. R. Locke & M. Romis, 2007, Global supply chain, MIT *Sloan Management Review*, 48(2): 54–62.

103. R. Amit & C. Zott, 2001, Value creation in e-business, *Strategic Management Journal*, 22 (Special Issue): 493–520; M. E. Porter, 2001, Strategy and the Internet, *Harvard Business Review*, 79(3): 62–78.

104. C. L. Luk, O. H. M. Yau, L. Y. M. Sin, A. C. B. Tse, R. P. M. Chow, & J. S. Y. Lee, 2008, The effects of social capital and organizational innovativeness in different institutional contexts, *Journal of International Business Studies*, 39: 589–612.

105. L .F. Mesquita, J. Anand, & T. H. Brush, 2008, Comparing the resource-based and relational views: Knowledge transfer and spillover in vertical alliances, *Strategic Management Journal*, 29: 913–941; A. Azadegan, K. J. Dooley, P. L. Carter, & J .R. Carter, 2008, Supplier innovativeness and the role of interorganizational learning in enhancing manufacturer capabilities, *Journal of Supply Chain Management*, 44(4): 14–35.

106. A. A. Lado, R. R. Dant, & A. G. Tekleab, 2008, Trust-opportunism paradox, relationalism, and performance in interfirm relationships: Evidence from the retail industry, *Strategic Management Journal*, 29: 401–423; S. N. Wasti & S. A. Wasti, 2008, Trust in buyer-supplier relations: The case of the Turkish automotive industry, *Journal of International Business Studies*, 39:118–131.

107. D. Faems, M. Janssens, A. Madhok, & B. Van Looy, 2008, Toward an integrative perspective on alliance governance: Connecting contract design, trust dynamics and contract application, *Academy of Management Journal*, 51:1053–1078.

108. M. J. Power, K. C. DeSouze, & C. Bonifazi, 2006, *The Outsourcing Handbook: How to Implement a Successful Outsourcing Process*, Philadelphia: Kogan Page.

109. P. W. Tam, 2007, Business technology: Outsourcing finds new niche, *Wall Street Journal*, April 17, B5.

110. S. Nambisan & M. Sawhney, 2007, A buyer's guide to the innovation bazaar, *Harvard Business Review*, 85(6): 109–118.

111. Y. Shi, 2007, Today's solution and tomorrow's problem: The business process outsourcing risk management puzzle, *California Management Review*, 49(3): 27–44.

112. C. C. De Fontenay & J. S. Gans, 2008, A bargaining perspective on strategic outsourcing and supply competition, *Strategic Management Journal*, 29: 819–839; A. Tiwana & M. Keil, 2007, Does peripheral knowledge complement control? An empirical test in technology outsourcing alliances, *Strategic Management Journal*, 28: 623–634.

113. A. Tiwana, 2008, Does interfirm modularity complement ignorance? A field study of software outsourcing alliances, *Strategic Management Journal*, 29: 1241–1252; J. C. Linder, S. Jarvenpaa, & T. H. Davenport, 2003, Toward an innovation sourcing strategy, MIT *Sloan Management Review*, 44(41): 43–49.

114. S. Lohr, 2007, At IBM, a smarter way to outsource, *New York Times Online*, July 5, http://nytimes.com.

115. C. Horng & W. Chen, 2008, From contract manufacturing to own brand management: The role of learning and cultural heritage identity, *Management and Organization Review*, 4: 109–133; M. Useem & J. Harder, 2000, Leading laterally in company outsourcing, *Sloan Management Review*, 41(2): 25–36.

116. R. C. Insinga & M. J. Werle, 2000, Linking outsourcing to business strategy, *Academy of Management Executive*, 14(41): 58–70.

117. B. Arrunada & X. H. Vazquez, 2006, When your contract manufacturer becomes your competitor, *Harvard Business Review*, 84(9): 135–144.

118. C. S. Katsikeas, D. Skarmeas, & D. C. Bello, 2009, Developing successful trust-based international exchange relationships, *Journal of International Business Studies*, 40: 132–155; E. Perez & J. Karp, 2007, U.S. to probe outsourcing after ITT case, *Wall Street Journal* (Eastern Edition), March 28, A3, A6.

119. C. Weigelt & M. B. Sarkar, 2009, Learning from supply-side agents: The impact of technology solution providers' experiential diversity on clients' innovation adoption, 52: 37–60; M. J. Mol, P. Pauwels, P. Matthyssens, & L. Quintens, 2004, A technological contingency perspective on the depth and scope of international outsourcing, *Journal of International Management*, 10: 287–305.

120. K. Couke & L. Sleuwaegen, 2008, Offshoring as a survival strategy: Evidence from manufacturing firms in Belgium, *Journal of International Business Studies*, 39: 1261–1277.

121. N. Heath, 2009, Outsourcing: The new hot spots, *BusinessWeek*, http://www.businessweek.com, February 20.

122. S. Hamm, 2009, IBM: Outsourcing at home, *BusinessWeek*, http://www.businessweek.com, January 16.

123. M. H. Safizadeh, J. M. Field, & L. P. Ritzman, 2008, Sourcing practices and boundaries of the firm in the financial services industry, *Strategic Management Journal*, 29: 79–91; M. A. Hitt, D. Ahlstrom, M. T. Dacin, E. Levitas, & L. Svobodina, 2004, The institutional effects on strategic alliance partner selection in transition economies: China versus Russia, *Organization Science*, 15: 173–185.

124. T. Felin & W. S. Hesterly, 2007, The knowledge-based view, nested heterogeneity, and new value creation: Philosophical considerations on the locus of knowledge, *Academy of Management Review*, 32: 195–218; Y. Mishina, T. G. Pollock, & J. F. Porac, 2004, Are more resources always better for growth? Resource stickiness in market and product expansion, *Strategic Management Journal*, 25: 1179–1197.

125. M. Gibbert, M. Hoegl, & L. Valikangas, 2007, In praise of resource constraints, *MIT Sloan Management Review*, 48(3): 15–17. 126. D. S. Elenkov & I. M. Manev, 2005, Top management leadership and influence on innovation: The role of sociocultural context, *Journal of Management*, 31: 381–402.

126. D. Kiley, 2007, The new heat on Ford, *BusinessWeek*, June 4, 32–37.

127. D. Welch, 2007, Staying paranoid at Toyota, *BusinessWeek*, July 2, 80–82.

128. L. Barton, Wellsprings of knowledge, 30–31.

PART 2

Strategic Actions: Strategy Formulation

CHAPTER 4

Business-Level
Strategy

*Studying this chapter should provide you with the strategic
management knowledge needed to:*

1. Define business-level strategy.

2. Discuss the relationship between customers and business-level
   strategies in terms of *who*, *what*, and *how*.

3. Explain the differences among business-level strategies.

4. Use the five forces of competition model to explain how above-
   average returns can be earned through each business-level strategy.

5. Describe the risks of using each of the business-level strategies.

ACER GROUP: USING A "BARE BONES" COST STRUCTURE TO SUCCEED IN GLOBAL PC MARKETS

Established in 1976, Acer Group uses four PC brands—Acer, Gateway, Packard Bell, and eMachines—as the foundation for its multi-brand global strategy. Currently the third largest PC seller in the world (behind only Hewlett-Packard and Dell), Acer employs over 6,000 and had 2008 revenues of $16.65 billion. Impressively, Acer's operating profit rose 38 percent from 2007 to 2008, to roughly $415 million. These performance data suggest that Acer was competing very successfully during the global recession.

There is little question as to the business-level strategy Acer uses. Noting that running a business with lower costs is good when markets are growing but that doing so is even better when markets are not growing (which was the case during the global recession), Acer's CEO Gianfranco Lanci remains strongly committed to the cost leadership strategy (this strategy is discussed later in the chapter) as the path to strategic competitiveness and above-average returns for his firm.

According to Lanci, a focus on controlling costs is part of Acer's culture. In his words: "We have always operated on the assumption that costs need to be kept under control. It's a kind of overall culture we have in the company. If you are used to it, you can run low costs without running into trouble." A decision to sell only through retailers and other outlets and to outsource all manufacturing and assembly operations are other actions Acer takes to reduce its costs as it uses the cost leadership strategy. Combined, the distribution channels Acer uses and

Richard Naude/Alamy

By diligently managing costs, Acer has offered consumers fully featured netbooks, such as their Aspire Timeline, at a price well below their major competitors.

its outsourcing of operations help to cut overhead costs—research and development and marketing and general and administrative expenses—to 8 percent of sales, well below HP's 15 percent and Dell's 14 percent. Lanci describes the cost savings in the following manner: "We focus 100% on indirect sales, while today most of the people are running direct and indirect at the same time. If you run direct and indirect, you need different setups; by definition, you add costs. We also focus only on consumers and small and midsize businesses. We never said we wanted to address the enterprise segment. This is another big difference."

Because of its lower overhead cost structure, Acer is able to price its products, such as netbooks, below those of competitors. Somewhat new to the PC market, netbooks are relatively small and inexpensive PCs with functionalities below those offered by laptops and desktops. However, their popularity continues to grow. Unlike Dell, HP, and Lenovo, Acer quickly entered the netbook market and sold 32 percent of all netbooks shipped worldwide at the end of 2008.

Acer uses its "bare bones" cost structure as the foundation for pricing its various products such as laptops very aggressively. The firm's new ultrathin laptop was expected to have a starting price of $650. For products with similar capabilities, the price for the HP product was around $1,800 and about $2,000 for the Dell product. After observing these prices, an analyst said that Acer was changing "… customers' perception of what you should pay for a computer."

Sources: 2009, Acer Group, http://www.acer.com, June 15; L. Chao, 2009, Acer expects low-cost laptops to lift shipments, *Wall Street Journal Online*, http://www.wsj.com, April 9; B. Einhorn, 2009, Acer closes in on Dell's No. 2 PC ranking, *BusinessWeek Online*, http://www.businessweek.com, January 15; B. Einhorn, 2009, How Acer is burning its PC rivals, *BusinessWeek Online*, http://www.businessweek.com, April 7; B. Einhorn, 2009, Acer boss Lanci takes aim at Dell and HP, *BusinessWeek Online*, http://www.businessweek.com, April 13; B. Einhorn, 2009, Acer's game-changing PC offensive, *BusinessWeek*, April 20, 65; S. Williams, 2009, Essentially cool: Acer's timeline notebooks, *New York Times Online*, http://www.nytimes.com, April 10.

Increasingly important to firm success,[1] strategy is concerned with making choices among two or more alternatives.[2] As we noted in Chapter 1, when choosing a strategy, the firm decides to pursue one course of action instead of others. The choices are influenced by opportunities and threats in the firm's external environment[3] (see Chapter 2) as well as the nature and quality of the resources, capabilities, and core competencies in its internal organization[4] (see Chapter 3). As we see in the Opening Case, Acer Group tries to drive its costs lower and lower as the foundation for how it competes in the global PC market. Recently, Acer's success has caused some of its competitors to renew their effort to reduce their costs. For example, Dell recently announced that it was committed to trimming $4 billion from its cost structure to improve its ability to compete against competitors such as Acer.[5]

The fundamental objective of using any type of strategy (see Figure 1.1) is to gain strategic competitiveness and earn above-average returns.[6] Strategies are purposeful, precede the taking of actions to which they apply, and demonstrate a shared understanding of the firm's vision and mission.[7] Acer's decisions to acquire Gateway and Packard Bell were quite purposeful. Acquiring Gateway helped the firm establish a better foothold in the U.S. market while acquiring Packard Bell helped it establish a stronger footprint in Europe.

An effectively formulated strategy marshals, integrates, and allocates the firm's resources, capabilities, and competencies so that it will be properly aligned with its external environment.[8] A properly developed strategy also rationalizes the firm's vision and mission along with the actions taken to achieve them.[9] Information about a host of variables including markets, customers, technology, worldwide finance, and the changing world economy must be collected and analyzed to properly form and use strategies. In the final analysis, sound strategic choices that reduce uncertainty regarding outcomes[10] are the foundation for building successful strategies.[11]

Business-level strategy, this chapter's focus, is an integrated and coordinated set of commitments and actions the firm uses to gain a competitive advantage by exploiting core competencies in specific product markets.[12] Business-level strategy indicates the choices the firm has made about how it intends to compete in individual product markets. The choices are important because long-term performance is linked to a firm's strategies.[13] Given the complexity of successfully competing in the global economy, the choices about how the firm will compete can be difficult.[14] For example, MySpace, a social networking site, recently reduced its workforce by almost one-third in order to "… rein in costs and contend with fast-growing rival Facebook Inc."[15] Competitive challenges in MySpace's U.S. and international operations contributed to the difficult decision to reduce the firm's workforce, partly with the purpose of operating more efficiently.[16] At the same time, competitor Facebook's recently announced strong move into additional international markets such as India challenged MySpace to further adjust or fine-tune its strategy as it engages its major competitor in various competitive battles.[17]

Every firm must form and use a business-level strategy. However, every firm may not use all the strategies—corporate-level, merger and acquisition, international, and cooperative—that we examine in Chapters 6 through 9. A firm competing in a single-product market area in a single geographic location does not need a corporate-level strategy to deal with product diversity or an international strategy to deal with geographic diversity. In contrast, a diversified firm will use one of the corporate-level strategies as well as a separate business-level strategy for each product market area in which it competes. Every firm—from the local dry cleaner to the multinational corporation—chooses at least one business-level strategy. Thus business-level strategy is the *core* strategy—the strategy that the firm forms to describe how it intends to compete in a product market.[18]

We discuss several topics to examine business-level strategies. Because customers are the foundation of successful business-level strategies and should never be taken for granted,[19] we present information about customers that is relevant to business-level strategies. In terms of customers, when selecting a business-level strategy the firm

A **business-level strategy** is an integrated and coordinated set of commitments and actions the firm uses to gain a competitive advantage by exploiting core competencies in specific product markets.

determines (1) *who* will be served, (2) *what* needs those target customers have that it will satisfy, and (3) *how* those needs will be satisfied. Selecting customers and deciding which of their needs the firm will try to satisfy, as well as how it will do so, are challenging tasks. Global competition has created many attractive options for customers, thus making it difficult to determine the strategy to best serve them. Effective global competitors have become adept at identifying the needs of customers in different cultures and geographic regions as well as learning how to quickly and successfully adapt the functionality of a firm's good or service to meet those needs.

Descriptions of the purpose of business-level strategies—and of the five business-level strategies—follow the discussion of customers. The five strategies we examine are called *generic* because they can be used in any organization competing in any industry.[20] Our analysis describes how effective use of each strategy allows the firm to favorably position itself relative to the five competitive forces in the industry (see Chapter 2). In addition, we use the value chain (see Chapter 3) to show examples of the primary and support activities necessary to implement specific business-level strategies. Because no strategy is risk-free,[21] we also describe the different risks the firm may encounter when using these strategies. In Chapter 11, we explain the organizational structures and controls linked with the successful use of each business-level strategy.

Customers: Their Relationship with Business-Level Strategies

Strategic competitiveness results only when the firm satisfies a group of customers by using its competitive advantages as the basis for competing in individual product markets.[22] A key reason firms must satisfy customers with their business-level strategy is that returns earned from relationships with customers are the lifeblood of all organizations.[23]

The most successful companies try to find new ways to satisfy current customers and/ or to meet the needs of new customers. Being able to do this can be even more difficult when firms and consumers face challenging economic conditions. During such times, firms may decide to reduce their workforce to control costs. As previously mentioned, MySpace has done this. This can lead to problems, however, when having fewer employees makes it harder for companies to meet individual customers' needs and expectations. In these instances, some suggest that firms should follow several courses of action, including "babying their best customers" by paying extra attention to them and developing a flexible workforce by cross-training employees so they can fill a variety of responsibilities on their jobs. Amazon.com, insurer USAA, and Lexus were recently identified as "customer service champs" because they devote extra care and attention to customer service during challenging economic times.[24]

Effectively Managing Relationships with Customers

The firm's relationships with its customers are strengthened when it delivers superior value to them. Strong interactive relationships with customers often provide the foundation for the firm's efforts to profitably serve customers' unique needs.

As the following statement shows, Harrah's Entertainment (the world's largest provider of branded casino entertainment) is committed to providing superior value to customers: "Harrah's Entertainment is focused on building loyalty and value with its customers through a unique combination of great service, excellent products, unsurpassed distribution, operational excellence and technology leadership."[25] Importantly, as Harrah's appears to anticipate, delivering superior value often results in increased customer loyalty. In turn, customer loyalty has a positive relationship with profitability. However, more choices and easily accessible information about the functionality of firms' products are creating increasingly sophisticated and knowledgeable customers, making it difficult to earn their loyalty.[26]

A number of companies have become skilled at the art of *managing* all aspects of their relationship with their customers.[27] For example, Amazon.com is widely recognized for the quality of information it maintains about its customers, the services it renders, and its ability to anticipate customers' needs. Using the information it has, Amazon tries to serve what it believes are the unique needs of each customer; and it has a strong reputation for being able to successfully do this.[28]

As we discuss next, firms' relationships with customers are characterized by three dimensions. Companies such as Acer and Amazon.com understand these dimensions and manage their relationships with customers in light of them.

Reach, Richness, and Affiliation

The *reach* dimension of relationships with customers is concerned with the firm's access and connection to customers. In general, firms seek to extend their reach, adding customers in the process of doing so.

Reach is an especially critical dimension for social networking sites such as Facebook and MySpace in that the value these firms create for users is to connect them with others. In mid-2009, traffic to MySpace was falling; at the same time, data showed that Facebook had matched MySpace in monthly U.S. visitors for the first time. Specifically, in May 2009, "MySpace attracted 70.2 million unique U.S. visitors...down 4.7% from a year ago while Facebook's U.S. audience nearly doubled to 70.3 million, according to comScore Media Metrix."[29] Reach is also important to Netflix. Fortunately for this firm, recent results indicate that its reach continues to expand: "Netflix ended the first quarter of 2009 with approximately 10,310,000 total subscribers, representing a 25 percent year-over-year growth from 8,234,000 total subscribers at the end of the first quarter of 2008 and a 10 percent sequential growth from 9,390,000 subscribers at the end of the fourth quarter of 2008."[30]

Richness, the second dimension of firms' relationships with customers, is concerned with the depth and detail of the two-way flow of information between the firm and the customer. The potential of the richness dimension to help the firm establish a competitive advantage in its relationship with customers leads many firms to offer online services in order to better manage information exchanges with their customers. Broader and deeper information-based exchanges allow firms to better understand their customers and their needs. Such exchanges also enable customers to become more knowledgeable about how the firm can satisfy them. Internet technology and e-commerce transactions have substantially reduced the costs of meaningful information exchanges with current and potential customers. As we have noted, Amazon is a leader in using the Internet to build relationships with customers. In fact, it bills itself as the most "customer-centric company" on earth. The firm's decision in June 2009 to launch "Your Amazon Ad Contest" demonstrates its belief in and focus on its customers. This contest asked Amazon customers to submit their vision of an Amazon television commercial to the firm. The winning entry was to receive $20,000 in Amazon.com gift cards.[31]

Affiliation, the third dimension, is concerned with facilitating useful interactions with customers. Viewing the world through the customer's eyes and constantly seeking ways to create more value for the customer have positive effects in terms of affiliation. Internet navigators such as Microsoft's MSN Autos helps online clients find and sort information. MSN Autos provides data and software to prospective car buyers that enable them to compare car models along multiple objective specifications. A prospective buyer who

Facebook's reach continues to grow rapidly, with the company announcing that it had surpassed 250 million users in July 2009. Much of the company's recent growth has come largely from outside the United States.

AP Photo/Press Association

has selected a specific car based on comparisons of different models can then be linked to dealers that meet the customer's needs and purchasing requirements. Information about other relevant issues such as financing and insurance and even local traffic patterns is also available at the site. Because its revenues come not from the final customer or end user but from other sources (such as advertisements on its Web site, hyperlinks, and associated products and services), MSN Autos represents the customer's interests, a service that fosters affiliation.[32]

As we discuss next, effectively managing customer relationships (along the dimensions of reach, richness, and affiliation) helps the firm answer questions related to the issues of *who*, *what*, and *how*.

Who: Determining the Customers to Serve

Deciding *who* the target customer is that the firm intends to serve with its business-level strategy is an important decision.[33] Companies divide customers into groups based on differences in the customers' needs (needs are discussed further in the next section) to make this decision. Dividing customers into groups based on their needs is called **market segmentation**, which is a process that clusters people with similar needs into individual and identifiable groups.[34] In the animal food products business, for example, the food-product needs of owners of companion pets (e.g., dogs and cats) differ from the needs for food and health-related products of those owning production animals (e.g., livestock). A subsidiary of Colgate-Palmolive, Hill's Pet Nutrition sells food products for pets. In fact, the company's mission is "to help enrich and lengthen the special relationship between people and their pets."[35] Schering-Plough sells "more than 15 animal medicine products including antibiotics, fertility treatments and a number of vaccines for livestock."[36] Thus, Hill and Schering-Plough target the needs of different segments of customers with the food products they sell for animals.

Almost any identifiable human or organizational characteristic can be used to subdivide a market into segments that differ from one another on a given characteristic. Common characteristics on which customers' needs vary are illustrated in Table 4.1.

Table 4.1 Basis for Customer Segmentation

Consumer Markets
1. Demographic factors (age, income, sex, etc.)
2. Socioeconomic factors (social class, stage in the family life cycle)
3. Geographic factors (cultural, regional, and national differences)
4. Psychological factors (lifestyle, personality traits)
5. Consumption patterns (heavy, moderate, and light users)
6. Perceptual factors (benefit segmentation, perceptual mapping)
Industrial Markets
1. End-use segments (identified by SIC code)
2. Product segments (based on technological differences or production economics)
3. Geographic segments (defined by boundaries between countries or by regional differences within them)
4. Common buying factor segments (cut across product market and geographic segments)
5. Customer size segments

Source: Adapted from S. C. Jain, 2000, *Marketing Planning and Strategy*, Cincinnati: South-Western College Publishing, 120.

Market segmentation is a process used to cluster people with similar needs into individual and identifiable groups.

In light of what it learned about its customers, Gap Inc. used *shopping experience* as a characteristic to subdivide its customers into different segments as a basis for serving their unique needs. Specifically, Gap learned from market research that its female and male customers want different shopping experiences. In a company official's words, "Research showed that men want to come and go easily, while women want an exploration."[37] In light of these research results, women's sections in Gap stores are organized by occasion (e.g., work, entertainment) with accessories for those occasions scattered throughout the section to facilitate browsing. The men's sections of Gap stores are more straightforward, with signs directing male customers to clothing items that are commonly stacked by size.

What: Determining Which Customer Needs to Satisfy

After the firm decides *who* it will serve, it must identify the targeted customer group's needs that its goods or services can satisfy. In a general sense, *needs (what)* are related to a product's benefits and features.[38] Successful firms learn how to deliver to customers what they want and when they want it.[39] Having close and frequent interactions with both current and potential customers helps the firm identify those individuals' and groups' current and future needs.[40]

From a strategic perspective, a basic need of all customers is to buy products that create value for them. The generalized forms of value that goods or services provide are either low cost with acceptable features or highly differentiated features with acceptable cost. In the recent global financial crisis, companies across industries recognized their customers' need to feel as secure as possible when making purchases. Allowing customers to return their cars if they lose their job within 12 months of the purchase is how Hyundai Motors decided to address this consumer need, creating value in the form of security.[41]

The most effective firms continuously strive to anticipate changes in customers' needs. The firm that fails to anticipate and certainly to recognize changes in its customers' needs may lose its customers to competitors whose products can provide more value to the focal firm's customers. For example, Ford Motor Company concluded that customers' needs across the global automobile market were becoming more similar. In response, the firm decided to build the Fiesta as a world car. While the car will be tailored somewhat to the needs of different customers in different markets, analysts believe that the firm "... is betting that it has figured out what has bedeviled mass-market automakers for decades, which is hitting a home run in every market with the same car."[42] Ford believes that changes have occurred resulting in more similarity in customers' needs for automotive transportation across multiple markets. If this assessment is correct, the firm may take customers away from automobile manufacturers failing to see the trend toward similarity rather than differences in customers' needs within multiple market segments.

Though there are exceptions like the perceived market for Ford's Fiesta, consumers' needs within individual market segments often vary a great deal.[43] Jason's Deli tries to address consumers' desires for high-quality, fresh sandwiches. In contrast, many large fast-food companies satisfy customer needs for lower-cost food items with acceptable quality that are delivered quickly. Diversified food and soft-drink producer PepsiCo believes that "any one consumer has different needs at different times of the day." Through its soft drinks (Pepsi products), snacks (Frito-Lay), juices (Tropicana), and cereals (Quaker), PepsiCo is developing new products from breakfast bars to healthier potato chips "to make certain that it covers all those needs."[44]

How: Determining Core Competencies Necessary to Satisfy Customer Needs

After deciding *who* the firm will serve and the specific *needs* of those customers, the firm is prepared to determine how to use its capabilities and competencies to develop products that can satisfy the needs of its target customers. As explained in

Chapters 1 and 3, *core competencies* are resources and capabilities that serve as a source of competitive advantage for the firm over its rivals. Firms use core competencies (*how*) to implement value-creating strategies and thereby satisfy customers' needs. Only those firms with the capacity to continuously improve, innovate, and upgrade their competencies can expect to meet and hopefully exceed customers' expectations across time.[45]

Companies draw from a wide range of core competencies to produce goods or services that can satisfy customers' needs. ProEnergy Services is an integrated service company operating seven business units in the energy industry. Superior client satisfaction is a core competence the firm relies on in competition with its competitors.[46]

SAS Institute is the world's largest privately owned software company and is the leader in business intelligence and analytics. Customers use SAS's programs for data warehousing, data mining, and decision support purposes. Allocating approximately 22 percent of revenues to research and development (R&D), a percentage that exceeds percentages allocated by its competitors, SAS relies on its core competence in R&D to satisfy the data-related needs of such customers as the U.S. Census Bureau and a host of consumer goods firms (e.g., hotels, banks, and catalog companies).[47] Kraft Foods relies on the capabilities of its sales force to create value for its customers,[48] while Safeway Inc. uses its competence to understand customers' unique needs to create its successful private-label brands such as O Organics and Eating Right.[49]

Sometimes, firms may find it necessary to use their core competencies as the foundation for producing new goods or services for new customers. This may be the case for some small automobile parts suppliers in the United States. Given that U.S. auto production in recent years declined about a third from more typical levels, a number of these firms are seeking to diversify their operations, perhaps exiting the auto parts supplier industry as a result of doing so. Some analysts believe that the first rule for these small manufacturers is to determine how their current capabilities and competencies might be used to produce value-creating products for different customers. One analyst gave the following example of how this might work: "There may be no reason that a company making auto door handles couldn't make ball-and-socket joints for artificial shoulders."[50]

Responding to the needs of customers concerned with food safety and quality, Safeway successfully launched the O Organics brand.

Our discussion about customers shows that all organizations must use their capabilities and core competencies (the *how*) to satisfy the needs (the *what*) of the target group of customers (the *who*) the firm has chosen to serve. Next, we describe the different business-level strategies that are available to firms to use to satisfy customers as the foundation for earning above-average returns.

The Purpose of a Business-Level Strategy

The purpose of a business-level strategy is to create differences between the firm's position and those of its competitors.[51] To position itself differently from competitors, a firm must decide whether it intends to *perform activities differently* or to *perform different activities*. In fact, "choosing to perform activities differently or to perform different activities than rivals" is the essence of business-level strategy.[52] Thus, the firm's business-level strategy is a deliberate choice about how it will perform the value chain's primary and support activities to create unique value. Indeed, in the complex twenty-first–century competitive landscape, successful use of a business-level strategy results only when the firm learns how to integrate the activities it performs in ways that create superior value for customers.

Firms develop an activity map to show how they integrate the activities they perform. We show Southwest Airlines's activity map in Figure 4.1. The manner in which

Figure 4.1 Southwest Airlines Activity System

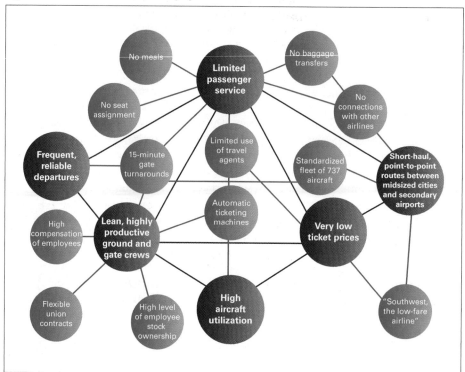

Southwest has integrated its activities is the foundation for the successful use of its cost leadership strategy (this strategy is discussed later in the chapter). The tight integration among Southwest's activities is a key source of the firm's ability to at least historically operate more profitably than its competitors.

As shown in Figure 4.1, Southwest Airlines has configured the activities it performs into six strategic themes—limited passenger service; frequent, reliable departures; lean, highly productive ground and gate crews; high aircraft utilization; very low ticket prices; and short-haul, point-to-point routes between mid-sized cities and secondary airports. Individual clusters of tightly linked activities make it possible for the outcome of a strategic theme to be achieved. For example, no meals, no seat assignments, and no baggage transfers form a cluster of individual activities that support the strategic theme of limited passenger service (see Figure 4.1).

Southwest's tightly integrated activities make it difficult for competitors to imitate the firm's cost leadership strategy. The firm's unique culture and customer service, both of which are sources of competitive advantages, are features that rivals have been unable to imitate, although some have tried. U.S. Airways's MetroJet subsidiary, United Airlines's United Shuttle, Delta's Song, and Continental Airlines's Continental Lite all failed in attempts to imitate Southwest's strategy. Hindsight shows that these competitors offered low prices to customers, but weren't able to operate at costs close to those of Southwest or to provide customers with any notable sources of differentiation, such as a unique experience while in the air. The key to Southwest's success has been its ability to continuously reduce its costs while providing customers with *acceptable* levels of differentiation such as an engaging culture. Firms using the cost leadership strategy must understand that in terms of sources of differentiation that accompany the cost leader's product, the customer defines *acceptable*.

Fit among activities is a key to the sustainability of competitive advantage for all firms, including Southwest Airlines. As Michael Porter comments, "Strategic fit among many activities is fundamental not only to competitive advantage but also to the sustainability of that advantage. It is harder for a rival to match an array of interlocked activities than it is merely to imitate a particular sales-force approach, match a process technology, or replicate a set of product features. Positions built on systems of activities are far more sustainable than those built on individual activities."[53]

Types of Business-Level Strategies

Firms choose from among five business-level strategies to establish and defend their desired strategic position against competitors: *cost leadership, differentiation, focused cost leadership, focused differentiation,* and *integrated cost leadership/differentiation* (see Figure 4.2). Each business-level strategy helps the firm to establish and exploit a particular *competitive advantage* within a particular *competitive scope.* How firms integrate the activities they perform within each different business-level strategy demonstrates how they differ from one another.[54] For example, firms have different activity maps, and thus, a Southwest Airlines activity map differs from those of competitors JetBlue, Continental, American Airlines, and so forth. Superior integration of activities increases the likelihood of being able to gain an advantage over competitors and to earn above-average returns.

When selecting a business-level strategy, firms evaluate two types of potential competitive advantages: "lower cost than rivals, or the ability to differentiate and command a premium price that exceeds the extra cost of doing so."[55] Having lower cost derives from the firm's ability to perform activities differently than rivals; being able to differentiate indicates the firm's capacity to perform different (and valuable) activities.[56] Thus, based on the nature and quality of its internal resources, capabilities, and core competencies,

Figure 4.2 Five Business-Level Strategies

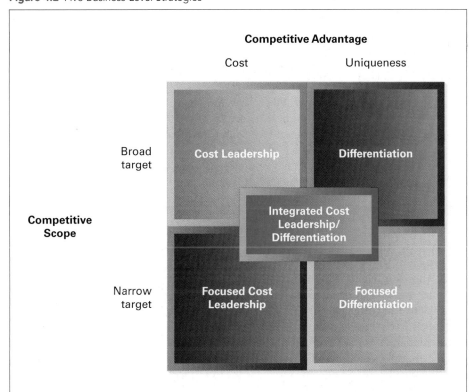

Source: Adapted with the permission of The Free Press, an imprint of Simon & Schuster Adult Publishing Group, from *Competitive Advantage: Creating and Sustaining Superior Performance,* by Michael E. Porter, 12. Copyright © 1985, 1998 by Michael E. Porter.

a firm seeks to form either a cost competitive advantage or a uniqueness competitive advantage as the basis for implementing its business-level strategy.

Two types of competitive scopes are broad target and narrow target (see Figure 4.2). Firms serving a broad target market seek to use their competitive advantage on an industry-wide basis. A narrow competitive scope means that the firm intends to serve the needs of a narrow target customer group. With focus strategies, the firm "selects a segment or group of segments in the industry and tailors its strategy to serving them to the exclusion of others."[57] Buyers with special needs and buyers located in specific geographic regions are examples of narrow target customer groups.[58] As shown in Figure 4.2, a firm could also strive to develop a combined cost/uniqueness competitive advantage as the foundation for serving a target customer group that is larger than a narrow segment but not as comprehensive as a broad (or industry-wide) customer group. In this instance, the firm uses the integrated cost leadership/differentiation strategy.

None of the five business-level strategies shown in Figure 4.2 is inherently or universally superior to the others.[59] The effectiveness of each strategy is contingent both on the opportunities and threats in a firm's external environment and on the strengths and weaknesses derived from the firm's resource portfolio. It is critical, therefore, for the firm to select a business-level strategy that is based on a match between the opportunities and threats in its external environment and the strengths of its internal organization as shown by its core competencies.[60] And, once the firm chooses its strategy, it should consistently emphasize actions that are required to successfully use it. Wal-Mart's continuous emphasis on driving its costs lower is thought to be a key to the firm's effective cost leadership strategy.[61]

Cost Leadership Strategy

The **cost leadership strategy** is an integrated set of actions taken to produce goods or services with features that are acceptable to customers at the lowest cost, relative to that of competitors.[62] Firms using the cost leadership strategy commonly sell standardized goods or services (but with competitive levels of differentiation) to the industry's most typical customers. Process innovations, which are newly designed production and distribution methods and techniques that allow the firm to operate more efficiently, are critical to successful use of the cost leadership strategy.[63]

As noted, cost leaders' goods and services must have competitive levels of differentiation that create value for customers. Recently, Kia Motors decided to emphasize the design of its cars in the U.S. market as a source of differentiation while implementing its cost leadership strategy. Called "cheap chic," some analysts had a positive view of this decision, saying that "When they're done, Kia's cars will still be low-end (in price), but they won't necessarily look like it."[64] It is important for firms using the cost leadership strategy, such as Kia, to do so in this way because concentrating only on reducing costs could result in the firm efficiently producing products that no customer wants to purchase. In fact, such extremes could lead to limited potential for all-important process innovations, employment of lower-skilled workers, poor conditions on the production line, accidents, and a poor quality of work life for employees.[65]

As shown in Figure 4.2, the firm using the cost leadership strategy targets a broad customer segment or group. Cost leaders concentrate on finding ways to lower their costs relative to competitors by constantly rethinking how to complete their primary and support activities to reduce costs still further while maintaining competitive levels of differentiation.[66]

For example, cost leader Greyhound Lines Inc. continuously seeks ways to reduce the costs it incurs to provide bus service while offering customers an acceptable level of differentiation. Greyhound is offering new services to customers as a way of improving the quality of the experience customers have when paying the firm's low prices for its services. Changes in the economic segment of the general environment (see Chapter 2) are creating an opportunity for Greyhound to do this. Specifically, the recent recession

The **cost leadership strategy** is an integrated set of actions taken to produce goods or services with features that are acceptable to customers at the lowest cost, relative to that of competitors.

found more people seeking to travel by bus instead of by planes and trains. However, these new customers "... insist on certain amenities they've grown accustomed to on planes and trains—such as Internet access and cushier seats, not to mention cleanliness." To maintain competitive levels of differentiation while using the cost leadership strategy, Greyhound recently starting using over 100 "motor coaches" that have leather seats, additional legroom, Wi-Fi access, and power outlets in every row.[67]

Greyhound enjoys economies of scale by serving more than 25 million passengers annually with about 2,300 destinations in the United States and operating approximately 1,250 buses. These scale economies allow the firm to keep its costs low while offering some of the differentiated services today's customers seek from the company. Demonstrating the firm's commitment to the physical environment segment of the general environment is the fact that "one Greyhound bus takes an average of 34 cars off the road."[68]

As primary activities, inbound logistics (e.g., materials handling, warehousing, and inventory control) and outbound logistics (e.g., collecting, storing, and distributing products to customers) often account for significant portions of the total cost to produce some goods and services. Research suggests that having a competitive advantage in terms of logistics creates more value when using the cost leadership strategy than when using the differentiation strategy.[69] Thus, cost leaders seeking competitively valuable ways to reduce costs may want to concentrate on the primary activities of inbound logistics and outbound logistics. In so doing many firms choose to outsource their manufacturing operations to low-cost firms with low-wage employees (e.g., China).[70]

Cost leaders also carefully examine all support activities to find additional sources of potential cost reductions. Developing new systems for finding the optimal combination of low cost and acceptable levels of differentiation in the raw materials required to produce the firm's goods or services is an example of how the procurement support activity can facilitate successful use of the cost leadership strategy.

Big Lots Inc. uses the cost leadership strategy. With its vision of being "The World's Best Bargain Place," Big Lots is the largest closeout retailer in the United States with annual sales of over $4.5 billion. For Big Lots, closeout goods "are the same first-quality, brand-name products found at other retailers, but at substantially lower prices."[71] The firm relies on a disciplined merchandise cost and inventory management system to continuously drive its costs lower.[72] The firm's stores sell name-brand products at prices that are 20 to 40 percent below those of discount retailers and roughly 70 percent below those of traditional retailers. Big Lots's buyers search for manufacturer overruns and discontinued styles to find goods priced well below wholesale prices. In addition, the firm buys from overseas suppliers. Big Lots satisfies the customers' need to access the differentiated features of brand-name products, but at a fraction of their initial cost. Tightly integrating its purchasing and inventory management activities across its stores is the main core competence Big Lots uses to satisfy its customers' needs.

As described in Chapter 3, firms use value-chain analysis to identify the parts of the company's operations that create value and those that do not. Figure 4.3 demonstrates the primary and support activities that allow a firm to create value through the cost leadership strategy. Companies unable to link the activities shown in this figure through the activity map they form typically lack the core competencies needed to successfully use the cost leadership strategy.

Effective use of the cost leadership strategy allows a firm to earn above-average returns in spite of the presence of strong competitive forces (see Chapter 2). The next sections (one for each of the five forces) explain how firms implement a cost leadership strategy.

Rivalry with Existing Competitors

Having the low-cost position is valuable to deal with rivals. Because of the cost leader's advantageous position, rivals hesitate to compete on the basis of price, especially before evaluating the potential outcomes of such competition.[73] Wal-Mart is known for its ability to continuously reduce its costs, creating value for customers in the process of doing so.

Figure 4.3 Examples of Value-Creating Activities Associated with the Cost Leadership Strategy

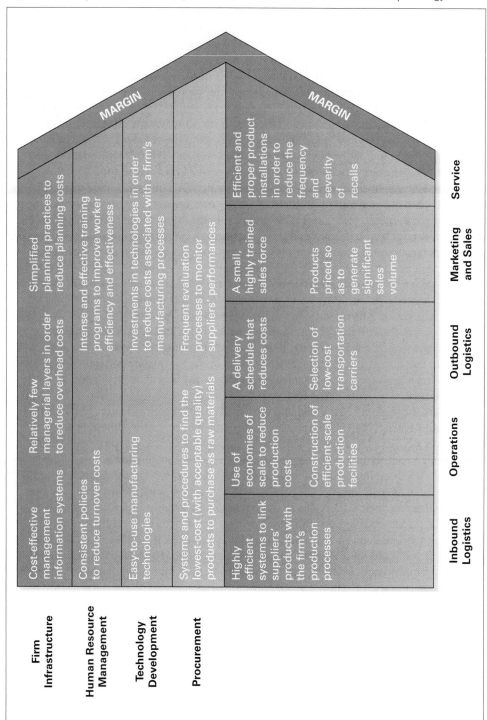

Source: Adapted with the permission of The Free Press, an imprint of Simon & Schuster Adult Publishing Group, from *Competitive Advantage: Creating and Sustaining Superior Performance*, by Michael E. Porter, 47. Copyright © 1985, 1998 by Michael E. Porter.

In light of this ability, rivals such as Costco and Target hesitate to compete against Wal-Mart strictly on the basis of costs and, subsequently, prices to consumers. Recently, Wal-Mart decided to expand "... its private-label line of food and household cleaners to take advantage of recession-pinched consumers' increasing desire to buy cheaper store brands rather than more expensive brand-name products." Because it controls the costs associated with producing its private-label products (Great Value is the name of Wal-Mart's private-label offerings), the firm is able to drive its costs lower when manufacturing and distributing its own products.

Bargaining Power of Buyers (Customers)

Powerful customers can force a cost leader to reduce its prices, but not below the level at which the cost leader's next-most-efficient industry competitor can earn average returns. Although powerful customers might be able to force the cost leader to reduce prices even below this level, they probably would not choose to do so. Prices that are low enough to prevent the next-most-efficient competitor from earning average returns would force that firm to exit the market, leaving the cost leader with less competition and in an even stronger position. Customers would thus lose their power and pay higher prices if they were forced to purchase from a single firm operating in an industry without rivals.

Bargaining Power of Suppliers

The cost leader operates with margins greater than those of competitors. Cost leaders want to constantly increase their margins by driving their costs lower. Big Lots's gross margin increased from 39.7 percent in 2008 to 40.4 percent in 2009,[74] an indication the firm was effectively using the cost leadership strategy. Among other benefits, higher gross margins relative to those of competitors make it possible for the cost leader to absorb its suppliers' price increases. When an industry faces substantial increases in the cost of its supplies, only the cost leader may be able to pay the higher prices and continue to earn either average or above-average returns. Alternatively, a powerful cost leader may be able to force its suppliers to hold down their prices, which would reduce the suppliers' margins in the process.

Wal-Mart uses its power with suppliers (gained because it buys such large quantities from many suppliers) to extract lower prices from them. These savings are then passed on to customers in the form of lower prices, which further strengthens Wal-Mart's position relative to competitors lacking the power to extract lower prices from suppliers. The fact that Wal-Mart is the largest retailer in North America is a key reason the firm has a great deal of power with its suppliers. Another indicator of this power is that with 25 percent of the total market, Wal-Mart is the largest supermarket operator in the United States; and its Sam's Club division is the second largest warehouse club in the United States. Collectively, this sales volume and the market penetration it suggests (over 100 million people visit a Wal-Mart store each week) create the ability for Wal-Mart to gain access to low prices from its suppliers.

Potential Entrants

Through continuous efforts to reduce costs to levels that are lower than competitors', a cost leader becomes highly efficient. Because ever-improving levels of efficiency (e.g., economies of scale) enhance profit margins, they serve as a significant entry barrier to potential competitors.[75] New entrants must be willing and able to accept no-better-than-average returns until they gain the experience required to approach the cost leader's efficiency. To earn even average returns, new entrants must have the competencies required to match the cost levels of competitors other than the cost leader. The low profit margins (relative to margins earned by firms implementing the differentiation strategy) make it necessary for the cost leader to sell large volumes of its product to earn above-average returns. However, firms striving to be the cost leader must avoid pricing their products so low that their ability to operate profitably is reduced, even though volume increases.

Product Substitutes

Compared with its industry rivals, the cost leader also holds an attractive position in terms of product substitutes. A product substitute becomes an issue for the cost leader when its features and characteristics, in terms of cost and differentiated features, are potentially attractive to the firm's customers. When faced with possible substitutes, the cost leader has more flexibility than its competitors. To retain customers, it can reduce the price of its good or service. With still lower prices and competitive levels of differentiation, the cost leader increases the probability that customers will prefer its product rather than a substitute.

Competitive Risks of the Cost Leadership Strategy

The cost leadership strategy is not risk free. One risk is that the processes used by the cost leader to produce and distribute its good or service could become obsolete because of competitors' innovations. These innovations may allow rivals to produce at costs lower than those of the original cost leader, or to provide additional differentiated features without increasing the product's price to customers.

A second risk is that too much focus by the cost leader on cost reductions may occur at the expense of trying to understand customers' perceptions of "competitive levels of differentiation." Wal-Mart, for example, has been criticized for having too few salespeople available to help customers and too few individuals at checkout registers. These complaints suggest that there might be a discrepancy between how Wal-Mart's customers define "minimal levels of service" and the firm's attempts to drive its costs lower and lower.

Imitation is a final risk of the cost leadership strategy. Using their own core competencies, competitors sometimes learn how to successfully imitate the cost leader's strategy. When this happens, the cost leader must increase the value its good or service provides to customers. Commonly, value is increased by selling the current product at an even lower price or by adding differentiated features that create value for customers while maintaining price.

Netflix may be encountering this risk from Redbox, which is the largest operator of DVD-rental kiosks in the United States. Using vending machines that Redbox has established in supermarkets and discount stores, customers pay $1 per day for DVDs. In contrast, Netflix's cheapest plan is $5 per month (the customer receives two DVDs by mail per month with this plan). An analyst using the following words to describe this situation: "Netflix CEO Reed Hastings has something to worry about: an even cheaper DVD rental service run by one of his former lieutenants."[76]

Differentiation Strategy

The **differentiation strategy** is an integrated set of actions taken to produce goods or services (at an acceptable cost) that customers perceive as being different in ways that are important to them.[77] While cost leaders serve a typical customer in an industry, differentiators target customers for whom value is created by the manner in which the firm's products differ from those produced and marketed by competitors. Product innovation, which is "the result of bringing to life a new way to solve the customer's problem—through a new product or service development—that benefits both the customer and the sponsoring company"[78] is critical to successful use of the differentiation strategy.[79]

Firms must be able to produce differentiated products at competitive costs to reduce upward pressure on the price that customers pay. When a product's differentiated features are produced at noncompetitive costs, the price for the product can exceed what the firm's target customers are willing to pay. When the firm has a thorough understanding of what its target customers value, the relative importance they attach to the satisfaction of different needs, and for what they are willing to pay a premium, the differentiation strategy can be effective in helping it earn above-average returns.

Through the differentiation strategy, the firm produces nonstandardized (that is, unique) products for customers who value differentiated features more than they value low cost. For example, superior product reliability and durability and high-performance sound systems are among the differentiated features of Toyota Motor Corporation's Lexus products. The Lexus promotional statement—"We pursue perfection, so you can

The **differentiation strategy** is an integrated set of actions taken to produce goods or services (at an acceptable cost) that customers perceive as being different in ways that are important to them.

pursue living"—suggests a strong commitment to overall product quality as a source of differentiation. However, Lexus offers its vehicles to customers at a competitive purchase price. As with Lexus products, a good's or service's unique attributes, rather than its purchase price, provide the value for which customers are willing to pay.

Continuous success with the differentiation strategy results when the firm consistently upgrades differentiated features that customers value and/or creates new valuable features (innovates) without significant cost increases.[80] This approach requires firms to constantly change their product lines.[81] These firms may also offer a portfolio of products that complement each other, thereby enriching the differentiation for the customer and perhaps satisfying a portfolio of consumer needs.[82] Because a differentiated product satisfies customers' unique needs, firms following the differentiation strategy are able to charge premium prices. Customers are willing to pay a premium price for a product only when a "firm (is) truly unique at something or be perceived as unique."[83] The ability to sell a good or service at a price that substantially exceeds the cost of creating its differentiated features allows the firm to outperform rivals and earn above-average returns. For example, shirt and neckwear manufacturer Robert Talbott follows stringent standards of craftsmanship and pays meticulous attention to every detail of production. The firm imports exclusive fabrics from the world's finest mills to make men's dress shirts and neckwear. Single-needle tailoring is used, and precise collar cuts are made to produce shirts. According to the company, customers purchasing one of its products can be assured that they are being provided with the finest fabrics available.[84] Thus, Robert Talbott's success rests on the firm's ability to produce and sell its differentiated products at a price exceeding the costs of imported fabrics and its unique manufacturing processes.

Rather than costs, a firm using the differentiation strategy always concentrates on investing in and developing features that differentiate a product in ways that create value for customers. Robert Talbott uses the finest silks from Europe and Asia to produce its "Best of Class" collection of ties. Overall, a firm using the differentiation strategy seeks to be different from its competitors on as many dimensions as possible. The less similarity between a firm's goods or services and those of competitors, the more buffered it is from rivals' actions. Commonly recognized differentiated goods include Toyota's Lexus, Ralph Lauren's wide array of product lines, and Caterpillar's heavy-duty earth-moving equipment. McKinsey & Co. is a well-known example of a firm that offers differentiated services.

A good or service can be differentiated in many ways. Unusual features, responsive customer service, rapid product innovations and technological leadership, perceived prestige and status, different tastes, and engineering design and performance are examples of approaches to differentiation.[85] While the number of ways to reduce costs may be finite, virtually anything a firm can do to create real or perceived value is a basis for differentiation. Consider product design as a case in point. Because it can create a positive experience for customers, design is becoming an increasingly important source of differentiation (even for cost leaders seeking to find ways to add functionalities to their low-cost products as a way of differentiating their products from competitors) and hopefully, for firms emphasizing it, of competitive advantage.[86] As we noted, design is a way Kia Motors is now trying to create some uniqueness for its products that are manufactured and sold as part of the firm's cost leadership strategy. Apple is often cited as the firm that sets the standard in design, with the iPod and the iPhone demonstrating Apple's product design capabilities.[87]

The value chain can be analyzed to determine if a firm is able to link the activities required to create value by using the differentiation strategy. Examples of primary and support activities that are commonly used to differentiate a good or service are shown in Figure 4.4. Companies without the skills needed to link these activities cannot expect to successfully use the differentiation strategy. Next, we explain how firms using the differentiation strategy can successfully position themselves in terms of the five forces of competition (see Chapter 2) to earn above-average returns.

Figure 4.4 Examples of Value-Creating Activities Associated with the Differentiation Strategy

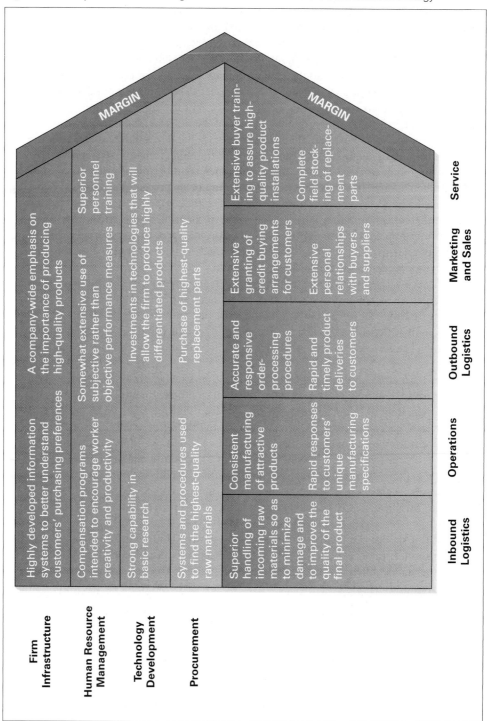

Source: Adapted with the permission of The Free Press, an imprint of Simon & Schuster Adult Publishing Group, from *Competitive Advantage: Creating and Sustaining Superior Performance*, by Michael E. Porter, 47. Copyright © 1985, 1998 by Michael E. Porter.

Rivalry with Existing Competitors

Customers tend to be loyal purchasers of products differentiated in ways that are meaningful to them. As their loyalty to a brand increases, customers' sensitivity to price increases is reduced. The relationship between brand loyalty and price sensitivity insulates a firm from competitive rivalry. Thus, Robert Talbott's "Best of Class" neckwear line is insulated from competition, even on the basis of price, as long as the company continues to satisfy the differentiated needs of its target customer group with the unique qualities of this line of ties. Likewise, Bose is insulated from intense rivalry as long as customers continue to perceive that its stereo equipment offers superior sound quality at a competitive purchase price. Both Robert Talbott and Bose have strong positive reputations for the high-quality and unique products that they provide. Thus, reputations can sustain the competitive advantage of firms following a differentiation strategy.[88]

Bargaining Power of Buyers (Customers)

The uniqueness of differentiated goods or services reduces customers' sensitivity to price increases. Customers are willing to accept a price increase when a product still satisfies their perceived unique needs better than does a competitor's offering. Thus, the golfer whose needs are uniquely satisfied by Callaway golf clubs will likely continue buying those products even if their cost increases. Similarly, the customer who has been highly satisfied with a Louis Vuitton wallet will probably replace that wallet with another one made by the same company even though the purchase price is higher than the original one. Purchasers of brand-name food items (e.g., Heinz ketchup and Kleenex tissues) will accept price increases in those products as long as they continue to perceive that the product satisfies their unique needs at an acceptable cost. In all of these instances, the customers are relatively insensitive to price increases because they do not think that an acceptable product alternative exists.

Bargaining Power of Suppliers

Because the firm using the differentiation strategy charges a premium price for its products, suppliers must provide high-quality components, driving up the firm's costs. However, the high margins the firm earns in these cases partially insulate it from the influence of suppliers in that higher supplier costs can be paid through these margins. Alternatively, because of buyers' relative insensitivity to price increases, the differentiated firm might choose to pass the additional cost of supplies on to the customer by increasing the price of its unique product.

Potential Entrants

Customer loyalty and the need to overcome the uniqueness of a differentiated product present substantial barriers to potential entrants. Entering an industry under these conditions typically demands significant investments of resources and patience while seeking customers' loyalty.

Product Substitutes

Firms selling brand-name goods and services to loyal customers are positioned effectively against product substitutes. In contrast, companies without brand loyalty face a higher probability of their customers switching either to products that offer differentiated features that serve the same function (particularly if the substitute has a lower price) or to products that offer more features and perform more attractive functions.

Competitive Risks of the Differentiation Strategy

One risk of the differentiation strategy is that customers might decide that the price differential between the differentiator's product and the cost leader's product is too large. In this instance, a firm may be offering differentiated features that exceed target customers' needs. The firm then becomes vulnerable to competitors that are able to offer customers a combination of features and price that is more consistent with their needs.

This risk is generalized across a number of companies producing different types of products during the recent global economic crisis—a time when forecasters suggested that "Sales of luxury goods, everything from apparel, to jewelry and leather goods, could plunge globally by 10% ... "[89] in 2009. The decline was expected to be more severe in the United States compared to Europe and Japan. A decision made during this time by

Coach Inc., a maker of high-quality, luxurious accessories and gifts for women and men, demonstrates one firm's reaction to the predicted decline in the sales of luxury goods. With an interest of providing products to increasingly cost-conscious customers without "cheapening" the firm's image, Coach chose to introduce a new line of its products called "Poppy"; the average price of items in this line is approximately 20 percent lower than the average price of Coach's typical products.[90]

Another risk of the differentiation strategy is that a firm's means of differentiation may cease to provide value for which customers are willing to pay. A differentiated product becomes less valuable if imitation by rivals causes customers to perceive that competitors offer essentially the same good or service, but at a lower price.[91] A third risk of the differentiation strategy is that experience can narrow customers' perceptions of the value of a product's differentiated features. For example, customers having positive experiences with generic tissues may decide that the differentiated features of the Kleenex product are not worth the extra cost. Similarly, while a customer may be impressed with the quality of a Robert Talbott "Best of Class" tie, positive experiences with less expensive ties may lead to a conclusion that the price of the "Best of Class" tie exceeds the benefit. To counter this risk, firms must continue to meaningfully differentiate their product for customers at a price they are willing to pay.

Counterfeiting is the differentiation strategy's fourth risk. "Counterfeits are those products bearing a trademark that is identical to or indistinguishable from a trademark registered to another party, thus infringing the rights of the older of the trademark."[92] We describe actions companies such as Hewlett-Packard take to deal with the problems counterfeit goods create for firms whose rights are infringed upon in the Strategic Focus.

Focus Strategies

The **focus strategy** is an integrated set of actions taken to produce goods or services that serve the needs of a particular competitive segment. Thus, firms use a focus strategy when they utilize their core competencies to serve the needs of a particular industry segment or niche to the exclusion of others. Examples of specific market segments that can be targeted by a focus strategy include (1) a particular buyer group (e.g., youths or senior citizens), (2) a different segment of a product line (e.g., products for professional painters or the do-it-yourself group), or (3) a different geographic market (e.g., northern or southern Italy).[93]

There are many specific customer needs firms can serve by using a focus strategy. For example, Los Angeles–based investment banking firm Greif & Company positions itself as "The Entrepreneur's Investment Bank." Greif & Company is a leader in providing merger and acquisition advice to medium-sized businesses located in the western United States.[94] Goya Foods is the largest U.S.-based Hispanic-owned food company in the United States. Segmenting the Hispanic market into unique groups, Goya offers more than 1,500 products to consumers. The firm seeks "to be the be-all for the Latin community."[95] Electronics retailer Conn's Inc., operating stores in Texas, Louisiana, and Oklahoma, uses a commissioned sales staff, which is "trained to explain increasingly complex televisions and washing machines," and its own financing business to help local citizens who dislike receiving what they perceive to be "impersonal" service from large national chains.[96] By successfully using a focus strategy, firms such as these gain a competitive advantage in specific market niches or segments, even though they do not possess an industry-wide competitive advantage.

Although the breadth of a target is clearly a matter of degree, the essence of the focus strategy "is the exploitation of a narrow target's differences from the balance of the industry."[97] Firms using the focus strategy intend to serve a particular segment of an industry more effectively than can industry-wide competitors. They succeed when they effectively serve a segment whose unique needs are so specialized that broad-based competitors choose not to serve that segment or when they satisfy the needs of a segment being served poorly by industry-wide competitors.[98]

The **focus strategy** is an integrated set of actions taken to produce goods or services that serve the needs of a particular competitive segment.

DECLARING WAR AGAINST COUNTERFEITERS TO PROTECT PRODUCT INTEGRITY AND PROFITABILITY

Many of us have seen them and some of us may own one or two of them—products that are intended to look like well-known branded items. Callaway golf clubs, Louis Vuitton purses and shoes, Coach handbags, and Rolex watches are but a few of the items that are counterfeited throughout the world. Counterfeiting is big business; regarded by some as "…one of the most significant threats to the free market." Supporting this assertion is the fact that according to the International Chamber of Commerce, counterfeit goods accounted for about $600 billion in sales in 2007, which is roughly 6 percent of global trade.

Producing and selling counterfeit products negatively affects societies and individual firms. Jobs are lost in companies making the "legitimate" versions of products that are sold by firms using the differentiation strategy. In turn, lost jobs mean lost tax revenues for local and national taxing agencies. While some work is created for those manufacturing the counterfeit goods, these jobs pay less and the companies and their employees typically pay few if any taxes on unreported sales at the firm level and unreported income at the individual employee level.

The selling of counterfeit ink demonstrates the problems individual firms encounter. In 2008 alone, analysts estimate that Hewlett-Packard's (HP) imaging and printing group lost over $1 billion in revenue to counterfeit ink cartridges. In addition to losing sales revenue, HP is concerned that counterfeit cartridges lack product quality and integrity and may hurt the firm's reputation.

Adrian Brown/TCPI/The Canadian Press

In light of the problems counterfeiting creates, HP has gone to war against counterfeiters. The firm employs teams of people to roam the globe looking for counterfeit versions of its products. Often, customers contact these teams if they suspect that a shipment of cartridges they purchased from a wholesaler is counterfeit. If HP's detectives discover that products are indeed counterfeit, "They take their findings to law enforcement to help nab big distributors of counterfeit ink supplies." HP views these actions as critical to the firm's efforts to earn revenues and profits from its products.

Sources: C. Edwards, 2009, HP declares war on counterfeiters, *BusinessWeek*, June 8, 44–45; P. E. Chaudhry, A. Zimmerman, J. R. Peters, & V. V. Cordell, 2009, Preserving intellectual property rights: Managerial insight into the escalating counterfeit market quandary, *Business Horizons*, 52: 57–66; I. Phau & M. Teah, 2009, Devil wears (counterfeit) Prada: A study of antecedents and outcomes of attitudes towards counterfeits of luxury brands, *Journal of Consumer Marketing*, 26: 15–27; J. Abelson, 2008, Grim competition with counterfeiters, *Boston Globe Online*, http://www.boston.com, August 21.

Firms can create value for customers in specific and unique market segments by using the focused cost leadership strategy or the focused differentiation strategy.

Focused Cost Leadership Strategy

Based in Sweden, IKEA, a global furniture retailer with locations in 24 countries and territories and sales revenue of 21.1 billion euros in 2008, uses the focused cost leadership strategy. Young buyers desiring style at a low cost are IKEA's target customers.[99] For these customers, the firm offers home furnishings that combine good design, function, and acceptable quality with low prices. According to the firm, "Low cost is always in focus. This applies to every phase of our activities."[100]

IKEA emphasizes several activities to keep its costs low. For example, instead of relying primarily on third-party manufacturers, the firm's engineers design low-cost, modular furniture ready for assembly by customers. To eliminate the need for sales associates or decorators, IKEA positions the products in its stores so that customers can view different living combinations (complete with sofas, chairs, tables, etc.) in a single room-like setting, which helps the customer imagine how a grouping of furniture will look in the home. A third practice that helps keep IKEA's costs low is requiring customers to transport their own purchases rather than providing delivery service.

Although it is a cost leader, IKEA also offers some differentiated features that appeal to its target customers, including its unique furniture designs, in-store playrooms for children, wheelchairs for customer use, and extended hours. IKEA believes that these services and products "are uniquely aligned with the needs of [its] customers, who are young, are not wealthy, are likely to have children (but no nanny), and, because they work, have a need to shop at odd hours."[101] Thus, IKEA's focused cost leadership strategy also includes some differentiated features with its low-cost products.

Focused Differentiation Strategy

Other firms implement the focused differentiation strategy. As noted earlier, there are many dimensions on which firms can differentiate their good or service. For example, New Look Laser Tattoo Removal, located in Houston, Texas, specializes in removing tattoos that customers no longer desire. According to the firm, some of its customers want to remove tattoos prior to interviewing for jobs while others believe that removing them can benefit their careers. As one of the firm's customers said, "Tattoos make you look a little rougher. I don't want to worry about what people are thinking about me."[102]

The new generation of lunch trucks populating cities such as New York, San Franciso, and Los Angeles also use the focused differentiation strategy. Serving "high-end fare such as grass-fed hamburgers, escargot and crème brulee," highly trained chefs and well-known restaurateurs own and operate many of these trucks. In fact, "the new breed of lunch truck is aggressively gourmet, tech-savvy and politically correct." Selling sustainably harvested fish tacos in a vehicle that is fueled by vegetable oil, the Green Truck, located in Los Angeles, demonstrates these characteristics. Moreover, the owners of these trucks often use Twitter and Facebook to inform customers of their locations as they move from point to point in their focal city.[103]

Denver-based Kazoo Toys uses the focused differentiation strategy to create value for parents and children interested in purchasing unique toys while simultaneously having access to unique services. As we explain in the Strategic Focus, continuously concentrating on ways to create unique value for its customers seems to be the foundation of the firm's continuing success.

With a focus strategy, firms such as Kazoo Toys must be able to complete various primary and support activities in a competitively superior manner to develop and sustain a competitive advantage and earn above-average returns. The activities required to use the focused cost leadership strategy are virtually identical to those of the industry-wide cost leadership strategy (Figure 4.3), and activities required to use the focused differentiation strategy are largely identical to those of the industry-wide differentiation strategy

KAZOO TOYS: CRISP DIFFERENTIATION AS A MEANS OF CREATING VALUE FOR A CERTAIN SET OF CUSTOMERS

Kazoo Toys is a full-service toy store in Denver, Colorado. Offering over 60,000 unique toys for kids of all ages in the brick and mortar location and an additional 6,000 products online at http://www.kazootoys.com, the firm is the world's largest seller of educational, non-violent toys. Children from birth to age 12 are the firm's target market. The essence of the differentiation Kazoo Toys provides its customers is described in the following words: "We know our toys, we know your kids, and we love good customer service. We remain dedicated to providing the best possible tools for your child's healthy play." With respect to toys specifically, the firm's slogan ("Toys That Play with Imagination!") captures the educational aspects of its products.

Kazoo Toys differs from competitors in a number of ways. For example, in terms of inventory, the firm does not stock well-known toy brands (e.g., Mattel and Fisher-Price) that are available from most large retailers. In contrast, Kazoo stocks harder-to-find products such as German-made, Gotz Dolls as well as a range of unique toys that are made in the United States, France, and many other countries. Stocking unique toys allows Kazoo to avoid competing on the price variable and to earn margins required to support the differentiated products and services the firm provides to its customers. Another source of differentiation is Kazoo's exclusive contract with the U.S. Army & Air Force Exchange Service (AAFES)—a contract in which Kazoo is the toy site of choice on military shopping sites.

The firm's open invitation to professionals is another way Kazoo differs from competitors. Speech therapists are welcomed to the store to try to locate toys that might help their patients. Although the store continues to expand to accommodate its success, the design remains unique in that it features smaller departments. For example, there is a "Thomas the Tank Engine" department and a Playmobil department. The inventory is freshened frequently to expose customers to the latest, most innovative, educational, and nonviolent toys. The company's online store (which now generates roughly 50 percent of the firm's revenue) is also known for its strong customer service. Here is how one customer described the online service she received: "Old-fashioned friendly service. When I called

Courtesy of Kazoo & Company Toys

Differentiating itself in terms of product lines and overall customer experience from its big box competitors has allowed CEO Diana Nelson to offer her customers at Kazoo Toys a unique toy shopping experience.

to check the delivery date of a little piano I had ordered for my grandson, I was actually speaking to a person that was friendly, polite, courteous, and just delightful. I will continue to buy from this company. They have a real interest in giving top-quality service. It has been a most enjoyable experience." As this comment suggests, excellent customer service is an important source of differentiation for Kazoo Toys.

Sources: B. Ruggiero, 2009, Super staff and creative expansion keep toy store, Kazoo Toys blog, http://www.kazootoys. blogspot.com, March 11; E. Aguilera, 2008, Kazoo & Co. toys with growth, *Denver Post Online*, http://www.denverpost. com, July 3; B. R. Barringer & R. D. Ireland, 2008, *Entrepreneurship: Successfully launching new ventures*, 2nd ed., Prentice-Hall; T. Polanski, 2008, Diana Nelson, CEO of Kazoo Toys discusses business trials and triumphs with Tom Polanski, *eBizine.com*, http://www.ebizine.com, July 30.

(Figure 4.4). Similarly, the manner in which each of the two focus strategies allows a firm to deal successfully with the five competitive forces parallels those of the two broad strategies. The only difference is in the firm's competitive scope; the firm focuses on a narrow industry segment. Thus, Figures 4.3 and 4.4 and the text regarding the five competitive forces also describe the relationship between each of the two focus strategies and competitive advantage.

Competitive Risks of Focus Strategies

With either focus strategy, the firm faces the same general risks as does the company using the cost leadership or the differentiation strategy, respectively, on an industry-wide basis. However, focus strategies have three additional risks.

First, a competitor may be able to focus on a more narrowly defined competitive segment and "outfocus" the focuser. This would happen to IKEA if another firm found a way to offer IKEA's customers (young buyers interested in stylish furniture at a low cost) additional sources of differentiation while charging the same price or to provide the same service with the same sources of differentiation at a lower price. Second, a company competing on an industry-wide basis may decide that the market segment served by the firm using a focus strategy is attractive and worthy of competitive pursuit. For example, women's clothiers such as Chico's, Ann Taylor, and Liz Claiborne might conclude that the profit potential in the narrow segment being served by Anne Fontaine is attractive and to design and sell competitively similar clothing items. Initially, Anne Fontaine designed and sold only white shirts for women. Quite differentiated on the basis of their design, craftsmanship, and high quality of raw materials, one customer describes her reaction to wearing an Anne Fontaine shirt in this manner: "Once you put on a Fontaine design, you'll find that not one other white shirt can compare as far as design and quality craftsmanship are concerned."[104] The third risk involved with a focus strategy is that the needs of customers within a narrow competitive segment may become more similar to those of industry-wide customers as a whole over time. As a result, the advantages of a focus strategy are either reduced or eliminated. At some point, for example, the needs of Anne Fontaine's customers for high-quality, uniquely designed white shirts may dissipate. If this were to happen, Anne Fontaine's customers might choose to buy white shirts from chains such as Liz Claiborne that sell clothing items with some differentiation, but at a lower cost.

Integrated Cost Leadership/Differentiation Strategy

Most consumers have high expectations when purchasing a good or service. In general, it seems that most consumers want to pay a low price for products with somewhat highly differentiated features. Because of these customer expectations, a number of firms engage in primary and support activities that allow them to simultaneously pursue low cost and differentiation. Firm seeking to do this use the **integrated cost leadership/differentiation strategy**. The objective of using this strategy is to efficiently produce products with some differentiated features. Efficient production is the source of maintaining low costs while differentiation is the source of creating unique value. Firms that successfully use the integrated cost leadership/differentiation strategy usually adapt quickly to new technologies and rapid changes in their external environments. Simultaneously concentrating on developing two sources of competitive advantage (cost and differentiation) increases the number of primary and support activities in which the firm must become competent. Such firms often have strong networks with external parties that perform some of the primary and support activities.[105] In turn, having skills in a larger number of activities makes a firm more flexible.

Concentrating on the needs of its core customer group (higher-income, fashion-conscious discount shoppers), Target Stores uses an integrated cost leadership/differentiation strategy as shown by its "Expect More. Pay Less" brand promise. Target's annual report describes this strategy: "To ensure our guests understand our unique ability to meet their

The **integrated cost leadership/differentiation strategy** involves engaging in primary and support activities that allow a firm to simultaneously pursue low cost and differentiation.

desire for everyday essentials and affordable indulgences, we elevated the prominence of the 'Pay Less' half of our brand promise in both our merchandising and marketing through in-store signing and presentation as well as new campaigns that emphasize our outstanding value. At the same time, we continued to deliver differentiation and newness on the 'Expect More' side of our brand promise with the introduction of Converse One Star in apparel and shoes, the launch of upscale beauty brands, an expanded owned brand presence and a continuous flow of designer collections at exceptional prices."[106] To implement this strategy, Target relies on its relationships with various companies to offer differentiated products at discounted prices. Collections from eco-conscious Rogan Gregory in apparel, Anya Hindmarch in handbags, Sigerson Morrison in shoes, and John Derian and Sami Hayek in home décor are some of the products available in Target's stores. While implementing its strategy, "Target strives to be a responsible steward of the environment."[107] To protect the physical environment, the firm takes several actions annually including recycling 47,600 broken shopping carts, 2.1 million pounds of plastic, and 153,000 pounds of metal from broken hangers.

European-based Zara, which pioneered "cheap chic" in clothing apparel, is another firm using the integrated cost leadership/differentiation strategy. Zara offers current and desirable fashion goods at relatively low prices. To implement this strategy effectively requires sophisticated designers and effective means of managing costs, which fits Zara's capabilities. Zara can design and begin manufacturing a new fashion in three weeks, which suggests a highly flexible organization that can adapt easily to changes in the market or with competitors.[108]

Flexibility is required for firms to complete primary and support activities in ways that allow them to use the integrated cost leadership/differentiation strategy in order to produce somewhat differentiated products at relatively low costs. Flexible manufacturing systems, information networks, and total quality management systems are three sources of flexibility that are particularly useful for firms trying to balance the objectives of continuous cost reductions and continuous enhancements to sources of differentiation as called for by the integrated strategy.

Zara has been successful at offering its customers the latest fashions at reasonable prices while also carefully managing their costs.

Flexible Manufacturing Systems

A flexible manufacturing system (FMS) increases the "flexibilities of human, physical, and information resources"[109] that the firm integrates to create relatively differentiated products at relatively low costs. A significant technological advance, FMS is a computer-controlled process used to produce a variety of products in moderate, flexible quantities with a minimum of manual intervention.[110] Often the flexibility is derived from modularization of the manufacturing process (and sometimes other value chain activities as well).[111]

The goal of an FMS is to eliminate the "low cost versus product variety" trade-off that is inherent in traditional manufacturing technologies. Firms use an FMS to change quickly and easily from making one product to making another. Used properly, an FMS allows the firm to respond more effectively to changes in its customers' needs, while retaining low-cost advantages and consistent product quality.[112] Because an FMS also enables the firm to reduce the lot size needed to manufacture a product efficiently, the firm's capacity to serve the unique needs of a narrow competitive scope is higher. In industries of all types, effective mixes of the firm's tangible assets (e.g., machines) and intangible assets (e.g., people's skills) facilitate implementation of complex competitive strategies, especially the integrated cost leadership/differentiation strategy.[113]

Information Networks

By linking companies with their suppliers, distributors, and customers, information networks provide another source of flexibility. These networks, when used effectively, help the firm satisfy customer expectations in terms of product quality and delivery speed.[114]

STRATEGY RIGHT NOW

Following similar principles to the integrated cost leadership/differentiation strategy, read how companies are creating uncontested market space employing the Blue Ocean Strategy.

www.cengage.com/management/hitt

Earlier, we discussed the importance of managing the firm's relationships with its customers in order to understand their needs. Customer relationship management (CRM) is one form of an information-based network process that firms use for this purpose.[115] An effective CRM system provides a 360-degree view of the company's relationship with customers, encompassing all contact points, business processes, and communication media and sales channels.[116] The firm can then use this information to determine the trade-offs its customers are willing to make between differentiated features and low cost—an assessment that is vital for companies using the integrated cost leadership/differentiation strategy.

Thus, to make comprehensive strategic decisions with effective knowledge of the organization's context, good information flow is essential. Better quality managerial decisions require accurate information on the firm's environment.[117]

Total Quality Management Systems

Total quality management (TQM) is a "managerial innovation that emphasizes an organization's total commitment to the customer and to continuous improvement of every process through the use of data-driven, problem-solving approaches based on empowerment of employee groups and teams."[118] Firms develop and use TQM systems in order to (1) increase customer satisfaction, (2) cut costs, and (3) reduce the amount of time required to introduce innovative products to the marketplace.[119]

Firms able to simultaneously reduce costs while enhancing their ability to develop innovative products increase their flexibility, an outcome that is particularly helpful to firms implementing the integrated cost leadership/differentiation strategy. Exceeding customers' expectations regarding quality is a differentiating feature, and eliminating process inefficiencies to cut costs allows the firm to offer that quality to customers at a relatively low price. Thus, an effective TQM system helps the firm develop the flexibility needed to spot opportunities to simultaneously increase differentiation and reduce costs. Yet, TQM systems are available to all competitors. So they may help firms maintain competitive parity, but rarely alone will they lead to a competitive advantage.[120]

Competitive Risks of the Integrated Cost Leadership/Differentiation Strategy

The potential to earn above-average returns by successfully using the integrated cost leadership/differentiation strategy is appealing. However, it is a risky strategy, because firms find it difficult to perform primary and support activities in ways that allow them to produce relatively inexpensive products with levels of differentiation that create value for the target customer. Moreover, to properly use this strategy across time, firms must be able to simultaneously reduce costs incurred to produce products (as required by the cost leadership strategy) while increasing products' differentiation (as required by the differentiation strategy).

Firms that fail to perform the primary and support activities in an optimum manner become "stuck in the middle."[121] Being stuck in the middle means that the firm's cost structure is not low enough to allow it to attractively price its products and that its products are not sufficiently differentiated to create value for the target customer. These firms will not earn above-average returns and will earn average returns only when the structure of the industry in which it competes is highly favorable.[122] Thus, companies implementing the integrated cost leadership/differentiation strategy must be able to perform the primary and support activities in ways that allow them to produce products that offer the target customer some differentiated features at a relatively low cost/price.

Firms can also become stuck in the middle when they fail to successfully implement *either* the cost leadership *or* the differentiation strategy. In other words, industry-wide competitors too can become stuck in the middle. Trying to use the integrated strategy is costly in that firms must pursue both low costs and differentiation. Firms may need

Total quality management (TQM) is a managerial innovation that emphasizes an organization's total commitment to the customer and to continuous improvement of every process through the use of data-driven, problem-solving approaches based on empowerment of employee groups and teams.

to form alliances with other firms to achieve differentiation, yet alliance partners may extract prices for the use of their resources that make it difficult to meaningfully reduce costs.[123] Firms may be motivated to make acquisitions to maintain their differentiation through innovation or to add products to their portfolio not offered by competitors.[124] Recent research suggests that firms using "pure strategies," either cost leadership or differentiation, often outperform firms attempting to use a "hybrid strategy" (i.e., integrated cost leadership/differentiation strategy). This research suggests the risky nature of using an integrated strategy.[125] However, the integrated strategy is becoming more common and perhaps necessary in many industries because of technological advances and global competition.

SUMMARY

- A business-level strategy is an integrated and coordinated set of commitments and actions the firm uses to gain a competitive advantage by exploiting core competencies in specific product markets. Five business-level strategies (cost leadership, differentiation, focused cost leadership, focused differentiation, and integrated cost leadership/differentiation) are examined in the chapter.

- Customers are the foundation of successful business-level strategies. When considering customers, a firm simultaneously examines three issues: *who*, *what*, and *how*. These issues, respectively, refer to the customer groups to be served, the needs those customers have that the firm seeks to satisfy, and the core competencies the firm will use to satisfy customers' needs. Increasing segmentation of markets throughout the global economy creates opportunities for firms to identify more unique customer needs they can serve with one of the business-level strategies.

- Firms seeking competitive advantage through the cost leadership strategy produce no-frills, standardized products for an industry's typical customer. However, these low-cost products must be offered with competitive levels of differentiation. Above-average returns are earned when firms continuously emphasize efficiency such that their costs are lower than those of their competitors, while providing customers with products that have acceptable levels of differentiated features.

- Competitive risks associated with the cost leadership strategy include (1) a loss of competitive advantage to newer technologies, (2) a failure to detect changes in customers' needs, and (3) the ability of competitors to imitate the cost leader's competitive advantage through their own unique strategic actions.

- Through the differentiation strategy, firms provide customers with products that have different (and valued) features. Differentiated products must be sold at a cost that customers believe is competitive relative to the product's features as compared to the cost/feature combinations available from competitors' goods. Because of their uniqueness, differentiated goods or services are sold at a premium price. Products can be differentiated along any dimension that some customer group values.

Firms using this strategy seek to differentiate their products from competitors' goods or services along as many dimensions as possible. The less similarity to competitors' products, the more buffered a firm is from competition with its rivals.

- Risks associated with the differentiation strategy include (1) a customer group's decision that the differences between the differentiated product and the cost leader's goods or services are no longer worth a premium price, (2) the inability of a differentiated product to create the type of value for which customers are willing to pay a premium price, (3) the ability of competitors to provide customers with products that have features similar to those of the differentiated product, but at a lower cost, and (4) the threat of counterfeiting, whereby firms produce a cheap "knockoff" of a differentiated good or service.

- Through the cost leadership and the differentiated focus strategies, firms serve the needs of a narrow competitive segment (e.g., a buyer group, product segment, or geographic area). This strategy is successful when firms have the core competencies required to provide value to a specialized market segment that exceeds the value available from firms serving customers on an industry-wide basis.

- The competitive risks of focus strategies include (1) a competitor's ability to use its core competencies to "outfocus" the focuser by serving an even more narrowly defined market segment, (2) decisions by industry-wide competitors to focus on a customer group's specialized needs, and (3) a reduction in differences of the needs between customers in a narrow market segment and the industry-wide market.

- Firms using the integrated cost leadership/differentiation strategy strive to provide customers with relatively low-cost products that also have valued differentiated features. Flexibility is required for the firm to learn how to use primary and support activities in ways that allow them to produce differentiated products at relatively low costs. The primary risk of this strategy is that a firm might produce products that do not offer sufficient value in terms of either low cost or differentiation. In such cases, the company is "stuck in the middle." Firms stuck in the middle compete at a disadvantage and are unable to earn more than average returns.

1. What is a business-level strategy?

2. What is the relationship between a firm's customers and its business-level strategy in terms of *who, what,* and *how*? Why is this relationship important?

3. What are the differences among the cost leadership, differentiation, focused cost leadership, focused differentiation, and integrated cost leadership/differentiation business-level strategies?

4. How can each one of the business-level strategies be used to position the firm relative to the five forces of competition in a way that helps the firm earn above-average returns?

5. What are the specific risks associated with using each business-level strategy?

EXPERIENTIAL | EXERCISES

EXERCISE 1: CUSTOMER NEEDS AND STOCK TRADING

Nearly 100 million Americans have investments in the stock market through shares of individual companies or positions in mutual funds. At its peak volume, the New York Stock Exchange has traded more than 3.5 billion shares in a single day. Stock brokerage firms are the conduit to help individuals plan their portfolios and manage transactions. Given the scope of this industry, there is no single definition of what customers consider as "superior value" from a brokerage operation.

Part One

After forming small teams, the instructor will ask the teams to count off by threes. The teams will study three different brokerage firms, with team 1 examining TD Ameritrade (ticker: AMTD), team 2 E*TRADE (ticker: ETFC), and team 3, Charles Schwab (ticker: SCHW).

Part Two

Each team should research its target company to answer the following questions:

- Describe the "who, what, and how" for your firm. How stable is this focus? How much have these elements changed in the last five years?
- Describe your firm's strategy.
- How does your firm's strategy offer protection against each of the five forces?

Part Three

In class, the instructor will ask two teams for each firm to summarize their results. Next, the whole class will discuss which firm is most effective at meeting the needs of its customer base.

EXERCISE 2: CREATE A BUSINESS-LEVEL STRATEGY

This assignment brings together elements from the previous chapters. Accordingly, you and your team will create a business-level strategy for a firm of your own creation. The instructor will assign you an industry for which you will create an entry strategy using one of the five business-level strategies.

Each team is assigned one of the business-level strategies described in the chapter:

- Cost leadership
- Differentiation
- Focused cost leadership
- Focused differentiation
- Integrated cost leadership/differentiation

Part One

Research your industry and describe the general environment. Using the segments of the general environment, identify some factors for each segment that are influential for your industry. Next, describe the industry environment using Porter's five-forces model. Database services like Mint Global, Datamonitor, or IBISWorld can be helpful in this regard. If those are not available, consult your local librarian for assistance. After this, you should be able to clearly articulate the opportunities and the threats that exist.

Part Two

Create on a poster the business-level strategy assigned to your team. Be prepared to describe the following:

- Vision statement and mission statement
- Description of your target customer
- Picture of your business—for example, where is it located (downtown, suburb, rural, etc)?
- Describe trends that provide opportunities and threats for your intended strategy.
- List the resources, both tangible and intangible, required to compete successfully in this market.
- How will you go about creating a sustainable competitive advantage?

THE COUNTERINTUITIVE STRATEGY

William Johnson Chairman, president, and chief executive officer/H. J. Heinz Company

William Johnson discusses the rationalization of business segments that the company found itself holding in 2002.

Before you watch the video consider the following concepts and questions and be prepared to discuss them in class:

Concepts
- Customers
- Strategy
- Focusing on capabilities
- Portfolio of businesses
- Business-level strategy

Questions
1. Research H. J. Heinz Company and describe its portfolio of businesses and its business-level strategy.
2. Do you think the goal of any company should be to grow and get bigger—particularly a publicly-traded one like Heinz?
3. In any corporation, should underperforming business segments be sold?

NOTES

1. D. J. Collis & M. G. Rukstad, 2008, Can you say what your strategy is? *Harvard Business Review*, 86(4): 82–90.
2. H. Greve, 2009, Bigger and safer: The diffusion of competitive advantage, *Strategic Management Journal*, 30: 1–23.
3. M. A. Delmas & M. W. Toffel, 2008, Organizational responses to environmental demands: Opening the black box, *Strategic Management Journal*, 29: 1027–1055; S. Elbanna & J. Child, 2007, The influence of decision, environmental and firm characteristics on the rationality of strategic decision-making, *Journal of Management Studies*, 44: 561–591; T. Yu & A. A. Cannella, Jr., 2007, Rivalry between multinational enterprises: An event history approach, *Academy of Management Journal*, 50: 665–686.
4. S. L. Newbert, 2008, Value, rareness, competitive advantage, and performance: A conceptual-level empirical investigation of the resource-based view of the firm, *Strategic Management Journal*, 29: 745–768.
5. M. V. Copeland, 2009, Dell's bread-and-butter puts it in a jam, *CNNMoney.com*, http://www.cnnmoney.com, February 27.
6. N. A. Morgan & L. L. Rego, 2009, Brand portfolio strategy and firm performance, *Journal of Marketing*, 73: 59–74; C. Zott & R. Amit, 2008, The fit between product market strategy and business model: Implications for firm performance, *Strategic Management Journal*, 29: 1–26.
7. S. Kaplan, 2008, Framing contests: Strategy making under uncertainty, *Organization Science*, 19: 729–752.
8. S. Maxfield, 2008, Reconciling corporate citizenship and competitive strategy: Insights from economic theory, *Journal of Business Ethics*, 80: 367–377; K. Shimizu & M. A. Hitt, 2004, Strategic flexibility: Organizational preparedness to reverse ineffective strategic decisions, *Academy of Management Executive*, 18(4): 44–59.
9. B. Chakravarthy & P. Lorange, 2008, Driving renewal: The entrepreneur-manager, *Journal of Business Strategy*, 29: 14–21.
10. R. Oriani & M. Sobrero, 2008, Uncertainty and the market valuation of R&D within a real options logic, *Strategic Management Journal*, 29: 343–361.
11. J. A. Lamberg, H. Tikkanen, T. Nokelainen, & H. Suur-Inkeroinen, 2009, Competitive dynamics, strategic consistency, and organizational survival, *Strategic Management Journal*, 30: 45–60; R. D. Ireland & C. C. Miller, 2005, Decision-making and firm success, *Academy of Management Executive*, 18(4): 8–12.
12. I. Goll, N. B. Johnson, & A. A. Rasheed, 2008, Top management team demographic characteristics, business strategy, and firm performance in the US airline industry: The role of managerial discretion, *Management Decision*, 46: 201–222; J. R. Hough, 2006, Business segment performance redux: A multilevel approach, *Strategic Management Journal*, 27: 45–61.
13. P. Ozcan & K. M. Eisenhardt, 2009, Origin of alliance portfolios: Entrepreneurs, network strategies, and firm performance, *Academy of Management Journal*, 52: 246–279; B. Choi, S. K. Poon, & J. G. Davis, 2008, Effects of knowledge management strategy on organizational performance: A complementarity theory-based approach, *Omega*, 36: 235–251.
14. J. W. Spencer, 2008, The impact of multinational enterprise strategy on indigenous enterprises: Horizontal spillovers and crowding out in developing countries, *Academy of Management Review*, 33: 341–361.
15. E. Steel, 2009, MySpace slashes jobs as growth slows down, *Wall Street Journal Online*, http://www.wsj.com, June 17.
16. R. Grover, 2009, Van Natta cuts jobs at MySpace, *Wall Street Journal Online*, http://www.wsj.com, June 16.
17. B. Einhorn & M. Srivastava, 2009, Social networking: Facebook looks to India, *Wall Street Journal Online*, http://www.wsj.com, June 15.
18. D. Lei & J. W. Slocum, 2009, The tipping points of business strategy: The rise and decline of competitiveness, *Organizational Dynamics*, 38: 131–147.
19. R. J. Harrington & A. K. Tjan, 2008, Transforming strategy one customer at a time, *Harvard Business Review*, 86(3): 62–72; R. Priem, 2007, A consumer perspective on value creation, *Academy of Management Review*, 32: 219–235.
20. M. E. Porter, 1980, *Competitive Strategy*, New York: Free Press.
21. M. Baghai, S. Smit, & P. Viguerie, 2009, Is your growth strategy flying blind? *Harvard Business Review*, 87(5): 86–96.
22. D. G. Sirmon, S. Gove, & M. A. Hitt, 2008, Resource management in dyadic competitive rivalry: The effects of resource bundling and deployment, *Academy of Management Journal*, 51: 919–935; D. G. Sirmon, M. A. Hitt, & R. D. Ireland, 2007, Managing firm resources in dynamic environments to create value: Inside the black box, *Academy of Management Review*, 32: 273–292.
23. A. Wetergins & R. Boschma, 2009, Does spatial proximity to customers matter for innovative performance? Evidence

from the Dutch software sector, *Research Policy*, 38: 746–755.

24. J. McGregor, 2009, When service means survival, *BusinessWeek*, March 2: 26–33.

25. 2009, Company information, http://www.harrahs.com, June 17.

26. Y. Liu & R. Yang, 2009, Competing loyalty programs: Impact of market saturation, market share, and category expandability, *Journal of Marketing*, 73: 93–108; P. R. Berthon, L. F. Pitt, I. McCarthy, & S. M. Kates, 2007, When customers get clever: Managerial approaches to dealing with creative customers, *Business Horizons*, 50(1): 39–47.

27. P. E. Frown & A. F. Payne, 2009, Customer relationship management: A strategic perspective, *Journal of Business Market Management*, 3: 7–27.

28. H. Green, 2009, How Amazon aims to keep you clicking, *BusinessWeek*, March 2: 34–35.

29. E. Steel, 2009, MySpace slashes jobs as growth slows down, *Wall Street Journal Online*, http://www.wsj.com, June 17.

30. 2009, Netflix announces Q1 2009 financial results, http://www.netflix.com, April 23.

31. 2009, Amazon turns to customers for new TV advertising campaign, http://www.amazon.com, June 8.

32. 2009, http://www.autos.msn.com, June 17.

33. I. C. MacMillan & L. Selden, 2008, The incumbent's advantage, *Harvard Business Review*, 86(10): 111–121; G. Dowell, 2006, Product-line strategies of new entrants in an established industry: Evidence from the U. S. bicycle industry, *Strategic Management Journal*, 27: 959–979.

34. J. Zhang & M. Wedel, 2009, The effectiveness of customized promotions in online and offline stores, *Journal of Marketing Research*, 46: 190–206; C. W. Lamb Jr., J. F. Hair Jr., & C. McDaniel, 2006, *Marketing*, 8th ed., Mason, OH: Thomson South-Western, 224.

35. 2009, About Hill's pet nutrition, http://www.hillspet.com, June 17.

36. 2009, Merck mulls selling off veterinary products, its own or Schering-Plough's before $41 merger, http://www.blog.taragana.com, June 3.

37. S. Hamner, 2005, Filling the gap, *Business 2.0*, July, 30.

38. S. French, 2009, Re-framing strategic thinking: The research-aims and outcomes, *Journal of Management Development*, 28: 205–224.

39. R. J. Brodie, J. R. M. Whittome, & G. J. Brush, 2009, Investigating the service brand: A customer value perspective, *Journal of Business Research*, 62: 345–355; P. D. Ellis, 2006, Market orientation and performance: A meta-analysis and cross-national comparisons, *Journal of Management Studies*, 43: 1089–1107.

40. L. A. Bettencourt & A. W. Ulwick, 2008, The customer-centered innovation map, *Harvard Business Review*, 86(5): 109–114.

41. A. Feldman, 2009, Wooing the worried, *BusinessWeek*, April 27, 24.

42. D. Kiley, 2009, One Ford for the whole wide world, *BusinessWeek*, June 15, 58–59.

43. E. A. Borg, 2009, The marketing of innovations in high-technology companies:

A network approach, *European Journal of Marketing*, 43: 364–70.

44. D. Foust, F. F. Jespersen, F. Katzenberg, A. Barrett, & R. O. Crockett, 2003, The best performers, *BusinessWeek Online*, http://www.businessweek.com, March 24.

45. T. Y. Eng & J. G. Spickett-Jones, 2009, An investigation of marketing capabilities and upgrading performance of manufacturers in Mainland China and Hong Kong, *Journal of World Business*, in press; M. B. Heeley & R. Jacobson, 2008, The recency of technological inputs and financial performance, *Strategic Management Journal*, 29: 723–744.

46. 2009, Experience our energy, http://www.proenergyservices.com, June 17.

47. 2009, SAS honored with 2009 Asia Pacific Forst & Sullivan ICT aware for business intelligence, http://www.sas.com, June 9.

48. 2009, Strategies, http://www.kraft.com, June 17.

49. T. W. Martin, 2009, Safeway cultivates its private labels as brands to be sold by other chains, *Wall Street Journal Online*, http://www.wsj.com, May 7.

50. K. E. Klein, 2009, Survival advice for auto parts suppliers, *Wall Street Journal Online*, http://www.wsj.com, June 16.

51. M. E. Porter, 1985, *Competitive Advantage*, New York: Free Press, 26.

52. M. E. Porter, 1996, What is strategy? *Harvard Business Review*, 74(6): 61–78.

53. Porter, What is strategy?

54. M. Reitzig & P. Puranam, 2009, Value appropriation as an organizational capability: The case of IP protection through patents, *Strategic Management Journal*, 30: 765–789; C. Zott, 2003, Dynamic capabilities and the emergence of intraindustry differential firm performance: Insights from a simulation study, *Strategic Management Journal*, 24: 97–125.

55. M. E. Porter, 1994, Toward a dynamic theory of strategy, in R. P. Rumelt, D. E. Schendel, & D. J. Teece (eds.), *Fundamental Issues in Strategy*, Boston: Harvard Business School Press: 423–461.

56. Porter, What is strategy? 62.

57. Porter, *Competitive Advantage*, 15.

58. S. Sun, 2009, An analysis on the conditions and methods of market segmentation, *International Journal of Business and Management*, 4: 63–70.

59. J. Gonzales-Benito & I. Suarez-Gonzalez, 2009, A study of the role played by manufacturing strategic objectives and capabilities in understanding the relationship between Porter's generic strategies and business performance, *British Journal of Management*, in press.

60. G. B. Voss, D. Sirdeshmukh, & Z. G. Voss, 2008, The effects of slack resources and environmental threat on product exploration and exploitation, *Academy of Management Journal*, 51: 147–158.

61. S. McKee, 2009, Customers your company doesn't want, *Wall Street Journal Online*, http://www.wsj.com, June 12.

62. Porter, *Competitive Strategy*, 35–40.

63. M. J. Gehlhar, A. Regmi, S. E. Stefanou, & B. L. Zoumas, 2009, Brand leadership and product innovation as firm strategies in

global food markets, *Journal of Product & Brand Management*, 18: 115–126.

64. M. Ihlwan, 2009, Kia Motors: Still cheap, now chic, *BusinessWeek*, June 1, 58.

65. D. Mehri, 2006, The dark side of lean: An insider's perspective on the realities of the Toyota production system, *Academy of Management Perspectives*, 20(2): 21–42.

66. N. T. Sheehan & G. Vaidyanathan, 2009, using a value creation compass to discover "Blue Oceans," *Strategy & Leadership*, 37: 13-20; D. F. Spulber, 2004, *Management Strategy*, New York: McGraw Hill/Irwin, 175.

67. A. M. Chaker, 2009, Planes, trains ... and buses? *Wall Street Journal Online*, http://www.wsj.com, June 18.

68. 2009, About Greyhound, http://www.greyhound.com, June 17.

69. M. Kotabe & R. Mudambi, 2009, Global sourcing and value creation: Opportunities and challenges, *Journal of International Management*, 15: 121–125; D. F. Lynch, S. B. Keller, & J. Ozment, 2000, The effects of logistics capabilities and strategy on firm performance, *Journal of Business Logistics*, 21(2): 47–68.

70. J. Hatonen & T. Erikson, 2009, 30+ years of research and practice of outsourcing—Exploring the past and anticipating the future, *Journal of International Management*, 15: 142–155; P. Edwards & M. Ram, 2006, Surviving on the margins of the economy: Working relationships in small, low-wage firms, *Journal of Management Studies*, 43: 895–916.

71. 2009, What is a closeout? http://www.biglots.com, June 18.

72. 2009, Big Lots, *Standard & Poor's Stock Reports*, http://www.standardandpoors.com, June 13.

73. J. Morehouse, B. O'Mera, C. Hagen, & T. Huseby, 2008, Hitting back: Strategic responses to low-cost rivals, *Strategy & Leadership*, 36: 4–13; L. K. Johnson, 2003, Dueling pricing strategies, *The McKinsey Quarterly*, 44(3): 10–11.

74. K. E. Grace, 2009, Big Lots net falls 14%, expects 2009 earnings above views, *Wall Street Journal Online*, http://www.wsj.com, March 4.

75. O. Ormanidhi & O. Stringa, 2008, Porter's model of generic competitive strategies, *Business Economics*, 43: 55–64; J. Bercovitz & W. Mitchell, 2007, When is more better? The impact of business scale and scope on long-term business survival, while controlling for profitability, *Strategic Management Journal*, 28: 61–79.

76. J. Mintz, 2009, Redbox's kiosks take on Netflix's red envelopes, *The Eagle*, June 21, A14.

77. Porter, *Competitive Strategy*, 35–40.

78. 2009, Product innovation, http://www.1000ventures.com, June 19.

79. R. Cowan & N. Jonard, 2009, Knowledge portfolios and the organization of innovation networks, *Academy of Management Review*, 34: 320–342.

80. D. Ashmos Plowman, L. T. Baker, T. E. Beck, M. Kulkarni, S. Thomas-Solansky, & D. V. Travis, 2007, Radical change accidentally: The emergence and amplification of small change, *Academy of*

Management Journal, 50: 515–543; A. Wadhwa & S. Kotha, 2006, Knowledge creation through external venturing: Evidence from the telecommunications equipment manufacturing industry, *Academy of Management Journal*, 49: 819–835.

81. D. W. Baack & D. J. Boggs, 2008, The difficulties in using a cost leadership strategy in emerging markets, *International Journal of Emerging Markets*, 3: 125–139; M. J. Benner, 2007, The incumbent discount: Stock market categories and response to radical technological change, *Academy of Management Review*, 32: 703–720.

82. F. T. Rothaermel, M. A. Hitt, & L. A. Jobe, 2006, Balancing vertical integration and strategic outsourcing: Effects on product portfolio, product success and firm performance, *Strategic Management Journal*, 27: 1033–1056; A. V. Mainkar, M. Lubatkin, & W. S. Schulze, 2006, Toward a product-proliferation theory of entry barriers, *Academy of Management Review*, 31: 1062–1075.

83. Porter, *Competitive Advantage*, 14.

84. 2009, History, http://www.roberttalbott.com, June 19.

85. L. A. Bettencourt & A. W. Ulwick, 2008, The customer-centered innovation map, *Harvard Business Review*, 86(5): 109–114; W. C. Bogner & P. Bansal, 2007, Knowledge management as a basis for sustained high performance, *Journal of Management Studies*, 44:165–188; M. Semadeni, 2006, Minding your distance: How management consulting firms use service marks to position competitively, *Strategic Management Journal*, 27: 169–187.

86. M. Abbott, R. Holland, J. Giacomin, & J. Shackleton, 2009, Changing affective content in brand and product attributes, *Journal of Product & Brand Management*, 18: 17–26; P. Best, Using design to drive innovation, *BusinessWeek Online*, http://www.businessweek.com, June 29.

87. B. Charny & J. A. Dicolo, 2009, Apple debuts new iPhones to long lines, *Wall Street Journal Online*, http://www.wsj.com, June 19.

88. M. Jensen & A. Roy, 2008, Staging exchange partner choices: When do status and reputation matter? *Academy of Management Journal*, 51: 495–516; V. P. Rindova, T. G. Pollock, & M. A. Hayward, 2006, Celebrity firms: The social construction of market popularity, *Academy of Management Review*, 31: 50–71.

89. V. O'Connell, 2009, Sales of luxury goods seen falling by 10%, *Wall Street Journal Online*, http://www.wsj.com, April 11.

90. S. Berfield, 2009, Coach's new bag, *BusinessWeek*, June 29: 41-43; S. Berfield, 2009, Coach's Poppy line is luxury for recessionary times, *BusinessWeek Online*, http://www.wsj.com, June 18.

91. D. G. Sirmon, J.-L. Arregle, M. A. Hitt, & J. W. Webb, 2008, The role of family influence in firms' strategic responses to threat of imitation, *Entrepreneurship Theory and Practice*, 32: 979–998;

F. K. Pil & S. K. Cohen, 2006, Modularity: Implications for imitation, innovation, and sustained advantage, *Academy of Management Review*, 31: 995–1011.

92. X. Bian & L. Moutinho, 2009, An investigation of determinants of counterfeit purchase consideration, *Journal of Business Research*, 62: 368–378.

93. Porter, *Competitive Strategy*, 98.

94. 2009, Greif & Co., http://www.greifco.com, June 19.

95. 2009, About Goya foods, http://www.goyafoods.com, June 20.

96. M. Bustillo, 2009, Small electronics chains thrive in downturn, *Wall Street Journal Online*, http://www.wsj.com, May 27.

97. Porter, *Competitive Advantage*, 15.

98. Ibid., 15–16.

99. K. Kling & I. Goteman, 2003, IKEA CEO Andres Dahlvig on international growth and IKEA's unique corporate culture and brand identity, *Academy of Management Executive*, 17(1): 31–37.

100. 2009, About IKEA, http://www.ikea.com, June 21.

101. G. Evans, 2003, Why some stores strike me as special, *Furniture Today*, 27(24): 91; Porter, What is strategy?, 65.

102. J. Latson, 2009, Tattoo removal makes mark in slow economy, *Houston Chronicle Online*, http://www.chron.com, April 25.

103. K. McLaughlin, 2009, Food truck nation, *Wall Street Journal Online*, http://www.wsj.com, June 5.

104. 2009, Woman of style: CEO Anne Fontaine, http://www.factio-magazine.com, June 20.

105. O. Furrer, D. Sudharshan, H. Thomas, & M. T. Zlexandre, 2008, Resource configurations, generic strategies, and firm performance: Exploring the parallels between resource-based and competitive strategy theories in a new industry, *Journal of Strategy and Management*, 1: 15–40; J. H. Dyer & N. W. Hatch, 2006, Relation-specific capabilities and barriers to knowledge transfers: Creating advantage through network relationships, *Strategic Management Journal*, 27: 701–719.

106. 2008, Letter to our shareholders, http://www.target.com, June 20.

107. 2009, Environment, http://www.target.com, June 21.

108. K. Capell, 2008, Zara thrives by breaking all the rules, *BusinessWeek*, October 20, 66.

109. R. Sanchez, 1995, Strategic flexibility in product competition, *Strategic Management Journal*, 16 (Special Issue): 140.

110. M. I. M. Wahab, D. Wu, and C.-G. Lee, 2008, A generic approach to measuring the machine flexibility of manufacturing systems, *European Journal of Operational Research*, 186: 137–149.

111. M. Kotabe, R. Parente, & J. Y. Murray, 2007, Antecedents and outcomes of modular production in the Brazilian automobile industry: A grounded theory approach, *Journal of International Business Studies*, 38: 84–106.

112. T. Raj, R. Shankar, & M. Sunhaib, 2009, An ISM approach to analyse interaction

between barriers of transition to Flexible Manufacturing Systems, *International Journal of Manufacturing Technology and Management*, 16: 417–438. E. K. Bish, A. Muriel, & S. Biller, 2005, Managing flexible capacity in a make-to-order environment, *Management Science*, 51: 167–180.

113. S. M. Iravani, M. P. van Oyen, & K. T. Sims, 2005, Structural flexibility: A new perspective on the design of manufacturing and service operations, *Management Science*, 51: 151–166.

114. P. Theodorou & G. Florou, 2008, Manufacturing strategies and financial performance—the effect of advanced information Technology: CAD/CAM systems, *Omega*, 36: 107–121.

115. N. A. Morgan & L. L. Rego, 2009, Brand portfolio strategy and firm performance, *Journal of Marketing*, 73: 59–74.

116. D. Elmuti, H. Jia, & D. Gray, 2009, Customer relationship management strategic application and organizational effectiveness: An empirical investigation, *Journal of Strategic Marketing*, 17: 75–96.

117. D. P. Forbes, 2007, Reconsidering the strategic implications of decision comprehensiveness, *Academy of Management Review*, 32: 361–376.

118. J. D. Westphal, R. Gulati, & S. M. Shortell, 1997, Customization or conformity: An institutional and network perspective on the content and consequences of TQM adoption, *Administrative Science Quarterly*, 42: 366–394.

119. S. Modell, 2009, Bundling management control innovations: A field study of organisational experimenting with total quality management and the balanced scorecard, *Accounting, Auditing & Accountability Journal*, 22: 59–90.

120. A. Keramati & A. Albadvi, 2009, Exploring the relationship between use of information technology in total quality management and SMEs performance using canonical correlation analysis: A survey on Swedish car part supplier sector, *International Journal of Information Technology and Management*, 8: 442–462; R. J. David & S. Strang, 2006, When fashion is fleeting: Transitory collective beliefs and the dynamics of TQM consulting, *Academy of Management Journal*, 49: 215–233.

121. Porter, *Competitive Advantage*, 16.

122. Ibid., 17.

123. M. A. Hitt, L. Bierman, K. Uhlenbruck, & K. Shimizu, 2006, The importance of resources in the internationalization of professional service firms: The good, the bad, and the ugly, *Academy of Management Journal*, 49: 1137–1157.

124. P. Puranam, H. Singh, & M. Zollo, 2006, Organizing for innovation: Managing the coordination-autonomy dilemma in technology acquisitions, *Academy of Management Journal*, 49: 263–280.

125. S. Thornhill & R. E. White, 2007, Strategic purity: A multi-industry evaluation of pure vs. hybrid business strategies, *Strategic Management Journal*, 28: 553–561.

CHAPTER 5

Competitive Rivalry and Competitive Dynamics

Studying this chapter should provide you with the strategic management knowledge needed to:

1. Define competitors, competitive rivalry, competitive behavior, and competitive dynamics.

2. Describe market commonality and resource similarity as the building blocks of a competitor analysis.

3. Explain awareness, motivation, and ability as drivers of competitive behaviors.

4. Discuss factors affecting the likelihood a competitor will take competitive actions.

5. Describe factors affecting the likelihood a competitor will respond to actions taken against it.

6. Explain the competitive dynamics in each of slow-cycle, fast-cycle, and standard-cycle markets.

COMPETITION IN RECESSIONS: LET THE BAD TIMES ROLL

Competitive rivalry often increases significantly during recessions, and some selected businesses in particular industries actually experience heightened demand. When economic times are bad, many people change their shopping behavior. In particular, people buy what they need in goods but also search for ways to escape their daily negative environment (e.g., through entertainment) and find ways to experience some form of enjoyment (e.g., eat sweets). For these reasons, staple goods manufacturers; retailers that sell consumer staple goods, health care products, and pharmaceuticals; movie studios and theaters; video game developers and distributors; candy manufacturers; and those making and distributing tobacco and alcohol tend to do well during recessionary times. For example, box-office receipts for movies increased by 20 percent in 2008 and sales were up over 17 percent in the first two months of 2009. Home viewing of movies increased as well. Netflix experienced an increase of 600,000 new subscribers in the first 1.5 months of 2009 alone. Parents can afford to take their children to the movies or rent them for viewing at home, substituting this form of entertainment for taking the children on major trips to Disneyland and similar more expensive adventures.

People frequently will reduce major expenses where possible (e.g., increase carpooling to work, use coupons for purchases) but will also spend extra money for some enjoyment, such as candy. Consumers in the United States spend billions of dollars for candy each year, with an approximate increase of 3 percent in 2008. A Nielsen survey revealed that pasta, candy, and beer were relatively immune from the negative effects of a recession. Dylan Lauren, owner of Dylan's Candy Bar, noted that her company has experienced sales increases during bad times such as 9/11, war, and the falling stock market. In fact, she is currently expanding her business with plans to open new outlets in Los Angeles and Las Vegas and adding a candy cocktail bar to her headquarters in New York City. Of course, she has to compete with other specialty candy companies (e.g., Rocky Mountain Chocolate Factory) and even large candy manufacturers such as Hershey and Mars.

Water is a necessity, which draws increased attention even during bad economic times. While the bottled water industry suffered a little during the last recession (sales decreased by 2 percent in 2008), Coca-Cola, PepsiCo, and Nestle, three major bottled water distributors, are fighting to gain enhanced market shares by introducing lower-cost versions,

Bryan Bedder/Getty Images

While consumers frequently reduce spending on large ticket items during periods of economic strain, some businesses actually experience growth as people adjust their priorities.

flavored-water varieties, and even vitamin-enhanced versions. In addition, they must deal with the environmental concerns about the plastic bottles in which their product is distributed. Interestingly, the economic decline has increased the number and type of competitors with which Coke, Pepsi, and Nestle must contend. For example, water filter manufacturers and distributors have experienced a growing demand for their products (replacing purchases of bottled water with filtered tap water). Clean drinking water is an increasing global concern, causing companies such as IBM to enter the market with new "water-management services." IBM projects the water-management services market to reach $20 billion by 2014. In addition, major firms such as GE, Siemens, and Veolia Environment (France) are developing significant plans to help provide clean water in different parts of the world.

Thus, we can conclude that competitive dynamics within industries vary considerably and not all are affected negatively by economic recessions. Yet, changes in the market can be quite challenging as markets are complex—new competitors enter and consumer tastes change, with some of the changes likely to be long term, continuing even after good economic times return.

Sources: 2008, Nielsen reveals consumer goods categories among those most immune, most vulnerable to recession, *Progressive Grocer*, http://www.progressivegrocer.com, June 5; J. Flanigan, 2008, Keeping the water pure is suddenly in demand, *The New York Times*, http://www.nytimes.com, June 19; M. Irvine, 2008, Candy a sweet spot in sour economy, *Newsvine*, http://www.newsvine.com, June 23; F. C. Gil, 2008, Industry insiders: Dylan Lauren, candy princess, *BlackBook*, http://www.blackbookmag.com, October 22; C. Palmer & N. Byrnes, 2009, Coke and Pepsi try reinventing water, *BusinessWeek*, http://www.businessweek.com, February 19; P. Huguenin, 2009. 10 industries going strong—despite the recession, *New York Daily News*, http://www.nydailynews.com, February 19; M. Cieply & B. Barnes, 2009, In downturn, Americans flock to the movies, *The New York Times*, http://www.nytimes.com, March 1; J. Robertson, 2009, IBM launches water-management services operation, *BusinessWeek*, http://www.businessweek.com, March 13.

Firms operating in the same market, offering similar products, and targeting similar customers are **competitors**.[1] Southwest Airlines, Delta, United, Continental, and JetBlue are competitors, as are PepsiCo and Coca-Cola Company. As described in the Opening Case, PepsiCo and Coca-Cola are currently engaging in a heated competitive battle in the market for bottled water with sales slipping and the two companies trying to maintain or even increase their market share. And, even though the candy market is growing in the recession, small candy retailers such as Dylan's Candy Bar must compete for the expanding market with other specialty candy retailers (e.g., Rocky Mountain Chocolate Factory) and large candy manufacturers (e.g., Hershey and Mars).

Firms interact with their competitors as part of the broad context within which they operate while attempting to earn above-average returns.[2] The decisions firms make about their interactions with their competitors significantly affect their ability to earn above-average returns.[3] Because 80 to 90 percent of new firms fail, learning how to select the markets in which to compete and how to best compete within them is highly important.[4]

Competitive rivalry is the ongoing set of competitive actions and competitive responses that occur among firms as they maneuver for an advantageous market position.[5] Especially in highly competitive industries, firms constantly jockey for advantage as they launch strategic actions and respond or react to rivals' moves.[6] It is important for those leading organizations to understand competitive rivalry, in that "the central, brute empirical fact in strategy is that some firms outperform others,"[7] meaning that competitive rivalry influences an individual firm's ability to gain and sustain competitive advantages.[8]

A sequence of firm-level moves, rivalry results from firms initiating their own competitive actions and then responding to actions taken by competitors.[9] **Competitive behavior** is the set of competitive actions and responses the firm takes to build or defend its competitive advantages and to improve its market position.[10] Through competitive behavior, the firm tries to successfully position itself relative to the five forces of competition (see Chapter 2) and to defend current competitive advantages while building advantages for the future (see Chapter 3). Increasingly, competitors engage in competitive actions and responses in more than one market.[11] Firms competing against each other in several product or geographic markets are engaged in **multimarket competition**.[12]

Competitors are firms operating in the same market, offering similar products, and targeting similar customers.

Competitive rivalry is the ongoing set of competitive actions and competitive responses that occur among firms as they maneuver for an advantageous market position.

Competitive behavior is the set of competitive actions and competitive responses the firm takes to build or defend its competitive advantages and to improve its market position.

Multimarket competition occurs when firms compete against each other in several product or geographic markets.

Figure 5.1 From Competitors to Competitive Dynamics

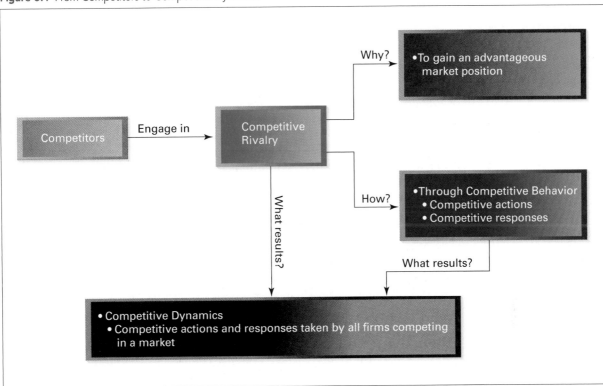

Source: Adapted from M. J. Chen, 1996, Competitor analysis and interfirm rivalry: Toward a theoretical integration, *Academy of Management Review*, 21: 100–134.

All competitive behavior—that is, the total set of actions and responses taken by all firms competing within a market—is called **competitive dynamics**. The relationships among these key concepts are shown in Figure 5.1.

This chapter focuses on competitive rivalry and competitive dynamics. A firm's strategies are dynamic in nature because actions taken by one firm elicit responses from competitors that, in turn, typically result in responses from the firm that took the initial action.[13] As explained in the Opening Case, Coca-Cola and PepsiCo are changing how they compete because of the recession, out of concern for the environment, and in response to each other and Nestle, another major competitor. Also, Dylan's Candy Bar is responding to increased demand by adding more outlets in additional cities. Yet, it must also be sensitive to how competitors such as the Rocky Mountain Chocolate Factory respond and actions taken by large, well-known candy manufacturers (e.g., Hershey).[14]

Competitive rivalry's effect on the firm's strategies is shown by the fact that a strategy's success is determined not only by the firm's initial competitive actions but also by how well it anticipates competitors' responses to them *and* by how well the firm anticipates and responds to its competitors' initial actions (also called attacks).[15] Although competitive rivalry affects all types of strategies (e.g., corporate-level, acquisition, and international), its dominant influence is on the firm's business-level strategy or strategies. Indeed, firms' actions and responses to those of their rivals are the basic building blocks of business-level strategies.[16] Recall from Chapter 4 that business-level strategy is concerned with what the firm does to successfully use its competitive advantages in specific product markets. In the global economy, competitive rivalry is intensifying,[17] meaning that the significance of its effect on firms' business-level strategies is increasing. However, firms that develop and use effective business-level strategies tend to outperform competitors in individual product markets, even when experiencing intense competitive rivalry that price cuts bring about.[18]

Competitive dynamics refer to all competitive behaviors—that is, the total set of actions and responses taken by all firms competing within a market.

A Model of Competitive Rivalry

Competitive rivalry evolves from the pattern of actions and responses as one firm's competitive actions have noticeable effects on competitors, eliciting competitive responses from them.[19] This pattern suggests that firms are mutually interdependent, that they are affected by each other's actions and responses, and that marketplace success is a function of both individual strategies and the consequences of their use.[20] Increasingly, too, executives recognize that competitive rivalry can have a major effect on the firm's financial performance[21] Research shows that intensified rivalry within an industry results in decreased average profitability for the competing firms.[22]

Figure 5.2 presents a straightforward model of competitive rivalry at the firm level; this type of rivalry is usually dynamic and complex.[23] The competitive actions and responses the firm takes are the foundation for successfully building and using its capabilities and core competencies to gain an advantageous market position.[24] The model in Figure 5.2 presents the sequence of activities commonly involved in competition between a particular firm and each of its competitors. Companies can use the model to understand how to be able to predict competitors' behavior (actions and responses) and reduce the uncertainty associated with competitors' actions.[25] Being able to predict competitors' actions and responses has a positive effect on the firm's market position and its subsequent financial performance.[26] The sum of all the individual rivalries modeled in Figure 5.2 that occur in a particular market reflects the competitive dynamics in that market.

The remainder of the chapter explains components of the model shown in Figure 5.2. We first describe market commonality and resource similarity as the building blocks of a competitor analysis. Next, we discuss the effects of three organizational characteristics— awareness, motivation, and ability—on the firm's competitive behavior. We then examine competitive rivalry between firms, or interfirm rivalry, in detail by describing the factors that affect the likelihood a firm will take a competitive action and the factors that affect the likelihood a firm will respond to a competitor's action. In the chapter's final section, we turn our attention to competitive dynamics to describe how market characteristics affect competitive rivalry in slow-cycle, fast-cycle, and standard-cycle markets.

Figure 5.2 A Model of Competitive Rivalry

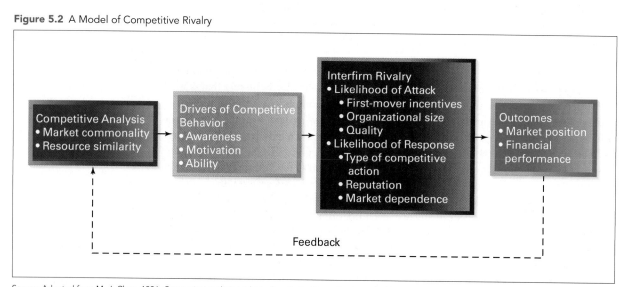

Source: Adapted from M. J. Chen, 1996, Competitor analysis and interfirm rivalry: Toward a theoretical integration, *Academy of Management Review*, 21: 100–134.

Competitor Analysis

As previously noted, a competitor analysis is the first step the firm takes to be able to predict the extent and nature of its rivalry with each competitor. The number of markets in which firms compete against each other (called market commonality, defined on the following pages) and the similarity in their resources (called resource similarity, also defined in the following section) determine the extent to which the firms are competitors. Firms with high market commonality and highly similar resources are "clearly direct and mutually acknowledged competitors."[27] The drivers of competitive behavior—as well as factors influencing the likelihood that a competitor will initiate competitive actions and will respond to its competitor's actions—influence the intensity of rivalry, even for direct competitors.[28]

In Chapter 2, we discussed competitor analysis as a technique firms use to understand their competitive environment. Together, the general, industry, and competitive environments comprise the firm's external environment. We also described how competitor analysis is used to help the firm *understand* its competitors. This understanding results from studying competitors' future objectives, current strategies, assumptions, and capabilities (see Figure 2.3 on page **60**). In this chapter, the discussion of competitor analysis is extended to describe what firms study to be able to *predict* competitors' behavior in the form of their competitive actions and responses. The discussions of competitor analysis in Chapter 2 and in this chapter are complementary in that firms must first *understand* competitors (Chapter 2) before their competitive actions and competitive responses can be *predicted* (this chapter). These analyses are highly important because they help managers to avoid "competitive blind spots," in which managers are unaware of specific competitors or their capabilities. If managers have competitive blind spots, they may be surprised by a competitor's actions, thereby allowing the competitor to increase its market share at the expense of the manager's firm.[29] Competitor analyses are especially important when a firm enters a foreign market. Managers need to understand the local competition and foreign competitors currently operating in the market.[30] Without such analyses, they are less likely to be successful.

Market Commonality

Each industry is composed of various markets. The financial services industry has markets for insurance, brokerage services, banks, and so forth. To concentrate on the needs of different, unique customer groups, markets can be further subdivided. The insurance market, for example, could be broken into market segments (such as commercial and consumer), product segments (such as health insurance and life insurance), and geographic markets (such as Western Europe and Southeast Asia). In general, the capabilities the Internet's technologies generate help to shape the nature of industries' markets along with the competition among firms operating in them.[31] For example, widely available electronic news sources affect how traditional print news distributors such as newspapers conduct their business.

Competitors tend to agree about the different characteristics of individual markets that form an industry.[32] For example, in the transportation industry, the commercial air travel market differs from the ground transportation market, which is served by such firms as YRC Worldwide (one of the largest transportation service providers in the world)[33] and major YRC competitors Arkansas Best, Con-way Inc., and FedEx Freight.[34] Although differences exist, many industries' markets are partially related in terms of technologies used or core competencies needed to develop a competitive advantage. For example, different types of transportation companies need to provide reliable and timely service. Commercial air carriers such as Southwest, Continental, and JetBlue must therefore develop service competencies to satisfy their passengers, while YRC and its major competitors must develop such competencies to serve the needs of those using their fleets to ship goods.

Firms sometimes compete against each other in several markets that are in different industries. As such these competitors interact with each other several times, a condition called market commonality. More formally, **market commonality** is concerned with the number of markets with which the firm and a competitor are jointly involved and the degree of importance of the individual markets to each.[35] When firms produce similar products and compete for the same customers, the competitive rivalry is likely to be high.[36] Firms competing against one another in several or many markets engage in multimarket competition.[37] Coca-Cola and PepsiCo compete across a number of product (e.g., soft drinks, bottled water) and geographic markets (throughout the United States and in many foreign markets) as suggested in the Opening Case. Even smaller firms, such as Dylan's Candy Bar, are likely to compete with some competitors in several geographic markets as they enter new cities. Airlines, chemicals, pharmaceuticals, and consumer foods are examples of other industries in which firms often simultaneously compete against each other in multiple markets.

Firms competing in several markets have the potential to respond to a competitor's actions not only within the market in which the actions are taken, but also in other markets where they compete with the rival. This potential creates a complicated competitive mosaic in which "the moves an organization makes in one market are designed to achieve goals in another market in ways that aren't immediately apparent to its rivals."[38]

MICHAEL URBAN/AFP/GETTY Images

In order to grow, DHL Express is tasked with competing against UPS and FEDEX, much larger rivals with similar resources.

This potential complicates the rivalry between competitors. In fact, research suggests that "a firm with greater multimarket contact is less likely to initiate an attack, but more likely to move (respond) aggressively when attacked."[39] Thus, in general, multimarket competition reduces competitive rivalry, but some firms will still compete when the potential rewards (e.g., potential market share gain) are high.[40]

Resource Similarity

Resource similarity is the extent to which the firm's tangible and intangible resources are comparable to a competitor's in terms of both type and amount.[41] Firms with similar types and amounts of resources are likely to have similar strengths and weaknesses and use similar strategies.[42] The competition between FedEx and United Parcel Service (UPS) in using information technology to improve the efficiency of their operations and to reduce costs demonstrates these expectations. Pursuing similar strategies that are supported by similar resource profiles, personnel in these firms work at a feverish pace to receive, sort, and ship packages. At a UPS hub, for example, "workers have less than four hours (on a peak night) to process more than a million packages from at least 100 planes and probably 160 trucks."[43] FedEx and UPS are both spending more than $1 billion annually on research and development (R&D) to find ways to improve efficiency and reduce costs. Rival DHL Express is trying to compete with the two global giants supported by the privatized German postal service, Deutsche Post World Net, which acquired it in 2002. While DHL has made impressive gains in recent years (e.g., increasing its brand awareness and building impressive operations in the United States), it still must struggle to compete against its stronger rivals with similar resources. To survive, it has negotiated a partnership agreement with UPS in which UPS will handle DHL's air shipments. Such arrangements are often referred to as "coopetition" (cooperation between competitors).[44]

When performing a competitor analysis, a firm analyzes each of its competitors in terms of market commonality and resource similarity. The results of these analyses can be mapped for visual comparisons. In Figure 5.3, we show different hypothetical intersections

Market commonality is concerned with the number of markets with which the firm and a competitor are jointly involved and the degree of importance of the individual markets to each.

Resource similarity is the extent to which the firm's tangible and intangible resources are comparable to a competitor's in terms of both type and amount.

Figure 5.3 A Framework of Competitor Analysis

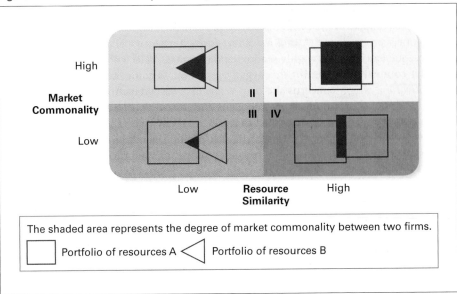

The shaded area represents the degree of market commonality between two firms.

☐ Portfolio of resources A   ◁ Portfolio of resources B

Source: Adapted from M. J. Chen, 1996, Competitor analysis and interfirm rivalry: Toward a theoretical integration, *Academy of Management Review*, 21: 100–134.

between the firm and individual competitors in terms of market commonality and resource similarity. These intersections indicate the extent to which the firm and those with which it is compared are competitors. For example, the firm and its competitor displayed in quadrant I have similar types and amounts of resources (i.e., the two firms have a similar portfolio of resources). The firm and its competitor in quadrant I would use their similar resource portfolios to compete against each other in many markets that are important to each. These conditions lead to the conclusion that the firms modeled in quadrant I are direct and mutually acknowledged competitors (e.g., FedEx and UPS). In contrast, the firm and its competitor shown in quadrant III share few markets and have little similarity in their resources, indicating that they aren't direct and mutually acknowledged competitors. Thus, a small local, family-owned Italian restaurant does not compete directly against Olive Garden nor does it have resources that are similar to those of Darden Restaurants, Inc. (Olive Garden's owner). The firm's mapping of its competitive relationship with rivals is fluid as firms enter and exit markets and as companies' resources change in type and amount. Thus, the companies with which the firm is a direct competitor change across time.

Drivers of Competitive Actions and Responses

As shown in Figure 5.2 (on page **132**) market commonality and resource similarity influence the drivers (awareness, motivation, and ability) of competitive behavior. In turn, the drivers influence the firm's competitive behavior, as shown by the actions and responses it takes while engaged in competitive rivalry.[45]

Awareness, which is a prerequisite to any competitive action or response taken by a firm, refers to the extent to which competitors recognize the degree of their mutual interdependence that results from market commonality and resource similarity.[46] Awareness tends to be greatest when firms have highly similar resources (in terms of types and amounts) to use while competing against each other in multiple markets. Komatsu Ltd., Japan's top construction machinery maker and U.S.-based Caterpillar Inc. have similar resources and are certainly aware of each other's actions.[47] The same is true for Wal-Mart and France's Carrefour, the two largest supermarket groups in the world as noted in the Strategic Focus. The last two firms' joint awareness has increased as they use similar resources to compete against each other for dominant positions in multiple European and South American markets.[48] Awareness affects the extent to which the firm understands the consequences of its competitive actions and responses. A lack of awareness can lead to excessive competition, resulting in a negative effect on all competitors' performance.[49]

Motivation, which concerns the firm's incentive to take action or to respond to a competitor's attack, relates to perceived gains and losses. Thus, a firm may be aware of competitors but may not be motivated to engage in rivalry with them if it perceives that its position will not improve or that its market position won't be damaged if it doesn't respond.[50] In some cases, firms may locate near competitors in order to more easily access suppliers and customers. For example, Latin American banks have located operations in Miami, Florida, to reach customers from a similar culture and to access employees who understand this culture as well. In Miami, there are several Latin American banks that direct most of their competitive actions at U.S. financial institutions.[51]

Market commonality affects the firm's perceptions and resulting motivation. For example, the firm is generally more likely to attack the rival with whom it has low market commonality than the one with whom it competes in multiple markets. The primary reason is the high stakes involved in trying to gain a more advantageous position over a rival with whom the firm shares many markets. As mentioned earlier, multimarket competition can find a competitor responding to the firm's action in a market different from the one in which the initial action was taken. Actions and responses of this type can cause both firms to lose focus on core markets and to battle each other with resources that had been allocated for other purposes. Because of the high stakes of competition under the condition of market commonality, the probability is high that the attacked firm will respond to its competitor's action in an effort to protect its position in one or more markets.[52]

In some instances, the firm may be aware of the markets it shares with a competitor and be motivated to respond to an attack by that competitor, but lack the ability to do so. *Ability* relates to each firm's resources and the flexibility they provide. Without available resources (such as financial capital and people), the firm lacks the ability to attack a competitor or respond to its actions. For example, smaller and newer firms tend to be more innovative but generally have fewer resources to attack larger and established competitors. Likewise, foreign firms often are at a disadvantage against local firms because of the local firms' social capital (relationships) with consumers, suppliers, and government officials.[53] However, similar resources suggest similar abilities to attack and respond. When a firm faces a competitor with similar resources, careful study of a possible attack before initiating it is essential because the similarly resourced competitor is likely to respond to that action.[54]

Resource *dissimilarity* also influences competitive actions and responses between firms, in that "the greater is the resource imbalance between the acting firm and competitors or potential responders, the greater will be the delay in response"[55] by the firm with a resource disadvantage. For example, Wal-Mart initially used a focused cost leadership strategy to compete only in small communities (those with a population of 25,000 or less). Using sophisticated logistics systems and extremely efficient purchasing practices, among others, to gain competitive advantages, Wal-Mart created a new type of value (primarily in the form of wide selections of products at the lowest competitive prices) for customers in small retail markets. Local competitors lacked the ability to marshal needed resources at the pace required to respond quickly and effectively. However, even when facing competitors with greater resources (greater ability) or more attractive market positions, firms should eventually respond, no matter how daunting the task seems. Choosing not to respond can ultimately result in failure, as happened with at least some local retailers who didn't respond to Wal-Mart's competitive actions. Of course, the actions taken by Wal-Mart were only the beginning. Wal-Mart has become the largest retailer in the world and feared by all competitors, large and small as explained in the Strategic Focus.

STRATEGY
RIGHT NOW

In addition to delivering low prices, Wal-Mart is catering to their cash-strapped customers with financial services.

www.cengage.com/
management/hitt

THE COMPETITIVE BATTLE AMONG BIG BOX RETAILERS: WAL-MART VERSUS ALL THE OTHERS

When Wal-Mart enters a new market, the incumbent competitors commonly experience declines in their sales of 5 to 17 percent. Wal-Mart is the largest retailer in the world, with annual sales of more than $400 billion. As such, it buys in huge quantities and can command a very low price from all suppliers. Its low costs for goods and its highly efficient distribution system allow it to offer the lowest price on any goods it sells. If this is not enough, the severe global economic recession experienced in 2008 and 2009 attracted more customers to Wal-Mart and away from competitors such as Target and Carrefour. In fact, both Target and Carrefour experienced major reductions in their sales while Wal-Mart had small increases. For example, in December 2008, Target had a 4.1 percent decline in sales and Wal-Mart enjoyed a 2.5 percent increase. J. C. Penney's sales declined even more—8.8 percent. Wal-Mart's sales also increased in the first two months of 2009.

Target matches Wal-Mart's prices on approximately 25 percent of its products but cannot with more products because its cost structure is not as favorable. Carrefour tried to match Wal-Mart and other competitors by severely dropping its prices during the recession with the intent of keeping its customers, but it suffered from the lost margins. Through the worst stock market in many years, Wal-Mart's stock price only declined 2 percent while Carrefour's stock price decreased by 45 percent. Wal-Mart has a reputation for selling high-quality goods at the lowest possible prices. So, during the recession, many people shopped at Wal-Mart even when competitors matched Wal-Mart's prices. In fact, many families purposely "traded down" during the bad economic times. Even Sam's Club, Wal-Mart's warehouse retailer operations, performed well. Costco, its primary competitor, had outperformed Sam's for several years prior to the recession. However, during the recession Sam's passed Costco with sales increases of 5.9 percent in same-store sales compared to Costco's 4 percent increase.

James Leynse/CORBIS

Wal-Mart's consistently low prices and good quality have brought in new customers during the recession who might have otherwise shopped at a competitor.

The only way that competitors can usually survive in markets with Wal-Mart is to add differentiated products in niches where Wal-Mart is not strong. In fact, Target successfully positioned itself as an "upscale discounter" trying to avoid direct competition with Wal-Mart. However, during recessions, discounts on upscale goods are not as valuable. Thus, even Target tried to add more basic goods and add to its food lines. Interestingly, both Target and Wal-Mart planned to open a number of stores during 2009 even with the economic downturn. But, Target simultaneously downsized its headquarters' staff by 1,000 positions. The main concern of many Wal-Mart competitors now is how to regain the market share they lost in the recession when the economy recovers. The challenges ahead for Wal-Mart's competitors are substantial.

Sources: 2008, Wal-Mart, Wikipedia, http://www.wikipedia.org; S. Rosenbloom, 2008, For Wal-Mart, a Christmas that's made to order, *The New York Times*, http://www.nytimes.com, November 6; F. Forrest, 2009, What happens when Wal-Mart enters, *Insights*, Marketing Science Institute, Winter; J. Birchall, 2009, Target to cut 1,000 HQ positions, *Financial Times*, http://www.ft.com, January 27; M. Bustillo, 2009, New chief at Wal-Mart looks abroad for growth, *The Wall Street Journal*, http://www.wsj.com, February 2; J. Birchall, 2009, Wal-Mart's U.S. sales surge ahead, *Financial Times*, http://www.ft.com, March 5; A. Zimmerman, 2009, Wal-Mart tosses a PR "jump ball," *The Wall Street Journal*, http://www.wsj.com, March 12; M. Neal, 2009, Carrefour's no Wal-Mart, *The Wall Street Journal*, http://www.wsj.com, March 12; S. Gregory, 2009, Wal-Mart vs. Target: No contest in the recession, *Time*, http://www.time.com, March 14.

Competitive Rivalry

The ongoing competitive action/response sequence between a firm and a competitor affects the performance of both firms;[56] thus it is important for companies to carefully analyze and understand the competitive rivalry present in the markets they serve to select and implement successful strategies.[57] Understanding a competitor's awareness, motivation, and ability helps the firm to predict the likelihood of an attack by that competitor and the probability that a competitor will respond to actions taken against it.

As we described earlier, the predictions drawn from studying competitors in terms of awareness, motivation, and ability are grounded in market commonality and resource similarity. These predictions are fairly general. The value of the final set of predictions the firm develops about each of its competitors' competitive actions and responses is enhanced by studying the "Likelihood of Attack" factors (such as first-mover incentives and organizational size) and the "Likelihood of Response" factors (such as the actor's reputation) that are shown in Figure 5.2. Evaluating and understanding these factors allow the firm to refine the predictions it makes about its competitors' actions and responses.

In response to shrinking market share, executives at Guess, Inc. made the decision to take the brand upscale rather than cut prices and potentially see their brand equity decline.

Strategic and Tactical Actions

Firms use both strategic and tactical actions when forming their competitive actions and competitive responses in the course of engaging in competitive rivalry.[58] A **competitive action** is a strategic or tactical action the firm takes to build or defend its competitive advantages or improve its market position. A **competitive response** is a strategic or tactical action the firm takes to counter the effects of a competitor's competitive action. A **strategic action** or a **strategic response** is a market-based move that involves a significant commitment of organizational resources and is difficult to implement and reverse. A **tactical action** or a **tactical response** is a market-based move that is taken to fine-tune a strategy; it involves fewer resources and is relatively easy to implement and reverse.

The decision a few years ago by newly installed leaders at Guess Inc. to take their firm's brand of denims and related products upscale rather than dilute the brand more by lowering prices when Guess was losing market share is an example of a strategic response.[59] And Boeing's decision to commit the resources required to build the super-efficient 787 midsized jetliner with its first deliveries in 2007 and 2008[60] demonstrates a strategic action. Changes in airfares are somewhat frequently announced by airlines. As tactical actions that are easily reversed, pricing decisions are often taken by these firms to increase demand in certain markets during certain periods.

As discussed in the Strategic Focus, Wal-Mart prices aggressively as a means of increasing revenues and gaining market share at the expense of competitors. But discounted prices with high expenses (as implemented by Carrefour) weigh on margins and slow profit growth (or possibly even produce losses). Although pricing aggressively is at the core of what Wal-Mart is and how it competes, can the tactical action of aggressive pricing continue to lead to the competitive success the firm has enjoyed historically? Is Wal-Mart achieving the type of balance between strategic and tactical competitive actions and competitive responses that is a foundation for all firms' success in marketplace competitions?

When engaging rivals in competition, firms must recognize the differences between strategic and tactical actions and responses and should develop an effective balance between the two types of competitive actions and responses. Airbus, Boeing's major competitor in commercial airliners, is aware that Boeing is strongly committed to taking

A **competitive action** is a strategic or tactical action the firm takes to build or defend its competitive advantages or improve its market position.

A **competitive response** is a strategic or tactical action the firm takes to counter the effects of a competitor's competitive action.

A **strategic action** or a **strategic response** is a market-based move that involves a significant commitment of organizational resources and is difficult to implement and reverse.

A **tactical action** or a **tactical response** is a market-based move that is taken to fine-tune a strategy; it involves fewer resources and is relatively easy to implement and reverse.

actions it believes are necessary to successfully launch the 787 jetliner, because deciding to design, build, and launch the 787 is a major strategic action. In fact, many analysts believe that Boeing's development of the 787 airliner was a strategic response to Airbus's new A380 aircraft.

Likelihood of Attack

In addition to market commonality, resource similarity, and the drivers of awareness, motivation, and ability, other factors affect the likelihood a competitor will use strategic actions and tactical actions to attack its competitors. Three of these factors—first-mover incentives, organizational size, and quality—are discussed next.

First-Mover Incentives

A **first mover** is a firm that takes an initial competitive action in order to build or defend its competitive advantages or to improve its market position. The first-mover concept has been influenced by the work of the famous economist Joseph Schumpeter, who argued that firms achieve competitive advantage by taking innovative actions[61] (innovation is defined and described in detail in Chapter 13). In general, first movers "allocate funds for product innovation and development, aggressive advertising, and advanced research and development."[62]

The benefits of being a successful first mover can be substantial.[63] Especially in fast-cycle markets (discussed later in the chapter), where changes occur rapidly and where it is virtually impossible to sustain a competitive advantage for any length of time, a first mover can experience many times the valuation and revenue of a second mover.[64] This evidence suggests that although first-mover benefits are never absolute, they are often critical to a firm's success in industries experiencing rapid technological developments and relatively short product life cycles.[65] In addition to earning above-average returns until its competitors respond to its successful competitive action, the first mover can gain (1) the loyalty of customers who may become committed to the goods or services of the firm that first made them available, and (2) market share that can be difficult for competitors to take during future competitive rivalry.[66] The general evidence that first movers have greater survival rates than later market entrants[67] is perhaps the culmination of first-mover benefits.

The firm trying to predict its competitors' competitive actions might conclude that they will take aggressive strategic actions to gain first movers' benefits. However, even though a firm's competitors might be motivated to be first movers, they may lack the ability to do so. First movers tend to be aggressive and willing to experiment with innovation and take higher, yet reasonable, levels of risk.[68] To be a first mover, the firm must have readily available the resources to significantly invest in R&D as well as to rapidly and successfully produce and market a stream of innovative products.[69]

Organizational slack makes it possible for firms to have the ability (as measured by available resources) to be first movers. *Slack* is the buffer or cushion provided by actual or obtainable resources that aren't currently in use and are in excess of the minimum resources needed to produce a given level of organizational output.[70] As a liquid resource, slack can quickly be allocated to support competitive actions, such as R&D investments and aggressive marketing campaigns that lead to first-mover advantages. This relationship between slack and the ability to be a first mover allows the firm to predict that a first mover competitor likely has available slack and will probably take aggressive competitive actions to continuously introduce innovative products. Furthermore, the firm can predict that as a first mover, a competitor will try to rapidly gain market share and customer loyalty in order to earn above-average returns until its competitors are able to effectively respond to its first move.

Firms evaluating their competitors should realize that being a first mover carries risk. For example, it is difficult to accurately estimate the returns that will be earned from introducing product innovations to the marketplace.[71] Additionally, the first mover's

A **first mover** is a firm that takes an initial competitive action in order to build or defend its competitive advantages or to improve its market position.

cost to develop a product innovation can be substantial, reducing the slack available to support further innovation. Thus, the firm should carefully study the results a competitor achieves as a first mover. Continuous success by the competitor suggests additional product innovations, while lack of product acceptance over the course of the competitor's innovations may indicate less willingness in the future to accept the risks of being a first mover.[72]

A **second mover** is a firm that responds to the first mover's competitive action, typically through imitation. More cautious than the first mover, the second mover studies customers' reactions to product innovations. In the course of doing so, the second mover also tries to find any mistakes the first mover made so that it can avoid them and the problems they created. Often, successful imitation of the first mover's innovations allows the second mover to avoid the mistakes and the major investments required of the pioneers (first movers).[73]

Second movers also have the time to develop processes and technologies that are more efficient than those used by the first mover or that create additional value for consumers.[74] The most successful second movers rarely act too fast (so they can fully analyze the first mover's actions) nor too slow (so they do not give the first mover time to correct its mistakes and "lock in" customer loyalty).[75] Overall, the outcomes of the first mover's competitive actions may provide an effective blueprint for second and even late movers (discussed below) as they determine the nature and timing of their competitive responses.[76] Determining whether a competitor is an effective second mover (based on its past actions) allows a first-mover firm to predict that the competitor will respond quickly to successful, innovation-based market entries. The first mover can expect a successful second-mover competitor to study its market entries and to respond with a new entry into the market within a short time period. As a second mover, the competitor will try to respond with a product that provides greater customer value than does the first mover's product. The most successful second movers are able to rapidly and meaningfully interpret market feedback to respond quickly, yet successfully, to the first mover's successful innovations.

A **late mover** is a firm that responds to a competitive action a significant amount of time after the first mover's action and the second mover's response. Typically, a late response is better than no response at all, although any success achieved from the late competitive response tends to be considerably less than that achieved by first and second movers. However, on occasion, late movers can be successful if they develop a unique way to enter the market and compete.[77]

The firm competing against a late mover can predict that the competitor will likely enter a particular market only after both the first and second movers have achieved success in that market. Moreover, on a relative basis, the firm can predict that the late mover's competitive action will allow it to earn average returns only after the considerable time required for it to understand how to create at least as much customer value as that offered by the first and second movers' products.

Organizational Size

An organization's size affects the likelihood it will take competitive actions as well as the types and timing of those actions.[78] In general, small firms are more likely than large companies to launch competitive actions and tend to do it more quickly. Smaller firms are thus perceived as nimble and flexible competitors who rely on speed and surprise to defend their competitive advantages or develop new ones while engaged in competitive rivalry, especially with large companies, to gain an advantageous market position.[79] Small firms' flexibility and nimbleness allow them to develop variety in their competitive actions; large firms tend to limit the types of competitive actions used.[80]

Large firms, however, are likely to initiate more competitive actions along with more strategic actions during a given period.[81] Thus, when studying its competitors in terms of organizational size, the firm should use a measurement such as total sales revenue or

A **second mover** is a firm that responds to the first mover's competitive action, typically through imitation.

A **late mover** is a firm that responds to a competitive action a significant amount of time after the first mover's action and the second mover's response.

total number of employees. The competitive actions the firm likely will encounter from competitors larger than it is will be different from the competitive actions it will encounter from smaller competitors.

The organizational size factor adds another layer of complexity. When engaging in competitive rivalry, the firm often prefers a large number of unique competitive actions. Ideally, the organization has the amount of slack resources held by a large firm to launch a greater *number* of competitive actions and a small firm's flexibility to launch a greater *variety* of competitive actions. Herb Kelleher, cofounder and former CEO of Southwest Airlines, addressed this matter: "Think and act big and we'll get smaller. Think and act small and we'll get bigger."[82]

In the context of competitive rivalry, Kelleher's statement can be interpreted to mean that relying on a limited number or types of competitive actions (which is the large firm's tendency) can lead to reduced competitive success across time, partly because competitors learn how to effectively respond to the predictable. In contrast, remaining flexible and nimble (which is the small firm's tendency) in order to develop and use a wide variety of competitive actions contributes to success against rivals.

As explained in the Strategic Focus, Wal-Mart is a huge firm and generates annual sales revenue that makes it the world's largest company. Because of its size, scale, and resources, Wal-Mart has the flexibility required to take many types of competitive actions that few—if any—of its competitors can undertake. Demonstrating this type of flexibility in terms of competitive actions may prove critical to Wal-Mart's battles with competitors such as Costco and Target, among others.

Quality

Quality has many definitions, including well-established ones relating it to the production of goods or services with zero defects[83] and as a cycle of continuous improvement.[84] From a strategic perspective, we consider quality to be the outcome of how a firm completes primary and support activities (see Chapter 3). Thus, **quality** exists when the firm's goods or services meet or exceed customers' expectations. Some evidence suggests that quality may be the most critical component in satisfying the firm's customers.[85]

In the eyes of customers, quality is about doing the right things relative to performance measures that are important to them.[86] Customers may be interested in measuring the quality of a firm's goods and services against a broad range of dimensions. Sample quality dimensions in which customers commonly express an interest are shown in Table 5.1. Quality is possible only when top-level managers support it and when its importance is institutionalized throughout the entire organization and its value chain.[87] When quality is institutionalized and valued by all, employees and managers alike become vigilant about continuously finding ways to improve quality.[88]

Quality is a universal theme in the global economy and is a necessary but not sufficient condition for competitive success.[89] Without quality, a firm's products lack credibility, meaning that customers don't think of them as viable options. Indeed, customers won't consider buying a product until they believe that it can satisfy at least their base-level expectations in terms of quality dimensions that are important to them. Boeing's new 787 aircraft may have problems in the marketplace because of quality concerns. For example, Chi Zhou, Chairman of Shanghai Airlines, suggested that the 787 does not "fully meet the quality that Boeing touted earlier." As such Zhou stated that his airline may cancel or postpone delivery of its order for nine aircraft.[90]

Quality affects competitive rivalry. The firm evaluating a competitor whose products suffer from poor quality can predict declines in the competitor's sales revenue until the quality issues are resolved. In addition, the firm can predict that the competitor likely won't be aggressive in its competitive actions until the quality problems are corrected in order to gain credibility with customers. However, after the problems are corrected, that competitor is likely to take more aggressive competitive actions.

Quality exists when the firm's goods or services meet or exceed customers' expectations.

Table 5.1 Quality Dimensions of Goods and Services

Product Quality Dimensions
1. *Performance*—Operating characteristics
2. *Features*—Important special characteristics
3. *Flexibility*—Meeting operating specifications over some period of time
4. *Durability*—Amount of use before performance deteriorates
5. *Conformance*—Match with preestablished standards
6. *Serviceability*—Ease and speed of repair
7. *Aesthetics*—How a product looks and feels
8. *Perceived quality*—Subjective assessment of characteristics (Product image)
Service Quality Dimensions
1. *Timeliness*—Performed in the promised period of time
2. *Courtesy*—Performed cheerfully
3. *Consistency*—Giving all customers similar experiences each time
4. *Convenience*—Accessibility to customers
5. *Completeness*—Fully serviced, as required
6. *Accuracy*—Performed correctly each time

Source: Adapted from J. Evans, 2008, *Managing for Quality and Performance*, 7th ed., Mason, OH: Thomson Publishing.

Likelihood of Response

The success of a firm's competitive action is affected by the likelihood that a competitor will respond to it as well as by the type (strategic or tactical) and effectiveness of that response. As noted earlier, a competitive response is a strategic or tactical action the firm takes to counter the effects of a competitor's competitive action. In general, a firm is likely to respond to a competitor's action when (1) the action leads to better use of the competitor's capabilities to gain or produce stronger competitive advantages or an improvement in its market position, (2) the action damages the firm's ability to use its capabilities to create or maintain an advantage, or (3) the firm's market position becomes less defensible.[91]

In addition to market commonality and resource similarity and awareness, motivation, and ability, firms evaluate three other factors—type of competitive action, reputation, and market dependence—to predict how a competitor is likely to respond to competitive actions (see Figure 5.2 on page **133**).

Type of Competitive Action

Competitive responses to strategic actions differ from responses to tactical actions. These differences allow the firm to predict a competitor's likely response to a competitive action that has been launched against it. Strategic actions commonly receive strategic responses and tactical actions receive tactical responses. In general, strategic actions elicit fewer total competitive responses because strategic responses, such as market-based moves, involve a significant commitment of resources and are difficult to implement and reverse.[92]

Another reason that strategic actions elicit fewer responses than do tactical actions is that the time needed to implement a strategic action and to assess its effectiveness can delay the competitor's response to that action.[93] In contrast, a competitor likely will respond quickly to a tactical action, such as when an airline company almost immediately matches a competitor's tactical action of reducing prices in certain markets. Either strategic actions or tactical actions that target a large number of a rival's customers are likely to elicit strong responses.[94] In fact, if the effects of a competitor's strategic action on the focal firm are significant (e.g., loss of market share, loss of major resources such as critical employees), a response is likely to be swift and strong.[95]

Actor's Reputation

In the context of competitive rivalry, an *actor* is the firm taking an action or a response while *reputation* is "the positive or negative attribute ascribed by one rival to another based on past competitive behavior."[96] A positive reputation may be a source of above-average returns, especially for consumer goods producers.[97] Thus, a positive corporate reputation is of strategic value[98] and affects competitive rivalry. To predict the likelihood of a competitor's response to a current or planned action, firms evaluate the responses that the competitor has taken previously when attacked—past behavior is assumed to be a predictor of future behavior.

AP Photo/Ng Han Guan

While IBM's initial success in the PC market may have inspired a host of competitors, the competitive landscape has continued to shift with the acquisitions of Gateway by Acer, Compaq by HP, and IBM's PC division by Lenovo.

Competitors are more likely to respond to strategic or tactical actions when they are taken by a market leader.[99] In particular, evidence suggests that commonly successful actions, especially strategic actions, will be quickly imitated. For example, although a second mover, IBM committed significant resources to enter the PC market. When IBM was immediately successful in this endeavor, competitors such as Dell, Compaq, HP, and Gateway responded with strategic actions to enter the market. IBM's reputation as well as its successful strategic action strongly influenced entry by these competitors. However, the competitive landscape has changed dramatically over time. For example, Lenovo, a Chinese firm, paid $1.75 billion in 2005 to buy IBM's PC division.

In contrast to a firm with a strong reputation such as IBM, competitors are less likely to take responses against a company with a reputation for competitive behavior that is risky, complex, and unpredictable. The firm with a reputation as a price predator (an actor that frequently reduces prices to gain or maintain market share) generates few responses to its pricing tactical actions because price predators, which typically increase prices once their market share objective is reached, lack credibility with their competitors.[100] Occasionally, a firm with a minor reputation can sneak up on larger, more resourceful competitors and take market share from them. In recent years, for example, firms from emerging markets have taken market share from major competitors based in developed markets.[101]

Dependence on the Market

Market dependence denotes the extent to which a firm's revenues or profits are derived from a particular market.[102] In general, competitors with high market dependence are likely to respond strongly to attacks threatening their market position.[103] Interestingly, the threatened firm in these instances may not always respond quickly, even though an effective response to an attack on the firm's position in a critical market is important.

Sargento Foods is a family-owned company based in Wisconsin. The firm is a leading packager and marketer of "shredded, snack and specialty cheeses (that are) sold under the Sargento brand, cheese and non-cheese snack food items and ethnic sauces." With sales exceeding $600 million annually, Sargento's business is founded on a passion for cheese. Because Sargento's business operations revolve strictly around cheese products, it is totally dependent on the market for cheese. As such, any competitor that chooses to attack Sargento and its market positions can anticipate a strong response to its competitive actions.

Competitive Dynamics

Whereas competitive rivalry concerns the ongoing actions and responses between a firm and its direct competitors for an advantageous market position, competitive dynamics concern the ongoing actions and responses among *all* firms competing within a market for advantageous positions. Building and sustaining competitive advantages are at the core of competitive rivalry, in that advantages are the key to creating value for shareholders.[104]

To explain competitive dynamics, we explore the effects of varying rates of competitive speed in different markets (called slow-cycle, fast-cycle, and standard-cycle markets) on the behavior (actions and responses) of all competitors within a given market. Competitive behaviors as well as the reasons for taking them are similar within each market type, but differ across types of markets.[105] Thus, competitive dynamics differ in slow-cycle, fast-cycle, and standard-cycle markets. The sustainability of the firm's competitive advantages differs across the three market types.

As noted in Chapter 1, firms want to sustain their competitive advantages for as long as possible, although no advantage is permanently sustainable. The degree of sustainability is affected by how quickly competitive advantages can be imitated and how costly it is to do so.

Slow-Cycle Markets

Slow-cycle markets are those in which the firm's competitive advantages are shielded from imitation commonly for long periods of time and where imitation is costly.[106] Thus, competitive advantages are sustainable over longer periods of time in slow-cycle markets.

Building a unique and proprietary capability produces a competitive advantage and success in a slow-cycle market. This type of advantage is difficult for competitors to understand. As discussed in Chapter 3, a difficult-to-understand and costly-to-imitate resource or capability usually results from unique historical conditions, causal ambiguity, and/or social complexity. Copyrights, geography, patents, and ownership of an information resource are examples of resources.[107] After a proprietary advantage is developed, the firm's competitive behavior in a slow-cycle market is oriented to protecting, maintaining, and extending that advantage. Thus, the competitive dynamics in slow-cycle markets usually concentrate on competitive actions and responses that enable firms to protect, maintain, and extend their competitive advantage. Major strategic actions in these markets, such acquisitions, usually carry less risk than in faster-cycle markets.[108]

Walt Disney Co. continues to extend its proprietary characters, such as Mickey Mouse, Minnie Mouse, and Goofy. These characters have a unique historical development as a result of Walt and Roy Disney's creativity and vision for entertaining people. Products based on the characters seen in Disney's animated films are sold through Disney's theme park shops as well as freestanding retail outlets called Disney Stores. Because copyrights shield it, the proprietary nature of Disney's advantage in terms of animated character trademarks protects the firm from imitation by competitors.

Consistent with another attribute of competition in a slow-cycle market, Disney protects its exclusive rights to its characters and their use. As with all firms competing in slow-cycle markets, Disney's competitive actions (such as building theme parks in France, Japan, and China) and responses (such as lawsuits to protect its right to fully control use of its animated characters) maintain and extend its proprietary competitive advantage while protecting it.

Patent laws and regulatory requirements such as those in the United States requiring FDA (Food and Drug Administration) approval to launch new products shield pharmaceutical companies' positions. Competitors in this market try to extend patents on their

Slow-cycle markets are those in which the firm's competitive advantages are shielded from imitation commonly for long periods of time and where imitation is costly.

drugs to maintain advantageous positions that the patents provide. However, after a patent expires, the firm is no longer shielded from competition, allowing generic imitations and usually leading to a loss of sales.

The competitive dynamics generated by firms competing in slow-cycle markets are shown in Figure 5.4. In slow-cycle markets, firms launch a product (e.g., a new drug) that has been developed through a proprietary advantage (e.g., R&D) and then exploit it for as long as possible while the product is shielded from competition. Eventually, competitors respond to the action with a counterattack. In markets for drugs, this counterattack commonly occurs as patents expire or are broken through legal means, creating the need for another product launch by the firm seeking a protected market position.

Fast-Cycle Markets

Fast-cycle markets are markets in which the firm's capabilities that contribute to competitive advantages aren't shielded from imitation and where imitation is often rapid and inexpensive. Thus, competitive advantages aren't sustainable in fast-cycle markets. Firms competing in fast-cycle markets recognize the importance of speed; these companies appreciate that "time is as precious a business resource as money or head count—and that the costs of hesitation and delay are just as steep as going over budget or missing a financial forecast."[109] Such high-velocity environments place considerable pressures on top managers to quickly make strategic decisions that are also effective.[110] The often substantial competition and technology-based strategic focus make the strategic decision complex, increasing the need for a comprehensive approach integrated with decision speed, two often-conflicting characteristics of the strategic decision process.[111]

Reverse engineering and the rate of technology diffusion in fast-cycle markets facilitate rapid imitation. A competitor uses reverse engineering to quickly gain the knowledge required to imitate or improve the firm's products. Technology is diffused rapidly in fast-cycle markets, making it available to competitors in a short period. The technology often used by fast-cycle competitors isn't proprietary, nor is it protected by patents as is the technology used by firms competing in slow-cycle markets. For example, only a few hundred parts, which are readily available on the open market, are required to build a PC. Patents protect only a few of these parts, such as microprocessor chips.[112]

Figure 5.4 Gradual Erosion of a Sustained Competitive Advantage

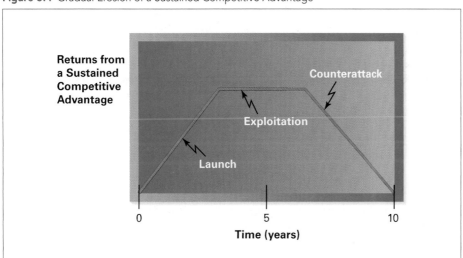

Source: Adapted from I. C. MacMillan, 1988, Controlling competitive dynamics by taking strategic initiative, *Academy of Management Executive,* II(2): 111–118.

Fast-cycle markets are markets in which the firm's capabilities that contribute to competitive advantages aren't shielded from imitation and where imitation is often rapid and inexpensive.

Fast-cycle markets are more volatile than slow-cycle and standard-cycle markets. Indeed, the pace of competition in fast-cycle markets is almost frenzied, as companies rely on innovations as the engines of their growth. Because prices often decline quickly in these markets, companies need to profit quickly from their product innovations. Imitation of many fast-cycle products is relatively easy, as demonstrated by Dell and HP, along with many other PC vendors that have partly or largely imitated the original PC design to create their products. Continuous reductions in the costs of parts, as well as the fact that the information required to assemble a PC isn't especially complicated and is readily available, make it possible for additional competitors to enter this market without significant difficulty.[113]

The fast-cycle market characteristics just described make it virtually impossible for companies in this type of market to develop sustainable competitive advantages. Recognizing this reality, firms avoid "loyalty" to any of their products, preferring to cannibalize their own before competitors learn how to do so through successful imitation. This emphasis creates competitive dynamics that differ substantially from those found in slow-cycle markets. Instead of concentrating on protecting, maintaining, and extending competitive advantages, as in slow-cycle markets, companies competing in fast-cycle markets focus on learning how to rapidly and continuously develop new competitive advantages that are superior to those they replace. They commonly search for fast and effective means of developing new products. For example, it is common in some industries for firms to use strategic alliances to gain access to new technologies and thereby develop and introduce more new products into the market.[114] In recent years, many of these alliances have been offshore (with partners in foreign countries) in order to access appropriate skills while maintaining lower costs to compete.[115]

The competitive behavior of firms competing in fast-cycle markets is shown in Figure 5.5. As suggested by the figure, competitive dynamics in this market type entail actions and responses that are oriented to rapid and continuous product introductions and the development of a stream of ever-changing competitive advantages. The firm launches a product to achieve a competitive advantage and then exploits the advantage for as long as possible. However, the firm also tries to develop another temporary competitive advantage before competitors can respond to the first one (see Figure 5.5). Thus, competitive dynamics in fast-cycle markets often result in rapid product upgrades as well as quick product innovations.[116]

Figure 5.5 Developing Temporary Advantages to Create Sustained Advantage

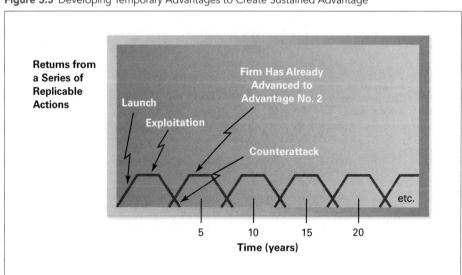

Source: Adapted from I. C. MacMillan, 1988, Controlling competitive dynamics by taking strategic initiative, *Academy of Management Executive*, II(2): 111–118.

STRATEGIC FOCUS

SOOTHING THE SOUL WITH KISSES—CANDY KISSES THAT IS

As explained in the Opening Case, candy seems to be recession proof. For example, in the depression of the 1930s, candy companies actually performed well. In fact, several candy products that remain popular today were developed and introduced during the 1930s. For example, Snickers was introduced in 1930, Tootsie Roll Pops in 1931, and Mars Bars in 1932. During tough economic times, people spend more time at home and look for ways they can reduce their stress. Eating candy is an enjoyable way to relax and it is inexpensive compared to many other outlets one may seek. It is an affordable luxury. Eating candy makes people think of better times and may even remind them of enjoyable times as a child. One person who works in his father's candy store on the weekend says that he likes to do so because people are happy when they are buying candy.

For these reasons, the performance of candy manufacturers has been one of the few bright spots in the recession of 2008–2009. For example, the Hershey Company experienced a 3.8 percent sales increase in 2008 compared to 2007 as well as an increase in profits. Few companies in other industries had such a positive experience. In fact, Hershey announced plans to increase its advertising by almost 17 percent in 2009. Many of the best-selling candies during the recession are cheaper and old fashioned, which has also helped Hershey. However, even some of the more exclusive candy companies had performance gains during the recession. Godiva Chocolatier, Inc., expects continued growth, while Lindt & Sprungli AG, maker of premium candies, had a 5.8 percent increase in sales during 2008. Cadbury achieved a 30 percent increase in its annual profits. Nestle's profits were 10.9 percent higher in 2008 as well.

Hershey took several actions in recent years that have aided its performance gains. For example, it finally responded to its competitors' premium product lines (e.g., Godiva, Cadbury) with a premium line of its own, Bliss Chocolates. In addition, it developed a line of chocolates for Starbucks that are sold as premium candies. However, Hershey's best sales have come from its basic product lines such as Hershey Bars, Kisses, and Reese's Peanut Butter Cups. Thus, Hershey placed a renewed emphasis on these product lines. Hershey also experienced increased sales through discount retailers and at convenience stores (especially after the price of gasoline declined significantly).

Mark Savage/CORBIS

Not only have candy manufacturers seen sales increase during the recession, brands such as Hershey are investing more in marketing and launching new product lines to take on more upscale competitors.

Sources: S. Grimmett, 2008, Hershey (HSY): Kisses sweeten the recession, *Today's Financial News*, http://www.todaysfinancialnews.com, October 8; J. Gordon, 2008, Prospecting in the recession? Think chocolate, The Customer Collective, http://www.thecustomercollective.com, November 3; D. Hockens, 2009, Hershey's profits rise as economy slumps, *Pennlive Blog*, http://www.pennlive.com/blogs, January 27; J. Jargon & A. Cordeiro, 2009, Recession puts Hershey in sweet spot, *The Wall Street Journal*, http://www.wsj.com, January 28; 2009, Cadbury chocolate sales soar in recession, *YumSugar*, http://www.yumsugar.com, February 26; C. Haughney, 2009, When economy sours, tootsie rolls soothe souls, *The New York Times*, http://www.nytimes.com, March 24.

As our discussion suggests, innovation plays a critical role in the competitive dynamics in fast-cycle markets. For individual firms, then, innovation is a key source of competitive advantage. Through innovation, the firm can cannibalize its own products before competitors successfully imitate them.

Candy products represent a standard-cycle market. The firms in the industry take actions to build customer loyalty, seek high market shares and try to build positive brand names. We discuss standard-cycle markets such as this one in the next section.

Standard-Cycle Markets

Standard-cycle markets are markets in which the firm's competitive advantages are partially shielded from imitation and imitation is moderately costly. Competitive advantages are partially sustainable in standard-cycle markets, but only when the firm is able to continuously upgrade the quality of its capabilities to stay ahead of competitors. The competitive actions and responses in standard-cycle markets are designed to seek large market shares, to gain customer loyalty through brand names, and to carefully control a firm's operations in order to consistently provide the same positive experience for customers.[117]

Standard-cycle companies serve many customers in competitive markets. Because the capabilities and core competencies on which their competitive advantages are based are less specialized, imitation is faster and less costly for standard-cycle firms than for those competing in slow-cycle markets. However, imitation is slower and more expensive in these markets than in fast-cycle markets. Thus, competitive dynamics in standard-cycle markets rest midway between the characteristics of dynamics in slow-cycle and fast-cycle markets. Imitation comes less quickly and is more expensive for standard-cycle competitors when a firm is able to develop economies of scale by combining coordinated and integrated design and manufacturing processes with a large sales volume for its products.

Because of large volumes, the size of mass markets, and the need to develop scale economies, the competition for market share is intense in standard-cycle markets. This form of competition is readily evident in the battles among consumer foods' producers, such as the candy makers described in the Strategic Focus. Hershey competes in different market segments with Mars, Cadbury, Nestle, and Godiva. In addition, similar to other consumer food manufacturers, some candy makers have kept prices constant selling downsized packages (others, like Hershey, have increased their prices). Package design and ease of availability are the competitive dimensions on which these firms sometimes compete to outperform their rivals in this market.

Innovation can also drive competitive actions and responses in standard-cycle markets, especially when rivalry is intense. Some innovations in standard-cycle markets are incremental rather than radical in nature (incremental and radical innovations are discussed in Chapter 13). For example, consumer foods' producers are innovating in terms of healthy products. Overall, many firms are relying on innovation as a means of competing in standard-cycle markets and to earn above-average returns.

Overall, innovation has a substantial influence on competitive dynamics as it affects the actions and responses of all companies competing within a slow-cycle, fast-cycle, or standard-cycle market. We have emphasized the importance of innovation to the firm's strategic competitiveness in earlier chapters and do so again in Chapter 13. These discussions highlight the importance of innovation in most types of markets.

Standard-cycle markets are markets in which the firm's competitive advantages are moderately shielded from imitation and where imitation is moderately costly.

SUMMARY

- Competitors are firms competing in the same market, offering similar products, and targeting similar customers. Competitive rivalry is the ongoing set of competitive actions and competitive responses occurring between competitors as they compete against each other for an advantageous market position. The outcomes of competitive rivalry influence the firm's ability to sustain its competitive advantages as well as the level (average, below average, or above average) of its financial returns.

- The set of competitive actions and responses that an individual firm takes while engaged in competitive rivalry is called competitive behavior. Competitive dynamics is the set of actions and responses taken by all firms that are competitors within a particular market.

- Firms study competitive rivalry in order to predict the competitive actions and responses that each of their competitors likely will take. Competitive actions are either strategic or tactical in nature. The firm takes competitive actions to defend or build its competitive advantages or to improve its market position. Competitive responses are taken to counter the effects of a competitor's competitive action. A strategic action or a strategic response requires a significant commitment of organizational resources, is difficult to successfully implement, and is difficult to reverse. In contrast, a tactical action or a tactical response requires fewer organizational resources and is easier to implement and reverse. For example, for an airline company, entering major new markets is an example of a strategic action or a strategic response; changing its prices in a particular market is an example of a tactical action or a tactical response.

- A competitor analysis is the first step the firm takes to be able to predict its competitors' actions and responses. In Chapter 2, we discussed what firms do to *understand* competitors. This discussion was extended in this chapter to describe what the firm does to *predict* competitors' market-based actions. Thus, understanding precedes prediction. Market commonality (the number of markets with which competitors are jointly involved and their importance to each) and resource similarity (how comparable competitors' resources are in terms of type and amount) are studied to complete a competitor analysis. In general, the greater the market commonality and resource similarity, the more firms acknowledge that they are direct competitors.

- Market commonality and resource similarity shape the firm's awareness (the degree to which it and its competitors understand their mutual interdependence), motivation (the firm's incentive to attack or respond), and ability (the quality of the resources available to the firm to attack and respond). Having knowledge of these characteristics of a competitor increases the quality of the firm's predictions about that competitor's actions and responses.

- In addition to market commonality and resource similarity and awareness, motivation, and ability, three more specific factors affect the likelihood a competitor will take competitive actions. The first of these concerns first-mover incentives. First movers, those taking an initial competitive action, often gain loyal customers and earn above-average returns until competitors can successfully respond to their action. Not all firms can be first movers in that they may lack the awareness, motivation, or ability required to engage in this type of competitive behavior. Moreover, some firms prefer to be a second mover (the firm responding to the first mover's action). One reason for this is that second movers, especially those acting quickly, can successfully compete against the first mover. By evaluating the first mover's product, customers' reactions to it, and the responses of other competitors to the first mover, the second mover can avoid the early entrant's mistakes and find ways to improve upon the value created for customers by the first mover's good or service. Late movers (those that respond a long time after the original action was taken) commonly are lower performers and are much less competitive.

- Organizational size, the second factor, tends to reduce the variety of competitive actions that large firms launch while it increases the variety of actions undertaken by smaller competitors. Ideally, the firm would prefer to initiate a large number of diverse actions when engaged in competitive rivalry. The third factor, quality, is a base denominator to competing successfully in the global economy. It is a necessary prerequisite to achieve competitive parity. It is a necessary but insufficient condition for gaining an advantage.

- The type of action (strategic or tactical) the firm took, the competitor's reputation for the nature of its competitor behavior, and that competitor's dependence on the market in which the action was taken are studied to predict a competitor's response to the firm's action. In general, the number of tactical responses taken exceeds the number of strategic responses. Competitors respond more frequently to the actions taken by the firm with a reputation for predictable and understandable competitive behavior, especially if that firm is a market leader. In general, the firm can predict that when its competitor is highly dependent for its revenue and profitability in the market in which the firm took a competitive action, that competitor is likely to launch a strong response. However, firms that are more diversified across markets are less likely to respond to a particular action that affects only one of the markets in which they compete.

- In slow-cycle markets, where competitive advantages can be maintained for at least a period of time, the competitive dynamics often include firms taking actions and responses intended to protect, maintain, and extend their proprietary advantages. In fast-cycle markets, competition is substantial as firms concentrate on developing a series of temporary competitive advantages. This emphasis is necessary because firms' advantages in fast-cycle markets aren't proprietary and, as such, are subject to rapid and relatively inexpensive imitation. Standard-cycle markets have a level of competition between that in slow-cycle and fast-cycle markets; firms are moderately shielded from competition in these markets as they use capabilities that produce competitive advantages that are moderately sustainable. Competitors in standard-cycle markets serve mass markets and try to develop economies of scale to enhance their profitability. Innovation is vital to competitive success in each of the three types of markets. Companies should recognize that the set of competitive actions and responses taken by all firms differs by type of market.

REVIEW QUESTIONS

1. Who are competitors? How are competitive rivalry, competitive behavior, and competitive dynamics defined in the chapter?

2. What is market commonality? What is resource similarity? What does it mean to say that these concepts are the building blocks for a competitor analysis?

3. How do awareness, motivation, and ability affect the firm's competitive behavior?

4. What factors affect the likelihood a firm will take a competitive action?

5. What factors affect the likelihood a firm will initiate a competitive response to the action taken by a competitor?

6. What competitive dynamics can be expected among firms competing in slow-cycle markets? In fast-cycle markets? In standard-cycle markets?

EXPERIENTIAL EXERCISES

EXERCISE 1: WIN-WIN, WIN-LOSE, OR LOSE-LOSE?

A key aspect of company strategy concerns the interactions between two or more firms. When a new market segment emerges, should a firm strive for a first-mover advantage or wait to see how the market takes shape? Diversified firms compete against one another in multiple market segments and must often consider how actions in one market might be subject to retaliation by a competitor in another segment. Similarly, when a competitor initiates a price war, a firm must decide whether it should respond in kind or not.

Game theory is helpful for understanding the strategic interaction between firms. Game theory uses assumptions about the behavior of rivals to help a company choose a specific strategy that maximizes its return. In this exercise, you will use game theory to help analyze business decisions.

Individual

One of the classic illustrations of game theory can be found in the prisoner's dilemma. Two criminals have been apprehended by the police for suspicion of a robbery. The police separate the thieves and offer them the same deal: Inform on your peer and receive a lesser sentence. Let your peer inform on you, and receive a harsher sentence. What should you tell the police?

Visit http://www.gametheory.net where you can play the prisoner's dilemma against a computer. Play the dilemma using different parameters, and make notes of your experience.

Groups

There are many examples of game theory in popular culture, from the reality show *Survivor* to episodes of *The Simpsons*. Revisit http://www.gametheory.net and select either a television or movie illustration. Discuss the applications of game theory with your team.

As a group, prepare a one-page summary of how game theory can be applied to competitive interactions between firms.

EXERCISE 2: DOES THE FIRST MOVER TRULY HAVE AN ADVANTAGE?

Henry Ford is often credited with saying that he would rather be the first person to be second. This is strange coming from the innovator of the mass-produced automobile in the United States. So is the first-mover advantage a myth, or is it something that every firm should strive for?

First movers are considered to be the ones that initially introduce an innovative product or service into a market segment. The theory is that doing so creates an almost impenetrable competitive advantage that later entrants find difficult to overcome. However, history is replete with situations where second or later movers find success. If the best way to succeed in the future is to understand the past, then an understanding of why certain first movers succeeded and others failed should be instructive. This exercise requires you to investigate a first mover and identify specifically why, or why not, it was able to hold onto its first-mover advantage.

Part One

Pick an industry that you find of interest. This assignment can be done individually or in a team. Research that industry and identify one or two instances of a first mover—the introduction of new offering into new market segments. For example, you might pick consumer electronics and look for firms that initiated new products in new market segments. Your choice of industry must be approved in advance by your instructor as duplication of industry is to be avoided.

Part Two

Each individual or team is to present their findings with the discussion centering on the following:

- Provide a brief history and description of the industry chosen. Was this a fast-, standard-, or slow-cycle market at the time the first mover initiated its strategic action?

- How has innovation of new products been accomplished traditionally in this industry: through new firms entering the market or existing firms launching new offerings?
- Identify one or two first movers and provide a review of what happened when they entered that industry. Describe why the product or offering has been successful or why it failed.
- What did you learn as a result of this exercise? Do you consider the first mover a wise strategy; is your answer dependent on industry, timing, or luck?

VIDEO CASE

THE BIRTH OF NETJETS

Richard Santulli/Chairman and CEO/NetJets

In 1986, NetJets founder Richard Santulli created the fractional airline ownership business model. Today his airline flies over 390,000 flights annually to more than 173 different countries. With 800 planes under its management, NetJets is the second largest airline in the world.

Be prepared to discuss the following concepts and questions in class:

Concepts

- First mover

- Reputation
- Segmentation
- Industry competitive dynamics
- Standard-cycle markets

Questions

1. Think about the airline industry in terms of standard-cycle markets. What does being in this type of industry mean for most aviation transportation competitors?
2. Think through the benefits to being a first mover. Why is this many times not a sustainable advantage?
3. Why do you think Continental Airlines or American Airlines did not invent the concept of fractional ownership?

NOTES

1. D. F. Spulber, 2004, *Management Strategy*, Boston: McGraw-Hill/Irwin, 87–88; M.-J. Chen, 1996, Competitor analysis and interfirm rivalry: Toward a theoretical integration, *Academy of Management Review*, 21: 100–134.

2. M. Schrage, 2007, The myth of commoditization, *MIT Sloan Management Review*, 48(2): 10–14; T. Galvin, 2002, Examining institutional change: Evidence from the founding dynamics of U.S. health care interest associations, *Academy of Management Journal*, 45: 673–696.

3. R. D. Ireland & J. W. Webb, 2007, Strategic entrepreneurship: Creating competitive advantage through streams of innovation, *Business Horizons*, 50: 49–59.

4. B. R. Barringer & R. D. Ireland, 2008, *Entrepreneurship: Successfully Launching New Ventures*, 2nd ed., Upper Saddle River, NJ: Prentice Hall; A. M. Knott & H. E. Posen, 2005, Is failure good? *Strategic Management Journal*, 26: 617–641.

5. P. J. Derfus, P. G. Maggitti, C. M. Grimm, & K. G. Smith, 2008, The red queen effect: Competitive actions and firm performance, *Academy of Management Journal*, 51; 61–80; C. M. Grimm, H. Lee, & K. G. Smith, 2006, *Strategy as Action: Competitive Dynamics and Competitive Advantage*, New York: Oxford University Press.

6. J. W. Selsky, J. Goes, & O. N. Baburoglu, 2007, Contrasting perspectives of strategy making: Applications in "hyper" environments, *Organization Studies*, 28(1): 71–94; A. Nair & L. Filer, 2003, Cointegration of firm strategies within groups: A long-run analysis of firm behavior in the Japanese steel industry, *Strategic Management Journal*, 24: 145–159.

7. T. C. Powell, 2003, Varieties of competitive parity, *Strategic Management Journal*, 24: 61–86.

8. D. G. Sirmon, S. Gove, & M. A. Hitt, 2008, Resource management in dyadic competitive rivalry: The effects of resource bundling and deployment, *Academy of Management Journal*, 51: 919–935; J. Rodriguez-Pinto, J. Gutierrez-Cillan, & A. I. Rodriguez-Escudero, 2007, Order and scale market entry, firm resources, and performance, *European Journal of Marketing*, 41: 590–607.

9. S. K. Ethitaj & D. H. Zhu, 2008, Performance effects of imitative entry, *Strategic Management Journal*, 29: 797–817.

10. Grimm, Lee, & Smith, *Strategy as Action*; G. Young, K. G. Smith, C. M. Grimm, & D. Simon, 2000, Multimarket contact and resource dissimilarity: A competitive dynamics perspective, *Journal of Management*, 26: 1217–1236.

11. E. I. Rose & K. Ito, 2008, Competitive interactions: The international investment patterns of Japanese automobile manufacturers, *Journal of International Business Studies*, 39: 864–879; T. L. Sorenson, 2007, Credible collusion in multimarket oligopoly, *Managerial and Decision Economics*, 28(2): 115–128.

12. T. Yu, M. Subramaniam, & A. A. Cannella, 2009, Rivalry deterrence in international markets: Contingencies governing the mutual forbearance hypothesis, *Academy of Management Journal*, 52: 127–147; K. G. Smith, W. J. Ferrier, & H. Ndofor, 2001, Competitive dynamics research: Critique and future directions, in M. A. Hitt, R. E. Freeman, & J. S. Harrison (eds.), *Handbook of Strategic Management*, Oxford, UK: Blackwell Publishers, 326.

13. G. Young, K. G. Smith, & C. M. Grimm, 1996, "Austrian" and industrial organization perspectives on firm-level competitive activity and performance, *Organization Science*, 73: 243–254.

14. 2007, Dell to sell PCs at Wal-Mart in retail drive, http://www.reuters.com, May 24.

15. H. D. Hopkins, 2003, The response strategies of dominant U.S. firms to Japanese challengers, *Journal of Management*, 29: 5–25; G. S. Day & D. J. Reibstein, 1997, The dynamic challenges for theory and practice, in G. S. Day & D. J. Reibstein (eds.), *Wharton on Competitive Strategy*, New York: John Wiley & Sons, 2.

16. J. J. Li, K. Z. Zhou, & A. T. Shao, 2009, Competitive position, managerial ties & profitability of foreign firms in China: An interactive perspective, *Journal of International Business Studies*, 40: 339–352; M.-J. Chen & D. C. Hambrick, 1995, Speed, stealth, and selective attack: How small firms differ from large firms in competitive behavior, *Academy of Management Journal*, 38: 453–482.

17. T. Dewett & S. David, 2007, Innovators and imitators in novelty-intensive markets: A research agenda, *Creativity and Innovation Management*, 16(1): 80–92.

18. A. Sahay, 2007, How to reap higher profits with dynamic pricing, *MIT Sloan Management Review*, 48(4): 53–60; T. J. Douglas & J. A. Ryman, 2003, Understanding competitive advantage in the general hospital industry: Evaluating strategic competencies, *Strategic Management Journal*, 24: 333–347.

19. T. Yu & A. A. Cannella, Jr., 2007, Rivalry between multinational enterprises: An event history approach, *Academy of Management Journal*, 50: 665–686; W. J. Ferrier, 2001, Navigating the competitive landscape: The drivers and consequences of competitive aggressiveness, *Academy of Management Journal*, 44: 858–877.

20. Smith, Ferrier, & Ndofor, Competitive dynamics research, 319.

21. E. G. Olson & D. Sharma, 2008, Beating the commoditization trend: A framework from the electronics industry, *Journal of Business Strategy*, 29(4): 22–28; J. Shamsie, 2003, The context of dominance: An industry-driven framework for exploiting reputation, *Strategic Management Journal*, 24: 199–215.

22. J. Li, 2008, Asymmetric interactions between foreign and domestic banks: Effects on market entry, *Strategic Management Journal*, 29: 873–893; K. Cool, L. H. Roller, & B. Leleux, 1999, The relative impact of actual and potential rivalry on firm profitability in the pharmaceutical industry, *Strategic Management Journal*, 20: 1–14.

23. G. Leask & D. Parker, 2007, Strategic groups, competitive groups and performance within the U.K. pharmaceutical industry: Improving our understanding of the competitive process, *Strategic Management Journal*, 28: 723–745; D. R. Gnyawali & R. Madhavan, 2001, Cooperative networks and competitive dynamics: A structural embeddedness perspective, *Academy of Management Review*, 26: 431–445.

24. V. La, P. Patterson & C. Styls, 2009, Client-perceived performance and value in professional B2B services: An international perspective, *Journal of International Business Studies*, 40: 274–300; Y. Y. Kor & J. T. Mahoney, 2005, How dynamics, management, and governance of resource deployments influence firm-level performance, *Strategic Management Journal*, 26: 489–496.

25. R. L. Priem, L. G. Love, & M. A. Shaffer, 2002, Executives' perceptions of uncertainty scores: A numerical taxonomy and underlying dimensions, *Journal of Management*, 28: 725–746.

26. J. C. Bou & A. Satorra, 2007, The persistence of abnormal returns at industry and firm levels: Evidence from Spain, *Strategic Management Journal*, 28: 707–722.

27. Chen, Competitor analysis, 108.

28. Chen, Competitor analysis, 109.

29. D. Ng, R. Westgren, & S. Sonka, 2009, Competitive blind spots in an institutional field, *Strategic Management Journal*, 30: 349–369.

30. S. J. Chang & D. Xu, 2008, Spillovers and competition among foreign and local firms in China, *Strategic Management Journal*, 29: 495–518.

31. K. Uhlenbruck, M. A. Hitt, & M. Semadeni, 2005, Market value effects of acquisitions of Internet firms: A resource-based analysis, working paper, University of Montana; A. Afuah, 2003, Redefining firm boundaries in the face of the Internet: Are firms really shrinking? *Academy of Management Review*, 28: 34–53.

32. H. Gebauer, 2007, Entering low-end markets: A new strategy for Swiss companies, *Journal of Business Strategy*, 27(5): 23–31.

33. 2007, YRC Worldwide, http://www.yrcw.com, July 30.

34. 2007, YRC Worldwide, *Hoovers*, http://www.hoovers.com/yrc-worldwide, July 30.

35. Chen, Competitor analysis, 106.

36. A. Kachra & R. E. White, 2008, Know-how transfer: The role of social, economic/competitive, and firm boundary factors, *Strategic Management Journal*, 29: 425–445.

37. M. J. Chen, K.-H. Su, & W. Tsai, 2007, Competitive tension: The awareness-motivation-capability perspective, *Academy of Management Journal*, 50: 101–118; J. Gimeno & C. Y. Woo, 1999, Multimarket contact, economies of scope, and firm performance, *Academy of Management Journal*, 42: 239–259.

38. I. C. MacMillan, A. B. van Putten, & R. S. McGrath, 2003, Global gamesmanship, *Harvard Business Review*, 81(5): 62–71.

39. Young, Smith, Grimm, & Simon, Multimarket contact, 1230.

40. H. R. Greve, 2008, Multimarket contact and sales growth: Evidence from insurance, *Strategic Management Journal*, 29: 229–249; J. Gimeno, 1999, Reciprocal threats in multimarket rivalry: Staking out "spheres of influence" in the U.S. airline industry, *Strategic Management Journal*, 20: 101–128.

41. S. Jayachandran, J. Gimeno, & P. R. Varadarajan, 1999, Theory of multimarket competition: A synthesis and implications for marketing strategy, *Journal of Marketing*, 63: 49–66; Chen, Competitor analysis, 107.

42. H. Schiele, 2008, Location, location: The geography of industry clusters, *Journal of Business Strategy*, 29(3): 29–36; J. Gimeno & C. Y. Woo, 1996, Hypercompetition in a multimarket environment: The role of strategic similarity and multimarket contact on competitive de-escalation, *Organization Science*, 7: 322–341.

43. C. H. Deutsch, 2007, UPS embraces high-tech delivery methods, *New York Times Online*, http://www.nytimes.com, July 12.

44. S. MacMillan, 2008, The issue: DHL turns to rival UPS, *BusinessWeek*, http//:www.businessweek.com, June.

45. Chen, Su, & Tsai, Competitive tension; Chen, Competitor analysis, 110.

46. Ibid.; W. Ocasio, 1997, Towards an attention-based view of the firm, *Strategic Management Journal*, 18 (Special Issue): 187–206; Smith, Ferrier, & Ndofor, Competitive dynamics research, 320.

47. 2007, Komatsu lifts outlook, outdoes rival Caterpillar, *New York Times Online*, http://www.nytimes.com, July 30.

48. M. Neal, 2009, Carrefour's no Wal-Mart, *Wall StreetJjournal*, //:www.wsj.com, March 12; 2007, Carrefour battles Wal-Mart in South America, Elsevier Food International, http://www.foodinternational.net, July 31.

49. S. Tallman, M. Jenkins, N. Henry, & S. Pinch, 2004, Knowledge, clusters and competitive advantage, *Academy of Management Review*, 29: 258–271; J. F. Porac & H. Thomas, 1994, Cognitive categorization and subjective rivalry among retailers in a small city, *Journal of Applied Psychology*, 79: 54–66.

50. S. H. Park & D. Zhou, 2005, Firm heterogeneity and competitive dynamics in alliance formation, *Academy of Management Review*, 30: 531–554.

51. S. R. Miller, D. E. Thomas, L. Eden & M. A. Hitt, 2008, Knee deep in the big muddy: The survival of emerging market firms in developed markets, *Management International Review*, 48: 645–666.

52. Chen, Competitor analysis, 113.

53. M. Leiblein & T. Madsen, 2009, Unbundling competitive heterogeneity: Incentive structures and capability influences on technological innovation, *Strategic Management Journal*, 30: in press; J. J. Li, L. Poppo, & K. Z. Zhou, 2008, Do managerial ties in China always produce value? Competition, uncertainty and domestic vs. foreign competition, *Strategic Management Journal*, 29: 383–400.

54. R. Belderbos & L. Sleuwaegen, 2005, Competitive drivers and international plant configuration strategies: A product-

level test, *Strategic Management Journal*, 26: 577–593.

55. C. M. Grimm & K. G. Smith, 1997, *Strategy as Action: Industry Rivalry and Coordination*, Cincinnati: South-Western Publishing Co., 125.

56. B. Webber, 2007, Volatile markets, *Business Strategy Review*, 18(2): 60–67; K. G. Smith, W. J. Ferrier, & C. M. Grimm, 2001, King of the hill: Dethroning the industry leader, *Academy of Management Executive*, 15(2): 59–70.

57. S. E. Jackson, 2008, Grow your business without leaving your competitive stronghold, *Journal of Business Strategy*, 29(4): 60–62.

58. W. J. Ferrier & H. Lee, 2003, Strategic aggressiveness, variation, and surprise: How the sequential pattern of competitive rivalry influences stock market returns, *Journal of Managerial Issues*, 14: 162–180.

59. C. Palmeri, 2007, How Guess got its groove back, *BusinessWeek*, July 23, 126.

60. S. Holmes, 2007, Better living at 30,000 feet, *BusinessWeek*, August 6, 76–77.

61. J. Schumpeter, 1934, *The Theory of Economic Development*, Cambridge, MA: Harvard University Press.

62. J. L. C. Cheng & I. F. Kesner, 1997, Organizational slack and response to environmental shifts: The impact of resource allocation patterns, *Journal of Management*, 23: 1–18.

63. F. F. Suarez & G. Lanzolla, 2007, The role of environmental dynamics in building a first mover advantage theory, *Academy of Management Review*, 32: 377–392.

64. G. M. McNamara, J. Haleblian, & B. J. Dykes, 2008, The performance implications of participating in an acquisition wave: Early mover advantages, bandwagon effects, and the moderating influence of industry characteristics and acquirer tactics, *Academy of Management Journal*, 51, 113–130; F. Wang, 2000, Too appealing to overlook, *America's Network*, December, 10–12.

65. R. K. Sinha & C. H. Noble, 2008, The adoption of radical manufacturing technologies and firm survival, *Strategic Management Journal*, 29: 943–962; D. P. Forbes, 2005, Managerial determinants of decision speed in new ventures, *Strategic Management Journal*, 26: 355–366.

66. H. R. Greve, 2009, Bigger and safer: The diffusion of competitive advantage, *Strategic Management Journal*, 30: 1–23; W. T. Robinson & S. Min, 2002, Is the first to market the first to fail? Empirical evidence for industrial goods businesses, *Journal of Marketing Research*, 39: 120–128.

67. T. Cottrell & B. R. Nault, 2004, *Strategic Management Journal*, 25: 1005–1025; R. Agarwal, M. B. Sarkar, & R. Echambadi, 2002, The conditioning effect of time on firm survival: An industry life cycle approach, *Academy of Management Journal*, 45: 971–994.

68. A. Srivastava & H. Lee, 2005, Predicting order and timing of new product moves: The role of top management in corporate entrepreneurship, *Journal of Business Venturing*, 20: 459–481.

69. M. S. Giarratana & A. Fosfuri, 2007, Product strategies and survival in Schumpeterian environments: Evidence from the U.S. security software industry, *Organization Studies*, 28(6): 909–929; J. W. Spencer & T. P. Murtha, 2005, How do governments matter to new industry creation? *Academy of Management Review*, 30: 321–337.

70. Z. Simsek, J. F. Veiga, & M. H. Lubatkin, 2007, The impact of managerial environmental perceptions on corporate entrepreneurship: Toward understanding discretionary slack's pivotal role, *Journal of Management Studies*, 44:1398–1424; S. W. Geiger & L. H. Cashen, 2002, A multidimensional examination of slack and its impact on innovation, *Journal of Managerial Issues*, 14: 68–84.

71. B. S. Teng, 2007, Corporate entrepreneurship activities through strategic alliances: A resource-based approach toward competitive advantage, *Journal of Management Studies*, 44: 119–142; M. B. Lieberman & D. B. Montgomery, 1988, First-mover advantages, *Strategic Management Journal*, 9: 41–58.

72. D. Lange, S. Boivie, & A. D. Henderson, 2009, The parenting paradox: How multibusiness diversifiers endorse disruptive technologies while their corporate children struggle, *Academy of Management Journal*, 52: 179–198.

73. S. Jonsson & P. Regner, 2009, Normative barriers to imitation: Social complexity of core competences in a mutual fund industry, *Strategic Management Journal*, 30: 517–536; 2001, Older, wiser, webbier, *The Economist*, June 30, 10.

74. M. Shank, 2002, Executive strategy report, IBM business strategy consulting, http://www.ibm.com, March 14; W. Boulding & M. Christen, 2001, First-mover disadvantage, *Harvard Business Review*, 79(9): 20–21.

75. J. L. Boyd & R. K. F. Bresser, 2008, Performance implications of delayed competitive responses: Evidence from the U.S. retail industry, *Strategic Management Journal*, 29: 1077–1096.

76. J. Gimeno, R. E. Hoskisson, B. B. Beal, & W. P. Wan, 2005, Explaining the clustering of international expansion moves: A critical test in the U.S. telecommunications industry, *Academy of Management Journal*, 48: 297–319; K. G. Smith, C. M. Grimm, & M. J. Gannon, 1992, *Dynamics of Competitive Strategy*, Newberry Park, CA.: Sage Publications.

77. J. Li & R. K. Koxhikode, 2008, Knowledge management and innovation strategy: The challenge for latecomers in emerging economies, *Asia Pacific Journal of Management*, 25: 429–450.

78. S. D. Dobrev & G. R. Carroll, 2003, Size (and competition) among organizations: Modeling scale-based selection among automobile producers in four major countries, 1885–1981, *Strategic Management Journal*, 24: 541–558.

79. L. F. Mesquita & S. G. Lazzarini, 2008, Horizontal and vertical relationships in developing economies: Implications for SMEs access to global markets, *Academy of Management Journal*, 51: 359–380; F. K. Pil & M. Hoiweg, 2003, Exploring scale: The advantage of thinking small, *The McKinsey Quarterly*, 44(2): 33–39.

80. M. A. Hitt, L. Bierman, & J. D. Collins, 2007, The strategic evolution of U.S. law firms, *Business Horizons*, 50: 17–28; D. Miller & M. J. Chen, 1996, The simplicity of competitive repertoires: An empirical analysis, *Strategic Management Journal*, 17: 419–440.

81. Young, Smith, & Grimm, "Austrian" and industrial organization perspectives.

82. B. A. Melcher, 1993, How Goliaths can act like Davids, *BusinessWeek*, Special Issue, 193.

83. P. B. Crosby, 1980, *Quality Is Free*, New York: Penguin.

84. W. E. Deming, 1986, *Out of the Crisis*, Cambridge, MA: MIT Press.

85. D. A. Mollenkopf, E. Rabinovich, T. M. Laseter, & K. K. Boyer, 2007, Managing Internet product returns: A focus on effective service operations, *Decision Sciences*, 38: 215–250; L. B. Crosby, R. DeVito, & J. M. Pearson, 2003, Manage your customers' perception of quality, *Review of Business*, 24(1): 18–24.

86. K. Watanabe, 2007, Lessons from Toyota's long drive, *Harvard Business Review*, 85(7/8): 74–83; R. S. Kaplan & D. P. Norton, 2001, *The Strategy-Focused Organization*, Boston: Harvard Business School Press.

87. A. Azadegan, K. J. Dooley, P. L. Carter, & J. R. Carter, 2008, Supplier innovativeness and the role of interorganizational learning in enhancing manufacturing capabilities, *Journal of Supply Chain Management*, 44(4): 14–5; O. Bayazit & B. Karpak, 2007, An analytical network process-based framework for successful total quality management (TQM): An assessment of Turkish manufacturing industry readiness, *International Journal of Production Economics*, 105(1) 79–96.

88. K. E. Weick & K. M. Sutcliffe, 2001, *Managing the Unexpected*, San Francisco: Jossey-Bass, 81–82.

89. G. Macintosh, 2007, Customer orientation, relationship quality, and relational benefits to the firm, *Journal of Services Marketing*, 21(3): 150–159; G. Yeung & V. Mok, 2005, What are the impacts of implementing ISOs on the competitiveness of manufacturing industry in China, *Journal of World Business*, 40: 139–157.

90. J Wallace, 2009, Boeing at risk of losing more 787 orders, *Seattle-Post-Intelligencer*, http//:www.seattlepi.nwsource.com, March 13.

91. T. R. Cook, D. J. Ketchen, J. G. Combs, & S. Y. Todd, 2008, Strategic resources and performance: A meta-analysis, *Strategic Management Journal*, 29: 1141–1154;

Smith, Ferrier, & Ndofor, Competitive dynamics research, 323.

92. M. J. Chen & I. C. MacMillan, 1992, Nonresponse and delayed response to competitive moves, *Academy of Management Journal*, 35: 539–570; Smith, Ferrier, & Ndofor, Competitive dynamics research, 335.

93. M. J. Chen, K. G. Smith, & C. M. Grimm, 1992, Action characteristics as predictors of competitive responses, *Management Science*, 38: 439–455.

94. M. J. Chen & D. Miller, 1994, Competitive attack, retaliation and performance: An expectancy-valence framework, *Strategic Management Journal*, 15: 85–102.

95. T. Gardner, 2005, Interfirm competition for human resources: Evidence from the software industry, *Academy of Management Journal*, 48: 237–258; N. Huyghebaert & L. M. van de Gucht, 2004, Incumbent strategic behavior in financial markets and the exit of entrepreneurial start-ups, *Strategic Management Journal*, 25: 669–688.

96. Smith, Ferrier, & Ndofor, Competitive dynamics research, 333.

97. V. P. Rindova, A. P. Petkova, & S. Kotha, 2007, Standing out: How firms in emerging markets build reputation, *Strategic Organization*, 5: 31–70; J. Shamsie, 2003, The context of dominance: An industry-driven framework for exploiting reputation, *Strategic Management Journal*, 24: 199–215.

98. A. D. Smith, 2007, Making the case for the competitive advantage of corporate social responsibility, *Business Strategy Series*, 8(3): 186–195; P. W. Roberts & G. R. Dowling, 2003, Corporate reputation and sustained superior financial performance, *Strategic Management Journal*, 24: 1077–1093.

99. W. J. Ferrier, K. G. Smith, & C. M. Grimm, 1999, The role of competitive actions in market share erosion and industry dethronement: A study of industry leaders and challengers, *Academy of Management Journal*, 42: 372–388.

100. Smith, Grimm, & Gannon, *Dynamics of Competitive Strategy*.

101. L. Li, L. Zhang, & B. Arys, 2008, The turtle–hare story revisited: Social capital and resource accumulation for firms from emerging economies, *Asia Pacific Journal of Management*, 25: 251–275.

102. A. Karnani & B. Wernerfelt, 1985, Multiple point competition, *Strategic Management Journal*, 6: 87–97.

103. Smith, Ferrier, & Ndofor, Competitive dynamics research, 330.

104. S. L. Newbert, 2007, Empirical research on the resource-based view of the firm: An assessment and suggestions for future research, *Strategic Management Journal*, 28: 121–146; G. McNamara, P. M. Vaaler, & C. Devers, 2003, Same as it ever was: The search for evidence of increasing hypercompetition, *Strategic Management Journal*, 24: 261–278.

105. M. F. Wiersema & H. P. Bowen, 2008, Corporate diversification: The impact of foreign competition, industry globalization and product diversification, *Strategic Management Journal*, 29: 115–132; A. Kalnins & W. Chung, 2004, Resource-seeking agglomeration: A study of market entry in the lodging industry, *Strategic Management Journal*, 25: 689–699.

106. J. R. Williams, 1992, How sustainable is your competitive advantage? *California Management Review*, 34(3): 29–51.

107. J. A. Lamberg, H. Tikkanen, & T. Nokelainen, 2009, Competitive dynamics, strategic consistency and organizational survival, *Strategic Management Journal*, 30: 45–60; D. A. Chmielewski & A. Paladino, 2007, Driving a resource orientation: Reviewing the role of resources and capability characteristics, *Management Decision*, 45: 462–483.

108. N. Pangarkar & J. R. Lie, 2004, The impact of market cycle on the performance of Singapore acquirers, *Strategic Management Journal*, 25: 1209–1216.

109. 2003, How fast is your company? *Fast Company*, June, 18.

110. D. P. Forbes, 2007, Reconsidering the strategic implications of decision comprehensiveness, *Academy of Management Review*, 32: 361–376; T. Talaulicar, J. Grundei, & A. V. Werder, 2005, Strategic decision making in startups: The effect of top management team organization and processes on speed and comprehensiveness, *Journal of Business Venturing*, 20: 519–541.

111. A. H. Ang, 2008, Competitive intensity and collaboration: Impact on firm growth across technological environments, *Strategic Management Journal*, 29: 1057–1075; M. Song, C. Droge, S. Hanvanich, & R. Calantone, 2005, Marketing and technology resource complementarity: An analysis of their interaction effect in two environmental contexts, *Strategic Management Journal*, 26: 259–276.

112. R. Williams, 1999, Renewable advantage: Crafting strategy through economic time, New York: Free Press, 8.

113. Ibid.

114. D. Li, L. E. Eden, M. A. Hitt, & R. D. Ireland, 2008, Friends, acquaintances or strangers? Partner selection in R&D alliances, *Academy of Management Journal*, 51: 315–334; D. Gerwin, 2004, Coordinating new product development in strategic alliances, *Academy of Management Review*, 29: 241–257.

115. K. Coucke & L. Sleuwaegen, 2008, Offshoring as a survival strategy: Evidence from manufacturing firms in Belgium, *Journal of international Business Studies*, 39: 1261–1277.

116. P. Carbonell & A. I. Rodriguez, 2006, The impact of market characteristics and innovation speed on perceptions of positional advantage and new product performance, *International Journal of Research in Marketing*, 23(1): 1–12; R. Sanchez, 1995, Strategic flexibility in production competition, *Strategic Management Journal*, 16 (Special Issue): 9–26.

117. R. Adner & D. Levinthal, 2008, Doing versus seeing: Acts of exploitation and perceptions of exploration, *Strategic Entrepreneurship Journal*, 2: 43–52; Williams, *Renewable Advantage*, 7.

CHAPTER 6

Corporate-Level Strategy

Studying this chapter should provide you with the strategic management knowledge needed to:

1. Define corporate-level strategy and discuss its purpose.

2. Describe different levels of diversification with different corporate-level strategies.

3. Explain three primary reasons firms diversify.

4. Describe how firms can create value by using a related diversification strategy.

5. Explain the two ways value can be created with an unrelated diversification strategy.

6. Discuss the incentives and resources that encourage diversification.

7. Describe motives that can encourage managers to overdiversify a firm.

FOSTER'S GROUP DIVERSIFICATION INTO THE WINE BUSINESS

Foster's Group's slogan "Australian for beer" is fitting, given that it produces some of Australia's top beers, including Foster's Lager and Victoria beer. However, in 2008, wine contributed 76 percent of the company's sale earnings. Although Foster's was traditionally a brewer and distributor of beer products, it foresaw more growth prospects with the sales of wine than beer. It also perceived an opportunity to commingle the marketing and distribution of these two spirit products to create economies of scope (a concept defined later in the chapter). In 2001, Foster's bought Beringer Wine Estates, a leading California winery with approximately $1.2 billion in sales. Then in 2005, Foster's acquired another premium winemaker, Southcorp; the acquisition of these companies made Foster's one of the world's biggest global wine companies.

In order to create synergy between the beer and wine assets, Foster's used one sales force to focus on the mass marketing of beer and cheap spirits, as well as selling high-priced wine to specialized restaurants and liquor stores selling to wine connoisseurs with more sophisticated tastes. The sharing of these activities between businesses that focus on low-cost mass marketing and focused differentiation (premium wines) turned out to be a significant mistake. Furthermore, the assets, especially Southcorp, were purchased at a distinct premium. Although the higher growth rate potential for wine sales seemed like the perfect strategic fit with the low growth rate of beer sales, the synergy between these two businesses was apparently not realized. Furthermore, currency problems contributed to the performance problem; the Southcorp assets were devalued as the U.S. dollar depreciated relative to the Australian dollar. One analyst said "they [Foster's] paid too much and they bought at the wrong time in the cycle."

Christian Heeb/laif/Redux

Despite perceived opportunities to leverage their existing brewery-focused marketing and distribution operations, Foster's encountered numerous problems in the integration of the Beringer and Southcorp wineries.

To correct the problem Foster's has recently been separating these businesses and creating a new marketing group for the wine business while maintaining its current expertise in the brewing and distribution of beer. Because the separation of these businesses is crucial for Foster's to remain profitable, it may be willing to divest one of these businesses, most likely the wine segment because its basic expertise among the key leaders and other personnel is in the beer business.

This is an example of related constrained diversification being poorly executed. Interestingly, a new CEO was appointed after the strategic mistakes occurred. Related constrained diversification, as defined later in the chapter, focuses on managing different businesses, which are potentially highly related in regard to the manufacturing, sales, and distribution activities among the firm's related business portfolio. Unfortunately, Foster's focused on the growth cycle differences and not the detailed implementation differences related to the sharing of actual activities between beer and premium wine, which were not as great a fit as earlier suspected.

Sources: C. Koons, 2009, Earnings: Foster's to retain, revamp struggling wine business, *Wall Street Journal*, February 18, B6; 2009, Foster's Company limited, 2009, *Hoovers Company Records*, http://www.hoovers.com, March 15, 42414; E. Ellis, 2008, What'll you have mate? *Barron's*, October 27, 34–36; S. Murdoch, 2008, Corporate news: Foster's Group names Johnston to be CEO, *Wall Street Journal*, September 27, D6; G. Charles, 2007, Foster's Group plans global wine brands relaunch, *Marketing*, November 29, 3.

Our discussions of business-level strategies (Chapter 4) and the competitive rivalry and competitive dynamics associated with them (Chapter 5) concentrate on firms competing in a single industry or product market.[1] In this chapter, we introduce you to corporate-level strategies, which are strategies firms use to *diversify* their operations from a single business competing in a single market into several product markets and, most commonly, into several businesses. Thus, a **corporate-level strategy** specifies actions a firm takes to gain a competitive advantage by selecting and managing a group of different businesses competing in different product markets. Corporate-level strategies help companies select new strategic positions—positions that are expected to increase the firm's value.[2] As explained in the Opening Case, Foster's Group Ltd., an Australian beverage company, competes in several different beverage segments dominated by beer and wine brands.

Another example is Interpublic Group, a marketing and advertising firm. It is taking advantage of the economic downturn to acquire companies at a decreased price and increase its portfolio of businesses. It is currently seeking to acquire firms in the digital and mobile sector to grow its Media Brands operations to help achieve its goal of being one of the top three players in its respective market by the year 2011.[3]

As is the case with Foster's, firms use corporate-level strategies as a means to grow revenues and profits. But there can be different strategic intents beside growth. Firms can pursue defensive or offensive strategies that realize growth but have different strategic intents. Firms can also pursue market development by moving into different geographic markets (this approach will be discussed in Chapter 8). Firms can acquire competitors (horizontal integration) or buy a supplier or customer (vertical integration). These strategies will be discussed in Chapter 7. The basic corporate strategy, the topic of this chapter, focuses on diversification.

The decision to take actions to pursue growth is never a risk-free choice for firms. Indeed, as the Opening Case illustrated, Foster's Group experienced difficulty in integrating the beer and wine marketing and sales operations to share these activities. Also, Luxottica Group, a leader in the fashion sunglasses industry, has faced risks associated with its acquisition of Oakley, a firm focused on producing sporty sunglasses. Can a luxury goods manufacturer successfully integrate a sporting goods manufacturing company?[4] Effective firms carefully evaluate their growth options (including the different corporate-level strategies) before committing firm resources to any of them.[5]

Because the diversified firm operates in several different and unique product markets and likely in several businesses, it forms two types of strategies: corporate-level (or company-wide) and business-level (or competitive).[6] Corporate-level strategy is concerned with two key issues: in what product markets and businesses the firm should compete and how corporate headquarters should manage those businesses.[7] For the diversified corporation, a business-level strategy (see Chapter 4) must be selected for each of the businesses in which the firm has decided to compete. In this regard, each of Foster's product divisions uses different business-level strategies; while both focus on differentiation, the beer business is focused more on differentiation by a mass market approach while the high-end of the wine business targets unique customers based on individual tastes desired by marketing "its pricey wines to chic restaurants and liquor stores catering to connoisseurs."[8]

As is the case with a business-level strategy, a corporate-level strategy is expected to help the firm earn above-average returns by creating value.[9] Some suggest that few corporate-level strategies actually create value.[10] As the Opening Case indicates, realizing value through a corporate strategy can be difficult to achieve. In fact, the degree to which corporate-level strategies create value beyond the sum of the value created by all of a firm's business units remains an important research question.[11]

Evidence suggests that a corporate-level strategy's value is ultimately determined by the degree to which "the businesses in the portfolio are worth more under the management of the company than they would be under any other ownership."[12] Thus, an effective

A **corporate-level strategy** specifies actions a firm takes to gain a competitive advantage by selecting and managing a group of different businesses competing in different product markets.

corporate-level strategy creates, across all of a firm's businesses, aggregate returns that exceed what those returns would be without the strategy[13] and contributes to the firm's strategic competitiveness and its ability to earn above-average returns.[14]

Product diversification, a primary form of corporate-level strategies, concerns the scope of the markets and industries in which the firm competes as well as "how managers buy, create and sell different businesses to match skills and strengths with opportunities presented to the firm."[15] Successful diversification is expected to reduce variability in the firm's profitability as earnings are generated from different businesses.[16] Because firms incur development and monitoring costs when diversifying, the ideal portfolio of businesses balances diversification's costs and benefits. CEOs and their top-management teams are responsible for determining the ideal portfolio for their company.[17]

We begin this chapter by examining different levels of diversification (from low to high). After describing the different reasons firms diversify their operations, we focus on two types of related diversification (related diversification signifies a moderate to high level of diversification for the firm). When properly used, these strategies help create value in the diversified firm, either through the sharing of resources (the related constrained strategy) or the transferring of core competencies across the firm's different businesses (the related linked strategy). We then discuss unrelated diversification, which is another corporate-level strategy that can create value. The chapter then shifts to the topic of incentives and resources that may stimulate diversification which is value neutral. However, managerial motives to diversify, the final topic in the chapter, can actually destroy some of the firm's value.

Levels of Diversification

Diversified firms vary according to their level of diversification and the connections between and among their businesses. Figure 6.1 lists and defines five categories of businesses according to increasing levels of diversification. The single- and dominant-business categories denote relatively low levels of diversification; more fully diversified firms are classified into related and unrelated categories. A firm is related through its diversification when its businesses share several links; for example, businesses may share products (goods or services), technologies, or distribution channels. The more links among businesses, the more "constrained" is the relatedness of diversification. Unrelatedness refers to the absence of direct links between businesses.

Low Levels of Diversification

A firm pursuing a low level of diversification uses either a single- or a dominant-business, corporate-level diversification strategy. A *single-business diversification strategy* is a corporate-level strategy wherein the firm generates 95 percent or more of its sales revenue from its core business area.[18] For example, Wm. Wrigley Jr. Company, the world's largest producer of chewing and bubble gums, historically used a single-business strategy while operating in relatively few product markets. Wrigley's trademark chewing gum brands include Spearmint, Doublemint, and Juicy Fruit, although the firm produces other products as well. Sugar-free Extra, which currently holds the largest share of the U.S. chewing gum market, was introduced in 1984.

In 2005, Wrigley shifted from its traditional focused strategy when it acquired the confectionary assets of Kraft Foods Inc., including the well-known brands Life Savers and Altoids. As Wrigley expanded, it may have intended to use the dominant-business strategy with the diversification of its product lines beyond gum; however, Wrigley was acquired in 2008 by Mars, a privately held global confection company (the maker of Snickers and M&Ms).[19]

Figure 6.1 Levels and Types of Diversification

Low Levels of Diversification

Single business: 95% or more of revenue comes from a single business.

Dominant business: Between 70% and 95% of revenue comes from a single business.

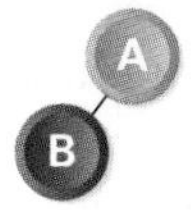

Moderate to High Levels of Diversification

Related constrained: Less than 70% of revenue comes from the dominant business, and all businesses share product, technological, and distribution linkages.

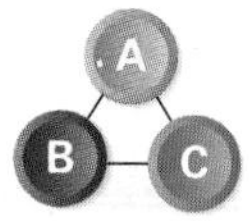

Related linked (mixed related and unrelated): Less than 70% of revenue comes from the dominant business, and there are only limited links between businesses.

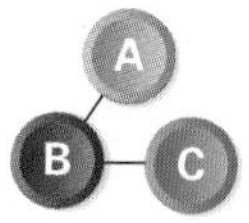

Very High Levels of Diversification

Unrelated: Less than 70% of revenue comes from the dominant business, and there are no common links between businesses.

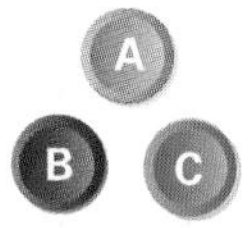

Source: Adapted from R. P. Rumelt, 1974, *Strategy, Structure and Economic Performance*, Boston: Harvard Business School.

With the *dominant-business diversification strategy,* the firm generates between 70 and 95 percent of its total revenue within a single business area. United Parcel Service (UPS) uses this strategy. Recently UPS generated 61 percent of its revenue from its U.S. package delivery business and 22 percent from its international package business, with the remaining 17 percent coming from the firm's non-package business.[20] Though the U.S. package delivery business currently generates the largest percentage of UPS's sales revenue, the firm anticipates that in the future its other two businesses will account for the majority of revenue growth. This expectation suggests that UPS may become more diversified, both in terms of its goods and services and in the number of countries in which those goods and services are offered.

Moderate and High Levels of Diversification

A firm generating more than 30 percent of its revenue outside a dominant business and whose businesses are related to each other in some manner uses a related diversification corporate-level strategy. When the links between the diversified firm's businesses are rather direct, a *related constrained diversification strategy* is being used. Campbell Soup, Procter & Gamble, and Merck & Company all use a related constrained strategy, as do some large cable companies. With a related constrained strategy, a firm shares resources and activities between its businesses.

The diversified company with a portfolio of businesses that have only a few links between them is called a mixed related and unrelated firm and is using the *related linked diversification strategy* (see Figure 6.1). General Electric (GE) uses this corporate-level diversification strategy. Compared with related constrained firms, related linked firms share fewer resources and assets between their businesses, concentrating instead on transferring knowledge and core competencies between the businesses. As with firms using each type of diversification strategy, companies implementing the related linked strategy constantly adjust the mix in their portfolio of businesses as well as make decisions about how to manage these businesses.

A highly diversified firm that has no relationships between its businesses follows an *unrelated diversification strategy.* United Technologies, Textron, Samsung, and Hutchison Whampoa Limited (HWL) are examples of firms using this type of corporate-level strategy. Commonly, firms using this strategy are called *conglomerates.*

HWL is a leading international corporation committed to innovation and technology with businesses spanning the globe.[21] Ports and related services, telecommunications, property and hotels, retail and manufacturing, and energy and infrastructure are HWL's five core businesses. These businesses are not related to each other, and the firm makes no efforts to share activities or to transfer core competencies between or among them. Each of these five

businesses is quite large; for example, the retailing arm of the retail and manufacturing business has more than 6,200 stores in 31 countries. Groceries, cosmetics, electronics, wine, and airline tickets are some of the product categories featured in these stores. This firm's size and diversity suggest the challenge of successfully managing the unrelated diversification strategy. However, Hutchison's CEO Li Ka-shing has been successful at not only making smart acquisitions, but also at divesting businesses with good timing.[22]

Hutchison's CEO Li Ka-shing successfully manages a highly diverse organization with five core businesses, which operate with minimal interdependency.

MIKE CLARKE/AFP/Getty Images

Reasons for Diversification

A firm uses a corporate-level diversification strategy for a variety of reasons (see Table 6.1). Typically, a diversification strategy is used to increase the firm's value by improving its

Table 6.1 Reasons for Diversification

Value-Creating Diversification
- Economies of scope (related diversification)
  - Sharing activities
  - Transferring core competencies
- Market power (related diversification)
  - Blocking competitors through multipoint competition
  - Vertical integration
- Financial economies (unrelated diversification)
  - Efficient internal capital allocation
  - Business restructuring

Value-Neutral Diversification
- Antitrust regulation
- Tax laws
- Low performance
- Uncertain future cash flows
- Risk reduction for firm
- Tangible resources
- Intangible resources

Value-Reducing Diversification
- Diversifying managerial employment risk
- Increasing managerial compensation

overall performance. Value is created either through related diversification or through unrelated diversification when the strategy allows a company's businesses to increase revenues or reduce costs while implementing their business-level strategies.

Other reasons for using a diversification strategy may have nothing to do with increasing the firm's value; in fact, diversification can have neutral effects or even reduce a firm's value. Value-neutral reasons for diversification include a desire to match and thereby neutralize a competitor's market power (such as to neutralize another firm's advantage by acquiring a similar distribution outlet). Decisions to expand a firm's portfolio of businesses to reduce managerial risk can have a negative effect on the firm's value. Greater amounts of diversification reduce managerial risk in that if one of the businesses in a diversified firm fails, the top executive of that business does not risk total failure by the corporation. As such, this reduces the top executives' employment risk. In addition, because diversification can increase a firm's size and thus managerial compensation, managers have motives to diversify a firm to a level that reduces its value.[23] Diversification rationales that may have a neutral or negative effect on the firm's value are discussed later in the chapter.

Operational relatedness and corporate relatedness are two ways diversification strategies can create value (see Figure 6.2). Studies of these independent relatedness dimensions show the importance of resources and key competencies.[24] The figure's vertical dimension depicts opportunities to share operational activities between businesses (operational relatedness) while the horizontal dimension suggests opportunities for transferring corporate-level core competencies (corporate relatedness). The firm with a strong capability in managing operational synergy, especially in sharing assets between its businesses, falls in the upper left quadrant, which also represents vertical sharing of assets through vertical integration. The lower right quadrant represents a highly developed corporate capability for transferring one or more core competencies across businesses.

Figure 6.2 Value-Creating Diversification Strategies: Operational and Corporate Relatedness

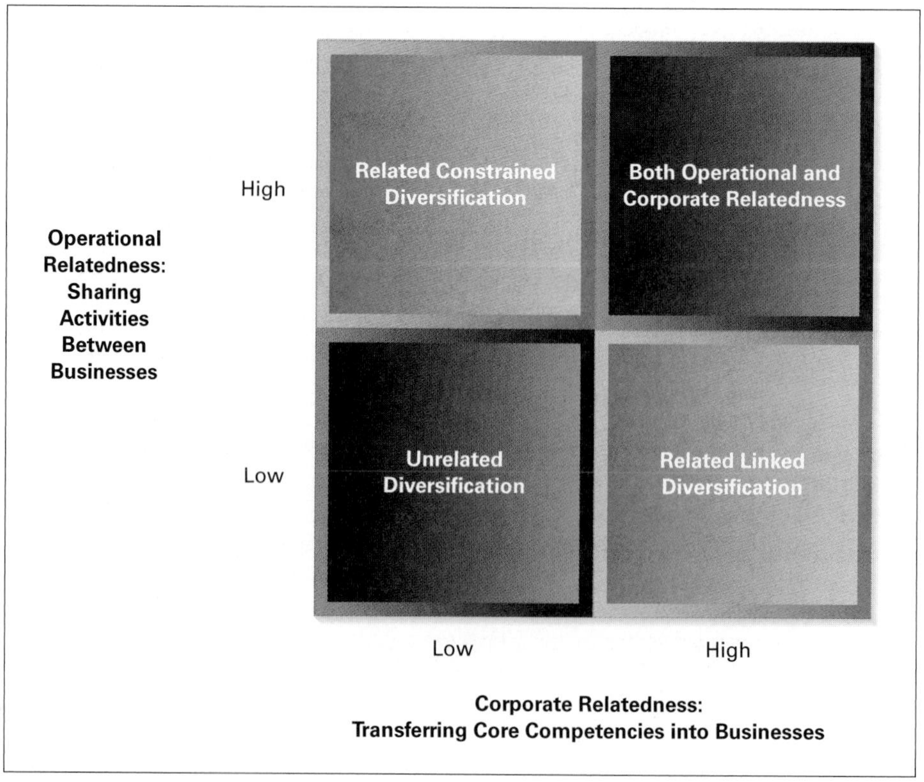

This capability is located primarily in the corporate headquarters office. Unrelated diversification is also illustrated in Figure 6.2 in the lower left quadrant. Financial economies (discussed later), rather than either operational or corporate relatedness, are the source of value creation for firms using the unrelated diversification strategy.

Value-Creating Diversification: Related Constrained and Related Linked Diversification

With the related diversification corporate-level strategy, the firm builds upon or extends its resources and capabilities to create value.[25] The company using the related diversification strategy wants to develop and exploit economies of scope between its businesses.[26] Available to companies operating in multiple product markets or industries,[27] **economies of scope** are cost savings that the firm creates by successfully sharing some of its resources and capabilities or transferring one or more corporate-level core competencies that were developed in one of its businesses to another of its businesses.

As illustrated in Figure 6.2, firms seek to create value from economies of scope through two basic kinds of operational economies: sharing activities (operational relatedness) and transferring corporate-level core competencies (corporate relatedness). The difference between sharing activities and transferring competencies is based on how separate resources are jointly used to create economies of scope. To create economies of scope tangible resources, such as plant and equipment or other business-unit physical assets, often must be shared. Less tangible resources, such as manufacturing know-how, can also be shared. However, know-how transferred between separate activities with no physical or tangible resource involved is a transfer of a corporate-level core competence, not an operational sharing of activities.[28]

Operational Relatedness: Sharing Activities

Firms can create operational relatedness by sharing either a primary activity (such as inventory delivery systems) or a support activity (such as purchasing practices)—see Chapter 3's discussion of the value chain. Firms using the related constrained diversification strategy share activities in order to create value. Procter & Gamble (P&G) uses this corporate-level strategy. P&G's paper towel business and baby diaper business both use paper products as a primary input to the manufacturing process. The firm's paper production plant produces inputs for both businesses and is an example of a shared activity. In addition, because they both produce consumer products, these two businesses are likely to share distribution channels and sales networks.

As noted in the Opening Case, Foster's Group sought to create operational relatedness between the beer and wine business. Firms expect activity sharing among units to result in increased strategic competitiveness and improved financial returns. Through its shared product approach, Foster's Group was unable to improve its market share position, especially in the wine business. As previously mentioned, pursuing operational relatedness is not easy, and often synergies are not realized as planned.

Activity sharing is also risky because ties among a firm's businesses create links between outcomes. For instance, if demand for one business's product is reduced, it may not generate sufficient revenues to cover the fixed costs required to operate the shared facilities. These types of organizational difficulties can reduce activity-sharing success. This problem occurred in the Foster's Group in the Opening Case because there were problems in the sharing of activities between the beer and wine businesses, especially in the marketing and distribution.

Although activity sharing across businesses is not risk-free, research shows that it can create value. For example, studies that acquisitions of firms in the same industry (horizontal

Economies of scope are cost savings that the firm creates by successfully sharing some of its resources and capabilities or transferring one or more corporate-level core competencies that were developed in one of its businesses to another of its businesses.

acquisitions), such as the banking industry and software (see the Oracle Strategic Focus), found that sharing resources and activities and thereby creating economies of scope contributed to postacquisition increases in performance and higher returns to share-holders.[29] Additionally, firms that sold off related units in which resource sharing was a possible source of economies of scope have been found to produce lower returns than those that sold off businesses unrelated to the firm's core business.[30] Still other research discovered that firms with closely related businesses have lower risk.[31] These results suggest that gaining economies of scope by sharing activities across a firm's businesses may be important in reducing risk and in creating value. Further, more attractive results are obtained through activity sharing when a strong corporate headquarters office facilitates it.[32]

The Strategic Focus on Oracle's acquisition strategy of other software firms represents an attempt to implement a related constrained strategy. However, as the example indicates it still remains to be seen how successful the strategy will be.

Corporate Relatedness: Transferring of Core Competencies

Over time, the firm's intangible resources, such as its know-how, become the foundation of core competencies. **Corporate-level core competencies** are complex sets of resources and capabilities that link different businesses, primarily through managerial and technological knowledge, experience, and expertise.[33] Firms seeking to create value through corporate relatedness use the related linked diversification strategy.

In at least two ways, the related linked diversification strategy helps firms to create value.[34] First, because the expense of developing a core competence has already been incurred in one of the firm's businesses, transferring this competence to a second business eliminates the need for that business to allocate resources to develop it. Such is the case at Hewlett-Packard (HP), where the firm transferred its competence in ink printers to high-end copiers. Rather than the standard laser printing technology in most high-end copiers, HP is using ink-based technology. One manager liked the product because, as he noted, "We are able to do a lot better quality at less price."[35] This capability will also give HP the opportunity to sell more ink products, which is how it has been able to create higher profit margins.

Resource intangibility is a second source of value creation through corporate relatedness. Intangible resources are difficult for competitors to understand and imitate. Because of this difficulty, the unit receiving a transferred corporate-level competence often gains an immediate competitive advantage over its rivals.[36]

A number of firms have successfully transferred one or more corporate-level core competencies across their businesses. Virgin Group Ltd. transfers its marketing core competence across airlines, cosmetics, music, drinks, mobile phones, health clubs, and a number of other businesses.[37] Honda has developed and transferred its competence in engine design and manufacturing among its businesses making products such as motorcycles, lawnmowers, and cars and trucks. Company officials indicate that "Honda is the world's largest manufacturer of engines and has earned its reputation for unsurpassed quality, performance and reliability."[38]

One way managers facilitate the transfer of corporate-level core competencies is by moving key people into new management positions.[39] However, the manager of an older business may be reluctant to transfer key people who have accumulated knowledge and experience critical to the business's success. Thus, managers with the ability to facilitate the transfer of a core competence may come at a premium, or the key people involved may not want to transfer. Additionally, the top-level managers from the transferring business may not want the competencies transferred to a new business to fulfill the firm's diversification objectives. Research also suggests too much dependence on outsourcing can lower the usefulness of core competencies and thereby reduce their useful transferability to other business units in the diversified firm.[40]

Corporate-level core competencies are complex sets of resources and capabilities that link different businesses, primarily through managerial and technological knowledge, experience, and expertise.

ORACLE'S RELATED CONSTRAINED DIVERSIFICATION STRATEGY

Oracle has been diversifying its software business in a related way through a significant acquisition program. In 2008 alone, it made 10 acquisitions of smaller software producers and companies that develop software production tools. Despite the economic downturn, by the end of 2008 Oracle had retained $13 billion, allowing it to pursue its acquisition strategy.

Historically, Oracle has been the largest player by market share in the "database" management software industry. Nonetheless, in 2003, it started buying large software makers including PeopleSoft (this was a hostile takeover bid, which did not close until January 2005). It also bought Siebel Systems, Hyperion Solutions, and in early 2008 acquired BEA Systems for approximately $8.5 billion. From 2004–2008 the company collectively spent approximately $25 billion on acquisitions. Oracle's positioning has also changed such that it derives more from enterprise resource planning (ERP) software (its largest acquisitions—for example, PeopleSoft, Siebel Systems, and BEA Systems) and less from database management as it seeks to combine the whole company and its different segments to position itself as a stronger competitor against SAP—the largest player in the ERP industry. Additionally, Oracle's maintenance contracts have helped offset some of its lower sales in basic software in the down cycle. However, over time customers might protest the large margins associated with these maintenance contracts and seek to cut back on them during the recession.

In order to manage its strategy and to compete in a more focused way, Oracle has targeted specific industries to allow it to compete more effectively with competitors such as SAP. These industries include financial services, insurance, retail, and telecommunications. It set a goal to be the number one or number two software supplier in each of these industry segments.

However, the difficulty is to organize and coordinate these acquisitions into a cohesive set of businesses by which Oracle can create economies of scope through more efficient management techniques. This is somewhat hindered by the differences in cultures and structures of its acquisitions. The benefit has been that the assets have been purchased at lower prices because private equity investors' (i.e., venture capitalists) funding has decreased 80 percent, and thus Oracle has been the primary means for these firms to obtain funding. Corporate venture capital has been a mainstay for firms in the Silicon Valley, in which Oracle has done much acquisition activity.

In summary, the organizational integration aspects have prevented much of the possible sharing of activities that this strategy requires to be successful. Oracle's continued success will be determined by how far its stock price falls relative to its costs of acquisition of

Oracle's acquisition of companies such as BEA Systems has positioned it to compete in the ERP industry with SAP; however, its performance will rely on how successfully it integrates these new businesses.

these new businesses and its ability to integrate these acquisitions into a cohesive structure that will allow the sharing of activities to take place more efficiently. It is important that central headquarters implement controls to foster the sharing of activities between related divisions for success to occur.

Sources: B. Worthen, 2009, Cash-rich Oracle scoops up bargains in recession spree, *Wall Street Journal*, February 17, A1, A12; J. Hodgson, 2009, Rethinking software support: Recession puts new focus on Oracle maintenance contracts, *Wall Street Journal*, March 12, B8; 2009, Oracle Corporation, *Hoovers Company Records*, March 15, 14337; M. V. Copeland, 2008, Big tech goes bargain hunting, *Fortune*, November 10, 43; B. Vara & B. Worthen, 2007, As software firms merge, synergy is elusive: Shareholders may prosper from trend, but customers see scant benefits so far, *Wall Street Journal*, November 20, B1.

Market Power

Firms using a related diversification strategy may gain market power when successfully using their related constrained or related linked strategy. **Market power** exists when a firm is able to sell its products above the existing competitive level or to reduce the costs of its primary and support activities below the competitive level, or both.[41] Mars' acquisition of the Wrigley assets was part of its related constrained diversification strategy and added market share to the Mars/Wrigley integrated firm, as it realized 14.4 percent of the market share. This catapulted Mars/Wrigley above Cadbury and Nestle, which have 10.1 and 7.7 percent of the market share, respectively, and left Hershey with only 5.5 percent of the market.[42]

In addition to efforts to gain scale as a means of increasing market power, as Mars did when it acquired Wrigley, firms can create market power through multipoint competition and vertical integration. **Multipoint competition** exists when two or more diversified firms simultaneously compete in the same product areas or geographic markets.[43] The actions taken by UPS and FedEx in two markets, overnight delivery and ground shipping, illustrate multipoint competition. UPS has moved into overnight delivery, FedEx's stronghold; FedEx has been buying trucking and ground shipping assets to move into ground shipping, UPS's stronghold. Moreover, geographic competition for markets increases. The strongest shipping company in Europe is DHL. All three competitors (UPS, FedEx, and DHL) are trying to move into large foreign markets to either gain a stake or to expand their existing share. For instance, because the area of China that is close to Hong Kong is becoming a top destination for shipping throughout Asia, competition is raging among these three international shippers.[44] If one of these firms successfully gains strong positions in several markets while competing against its rivals, its market power may increase. Interestingly, DHL had to exit the U.S. market because it was too difficult to compete against UPS and FedEx, which are dominant in the United States.

Some firms using a related diversification strategy engage in vertical integration to gain market power. **Vertical integration** exists when a company produces its own inputs (backward integration) or owns its own source of output distribution (forward integration). In some instances, firms partially integrate their operations, producing and selling their products by using company businesses as well as outside sources.[45]

Vertical integration is commonly used in the firm's core business to gain market power over rivals. Market power is gained as the firm develops the ability to save on its operations, avoid market costs, improve product quality, and, possibly, protect its technology from imitation by rivals.[46] Market power also is created when firms have strong ties between their assets for which no market prices exist. Establishing a market price would result in high search and transaction costs, so firms seek to vertically integrate rather than remain separate businesses.[47]

Vertical integration has its limitations. For example, an outside supplier may produce the product at a lower cost. As a result, internal transactions from vertical integration may be expensive and reduce profitability relative to competitors.[48] Also, bureaucratic costs may occur with vertical integration. And, because vertical integration can require substantial

Market power exists when a firm is able to sell its products above the existing competitive level or to reduce the costs of its primary and support activities below the competitive level, or both.

Multipoint competition exists when two or more diversified firms simultaneously compete in the same product areas or geographical markets.

Vertical integration exists when a company produces its own inputs (backward integration) or owns its own source of output distribution (forward integration).

investments in specific technologies, it may reduce the firm's flexibility, especially when technology changes quickly. Finally, changes in demand create capacity balance and coordination problems. If one business is building a part for another internal business but achieving economies of scale requires the first division to manufacture quantities that are beyond the capacity of the internal buyer to absorb, it would be necessary to sell the parts outside the firm as well as to the internal business. Thus, although vertical integration can create value, especially through market power over competitors, it is not without risks and costs.[49]

For example, CVS, a drugstore competitor to Walgreens, recently merged with Caremark, a large pharmaceutical benefits manager (PBM). For CVS this merger represents a forward vertical move broadening its business from retail into health care management. However, Medco, a competitor to Caremark, indicates that companies competing with CVS "are more comfortable with [their] neutral position than they are with the concept of a combination" between CVS and Caremark.[50] Thus, although CVS may gain some market power, it risks alienating rivals such as Walgreens, which may choose to collaborate with other benefit managers such as Medco or Express Scripts. Likewise, many health care insurance providers have vertically integrated into PBMs. However, as the larger PBMs such as Express Scripts, CVS/Caremark, and Medco Health Solutions increase in size, PBMs associated with particular insurance providers have not been able to compete successfully. This has led some large insurance providers to consider divestiture. For example, WellPoint announced recently that its in-house benefits management business, NextRx, is going to be sold.[51] In fact, Express Scripps was able to win the bidding for NextRx.[52] This could spur other insurance companies such as Aetna Inc. and Cigna Corp. to spin off their PBM businesses as well. The larger PBMs may be able to leverage their size and obtain cheaper drug prices from manufacturers and manage insurers' drug benefits at a lower cost.

Many manufacturing firms have been reducing vertical integration as a means of gaining market power.[53] In fact, deintegration is the focus of most manufacturing firms, such as Intel and Dell, and even some large auto companies, such as Ford and General Motors, as they develop independent supplier networks.[54] Flextronics, an electronics contract manufacturer, represents a new breed of large contract manufacturers that is helping to foster this revolution in supply-chain management.[55] Such firms often manage their customers' entire product lines and offer services ranging from inventory management to delivery and after-sales service. Conducting business through e-commerce also allows vertical integration to be changed into "virtual integration."[56] Thus, closer relationships are possible with suppliers and customers through virtual integration or electronic means of integration, allowing firms to reduce the costs of processing transactions while improving their supply-chain management skills and tightening the control of their inventories. This evidence suggests that *virtual integration* rather than *vertical integration* may be a more common source of market power gains for firms today.

Simultaneous Operational Relatedness and Corporate Relatedness

As Figure 6.2 suggests, some firms simultaneously seek operational and corporate relatedness to create economies of scope.[57] The ability to simultaneously create economies of scope by sharing activities (operational relatedness) and transferring core competencies (corporate relatedness) is difficult for competitors to understand and learn how to imitate. However, if the cost of realizing both types of relatedness is not offset by the benefits created, the result is diseconomies because the cost of organization and incentive structure is very expensive.[58]

As the Strategic Focus on Johnson & Johnson illustrates, this company uses a strategy that combines operational and corporate relatedness with some success. Likewise, Walt Disney Co. uses a related diversification strategy to simultaneously create economies of scope through operational and corporate relatedness. Within the firm's Studio Entertainment business, for example, Disney can gain economies of scope by sharing activities among its different movie distribution companies such as Touchstone Pictures, Hollywood Pictures, and Dimension Films. Broad and deep knowledge about its customers is a capability on which Disney relies to develop corporate-level core competencies in terms of advertising and marketing. With these competencies, Disney is able to create economies of scope through corporate relatedness as it cross-sells products that are highlighted in its movies through the distribution channels that are part of its Parks and Resorts and Consumer Products businesses. Thus, characters created in movies become figures that are marketed through Disney's retail stores (which are part of the Consumer Products business). In addition, themes established in movies become the source of new rides in the firm's theme parks, which are part of the Parks and Resorts business and provide themes for clothing and other retail business products.[59]

As we described, Johnson & Johnson and Walt Disney Co. have been able to successfully use related diversification as a corporate-level strategy through which they create economies of scope by sharing some activities and by transferring core competencies. However, it can be difficult for investors to actually observe the value created by a firm (such as Walt Disney Co.) as it shares activities and transfers core competencies. For this reason, the value of the assets of a firm using a diversification strategy to create economies of scope in this manner tends to be discounted by investors. For example, analysts have complained that both Citibank and UBS, two large multiplatform banks, have underperformed their more focused counterparts in regard to stock market appreciation. In fact, both banks have heard calls for breaking up their separate businesses in insurance, hedge funds, consumer lending, and investment banking.[60] One analyst speaking of Citigroup suggested that "creating real synergy between its divisions has been hard," implying that Citigroup's related diversification strategy suffered from some possible diseconomies of scale.[61] Due to its diseconomies and other losses related to the economic downturn, Citigroup has recently considered selling some of its foreign divisions, such as its Japanese investment bank and brokerage service.[62] USB is changing its strategy as well. The bank's three divisions—private banking, investment banking, and asset management—will be reorganized into a more centralized unit to reduce costs. Previously each segment was given more autonomy over its operations; this model proved too costly and the new CEO, Oswald Grubel, is seeking to reduce possible diseconomies of scale through the centralization, especially in regard to information technology.[63]

Unrelated Diversification

Firms do not seek either operational relatedness or corporate relatedness when using the unrelated diversification corporate-level strategy. An unrelated diversification strategy (see Figure 6.2) can create value through two types of financial economies. **Financial economies** are cost savings realized through improved allocations of financial resources based on investments inside or outside the firm.[64]

Efficient internal capital allocations can lead to financial economies. Efficient internal capital allocations reduce risk among the firm's businesses—for example, by leading to the development of a portfolio of businesses with different risk profiles. The second type of financial economy concerns the restructuring of acquired assets. Here, the diversified firm buys another company, restructures that company's assets in ways that allow it to operate more profitably, and then sells the company for a profit in the external market.[65] Next, we discuss the two types of financial economies in greater detail.

Efficient Internal Capital Market Allocation

In a market economy, capital markets are thought to efficiently allocate capital. Efficiency results as investors take equity positions (ownership) with high expected future cash-flow values. Capital is also allocated through debt as shareholders and debtholders try to improve the value of their investments by taking stakes in businesses with high growth and profitability prospects.

Financial economies are cost savings realized through improved allocations of financial resources based on investments inside or outside the firm.

JOHNSON & JOHNSON USES BOTH OPERATIONAL AND CORPORATE RELATEDNESS

Johnson & Johnson (J&J) is a widely diversified business. It is the world's seventh largest pharmaceutical company, fourth largest biologics company, the premier consumer health products company, and the largest medical devices and diagnostics company. These businesses are combined into three main groups: consumer health care, medical devices and diagnostics, and pharmaceuticals. The consumer health care business produces products for hair, skin, teeth, and babies. The medical devices and diagnostics business develops stents and many other products focused on cardiovascular care and equipment for surgical settings. The pharmaceutical business is focused on the central nervous system and internal medicines for helping with such disorders as schizophrenia, epilepsy, diabetes, and cardiovascular and infectious diseases. Within the pharmaceutical business, another unit focuses on biotechnology to treat autoimmune disorders such as rheumatoid arthritis, psoriasis, and Crohn's disease. Yet another unit, the neurology unit, focuses on developing drugs for HIV/AIDS, hepatitis C, and tuberculosis. Traditionally these businesses were managed with a mixed related and unrelated strategy. Associated with this strategy was a definite approach focused on decentralization.

More recently, J&J aspired to not only have relatedness within the major businesses, but also to have corporate relatedness across all of its business units. CEO William Bolden has sought to propel growth by getting autonomous divisions to work more closely together. "The move suggests the desire to increase interaction to squeeze more value from areas where they overlap." The integrated approach aims to harness expertise from various units to harness and use its diagnostics testing equipment in diagnosing disease earlier than other products on the market. It is also seeking to harness expertise to better assist its glucose monitoring segment to more effectively monitor diabetes.

Other drug companies have been focused on either pharmaceuticals or consumer products and have been reducing the overlap. J&J has taken advantage of both positions and as a result has been more profitable during the current economic downturn than the more focused pharmaceutical or principal products companies. One major innovation between the pharmaceuticals and the device business was the drug-coated stent, which was originally created by Cordis, a division of its medical equipment business. This spurred competition in this industry with other stent makers, including Boston Scientific and Abbott Laboratories. J&J also increased the competition with its new device, Nevo, "a totally redesigned product" in the stent business.

Stephen Hepworth/Alamy

Johnson & Johnson's development of the drug-coated stent was made possible through the coordinated efforts of both their pharmaceutical and medical device businesses.

Besides innovation where the expertise of previously decentralized businesses is combined, J&J is seeking to pursue corporate relatedness in regard to marketing by completing a massive consolidation of its contracted media and advertising agencies. It has settled on a large involvement of several companies such as WPP and Interpublic Group. It is therefore pursuing a single brand according to market and channels and is forcing a consolidation of marketing across its businesses. The purpose for this strategic change is to create a more unified brand and decrease the high costs that are associated with each business unit handling its own media and advertising concepts.

In summary, J&J moved from a related linked strategy focused only on operational relatedness to a strategy that is focused more on pursuing both operational relatedness (with its separate businesses sharing operation activities) and corporate relatedness across its business units. It has strived to achieve greater innovation and management of the regulatory process as well as much better coordination across its businesses in marketing. There are other areas in which it is trying to develop more efficiencies, such as the production process. As such, it is pursuing both operational and corporate relatedness.

Sources: M. Arnold, 2009, J&J shows the way, *Medical Marketing and Media*, January, 39, 41, 43; 2008, J&J perks up, *Financial Times*, http://www.ft.com, December 1; J. Bennett, 2008, J&J: A balm for your portfolio, *Barron's*, October 27, 39; C. Bowe, 2008, Cautious chief with an impulse for innovation, *Financial Times*, http://www.ft.com, January 14, 14; P. Loftus & S. Wang, 2008, Earnings digest—pharmaceuticals: Diversified strategy buoys J&J's results, *Wall Street Journal*, July 16, B4; S. Wang, 2008, Corporate news: J&J acquires wellness firm, widening scope, *Wall Street Journal*, October 28, B3; A. Johnson, 2007, J&J realigns managers, revamps units; move calls for divisions to integrate their work, *Wall Street Journal*, November 16, A10.

STRATEGY
RIGHT NOW

Read more about the corporate-level strategies that guide decision-making at Johnson & Johnson.

www.cengage.com/ management/hitt

In large diversified firms, the corporate headquarters office distributes capital to its businesses to create value for the overall corporation. The nature of these distributions may generate gains from internal capital market allocations that exceed the gains that would accrue to shareholders as a result of capital being allocated by the external capital market.[66] Because those in a firm's corporate headquarters generally have access to detailed and accurate information regarding the actual and prospective performance of the company's portfolio of businesses, they have the best information to make capital distribution decisions.

Compared with corporate office personnel, external investors have relatively limited access to internal information and can only estimate the performances of individual businesses as well as their future prospects. Moreover, although businesses seeking capital must provide information to potential suppliers (such as banks or insurance companies), firms with internal capital markets may have at least two informational advantages. First, information provided to capital markets through annual reports and other sources may not include negative information, instead emphasizing positive prospects and outcomes. External sources of capital have limited ability to understand the operational dynamics of large organizations. Even external shareholders who have access to information have no guarantee of full and complete disclosure.[67] Second, although a firm must disseminate information, that information also becomes simultaneously available to the firm's current and potential competitors. With insights gained by studying such information, competitors might attempt to duplicate a firm's value-creating strategy. Thus, an ability to efficiently allocate capital through an internal market may help the firm protect the competitive advantages it develops while using its corporate-level strategy as well as its various business-unit level strategies.

If intervention from outside the firm is required to make corrections to capital allocations, only significant changes are possible, such as forcing the firm into bankruptcy or changing the top management team. Alternatively, in an internal capital market, the corporate headquarters office can fine-tune its corrections, such as choosing to adjust managerial incentives or suggesting strategic changes in one of the firm's businesses. Thus, capital can be allocated according to more specific criteria than is possible with external market allocations. Because it has less accurate information, the external capital market may fail to allocate resources adequately to high-potential investments. The corporate headquarters office of a diversified company can more effectively perform such tasks as disciplining underperforming management teams through resource allocations.[68]

Large, highly diversified businesses often face what is known as the "conglomerate discount." This discount results from analysts not knowing how to value a vast array of large businesses with complex financial reports. For instance, one analyst suggested in regard to figuring out GE's financial results in its quarterly report, "A Rubik's cube may in fact be easier to figure out."[69] To overcome this discount, many unrelated diversified or industrial conglomerates have sought to establish a brand for the parent company. For instance, recent advertisements by GE "moved its focus from customer comfort and convenience ("We Bring Good Things to Life") to a more future-oriented mantra ("Imagination at Work") that promises creative and innovative products."[70] More recently, United Technologies initiated a brand development approach with the slogan "United Technologies. You can see everything from here." United Technologies suggested that its earnings multiple (PE ratio) compared to its stock price is only average even though its performance has been better than other conglomerates in its group. It is hoping that the "umbrella" brand advertisement will raise its PE to a level comparable to its competitors.[71]

In spite of the challenges associated with it, a number of corporations continue to use the unrelated diversification strategy, especially in Europe and in emerging markets. Siemens, for example, is a large German conglomerate with a highly diversified approach. Its former CEO argued that "When you are in an up-cycle and the capital markets have plenty of opportunities to invest in single-industry companies … investors savor those opportunities. But when things change pure plays go down faster than you can look."[72] In the current downturn, diversification is helping some companies improve future performance,[73] as the Oracle Strategic Focus illustrates.

The Achilles' heel for firms using the unrelated diversification strategy in a developed economy is that competitors can imitate financial economies more easily than they can replicate the value gained from the economies of scope developed through operational relatedness and corporate relatedness. This issue is less of a problem in emerging economies, where the absence of a "soft infrastructure" (including effective financial intermediaries, sound regulations, and contract laws) supports and encourages use of the unrelated diversification strategy.[74] In fact, in emerging economies such as those in Korea, India, and Chile, research has shown that diversification increases the performance of firms affiliated with large diversified business groups.[75]

Restructuring of Assets

Financial economies can also be created when firms learn how to create value by buying, restructuring, and then selling the restructured companies' assets in the external market.[76] As in the real estate business, buying assets at low prices, restructuring them, and selling them at a price that exceeds their cost generates a positive return on the firm's invested capital.

As the ensuing Strategic Focus on unrelated diversified companies that pursue this strategy suggests, creating financial economies by acquiring and restructuring other companies' assets involves significant trade-offs. For example, Danaher's success requires a focus on mature, manufacturing businesses because of the uncertainty of demand for high-technology products. In high-technology businesses, resource allocation decisions become too complex, creating information-processing overload on the small corporate headquarters offices that are common in unrelated diversified firms. High-technology businesses are often human-resource dependent; these people can leave or demand higher pay and thus appropriate or deplete the value of an acquired firm.[77]

Buying and then restructuring service-based assets so they can be profitably sold in the external market is also difficult. Sales in such instances are often a product of close personal relationships between a client and the representative of the firm being restructured. Thus, for both high-technology firms and service-based companies, relatively few tangible assets can be restructured to create value and sell profitably. It is difficult to restructure intangible assets such as human capital and effective relationships that have evolved over time between buyers (customers) and sellers (firm personnel). As the Strategic Focus Segment also indicates, care must be taken in a downturn to restructure

STRATEGIC FOCUS

DANAHER AND ITW: SERIAL ACQUIRERS OF DIVERSIFIED INDUSTRIAL MANUFACTURING BUSINESSES

Danaher has four broad industrial strategic business units, including professional instrumentation (test and measurement, and environmental instrumentation), medical technologies (dental equipment and consumables, life sciences and acute care, and diagnostics), industrial technologies (including motion and product identification, aerospace and defense, water quality, and censors and controls), and tools and components (Craftsman Hand Tools, Jacobs Chuck Manufacturing and Jacobs Vehicle Systems, Delta Consolidated Industries, and Hennessy Industries). Each set of businesses is quite broad and relatively diversified across the strategic business unit. Danaher's strategy is focused on acquisitions and restructuring of the acquired businesses.

Once a business is acquired, experts from the Danaher corporate headquarters visit the new subsidiary and seek to establish the firm's philosophy and value set and improve productivity through proven lean manufacturing techniques and processes. The processes are focused on improved quality, delivery of products, and cost improvement, as well as product and process innovation. Although its acquisition activity slowed down in 2008, Danaher generated $1.6 billion in free cash flow, which will allow it to pursue more acquisitions when opportunities arise. The company's largest deal occurred in 2007 when it purchased Tektronix, adding $1.2 billion in revenue to its overall $12.7 billion revenue in 2008.

GIPhotoStock Z/Alamy

Interestingly, Danaher also sold off its power quality business to Thomas & Betts Corporation in 2007, illustrating that it also makes timely divestitures.

Illinois Tool Works (ITW), a similar serial acquirer, has bid against Danaher for deals in the past. It too slowed its M&A activity in 2008. ITW started out as a toolmaker and tripled its size in the past decade to 750 business units worldwide. Its acquisition and diversification strategy focuses on small, low-margin but mature industrial businesses. Examples of its products include screws, auto parts, deli-slicers, and the plastic rings that hold together soft drink cans. It seeks to restructure each business it acquires in order to increase the business unit's profit margins by focusing on a narrowly defined product range and targeting the most lucrative products and customers using the 80/20 concept, where 80 percent of the revenues are derived from 20 percent of the customers. Most of its acquisitions are under $100 million. These firms seek to buy low, restructure, and operate, as well as selectively divest after the restructuring.

Although no company is immune, Danaher has done better in the recession than other similar highly diversified industrial firms, such as General Electric, because it sells many of its products to universities and hospitals, which have not had drastic budget cuts as have other commercial businesses in the downturn.

Sources: B. Tita, 2009, Danaher defies skeptics, stands by 2009 forecast, *Wall Street Journal*, March 4, B7; 2008, Comparing the machinery companies, *Shareowner*, March 2008, 15–21; 2008, Danaher business system, http://www.danaher.com, March 21; D. K. Berman, 2007, Danaher is set to buy Tektronix: Purchase for $2.8 billion would be firm's largest: Big boost in test division, *Wall Street Journal*, October 15, A3; R. Brat, 2007, Turning managers into takeover artists: How conglomerate ITW mints new deal makers to fuel its expansion, *Wall Street Journal*, April 6, A1, A8.

and buy and sell at appropriate times. The downturn can also present opportunities as the Oracle Strategic Focus notes. Ideally, executives will follow a strategy of buying businesses when prices are lower, such as in the midst of a recession and selling them at late stages in an expansion.[78]

Value-Neutral Diversification: Incentives and Resources

The objectives firms seek when using related diversification and unrelated diversification strategies all have the potential to help the firm create value by using a corporate-level strategy. However, these strategies, as well as single- and dominant-business diversification strategies, are sometimes used with value-neutral rather than value-creating objectives in mind. As we discuss next, different incentives to diversify sometimes exist, and the quality of the firm's resources may permit only diversification that is value neutral rather than value creating.

Incentives to Diversify

Incentives to diversify come from both the external environment and a firm's internal environment. External incentives include antitrust regulations and tax laws. Internal incentives include low performance, uncertain future cash flows, and the pursuit of synergy and reduction of risk for the firm.

Antitrust Regulation and Tax Laws

Government antitrust policies and tax laws provided incentives for U.S. firms to diversify in the 1960s and 1970s.[79] Antitrust laws prohibiting mergers that created increased market power (via either vertical or horizontal integration) were stringently enforced during that period.[80] Merger activity that produced conglomerate diversification was encouraged primarily by the Celler-Kefauver Antimerger Act (1950), which discouraged horizontal and vertical mergers. As a result, many of the mergers during the 1960s and 1970s were "conglomerate" in character, involving companies pursuing different lines of business. Between 1973 and 1977, 79.1 percent of all mergers were conglomerate in nature.[81]

During the 1980s, antitrust enforcement lessened, resulting in more and larger horizontal mergers (acquisitions of target firms in the same line of business, such as a merger between two oil companies).[82] In addition, investment bankers became more open to the kinds of mergers facilitated by regulation changes; as a consequence, takeovers increased to unprecedented numbers.[83] The conglomerates, or highly diversified firms, of the 1960s and 1970s became more "focused" in the 1980s and early 1990s as merger constraints were relaxed and restructuring was implemented.[84]

In the late 1990s and early 2000s, antitrust concerns emerged again with the large volume of mergers and acquisitions (see Chapter 7).[85] Mergers are now receiving more scrutiny than they did in the 1980s and through the early 1990s.[86] For example, in the merger between P&G and Gillette, regulators required that each firm divest certain businesses before they were allowed to secure the deal.

The tax effects of diversification stem not only from corporate tax changes, but also from individual tax rates. Some companies (especially mature ones) generate more cash from their operations than they can reinvest profitably. Some argue that *free cash flows* (liquid financial assets for which investments in current businesses are no longer economically viable) should be redistributed to shareholders as dividends.[87] However, in the 1960s and 1970s, dividends were taxed more heavily than were capital gains. As a result, before 1980, shareholders preferred that firms use free cash flows to buy and build companies in high-performance industries. If the firm's stock value appreciated over the long term, shareholders might receive a better return on those funds than if the funds had been redistributed as dividends, because returns from stock sales would be taxed more lightly than would dividends.

Under the 1986 Tax Reform Act, however, the top individual ordinary income tax rate was reduced from 50 to 28 percent, and the special capital gains tax was changed to treat capital gains as ordinary income. These changes created an incentive for shareholders to stop encouraging firms to retain funds for purposes of diversification. These tax law changes also influenced an increase in divestitures of unrelated business units after 1984. Thus, while individual tax rates for capital gains and dividends created a shareholder incentive to increase diversification before 1986, they encouraged less diversification after 1986, unless it was funded by tax-deductible debt. The elimination of personal interest deductions, as well as the lower attractiveness of retained earnings to shareholders, might prompt the use of more leverage by firms (interest expenses are tax deductible).

Corporate tax laws also affect diversification. Acquisitions typically increase a firm's depreciable asset allowances. Increased depreciation (a non-cash-flow expense) produces lower taxable income, thereby providing an additional incentive for acquisitions. Before 1986, acquisitions may have been the most attractive means for securing tax benefits,[88] but the 1986 Tax Reform Act diminished some of the corporate tax advantages of diversification.[89] The recent changes recommended by the Financial Accounting Standards Board eliminated the "pooling of interests" method to account for the acquired firm's assets and it also eliminated the write-off for research and development in process, and thus reduced some of the incentives to make acquisitions, especially acquisitions in related high-technology industries (these changes are discussed further in Chapter 7).[90]

Although federal regulations were loosened somewhat in the 1980s and then retightened in the late 1990s, a number of industries experienced increased merger activity due to industry-specific deregulation activity, including banking, telecommunications, oil and gas, and electric utilities. For instance, in banking the Garns–St. Germain Deposit Institutions Act of 1982 (GDIA) and the Competitive Equality Banking Act of 1987 (CEBA) reshaped the acquisition frequency in banking by relaxing the regulations that limited interstate bank acquisitions.[91] Regulation changes have also affected convergence between media and telecommunications industries, which has allowed a number of mergers, such as the successive Time Warner and AOL mergers. The Federal Communications Commission (FCC) made a highly contested ruling "allowing broadcasters to own TV stations that reach 45 percent of U.S. households (up from 35 percent), own three stations in the largest markets (up from two), and own a TV station and newspaper in the same town."[92] Thus, regulatory changes such as the ones we have described create incentives or disincentives for diversification. Interestingly, European antitrust laws have historically been stricter regarding horizontal mergers than those in the United States, but more recently have become similar.[93]

Low Performance

Some research shows that low returns are related to greater levels of diversification.[94] If "high performance eliminates the need for greater diversification,"[95] then low performance may provide an incentive for diversification. In 2005, eBay acquired Skype for $3.1 billion in hopes that it would create synergies and improve communication between buyers and sellers. However, in 2008 eBay announced that it would sell Skype if the opportunity presents itself because it has failed to increase cash flow for its core e-commerce business and the synergies have not been realized. Some critics have even urged eBay to rid itself of PayPal in order to boost its share price.[96]

Research evidence and the experience of a number of firms suggest that an overall curvilinear relationship, as illustrated in Figure 6.3, may exist between diversification and performance.[97] Although low performance can be an incentive to diversify, firms that are more broadly diversified compared to their competitors may have overall lower performance. Further, broadly based banks, such as Citigroup and UBS as noted earlier, have been under pressure to "break up" because they seem to underperform compared to their peers. Additionally, before being acquired by Barclays in 2009, Lehman Brothers

Figure 6.3 The Curvilinear Relationship between Diversification and Performance

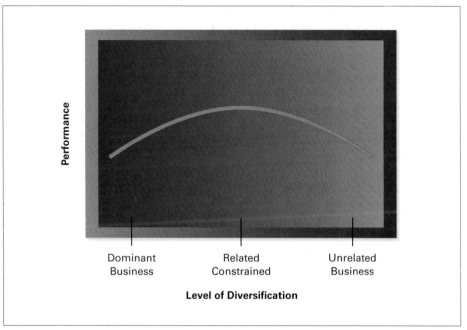

divested much of its asset management and commercial mortgage businesses to improve the company's cash flow.[98]

Uncertain Future Cash Flows

As a firm's product line matures or is threatened, diversification may be an important defensive strategy.[99] Small firms and companies in mature or maturing industries sometimes find it necessary to diversify for long-term survival.[100] For example, auto-industry suppliers have been slowly diversifying into other more promising businesses such as "green" businesses and medical supplies as the auto industry has declined. Dephi, for instance, once part of General Motors, has been expanding its electric car battery expertise into residential energy systems. Abbott Workholding Products, Inc. has been expanding its industrial tools business into tools for making artificial knee and bone replacements.[101]

Diversifying into other product markets or into other businesses can reduce the uncertainty about a firm's future cash flows. Merck looked to expand into the biosimilars business (production of drugs which are similar to approved drugs) in hopes of stimulating its prescription drug business due to lower expected results as many of its drug patents expire.[102] For example, in 2009 it purchased Insmed's portfolio of follow-on biologics for $130 million. It will carry out the development of biologics that prevent infections in cancer patients receiving chemotherapy. Such drugs include, INS-19 is in late-stage trials while INS-20 is in early-stage development.[103]

Synergy and Firm Risk Reduction

Diversified firms pursuing economies of scope often have investments that are too inflexible to realize synergy between business units. As a result, a number of problems may arise. **Synergy** exists when the value created by business units working together exceeds the value that those same units create working independently. But as a firm increases its relatedness between business units, it also increases its risk of corporate failure, because synergy produces joint interdependence between businesses that constrains the firm's flexibility to respond. This threat may force two basic decisions.

Synergy exists when the value created by business units working together exceeds the value that those same units create working independently.

First, the firm may reduce its level of technological change by operating in environments that are more certain. This behavior may make the firm risk averse and thus uninterested in pursuing new product lines that have potential, but are not proven. Alternatively, the firm may constrain its level of activity sharing and forgo synergy's potential benefits. Either or both decisions may lead to further diversification.[104] The former would lead to related diversification into industries in which more certainty exists. The latter may produce additional, but unrelated, diversification.[105] Research suggests that a firm using a related diversification strategy is more careful in bidding for new businesses, whereas a firm pursuing an unrelated diversification strategy may be more likely to overprice its bid, because an unrelated bidder may not have full information about the acquired firm.[106] However, firms using either a related or an unrelated diversification strategy must understand the consequences of paying large premiums.[107] In the situation with eBay, former CEO Meg Whitman received heavy criticism for paying such a high price for Skype, especially when the firm did not realize the synergies it was seeking.

Resources and Diversification

As already discussed, firms may have several value-neutral incentives as well as value-creating incentives (such as the ability to create economies of scope) to diversify. However, even when incentives to diversify exist, a firm must have the types and levels of resources and capabilities needed to successfully use a corporate-level diversification strategy.[108] Although both tangible and intangible resources facilitate diversification, they vary in their ability to create value. Indeed, the degree to which resources are valuable, rare, difficult to imitate, and nonsubstitutable (see Chapter 3) influences a firm's ability to create value through diversification. For instance, free cash flows are a tangible financial resource that may be used to diversify the firm. However, compared with diversification that is grounded in intangible resources, diversification based on financial resources only is more visible to competitors and thus more imitable and less likely to create value on a long-term basis.[109]

Tangible resources usually include the plant and equipment necessary to produce a product and tend to be less-flexible assets. Any excess capacity often can be used only for closely related products, especially those requiring highly similar manufacturing technologies. For example, Acer Inc. hopes to benefit during the current economic downturn and build market share through a related diversification move. Acer believes that the large computer makers such as Dell and Hewlett-Packard have underestimated the demand for mini-notebook or "netbook" computers. Acer diversified into these compact machines and now has about 30 percent of the market share. These smaller and less expensive machines are expected to become 15 to 20 percent of the overall PC market. It has also expanded into "smart phones" and at the same time has created seamless integration between such phones and PCs for data transfer. There are obvious manufacturing and sales integration opportunities between its basic tangible assets and these related diversification moves.[110]

Excess capacity of other tangible resources, such as a sales force, can be used to diversify more easily. Again, excess capacity in a sales force is more effective with related diversification, because it may be utilized to sell similar products. The sales force would be more knowledgeable about related-product characteristics, customers, and distribution channels.[111] Tangible resources may create resource interrelationships in production, marketing, procurement, and technology, defined earlier as activity sharing. Intangible resources are more flexible than tangible physical assets in facilitating diversification. Although the sharing of tangible resources may induce diversification, intangible resources such as tacit knowledge could encourage even more diversification.[112]

The small "EEE" Acer notebook computer (shown here in white) facilitates Acer's related diversification strategy.

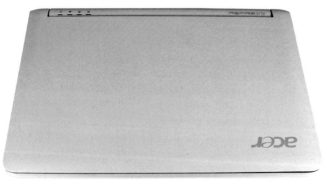

Sometimes, however, the benefits expected from using resources to diversify the firm for either value-creating or value-neutral reasons are not gained.[113] For example, as noted in the Opening Case, implementing operational relatedness has been difficult for the Foster's Group in integrating the wine and beer businesses; the joint marketing operation was a failure. Also, Sara Lee executives found that they could not realize synergy between elements of its diversified portfolio, and subsequently shed businesses accounting for 40 percent of is revenue to focus on food and food-related products to more readily achieve synergy. The downturn has caused Sara Lee to continue this process in order to more sharply focus possible synergies between businesses.[114]

Value-Reducing Diversification: Managerial Motives to Diversify

Managerial motives to diversify can exist independent of value-neutral reasons (i.e., incentives and resources) and value-creating reasons (e.g., economies of scope). The desire for increased compensation and reduced managerial risk are two motives for top-level executives to diversify their firm beyond value-creating and value-neutral levels.[115] In slightly different words, top-level executives may diversify a firm in order to diversify their own employment risk, as long as profitability does not suffer excessively.[116]

Diversification provides additional benefits to top-level managers that shareholders do not enjoy. Research evidence shows that diversification and firm size are highly correlated, and as firm size increases, so does executive compensation.[117] Because large firms are complex, difficult-to-manage organizations, top-level managers commonly receive substantial levels of compensation to lead them.[118] Greater levels of diversification can increase a firm's complexity, resulting in still more compensation for executives to lead an increasingly diversified organization. Governance mechanisms, such as the board of directors, monitoring by owners, executive compensation practices, and the market for corporate control, may limit managerial tendencies to overdiversify. These mechanisms are discussed in more detail in Chapter 10.

In some instances, though, a firm's governance mechanisms may not be strong, resulting in a situation in which executives may diversify the firm to the point that it fails to earn even average returns.[119] The loss of adequate internal governance may result in poor relative performance, thereby triggering a threat of takeover. Although takeovers may improve efficiency by replacing ineffective managerial teams, managers may avoid takeovers through defensive tactics, such as "poison pills," or may reduce their own exposure with "golden parachute" agreements.[120] Therefore, an external governance threat, although restraining managers, does not flawlessly control managerial motives for diversification.[121]

Most large publicly held firms are profitable because the managers leading them are positive stewards of firm resources, and many of their strategic actions, including those related to selecting a corporate-level diversification strategy, contribute to the firm's success.[122] As mentioned, governance mechanisms should be designed to deal with exceptions to the managerial norms of making decisions and taking actions that will increase the firm's ability to earn above-average returns. Thus, it is overly pessimistic to assume that managers usually act in their own self-interest as opposed to their firm's interest.[123]

Top-level executives' diversification decisions may also be held in check by concerns for their reputation. If a positive reputation facilitates development and use of managerial power, a poor reputation may reduce it. Likewise, a strong external market for managerial talent may deter managers from pursuing inappropriate diversification.[124] In addition, a diversified firm may police other firms by acquiring those that are poorly managed in order to restructure its own asset base. Knowing that their firms could be acquired if they are not managed successfully encourages executives to use value-creating, diversification strategies.

As shown in Figure 6.4, the level of diversification that can be expected to have the greatest positive effect on performance is based partly on how the interaction of resources, managerial motives, and incentives affects the adoption of particular diversification strategies. As indicated earlier, the greater the incentives and the more flexible the resources, the higher the level of expected diversification. Financial resources (the most flexible) should have a stronger relationship to the extent of diversification than either tangible or intangible resources. Tangible resources (the most inflexible) are useful primarily for related diversification.

As discussed in this chapter, firms can create more value by effectively using diversification strategies. However, diversification must be kept in check by corporate governance (see Chapter 10). Appropriate strategy implementation tools, such as organizational structures, are also important (see Chapter 11).

We have described corporate-level strategies in this chapter. In the next chapter, we discuss mergers and acquisitions as prominent means for firms to diversify and to grow profitably. These trends toward more diversification through acquisitions, which have been partially reversed due to restructuring (see Chapter 7), indicate that learning has taken place regarding corporate-level diversification strategies.[125] Accordingly, firms that diversify should do so cautiously, choosing to focus on relatively few, rather than many, businesses. In fact, research suggests that although unrelated diversification has

Figure 6.4 Summary Model of the Relationship between Diversification and Firm Performance

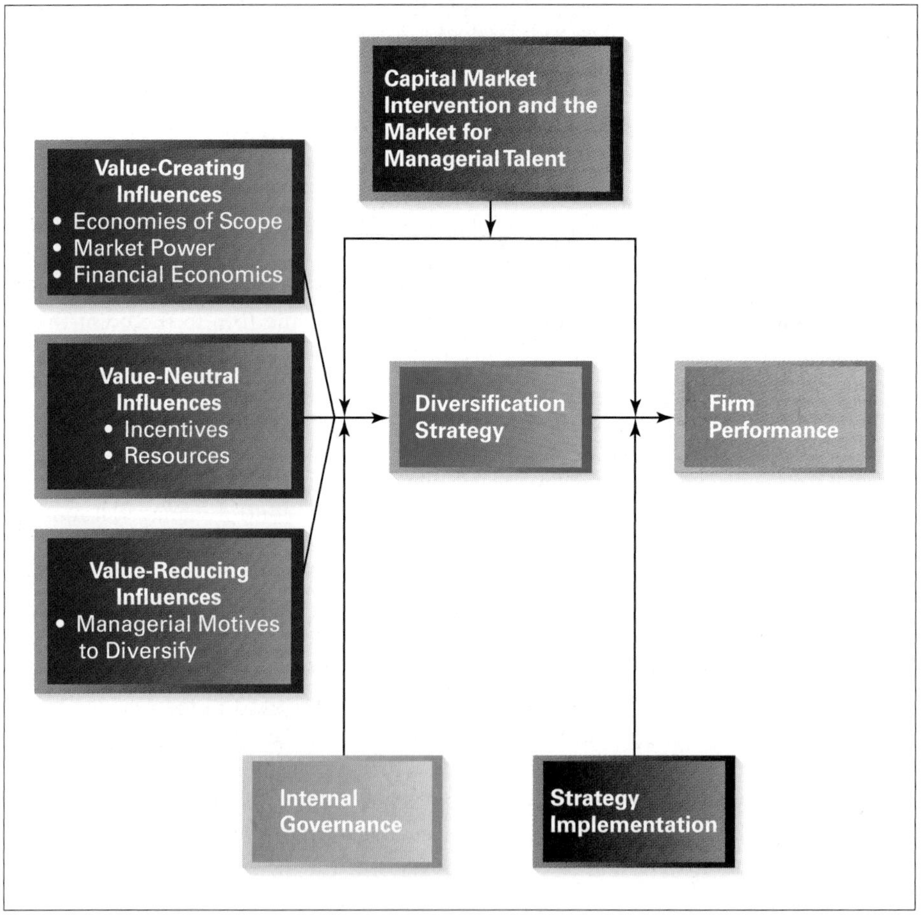

Source: Adapted from R. E. Hoskisson & M. A. Hitt, 1990, Antecedents and performance outcomes of diversification: A review and critique of theoretical perspectives, *Journal of Management*, 16: 498.

decreased, related diversification has increased, possibly due to the restructuring that continued into the 1990s and early twenty-first century. This sequence of diversification followed by restructuring is now taking place in Europe and other places such as Korea, mirroring actions of firms in the United States and the United Kingdom.[126] Firms can improve their strategic competitiveness when they pursue a level of diversification that is appropriate for their resources (especially financial resources) and core competencies and the opportunities and threats in their country's institutional and competitive environments.[127]

SUMMARY

- The primary reason a firm uses a corporate-level strategy to become more diversified is to create additional value. Using a single- or dominant-business corporate-level strategy may be preferable to seeking a more diversified strategy, unless a corporation can develop economies of scope or financial economies between businesses, or unless it can obtain market power through additional levels of diversification. Economies of scope and market power are the main sources of value creation when the firm diversifies by using a corporate-level strategy with moderate to high levels of diversification.

- The related diversification corporate-level strategy helps the firm create value by sharing activities or transferring competencies between different businesses in the company's portfolio.

- Sharing activities usually involves sharing tangible resources between businesses. Transferring core competencies involves transferring core competencies developed in one business to another business. It also may involve transferring competencies between the corporate headquarters office and a business unit.

- Sharing activities is usually associated with the related constrained diversification corporate-level strategy. Activity sharing is costly to implement and coordinate, may create unequal benefits for the divisions involved in the sharing, and may lead to fewer managerial risk-taking behaviors.

- Transferring core competencies is often associated with related linked (or mixed related and unrelated) diversification,

although firms pursuing both sharing activities and transferring core competencies can also use the related linked strategy.

- Efficiently allocating resources or restructuring a target firm's assets and placing them under rigorous financial controls are two ways to accomplish successful unrelated diversification. Firms using the unrelated diversification strategy focus on creating financial economies to generate value.

- Diversification is sometimes pursued for value-neutral reasons. Incentives from tax and antitrust government policies, performance disappointments, or uncertainties about future cash flow are examples of value-neutral reasons that firms may choose to become more diversified.

- Managerial motives to diversify (including to increase compensation) can lead to overdiversification and a subsequent reduction in a firm's ability to create value. Evidence suggests, however, that the majority of top-level executives seek to be good stewards of the firm's assets and avoid diversifying the firm in ways and amounts that destroy value.

- Managers need to pay attention to their firm's internal organization and its external environment when making decisions about the optimum level of diversification for their company. Of course, internal resources are important determinants of the direction that diversification should take. However, conditions in the firm's external environment may facilitate additional levels of diversification, as might unexpected threats from competitors.

REVIEW QUESTIONS

1. What is corporate-level strategy and why is it important?

2. What are the different levels of diversification firms can pursue by using different corporate-level strategies?

3. What are three reasons firms choose to diversify their operations?

4. How do firms create value when using a related diversification strategy?

5. What are the two ways to obtain financial economies when using an unrelated diversification strategy?

6. What incentives and resources encourage diversification?

7. What motives might encourage managers to overdiversify their firm?

EXPERIENTIAL EXERCISES

EXERCISE 1: COMPARISON OF DIVERSIFICATION STRATEGIES

The use of diversification varies both across and within industries. In some industries, most firms may follow a single- or dominant-product approach. Other industries are characterized by a mix of both single-product and heavily diversified firms. The purpose of this exercise is to learn how the use of diversification varies across firms in an industry, and the implications of such use.

Part One

Working in small teams of four to seven people, choose an industry to research. You will then select two firms in that industry for further analysis. Many resources can aid you in identifying specific firms in an industry for analysis. One option is to visit the Web site of the New York Stock Exchange (http://www.nyse.com), which has an option to screen firms by industry group. A second option is http://www.hoovers.com, which offers similar listings. Identify two public firms based in the United States. (Note that Hoovers includes some private firms, and the NYSE includes some foreign firms. Data for the exercise are often unavailable for foreign or private companies.)

Once a target firm is identified, you will need to collect business segment data for each company. Segment data break down the company's revenues and net income by major lines of business. These data are reported in the firm's SEC 10-K filing and may also be reported in the annual report. Both the annual report and 10-K are usually found on the company's Web site; both the Hoovers and NYSE listings include company homepage information. For the most recent three-year period available, calculate the following:

- Percentage growth in segment sales
- Net profit margin by segment

- Bonus item: compare profitability to industry averages (*Industry Norms and Key Business Ratios* publishes profit norms by major industry segment)

Next, based on your reading of the company filings and these statistics, determine whether the firm is best classified as:

- Single product
- Dominant product
- Related diversified
- Unrelated diversified

Part Two

Prepare a brief PowerPoint presentation for use in class discussion. Address the following in the presentation:

- Describe the extent and nature of diversification used at each firm.
- Can you provide a motive for the firm's diversification strategy, given the rationales for diversification put forth in the chapter?
- Which firm's diversification strategy appears to be more effective? Try to justify your answer by explaining why you think one firm's strategy is more effective than the other.

EXERCISE 2: HOW DOES THE FIRM'S PORTFOLIO STACK UP?

The BCG (Boston Consulting Group) product portfolio matrix has been around for decades and was introduced by the BCG as a way for firms to understand the priorities that should be given to the various segments within their mix of businesses. It is based on a matrix with two vertices: firm market share and projected market growth rate, as shown below:

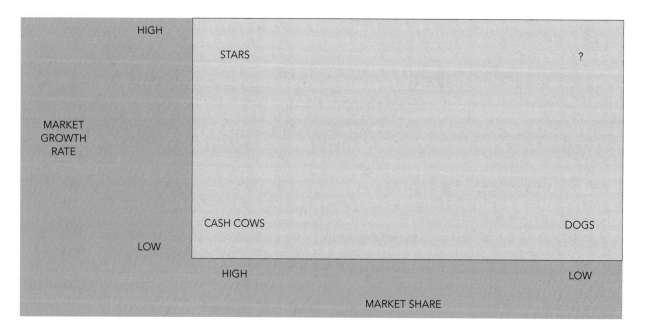

Each firm therefore can categorize its business units as follows:

- Stars: High growth and high market share. These business units generate large amounts of cash but also use large amounts of cash. These are often the focus of the firm's priorities as these segments have a potentially bright future.
- Cash Cows: Low market growth coupled with high market share. Profits and cash generated are high; the need for new cash is low. Provides a foundation for the firm from which it can launch new initiatives.
- Dogs: Low market growth and low market share. This is usually a situation firms seek to avoid. This is quite often the target of a turnaround plan or liquidation effort.
- Question Marks: High market growth but low market share. Creates a need to move strategically because of high demands on cash due to market needs yet low cash returns because of the low firm market share.

This way to analyze a firm's corporate level strategy or the way in which it rewards and prioritizes its business units has come under some criticism. For one, market share is not the only way in which a firm should view success or potential success; second, market growth is not the only indicator for the attractiveness of a market; and third, sometimes "dogs" can earn as much cash as "cows."

Part One

Pick a publicly traded firm that has a diversified corporate-level strategy. The more unrelated the segments the better.

Part Two

Analyze the firm using the BCG matrix. In order to do this you will need to develop market share ratings for each operating unit and assess the overall market attractiveness for that segment.

VIDEO CASE

THE RISKS OF DIVERSIFICATION

Sir Mark Weinberg President/St. James's Place Capital

Sir Mark Weinberg discusses the wisdom, or lack thereof, in firms that diversify their portfolio of businesses. Having been a director of a firm (British American Tobacco) that implemented an unrelated diversification strategy to reduce risk in the company's core business units, Sir Weinberg has keen insights into the wisdom of this strategy.

Before you watch the video consider the following concepts and questions and be prepared to discuss them in class:

Concepts

- Executive hubris
- Diversification
- Risk

- Unrelated acquisition
- Core competency

Questions

1. Think about firms that implement an unrelated diversification strategy. Why are some firms able to implement this corporate level strategy effectively while others struggle?
2. Read the history of British American Tobacco since 1969 from the company's Web site. What impressions do you take away from this?
3. British American Tobacco utilized the concept of risk minimization as a reason for diversification away from its core business. Do you consider this to be a valid rationale for implementing an unrelated diversification strategy?
4. How do public equity markets value unrelated diversification strategies and why do you think they do so?

NOTES

1. M. E. Porter, 1980, *Competitive Strategy*, New York: The Free Press, xvi.
2. M. D. R. Chari, S. Devaraj, & P. David, 2008, The impact of information technology investments and diversification strategies on firm performance, *Management Science*, 54: 224–234; A. Pehrsson, 2006, Business relatedness and performance: A study of managerial perceptions, *Strategic Management Journal*, 27: 265–282.
3. A. Hargrave-Silk, 2008, Media Brands moves to diversify, Media 3, November.
4. S. Walters & R. Stone, 2007, The trouble with rose-colored glasses, *Barron's*, June 25, M10.
5. A. O'Connell, 2009, Lego CEO Jørgen Vig Knudstorp on leading through survival and growth, *Harvard Business Review*, 87(1): 1–2.
6. M. E. Porter, 1987, From competitive advantage to corporate strategy, *Harvard Business Review*, 65(3): 43–59.
7. Ibid.; M. E. Raynor, 2007, What is corporate strategy, really? *Ivey Business Journal*, 71(8): 1–3.
8. E. Ellis, 2008, What'll you have, mate? *Barron's*, October 27, 34–36.
9. A. A. Calart & J. E. Ricart, 2007, Corporate strategy: An agent-based approach, *European Management Review*, 4: 107–120; M. Kwak, 2002, Maximizing value through diversification, *MIT Sloan Management Review*, 43(2): 10.
10. K. Lee, M. W. Peng, & K. Lee, 2008, From diversification premium to diversification discount during institutional transitions, *Journal of World Business*, 43(1): 47–65; M. Ammann & M. Verhofen, 2006, The conglomerate discount: A new explanation based on credit risk, *International Journal of Theoretical & Applied Finance*, 9(8): 1201–1214; S. A. Mansi & D. M. Reeb, 2002, Corporate diversification: What gets discounted? *Journal of Finance*, 57: 2167–2183.
11. N. M. Schmid & I. Walter, 2009, Do financial conglomerates create or

destroy economic value? *Journal of Financial Intermediation*, 18(2): 193–216; C. E. Helfat & K. M. Eisenhardt, 2004, Intertemporal economies of scope organizational modularity, and the dynamics of diversification, *Strategic Management Journal*, 25: 1217–1232.

12. A. Campbell, M. Goold, & M. Alexander, 1995, Corporate strategy: The question for parenting advantage, *Harvard Business Review*, 73(2): 120–132.

13. D. Collis, D. Young, & M. Goold, 2007, The size, structure, and performance of corporate headquarters, *Strategic Management Journal*, 28: 283–405; M. Goold & A. Campbell, 2002, Parenting in complex structures, *Long Range Planning*, 35(3): 219–243; T. H. Brush, P. Bromiley, & M. Hendrickx, 1999, The relative influence of industry and corporation on business segment performance: An alternative estimate, *Strategic Management Journal*, 20: 519–547.

14. H. Chesbrough, 2007, The market for innovation: Implications for corporate strategy, *California Management Review*, 49(3): 45–66; D. Miller, 2006, Technological diversity, related diversification, and firm performance, *Strategic Management Journal*, 27: 601–619; D. J. Miller, 2004, Firms' technological resources and the performance effects of diversification: A longitudinal study, *Strategic Management Journal*, 25: 1097–1119.

15. D. D. Bergh, 2001, Diversification strategy research at a crossroads: Established, emerging and anticipated paths, in M. A. Hitt, R. E. Freeman, & J. S. Harrison (eds.), *Handbook of Strategic Management*, Oxford, UK: Blackwell Publishers, 363–383.

16. H. C. Wang & J. B. Barney, 2006, Employee incentives to make firm-specific investments: Implications for resource-based theories of corporate diversification, *Academy of Management Journal*, 31: 466–476.

17. J. J. Marcel, 2009, Why top management team characteristics matter when employing a chief operating officer: A strategic contingency perspective, *Strategic Management Journal*, 30(6): 647–658; A. J. Ward, M. J. Lankau, A. C. Amason, J. A. Sonnenfeld, & B. R. Agle, 2007, Improving the performance of top management teams, *MIT Sloan Management Review*, 48(3): 85–90.

18. R. P. Rumelt, *Strategy, Structure, and Economic Performance*, Boston: Harvard Business School, 1974; L. Wrigley, 1970, *Divisional Autonomy and Diversification* (Ph.D. dissertation), Harvard Business School.

19. P. Gogoi, N. Arndt, & J. Crown, 2008, A bittersweet deal for Wrigley: Selling the family business wasn't William Wrigley Jr.'s plan, but the Mars offer was too good to refuse, *BusinessWeek*, May 12, 34.

20. 2009, United Parcel Service 2008 Annual Report, http://www.ups.com, June 14.

21. 2009, Hutchison Whampoa Limited, http://www.hoovers.com, March 15; J. Spencer, 2007, Hutchison's Li looks to make well-timed exit; Indian wireless assets may yield a windfall; a bigger risk to buyers, *Wall Street Journal*, January 29, B4.

22. M. Lee, 2008, Hutch Telecom to pay special dividend; shares surge (update2), http://www.bloomberg.com, November 12; 2007, What has Superman got up his sleeve? *Euroweek*, February 23, 1.

23. M. A. Williams, T. B. Michael, & E. R. Waller, 2008, Managerial incentives and acquisitions: A survey of the literature. *Managerial Finance*, 34(5): 328–341; S. W. Geiger & L. H. Cashen, 2007, Organizational size and CEO compensation: The moderating effect of diversification in downscoping organizations, *Journal of Managerial Issues*, 9(2): 233–252; R. K. Aggarwal & A. A. Samwick, 2003, Why do managers diversify their firms? Agency reconsidered, *Journal of Finance*, 58: 71–118.

24. D. J. Miller, M. J. Fern, & L. B. Cardinal, 2007, The use of knowledge for technological innovation within diversified firms, *Academy of Management Journal*, 50: 308–326.

25. H. Tanriverdi & C. -H. Lee, 2008, Within-industry diversification and firm performance in the presence of network externalities: Evidence from the software industry, *Academy of Management Journal*, 51(2): 381–397; H. Tanriverdi & N. Venkatraman, 2005, Knowledge relatedness and the performance of multibusiness firms, *Strategic Management Journal*, 26: 97–119.

26. M. D. R. Chari, S. Devaraj, & P. David, 2008, The impact of information technology investments and diversification strategies on firm performance, *Management Science*, 54(1): 224–234; H. Tanriverdi, 2006, Performance effects of information technology synergies in multibusiness firms, *MIS Quarterly*, 30(1): 57–78.

27. M. E. Porter, 1985, *Competitive Advantage*, New York: Free Press, 328.

28. N. Shin, 2009, Information technology and diversification: How their relationship affects firm performance. *International Journal of E-Collaboration*, 5(1): 69–83; D. Miller, 2006, Technological diversity, related diversification, and firm performance, *Strategic Management Journal*, 27: 601–619.

29. Tanriverdi & Lee, Within-industry diversification and firm performance in the presence of network externalities: Evidence from the software industry; P. Puranam & K. Srikanth, 2007, What they know vs. what they do: How acquirers leverage technology acquisitions, *Strategic Management Journal*, 28: 805–825; C. Park, 2003, Prior performance characteristics of related and unrelated acquirers, *Strategic Management Journal*, 24: 471–480; G. Delong, 2001, Stockholder gains from focusing versus diversifying bank mergers, *Journal of Financial Economics*, 2: 221–252; T. H. Brush, 1996, Predicted change in operational synergy and post-acquisition performance of acquired businesses, *Strategic Management Journal*, 17.

30. D. D. Bergh, 1995, Size and relatedness of units sold: An agency theory and resource-based perspective, *Strategic Management Journal*, 16: 221–239.

31. M. Lubatkin & S. Chatterjee, 1994, Extending modern portfolio theory into the domain of corporate diversification: Does it apply? *Academy of Management Journal*, 37: 109–136.

32. E. Dooms & A. A. Van Oijen, 2008, The balance between tailoring and standardizing control, *European Management Review*, 5(4): 245–252; T. Kono, 1999, A strong head office makes a strong company, *Long Range Planning*, 32(2): 225.

33. I. -C. Hsu & Y. -S. Wang, 2008, A model of intraorganizational knowledge sharing: Development and initial test. *Journal of Global Information Management*, 16(3): 45–73; Puranam & Srikanth, What they know vs. what they do; F. T. Rothaermel, M. A. Hitt, & L. A. Jobe, 2006, Balancing vertical integration and strategic outsourcing: Effects on product portfolio, product success, and firm performance, *Strategic Management Journal*, 27: 1033–1056; S. Chatterjee & B. Wernerfelt, 1991, The link between resources and type of diversification: Theory and evidence, *Strategic Management Journal*, 12: 33–48.

34. A. Rodríguez-Duarte, F. D. Sandulli, B. Minguela-Rata, & J. I. López-Sánchez, 2007, The endogenous relationship between innovation and diversification, and the impact of technological resources on the form of diversification, *Research Policy*, 36: 652–664; L. Capron & N. Pistre, 2002, When do acquirers earn abnormal returns? *Strategic Management Journal*, 23: 781–794.

35. C. Lawton, 2007, H-P begins push into high-end copiers, *Wall Street Journal*, April 24, B3.

36. Miller, Fern, & Cardinal, The use of knowledge for technological innovation within diversified firms; J. W. Spencer, 2003, Firms' knowledge-sharing strategies in the global innovation system: Empirical evidence from the flat panel display industry, *Strategic Management Journal*, 24: 217–233.

37. J. Thottam, 2008, Branson's flight plan, *Time*, April 28, 40.

38. 2009, Honda engines, Honda motor company, http://www.honda.com, March 30.

39. L. C. Thang, C. Rowley, T. Quang, & M. Warner, 2007, To what extent can management practices be transferred between countries?: The case of human resource management in Vietnam, *Journal of World Business*, 42(1): 113–127; G. Stalk Jr., 2005, Rotate the core, *Harvard Business Review*, 83(3): 18–19.

40. S. Gupta, A. Woodside, C. Dubelaar, & D. Bradmore, 2009, Diffusing knowledge-based core competencies for leveraging

innovation strategies: Modeling outsourcing to knowledge process organizations (KPOs) in pharmaceutical networks, *Industrial Marketing Management*, 38(2): 219–227.

41. S. Chatterjee & J. Singh, 1999, Are trade-offs inherent in diversification moves? A simultaneous model for type of diversification and mode of expansion decisions, *Management Science*, 45: 25–41.

42. J. Wiggins, 2008, Mars' move for Wrigley leaves rivals trailing, *Financial Times*, April 29, 24.

43. L. Fuentelsaz & J. Gomez, 2006, Multi-point competition, strategic similarity and entry into geographic markets, *Strategic Management Journal*, 27: 477–499; J. Gimeno & C. Y. Woo, 1999, Multimarket contact, economies of scope, and firm performance, *Academy of Management Journal*, 42: 239–259.

44. B. P. Biederman, 2008, Preparing for take-off, *Journal of Commerce*, July 28; R. Kwong, 2007, Big four hope expansion will deliver the goods, *Financial Times*, May 23, 15.

45. T. A. Shervani, G. Frazier, & G. Challagalla, 2007, The moderating influence of firm market power on the transaction cost economics model: An empirical test in a forward channel integration context, *Strategic Management Journal*, 28: 635–652; R. Gulati, P. R. Lawrence, & P. Puranam, 2005, Adaptation in vertical relationships: Beyond incentive conflict, *Strategic Management Journal*, 26: 415–440.

46. P. Broedner, S. Kinkel, & G. Lay, 2009, Productivity effects of outsourcing: New evidence on the strategic importance of vertical integration decisions, *International Journal of Operations & Production Management*, 29(2): 127–150; D. A. Griffin, A. Chandra, & T. Fealey, 2005, Strategically employing natural channels in an emerging market, *Thunderbird International Business Review*, 47(3): 287–311.

47. R. Carter & G. M. Hodgson, 2006, The impact of empirical tests of transaction cost economics on the debate on the nature of the firm, *Strategic Management Journal*, 27: 461–484; O. E. Williamson, 1996, Economics and organization: A primer, *California Management Review*, 38(2): 131–146.

48. S. Novak & S. Stern, 2008, How does outsourcing affect performance dynamics? Evidence from the automobile industry, *Management Science*, 54(12): 1963–1979.

49. C. Wolter & F. M. Veloso, 2008, The effects of innovation on vertical structure: Perspectives on transaction costs and competences, *Academy of Management Review*, 33(3): 586–605; M. G. Jacobides, 2005, Industry change through vertical disintegration: How and why markets emerged in mortgage banking, *Academy of Management Journal*, 48: 465–498.

50. W. D. Brin, 2007, Earnings digest—Health care: As rivals tussle, Medco sees gains; drug-benefit manager cites competitive

edge due to business model, *Wall Street Journal*, February 22, C6.

51. V. Fuhmans & M. Karnitschnig, 2009, Corporate news: WellPoint puts NextRx on the auction block, *Wall Street Journal*, March 6, B3.

52. A. R. Sorkin & M. J. de le Merced, 2009, Express Scripts is said to be near a deal for WellPoint's pharmacy unit, *New York Times*, http://www.nytimes.com, April 13.

53. L. R. Kopczak & M. E. Johnson, 2003, The supply-chain management effect, *MIT Sloan Management Review*, 3: 27–34; K.R. Harrigan, 2001, Strategic flexibility in the old and new economies, in M. A. Hitt, R. E. Freeman, & J. S. Harrison (eds.), *Handbook of Strategic Management*, Oxford, UK: Blackwell Publishers, 97–123.

54. T. Hutzschenreuter & F. Gröne, 2009, Changing vertical integration strategies under pressure from foreign competition: The case of U.S. and German multinationals, *Journal of Management Studies*, 46(2): 269–307.

55. 2009, Flextronics International Ltd., http://www.hoovers.com, March 15.

56. P. Kothandaraman & D. T. Wilson, 2001, The future of competition: Value-creating networks, *Industrial Marketing Management*, 30: 379–389.

57. K. M. Eisenhardt & D. C. Galunic, 2000, Coevolving: At last, a way to make synergies work, *Harvard Business Review*, 78(1): 91–111.

58. J. A. Nickerson & T. R. Zenger, 2008, Envy, comparison costs, and the economic theory of the firm, *Strategic Management Journal*, 13: 1429–1449.

59. L Greene, 2009, Adult nostalgia for childhood brands, *Financial Times*. http://www.ft.com, February 14; M. Marr, 2007, The magic kingdom looks to hit the road, *Wall Street Journal*, http://www.wsj.com, February 8.

60. E. Taylor & J. Singer, 2007, New UBS chief keeps strategy intact, *Wall Street Journal*, July 7, A3.

61. 2009, Breaking up the Citi, *Wall Street Journal*, January 14, A12; 2007, http://www.breakingviews.com: Citi to world: Drop "group," *Wall Street Journal*, January 17, C16.

62. 2009, Citigroup may sell Japanese units to raise cash, *Business 24-7*, http://www.business24-7.ae, February 26.

63. K. Bart, 2009, International finance: He cut costs at Credit Suisse; now he'll do it at UBS, *Wall Street Journal*, April 2, C2.

64. D. W. Ng, 2007, A modern resource based approach to unrelated diversification. *Journal of Management Studies*, 44(8): 1481–1502; D. D. Bergh, 1997, Predicting divestiture of unrelated acquisitions: An integrative model of ex ante conditions, *Strategic Management Journal*, 18: 715–731; C. W. L. Hill, 1994, Diversification and economic performance: Bringing structure and corporate management back into the picture, in R. P. Rumelt, D. E. Schendel, & D. J. Teece (eds.), *Fundamental Issues in*

Strategy, Boston: Harvard Business School Press, 297–321.

65. Porter, *Competitive Advantage*.

66. S. Lee, K. Park, H. H. Shin, 2009, Disappearing internal capital markets: Evidence from diversified business groups in Korea. *Journal of Banking & Finance*, 33(2): 326–334; D. Collis, D. Young, & M. Goold, 2007, The size, structure, and performance of corporate headquarters, *Strategic Management Journal*, 28: 283–405; O. E. Williamson, 1975, *Markets and Hierarchies: Analysis and Antitrust Implications*, New York: Macmillan Free Press.

67. R. Aggarwal & N. A. Kyaw, 2009, International variations in transparency and capital structure: Evidence from european firms. *Journal of International Financial Management & Accounting*, 20(1): 1–34; R. J. Indjejikian, 2007, Discussion of accounting information, disclosure, and the cost of capital, *Journal of Accounting Research*, 45(2): 421–426.

68. A. Mackey, 2008, The effect of CEOs on firm performance, *Strategic Management Journal*, 29(12): 1357–1367; Dooms & Van Oijen, The balance between tailoring and standardizing control; D. Miller, R. Eisenstat, & N. Foote, 2002, Strategy from the inside out: Building capability-creating organizations, *California Management Review*, 44(3): 37–54; M. E. Raynor & J. L. Bower, 2001, Lead from the center: How to manage divisions dynamically, *Harvard Business Review*, 79(5): 92–100.

69. K. Kranhold, 2007, GE report raises doubts, *Wall Street Journal*, January 20–21, A3.

70. R. Ettenson & J. Knowles, 2008, Don't confuse reputation with brand. *MIT Sloan Management Review*, 49(2): 21.

71. P. Engardio & M. Arndt, 2007, What price reputation: Many savvy companies are starting to realize that a good name can be their most important asset—and actually boost the stock price. *Business Week*, July 8, 70–79; J. Lunsford & B. Steinberg, 2006, Conglomerates' conundrum, *Wall Street Journal*, B1, B7.

72. F. Guerrera, 2007, Siemens chief makes the case for conglomerates, *Financial Times*, http://www.ft.com, February 5.

73. B. Quint, 2009, Companies deal with tough times through diversification. *Information Today*, 26(3): 7–8.

74. A. Delios, D. Xu, & P. W. Beamish, 2008, Within-country product diversification and foreign subsidiary performance, *Journal of International Business Studies*, 39(4): 706–724; M. W. Peng & A. Delios, 2006, What determines the scope of the firm over time and around the world? An Asia Pacific perspective, *Asia Pacific Journal of Management*, 23: 385–405; T. Khanna, K. G. Palepu, & J. Sinha, 2005, Strategies that fit emerging markets, *Harvard Business Review*, 83(6): 63–76.

75. Lee, Park, Shin, Disappearing internal capital markets: Evidence from diversified business groups in Korea; A. Chakrabarti, K. Singh, & I. Mahmood, 2006, Diversification and performance:

Evidence from East Asian firms, *Strategic Management Journal*, 28: 101–120; T. Khanna & K. Palepu, 2000, Is group affiliation profitable in emerging markets? An analysis of diversified Indian business groups, *Journal of Finance*, 55: 867–892; T. Khanna & K. Palepu, 2000, The future of business groups in emerging markets: Long-run evidence from Chile, *Academy of Management Journal*, 43: 268–285.

76. D. D. Bergh, R. A. Johnson, & R. L. Dewitt, 2008, Restructuring through spin-off or sell-off: Transforming information asymmetries into financial gain, *Strategic Management Journal*, 29(2): 133–148; C. Decker & M. Mellewigt, 2007, Thirty years after Michael E. Porter: What do we know about business exit? *Academy of Management Perspectives*, 2: 41–55; S. J. Chang & H. Singh, 1999, The impact of entry and resource fit on modes of exit by multibusiness firms, *Strategic Management Journal*, 20: 1019–1035.

77. R. Coff, 2003, Bidding wars over R&D-intensive firms: Knowledge, opportunism, and the market for corporate control, *Academy of Management Journal*, 46: 74–85.

78. P. Navarro, 2009, Recession-proofing your organization, *MIT Sloan Management Review*, 50(3): 45–51.

79. M. Lubatkin, H. Merchant, & M. Srinivasan, 1997, Merger strategies and shareholder value during times of relaxed antitrust enforcement: The case of large mergers during the 1980s, *Journal of Management*, 23: 61–81.

80. D. P. Champlin & J. T. Knoedler, 1999, Restructuring by design? Government's complicity in corporate restructuring, *Journal of Economic Issues*, 33(1): 41–57.

81. R. M. Scherer & D. Ross, 1990, *Industrial Market Structure and Economic Performance*, Boston: Houghton Mifflin.

82. A. Shleifer & R. W. Vishny, 1994, Takeovers in the 1960s and 1980s: Evidence and implications, in R. P. Rumelt, D. E. Schendel, & D. J. Teece (eds.), *Fundamental Issues in Strategy*, Boston: Harvard Business School Press, 403–422.

83. S. Chatterjee, J. S. Harrison, & D. D. Bergh, 2003, Failed takeover attempts, corporate governance and refocusing, *Strategic Management Journal*, 24: 87–96; Lubatkin, Merchant, & Srinivasan, Merger strategies and shareholder value; D. J. Ravenscraft & R. M. Scherer, 1987, *Mergers, Sell-Offs and Economic Efficiency*, Washington, DC: Brookings Institution, 22.

84. D. A. Zalewski, 2001, Corporate takeovers, fairness, and public policy, *Journal of Economic Issues*, 35: 431–437; P. L. Zweig, J. P. Kline, S. A. Forest, & K. Gudridge, 1995, The case against mergers, *BusinessWeek*, October 30, 122–130; J. R. Williams, B. L. Paez, & L. Sanders, 1988, Conglomerates revisited, *Strategic Management Journal*, 9: 403–414.

85. E. J. Lopez, 2001, New anti-merger theories: A critique, *Cato Journal*, 20: 359–378; 1998, The trustbusters' new tools, *The Economist*, May 2, 62–64.

86. R. Croyle & P. Kager, 2002, Giving mergers a head start, *Harvard Business Review*, 80(10): 20–21.

87. M. C. Jensen, 1986, Agency costs of free cash flow, corporate finance, and takeovers, *American Economic Review*, 76: 323–329.

88. R. Gilson, M. Scholes, & M. Wolfson, 1988, Taxation and the dynamics of corporate control: The uncertain case for tax motivated acquisitions, in J. C. Coffee, L. Lowenstein, & S. Rose-Ackerman (eds.), *Knights, Raiders, and Targets: The Impact of the Hostile Takeover*, New York: Oxford University Press, 271–299.

89. C. Steindel, 1986, Tax reform and the merger and acquisition market: The repeal of the general utilities, *Federal Reserve Bank of New York Quarterly Review*, 11(3): 31–35.

90. M. A. Hitt, J. S. Harrison, & R. D. Ireland, 2001, *Mergers and Acquisitions: A Guide to Creating Value for Stakeholders*, New York: Oxford University Press.

91. J. Haleblian; J.-Y. Kim, & N. Rajagopalan, 2006, The influence of acquisition experience and performance on acquisition behavior: Evidence from the U.S. commercial banking industry, *Academy of Management Journal*, 49: 357–370.

92. D. B. Wilkerson & R. Britt, 2003, It's showtime for media deals: Radio lessons fuel debate over control of TV, newspapers, *MarketWatch*, http://www.marketwatch.com, May 30.

93. M. T. Brouwer, 2008, Horizontal mergers and efficiencies; theory and antitrust practice, *European Journal of Law and Economics*, 26(1): 11–26.

94. T. Afza, C. Slahudin, & M. S. Nazir, 2008, Diversification and corporate performance: An evaluation of Pakistani firms, *South Asian Journal of Management*, 15(3): 7–18; J. M. Shaver, 2006, A paradox of synergy: Contagion and capacity effects in mergers and acquisitions, *Academy of Management Journal*, 31: 962–976; C. Park, 2002, The effects of prior performance on the choice between related and unrelated acquisitions: Implications for the performance consequences of diversification strategy, *Journal of Management Studies*, 39: 1003–1019.

95. Rumelt, *Strategy, Structure and Economic Performance*, 125.

96. R. Waters, 2008, eBay ready to sell Skype if strong synergies prove elusive, *Financial Times*, April 18, 17; A. Lashinsky, 2008, Is Skype on sale at eBay? *Fortune*, October 27, 158(8): 48.

97. L. E. Palich, L. B. Cardinal, & C. C. Miller, 2000, Curvilinearity in the diversification-performance linkage: An examination of over three decades of research, *Strategic Management Journal*, 21: 155–174.

98. P. Eavis, 2008, Lehman faces dilemma; signs of weakness abound with talk of Neuberger sale, *Wall Street Journal*, August 19, C14.

99. D. G. Sirmon, M. A. Hitt, & R. D. Ireland, 2007, Managing firm resources in dynamic environments to create value: Looking inside the black box, *Academy of Management Review*, 32: 273–292; A. E. Bernardo & B. Chowdhry, 2002, Resources, real options, and corporate strategy, *Journal of Financial Economics*, 63: 211–234.

100. W. H. Tsai, Y. C. Kuo, J.-H. Hung, 2009, Corporate diversification and CEO turnover in family businesses: Self-entrenchment or risk reduction? *Small Business Economics*, 32(1): 57–76; N. W. C. Harper & S. P. Viguerie, 2002, Are you too focused? *McKinsey Quarterly*, Mid-Summer, 29–38; J. C. Sandvig & L. Coakley, 1998, Best practices in small firm diversification, *Business Horizons*, 41(3): 33–40.

101. T. Aeppel, 2009, Auto suppliers attempt reinvention, *Wall Street Journal*, June 15, B1-B2.

102. L. Jarvis, 2008, Pharma strategies: Merck launches into the biosimilars business, *Chemical & Engineering News*, December, 86(50): 7.

103. J. Carroll, 2009, Merck acquires bio-similars in $130M pact, *Fierce Biotech*, http://www.fiercebiotech.com, February 12.

104. T. B. Folta & J. P. O'Brien, 2008, Determinants of firm-specific thresholds in acquisition decisions, *Managerial and Decision Economics*, 29(2/3): 209–225.

105. N. M. Kay & A. Diamantopoulos, 1987, Uncertainty and synergy: Towards a formal model of corporate strategy, *Managerial and Decision Economics*, 8: 121–130.

106. R. W. Coff, 1999, How buyers cope with uncertainty when acquiring firms in knowledge-intensive industries: Caveat emptor, *Organization Science*, 10: 144–161.

107. P. B. Carroll & C. Muim 2008, 7 ways to fail big, *Harvard Business Review*, 86(9): 82–91.

108. D. G. Sirmon, S. Gove, & M. A. Hitt, 2008, Resource management in dyadic competitive rivalry: The effects of resource bundling and deployment, *Academy of Management Journal*, 51(5): 919–935; S. J. Chatterjee & B. Wernerfelt, 1991, The link between resources and type of diversification: Theory and evidence, *Strategic Management Journal*, 12: 33–48.

109. E. N. K. Lim, S. S. Das, & A. Das, 2009, Diversification strategy, capital structure, and the Asian financial crisis (1997–1998): Evidence from Singapore firms, *Strategic Management Journal*, 30(6): 577–594; W. Keuslein, 2003, The Ebitda folly, *Forbes*, March 17, 165–167.

110. T.-I.Tsai & I. Johnson, 2009, Acer hopes to thrive in downturn, *Wall Street Journal*, February 17, B7.

111. L. Capron & J. Hulland, 1999, Redeployment of brands, sales forces, and

general marketing management expertise following horizontal acquisitions: A resource-based view, *Journal of Marketing,* 63(2): 41–54.

112. M. V. S. Kumar, 2009, The relationship between product and international diversification: The effects of short-run constraints and endogeneity. *Strategic Management Journal,* 30(1): 99–116; C. B. Malone & L. C. Rose, 2006. Intangible assets and firm diversification, *International Journal of Managerial Finance,* 2(2): 136–153; A. M. Knott, D. J. Bryce, & H. E. Posen, 2003, On the strategic accumulation of intangible assets, *Organization Science,* 14: 192–207.

113. Bergh, Johnson, & Dewitt, Restructuring through spin-off or sell-off: Transforming information asymmetries into financial gain; K. Shimizu & M. A. Hitt, 2005, What constrains or facilitates divestitures of formerly acquired firms? The effects of organizational inertia, *Journal of Management,* 31: 50–72.

114. D. Cimilluca & J. Jargon, 2009, Corporate news: Sara Lee weighs sale of European business, *Wall Street Journal,* March 13, B3; J. Jargon & J. Vuocolo, 2007, Sara Lee CEO challenged on antitakeover defenses, *Wall Street Journal,* May 11, B4.

115. M. A. Williams, T. B. Michael, & E. R. Waller, 2008, Managerial incentives and acquisitions: a survey of the literature. *Managerial Finance,* 34(5): 328–341; J. G. Combs & M. S. Skill, 2003, Managerialist and human capital explanation for key executive pay premiums: A contingency perspective, *Academy of Management Journal,* 46: 63–73; M. A. Geletkanycz, B. K. Boyd, & S. Finkelstein, 2001, The strategic value of CEO external directorate networks: Implications for CEO compensation, *Strategic Management Journal,* 9: 889–898; W. Grossman & R. E. Hoskisson, 1998, CEO pay at the crossroads of Wall Street and Main: Toward the strategic design of executive compensation, *Academy of Management Executive,* 12(1): 43–57.

116. R. E. Hoskisson, M. W. Castleton, & M. C. Withers, 2009, Complementarity in monitoring and bonding: More intense monitoring leads to higher executive compensation, *Academy of Management Perspectives,* 23(2): 57–74; Kaplan, S. N. 2008a. Are CEOs overpaid? *Academy of Management Perspectives,* 22(2): 5–20.

117. Geiger & Cashen, Organizational size and CEO compensation; J. J. Cordeiro & R. Veliyath, 2003, Beyond pay for performance: A panel study of the determinants of CEO compensation, *American Business Review,* 21(1): 56–66; Wright, Kroll, & Elenkov, Acquisition returns, increase in firm size, and chief executive officer compensation; S. R. Gray & A. A. Cannella Jr., 1997, The role of risk in executive compensation, *Journal of Management,* 23: 517–540.

118. Kaplan, Are CEOs overpaid?; R. Bliss & R. Rosen, 2001, CEO compensation and bank mergers, *Journal of Financial Economics,* 1: 107–138; W. G. Sanders & M. A. Carpenter, 1998, Internationalization and firm governance: The roles of CEO compensation, top team composition, and board structure, *Academy of Management Journal,* 41: 158–178.

119. J. Bogle, 2008, Reflections on CEO compensation, *Academy of Management Perspectives,* 22(2): 21–25; J. J. Janney, 2002, Eat or get eaten? How equity ownership and diversification shape CEO risk-taking, *Academy of Management Executive,* 14(4): 157–158; J. W. Lorsch, A. S. Zelleke, & K. Pick, 2001, Unbalanced boards, *Harvard Business Review,* 79(2): 28–30; R. E. Hoskisson & T. Turk, 1990, Corporate restructuring: Governance and control limits of the internal market, *Academy of Management Review,* 15: 459–477.

120. M. Kahan & E. B. Rock, 2002, How I learned to stop worrying and love the pill: Adaptive responses to takeover law, *University of Chicago Law Review,* 69(3): 871–915.

121. R. C. Anderson, T. W. Bates, J. M. Bizjak, & M. L. Lemmon, 2000, Corporate governance and firm diversification, *Financial Management,* 29(1): 5–22; J. D. Westphal, 1998, Board games: How CEOs adapt to increases in structural board independence from management, *Administrative Science Quarterly,* 43: 511–537; J. K. Seward & J. P. Walsh, 1996, The governance and control of voluntary corporate spin offs, *Strategic Management Journal,* 17: 25–39; J. P. Walsh & J. K. Seward, 1990, On the efficiency of internal and external corporate control mechanisms, *Academy of Management Review,* 15: 421–458.

122. S. M. Campbell, A. J. Ward, J. A. Sonnenfeld, & B. R. Agle, 2008, Relational ties that bind: Leader-follower relationship dimensions and charismatic attribution. *Leadership Quarterly,* 19(5): 556–568; M. Wiersema, 2002, Holes at the top: Why CEO firings backfire, *Harvard Business Review,* 80(12): 70–77.

123. J. M. Bizjak, M. L. Lemmon, & L. Naveen, 2008, Does the use of peer groups contribute to higher pay and less efficient compensation? *Journal of Financial Economics,* 90(2): 152–168; N. Wasserman, 2006, Stewards, agents, and the founder discount: Executive compensation in new ventures, *Academy of Management Journal,* 49: 960–976; V. Kisfalvi & P. Pitcher, 2003, Doing what feels right: The influence of CEO character and emotions on top management team dynamics, *Journal of Management Inquiry,* 12(10): 42–66; W. G. Rowe, 2001, Creating wealth in organizations: The role of strategic leadership, *Academy of Management Executive,* 15(1): 81–94.

124. E. F. Fama, 1980, Agency problems and the theory of the firm, *Journal of Political Economy,* 88: 288–307.

125. M. Y. Brannen & M. F. Peterson, 2009, Merging without alienating: Interventions promoting cross-cultural organizational integration and their limitations, *Journal of International Business Studies,* 40(3): 468–489; M. L. A. Hayward, 2002, When do firms learn from their acquisition experience? Evidence from 1990–1995, *Strategic Management Journal,* 23: 21–39; L. Capron, W. Mitchell, & A. Swaminathan, 2001, Asset divestiture following horizontal acquisitions: A dynamic view, *Strategic Management Journal,* 22: 817–844.

126. R. E. Hoskisson, R. A. Johnson, L. Tihanyi, & R. E. White, 2005, Diversified business groups and corporate refocusing in emerging economies, *Journal of Management,* 31: 941–965.

127. C. N. Chung & X. Luo, 2008, Institutional logics or agency costs: The influence of corporate governance models on business group restructuring in emerging economies, *Organization Science,* 19(5): 766–784; Chakrabarti, Singh, & Mahmood, Diversification and performance: Evidence from East Asian firms; W. P. Wan & R. E. Hoskisson, 2003, Home country environments, corporate diversification strategies, and firm performance, *Academy of Management Journal,* 46: 27–45.

CHAPTER 7

Merger and Acquisition Strategies

Studying this chapter should provide you with the strategic management knowledge needed to:

1. Explain the popularity of merger and acquisition strategies in firms competing in the global economy.

2. Discuss reasons why firms use an acquisition strategy to achieve strategic competitiveness.

3. Describe seven problems that work against achieving success when using an acquisition strategy.

4. Name and describe the attributes of effective acquisitions.

5. Define the restructuring strategy and distinguish among its common forms.

6. Explain the short- and long-term outcomes of the different types of restructuring strategies.

GLOBAL MERGER AND ACQUISITION ACTIVITY DURING A GLOBAL CRISIS

Mergers and acquisitions (M&A) are a primary means of firm growth. We define these terms and discuss a number of reasons firms use merger and acquisition strategies in this chapter.

Cross-border M&A activity (activity involving firms headquartered in different nations) increased during the 1990s and into the early part of the twenty-first century, largely because of the continuing globalization of the world's markets. A key advantage of mergers and acquisitions is that they can help firms grow rapidly in both domestic and international markets. For societies, mergers and acquisitions can be beneficial in that they "...are a critical tool for eliminating weaker players and wringing out excess capacity."

Merger and acquisition activity tends to be cyclical in nature flowing and ebbing in light of the opportunities and threats associated with a firm's external environment. In the very recent past, the global financial crisis has contributed to a sharp decline in M&A activity. The fact that "merger and acquisition volume worldwide dropped to $29 trillion in 2008, from $42 trillion the year before," demonstrates the caution firms exercised during 2008 in terms of using merger and acquisition strategies.

Evidence from the first part of 2009 suggests that the decline observed in 2008 continued, certainly with respect to cross-border M&A activity. "Global flows of foreign-direct investment halved during the first three months of 2009 as the value of cross-border mergers and acquisitions plummeted." Indeed, the value of cross-border M&A activity declined by 77 percent in the first quarter of 2009 compared to the same quarter a year earlier. The size of individual mergers and acquisitions also declined during 2008 and early 2009. In the first half of 2009, Pfizer's proposed $68 billion acquisition of Wyeth was the largest transaction. According to Dealogic, which tracks M&A activity, the U.S. federal government's $25 billion stake in Citigroup ranked as the fifth largest transaction during this six-month period. Uncertainty in the world's credit markets and possible political changes in different nations' orientation to M&A activity were among the causes of decline in global M&A activity during the recent financial crisis.

AP Photo/Eric Landwehr

Despite adverse economic conditions, in early 2009 Valero Energy became the first oil company to purchase a major ethanol producer when it bought the seven plants from the bankruptcy inventory of VeraSun.

In spite of the recent declines in M&A activity both globally and domestically, merger and acquisition strategies are still a very viable source of firm growth; as a result, they remain popular with many of the world's corporations. In the foreseeable future, M&A opportunities seem strong in several sectors such as energy and health care. In response to pushes toward greener, renewable energy sources, for example, major oil companies "...are eyeing players in alternative energy..." Fuel refiner Valero's purchase of ethanol producer VeraSun is an example of M&A activity taking place in this sector. Some of the major corporations in the health care industry have large amounts of cash that can be used to gain access to promising drugs and other firm's research and development skills. Pfizer's $68 billion acquisition of Wyeth demonstrates the type of activity taking place in this sector. (We further discuss this acquisition in a Strategic Focus in this chapter.) However, as is true for all strategies, firms in these two sectors and all other companies must carefully evaluate the "deal" (either a merger or an acquisition) they are contemplating to verify that completing the transaction will facilitate the firm's efforts to achieve strategic competitiveness and create value for stakeholders as a result of doing so.

Sources: P. Hannon, 2009, Foreign investing decreased by half earlier this year, *Wall Street Journal Online*, http://www.wsj.com, June 25; S. Jung-a, 2009, Mergers & acquisitions: Ambitious companies with war-chests look for value, *Financial Times Online*, http://www.ft.com, May 20; Z. Kouwe, 2009, Deals on ice in first half, with 40% drop in M.&A., *New York Times Online*, http://www.nytimes.com, July 1; J. Silver-Greenberg, 2009, Dealmakers test the waters, *BusinessWeek*, March 2, 18–20; 2008, Global M&A falls in 2008, *New York Times Online*, http://www.nytimes.com, December 22; L. Saigoi, 2008, Record number of M&A deals cancelled in 2008, *Financial Times Online*, http://www.ft.com, December 22.

We examined corporate-level strategy in Chapter 6, focusing on types and levels of product diversification strategies that firms derive from their core competencies to create competitive advantages and value for stakeholders. As noted in that chapter, diversification allows a firm to create value by productively using excess resources.[1] In this chapter, we explore merger and acquisition strategies. Firms throughout the world use these strategies, often in concert with diversification strategies, to become more diversified. As noted in the Opening Case, even though the amount of merger and acquisition activity completed in 2008 and through mid-2009 fell short of such activity in previous years, merger and acquisition strategies remain popular as a source of firm growth and hopefully, of above-average returns.

Most corporations are very familiar with merger and acquisition strategies. For example, the latter half of the twentieth century found major companies using these strategies to grow and to deal with the competitive challenges in their domestic markets as well as those emerging from global competitors. Today, smaller firms also use merger and acquisition strategies to grow in their existing markets and to enter new markets.[2]

Not unexpectedly, some mergers and acquisitions fail to reach their promise.[3] Accordingly, explaining how firms can successfully use merger and acquisition strategies to create stakeholder value[4] is a key purpose of this chapter. To do this we first explain the continuing popularity of merger and acquisition strategies as a choice firms evaluate when seeking growth and strategic competitiveness. As part of this explanation, we describe the differences between mergers, acquisitions, and takeovers. We next discuss specific reasons firms choose to use acquisition strategies and some of the problems organizations may encounter when implementing them. We then describe the characteristics associated with effective acquisitions before closing the chapter with a discussion of different types of restructuring strategies. Restructuring strategies are commonly used to correct or deal with the results of ineffective mergers and acquisitions.

The Popularity of Merger and Acquisition Strategies

Merger and acquisition strategies have been popular among U.S. firms for many years. Some believe that these strategies played a central role in the restructuring of U.S. businesses during the 1980s and 1990s and that they continue generating these types of benefits in the twenty-first century.[5]

Although popular and appropriately so as a means of growth with the potential to lead to strategic competitiveness, it is important to emphasize that changing conditions in the external environment influence the type of M&A activity firms pursue. During the recent financial crisis for example, tightening credit markets made it more difficult for firms to complete "megadeals" (those costing $10 billion or more). As a result, "... many acquirers are focusing on smaller targets with a niche focus that complements their existing business."[6] Additionally, the relatively weak U.S. dollar increased the interest of firms from other nations to acquire U.S. companies. For example, speculation surfaced in mid-2009 that Singapore's sovereign wealth fund, Temasek Holdings, was considering acquiring the aircraft-leasing unit of insurer AIG.

In the final analysis, firms use merger and acquisition strategies to improve their ability to create more value for all stakeholders including shareholders. As suggested by Figure 1.1, this reasoning applies equally to all of the other strategies (e.g., business-level, corporate-level, international and cooperative) a firm may formulate and then implement.

However, evidence suggests that using merger and acquisition strategies in ways that consistently create value is challenging. This is particularly true for acquiring firms in that some research results indicate that shareholders of acquired firms often earn above-average returns from acquisitions while shareholders of acquiring firms typically earn returns that are close to zero.[7] Moreover, in approximately two-thirds of all acquisitions, the acquiring firm's stock price falls immediately after the intended transaction is announced. This negative response reflects investors' skepticism about the likelihood that the acquirer will be able to achieve the synergies required to justify the premium.[8] Premiums can sometimes be excessive, as appears to be the case with NetApp's proposed acquisition of Data Domain in mid-2009: "On straightforward valuation measures, the (acquisition) price already looks in the stratosphere. At $33.50, the offer is 419 times Data Domain's consensus 2009 earnings, including the enormous cost of employee stock options."[9] Obviously, creating the amount of value required to account for this type of premium would be extremely difficult. Overall then, those leading firms that are using merger and acquisition strategies must recognize that creating more value for their stakeholders by doing so is indeed difficult.[10]

Mergers, Acquisitions, and Takeovers: What Are the Differences?

A **merger** is a strategy through which two firms agree to integrate their operations on a relatively coequal basis. Recently, Towers Perrin Forster & Crosby Inc. and Watson Wyatt Worldwide Inc., two large human-resources consulting firms, agreed to merge. Shareholders of each firm will own 50 percent of the newly formed company, which will be "…the world's biggest employee-benefits consultancy…."[11]

Even though the transaction between Towers Perrin and Watson Wyatt appears to be a merger, the reality is that few true mergers actually take place. The main reason for this is that one party to the transaction is usually dominant in regard to various characteristics such as market share, size, or value of assets. The transaction proposed between Xstrata and Anglo American appears to be an example of this.

In 2009, Swiss-based Xstrata (a global diversified mining group) proposed a friendly merger with London-based Anglo American (a diversified mining and natural resource group). While some analysts thought the proposed merger of equals "should create some value," they also concluded that the "…friendly merger with Anglo American (was) a pretty aggressive bear hug" given the terms Xstrata was seeking and its potential inability to pay the premium Anglo's shareholders expected. In this case too some felt that Anglo's assets were of higher quality, reducing the likelihood that the transaction was actually one of "equals."[12]

An **acquisition** is a strategy through which one firm buys a controlling, or 100 percent, interest in another firm with the intent of making the acquired firm a subsidiary business within its portfolio. After completing the transaction, the management of the acquired firm reports to the management of the acquiring firm.

In spite of the situation we described dealing with Xstrata and Anglo American, most of the mergers that are completed are friendly in nature. However, acquisitions can be friendly or unfriendly. A **takeover** is a special type of acquisition wherein the target firm does not solicit the acquiring firm's bid; thus, takeovers are unfriendly acquisitions. Research evidence showing "…that hostile acquirers deliver significantly higher shareholder value than friendly acquirers" for the acquiring firm[13] is a reason

A **merger** is a strategy through which two firms agree to integrate their operations on a relatively coequal basis.

An **acquisition** is a strategy through which one firm buys a controlling, or 100 percent, interest in another firm with the intent of making the acquired firm a subsidiary business within its portfolio.

A **takeover** is a special type of acquisition wherein the target firm does not solicit the acquiring firm's bid; thus, takeovers are unfriendly acquisitions.

some firms are willing to pursue buying another company even when that firm is not interested in being bought. Often, determining the price the acquiring firm is willing to pay to "take over" the target firm is the core issue in these transactions. In July 2009, for example, Exelon "…raised its hostile bid for rival power producer NRG Energy to nearly $7.5 billion in stock, marking the latest twist in the months-long takeover feud." At issue was NRG's position that Exelon's bids were inadequate. At the same time however, NRG "…said that it remained open to a deal at a fair price."[14]

On a comparative basis, acquisitions are more common than mergers and takeovers. Accordingly, we focus the remainder of this chapter's discussion on acquisitions.

Reasons for Acquisitions

In this section, we discuss reasons firms decide to acquire another company. Although each reason can provide a legitimate rationale, acquisitions are not always as successful as the involved parties want to be the case. Later in the chapter, we examine problems firms may encounter when seeking growth and strategic competitiveness through acquisitions.

Increased Market Power

Achieving greater market power is a primary reason for acquisitions.[15] Defined in Chapter 6, *market power* exists when a firm is able to sell its goods or services above competitive levels or when the costs of its primary or support activities are lower than those of its competitors. Market power usually is derived from the size of the firm and its resources and capabilities to compete in the marketplace;[16] it is also affected by the firm's share of the market. Therefore, most acquisitions that are designed to achieve greater market power entail buying a competitor, a supplier, a distributor, or a business in a highly related industry to allow the exercise of a core competence and to gain competitive advantage in the acquiring firm's primary market.

If a firm achieves enough market power, it can become a market leader, which is the goal of many firms. For example, having already acquired Gateway and Packard Bell (see the Strategic Focus in Chapter 4), Acer is contemplating acquiring other firms (perhaps Asustek of Taiwan or Lenovo of China) as a means of getting closer to its goal of being the leading maker and seller of personal computers.[17] Vertu, already the ninth-largest motor retailer in the United Kingdom, recently acquired some of the businesses and assets of Brooklyn Motor, a Ford and Mazda dealership. The transaction provided Vertu with its first Mazda franchise and facilitated the firm's intention of increasing its share of its core market in the Worcestershire area.[18]

Next, we discuss how firms use horizontal, vertical, and related types of acquisitions to increase their market power.

Horizontal Acquisitions

The acquisition of a company competing in the same industry as the acquiring firm is a *horizontal acquisition*. Horizontal acquisitions increase a firm's market power by exploiting cost-based and revenue-based synergies.[19] For example, National Australia Bank Ltd. recently acquired the wealth-management assets from Aviva PLC's Australian business. A company spokesman said that the acquisition would enhance National Australia's "…offering in key wealth-management segments including insurance and investment platforms, adding scale, efficiency and new capabilities to our operations."[20] Toys "R" Us Inc.'s acquisition of specialty toy retailer FAO Schwarz is another example of a horizontal acquisition. Toys "R" Us officials indicated that they intended to use their firm's "…buying clout to offer a slightly broader appeal to FAO's toy offerings…"[21] and to reduce the price FAO was paying to buy products for its stores.

Research suggests that horizontal acquisitions result in higher performance when the firms have similar characteristics,[22] such as strategy, managerial styles, and resource allocation patterns. Similarities in these characteristics support efforts to integrate the acquiring and the acquired firm. The similarity in the strategies they use should facilitate the integration of National Australia's and Aviva's wealth-management assets. Toys "R" Us and FAO Schwarz share similar product lines and allocate their resources similarly to buy and sell their products. Horizontal acquisitions are often most effective when the acquiring firm integrates the acquired firm's assets with its own assets, but only after evaluating and divesting excess capacity and assets that do not complement the newly combined firm's core competencies.[23]

Martin Sasse/laif/Redux Pictures

Toys "R" Us pursued an aggressive horizontal acquisitions strategy in 2009, with the acquisition of several small on-line toy retailers in early spring, FAO Schwarz in May, and the bankrupt KB Toys in the Fall.

Vertical Acquisitions

A *vertical acquisition* refers to a firm acquiring a supplier or distributor of one or more of its goods or services.[24] Through a vertical acquisition, the newly formed firm controls additional parts of the value chain (see Chapters 3 and 6),[25] which is how vertical acquisitions lead to increased market power.

CVS/Caremark, a firm that was formed as a result of a transaction completed in 2007, is a product of a vertical acquisition. In 2007, CVS Corporation (a retail pharmacy) acquired Caremark Rx, Inc. (a PBM or pharmacy benefits manager) to create CVS/Caremark, which is the largest integrated pharmacy services provider in the United States. In the firm's words: "Payers and patients count on CVS/Caremark for a broad range of services, from managing pharmacy benefits to filling prescriptions by mail or offering clinical expertise."[26] CVS/Caremark controls multiple parts of the value chain allowing it to use the size of its purchases to gain price concessions from those selling medicines and related products to it.

Related Acquisitions

Acquiring a firm in a highly related industry is called a *related acquisition*. Through a related acquisition, firms seek to create value through the synergy that can be generated by integrating some of their resources and capabilities. For example, Boeing recently acquired eXMeritus Inc., a company providing hardware and software to federal government and law enforcement agencies. eXMeritus's products are intended to help agencies securely share information across classified and unclassified networks and systems. eXMeritus is operating as part of Boeing's Integrated Defense Systems Network and Space Systems business unit. This related acquisition facilitates Boeing's intention of expanding its presence in the cyber and intelligence markets—markets that are related to other aspects of the firm's Integrated Defense Systems operations.[27]

Sometimes, firms fail to create value through a related acquisition. This is the case for FAO Schwarz's recent acquisition of Best Co., a fashion-oriented children's clothing company. The economic downturn that started around 2007 made it extremely difficult for FAO Schwarz to generate the type of operational synergies it expected to accrue through this related acquisition. Indeed, acquiring Best Co. weakened FAO, making it a target for Toys "R" Us as a horizontal acquisition.

Horizontal, vertical, and related acquisitions that firms complete to increase their market power are subject to regulatory review as well as to analysis by financial markets.[28] For example, Procter & Gamble (P&G) completed a horizontal acquisition of Gillette Co. in 2006. In announcing the transaction, P&G noted that integrating Gillette into P&G's operations would result in between $1 and $1.2 billion in annual cost synergies and a 1 percent incremental annual sales growth from revenue synergies for the first three years following the acquisition. However, before being finalized, this acquisition was subjected to a significant amount of government scrutiny as well as close examination by financial analysts. Ultimately, P&G had to sell off several businesses to gain the Federal Trade Commission's approval to acquire Gillette.[29] Thus, firms seeking growth and market power through acquisitions must understand the political/legal segment of the general environment (see Chapter 2) in order to successfully use an acquisition strategy.

Overcoming Entry Barriers

Barriers to entry (introduced in Chapter 2) are factors associated with a market or with the firms currently operating in it that increase the expense and difficulty new firms encounter when trying to enter that particular market. For example, well-established competitors may have economies of scale in the manufacture or service of their products. In addition, enduring relationships with customers often create product loyalties that are difficult for new entrants to overcome. When facing differentiated products, new entrants typically must spend considerable resources to advertise their products and may find it necessary to sell at prices below competitors' to entice new customers.

Facing the entry barriers that economies of scale and differentiated products create, a new entrant may find acquiring an established company to be more effective than entering the market as a competitor offering a product that is unfamiliar to current buyers. In fact, the higher the barriers to market entry, the greater the probability that a firm will acquire an existing firm to overcome them.

As this discussion suggests, a key advantage of using an acquisition strategy to overcome entry barriers is that the acquiring firm gains immediate access to a market. This advantage can be particularly attractive for firms seeking to overcome entry barriers associated with entering international markets.[30] Large multinational corporations from developed economies seek to enter emerging economies such as Brazil, Russia, India, and China (BRIC) because they are among the fastest-growing economies in the world.[31] As discussed next, completing a cross-border acquisition of a local target allows a firm to quickly enter fast-growing economies such as these.

Cross-Border Acquisitions

Acquisitions made between companies with headquarters in different countries are called *cross-border acquisitions*.[32] The purchase of U.K. carmakers Jaguar and Land Rover by India's Tata Motors is an example of a cross-border acquisition. We discuss this acquisition further later in this chapter.

We noted in the Opening Case that global M&A activity declined in the recent global financial crisis. The declines continued throughout the first half of 2009 largely because "…shrinking economies, volatile markets and scarce debt hammered corporate confidence."[33] This decline was in stark contrast to the significant increase in cross-border M&A activity during the 1990s. Nonetheless, as explained in the Opening Case, cross-border acquisitions remain popular as a viable path to firm growth and strategic competitiveness.

There are other interesting changes taking place in terms of cross-border acquisition activity. Historically, North American and European companies were the most active acquirers of companies outside their domestic markets. However, the current global competitive landscape is one in which firms from other nations may use an acquisition strategy more frequently than do their counterparts in North America and Europe. In this regard, some believe that "…the next wave of cross-border M&A may be led out of Asia. Chinese companies, in particular, are well positioned for cross-border acquisitions. Relative to their overseas peers, Chinese corporates are well capitalized with strong balance sheets and cash reserves."[34] In the Strategic Focus, we describe recent cross-border acquisitions some Chinese companies have completed or are evaluating. As you will see, the acquisitions we discuss involve natural resource companies and many are horizontal acquisitions through which the acquiring companies seek to increase their market power.

Firms headquartered in India are also completing more cross-border acquisitions than in the past. The weakening U.S. dollar and more favorable government policies toward cross-border acquisitions are supporting Indian companies' desire to rapidly become "global powerhouses."[35] In addition to rapid market entry, Indian companies typically seek access to product innovation capabilities and new brands and distribution channels when acquiring firms outside their domestic market.

Firms using an acquisition strategy to complete cross-border acquisitions should understand that these transactions are not risk free. For example, firms seeking to acquire companies in China must recognize that "…China remains a challenging environment for foreign investors. Cultural, regulatory, due diligence, and legal obstacles make acquisitions in China risky and difficult."[36] Thus, firms must carefully study the risks as well as the potential benefits when contemplating cross-border acquisitions.

STRATEGY RIGHT NOW

Learn more about how the recent global economic crisis changed the cross-border acquisition environment.

www.cengage.com/management/hitt

Cost of New Product Development and Increased Speed to Market

Developing new products internally and successfully introducing them into the marketplace often requires significant investment of a firm's resources, including time, making it difficult to quickly earn a profitable return.[37] Because an estimated 88 percent of innovations fail to achieve adequate returns, firm managers are also concerned with achieving adequate returns from the capital invested to develop and commercialize new products. Potentially contributing to these less-than-desirable rates of return is the successful imitation of approximately 60 percent of innovations within four years after the patents are obtained. These types of outcomes may lead managers to perceive internal product development as a high-risk activity.[38]

Acquisitions are another means a firm can use to gain access to new products and to current products that are new to the firm. Compared with internal product development processes, acquisitions provide more predictable returns as well as faster market entry. Returns are more predictable because the performance of the acquired firm's products can be assessed prior to completing the acquisition.[39]

Recently, America Online (AOL) acquired two online media companies, Patch Media Corp. and Going Inc. AOL acquired these firms to move more rapidly into the relatively fast-growing local online and advertising market. Patch operates Web sites to help local communities publish news and information while Going makes it possible for users to share information about local events. Access to these new products and services supports AOL's other products in the local online and advertising market space such as MapQuest and social networking site Bebo.[40]

STRATEGIC FOCUS

THE INCREASING USE OF ACQUISITION STRATEGIES BY CHINESE FIRMS AS A MEANS OF GAINING MARKET POWER IN A PARTICULAR INDUSTRY

Taking advantage of depressed prices for oil and gas assets and through the access to credit in their home country, Chinese state-owned companies have begun to use acquisitions as the path to securing "the resources needed to power China's growing economy" and to secure access to energy in future years. The belief that the recent global financial crisis has created an "unmatched buying opportunity" is also driving Chinese firms to acquire companies to gain access to their assets and to increase their market power.

The pace of Chinese firms' cross-border acquisitions quickened in 2009. By mid-2009, Chinese companies had completed 10 transactions in the oil and gas space. In contrast, these firms completed only 14 transactions in this space in all of 2008. Moreover, if outstanding bids were accepted by target companies, the amount Chinese firms will have spent on acquisitions would be 80 percent greater than the amount spent previously on a year-to-year basis.

Completed in mid-2009, state-owned Sinopec Group's acquisition of oil exploration company Addax Petroleum Corp. for $8.27 billion Canadian dollars was at the time the largest cross-border acquisition by a Chinese company. Calling the acquisition a "transformational transaction" that would accelerate its international growth, Sinopec paid a 16 percent premium for Addax. Based in Switzerland and listed in London and Toronto, Addax is one of the world's largest independent oil producers in West Africa and the Middle East on the basis of volume. Around the same time, CNOCC, China's top offshore oil and gas producer, hired Goldman Sachs to advise it on bidding to acquire a stake in Kosmos Energy, an Africa-focused oil and gas exploration company. CNOCC hired an investment advisory firm in anticipation of a bidding war breaking out for Kosmos, largely because of the attractiveness of the firm's assets.

Analysts studying these acquisitions and others that likely will be completed conclude that Chinese energy companies are becoming more confident in their ability to create value and gain market power through acquisitions. Business writers describe this confidence as follows: "...deals like the Addax acquisition show (that) they are gradually growing into international oil companies, capable of striking high-profile, cross-border deals. They are even expanding into countries, such as Syria, deemed too risky by Western oil companies."

The 2009 acquisition of Addax Petroleum Corp. with its holdings in Africa and the Middle East by the state-owned Sinopec Group represented at the time the largest Chinese cross-border oil and gas acquisition in history.

But not all of the cross-border acquisitions attempted by Chinese companies have been successful. For example, Anglo-American mining giant Rio Tinto Ltd. rejected Aluminum Corp. of China's (Chinalco) $19.5 billion bid to buy 18 percent of the company. Rio was attractive to Chinalco in that at the time, it was the world's third-largest miner and owned rich iron-ore and copper mines in locations throughout the world, including major facilities in

Australia. This acquisition would have given Chinalco a direct stake in mining assets—assets that were important to China's growth. In particular, iron ore is a crucial ingredient in China's steelmaking operations. Although disappointing, the rejection by Rio Tinto was not expected to slow China's commitment to allow its state-owned companies to pursue cross-border acquisitions as a means of improving their competitiveness in the global economy and as a means of gaining ownership of natural resources the nation believes are vital to its long-term growth.

Sources: 2009, Is China Inc. overpaying in its merger deals? *Wall Street Journal Online*, http://www.wsj.com, June 25; R. Carew, 2009, Chinalco acts to preserve its stake in Rio Tinto, *Wall Street Journal Online*, http://www.wsj.com, July 1; G. Chazan & S. Oster, 2009, Sinopec pact for Addax boosts China's buying binge, *Wall Street Journal Online*, http://www.wsj.com, June 25; E. Fry, 2009, Chinalco buys $1.5 bn Rio Tinto shares, *Financial Times Online*, http://www.ft.com, July 2; K. Maxwell, 2009, Shinsei and Aozora still talking, *Wall Street Journal Online*, http://www.wsj.com, June 26; S. Tucker, 2009, CNOCC considers Kosmos stake bid, *Financial Times Online*, http://www.ft.com, June 20.

A number of pharmaceutical firms use an acquisition strategy because of the cost of new product development. Acquisitions can enable firms to enter markets quickly and to increase the predictability of returns on their investments. To expand on these points, we discuss Pfizer's recently announced horizontal acquisition of Wyeth in the Strategic Focus.

Lower Risk Compared to Developing New Products

Because the outcomes of an acquisition can be estimated more easily and accurately than the outcomes of an internal product development process, managers may view acquisitions as being less risky.[41] However, firms should exercise caution when using acquisitions to reduce their risks relative to the risks the firm incurs when developing new products internally. Indeed, even though research suggests acquisition strategies are a common means of avoiding risky internal ventures (and therefore risky R&D investments), acquisitions may also become a substitute for innovation. Accordingly, acquisitions should always be strategic rather than defensive in nature. Thus, Pfizer's acquisition of Wyeth should be driven by strategic factors (e.g., cost and revenue synergies) instead of by defensive reasons (e.g., to gain sales revenue in the short term that will compensate for the revenue that will be lost when Lipitor goes off patent). Moreover, Pfizer should not reduce its emphasis on increasing the productivity from its R&D expenditures as a result of acquiring Wyeth.

Increased Diversification

Acquisitions are also used to diversify firms. Based on experience and the insights resulting from it, firms typically find it easier to develop and introduce new products in markets they are currently serving. In contrast, it is difficult for companies to develop products that differ from their current lines for markets in which they lack experience.[42] Thus, it is relatively uncommon for a firm to develop new products internally to diversify its product lines.[43]

Cisco Systems is an example of a firm that uses acquisitions to become more diversified. Historically, these acquisitions have helped the firm build its network components business that is focused on producing hardware. Recently, however, Cisco purchased IronPort Systems Inc., a company focused on producing security software for networks. This acquisition will help Cisco diversify its operations beyond its original expertise in network hardware and basic software. Cisco previously acquired technology in the security area through its purchase of Riverhead Networks Inc., Protego Networks Inc., and Perfigo Inc. However, the IronPort deal provides software service in networks that can help guard against spam and viruses that travel through e-mail and Web-based traffic.[44] In 2009, Cisco IronPort announced its "…new managed, hosted and hybrid hosted e-mail security systems that provide the industry's most versatile set of e-mail protection offerings."[45] Thus, the IronPort acquisition seems to be successful in terms of helping Cisco diversify its operations in ways that create value.

STRATEGIC FOCUS

PFIZER'S PROPOSED ACQUISITION OF WYETH: WILL THIS ACQUISITION BE SUCCESSFUL?

Pharmaceutical companies allocate significant amounts of money to research and development (R&D) in efforts to successfully develop new drugs. Pfizer Inc., for example, spends 15 percent of its sales revenue on R&D. As is the case for most if not all of its major competitors, Pfizer is committed to upholding the highest ethical standards when engaging in R&D. According to Pfizer, the firm is "… committed to the safety of patients who take part in our trials and upholds the highest ethical standards in all of (its) research initiatives."

In the words of a scholar who studies innovation: "R&D dollars by definition lead to uncertain outcomes." Because of the high levels of uncertainty associated with efforts to develop products internally, a number of pharmaceutical companies use acquisitions to gain access to new products and to a target firm's capabilities. At this time, some believe that the acquisitions taking place among these firms are "… reconfiguring the entire pharmaceutical sector."

Announced in early 2009, Pfizer's horizontal acquisition of Wyeth for roughly $68 billion was the largest transaction in the pharmaceutical industry in almost a decade. The purchase price meant that Pfizer would pay a premium of approximately 29 percent to acquire Wyeth. As a horizontal acquisition, this price suggested that Pfizer felt that the transaction would result in cost and revenue synergies that at least equaled the amount of the premium it was willing to pay.

Why did Pfizer conclude that this acquisition was in the best interests of its stakeholders—including its shareholders? A key reason was that Wyeth had been investing heavily in biotechnology and vaccines for about three decades. In fact, Wyeth had become the third-largest biotechnology company behind Amgen Inc. and Genentech Inc. Pfizer wanted to gain access to the new products that might flow from Wyeth's biotechnology-oriented R&D investments. Equally important is the contribution Wyeth would make to Pfizer's sales revenue—revenue that was expected to decline significantly after November 2011 when its hugely successful Lipitor drug (a drug for patients to control their high cholesterol) is scheduled to come off patent. The impact of generic drugs being produced to compete against Lipitor was potentially huge for Pfizer in that this drug alone generates about 25 percent of the firm's total revenue.

Libby Welch/Alamy

With the patent on Lipitor due to expire in 2011 and generic competitors lining up, Pfizer's acquisition of Wyeth and its pipeline of new products could help replace anticipated lost revenue.

Analysts' reactions to this acquisition were mixed to negative. Some said that the core problem is that although Wyeth's sales revenue would help Pfizer replace the revenue it will lose after Lipitor goes off patent, it does not deal with the fact that Pfizer is struggling to develop new products in-house. One analyst said that "Pfizer is spending $7.5 billion a year in research and producing almost nothing and now it has to buy Wyeth. If its pipeline were producing it wouldn't need to buy Wyeth."

Evidence suggests that acquisitions in the pharmaceutical industry do tend to generate cost savings through operational synergies. Accordingly, Pfizer's intended acquisition of Wyeth may achieve one of the benefits of a horizontal acquisition. Simultaneously though, Pfizer seeks to rely on Wyeth's capabilities in the biotechnology space to develop new products that the newly formed firm can quickly introduce to the market.

Sources: 2009, Pfizer's acquisition of Wyeth brings scale but will fail to deliver sustainable sales growth, *Trading Markets. com*, http://www.tradingmarkets.com, January 28; C. Arnst, 2009, The drug mergers' harsh side effects, *BusinessWeek Online*, http://www.businessweek.com, March 12; R. Jana, 2009, Do ideas cost too much? *BusinessWeek*, April 20, 46–58; J. Jannarone, 2009, Pfizer treatment is no cure, *Wall Street Journal Online*, http://www.wsj.com, January 24; S. Pettyprice, T. Randall, & Z. Mider, 2009, Pfizer's $68 billion Wyeth deal eases Lipitor loss, *Bloomberg.com*, http://www .bloomberg.com, January 26.

Acquisition strategies can be used to support use of both unrelated and related diversification strategies (see Chapter 6).[46] For example, United Technologies Corp. (UTC) uses acquisitions as the foundation for implementing its unrelated diversification strategy. Since the mid-1970s it has been building a portfolio of stable and noncyclical businesses including Otis Elevator Co. (elevators, escalators, and moving walkways) and Carrier Corporation (heating and air conditioning systems) in order to reduce its dependence on the volatile aerospace industry. Pratt & Whitney (aircraft engines), Hamilton Sundstrand (aerospace and industrial systems), Sikorsky (helicopters), UTC Fire & Security (fire safety and security products and services), and UTC Power (fuel cells and power systems) are the other businesses in which UTC competes as a result of using its acquisition strategy. While each business UTC acquires manufactures industrial and/or commercial products, many have a relatively low focus on technology (e.g., elevators, air conditioners, and security systems).[47] In contrast to UTC, Procter & Gamble (P&G) uses acquisitions to implement its related diversification strategy. Beauty, Health & Well-Being, and Household Care are P&G's core business segments. Gillette's products are included in the Beauty segment, where they are related to other products in this segment such as cosmetics, hair care, and skin care. As noted earlier in the chapter, P&G completed a horizontal acquisition of Gillette in 2006.

Firms using acquisition strategies should be aware that in general, the more related the acquired firm is to the acquiring firm, the greater is the probability the acquisition will be successful.[48] Thus, horizontal acquisitions and related acquisitions tend to contribute more to the firm's strategic competitiveness than do acquisitions of companies operating in product markets that are quite different from those in which the acquiring firm competes.[49]

Reshaping the Firm's Competitive Scope

As discussed in Chapter 2, the intensity of competitive rivalry is an industry characteristic that affects the firm's profitability.[50] To reduce the negative effect of an intense rivalry on their financial performance, firms may use acquisitions to lessen their dependence on one or more products or markets. Reducing a company's dependence on specific markets shapes the firm's competitive scope.

Each time UTC enters a new business (such as UTC Power, the firm's latest business segment), the corporation reshapes its competitive scope. In a more subtle manner, P&G's acquisition of Gillette reshaped its competitive scope by giving P&G a stronger presence in some products for whom men are the target market. By merging their operations, Towers Perrin and Watson Wyatt reshaped the scope of their formerly independent firms' operations in that Towers was stronger in health care consulting while Watson Wyatt was stronger in pension consulting. Thus, using an acquisition strategy reshaped the competitive scope of each of these firms.

Learning and Developing New Capabilities

Firms sometimes complete acquisitions to gain access to capabilities they lack. For example, acquisitions may be used to acquire a special technological capability. Research shows that firms can broaden their knowledge base and reduce inertia through acquisitions.[51]

For example, research suggests that firms increase the potential of their capabilities when they acquire diverse talent through cross-border acquisitions.[52] Of course, firms are better able to learn these capabilities if they share some similar properties with the firm's current capabilities. Thus, firms should seek to acquire companies with different but related and complementary capabilities in order to build their own knowledge base.[53]

A number of large pharmaceutical firms are acquiring the ability to create "large molecule" drugs, also known as biological drugs, by buying bio-technology firms. Thus, these firms are seeking access to both the pipeline of possible drugs and the capabilities that these firms have to produce them. Such capabilities are important for large pharmaceutical firms because these biological drugs are more difficult to duplicate by chemistry alone (the historical basis on which most pharmaceutical firms have expertise). These capabilities will allow generic drug makers to be more successful after chemistry-based drug patents expire. To illustrate the difference between these types of drugs, David Brennen, CEO of British drug maker AstraZeneca, suggested, "Some of these [biological-based drugs] have demonstrated that they're not just symptomatic treatments but that they actually alter the course of the disease."[54] Furthermore, biological drugs must clear more regulatory barriers or hurdles which, when accomplished, add more to the advantage the acquiring firm develops through successful acquisitions.

Problems in Achieving Acquisition Success

Acquisition strategies based on reasons described in this chapter can increase strategic competitiveness and help firms earn above-average returns. However, even when pursued for value-creating reasons, acquisition strategies are not problem-free. Reasons for the use of acquisition strategies and potential problems with such strategies are shown in Figure 7.1.

Research suggests that perhaps 20 percent of all mergers and acquisitions are successful, approximately 60 percent produce disappointing results, and the remaining 20 percent are clear failures.[55] In general, though, companies appear to be increasing their ability to effectively use acquisition strategies. An investment banker representing acquisition clients describes this improvement in the following manner: "I've been doing this work for 20-odd years, and I can tell you that the sophistication of companies going through transactions has increased exponentially."[56] Greater acquisition success accrues to firms able to (1) select the "right" target, (2) avoid paying too high a premium (doing appropriate due diligence), and (3) effectively integrate the operations of the acquiring and target firms.[57] In addition, retaining the target firm's human capital is foundational to efforts by employees of the acquiring firm to fully understand the target firm's operations and the capabilities on which those operations are based.[58] As shown in Figure 7.1, several problems may prevent successful acquisitions.

Integration Difficulties

The importance of a successful integration should not be underestimated.[59] As suggested by a researcher studying the process, "Managerial practice and academic writings show that the post-acquisition integration phase is probably the single most important determinant of shareholder value creation (and equally of value destruction) in mergers and acquisitions."[60]

Although critical to acquisition success, firms should recognize that integrating two companies following an acquisition can be quite difficult. Melding two corporate cultures, linking different financial and control systems, building effective working relationships (particularly when management styles differ), and resolving problems regarding the status of the newly acquired firm's executives are examples of integration challenges firms often face.[61]

Integration is complex and involves a large number of activities, which if overlooked can lead to significant difficulties. For example, when United Parcel Service (UPS) acquired Mail Boxes Etc., a large retail shipping chain, it appeared to be a merger that would generate benefits for both firms. The problem is that most of the Mail Boxes Etc.

Figure 7.1 Reasons for Acquisitions and Problems in Achieving Success

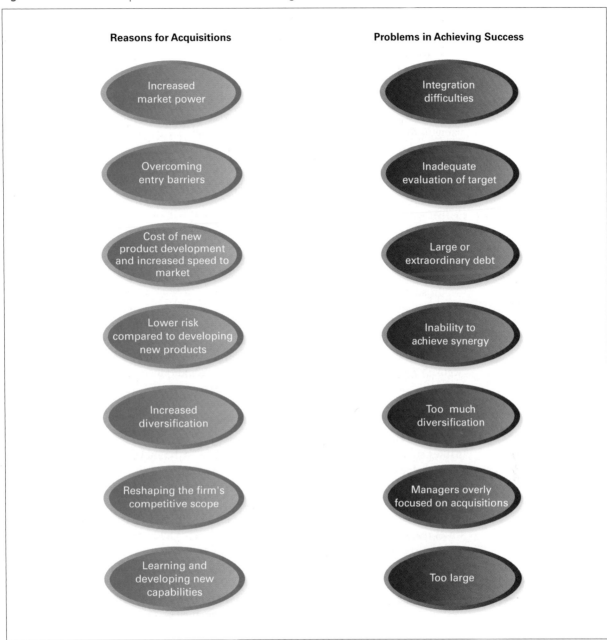

outlets were owned by franchisees. Following the merger, the franchisees lost the ability to deal with other shipping companies such as FedEx, which reduced their competitiveness. Furthermore, franchisees complained that UPS often built company-owned shipping stores close by franchisee outlets of Mail Boxes Etc. Additionally, a culture clash evolved between the free-wheeling entrepreneurs who owned the franchises of Mail Boxes Etc. and the efficiency-oriented corporate approach of the UPS operation, which focused on managing a large fleet of trucks and an information system to efficiently pick up and deliver packages. Also, Mail Boxes Etc. was focused on retail traffic, whereas UPS was focused more on the logistics of wholesale pickup and delivery. Although 87 percent of Mail Boxes Etc. franchisees decided to rebrand under the UPS name, many formed an owner's group and even filed suit against UPS in regard to the unfavorable nature of the franchisee contract.[62]

Inadequate Evaluation of Target

Due diligence is a process through which a potential acquirer evaluates a target firm for acquisition. In an effective due-diligence process, hundreds of items are examined in areas as diverse as the financing for the intended transaction, differences in cultures between the acquiring and target firm, tax consequences of the transaction, and actions that would be necessary to successfully meld the two workforces. Due diligence is commonly performed by investment bankers such as Deutsche Bank, Goldman Sachs, and Morgan Stanley, as well as accountants, lawyers, and management consultants specializing in that activity, although firms actively pursuing acquisitions may form their own internal due-diligence team.[63]

The failure to complete an effective due-diligence process may easily result in the acquiring firm paying an excessive premium for the target company. Interestingly, research shows that in times of high or increasing stock prices due diligence is relaxed; firms often overpay during these periods and long-run performance of the newly formed firm suffers.[64] Research also shows that without due diligence, "the purchase price is driven by the pricing of other 'comparable' acquisitions rather than by a rigorous assessment of where, when, and how management can drive real performance gains. [In these cases], the price paid may have little to do with achievable value."[65]

In addition, firms sometimes allow themselves to enter a "bidding war" for a target, even though they realize that their current bids exceed the parameters identified through due diligence. Earlier, we mentioned NetApp's bid for Data Domain that represents a 419 percent premium. Commenting about this, an analyst said that "… NetApp wouldn't be the first company to stay in a bidding war even when discretion was the better part of valor."[66] Rather than enter a bidding war, firms should only extend bids that are consistent with the results of their due diligence process.

Large or Extraordinary Debt

To finance a number of acquisitions completed during the 1980s and 1990s, some companies significantly increased their levels of debt. A financial innovation called junk bonds helped make this possible. *Junk bonds* are a financing option through which risky acquisitions are financed with money (debt) that provides a large potential return to lenders (bondholders). Because junk bonds are unsecured obligations that are not tied to specific assets for collateral, interest rates for these high-risk debt instruments sometimes reached between 18 and 20 percent during the 1980s.[67] Some prominent financial economists viewed debt as a means to discipline managers, causing them to act in the shareholders' best interests.[68] Managers holding this view are less concerned about the amount of debt their firm assumes when acquiring other companies.

Junk bonds are now used less frequently to finance acquisitions, and the conviction that debt disciplines managers is less strong. Nonetheless, firms sometimes still take on what turns out to be too much debt when acquiring companies. This may be the case for Tata Motors. Some analysts describe Tata's problems with debt this way: "Tata Motors' troubles began last year when it paid $2.3bn for Jaguar and Land Rover and borrowed $3bn to finance the transaction and provide additional working capital."[69] Because of this, some felt that the firm was less capable of providing the capital its various units required to remain competitive.

High debt can have several negative effects on the firm. For example, because high debt increases the likelihood of bankruptcy, it can lead to a downgrade in the firm's credit rating by agencies such as Moody's and Standard & Poor's.[70] In other instances, a firm may have to divest some assets to relieve its debt burden. South Korea's Kimho Asiana Group's decision to divest its Daewoo Engineering & Construction Co. may be an example of this in that the firm's liquidity was being questioned after acquiring both Daewoo and Korea Express within a short time period.[71] Thus, firms using an acquisition strategy must be certain that their purchases do not create a debt load that overpowers the company's ability to remain solvent.

Inability to Achieve Synergy

Derived from *synergos,* a Greek word that means "working together," *synergy* exists when the value created by units working together exceeds the value those units could create working independently (see Chapter 6). That is, synergy exists when assets are worth more when used in conjunction with each other than when they are used separately. For shareholders, synergy generates gains in their wealth that they could not duplicate or exceed through their own portfolio diversification decisions.[72] Synergy is created by the efficiencies derived from economies of scale and economies of scope and by sharing resources (e.g., human capital and knowledge) across the businesses in the merged firm.[73]

A firm develops a competitive advantage through an acquisition strategy only when a transaction generates private synergy. *Private synergy* is created when combining and integrating the acquiring and acquired firms' assets yield capabilities and core competencies that could not be developed by combining and integrating either firm's assets with another company. Private synergy is possible when firms' assets are complementary in unique ways; that is, the unique type of asset complementarity is not possible by combining either company's assets with another firm's assets.[74] Because of its uniqueness, private synergy is difficult for competitors to understand and imitate. However, private synergy is difficult to create.

A firm's ability to account for costs that are necessary to create anticipated revenue- and cost-based synergies affects its efforts to create private synergy. Firms experience several expenses when trying to create private synergy through acquisitions. Called transaction costs, these expenses are incurred when firms use acquisition strategies to create synergy.[75] Transaction costs may be direct or indirect. Direct costs include legal fees and charges from investment bankers who complete due diligence for the acquiring firm. Indirect costs include managerial time to evaluate target firms and then to complete negotiations, as well as the loss of key managers and employees following an acquisition.[76] Firms tend to underestimate the sum of indirect costs when the value of the synergy that may be created by combining and integrating the acquired firm's assets with the acquiring firm's assets is calculated.

Too Much Diversification

As explained in Chapter 6, diversification strategies can lead to strategic competitiveness and above-average returns. In general, firms using related diversification strategies outperform those employing unrelated diversification strategies. However, conglomerates formed by using an unrelated diversification strategy also can be successful, as demonstrated by United Technologies Corp.

At some point, however, firms can become overdiversified. The level at which overdiversification occurs varies across companies because each firm has different capabilities to manage diversification. Recall from Chapter 6 that related diversification requires more information processing than does unrelated diversification. Because of this additional information processing, related diversified firms become overdiversified with a smaller number of business units than do firms using an unrelated diversification strategy.[77] Regardless of the type of diversification strategy implemented, however, overdiversification leads to a decline in performance, after which business units are often divested.[78] Commonly, such divestments, which tend to reshape a firm's competitive scope, are part of a firm's restructuring strategy. (We discuss the strategy in greater detail later in the chapter.)

Even when a firm is not overdiversified, a high level of diversification can have a negative effect on its long-term performance. For example, the scope created by additional amounts of diversification often causes managers to rely on financial rather than strategic controls to evaluate business units' performance (we define and explain financial and strategic controls in Chapters 11 and 12). Top-level executives often rely on financial controls to assess the performance of business units when they do not have a rich understanding of business units' objectives and strategies. Using financial controls, such as return on investment (ROI), causes individual business-unit managers to focus on short-term outcomes at the expense of long-term investments. When long-term investments are reduced to increase short-term profits, a firm's overall strategic competitiveness may be harmed.[79]

Another problem resulting from too much diversification is the tendency for acquisitions to become substitutes for innovation. As we noted earlier, pharmaceutical firms such as Pfizer must be aware of this tendency as they acquire other firms to gain access to their products and capabilities. Typically, managers have no interest in acquisitions substituting for internal R&D efforts and the innovative outcomes that they can produce. However, a reinforcing cycle evolves. Costs associated with acquisitions may result in fewer allocations to activities, such as R&D, that are linked to innovation. Without adequate support, a firm's innovation skills begin to atrophy. Without internal innovation skills, the only option available to a firm to gain access to innovation is to complete still more acquisitions. Evidence suggests that a firm using acquisitions as a substitute for internal innovations eventually encounters performance problems.[80]

Managers Overly Focused on Acquisitions

Typically, a considerable amount of managerial time and energy is required for acquisition strategies to be used successfully. Activities with which managers become involved include (1) searching for viable acquisition candidates, (2) completing effective due-diligence processes, (3) preparing for negotiations, and (4) managing the integration process after completing the acquisition.

Top-level managers do not personally gather all of the data and information required to make acquisitions. However, these executives do make critical decisions on the firms to be targeted, the nature of the negotiations, and so forth. Company experiences show that participating in and overseeing the activities required for making acquisitions can divert managerial attention from other matters that are necessary for long-term competitive success, such as identifying and taking advantage of other opportunities and interacting with important external stakeholders.[81]

Both theory and research suggest that managers can become overly involved in the process of making acquisitions.[82] One observer suggested, "Some executives can become preoccupied with making deals—and the thrill of selecting, chasing and seizing a target."[83] The overinvolvement can be surmounted by learning from mistakes and by not having too much agreement in the boardroom. Dissent is helpful to make sure that all sides of a question are considered (see Chapter 10).[84] When failure does occur, leaders may be tempted to blame the failure on others and on unforeseen circumstances rather than on their excessive involvement in the acquisition process.

In response to a changing external environment, Liz Claiborne CEO William McComb made the decision to slow acquisitions and refocus on key brands and driving cost-efficiencies.

Brendan McDermid/Reuters/Landov

Actions taken at Liz Claiborne Inc. demonstrate the problem of being overly focused on acquisitions. Over time, Claiborne acquired a number of firms in sportswear apparel, growing from 16 to 36 brands in the process of doing so. However, while its managers were focused on making acquisitions, changes were taking place in the firm's external environment, including industry consolidation. Specifically, while most Claiborne sales were focused on traditional department stores, consolidation through acquisitions in this sector left less room for as many brands, given the purchasing practices of the large department stores. Additionally, competitors were gaining favor with customers, leaving fewer sales for Claiborne's products. In response to these problems, CEO William McComb announced in July 2007 a "... framework of a new organizational structure that was a crucial step in making Liz Claiborne Inc. into a more brand-focused and cost-effective business that (could) successfully navigate a rapidly changing retail environment." As a result of these actions, Claiborne is less diversified in terms of brands and less focused on acquisitions. Today, the firm has three distinct brand segments—domestic-based direct brands, international-based direct brands, and partnered brands.[85]

Too Large

Most acquisitions create a larger firm, which should help increase its economies of scale. These economies can then lead to more efficient operations—for example, two sales organizations can be integrated using fewer sales representatives because such sales personnel can sell the products of both firms (particularly if the products of the acquiring and target firms are highly related).[86]

Many firms seek increases in size because of the potential economies of scale and enhanced market power (discussed earlier). At some level, the additional costs required to manage the larger firm will exceed the benefits of the economies of scale and additional market power. The complexities generated by the larger size often lead managers to implement more bureaucratic controls to manage the combined firm's operations. *Bureaucratic controls* are formalized supervisory and behavioral rules and policies designed to ensure consistency of decisions and actions across different units of a firm. However, through time, formalized controls often lead to relatively rigid and standardized managerial behavior. Certainly, in the long run, the diminished flexibility that accompanies rigid and standardized managerial behavior may produce less innovation. Because of innovation's importance to competitive success, the bureaucratic controls resulting from a large organization (i.e., built by acquisitions) can have a detrimental effect on performance. As one analyst noted, "Striving for size per se is not necessarily going to make a company more successful. In fact, a strategy in which acquisitions are undertaken as a substitute for organic growth has a bad track record in terms of adding value."[87]

Effective Acquisitions

Earlier in the chapter, we noted that acquisition strategies do not always lead to above-average returns for the acquiring firm's shareholders.[88] Nonetheless, some companies are able to create value when using an acquisition strategy.[89] The probability of success increases when the firm's actions are consistent with the "attributes of successful acquisitions" shown in Table 7.1.

Cisco Systems is an example of a firm that appears to pay close attention to Table 7.1's attributes when using its acquisition strategy. In fact, Cisco is admired for its ability to complete successful acquisitions. A number of other network companies pursued acquisitions to build up their ability to sell into the network equipment binge, but only Cisco retained much of its value in the post-bubble era. Many firms, such as Lucent, Nortel, and Ericsson, teetered on the edge of bankruptcy after the dot-com bubble burst. When it makes an acquisition, "Cisco has gone much further in its thinking about integration. Not only is retention important, but Cisco also works to minimize the distractions caused by an acquisition. This is important, because the speed of change is so great, that even if the target firm's product development teams are distracted, they will be slowed, contributing to acquisition failure. So, integration must be rapid and reassuring."[90] For example, Cisco facilitates acquired employees' transitions to their new organization through a link on its Web site called "Connection for Acquired Employees." This Web site has been specifically designed for newly acquired employees and provides up-to-date materials tailored to their new jobs.[91]

Table 7.1 Attributes of Successful Acquisitions

Attributes	Results
1. Acquired firm has assets or resources that are complementary to the acquiring firm's core business	1. High probability of synergy and competitive advantage by maintaining strengths
2. Acquisition is friendly	2. Faster and more effective integration and possibly lower premiums
3. Acquiring firm conducts effective due diligence to select target firms and evaluate the target firm's health (financial, cultural, and human resources)	3. Firms with strongest complementarities are acquired and overpayment is avoided
4. Acquiring firm has financial slack (cash or a favorable debt position)	4. Financing (debt or equity) is easier and less costly to obtain
5. Merged firm maintains low to moderate debt position	5. Lower financing cost, lower risk (e.g., of bankruptcy), and avoidance of trade-offs that are associated with high debt
6. Acquiring firm has sustained and consistent emphasis on R&D and innovation	6. Maintain long-term competitive advantage in markets
7. Acquiring firm manages change well and is flexible and adaptable	7. Faster and more effective integration facilitates achievement of synergy

Results from a research study shed light on the differences between unsuccessful and successful acquisition strategies and suggest that a pattern of actions improves the probability of acquisition success.[92] The study shows that when the target firm's assets are complementary to the acquired firm's assets, an acquisition is more successful. With complementary assets, the integration of two firms' operations has a higher probability of creating synergy. In fact, integrating two firms with complementary assets frequently produces unique capabilities and core competencies. With complementary assets, the acquiring firm can maintain its focus on core businesses and leverage the complementary assets and capabilities from the acquired firm. In effective acquisitions, targets are often selected and "groomed" by establishing a working relationship prior to the acquisition.[93] As discussed in Chapter 9, strategic alliances are sometimes used to test the feasibility of a future merger or acquisition between the involved firms.[94]

The study's results also show that friendly acquisitions facilitate integration of the firms involved in an acquisition. Through friendly acquisitions, firms work together to find ways to integrate their operations to create synergy.[95] In hostile takeovers, animosity often results between the two top-management teams, a condition that in turn affects working relationships in the newly created firm. As a result, more key personnel in the acquired firm may be lost, and those who remain may resist the changes necessary to integrate the two firms.[96] With effort, cultural clashes can be overcome, and fewer key managers and employees will become discouraged and leave.[97]

Additionally, effective due-diligence processes involving the deliberate and careful selection of target firms and an evaluation of the relative health of those firms (financial health, cultural fit, and the value of human resources) contribute to successful acquisitions.[98] Financial slack in the form of debt equity or cash, in both the acquiring and acquired firms, also frequently contributes to acquisition success. Even though financial slack provides access to financing for the acquisition, it is still important to maintain a low or moderate level of debt after the acquisition to keep debt costs low. When substantial debt was used to finance the acquisition, companies with successful acquisitions reduced the debt quickly, partly by selling off assets from the acquired firm, especially noncomplementary or poorly performing assets. For these firms, debt costs do not prevent long-term investments such as R&D, and managerial discretion in the use of cash flow is relatively flexible.

Another attribute of successful acquisition strategies is an emphasis on innovation, as demonstrated by continuing investments in R&D activities. Significant R&D investments show a strong managerial commitment to innovation, a characteristic that is increasingly important to overall competitiveness in the global economy as well as to acquisition success.

Flexibility and adaptability are the final two attributes of successful acquisitions. When executives of both the acquiring and the target firms have experience in managing change and learning from acquisitions, they will be more skilled at adapting their capabilities to new environments.[99] As a result, they will be more adept at integrating the two organizations, which is particularly important when firms have different organizational cultures.

As we have learned, firms use an acquisition strategy to grow and achieve strategic competitiveness. Sometimes, though, the actual results of an acquisition strategy fall short of the projected results. When this happens, firms consider using restructuring strategies.

Restructuring

Restructuring is a strategy through which a firm changes its set of businesses or its financial structure.[100] Restructuring is a global phenomenon.[101] From the 1970s into the 2000s, divesting businesses from company portfolios and downsizing accounted for a large percentage of firms' restructuring strategies. Commonly, firms focus on a fewer number of products and markets following restructuring. The words of an executive describe this typical outcome: "Focus on your core business, but don't be distracted, let other people buy assets that aren't right for you."[102]

Although restructuring strategies are generally used to deal with acquisitions that are not reaching expectations, firms sometimes use these strategies because of changes they have detected in their external environment. For example, opportunities sometimes surface in a firm's external environment that a diversified firm can pursue because of the capabilities it has formed by integrating firms' operations. In such cases, restructuring may be appropriate to position the firm to create more value for stakeholders, given the environmental changes.[103]

As discussed next, firms use three types of restructuring strategies: downsizing, downscoping, and leveraged buyouts.

Downsizing

Downsizing is a reduction in the number of a firm's employees and, sometimes, in the number of its operating units, but it may or may not change the composition of businesses in the company's portfolio. Thus, downsizing is an intentional proactive management strategy whereas "decline is an environmental or organizational phenomenon that occurs involuntarily and results in erosion of an organization's resource base."[104] Downsizing is often a part of acquisitions that fail to create the value anticipated when the transaction was completed. Downsizing is often used when the acquiring firm paid too high of a premium to acquire the target firm.[105] Once thought to be an indicator of organizational decline, downsizing is now recognized as a legitimate restructuring strategy.

Reducing the number of employees and/or the firm's scope in terms of products produced and markets served occurs in firms to enhance the value being created as a result of

Restructuring is a strategy through which a firm changes its set of businesses or its financial structure.

completing an acquisition. When integrating the operations of the acquired firm and the acquiring firm, managers may not at first appropriately downsize. This is understandable in that "no one likes to lay people off or close facilities."[106] However, downsizing may be necessary because acquisitions often create a situation in which the newly formed firm has duplicate organizational functions such as sales, manufacturing, distribution, human resource management, and so forth. Failing to downsize appropriately may lead to too many employees doing the same work and prevent the new firm from realizing the cost synergies it anticipated. Managers should remember that as a strategy, downsizing will be far more effective when they consistently use human resource practices that ensure procedural justice and fairness in downsizing decisions.[107]

Downscoping

Downscoping refers to divestiture, spin-off, or some other means of eliminating businesses that are unrelated to a firm's core businesses. Downscoping has a more positive effect on firm performance than does downsizing[108] because firms commonly find that downscoping causes them to refocus on their core business.[109] Managerial effectiveness increases because the firm has become less diversified, allowing the top management team to better understand and manage the remaining businesses.[110]

In response to increasingly negative sales trends in print periodicals and to allow for more internal focus on growth-oriented services, McGraw-Hill is selling BusinessWeek which has been in publication since 1929.

Colin Young-Wolff/PhotoEdit

Motorola Inc. is a firm that has struggled recently. With an interest of refocusing on "technologies that can grow its business" as one path to reversing the firm's fortunes, Motorola is divesting assets that are not related to its core businesses. The recent sale of its fiber-to-the-node product line to Communications Test Design Inc., an engineering, repair, and logistics company, is an example of Motorola's use of a downscoping strategy.[111] In mid-2009, the McGraw-Hill Companies indicated that it was seeking a buyer for *BusinessWeek* magazine. This magazine was one of the products in McGraw's Information and Media business unit (the firm has two other business units). As was the case with many other magazines during the global financial crisis, *BusinessWeek* was being hurt "…by defections of readers and advertisers to the Internet" as well as by the oversupply of business magazine titles.[112] Divesting *BusinessWeek* would allow those leading McGraw's Information & Media unit to refocus on its other businesses, such as J.D. Power and Associates and the Aviation Week Group. Previous to the announcement, McGraw had already divested most of its periodicals.[113]

Firms often use the downscoping and the downsizing strategies simultaneously. However, when doing this, firms avoid layoffs of key employees, in that such layoffs might lead to a loss of one or more core competencies. Instead, a firm that is simultaneously downscoping and downsizing becomes smaller by reducing the diversity of businesses in its portfolio.[114]

In general, U.S. firms use downscoping as a restructuring strategy more frequently than do European companies—in fact, the trend in Europe, Latin America, and Asia has been to build conglomerates. In Latin America, these conglomerates are called *grupos*. Many Asian and Latin American conglomerates have begun to adopt Western corporate strategies in recent years and have been refocusing on their core businesses. This downscoping has occurred simultaneously with increasing globalization and with more open markets that have greatly enhanced competition. By downscoping, these firms have been able to focus on their core businesses and improve their competitiveness.[115]

Leveraged Buyouts

A *leveraged buyout* (LBO) is a restructuring strategy whereby a party (typically a private equity firm) buys all of a firm's assets in order to take the firm private. Once the transaction is completed, the company's stock is no longer traded publicly. Traditionally, leveraged buyouts were used as a restructuring strategy to correct for managerial mistakes or because the firm's managers were making decisions that primarily served their own interests rather than those of shareholders.[116] However, some firms use buyouts to build firm resources and expand rather than simply restructure distressed assets.[117]

Significant amounts of debt are commonly incurred to finance a buyout; hence, the term *leveraged* buyout. To support debt payments and to downscope the company to concentrate on the firm's core businesses, the new owners may immediately sell a number of assets.[118] It is not uncommon for those buying a firm through an LBO to restructure the firm to the point that it can be sold at a profit within a five- to eight-year period.

Management buyouts (MBOs), employee buyouts (EBOs), and whole-firm buyouts, in which one company or partnership purchases an entire company instead of a part of it, are the three types of LBOs. In part because of managerial incentives, MBOs, more so than EBOs and whole-firm buyouts, have been found to lead to downscoping, increased strategic focus, and improved performance.[119] Research shows that management buyouts can lead to greater entrepreneurial activity and growth.[120] As such, buyouts can represent a form of firm rebirth to facilitate entrepreneurial efforts and stimulate strategic growth.[121]

Restructuring Outcomes

The short- and long-term outcomes associated with the three restructuring strategies are shown in Figure 7.2. As indicated, downsizing typically does not lead to higher firm performance.[122] In fact, some research results show that downsizing contributes to lower returns for both U.S. and Japanese firms. The stock markets in the firms' respective

Figure 7.2 Restructuring and Outcomes

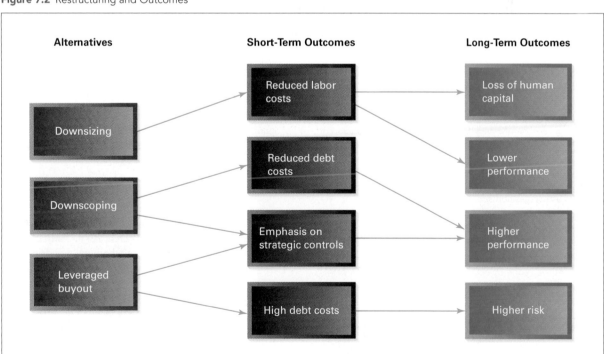

nations evaluated downsizing negatively, believing that it would have long-term negative effects on the firm's efforts to achieve strategic competitiveness. Investors also seem to conclude that downsizing occurs as a consequence of other problems in a company.[123] This assumption may be caused by a firm's diminished corporate reputation when a major downsizing is announced.[124]

The loss of human capital is another potential problem of downsizing (see Figure 7.2). Losing employees with many years of experience with the firm represents a major loss of knowledge. As noted in Chapter 3, knowledge is vital to competitive success in the global economy. Thus, in general, research evidence and corporate experience suggest that downsizing may be of more tactical (or short-term) value than strategic (or long-term) value,[125] meaning that firms should exercise caution when restructuring through downsizing.

Downscoping generally leads to more positive outcomes in both the short and long term than does downsizing or a leveraged buyout. Downscoping's desirable long-term outcome of higher performance is a product of reduced debt costs and the emphasis on strategic controls derived from concentrating on the firm's core businesses. In so doing, the refocused firm should be able to increase its ability to compete.[126]

Although whole-firm LBOs have been hailed as a significant innovation in the financial restructuring of firms, they can involve negative trade-offs.[127] First, the resulting large debt increases the firm's financial risk, as is evidenced by the number of companies that filed for bankruptcy in the 1990s after executing a whole-firm LBO. Sometimes, the intent of the owners to increase the efficiency of the bought-out firm and then sell it within five to eight years creates a short-term and risk-averse managerial focus.[128] As a result, these firms may fail to invest adequately in R&D or take other major actions designed to maintain or improve the company's core competence.[129] Research also suggests that in firms with an entrepreneurial mind-set, buyouts can lead to greater innovation, especially if the debt load is not too great.[130] However, because buyouts more often result in significant debt, most LBOs have been completed in mature industries where stable cash flows are possible.

SUMMARY

- Although the number of mergers and acquisitions completed declined in 2008 and early 2009, largely because of the global financial crisis, merger and acquisition strategies remain popular as a path to firm growth and earning of strategic competitiveness. Globalization and deregulation of multiple industries in many economies are two of the factors making mergers and acquisitions attractive to large corporations and small firms.

- Firms use acquisition strategies to (1) increase market power, (2) overcome entry barriers to new markets or regions, (3) avoid the costs of developing new products and increase the speed of new market entries, (4) reduce the risk of entering a new business, (5) become more diversified, (6) reshape their competitive scope by developing a different portfolio of businesses, and (7) enhance their learning as the foundation for developing new capabilities.

- Among the problems associated with using an acquisition strategy are (1) the difficulty of effectively integrating the firms involved, (2) incorrectly evaluating the target firm's value, (3) creating debt loads that preclude adequate long-term investments (e.g., R&D), (4) overestimating the potential for synergy, (5) creating a firm that is too diversified, (6) creating an internal environment in which managers devote increasing amounts of their time and energy to analyzing and completing the acquisition, and (7) developing a combined firm that is too large, necessitating extensive use of bureaucratic, rather than strategic, controls.

- Effective acquisitions have the following characteristics: (1) the acquiring and target firms have complementary resources that are the foundation for developing new capabilities; (2) the acquisition is friendly, thereby facilitating integration of the firms' resources; (3) the target firm is selected and purchased based on thorough due diligence; (4) the acquiring and target firms have considerable slack in the form of cash or debt capacity; (5) the newly formed firm maintains a low or moderate level of debt by selling off portions of the acquired firm or some of the acquiring firm's poorly performing units; (6) the acquiring and acquired firms have experience in terms of adapting to change; and (7) R&D and innovation are emphasized in the new firm.

- Restructuring is used to improve a firm's performance by correcting for problems created by ineffective management. Restructuring by downsizing involves reducing the number of employees and hierarchical levels in the firm. Although it can lead to short-term cost reductions, they may be realized at the expense of long-term success, because of the loss of valuable human resources (and knowledge) and overall corporate reputation.

- The goal of restructuring through downscoping is to reduce the firm's level of diversification. Often, the firm divests unrelated businesses to achieve this goal. Eliminating unrelated businesses makes it easier for the firm and its top-level managers to refocus on the core businesses.

- Through an LBO, a firm is purchased so that it can become a private entity. LBOs usually are financed largely through debt. Management buyouts (MBOs), employee buyouts (EBOs), and whole-firm LBOs are the three types of LBOs. Because they provide clear managerial incentives, MBOs have been the most successful of the three. Often, the intent of a buyout is to improve efficiency and performance to the point where the firm can be sold successfully within five to eight years.

- Commonly, restructuring's primary goal is gaining or reestablishing effective strategic control of the firm. Of the three restructuring strategies, downscoping is aligned most closely with establishing and using strategic controls and usually improves performance more on a comparative basis.

REVIEW QUESTIONS

1. Why are merger and acquisition strategies popular in many firms competing in the global economy?

2. What reasons account for firms' decisions to use acquisition strategies as a means to achieving strategic competitiveness?

3. What are the seven primary problems that affect a firm's efforts to successfully use an acquisition strategy?

4. What are the attributes associated with a successful acquisition strategy?

5. What is the restructuring strategy, and what are its common forms?

6. What are the short- and long-term outcomes associated with the different restructuring strategies?

EXPERIENTIAL EXERCISES

EXERCISE 1: HOW DID THE DEAL WORK OUT?

The text argues that mergers and acquisitions are a popular strategy for businesses both in the United States and abroad. However, returns for acquiring firms do not always live up to expectations. This exercise seeks to address this notion by analyzing, pre and post hoc, the results of actual acquisitions. By looking at the notifications of a deal beforehand, categorizing that deal, and then following it for a year, you will be able to learn about actual deals and their implications for strategic leaders and their firms.

Working in teams, identify a merger or acquisition that was completed in the last few years. This may be a cross-border acquisition or one centered in the United States. A couple of possible sources for this information are Reuters's Online M&A section or Yahoo! Finance's U.S. Mergers and Acquisitions Calendar. Each team must have its M&A choice approved in advance so as to avoid duplicates.

To complete this assignment you should be prepared to answer the following questions:

1. Describe the environment for the merger or acquisition you identified at the time it was completed. Using concepts discussed in the text, focus on management's representation to shareholders, industry environment, and the overall rationale for the transaction.

2. Did the acquirer pay a premium for the target firm? If so, how much? In addition, search for investor comments regarding the

wisdom of the transaction. Attempt to identify how the market reacted at the announcement of the transaction (LexisNexis often provides an article that will address this issue).

3. Describe the transaction going forward. Use concepts from the text such as, but not limited to:

- The reason for the transaction (i.e., market power, overcoming entry barriers, etc.)
- Any problems in achieving acquisition success
- Whether the transaction has been a success or not and why.

Prepare a 10- to 15-minute presentation for the class describing your findings. Organize the presentation as if you were updating the shareholders of the newly formed firm.

EXERCISE 2: CADBURY SCHWEPPES

Cadbury and Schweppes are two prominent and long-established companies. Cadbury was founded in 1824 and is the world's largest confectionary company. The bulk of Cadbury's sales are generated in Europe, with a substantially smaller presence in the Americas. Schweppes was founded in 1783, when its founder Jacob Schweppes invented a system to carbonate mineral water. Its brands include 7-Up, Dr Pepper, Sunkist, Snapple, Schweppes, and Mott's. Cadbury and Schweppes merged in 1969. In 2008, the combined firm posted approximately $32 billion in revenue and an $8.8 billion loss. The firm employed 160,000 people at this time. In what is termed a "demerger," the firm in 2008 spun off its North American beverage unit (Dr Pepper Snapple Group) and changed its name from Cadbury Schweppes to just Cadbury. Working in teams, prepare a brief PowerPoint presentation to address the following questions. You will need to consult the company's now separate Web sites http://www.drpeppersnapplegroup.com/ and http://www.cadbury.com, as well as news articles published about this event. Lexis Nexis is a good resource for news on topics such as this.

1. Why did Cadbury decide to divest itself of the beverage business?
2. What does it mean that Cadbury listed the separation as a demerger?
3. What factors hindered the success of a combined Cadbury Schweppes?
4. Do you feel that both the beverage and confectionary businesses are better or worse off being separated?

VIDEO CASE

FOCUS ON WHY A DEAL IS DONE, NOT HOW

Stuart Grief/Vice President of Strategy and Development/Textron

Stuart Grief, Vice President of Strategy and Development at Textron, talks about the art of the deal and how the company he represents goes through deal-making analysis. As you prepare for the video, consider the concepts of negotiation and deal-making; important ingredients of any M&A activity.

Before you watch the video consider the following concepts and questions and be prepared to discuss them in class:

Concepts
- M&A strategies
- Reasons for acquisition
- Problems in achieving success

Questions

1. Think through a deal or transaction you have recently made or considered making (i.e., purchased a car, bought a new computer, leased an apartment, took out a loan). Describe the deal-making process and why you ultimately decided to either make the deal or walk away from it.
2. How would you characterize Textron's corporate-level strategy? Visit the firm's Web site to see the various business units it manages. Describe what you think are the criteria the firm uses when evaluating targets for acquisition. Does it appear that Textron is willing to acquire any type of firm in any industry?
3. Overall, how should a company plan and undertake its merger and acquisition strategic initiatives?

NOTES

1. M. L. McDonald, J. D. Westphal, & M. E. Graebner, 2008, What do they know? The effects of outside director acquisition experience on firm acquisition performance, *Strategic Management Journal*, 29: 1155–1177; K. Uhlenbruck, M. A. Hitt, & M. Semadeni, 2006, Market value effects of acquisitions involving Internet firms: A resource-based analysis, *Strategic Management Journal*, 27: 899–913.
2. J. Wiklund & D. A. Shepherd, 2009, The effectiveness of alliances and acquisitions: The role of resource combination activities, *Entrepreneurship Theory and Practice*, 33: 193–212; C.-C. Lu, 2006, Growth strategies and merger patterns among small and medium sized enterprises: An empirical study, *International Journal of Management*, 23: 529–547.
3. M. A. Hitt, D. King, H. Krishnan, M. Makri, M. Schijven, K. Shimizu, & H. Zhu, 2009, Mergers and acquisitions: Overcoming pitfalls, building synergy and creating value, *Business Horizons*, in press.
4. G. M. McNamara, J. Haleblian, & B. J. Dykes, 2008, The performance implications of participating in an

acquisition wave: Early mover advantages, bandwagon effects, and the moderating influence of industry characteristics and acquirer tactics, *Academy of Management Journal*, 51: 113–130; J. Haleblian; J. Y. Kim, & N. Rajagopalan, 2006, The influence of acquisition experience and performance on acquisition behavior: Evidence from the U.S. commercial banking industry, *Academy of Management Journal*, 49: 357–370; M. A. Hitt, J. S. Harrison, & R. D. Ireland, 2001, *Mergers and Acquisitions: A Guide to Creating Value for Stakeholders*, New York: Oxford University Press.
5. R. Dobbs & V. Tortorici, 2007, Cool heads will bring in the best deals; Boardroom discipline is vital if the M&A boom is to benefit shareholders, *Financial Times*, February 28, 6.
6. J. Silver-Greenberg, 2009, Dealmakers test the waters, *BusinessWeek*, March 2, 18–20.
7. J. Y. Kim & S. Finkelstein, 2009, The effects of strategic and market complementarity on acquisition performance: Evidence from the U.S. commercial banking industry, 1989–2001;

Strategic Management Journal, 30: 617–646; J. J. Reuer, 2005, Avoiding lemons in M&A deals, *MIT Sloan Management Review*, 46(3).
8. M. Baker, X. Pan, & J. Wurgler, 2009, The psychology of pricing in mergers and acquisitions, Working Paper: http://www.papers.ssrn.com/so13/papers.cfm?abstract_id=1364152; K. Cool & M. Van de Laar, 2006, The performance of acquisitive companies in the U.S. In L. Renneboog (ed.), *Advances in Corporate Finance and Asset Pricing*, Amsterdam, Netherlands: Elsevier Science, 77–105.
9. M. Peers, 2009, NetApp should end Data Domain chase, *Wall Street Journal Online*, http://www.wsj.com, July 6.
10. K. J. Martijn Cremers, V. B. Nair, & K. John, 2009, Takeovers and the cross-section of returns, *Review of Financial Studies*, 22: 1409–1445; C. Tuch & N. O'Sullivan, 2007, The impact of acquisitions on firm performance: A review of the evidence, *International Journal of Management Review*, 9(2): 141–170.
11. J. McCracken & J. S. Lublin, 2009, Towers Perrin and Watson Wyatt to merge, *Wall*

Street Journal Online, http://www.wsj.com, June 29.

12. M. Curtin, 2009, Xstrata's well-timed bear hug, *Wall Street Journal Online,* http://www.wsj.com, June 22.

13. S. Sudarsanam & A. A. Mahate, 2006, Are friendly acquisitions too bad for shareholders and managers? Long-term value creation and top management turnover in hostile and friendly acquirers, *British Journal of Management: Supplement,* 17(1): S7–S30.

14. A. R. Sorkin, 2009, Exelon raises hostile bid for NRG, *New York Times Online,* http://www.nytimes.com, July 2.

15. E. Akdogu, 2009, Gaining a competitive edge through acquisitions: Evidence from the telecommunications industry, *Journal of Corporate Finance,* 15: 99–112; E. Devos, P.-R. Kadapakkam, & S. Krishnamurthy, 2009, How do mergers create value? A comparison of taxes, market power, and efficiency improvements as explanations for synergies, *Review of Financial Studies,* 22: 1179–1211.

16. J. Haleblian, C. E. Devers, G. McNamara, M. A. Carpenter, & R. B. Davison, 2009, Taking stock of what we know about mergers and acquisitions: A review and research agenda, *Journal of Management,* 35: 469–502; P. Wright, M. Kroll, & D. Elenkov, 2002, Acquisition returns, increase in firm size and chief executive officer compensation: The moderating role of monitoring, *Academy of Management Journal,* 45: 599–608.

17. A. Vance, 2009, Acer's chief urges more consolidation of the PC industry, *New York Times Online,* http://www.nytimes.com, July 7.

18. C. Tighe, 2009, Vertu buys up Brooklyn assets, *Financial Times Online,* http://www.ft.com, June 27;

19. K. E. Meyer, S. Estrin, S. K. Bhaumik, & M. W. Peng, 2009, Institutions, resources, and entry strategies in emerging economies, *Strategic Management Journal,* 30: 61–80; D. K. Oler, J. S. Harrison, & M. R. Allen, 2008, The danger of misinterpreting short-window event study findings in strategic management research: An empirical illustration using horizontal acquisitions, *Strategic Organization,* 6: 151–184.

20. A. Harrison, 2009, NAB buys Aviva assets, *Wall Street Journal Online,* http://www.wsj.com, June 23.

21. N. Casey, 2009, Toys "R" Us is purchasing retailer FAO Schwarz, *Wall Street Journal Online,* http://www.wsj.com, May 28.

22. C. E. Fee & S. Thomas, 2004, Sources of gains in horizontal mergers: Evidence from customer, supplier, and rival firms, *Journal of Financial Economics,* 74: 423–460.

23. T. Ushijima, 2009, R&D intensity and acquisition and divestiture of corporate assets: Evidence from Japan, *Journal of Economics and Business,* 61(5): 415–433; L. Capron, W. Mitchell, & A. Swaminathan, 2001, Asset divestiture following horizontal acquisitions: A dynamic view, *Strategic Management Journal,* 22: 817–844.

24. B. Gulbrandsen, K. Sandvik, & S. A. Haugland, 2009, Antecedents of vertical integration: Transaction cost economics and resource-based explanations, *Journal of Purchasing and Supply Management,* 15: 89–102; F. T. Rothaermel, M. A. Hitt, & L. A. Jobe, 2006, Balancing vertical integration and strategic outsourcing: Effects on product portfolio, product success, and firm performance, *Strategic Management Journal,* 27: 1033–1056.

25. A. Parmigiani, 2007, Why do firms both make and buy? An investigation of concurrent sourcing, *Strategic Management Journal,* 28: 285–311.

26. 2009, Our businesses, http://www.info.cvscaremark.com, July 7.

27. 2009, Boeing completes acquisition of eXMeritus Inc., http://www.boeing.mediaroom.com, June 22.

28. J. W. Brock & N. P. Obst, 2009, Market concentration, economic welfare, and antitrust policy, *Journal of Industry, Competition and Trade,* 9: 65–75; M. T. Brouwer, 2008, Horizontal mergers and efficiencies: Theory and antitrust practice, *European Journal of Law and Economics,* 26: 11–26.

29. 2008, Procter & Gamble Annual Report, http://www.pg.com, July.

30. K. E. Meyer, M. Wright, & S. Pruthi, 2009, Managing knowledge in foreign entry strategies: A resource-based analysis, *Strategic Management Journal,* 30: 557–574; S.-F. S. Chen & M. Zeng, 2004, Japanese investors' choice of acquisitions vs. startups in the U.S.: The role of reputation barriers and advertising outlays, *International Journal of Research in Marketing,* 21(2): 123–136.

31. C. Y. Tseng, 2009, Technological innovation in the BRIC economies, *Research-Technology Management,* 52: 29–35; S. McGee, 2007, Seeking value in BRICs, *Barron's,* July 9, L10–L11.

32. R. Chakrabarti, N. Jayaraman, & S. Mukherjee, 2009, Mars-Venus marriages: Culture and cross-border M&A, *Journal of International Business Studies,* 40: 216–237.

33. S. Jessop, 2009, "Brave" post-Lehman M&A rewarded by market—Study, *New York Times Online,* http://www.nytimes.com, July 5.

34. E. Zabinski, D. Freeman, & X. Jian, 2009, Navigating the challenges of cross-border M&A, *The Deal Magazine,* http://www.thedeal.com, May 29.

35. N. Kumar, 2009, *The Economic Times,* http://www.economictimes.indiatimes.com, March 27.

36. J. Chapman & W. Xu, 2008, Ten strategies for successful cross-border acquisitions in China, Nixon Peabody LLP Special Report, Mergers & Acquisitions, September, 30–35.

37. M. Makri, M. A. Hitt, & P. J. Lane, 2009, Complementary technologies, knowledge relatedness, and invention outcomes in high technology M&As, *Strategic Management Journal,* in press; C. Homburg & M. Bucerius, 2006, Is speed of integration really a success factor of mergers and acquisitions? An analysis of the role of internal and external relatedness, *Strategic Management Journal,* 27: 347–367.

38. H. K. Ellonen, P. Wilstrom, & A. Jantunen, 2009, Linking dynamic-capability portfolios and innovation outcomes, *Technovation,* in press; M. Song & C. A. De Benedetto, 2008, Supplier's involvement and success of radical new product development in new ventures, *Journal of Operations Management,* 26: 1–22; S. Karim, 2006, Modularity in organizational structure: The reconfiguration of internally developed and acquired business units, *Strategic Management Journal,* 27: 799–823.

39. R. E. Hoskisson & L. W. Busenitz, 2002, Market uncertainty and learning distance in corporate entrepreneurship entry mode choice, in M. A. Hitt, R. D. Ireland, S. M. Camp, & D. L. Sexton (eds.), *Strategic Entrepreneurship: Creating a New Mindset,* Oxford, U.K.: Blackwell Publishers, 151–172; M. A. Hitt, R. E. Hoskisson, R. A. Johnson, & D. D. Moesel, 1996, The market for corporate control and firm innovation, *Academy of Management Journal,* 39: 1084–1119.

40. E. Steel, 2009, AOL buys two companies specializing in local online media, *Wall Street Journal Online,* http://www.wsj.com, June 11.

41. W. P. Wan & D. W Yiu, 2009, From crisis to opportunity: Environmental jolt, corporate acquisitions, and firm performance, *Strategic Management Journal,* 30: 791–801; L. F. Hsieh & Y.-T. Tsai, 2005, Technology investment mode of innovative technological corporations: M&A strategy intended to facilitate innovation, *Journal of American Academy of Business,* 6(1): 185–194; G. Ahuja & R. Katila, 2001, Technological acquisitions and the innovation performance of acquiring firms: A longitudinal study, *Strategic Management Journal,* 22: 197–220.

42. F. Damanpour, R. M. Walker, & C. N. Avellaneda, 2009, Combinative effects of innovation types and organizational performance: A longitudinal study of service organizations, *Journal of Management Studies,* 46: 650–675.

43. F. Vermeulen, 2005, How acquisitions can revitalize companies, *MIT Sloan Management Review,* 46(4): 45–51; M. A. Hitt, R. E. Hoskisson, R. D. Ireland, & J. S. Harrison, 1991, Effects of acquisitions on R&D inputs and outputs, *Academy of Management Journal,* 34: 693–706.

44. B. White, 2007, Cisco to buy IronPort, a network-security firm, *Wall Street Journal,* January 4, A10.

45. 2009, Cisco breaks new ground in e-mail security, http://www.cisco.com, March 3.

46. H. Prechel, T. Morris, T. Woods, & R. Walden, 2008, Corporate diversification revisited: The political-legal environment, the multilayer-subsidiary form, and mergers and acquisitions, *The Sociological Quarterly*, 49: 849–878; C. E. Helfat & K. M. Eisenhardt, 2004, Inter-temporal economies of scope, organizational modularity, and the dynamics of diversification, *Strategic Management Journal*, 25: 1217–1232.

47. J. L. Lunsford, 2007, Boss talk: Transformer in transition; He turned UTC into giant; now, CEO George David carefully prepares successor, *Wall Street Journal*, May 17, B1.

48. T. Laamanen & T. Keil, 2008, Performance of serial acquirers: Toward an acquisition program perspective, *Strategic Management Journal*, 29: 663–672; D. J. Miller, M. J. Fern, & L. B. Cardinal, 2007, The use of knowledge for technological innovation within diversified firms, *Academy of Management Journal*, 50: 308–326.

49. J. Anand & H. Singh, 1997, Asset redeployment, acquisitions and corporate strategy in declining industries, *Strategic Management Journal*, 18 (Special Issue): 99–118.

50. T. Yu, M. Subramaniam, & A. A. Cannella, Jr., 2009, Rivalry deterrence in international markets: Contingencies governing the mutual forbearance hypothesis, *Academy of Management Journal*, 52: 127–147; D. G. Sirmon, S. Gove, & M. A. Hitt, 2008, Resource management in dyadic competitive rivalry: The effects of resource bundling and deployment, *Academy of Management Journal*, 51: 919–933.

51. H. Rui & G. S. Yip, 2008, Foreign acquisitions by Chinese firms: A strategic intent perspective, *Journal of World Business*, 43: 213–226; P. Puranam & K. Srikanth, 2007, What they know vs. what they do: How acquirers leverage technology acquisitions, *Strategic Management Journal*, 28: 805–825.

52. S. A. Zahra & J. C. Hayton, 2008, The effect of international venturing on firm performance: The moderating influence of absorptive capacity, *Journal of Business Venturing*, 23: 195–220.

53. J. S. Harrison, M. A. Hitt, R. E. Hoskisson, & R. D. Ireland, 2001, Resource complementarity in business combinations: Extending the logic to organizational alliances, *Journal of Management*, 27: 679–690.

54. J. Whalen, 2007, AstraZeneca thinks bigger; new chief increases commitment to 'large molecule' biological drugs, *Wall Street Journal*, May 22, A7.

55. J. A. Schmidt, 2002, Business perspective on mergers and acquisitions, in J. A. Schmidt (ed.), *Making Mergers Work*, Alexandria, VA: Society for Human Resource Management, 23–46.

56. Jessop, "Brave" post-Lehman M&A rewarded by market.

57. M. Cording, P. Christmann, & D. R. King, 2008, Reducing causal ambiguity in acquisition integration: Intermediate goals as mediators of integration decisions and acquisition performance, *Academy of Management Journal*, 51: 744–767; M. Zollo & H. Singh, 2004, Deliberate learning in corporate acquisitions: Post-acquisition strategies and integration capability in U.S. bank mergers, *Strategic Management Journal*, 25: 1233–1256.

58. N. Kumar, 2009, How emerging giants are rewriting the rules of M&A, *Harvard Business Review*, 87(5): 115–121; M. C. Sturman, 2008, The value of human capital specificity versus transferability, *Journal of Management*, 34: 290–316.

59. K. M. Ellis, T. H. Reus, & B. T. Lamont, 2009, The effects of procedural and informational justice in the integration of related acquisitions, *Strategic Management Journal*, 30: 137–161; F. Vermeulen, 2007, Business insight (a special report); bad deals: Eight warning signs that an acquisition may not pay off, *Wall Street Journal*, April 28, R10.

60. M. Zollo, 1999, M&A—The challenge of learning to integrate: Mastering strategy (part eleven), *Financial Times*, December 6, 14–15.

61. H. G. Barkema & M. Schijven, 2008, Toward unlocking the full potential of acquisitions: The role of organizational restructuring, *Academy of Management Journal*, 51: 696–722; J. Harrison, 2007, Why integration success eludes many buyers, *Mergers and Acquisitions*, 42(3): 18–20.

62. R. Gibson, 2006, Package deal; UPS's purchase of Mail Boxes Etc. looked great on paper. Then came the culture clash, *Wall Street Journal*, May 8, R13.

63. Z. Kouwe, 2009, Deals on ice in first half, with 40% drop in M&A, *New York Times Online*, http://www.nytimes.com, July 1.

64. T. B. Folta & J. P. O'Brien, 2008, Determinants of firm-specific thresholds in acquisition decisions, *Managerial and Decision Economics*, 29: 209–225; R. J. Rosen, 2006, Merger momentum and investor sentiment: The stock market reaction to merger announcements, *Journal of Business*, 79: 987–1017.

65. A. Rappaport & Sirower, Stock or cash? *Harvard Business Review*, 77(6): 149.

66. Peers, NetApp should end Data Domain chase.

67. G. Yago, 1991, *Junk Bonds: How High Yield Securities Restructured Corporate America*, New York: Oxford University Press, 146–148.

68. M. C. Jensen, 1986, Agency costs of free cash flow, corporate finance, and takeovers, *American Economic Review*, 76: 323–329.

69. J. Leahy & J. Reed, 2009, Tata strained by UK acquisitions, *Financial Times Online*, http://www.ft.com, May 21.

70. T. H. Noe & M. J. Rebello, 2006, The role of debt purchases in takeovers: A tale of two retailers, *Journal of Economics &*

Management Strategy, 15 (3): 609–648; M. A. Hitt & D. L. Smart, 1994, Debt: A disciplining force for managers or a debilitating force for organizations? *Journal of Management Inquiry*, 3: 144–152.

71. C. Jong-Woo, 2009, Kumho Asiana to sell Daewoo Engineering, *Fidelity.com*, http://www.fidelity.com, June 28.

72. S. W. Bauguess, S. B. Moeller, F. P. Schlingemann, & C. J. Zutter, 2009, Ownership structure and target returns, *Journal of Corporate Finance*, 15: 48–65; H. Donker & S. Zahir, 2008, Takeovers, corporate control, and return to target shareholders, *International Journal of Corporate Governance*, 1: 106–134.

73. A. B. Sorescu, R. K. Chandy, & J. C. Prabhu, 2007, Why some acquisitions do better than others: Product capital as a driver of long-term stock returns, *Journal of Marketing Research*, 44(1): 57–72; T. Saxton & M. Dollinger, 2004, Target reputation and appropriability: Picking and deploying resources in acquisitions, *Journal of Management*, 30: 123–147.

74. J. B. Barney, 1988, Returns to bidding firms in mergers and acquisitions: Reconsidering the relatedness hypothesis, *Strategic Management Journal*, 9 (Special Issue): 71–78.

75. O. E. Williamson, 1999, Strategy research: Governance and competence perspectives, *Strategic Management Journal*, 20: 1087–1108.

76. S. Chatterjee, 2007, Why is synergy so difficult in mergers of related businesses? *Strategy & Leadership*, 35(2): 46–52.

77. J. Santalo & M. Becerra, 2009, Competition from specialized firms and the diversification-performance linkage, *Journal of Finance*, 63: 851–883; C. W. L. Hill & R. E. Hoskisson, 1987, Strategy and structure in the multiproduct firm, *Academy of Management Review*, 12: 331–341.

78. M. L. A. Hayward & K. Shimizu, 2006, De-commitment to losing strategic action: Evidence from the divestiture of poorly performing acquisitions, *Strategic Management Journal*, 27: 541–557; R. A. Johnson, R. E. Hoskisson, & M. A. Hitt, 1993, Board of director involvement in restructuring: The effects of board versus managerial controls and characteristics, *Strategic Management Journal*, 14 (Special Issue): 33–50; C. C. Markides, 1992, Consequences of corporate refocusing: Ex ante evidence, *Academy of Management Journal*, 35: 398–412.

79. D. Marginso & L. McAulay, 2008, Exploring the debate on short-termism: A theoretical and empirical analysis, *Strategic Management Journal*, 29: 273–292; R. E. Hoskisson & R. A. Johnson, 1992, Corporate restructuring and strategic change: The effect on diversification strategy and R&D intensity, *Strategic Management Journal*, 13: 625–634.

80. T. Keil, M. V. J. Maula, H. Schildt, & S. A. Zahra, 2008, The effect of governance modes and relatedness of external business development activities on innovative performance, *Strategic Management Journal*, 29: 895–907; K. H. Tsai & J. C. Wang, 2008, External technology acquisition and firm performance: A longitudinal study, *Journal of Business Venturing*, 23: 91–112.

81. A. Kacperczyk, 2009, With greater power comes greater responsibility? Takeover protection and corporate attention to stakeholders, *Strategic Management Journal*, 30: 261–285; L. H. Lin, 2009, Mergers and acquisitions, alliances and technology development: An empirical study of the global auto industry, *International Journal of Technology Management*, 48: 295–307; M. L. Barnett, 2008, An attention-based view of real options reasoning, *Academy of Management Review*, 33: 606–628.

82. M. L. A. Hayward & D. C. Hambrick, 1997, Explaining the premiums paid for large acquisitions: Evidence of CEO hubris, *Administrative Science Quarterly* 42: 103–127; R. Roll, 1986, The hubris hypothesis of corporate takeovers, *Journal of Business*, 59: 197–216.

83. Vermeulen, Business insight (a special report); bad deals: Eight warning signs that an acquisition may not pay off.

84. L. A. Nemanich & D. Vera, 2009, Transformational leadership and ambidexterity in the context of an acquisition, *The Leadership Quarterly*, 20: 19–33.

85. 2009, Our company, http://www .lizclaiborne.com, July 12; R. Dobbs, 2007, Claiborne seeks to shed 16 apparel brands, *Wall Street Journal*, July 11, B1, B2.

86. V. Swaminathan, F. Murshed, & J. Hulland, 2008, Value creation following merger and acquisition announcements: The role of strategic emphasis alignment, *Journal of Marketing Research*, 45: 33–47.

87. Vermeulen, Business insight (a special report); bad deals: Eight warning signs that an acquisition may not pay off.

88. H. G. Barkema & M. Schijven, 2008, How do firms learn to make acquisitions? A review of past research and an agenda for the future, *Journal of Management*, 34: 594–634.

89. S. Chatterjee, 2009, The keys to successful acquisition programmes, *Long Range Planning*, 42: 137–163; C. M. Sanchez & S. R. Goldberg, 2009, Strategic M&As: Stronger in tough times? *Journal of Corporate Accounting & Finance*, 20: 3–7; C. Duncan & M. Mtar, 2006, Determinants of international acquisition success: Lessons from FirstGroup in North America, *European Management Journal*, 24: 396–410.

90. D. Mayer & M. Kenney, 2004, Economic action does not take place in a vacuum: Understanding Cisco's acquisition and development strategy, *Industry and Innovation*, 11(4): 299–325.

91. 2009, Connection for acquired employees, http://www.cisco.com, July 12.

92. M. A. Hitt, R. D. Ireland, J. S. Harrison, & A. Best, 1998, Attributes of successful and unsuccessful acquisitions of U.S. firms, *British Journal of Management*, 9: 91–114.

93. Uhlenbruck, Hitt, & Semadeni, Market value effects of acquisitions involving Internet firms: A resource-based analysis; J. Hagedoorn & G. Dysters, 2002, External sources of innovative capabilities: The preference for strategic alliances or mergers and acquisitions, *Journal of Management Studies*, 39: 167–188.

94. J. J. Reuer & R. Ragozzino, 2006, Agency hazards and alliance portfolios, *Strategic Management Journal*, 27: 27–43; P. Porrini, 2004, Can a previous alliance between an acquirer and a target affect acquisition performance? *Journal of Management*, 30: 545–562.

95. D. J. Kisgen, J. Qian, & W. Song, 2009, Are fairness opinions fair? The case of mergers and acquisitions, *Journal of Financial Economics*, 91: 179–207; R. J. Aiello & M. D. Watkins, 2000, The fine art of friendly acquisition, *Harvard Business Review*, 78(6): 100–107.

96. S. Chatterjee, 2009, Does increased equity ownership lead to more strategically involved boards? *Journal of Business Ethics*, 87: 267–277; D. D. Bergh, 2001, Executive retention and acquisition outcomes: A test of opposing views on the influence of organizational tenure, *Journal of Management*, 27: 603–622; J. P. Walsh, 1989, Doing a deal: Merger and acquisition negotiations and their impact upon target company top management turnover, *Strategic Management Journal*, 10: 307–322.

97. D. A. Waldman & M. Javidan, 2009, Alternative forms of charismatic leadership in the integration of mergers and acquisitions, *The Leadership Quarterly*, 20: 130–142; F. J. Froese, Y. S. Pak, & L. C. Chong, 2008, Managing the human side of cross-border acquisitions in South Korea, *Journal of World Business*, 43: 97–108.

98. M. E. Graebner, 2009, Caveat Venditor: Trust asymmetries in acquisitions of entrepreneurial firms, *Academy of Management Journal*, 52: 435–472; N. J. Morrison, G. Kinley, & K. L. Ficery, 2008, Merger deal breakers: When operational due diligence exposes risk, *Journal of Business Strategy*, 29: 23–28.

99. J. M. Shaver & J. M. Mezias, 2009, Diseconomies of managing in acquisitions: Evidence from civil lawsuits, *Organization Science*, 20: 206–222; M. L. McDonald, J. D. Westphal, & M. E. Graebner, What do they know? The effects of outside director acquisition experience on firm acquisition performance, *Strategic Management Journal*, 29: 1155–1177.

100. D. D. Bergh & E. N.-K. Lim, 2008, Learning how to restructure: Absorptive capacity and improvisational views of restructuring actions and performance, *Strategic Management Journal*, 29: 593–616; J. K. Kang, J. M. Kim, W. L. Liu, & S. Yi, 2006, Post-takeover restructuring and the sources of gains in foreign takeovers: Evidence from U.S. targets. *Journal of Business*, 79(5): 2503–2537.

101. Y. G. Suh & E. Howard, 2009, Restructuring retailing in Korea: The case of Samsung-Tesco, *Asia Pacific Business Review*, 15: 29–40; Z. Wu & A. Delios, 2009, The emergence of portfolio restructuring in Japan, *Management International Review*, 49: 313–335; R. E. Hoskisson, A. A. Cannella, L. Tihanyi, & R. Faraci, 2004. Asset restructuring and business group affiliation in French civil law countries, *Strategic Management Journal*, 25: 525–539.

102. S. Thurm, 2008, Who are the best CEOs of 2008, *Wall Street Journal Online*, http://www.wsj.com, December 15.

103. J. L. Morrow Jr., D. G. Sirmon, M. A. Hitt, & T. R. Holcomb, 2007, Creating value in the face of declining performance: Firm strategies and organizational recovery, *Strategic Management Journal*, 28: 271–283; J. L. Morrow Jr., R. A. Johnson, & L. W. Busenitz, 2004, The effects of cost and asset retrenchment on firm performance: The overlooked role of a firm's competitive environment, *Journal of Management*, 30: 189–208.

104. G. J. Castrogiovanni & G. D. Bruton, 2000, Business turnaround processes following acquisitions: Reconsidering the role of retrenchment, *Journal of Business Research*, 48: 25–34; W. McKinley, J. Zhao, & K. G. Rust, 2000, A sociocognitive interpretation of organizational downsizing, *Academy of Management Review*, 25: 227–243.

105. J. D. Evans & F. Hefner, 2009, Business ethics and the decision to adopt golden parachute contracts: Empirical evidence of concern for all stakeholders, *Journal of Business Ethics*, 86: 65–79; H. A. Krishnan, M. A. Hitt, & D. Park, 2007, Acquisition premiums, subsequent workforce reductions and post-acquisition performance, *Journal of Management*, 44: 709–732.

106. K. McFarland, 2008, Four mistakes leaders make when downsizing, *BusinessWeek Online*, http://www.businessweek.com, October 24.

107. C. O. Trevor & A. J. Nyberg, 2008, Keeping your headcount when all about you are losing theirs: Downsizing, voluntary turnover rates, and the moderating role of HR practices, *Academy of Management Journal*, 51: 259–276.

108. Berg & Lim, Learning how to restructure; R. E. Hoskisson & M. A. Hitt, 1994, *Downscoping: How to Tame the Diversified Firm*, New York: Oxford University Press.

109. Ushijima, R&D intensity and acquisition and divestiture of corporate assets; G. Benou, J. Madura, & T. Ngo, 2008, Wealth creation from high-tech divestitures, *The Quarterly Review of*

Economics and Finance, 48: 505–519;
L. Dranikoff, T. Koller, & A. Schneider,
2002, Divestiture: Strategy's missing link,
Harvard Business Review, 80(5): 74–83.

110. R. E. Hoskisson & M. A. Hitt, 1990,
Antecedents and performance outcomes
of diversification: A review and critique
of theoretical perspectives, Journal of
Management, 16: 461–509.

111. 2009, Motorola sells fiber-to-the-node
product line, New York Times Online,
http://www.nytimes.com, July 7.

112. M. Peers, 2009, Magazine business suffers
shakeout, Wall Street Journal Online,
http://www.wsj.com, July 13.

113. R. Perez-Pena, 2009, McGraw-Hill is said
to be seeking a buyer for BusinessWeek,
New York Times Online, http://www
.nytimes.com, July 14.

114. A. Kambil, 2008, What is your recession
playbook? Journal of Business Strategy,
29: 50–52; M. Rajand & M. Forsyth, 2002,
Hostile bidders, long-term performance,
and restructuring methods: Evidence from
the UK, American Business Review, 20:
71–81.

115. D. Hillier, P. McColgan, & S. Werema,
2008, Asset sales and firm strategy: An
analysis of divestitures by UK companies,
The European Journal of Finance, 15:
71–87; R. E. Hoskisson, R. A. Johnson,
L. Tihanyi, & R. E. White, 2005, Diversified
business groups and corporate refocusing
in emerging economies, Journal of
Management, 31: 941–965.

116. S. N. Kaplan & P. Stromberg, 2009,
Leveraged buyouts and private equity,
Journal of Economic Perspectives, 23:
121–146; C. Moschieri & J. Mair, 2008,
Research on corporate divestures: A
synthesis, Journal of Management &
Organization, 14: 399–422.

117. J. Mair & C. Moschieri, 2006, Unbundling
frees business for take off, Financial
Times, October 19, 2.

118. K. H. Wruck, 2009, Private equity,
corporate governance, and the
reinvention of the market for corporate
control, Journal of Applied Corporate
Finance, 20: 8–21; M. F. Wiersema &
J. P. Liebeskind, 1995, The effects of
leveraged buyouts on corporate growth
and diversification in large firms, Strategic
Management Journal, 16: 447–460.

119. R. Harris, D. S. Siegel, & M. Wright, 2005,
Assessing the impact of management
buyouts on economic efficiency: Plant-
level evidence from the United Kingdom,
Review of Economics and Statistics, 87:
148–153; A. Seth & J. Easterwood, 1995,
Strategic redirection in large management
buyouts: The evidence from post-
buyout restructuring activity, Strategic
Management Journal, 14: 251–274;
P. H. Phan & C. W. L. Hill, 1995,
Organizational restructuring and economic
performance in leveraged buyouts: An
ex-post study, Academy of Management
Journal, 38: 704–739.

120. M. Meuleman, K. Amess, M. Wright,
& L. Scholes, 2009, Agency, strategic
entrepreneurship, and the performance
of private equity-backed buyouts,
Entrepreneurship Theory and Practice, 33:
213–239; C. M. Daily, P. P. McDougall,
J. G. Covin, & D. R. Dalton, 2002,
Governance and strategic leadership
in entrepreneurial firms, Journal of
Management, 3: 387–412.

121. W. Kiechel III, 2007, Private equity's
long view, Harvard Business Review,
85(8): 18–20; M. Wright, R. E. Hoskisson,
& L. W. Busenitz, 2001, Firm rebirth:
Buyouts as facilitators of strategic growth
and entrepreneurship, Academy of
Management Executive, 15(1): 111–125.

122. E. G. Love & M. Kraatz, 2009, Character,
conformity, or the bottom line? How
and why downsizing affected corporate
reputation, Academy of Management
Journal, 52: 314–335; J. P. Guthrie & D.
K. Datta, 2008, Dumb and dumber: The
impact of downsizing on firm performance
as moderated by industry conditions,
Organization Science, 19: 108–123.

123. H. A. Krishnan & D. Park, 2002, The
impact of work force reduction on
subsequent performance in major mergers
and acquisitions: An exploratory study,
Journal of Business Research, 55(4):
285–292; P. M. Lee, 1997, A comparative
analysis of layoff announcements and
stock price reactions in the United States
and Japan, Strategic Management
Journal, 18: 879–894.

124. D. J. Flanagan & K. C. O'Shaughnessy,
2005, The effect of layoffs on firm reputation,
Journal of Management, 31: 445–463.

125. D. S. DeRue, J. R. Hollenbeck,
M. D. Johnson, D. R. Ilgen, &
D. K. Jundt, 2008, How different
team downsizing approaches
influence team-level adaptation and
performance, Academy of Management
Journal, 51: 182–196; C. D. Zatzick &
R. D. Iverson, 2006, High-involvement
management and workforce reduction:
Competitive advantage or disadvantage? Academy of Management Journal,
49: 999–1015; N. Mirabal & R. DeYoung,
2005, Downsizing as a strategic
intervention, Journal of American
Academy of Business, 6(1): 39–45.

126. K. Shimizu & M. A. Hitt, 2005, What
constrains or facilitates divestitures of
formerly acquired firms? The effects
of organizational inertia, Journal of
Management, 31: 50–72.

127. D. T. Brown, C. E. Fee, & S. E.
Thomas, 2009, Financial leverage
and bargaining power with suppliers:
Evidence from leveraged buyouts,
Journal of Corporate Finance, 15:
196–211; S. Toms & M. Wright, 2005,
Divergence and convergence within
Anglo-American corporate governance
systems: Evidence from the US and UK,
1950–2000, Business History, 47(2):
267–295.

128. G. Wood & M. Wright, 2009, Private
equity: A review and synthesis,
International Journal of Management
Reviews, in press; A.-L. Le Nadant &
F. Perdreau, 2006, Financial profile of
leveraged buy-out targets: Some French
evidence, Review of Accounting and
Finance, (4): 370–392.

129. G. D. Bruton, J. K. Keels, & E. L. Scifres,
2002, Corporate restructuring and
performance: An agency perspective on the
complete buyout cycle, Journal of Business
Research, 55: 709–724; W. F. Long & D. J.
Ravenscraft, 1993, LBOs, debt, and R&D
intensity, Strategic Management Journal,
14 (Special Issue): 119–135.

130. S. A. Zahra, 1995, Corporate
entrepreneurship and financial
performance: The case of management
leveraged buyouts, Journal of Business
Venturing, 10: 225–248.

CHAPTER 8

International
Strategy

Studying this chapter should provide you with the strategic management knowledge needed to:

1. Explain traditional and emerging motives for firms to pursue international diversification.

2. Identify the four major benefits of an international strategy.

3. Explore the four factors that provide a basis for international business-level strategies.

4. Describe the three international corporate-level strategies: multidomestic, global, and transnational.

5. Discuss the environmental trends affecting international strategy, especially liability of foreignness and regionalization.

6. Name and describe the five alternative modes for entering international markets.

7. Explain the effects of international diversification on firm returns and innovation.

8. Name and describe two major risks of international diversification.

ENTRY INTO CHINA BY FOREIGN FIRMS AND CHINESE FIRMS REACHING FOR GLOBAL MARKETS

Many foreign firms choose to operate in the Chinese market because it is so large and important. This is certainly the case for automobile firms that have used China as a base to both produce cars more cheaply and expand their market by selling in China. In particular General Motors (GM), through its partnership with Shanghai Automotive Industry Corporation (SAIC), has created successful joint ventures. Because this venture continues to be successful, Fritz Henderson, GM's CEO since its bankruptcy filing, has indicated that none of GM's operations in China are for sale. In fact, GM is seeking to extend its operations in China, possibly with new ventures. Volkswagen also has a joint venture with SAIC. Recently SAIC has sought to introduce its own automobiles domestically and plans to participate in global markets when possible. Similarly, another GM partner in China, Liuzhou Wuling Motors Co., is planning to develop its own vehicles rather than through a GM brand such as Chevrolet.

Because the U.S. auto market and other auto markets elsewhere in the world are experiencing substantially lower sales, the Chinese market is becoming more important. Porsche AG now owns 50.76 percent of Volkswagen and is launching the first exposure of its new model, the Panamera, in a Shanghai auto show in April 2009. Although the U.S. market still counts as the most important sale zone for Porsche, China is expected to have the largest auto market by sales volume in 2009.

The Chinese market is not only important for manufacturing such as the automobile industry, but also for service industries. For example, Google recently launched a music service supported by

Peter Parks/AFP/Getty Images

Models pose next to a Porsche Panamera, a new four-door sports car making its international debut at Auto Shanghai, China's largest auto show.

the world's four largest music labels: Warner Music Group Corp., Vivendi SA's Universal Music, EMI Group Ltd., and Sony Corp.'s Music Entertainment. Google and its partners hope to draw users away from Google's main Chinese competitors, especially Baidu Inc. Baidu is the dominant market share holder, with approximately 62 percent of the search market for Web downloads in China. Google increased its search engine market in China to 28 percent in 2008, up from 23 percent in 2007, but Baidu retained its dominance with a 62 percent market share, up from 59 percent in 2007.

Interestingly, some Chinese firms are more successful abroad than they are in their home market. Huawei Technologies Co. Ltd. is making inroads in the U.S. market. Huawei, a Chinese telecom equipment supplier, recently won a contract with Cox Communications, a U.S. TV cable provider. Huawei is also in the running for a potentially bigger contract with Clearwire Corporation. Clearwire is in the process of helping to build a wireless broadband network that would serve 120 million people in the United States by 2010. Other finalists for the contract include Motorola Inc., Samsung Electronics Co., and Nokia Siemens Networks. More generally, other competitors include Alcatel-Lucent and Telefon AB L.M. Ericsson. Another Chinese company, ZTE, competes with these firms as well. Although Huwaei and ZTE have had more success in developing regions of the world, Huawei has become a major vendor in Europe, where it has won numerous contracts with significant telecom providers such as Vodaphone Group PLC and France Telecom SA's Orange. Huawei also has a foothold in Canada, where it is building a third-generation (3G) network for BCE Inc.'s partners Bell Canada and Telus Corp.

Additionally, Huawei and ZTE were laggards in selling telephone equipment in their home market against Telefon AB L.M. Ericsson, Alcatel-Lucent, and Nokia Siemens

Networks (a joint venture of Nokia Corp. and Siemens AG), mainly because they were an unknown company when the first wireless networks were developed in China. However, thanks to government support for new wireless technology and an aggressive strategy of deeply undercutting competitors' prices, these two firms are beating out their rivals for an estimated $59 billion of spending over the next three years for new 3G wireless networks. China has approximately 659 million mobile subscribers, and the rollout of 3G is making sales growth for these markets even more important. It is expected that Huawei and ZTE will double their combined market share for 3G revenue with current wireless network growth. Although Ericsson's market share is remaining stable, market shares for Alcatel-Lucent and Nokia Siemens are expected to decline in China. Historically, Ericsson won the lion's share because Huawei and ZTE, as noted, were small when the existing network was built in the 1990s. Both companies have access to large credit lines from China's state-owned banks and other perks such as low cost land. This has allowed them to have more flexibility in pricing and to operate with lower margins without shareholder pressure. It will be interesting to see what happens when the fourth-generation (4G) networks are rolled out in a few years.

Sources: A. Back & L. Chao, 2009, Google begins China music service; Partnership with record labels gives users free access to licensed tracks, *Wall Street Journal*, March 30, B3; L. Chao, 2009, China's telecom-gear makers, once laggards at home, pass foreign rivals, *Wall Street Journal*, April 10, B1; K. Hille & A. Parker, 2009, Upwardly mobile Huawei, *Financial Times*, http://www.ft.com, March 20; K. Li, 2009, Google launches China service, *Financial Times*, March 31, 20; C. Rauwald, 2009, Porsche chooses the China road; four-door Panamera's Shanghai debut signals focus on emerging markets, *Wall Street Journal*, April 20, B2; A. Sharma & S. Silver, 2009, Huawei tries to crack U.S. market; Chinese telecom supplier wins Cox contract, is finalist for Clearwire deal, *Wall Street Journal*, March 26, B2; N. Shirouzu, P. J. Ho, & K. Rapoza, 2009, Corporate news: GM plans to retain China, Brazil units. *Wall Street Journal* June 3, B2; J. D. Stoll, 2009, Corporate news: GM pushes the throttle in China—affiliate's plan to expand into cars is seen as a key to growth in Asia, *Wall Street Journal*, April 27, B3; M. B. Teagarden & D. H. Cai, 2009, Learning from dragons who are learning from us; developmental lessons from China's global companies, *Organizational Dynamics*, 38(1): 73; C.-C. Tschang, 2009, Search engine squeeze? *BusinessWeek*, January 12, 21; E. Woyke, 2009, ZTE's smart phone ambitions, *Forbes*, http://www.forbes.com, March 16; B. Einhorn, 2008, Huawei, *BusinessWeek*, December 22, 51; S. Tucker, 2008, Case study: Huawei of China takes stock after frustrating year, *Financial Times*, http://www.ft.com, November 25.

As the Opening Case indicates, firms are entering China because of its large market, but China's firms are building their competitive capabilities and also seeking to enter foreign markets. China's entrance into the World Trade Organization (WTO) brought change not only to China and its trading partners but also to industries and firms throughout the world. Despite its developing market and institutional environment, Chinese firms such as Huawei Technologies Co. are taking advantage of the growing size of the Chinese market; they had previously learned new technologies and managerial capabilities from foreign partners and are now competing more strongly in domestic as well as foreign markets.[1]

Many firms choose direct investment in assets in foreign countries (e.g., establishing new subsidiaries, making acquisitions, or building joint ventures) over indirect investment because it provides better protection for their assets.[2] As indicated in the Opening Case, Chinese firms are developing their manufacturing capabilities and building their own branded products (e.g., Huawei and ZTE Corporation). As such, the potential global market power of Chinese firms is astounding.[3]

As foreign firms enter China and as Chinese firms enter into other foreign markets, both opportunities and threats for firms competing in global markets are exemplified. This chapter examines opportunities facing firms as they seek to develop and exploit core competencies by diversifying into global markets. In addition, we discuss different problems, complexities, and threats that might accompany a firm's international strategy.[4] Although national boundaries, cultural differences, and geographic distances all pose barriers to entry into many markets, significant opportunities motivate businesses to enter international markets. A business that plans to operate globally must formulate a successful strategy to take advantage of these global opportunities.[5] Furthermore, to mold their firms into truly global companies, managers must develop global mind-sets.[6] As firms move into international markets, they develop relationships with suppliers, customers, and partners and learning from these relationships. For example, as the Opening Case illustrates, SAIC learned new capabilities from its partnerships with GM and Volkswagen.

As illustrated in Figure 1.1, we discuss the importance of international strategy as a source of strategic competitiveness and above-average returns. This chapter focuses on the incentives to internationalize. After a firm decides to compete internationally, it must select its strategy and choose a mode of entry into international markets. It may enter international markets by exporting from domestic-based operations, licensing some of its products or services, forming joint ventures with international partners, acquiring a foreign-based firm, or establishing a new subsidiary. Such international diversification can extend product life cycles, provide incentives for more innovation, and produce above-average returns. These benefits are tempered by political and economic risks and the problems of managing a complex international firm with operations in multiple countries.

Figure 8.1 provides an overview of the various choices and outcomes of strategic competitiveness. The relationships among international opportunities, the resources and capabilities that result from such strategies, and the modes of entry that are based on core competencies are explored in this chapter.

Identifying International Opportunities: Incentives to Use an International Strategy

An **international strategy** is a strategy through which the firm sells its goods or services outside its domestic market.[7] One of the primary reasons for implementing an international strategy (as opposed to a strategy focused on the domestic market) is that international markets yield potential new opportunities.[8]

Raymond Vernon captured the classic rationale for international diversification.[9] He suggested that typically a firm discovers an innovation in its home-country market, especially in an advanced economy such as that of the United States. Often demand for

An **international strategy** is a strategy through which the firm sells its goods or services outside its domestic market.

Figure 8.1 Opportunities and Outcomes of International Strategy

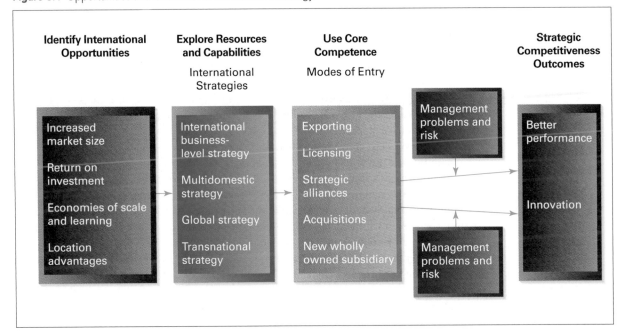

the product then develops in other countries, and exports are provided by domestic operations. Increased demand in foreign countries justifies making investments in foreign operations, especially to fend off foreign competitors. Vernon, therefore, observed that one reason why firms pursue international diversification is to extend a product's life cycle.

Another traditional motive for firms to become multinational is to secure needed resources. Key supplies of raw material—especially minerals and energy—are important in some industries. Other industries, such as clothing, electronics, and watchmaking, have moved portions of their operations to foreign locations in pursuit of lower production costs. Clearly one of the reasons for Chinese firms to expand internationally is to gain access to important resources.[10]

Although these traditional motives persist, other emerging motivations also drive international expansion (see Chapter 1). For instance, pressure has increased for a global integration of operations, mostly driven by more universal product demand. As nations industrialize, the demand for some products and commodities appears to become more similar. This borderless demand for globally branded products may be due to similarities in lifestyle in developed nations. Increases in global communication media also facilitate the ability of people in different countries to visualize and model lifestyles in different cultures.[11] IKEA, for example, has become a global brand by selling furniture in 44 countries through more than 300 stores that it owns and operates through franchisees. All of its furniture is sold in components that can be packaged in flat packs and assembled by the consumer after purchase. This arrangement has allowed for easier shipping and handling than fully assembled units and has facilitated the development of the global brand. Because of its low-cost approach, sales are increasing even during the economic downturn.[12]

In some industries, technology drives globalization because the economies of scale necessary to reduce costs to the lowest level often require an investment greater than that needed to meet domestic market demand. Companies also experience pressure for cost reductions, achieved by purchasing from the lowest-cost global suppliers. For instance, research and development expertise for an emerging business startup may not exist in the domestic market, but as foreign firms locate in the domestic market learning spillovers occur for domestic firms.[13]

New large-scale, emerging markets, such as China and India, provide a strong internationalization incentive based on their high potential demand for consumer products and services.[14] Because of currency fluctuations, firms may also choose to distribute their operations across many countries, including emerging ones, in order to reduce the risk of devaluation in one country.[15] However, the uniqueness of emerging markets presents both opportunities and challenges.[16] Even though India, for example, differs from Western countries in many respects, including culture, politics, and the precepts of its economic system, it also offers a huge potential market and its government is becoming more supportive of foreign direct investment.[17] However, the differences between China, India, and Western countries pose serious challenges to Western competitive paradigms that emphasize the skills needed to manage financial, economic, and political risks.[18]

Employment contracts and labor forces differ significantly in international markets. For example, it is more difficult to lay off employees in Europe than in the United States because of employment contract differences. In many cases, host governments demand joint ownership with a local company in order to invest in local operations; this allows the foreign firm to avoid tariffs. Also, host governments frequently require a high percentage of procurements, manufacturing, and R&D to use local sources.[19] These issues increase the need for local investment and responsiveness as opposed to seeking global economies of scale.

We've discussed incentives that influence firms to use international strategies. When these strategies are successful, firms can derive four basic benefits: (1) increased market size; (2) greater returns on major capital investments or on investments in new products and processes; (3) greater economies of scale, scope, or learning; and (4) a competitive advantage through location (e.g., access to low-cost labor, critical resources, or customers). We examine these benefits in terms of both their costs (such as higher coordination expenses and limited access to knowledge about host country political influences)[20] and their managerial challenges.

Increased Market Size

Firms can expand the size of their potential market—sometimes dramatically—by moving into international markets. Pharmaceutical firms have been doing significant foreign direct investment into both developed and emerging markets in an attempt to increase the market potential for new drugs. For example, when Japanese pharmaceutical firms made acquisitions of international rivals in 2008, one analyst noted: "One factor [driving the trend for outbound M&A] is that there are limited domestic growth opportunities… [These Japanese] companies are cash-rich and are in a good position to conduct acquisitions."[21] Indeed, Japan's large pharmaceutical firms collectively paid more than $20 billion during 2008 to buy overseas firms.

Although seeking to manage different consumer tastes and practices linked to cultural values or traditions is not simple, following an international strategy is a particularly attractive option to firms competing in domestic markets that have limited growth opportunities. For example, firms in the domestic soft drink industry have been searching for growth in foreign markets for some time now. Major competitors Pepsi and Coca-Cola have had relatively stable market shares in the United States for several years. Most of their sales growth has come from foreign markets. Coke, for instance, has used a strategy of buying overseas bottlers or expanding into other beverages such as fruit juice. However, a recent acquisition attempt of China's largest fruit-juice producer, China Huiyuan Juice Group Ltd., was turned down by Beijing regulators claiming that it would crowd out smaller players and increase consumer prices. China is Coke's fourth largest market by volume after the United States, Mexico, and Brazil. As with other emerging markets, it is growing faster than the U.S. market.[22]

The size of an international market also affects a firm's willingness to invest in R&D to build competitive advantages in that market. Larger markets usually offer higher potential returns and thus pose less risk for a firm's investments. The strength of the science base of the country in question also can affect a firm's foreign R&D investments.[23] Most firms prefer to invest more heavily in those countries with the scientific knowledge and talent to produce value-creating products and processes from their R&D activities.[24]

Return on Investment

Large markets may be crucial for earning a return on significant investments, such as plant and capital equipment or R&D. Therefore, most R&D-intensive industries such as electronics are international. In addition to the need for a large market to recoup heavy investment in R&D, the development pace for new technology is increasing. New products become obsolete more rapidly, and therefore investments need to be recouped more quickly. Moreover, firms' abilities to develop new technologies are expanding, and because of different patent laws across country borders, imitation by competitors is more likely. Through reverse engineering, competitors are able to disassemble a product, learn the new technology, and develop a similar product. Because competitors can imitate new technologies relatively quickly, firms need to recoup new product development costs even more rapidly. Consequently, the larger markets provided by international expansion are particularly attractive in many industries such as pharmaceutical firms, because they expand the opportunity for the firm to recoup significant capital investments and large-scale R&D expenditures.[25]

Regardless of other motives however, the primary reason for investing in international markets is to generate above-average returns on investments. Still, firms from different countries have different expectations and use different criteria to decide whether to invest in international markets, such as industry conditions and the potential for knowledge transfer.[26]

Economies of Scale and Learning

By expanding their markets, firms may be able to enjoy economies of scale, particularly in their manufacturing operations. To the extent that a firm can standardize its products across country borders and use the same or similar production facilities, thereby coordinating critical resource functions, it is more likely to achieve optimal economies of scale.[27]

Economies of scale are critical in the global auto industry. China's decision to join the World Trade Organization has allowed carmakers from other countries to enter their market and for lower tariffs to be charged (in the past, Chinese carmakers have had an advantage over foreign carmakers due to tariffs). Ford, Honda, General Motors, and Volkswagen are each producing an economy car to compete with the existing cars in China. Because of global economies of scale (allowing them to price their products competitively) and local investments in China, all of these companies are likely to obtain significant market share in China. Alternatively, SAIC is developing its branded vehicles to compete with the foreign automakers. SAIC's joint ventures with both GM and Volkswagen have been highly successful (as explained in the Opening Case). However, as also explained in the Opening Case, Porsche is seeking to market its vehicles in China to extend its scale economies, while Chinese firms are seeking to begin exporting vehicles overseas and perhaps enter foreign markets in other ways, such as through acquisitions.[28]

Firms may also be able to exploit core competencies in international markets through resource and knowledge sharing between units and network partners across country borders.[29] This sharing generates synergy, which helps the firm produce higher-quality goods or services at lower cost. In addition, working across international markets provides the firm with new learning opportunities.[30] Multinational firms have substantial occasions to learn from the different practices they encounter in separate international markets. However, research finds that to take advantage of international R&D investments, firms need to already have a strong R&D system in place to absorb the knowledge.[31]

Location Advantages

Firms may locate facilities in other countries to lower the basic costs of the goods or services they provide. These facilities may provide easier access to lower-cost labor, energy, and other natural resources. Other location advantages include access to critical supplies and to customers. Once positioned favorably with an attractive location, firms must manage their facilities effectively to gain the full benefit of a location advantage.[32]

Such location advantages can be influenced by costs of production and transportation requirements as well as by the needs of the intended customers.[33] Cultural influences may also affect location advantages and disadvantages. If there is a strong match between the cultures in which international transactions are carried out, the liability of foreignness is lower than if there is high cultural distance.[34] Research also suggests that regulation distances influence the ownership positions of multinational firms as well as their strategies for managing local and expatriate human resources.[35]

As suggested in the Opening Case, General Motors (GM) entered international markets to expand its market size. While GM has lost its position as the world's largest automaker after 76 years, even in bankruptcy it has expansion plans for its China ventures.[36] Still, GM faces a number of challenges from domestic Chinese competitors, such as its partners, SAIC and Liuzhou Wuling Motors Co., and from foreign competitors, such as Toyota and Volkswagen. It will have to formulate and implement a successful strategy for the Chinese market to maintain a competitive advantage there. Interestingly, given the downturn in sales, China may overtake the United States in domestic sales. An article in the *Wall Street Journal* noted: "China is expected to become the world's number one vehicle producer this year [2009], surpassing Japan. Mr. Young [chief financial officer of GM] said he is starting to think China could outmuscle the United States this year as the number one market for vehicle sales. GM had been predicting China would surpass the United States in 2015, but Chinese sales leapfrogged those in the United States in the first quarter [2009]."[37]

International Strategies

Firms choose to use one or both of two basic types of international strategies: business-level international strategy and corporate-level international strategy. At the business level, firms follow generic strategies: cost leadership, differentiation, focused cost leadership, focused differentiation, or integrated cost leadership/differentiation. The three corporate-level international strategies are multidomestic, global, or transnational (a combination of multidomestic and global). To create competitive advantage, each strategy must utilize a core competence based on difficult-to-imitate resources and capabilities.[38] As discussed in Chapters 4 and 6, firms expect to create value through the implementation of a business-level strategy and a corporate-level strategy.

International Business-Level Strategy

Each business must develop a competitive strategy focused on its own domestic market. We discussed business-level strategies in Chapter 4 and competitive rivalry and competitive dynamics in Chapter 5. International business-level strategies have some unique features. In an international business-level strategy, the home country of operation is often the most important source of competitive advantage.[39] The resources and capabilities established in the home country frequently allow the firm to pursue the strategy into markets located in other countries.[40] However, research indicates that as a firm continues its growth into multiple international locations, the country of origin is less important for competitive advantage.[41]

Michael Porter's model, illustrated in Figure 8.2, describes the factors contributing to the advantage of firms in a dominant global industry and associated with a specific home country or regional environment.[42] The first dimension in Porter's model is the factors of production. This dimension refers to the inputs necessary to compete in any industry—labor, land, natural resources, capital, and infrastructure (such as transportation, postal, and communication systems). There are basic factors (for example, natural and labor resources) and advanced factors (such as digital communication systems and a highly educated workforce). Other production factors are generalized (highway systems and the supply of debt capital) and specialized (skilled personnel in a specific industry, such as the workers in a port that specialize in handling bulk chemicals). If a country has both advanced and specialized production factors, it is likely to serve an industry well by spawning strong home-country competitors that also can be successful global competitors.

Ironically, countries often develop advanced and specialized factors because they lack critical basic resources. For example, some Asian countries, such as South Korea, lack abundant natural resources but offer a strong work ethic, a large number of engineers, and systems of large firms to create an expertise in manufacturing. Similarly, Germany developed a strong chemical industry, partially because Hoechst and BASF spent years creating a synthetic indigo dye to reduce their dependence on imports, unlike Britain, whose colonies provided large supplies of natural indigo.[43]

The second dimension in Porter's model, demand conditions, is characterized by the nature and size of buyers' needs in the home market for the industry's goods or services. A large market segment can produce the demand necessary to create scale-efficient facilities.

Figure 8.2 Determinants of National Advantage

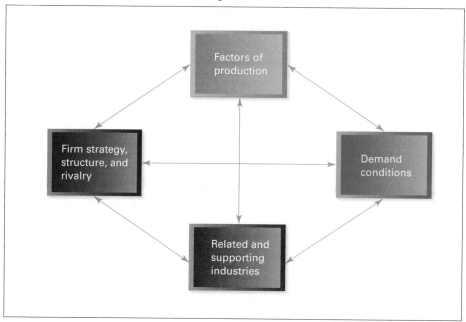

Chinese manufacturing companies have spent years focused on building their businesses in China, but are now beginning to look at markets beyond their borders, as described in the Opening Case about SAIC. As mentioned, SAIC (along with other Chinese firms) has begun the challenging process of building its brand equity in China but especially in other countries. In doing so, most Chinese firms begin in the Far East with the intention to move into Western markets when ready. Companies such as SAIC have been helped by China's entry to the World Trade Organization. Of course, companies such as SAIC are interested in entering international markets to increase their market share and profits.

Related and supporting industries are the third dimension in Porter's model. Italy has become the leader in the shoe industry because of related and supporting industries; a well-established leather-processing industry provides the leather needed to construct shoes and related products. Also, many people travel to Italy to purchase leather goods, providing support in distribution. Supporting industries in leather-working machinery and design services also contribute to the success of the shoe industry. In fact, the design services industry supports its own related industries, such as ski boots, fashion apparel, and furniture. In Japan, cameras and copiers are related industries. Similarly, it is argued that the creative resources associated with "popular cartoons such as Manga and the animation sector along with technological knowledge from the consumer electronics industry facilitated the emergence of a successful video game industry in Japan."[44]

Firm strategy, structure, and rivalry make up the final country dimension and also foster the growth of certain industries. The types of strategy, structure, and rivalry among firms vary greatly from nation to nation. The excellent technical training system in Germany fosters a strong emphasis on continuous product and process improvements. In Japan, unusual cooperative and competitive systems have facilitated the cross-functional management of complex assembly operations. In Italy, the national pride of the country's designers has spawned strong industries in sports cars, fashion apparel, and furniture. In the United States, competition among computer manufacturers and software producers has contributed to the development of these industries.

The four basic dimensions of the "diamond" model in Figure 8.2 emphasize the environmental or structural attributes of a national economy that contribute to national advantage. Government policy also clearly contributes to the success and failure of many firms and industries. For example, as illustrated in the Strategic Focus, the Chinese government has provided incentives for SunTech, a Chinese firm focused on creating solar power for utilities around the world, particularly in Europe.[45] SunTech is a "born global" firm that went directly into international markets that were emerging within the solar power industry. It has been successful so far because of the low-cost manufacturing and the high levels of engineering talent available in China. Likewise, Yandex in Russia (see the Strategic Focus) was successful because it found a way to meet the complexities of developing a search tool for the complex Russian language, which turned out to be an advantage in global competition.[46] Also, Yandex had strong demand conditions in Russia for Internet service and has been able to maintain its market share against strong competition from Google. Yandex is now entering the U.S. market and establishing a research base near Google's headquarters.

Although each firm must create its own success, not all firms will survive to become global competitors—not even those operating with the same country factors that spawned other successful firms. The actual strategic choices managers make

AP Photo/Ric Francis

NCsoft, a Korean game developer, has launched several successful online games featuring manga-inspired graphics.

may be the most compelling reasons for success or failure. Accordingly, the factors illustrated in Figure 8.2 are likely to produce competitive advantages only when the firm develops and implements an appropriate strategy that takes advantage of distinct country factors. Thus, these distinct country factors must be given thorough consideration when making a decision regarding the business-level strategy to use (i.e., cost leadership, differentiation, focused cost leadership, focused differentiation, and integrated cost leadership/differentiation, discussed in Chapter 4) in an international context. However, pursuing an international strategy leads to more adjustment and learning as the firm adjusts to competition in the host country. Such adjustments are continuous as illustrated by SunTech's operations, given the steep decline in demand for solar facilities in the economic downturn. It must adapt to the increasing competition from other startups and its major competitors in global markets.

International Corporate-Level Strategy

The international business-level strategies are based at least partially on the type of international corporate-level strategy the firm has chosen. Some corporate strategies give individual country units the authority to develop their own business-level strategies; other corporate strategies dictate the business-level strategies in order to standardize the firm's products and sharing of resources across countries.[47] International corporate-level strategy focuses on the scope of a firm's operations through both product and geographic diversification.[48] International corporate-level strategy is required when the firm operates in multiple industries and multiple countries or regions.[49] The headquarters unit guides the strategy, although business- or country-level managers can have substantial strategic

COUNTRY CONDITIONS SPAWN SUCCESSFUL HIGH TECH FIRMS IN EMERGING MARKETS

Few firms from large emerging economies have been more successful than SunTech Power Holdings, which manufactures solar panels in China for the global electric utilities industry. It was a "born global" firm founded in China and quickly began competing with large firms that dominated the industry such as Sharpe, Siemens, and BP Solar. It was initiated by Shi Zhengrong and he is still the CEO. He was allocated $6 million startup money from the government of Wuxi in China's Jiangsu province. Shi was trained in Australia at the University of New South Wales in Sydney, where he earned his Ph.D.

SunTech's biggest markets for solar panels and modules are in Europe, with German companies providing its largest amount of revenue. It is listed on the U.S. stock exchange with an all-time stock price high of $85 in 2007. There was overcapacity in the industry in 2009, partly because SunTech spawned lots of imitators; however, iSuppli, a research company that provides analytical data for the solar industry, suggests that there will be 11.1 gigawatts of panels produced in 2009, which is up 62 percent from 7.7 gigawatts in 2008. SunTech itself produces one gigawatt and hoped to produce 1.4 gigawatts by the end of 2009 and two gigawatts by 2010. However, SunTech's expansion plans are currently on hold until the financial crisis is over and the markets improve; in fact, SunTech had to lay off 800 employees in 2008.

Fomichev Mikhail/ITAR-TASS/Landov

The big advantage that SunTech has is its low-cost production system in China. It hopes to have "grid parity," which means that the cost of producing solar energy is at the point where there is no difference between competing fossil fuels such as coal and natural gas relative to that produced by solar panels. Currently SunTech is producing at a cost of $.35 per kilowatt hour whereas the grid parity cost is near $.14. Although this suggests that the firm has a long way to go to realize grid parity, Shi believes it can be realized in several years given its low cost of production and improvements in technological efficiency. The company has improved the collective power of its solar panels primarily through advancements in silicon technology. Shi predicts that with the new Obama administration the subsidies will improve and stimulate demand, and that striving to reach grid parity will also help the company as it moves toward a "post carbon" future.

Russia's largest online search company, Yandex, is equivalent to Google in the United States. Interestingly, Yandex started in the 1980s, long before Google's founders Sergey Brin and Larry Page had envisioned their company. Yandex arguably has superior search technology because of the peculiarities of the Russian language. Russian words often have 20 different endings that indicate their relationship to one another and make the language much more precise, but at the same time it makes searching for Russian words much more difficult than searching for English words. However, Yandex found a way to catch all of this phraseology and as such it controls 56 percent of the search engine market share in Russia compared to Google's 23 percent. More impressively, it has two thirds of all of the revenue from the search ads and draws three billion hits a month. Because of this FireFox has dropped Google as its default search engine in Russia in favor of Yandex.

Nonetheless, Yandex realizes that it must continue to innovate. For instance, it has an image search engine that eliminates repeated images and filters out faces, thus it provides better search capabilities for imaging. In addition, as mentioned in the chapter, Yandex has opened labs not far from Google's headquarters in Mountain View, California, with a staff of 20 or more engineers who index pages for a Russian audience but also keep abreast of technology developments that surface near Silicone Valley. According to Arkady Volozh, CEO of Yandex, Yahoo!, Microsoft, and Google have made repeated buyout offers for Yandex. Such offers suggest that Google and other companies would be interested in increasing their market share in Russia. One reason for this interest is that Russia has the fastest-growing Internet population in Europe. Google has increased its market share from 6 percent in 2001 to 23 percent in 2009; most likely because it hired engineers who understand the Russian language. One analyst indicated that due to the high demand for Internet service "Russia is a pivotal country for Google."

Yandex is one of the few high tech companies that was home-grown in Russia and is successful. The Russians are proud of this fact. The company hopes to continue to be successful and possibly even compete for market share in the United States. Yandex has been given the opportunity to list on the Nasdaq Exchange; however, it has put off doing an IPO because of the financial crisis.

Sources: J. Ioffe, 2009, The Russians are coming, *Fortune*, February 16, 36–38; B. Powell, 2009, China's new king of solar, *Fortune*, February 16, 94–97; G. L. White, 2009, Russia Web firm negotiates autonomy, *Wall Street Journal*, April 22, A10; 2008, China-based SunTech plans to triple U.S. sales through acquisitions, residential sales, *FinancialWire*, http://www.financialwire.net, October 2; J. Bush, 2008, Where Google isn't Goliath: Russia's Yandex—set to go public on Nasdaq—is innovating in a hurry to hold off the U.S. giant, *BusinessWeek*, http://www.businessweek.com, June 26; P. Ghemawat & T. Hout, 2008, Tomorrow's global giants: Not the usual suspects, *Harvard Business Review*, 86(11): 80–88.

input, depending on the type of international corporate-level strategy followed. The three international corporate-level strategies are multidomestic, global, and transnational, as shown in Figure 8.3.

Multidomestic Strategy

A **multidomestic strategy** is an international strategy in which strategic and operating decisions are decentralized to the strategic business unit in each country so as to allow that unit to tailor products to the local market.[50] A multidomestic strategy focuses on competition within each country. It assumes that the markets differ and therefore are segmented by country boundaries. The multidomestic strategy uses a highly decentralized approach, allowing each division to focus on a geographic area, region, or country.[51] In other words, consumer needs and desires, industry conditions (e.g., the number and type of competitors), political and legal structures, and social norms vary by country. With multidomestic strategies, the country managers have the autonomy to customize the firm's products as necessary to meet the specific needs and preferences of local customers. Therefore, these strategies should maximize a firm's competitive response to the idiosyncratic requirements of each market.[52]

The use of multidomestic strategies usually expands the firm's local market share because the firm can pay attention to the needs of the local clientele.[53] However, the use of these strategies results in less knowledge sharing for the corporation as a whole because of the differences across markets, decentralization, and the different strategies employed by local country units.[54] Moreover, multidomestic strategies do not allow the development of economies of scale and thus can be more costly. As a result, firms employing a multidomestic strategy decentralize their strategic and operating decisions

A **multidomestic strategy** is an international strategy in which strategic and operating decisions are decentralized to the strategic business unit in each country so as to allow that unit to tailor products to the local market.

Figure 8.3 International Corporate-Level Strategies

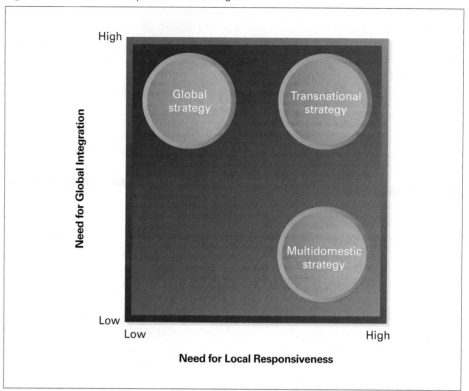

to the business units operating in each country. Historically, Unilever, a large European consumer products firm, has had a highly decentralized approach to managing its international operations. This approach allows regional managers considerable autonomy to adapt the product offerings to fit the market needs. However, more recently it has sought to have better coordination between its independent country subsidiaries and develop a strong global brand presence.[55]

Global Strategy

In contrast to a multidomestic strategy, a global strategy assumes more standardization of products across country markets.[56] As a result, a global strategy is centralized and controlled by the home office. The strategic business units operating in each country are assumed to be interdependent, and the home office attempts to achieve integration across these businesses.[57] The firm uses a **global strategy** to offer standardized products across country markets, with competitive strategy being dictated by the home office. Thus, a global strategy emphasizes economies of scale and offers greater opportunities to take innovations developed at the corporate level or in one country and utilize them in other markets.[58] Improvements in global accounting and financial reporting standards are facilitating this strategy.[59]

Although a global strategy produces lower risk, it may cause the firm to forgo growth opportunities in local markets, either because those markets are less likely to be identified as opportunities or because the opportunities require that products be adapted to the local market.[60] The global strategy is not as responsive to local markets and is difficult to manage because of the need to coordinate strategies and operating decisions across country borders. Yahoo! and eBay experienced these challenges when they moved into specific Asian markets. For example, eBay was unsuccessful in both the Japanese and Chinese markets when attempting to export its business model and approach from

A **global strategy** is an international strategy through which the firm offers standardized products across country markets, with competitive strategy being dictated by the home office.

North America to these two countries. It has reentered China but Meg Whitman, former CEO of eBay, suggested that she had no plans to reenter the Japanese market. Yahoo! has had rough times in China, going through several CEOs and trying to find the right formula to compete effectively in the Chinese market.[61] Also, as the Opening Case indicates, Google has had difficulty penetrating foreign markets such as China and competing against local competitors such as Baidu.

Achieving efficient operations with a global strategy requires sharing resources and facilitating coordination and cooperation across country boundaries, which in turn require centralization and headquarters control. Furthermore, research suggests that the performance of the global strategy is enhanced if it deploys in areas where regional integration among countries is occurring, such as the European Union.[62] Many Japanese firms have successfully used the global strategy.[63]

CEMEX is the third largest cement company in the world, behind France's Lafarge and Switzerland's Holcim, and is the largest producer of ready mix, a prepackaged product that contains all the ingredients needed to make localized cement products.

CEMEX has strong market power in the Americas as well as in Europe. CEMEX serves customers in more than 50 countries with more than 50,000 employees globally. Because CEMEX pursues a global strategy effectively, its centralization process has facilitated the integration of several businesses it acquired in the United States, Europe, and Asia. To integrate its businesses globally, CEMEX uses the Internet to improve logistics and manage an extensive supply network, thereby increasing revenue and reducing costs. Connectivity between the operations in different countries and universal standards dominates its approach. However, because of its recent acquisition of Ringer, a large Australian cement producer, it took on too much debt during the downturn and has had a very difficult time meeting its debt obligations.[64] Because of increasing global competition and the need to be cost efficient while simultaneously providing high-quality differentiated products, a number of firms have begun to pursue the transnational strategy, which is described next.

Transnational Strategy

A **transnational strategy** is an international strategy through which the firm seeks to achieve both global efficiency and local responsiveness. Realizing these goals is difficult: One requires close global coordination while the other requires local flexibility. "Flexible coordination"—building a shared vision and individual commitment through an integrated network—is required to implement the transnational strategy. Such integrated networks allow a firm to manage its connections with customers, suppliers, partners, and other parties more efficiently rather than using arm's-length transactions.[65] The transnational strategy is difficult to use because of its conflicting goals (see Chapter 11 for more on the implementation of this and other corporate-level international strategies). On the positive side, the effective implementation of a transnational strategy often produces higher performance than does the implementation of either the multidomestic or global international corporate-level strategies, although it is difficult to accomplish.[66]

Transnational strategies are challenging to implement but are becoming increasingly necessary to compete in international markets. The growing number of global competitors heightens the requirement to hold costs down. However, the increasing sophistication of markets with greater information flow (e.g., based on the diffusion of the Internet) and the desire for specialized products to meet consumers' needs pressures firms to differentiate and even customize their products in local markets. Differences in culture and institutional environments also require firms to adapt their products and approaches to local environments. However, some argue that most multinationals pursue more regional strategies and as such transnational strategies and structures may not be as necessary as once thought.[67]

A **transnational strategy** is an international strategy through which the firm seeks to achieve both global efficiency and local responsiveness.

Environmental Trends

Although the transnational strategy is difficult to implement, emphasis on global efficiency is increasing as more industries begin to experience global competition. To add to the problem, an increased emphasis on local requirements means that global goods and services often demand some customization to meet government regulations within particular countries or to fit customer tastes and preferences. In addition, most multinational firms desire coordination and sharing of resources across country markets to hold down costs, as illustrated by the CEMEX example.[68] Furthermore, some products and industries may be more suited than others for standardization across country borders.

As a result, some large multinational firms with diverse products employ a multidomestic strategy with certain product lines and a global strategy with others. Many multinational firms may require this type of flexibility if they are to be strategically competitive, in part due to trends that change over time. Two important trends are the liability of foreignness, which has increased since the terrorist attacks and the war in Iraq, and regionalization.

Liability of Foreignness

The dramatic success of Japanese firms such as Toyota and Sony in the United States and other international markets in the 1980s was a powerful jolt to U.S. managers and awakened them to the importance of international competition in markets that were rapidly becoming global markets. In the twenty-first century, China, India, Brazil, and Russia represent major international market opportunities for firms from many countries, including the United States, Japan, Korea, and the European Union.[69] However, there are legitimate concerns about the relative attractiveness of global strategies, due to the extra costs incurred to pursue internationalization, or the liability of foreignness relative to domestic competitors in a host country.[70] This is illustrated by the experience of Walt Disney Company in opening theme parks in foreign countries. For example, Disney suffered "lawsuits in France, at Disneyland Paris, because of the lack of fit between its transferred personnel policies and the French employees charged to enact them."[71] Disney executives learned from this experience in building the firm's newest theme park in Hong Kong.

Research shows that global strategies are not as prevalent as they once were and are still difficult to implement, even when using Internet-based strategies.[72] In addition, the amount of competition vying for a limited amount of resources and customers can limit firms' focus to regional rather than global markets. A regional focus allows firms to marshal their resources to compete effectively in regional markets rather than spreading their limited resources across many international markets.[73]

As such, firms may focus less on truly global markets and more on regional adaptation. Although parallel developments in the Internet and mobile telecommunication facilitate communications across the globe, as noted earlier, the implementation of Web-based strategies also requires local adaptation. The globalization of businesses with local strategies is demonstrated by the strategy that Google is using (see the Opening Case) by developing an online music download business in China.

Regionalization

Regionalization is a second trend that has become more common in global markets. Because a firm's location can affect its strategic competitiveness,[74] it must decide whether to compete in all or many global markets, or to focus on a particular region or regions. Competing in all markets provides economies that can be achieved because of the combined market size. Research suggests that firms that compete in risky emerging markets can also have higher performance.[75]

However, a firm that competes in industries where the international markets differ greatly (in which it must employ a multidomestic strategy) may wish to narrow its focus to a particular region of the world. In so doing, it can better understand the cultures, legal and social norms, and other factors that are important for effective competition in those markets. For example, a firm may focus on Far East markets only rather than competing simultaneously in the Middle East, Europe, and the Far East. Or the firm may choose a region of the world where the markets are more similar and some coordination and sharing of resources would be possible. In this way, the firm may be able not only to better understand the markets in which it competes, but also to achieve some economies, even though it may have to employ a multidomestic strategy. For instance, research suggests that most large retailers are better at focusing on a particular region rather than being truly global.[76] Firms commonly focus much of their international market entries into countries adjacent to their home country, which might be referred to as their home region.[77]

Countries that develop trade agreements to increase the economic power of their regions may promote regional strategies. The European Union (EU) and South America's Organization of American States (OAS) are country associations that developed trade agreements to promote the flow of trade across country boundaries within their respective regions.[78] Many European firms acquire and integrate their businesses in Europe to better coordinate pan-European brands as the EU creates more unity in European markets. With this process likely to continue as new countries are added to the agreement, some international firms may prefer to pursue regional strategies versus global strategies because the size of the market is increasing.[79]

The North American Free Trade Agreement (NAFTA), signed by the United States, Canada, and Mexico, facilitates free trade across country borders in North America. NAFTA loosens restrictions on international strategies within this region and provides greater opportunity for regional international strategies.[80] NAFTA does not exist for the sole purpose of U.S. businesses moving across its borders. In fact, Mexico is the number two trading partner of the United States, and NAFTA greatly increased Mexico's exports to the United States. Research suggests that managers of small- and medium-sized firms are influenced by the strategy they implement (those with a differentiation strategy are more positively disposed to the agreement than are those pursuing a cost leadership strategy) and by their experience and rivalry with exporting firms.[81]

Orlando Sierra/AFP/Getty Images

US Secretary of State Hillary Clinton and Hondoran President Manuel Zelaya meet with reporters following the 2009 general assembly meeting of the OAS in Honduras.

Most firms enter regional markets sequentially, beginning in markets with which they are more familiar. They also introduce their largest and strongest lines of business into these markets first, followed by their other lines of business once the first lines achieve success. They also usually invest in the same area as their original investment location.[82] However, research also suggests that the size of the market and industry characteristics can influence this decision.[83]

After the firm selects its international strategies and decides whether to employ them in regional or world markets, it must choose a market entry mode.[84]

Choice of International Entry Mode

International expansion is accomplished by exporting products, participating in licensing arrangements, forming strategic alliances, making acquisitions, and establishing new wholly owned subsidiaries. These means of entering international markets and their characteristics are shown in Table 8.1. Each means of market entry has its advantages and disadvantages. Thus, choosing the appropriate mode or path to enter international markets affects the firm's performance in those markets.

Exporting

Many industrial firms begin their international expansion by exporting goods or services to other countries.[85] Exporting does not require the expense of establishing operations in the host countries, but exporters must establish some means of marketing and distributing their products. Usually, exporting firms develop contractual arrangements with host-country firms.

The disadvantages of exporting include the often-high costs of transportation and tariffs placed on some incoming goods. Furthermore, the exporter has less control over the marketing and distribution of its products in the host country and must either pay the distributor or allow the distributor to add to the price to recoup its costs and earn a profit.

As a result, it may be difficult to market a competitive product through exporting or to provide a product that is customized to each international market.[86] However, evidence suggests that cost leadership strategies enhance the performance of exports in developed countries, whereas differentiation strategies with larger scale are more successful in emerging economies.[87]

Firms export mostly to countries that are closest to their facilities because of the lower transportation costs and the usually greater similarity between geographic neighbors. For example, United States' NAFTA partners Mexico and Canada account for more than half of the goods exported from Texas. The Internet has also made exporting easier. Even small firms can access critical information about foreign markets, examine a target market, research the competition, and find lists of potential customers.[88] Governments also use the Internet to facilitate applications for export and import licenses. Although terrorist threat is likely to slow its progress, high-speed technology is still the wave of the future.[89]

Small businesses are most likely to use the exporting mode of international entry; up to 50 percent of small U.S. firms will be involved in international trade by 2018, most of them through export.[90] Currency exchange rates are one of the most significant problems faced by small businesses. The United States in recent years has supported a weak dollar against the euro, which makes imports to the United States more expensive to U.S. consumers and U.S. goods less costly to foreign buyers, thus providing some economic relief for U.S. exporters.[91]

Licensing

Licensing is an increasingly common form of organizational network, particularly among smaller firms.[92] A licensing arrangement allows a foreign company to purchase the right

Table 8.1 Global Market Entry: Choice of Entry

Type of Entry	Characteristics
Exporting	High cost, low control
Licensing	Low cost, low risk, little control, low returns
Strategic alliances	Shared costs, shared resources, shared risks, problems of integration (e.g., two corporate cultures)
Acquisition	Quick access to new market, high cost, complex negotiations, problems of merging with domestic operations
New wholly owned subsidiary	Complex, often costly, time consuming, high risk, maximum control, potential above-average returns

to manufacture and sell the firm's products within a host country or set of countries.[93] The licensor is normally paid a royalty on each unit produced and sold. The licensee takes the risks and makes the monetary investments in facilities for manufacturing, marketing, and distributing the goods or services. As a result, licensing is possibly the least costly form of international expansion.

China is a large and growing market for cigarettes, while the U.S. market is shrinking due to health concerns. But U.S. cigarette firms have had trouble entering the Chinese market because state-owned tobacco firms have lobbied against such entry. As such, cigarette company Philip Morris International (PMI), which was separated from its former parent company Altria, had an incentive to form a deal with these state-owned firms. Such an agreement provides the state-owned firms access to the most famous brand in the world, Marlboro. Accordingly, both the Chinese firms and PMI have formed a licensing agreement to take advantage of the opportunity as China opens its markets more fully.[94] Because it is a licensing agreement rather than a foreign direct investment by PMI, China maintains control of the distribution. However, the Chinese state-owned tobacco monopoly, as part of the agreement, also gets to have PMI's help to distribute its own brands in select foreign markets. "The question is whether it can pluck three cigarette brands—RGD, Harmony and Dubliss—from relative obscurity and elevate them to an international, or at least regional, presence."[95]

Licensing is also a way to expand returns based on prior innovations.[96] Even if product life cycles are short, licensing may be a useful tool. For instance, because the toy industry faces relentless change and unpredictable buying patterns, licensing is used and contracts are often completed in foreign markets where labor may be less expensive.[97] Google, as the Opening Case illustrates, facilitated license agreements with the top four music producers in support of its strategy to gain more market share from Baidu in China.

Licensing also has disadvantages. For example, it gives the firm little control over the manufacture and marketing of its products in other countries. Thus, license deals must be structured properly.[98] In addition, licensing provides the least potential returns, because returns must be shared between the licensor and the licensee. Additionally, the international firm may learn the technology and produce and sell a similar competitive product after the license expires. Komatsu, for example, first licensed much of its technology from International Harvester, Bucyrus-Erie, and Cummins Engine to compete against Caterpillar in the earthmoving equipment business. Komatsu then dropped these licenses and developed its own products using the technology it had gained from the U.S. companies.[99] Like most global hotel chains, Starwood Hotels & Resorts Worldwide Inc. uses a franchise licensing arrangement and does not own most of its hotels. While focusing on other brands, it has let its Sheraton brand slip in quality. Given the current economic downturn, it is going to be difficult to get the owners to invest in needed design improvements and upgrades, especially given the owner differences in varying geographic markets.[100] Thus licensing can also lead to inflexibilities, and as such it is important that a firm think ahead and consider the consequences of each entry, especially in international markets.[101]

Strategic Alliances

In recent years, strategic alliances have become a popular means of international expansion.[102] Strategic alliances allow firms to share the risks and the resources required to enter international markets.[103] Moreover, strategic alliances can facilitate the development of new core competencies that contribute to the firm's future strategic competitiveness.[104]

As explained in the Opening Case, GM formed a joint venture with SAIC. This venture produced Buick and Cadillac automobiles for the Chinese market. The alliance has been highly successful for both firms. Similar to this example, most international strategic alliances are formed with a host-country firm that knows and understands the competitive conditions, legal and social norms, and cultural idiosyncrasies of the country, which helps the expanding firm manufacture and market a competitive product.

Often, firms in emerging economies want to form international alliances and ventures to gain access to sophisticated technologies that are new to them. Gaining access to new technologies and markets is one of ZTE's goals in seeking alliances with the mobile phone systems of Sprint, AT&T, and Verizon. ZTE, as introduced in the Opening Case, is a telecommunications network gear producer; it also produces mobile phones. It now is working on agreements with these three phone companies to produce "smartphones" for 3G and 4G systems to advance its product portfolio.[105] This type of arrangement can also benefit the non-emerging economy firm, in that it gains access to a new market and does not have to pay tariffs to do so (because it is partnering with a local company). In return, the host-country firm may find its new access to the expanding firm's technology and innovative products attractive.

Each partner in an alliance brings knowledge or resources to the partnership. Indeed, partners often enter an alliance with the purpose of learning new capabilities.[106] Common among those desired capabilities are technological skills. However, for technological knowledge to be transferred in an alliance usually requires trust between the partners.[107] Managing these expectations can facilitate improved performance.

The alliance between GM and SAIC has been successful over the years because of the way it is managed. In fact, both firms are pleased with the outcomes. Research suggests that company executives need to know their own firm well, understand factors that determine the norms in different countries, know how the firm is seen by other partners in the venture, and learn to adapt while remaining consistent with their own company cultural values. Such a multifaceted and versatile approach has helped the GM and SAIC alliance succeed.

Xinhua /Landov

ZTE Corporation, one of the largest Chinese telecommunication equipment manufacturers, has set the goal of becoming the third largest global provider of handsets by 2014 based on sales of its newly unveiled portfolio of smartphones and other wireless devices.

Not all alliances are successful; in fact, many fail.[108] The primary reasons for failure include incompatible partners and conflict between the partners. International strategic alliances are especially difficult to manage. Several factors may cause a relationship to sour. Trust between the partners is critical and is affected by at least four fundamental issues: the initial condition of the relationship, the negotiation process to arrive at an agreement, partner interactions, and external events.[109] Trust is also influenced by the country cultures involved in the alliance or joint venture.[110]

Research has shown that equity-based alliances, over which a firm has more control, tend to produce more positive returns.[111] (Strategic alliances are discussed in greater depth in Chapter 9.) However, if trust is required to develop new capabilities in a research collaboration, equity can serve as a barrier to the necessary relationship building. If conflict in a strategic alliance or joint venture is not manageable, an acquisition may be a better option.[112] Alliances can also lead to an acquisition, which is discussed next.

Acquisitions

As free trade has continued to expand in global markets, cross-border acquisitions have also been increasing significantly. In 2008, cross-border acquisitions comprised about 40 percent of all acquisitions completed worldwide, down from 45 percent in previous years.[113] As explained in Chapter 7, acquisitions can provide quick access to a new market. In fact, acquisitions often provide the fastest and the largest initial international expansion of any of the alternatives.[114] Thus, entry is much quicker than by other modes. For example, Wal-Mart entered Germany and the United Kingdom by acquiring local firms. Later, Wal-Mart withdrew from Germany.[115]

Although acquisitions have become a popular mode of entering international markets, they are not without costs. International acquisitions carry some of the disadvantages of domestic acquisitions (see Chapter 7). In addition, they can be expensive and also often require debt financing, which carries an extra cost. International negotiations for acquisitions can be exceedingly complex and are generally more complicated than domestic acquisitions. For example, acquisitions are being used by firms in emerging economies to enter developed economies. China has been buying firms in foreign countries that have assets in natural resources. For instance, China Minmetals, a state-owned mining firm, tried to acquire Oz Minerals, the world's second largest zinc miner based in Australia. However, this acquisition, like many others, has been opposed by the government because of the potential for a sovereign power to take control of important natural resources.[116]

Interestingly, acquirers make fewer acquisitions in countries with significant corruption. They choose to use international joint ventures instead. However, these ventures fail more often, although this is moderated by the acquiring firms' past experience with such deals. When acquisitions are made in such countries, acquirers commonly pay smaller premiums to buy the target firms.[117]

Dealing with the legal and regulatory requirements in the target firm's country and obtaining appropriate information to negotiate an agreement are frequent problems. Finally, the merging of the new firm into the acquiring firm is often more complex than in domestic acquisitions. The acquiring firm must deal not only with different corporate cultures, but also with potentially different social cultures and practices.[118] These differences make the integration of the two firms after the acquisition more challenging; it is difficult to capture the potential synergy when integration is slowed or stymied because of cultural differences.[119] Therefore, while international acquisitions have been popular because of the rapid access to new markets they provide, they also carry with them important costs and multiple risks.

SAIC acquired assets of the MG Rover Group, the British auto producer, which was insolvent at the time. This acquisition gave the Chinese firm an entry point into Europe and an opportunity to establish its own brand through the MG Rover label. SAIC previously considered a joint venture but decided to make the acquisition bid, worth $104 million. However, SAIC experienced formidable government opposition in the United Kingdom and had to clear extra regulatory hurdles to receive approval. By 2008 it had not produced one of the MG roadsters that it had intended because of "quality issues."[120]

New Wholly Owned Subsidiary

The establishment of a new wholly owned subsidiary is referred to as a **greenfield venture.** The process of creating such ventures is often complex and potentially costly, but it affords maximum control to the firm and has the most potential to provide above-average returns. This potential is especially true of firms with strong intangible capabilities that might be leveraged through a greenfield venture.[121] A firm maintains full control of its operations with a greenfield venture. More control is especially advantageous if the firm has proprietary technology. Research also suggests that "wholly owned subsidiaries and expatriate staff are preferred" in service industries where "close contacts with end customers" and "high levels of professional skills, specialized know-how, and customization" are required.[122] Other research suggests that greenfield investments are more prominent where physical capital-intensive plants are planned and that acquisitions are more likely preferred when a firm is human capital intensive—that is, where a strong local degree of unionization and high cultural distance would cause difficulty in transferring knowledge to a host nation through a greenfield approach.[123]

The risks are also high, however, because of the costs of establishing a new business operation in a new country. The firm may have to acquire the knowledge and expertise of the existing market by hiring either host-country nationals, possibly from competitors, or through consultants, which can be costly. Still, the firm maintains control over the technology, marketing, and distribution of its products. Furthermore, the company must build new manufacturing facilities, establish distribution networks, and learn and

The establishment of a new wholly owned subsidiary is referred to as a **greenfield venture.**

implement appropriate marketing strategies to compete in the new market.[124] Research also suggests that when the country risk is high, firms prefer to enter with joint ventures instead of greenfield investments in order to manage the risk. However, if they have previous experience in a country, they prefer to use a wholly owned greenfield venture rather than a joint venture.[125]

The globalization of the air cargo industry has implications for companies such as UPS and FedEx. The impact of this globalization is especially pertinent to China and the Asia Pacific region. China's air cargo market is expected to grow 11 percent per year through 2023. Accordingly, in 2008, both UPS and FedEx opened new hub operations in Shanghai and Gangzhou, respectively; each firm has about 6,000 employees in China. These hubs facilitated their distribution and logistics business during the Olympics in Beijing. These investments are wholly owned because these firms need to maintain the integrity of their IT and logistics systems in order to maximize efficiency. Greenfield ventures also help the firms to maintain the proprietary nature of their systems.[126]

Dynamics of Mode of Entry

A firm's mode of entry into international markets is affected by a number of factors.[127] Initially, market entry is often achieved through export, which requires no foreign manufacturing expertise and investment only in distribution. Licensing can facilitate the product improvements necessary to enter foreign markets, as in the Komatsu example. Strategic alliances have been popular because they allow a firm to connect with an experienced partner already in the targeted market. Strategic alliances also reduce risk through the sharing of costs. Therefore, all three modes—export, licensing, and strategic alliance—are good tactics for early market development. Also, the strategic alliance is often used in more uncertain situations, such as an emerging economy where there is significant risk, such as Venezuela or Colombia.[128] However, if intellectual property rights in the emerging economy are not well protected, the number of firms in the industry is growing fast, and the need for global integration is high, a joint venture or wholly owned subsidiary entry mode is preferred.[129]

To secure a stronger presence in international markets, acquisitions or greenfield ventures may be required. Aerospace firms Airbus and Boeing have used joint ventures, especially in large markets, to facilitate entry, while military equipment firms such as Thales SA have used acquisitions to build a global presence. Japanese auto manufacturers, such as Toyota, have gained a presence in the United States through both greenfield ventures and joint ventures. Because of Toyota's highly efficient manufacturing process, it wants to maintain control over its auto manufacturing when possible. It has engaged in a joint venture in the United States with General Motors,[130] but most of its manufacturing facilities are greenfield investments. It opened a new plant in Canada in 2008 and plans on opening a new plant in Mississippi in 2010, although this project may be delayed or postponed given the economic downturn.[131] Therefore, Toyota uses some form of foreign direct investment (e.g., greenfield ventures and joint ventures) rather than another mode of entry (although it may use exporting in new markets as it did in China). Both acquisitions and greenfield ventures are likely to come at later stages in the development of an international strategy.

Large diversified business groups, often found in emerging economies, not only gain resources through diversification but also have specialized abilities in managing differences in inward and outward flows of foreign direct investment.[132] For instance, in India such groups have facilitated the development of a thriving pharmaceutical industry.[133]

Thus, to enter a global market, a firm selects the entry mode that is best suited to the situation at hand. In some instances, the various options will be followed sequentially, beginning with exporting and ending with greenfield ventures. In other cases, the firm may use several, but not all, of the different entry modes, each in different markets. The decision regarding which entry mode to use is primarily a result of the industry's competitive conditions, the country's situation and government policies, and the firm's unique set of resources, capabilities, and core competencies.

Strategic Competitive Outcomes

After its international strategy and mode of entry have been selected, the firm turns its attention to implementation issues (see Chapter 11). Implementation is highly important, because international expansion is risky, making it difficult to achieve a competitive advantage (see Figure 8.1). The probability the firm will be successful with an international strategy increases when it is effectively implemented.

International Diversification and Returns

Firms have numerous reasons to diversify internationally.[134] **International diversification** is a strategy through which a firm expands the sales of its goods or services across the borders of global regions and countries into different geographic locations or markets. Because of its potential advantages, international diversification should be related positively to firms' returns. Research has shown that, as international diversification increases, firms' returns decrease initially but then increase quickly as firms learn to manage international expansion.[135] In fact, the stock market is particularly sensitive to investments in international markets. Firms that are broadly diversified into multiple international markets usually achieve the most positive stock returns, especially when they diversify geographically into core business areas.[136] Many factors contribute to the positive effects of international diversification, such as private versus government ownership, potential economies of scale and experience, location advantages, increased market size, and the opportunity to stabilize returns. The stabilization of returns helps reduce a firm's overall risk.[137] All of these outcomes can be achieved by smaller and newer ventures, as well as by larger and established firms.

Toyota has found that international diversification allows it to better exploit its core competencies, because sharing knowledge resources across subsidiaries can produce synergy. Also, a firm's returns may affect its decision to diversify internationally. For example, poor returns in a domestic market may encourage a firm to expand internationally in order to enhance its profit potential. In addition, internationally diversified firms may have access to more flexible labor markets, as the Japanese do in the United States, and may thereby benefit from scanning international markets for competition and market opportunities. Also, through global networks with assets in many countries, firms can develop more flexible structures to adjust to changes that might occur. "Offshore outsourcing" has created significant value-creation opportunities for firms engaged in it, especially as firms move into markets with more flexible labor markets. Furthermore, offshoring increases exports to firms that receive the offshoring contract.[138]

International Diversification and Innovation

In Chapter 1, we indicated that the development of new technology is at the heart of strategic competitiveness. As noted in Porter's model (see Figure 8.2), a nation's competitiveness depends, in part, on the capacity of its industry to innovate. Eventually and inevitably, competitors outperform firms that fail to innovate and improve their operations and products. Therefore, the only way to sustain a competitive advantage is to upgrade it continually.[139]

International diversification provides the potential for firms to achieve greater returns on their innovations (through larger or more numerous markets) and reduces the often substantial risks of R&D investments. Therefore, international diversification provides incentives for firms to innovate. Additionally, the firm uses its primary resources and capabilities to diversify internationally and thus earn further returns on these capabilities (e.g., capability to innovate).[140]

In addition, international diversification may be necessary to generate the resources required to sustain a large-scale R&D operation. An environment of rapid technological obsolescence makes it difficult to invest in new technology and the capital-intensive operations necessary to compete in this environment. Firms operating solely in domestic markets may find such investments difficult because of the length of time required to

International diversification is a strategy through which a firm expands the sales of its goods or services across the borders of global regions and countries into different geographic locations or markets.

recoup the original investment. If the time is extended, it may not be possible to recover the investment before the technology becomes obsolete. However, international diversification improves a firm's ability to appropriate additional returns from innovation before competitors can overcome the initial competitive advantage created by the innovation. In addition, firms moving into international markets are exposed to new products and processes. If they learn about those products and processes and integrate this knowledge into their operations, further innovation can be developed. To incorporate the learning into their own R&D processes, firms must manage those processes effectively in order to absorb and use the new knowledge to create further innovations.[141]

The relationship among international diversification, innovation, and returns is complex. Some level of performance is necessary to provide the resources to generate international diversification, which in turn provides incentives and resources to invest in research and development. The latter, if done appropriately, should enhance the returns of the firm, which then provides more resources for continued international diversification and investment in R&D. Of course, these relationships have to be managed well by a firm's top level managers. Evidence suggests that more culturally diverse top management teams often have a greater knowledge of international markets and their idiosyncrasies, but their orientation to expand internationally can be affected by the nature of their compensation.[142] (Top management teams are discussed further in Chapter 12.) Moreover, managing the diverse business units of a multinational firm requires skill, not only in managing a decentralized set of businesses, but also coordinating diverse points of view derived from regionalized businesses without descending into chaos. Firms that are able to do this will challenge the best global industry incumbents.[143] This topic will be addressed next.

Complexity of Managing Multinational Firms

Although firms can realize many benefits by implementing an international strategy, doing so is complex and can produce greater uncertainty.[144] For example, multiple risks are involved when a firm operates in several different countries. Firms can grow only so large and diverse before becoming unmanageable, or before the costs of managing them exceed their benefits. Managers are constrained by the complexity and sometimes by the culture and institutional systems within which they must operate.[145] The complexities involved in managing diverse international operations are shown in the problems experienced by even high-performing firms such as Toyota. Toyota became overly focused on sales in the North American market and began to experience quality problems (i.e., increased number of recalls) and reduced customer satisfaction. It also was late in entering the Chinese market with manufacturing and as a result, it was behind the market leaders, Volkswagen and GM. However, by 2008 it had recovered and actually was outselling both firms in China, but only in passenger cars.[146] Other complexities include the highly competitive nature of global markets, multiple cultural environments, potentially rapid shifts in the value of different currencies, and the instability of some national governments.

Risks in an International Environment

International diversification carries multiple risks. Because of these risks, international expansion is difficult to implement and manage. The chief risks are political and economic. Specific examples of political and economic risks are shown in Figure 8.4.

Political Risks

Political risks are risks related to instability in national governments and to war, both civil and international. Instability in a national government creates numerous problems, including economic risks and uncertainty created by government regulation; the existence of many, possibly conflicting, legal authorities or corruption; and the potential nationalization of private assets.[147] Foreign firms that invest in another country may have

Figure 8.4 Risk in the International Environment

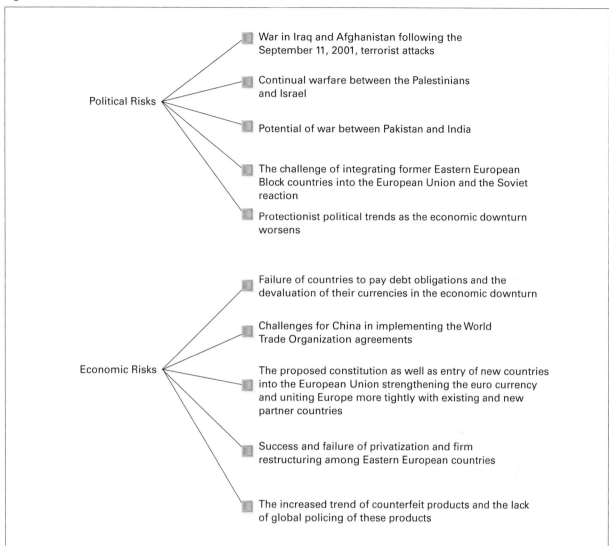

Political Risks

- War in Iraq and Afghanistan following the September 11, 2001, terrorist attacks
- Continual warfare between the Palestinians and Israel
- Potential of war between Pakistan and India
- The challenge of integrating former Eastern European Block countries into the European Union and the Soviet reaction
- Protectionist political trends as the economic downturn worsens

Economic Risks

- Failure of countries to pay debt obligations and the devaluation of their currencies in the economic downturn
- Challenges for China in implementing the World Trade Organization agreements
- The proposed constitution as well as entry of new countries into the European Union strengthening the euro currency and uniting Europe more tightly with existing and new partner countries
- Success and failure of privatization and firm restructuring among Eastern European countries
- The increased trend of counterfeit products and the lack of global policing of these products

Sources: 2009, Euro-Zone PPI posts biggest annual drop in 22 years, *Wall Street Journal*, http://www.online.wsj.com, May 5; 2009, The nuts and bolts come apart: As global demand contracts, trade is slumping and protectionism rising, *Economist*, http://www.economist.com, March 26; 2009, New fund, old fundamentals: Has the IMF changed or has the world? *Economist*, http://www.economist.com, April 30; 2009, Competitive devaluations, *Financial Times*, http://www.ft.com, March 14; D. Bilefsky, 2009, A crisis is separating Eastern Europe's strong from its weak, *New York Times*, http://www.nytimes.com, February 23; I. Dreyer, 2009, Mending EU-China trade ties, *Wall Street Journal*, http://www.online.wsj.com, May 6; J. Garten, 2009, The dangers of turning inward, *Wall Street Journal*, http://www.online.wsj.com, March 5; S. Levine, 2009, Emergency loans for European banks: Three international development banks pledged nearly $30 billion to shore up the troubled Eastern European banking system, *BusinessWeek*, http://www.businessweek.com, February 28; M. Singh, 2009, India launches a toy trade war with China, *Time*, http://www.time.com, February 6; 2008, The best way to do business with Russia, *Financial Times*, http://www.ft.com, August 21; 2008, Strong dollar, weak dollar, *Russia Today*, http://www.russiatoday.com, October 28; J. Barnham, 2008, China's pirates move up value chain, *Security Management*, June 44; L. Burkitt, 2008, Fighting fakes, *Forbes*, August 11, 44; B. Szlanko, 2008, Will the crisis spur Hungary to reform? *BusinessWeek*, http://www.businessweek.com, November, 13; B. Szlanko, Europe: Tougher than it looks on Russia, *BusinessWeek*, http://www.businessweek.com, September 4; C.-C. Tschang, 2008, Currency stalemate at U.S.-China meeting, *BusinessWeek*, http://www.businessweek.com, December 5.

concerns about the stability of the national government and the effects of unrest and government instability on their investments or assets.[148]

Russia has experienced a relatively high level of institutional instability in the years following its revolutionary transition to a more democratic government. Decentralized political control and frequent changes in policies created chaos for many, but especially for those in the business landscape. In an effort to regain more central control and reduce the chaos, Russian leaders took actions such as prosecuting powerful private firm executives, seeking to gain state control of firm assets, and not approving some foreign acquisitions of Russian businesses. The initial institutional instability, followed by the actions of the central government, caused some firms to have delayed or negated significant foreign direct investment in Russia. Although leaders in Russia have tried to reassure potential investors about their property rights, prior actions, the fact that other laws (e.g., environmental and employee laws) are weak, and the fact that government corruption is common makes firms leery of investing in Russia.[149]

Economic Risks

As illustrated in the example of Russian institutional instability and property rights, economic risks are interdependent with political risks. If firms cannot protect their intellectual property, they are highly unlikely to make foreign direct investments. Countries therefore need to create and sustain strong intellectual property rights and enforce them in order to attract desired foreign direct investment. As noted in the Strategic Focus, there is a growing problem with the continuing trend of counterfeit or fake products, especially as the market for these products becomes globalized. Firms like eBay get caught up in the struggle when authentic producers desire to punish the counterfeit producers for selling products on the Internet.

Another economic risk is the perceived security risk of a foreign firm acquiring firms that have key natural resources or firms that may be considered strategic in regard to intellectual property. For instance, many Chinese firms have been buying natural resource firms in Australia and Latin America as well as manufacturing assets in the United States. This has made the governments of the key resource firms nervous about such strategic assets falling under the control of state-owned Chinese firms.[150] Terrorism has also been of concern. Indonesia has difficulty competing for investment against China and India, countries that are viewed to have fewer security risks.

As noted earlier, foremost among the economic risks of international diversification are the differences and fluctuations in the value of different currencies.[151] The value of the dollar relative to other currencies determines the value of the international assets and earnings of U.S. firms; for example, an increase in the value of the U.S. dollar can reduce the value of U.S. multinational firms' international assets and earnings in other countries. Furthermore, the value of different currencies can also, at times, dramatically affect a firm's competitiveness in global markets because of its effect on the prices of goods manufactured in different countries.[152] An increase in the value of the dollar can harm U.S. firms' exports to international markets because of the price differential of the products. Thus, government oversight and control of economic and financial capital in the country affect not only local economic activity, but also foreign investments in the country. Certainly, the political and policy changes in Eastern Europe have stimulated much more FDI due to the significant changes there since the early 1990s.[153]

Google is the market leader in the Internet search markets in the United States and Europe. However, its expansion into Russia and Asian countries has experienced difficulties. As noted earlier, in the Strategic Focus, it has dominant competitors in Russia (Yandex) and China (Baidu). It learned from its previous difficulties and is managing with a persistent strategy, but these competitors are dominating, especially given the additional support that they receive from their local governments, formally and informally.

Limits to International Expansion: Management Problems

After learning how to operate effectively in international markets, firms tend to earn positive returns on international diversification. But, the returns often level off and become negative as the diversification increases past a certain point.[154] Several reasons explain the limits to the positive effects of international diversification. First, greater geographic dispersion across country borders increases the costs of coordination between units and the distribution of products. Second, trade barriers, logistical costs, cultural diversity, and other differences by country (e.g., access to raw materials and different employee skill levels) greatly complicate the implementation of an international diversification strategy.

Institutional and cultural factors can present strong barriers to the transfer of a firm's competitive advantages from one country to another. Marketing programs often have to be

THE CONTINUING THREAT TO LEGITIMATE COMPANIES FROM COUNTERFEIT OR FAKE PRODUCTS

The International Anti-Counterfeiting Coalition has estimated that counterfeit or fake products make up 7 percent of the world's goods. This is an issue of growing importance, especially for firms competing on a more global basis and for firms that have significant profit margins associated with intellectual property rights, such as software makers, entertainment content businesses (i.e., music producers), and branded products. As businesses or governments implement solutions to overcome counterfeit products, the "pirates" often move up the value chain to copy more high-tech, high-margin products. China's rock bottom production costs have turned it into the "world's workshop and [have] empowered an economic boom;" however, China's environment, because of lax legal enforcement, creates an incentive for counterfeit product makers to create fake products and software and also to supply "nonstandard" electronic components, which are less traceable.

For example, Philip Morris has filed a compliant with the International Trade Commission (ITC) to stop illegal import of "gray market" cigarettes from China and other regions bearing Philip Morris USA's trademarks, including Marlboro. Charlie Whitaker, the vice president of compliance and brand integrity for Philip Morris USA, suggests that "our brands are among our company's most valuable assets and we take many steps to protect them." The firm complains that Internet-based cigarette vendors are selling Philip Morris–labeled products in violation of U.S. intellectual property laws and the Lanham Act.

Many of the counterfeit products are sold on the Internet, similar to the cigarette example. French perfume producer L'Oréal has mounted a legal challenge to eBay for sales of fake products using its brand. L'Oréal argues that by failing to police fake products, eBay is in fact acting in concert with the sellers of those goods. Of course, eBay denies the claim saying that it is simply providing a trading platform and that the responsibility for looking after L'Oréal's trademarks should rest with L'Oréal. Interestingly, luxury good manufacturers LVMH and Hermes have won rulings in French courts on similar issues against eBay, but eBay has triumphed in other cases, such as one in a Belgium court.

Some counterfeit products are more than just a nuisance—they are dangerous. One firm identified bogus pesticides used to treat crops that could create health risks and reduce farmers' livelihoods. Additionally, the U.S. military is facing a growing threat from fatal equipment failures and even foreign espionage through computer components that might be embedded in war planes, ships, and communication networks. For instance, BEA Systems experienced field failures of some military equipment with bogus parts, and

Brooklyn district attorney displays seized counterfeit goods as evidence for court proceedings.

Mario Tama/Getty Images

some defense contractors have traced Chinese producers to fake microchips as well as tiny electronic circuits found in computer equipment and other electric gear. Because of these threats, the Pentagon has established more secure buying procedures to prevent the spread of counterfeit military-grade chips as aging equipment needs updating.

These and other problems illustrate the importance of protecting intellectual property and the risks associated with pursuing global trade and production. Firms might pursue legal challenges, but this is often difficult in emerging economies such as China and Russia, where there is weak legal protection. Some products such as fashion and clothing items can be protected with more sophisticated labels that guard against counterfeiters. As firms pursue international strategies by using strategies based on intellectual property and which require significant R&D investments, the loss of such intellectual property to counterfeiting increases and proactive strategies must be taken to protect against significant losses.

Sources: M. Murphy & N. Tait, 2009, L'Oréal mounts legal challenges over eBay sales, *Financial Times*, March 10, 4; J. Barnham, 2008, China's pirates move up value chain, *Security Management*, June 44; L. Burkitt, 2008, Fighting fakes, *Forbes*, August 11, 44; M. Fairley, 2008, Brand protection: Label makers become vital security link in anti-counterfeiting, *Converting Magazine*, August, 20; B. Grow, C.-C. Tschang, B. Burnsed, & K. Epstein, 2008, Dangerous fakes, *BusinessWeek*, October 13, 34–37; J. Slota & M. Humphreys, 2008, Connect the dots, *Pharmaceutical Executive*, July 67–70; 2008, Alarm at flood of bogus pesticides, *Financial Times*, May 20, 12.

STRATEGY RIGHT NOW

Learn how leading companies such as Unilever are using information technologies to help manage international diversification.

www.cengage.com/management/hitt

redesigned and new distribution networks established when firms expand into new countries. In addition, firms may encounter different labor costs and capital charges. In general, it is difficult to effectively implement, manage, and control a firm's international operations.

The amount of international diversification that can be managed varies from firm to firm and according to the abilities of each firm's managers. The problems of central coordination and integration are mitigated if the firm diversifies into more friendly countries that are geographically close and have cultures similar to its own country's culture. In that case, the firm is likely to encounter fewer trade barriers, the laws and customs are better understood, and the product is easier to adapt to local markets.[155] For example, U.S. firms may find it less difficult to expand their operations into Mexico, Canada, and Western European countries than into Asian countries.

Management must also be concerned with the relationship between the host government and the multinational corporation.[156] Although government policy and regulations are often barriers, many firms, such as Toyota and General Motors, have turned to strategic alliances, as they did in China, to overcome those barriers. By forming interorganizational networks, such as strategic alliances (see Chapter 9), firms can share resources and risks but also build flexibility. However, large networks can be difficult to manage.[157]

SUMMARY

- The use of international strategies is increasing. Traditional motives include extending the product life cycle, securing key resources, and having access to low-cost labor. Emerging motives include the integration of the Internet and mobile telecommunications, which facilitates global transactions. Also, firms experience increased pressure for global integration as the demand for commodities becomes borderless, and yet they feel simultaneous pressure for local country responsiveness.

- An international strategy is commonly designed primarily to capitalize on four benefits: increased market size; earning a return on large investments; economies of scale and learning; and advantages of location.

- International business-level strategies are usually grounded in one or more home-country advantages, as Porter's model suggests. Porter's model emphasizes four determinants: factors of production; demand conditions; related and supporting industries; and patterns of firm strategy, structure, and rivalry.

- There are three types of international corporate-level strategies. A multidomestic strategy focuses on competition within each country in which the firm competes. Firms using a multidomestic strategy decentralize strategic and operating decisions to the business units operating in each country, so that each unit can tailor its goods and services to the local market. A global strategy assumes more standardization of products across country boundaries; therefore, a competitive strategy is centralized and controlled by the home office. A transnational strategy seeks to integrate characteristics of both multidomestic and global strategies to emphasize both local responsiveness and global integration and coordination. This strategy is difficult to implement, requiring an integrated network and a culture of individual commitment.

- Although the transnational strategy's implementation is a challenge, environmental trends are causing many multinational firms to consider the need for both global efficiency and local responsiveness. Many large multinational firms, particularly those with many diverse products, use a multidomestic strategy with some product lines and a global strategy with others.

- The threat of wars and terrorist attacks increases the risks and costs of international strategies. Furthermore, research suggests that the liability of foreignness is more difficult to overcome than once thought.

- Some firms decide to compete only in certain regions of the world, as opposed to viewing all markets in the world as potential opportunities. Competing in regional markets allows firms and managers to focus their learning on specific markets, cultures, locations, resources, and other factors.

- Firms may enter international markets in one of several ways, including exporting, licensing, forming strategic alliances, making acquisitions, and establishing new wholly owned subsidiaries,

often referred to as greenfield ventures. Most firms begin with exporting or licensing, because of their lower costs and risks, but later they might use strategic alliances and acquisitions to expand internationally. The most expensive and risky means of entering a new international market is through the establishment of a new wholly owned subsidiary. On the other hand, such subsidiaries provide the advantages of maximum control by the firm and, if it is successful, the greatest returns.

- International diversification facilitates innovation in a firm, because it provides a larger market to gain more and faster returns from investments in innovation. In addition, international diversification may generate the resources necessary to sustain a large-scale R&D program.

- In general, international diversification is related to above-average returns, but this assumes that the diversification is effectively implemented and that the firm's international operations are well managed. International diversification provides greater economies of scope and learning which, along with greater innovation, help produce above-average returns.

- Several risks are involved with managing multinational operations. Among these are political risks (e.g., instability of national governments) and economic risks (e.g., fluctuations in the value of a country's currency).

- Some limits also constrain the ability to manage international expansion effectively. International diversification increases coordination and distribution costs, and management problems are exacerbated by trade barriers, logistical costs, and cultural diversity, among other factors.

REVIEW QUESTIONS

1. What are the traditional and emerging motives that cause firms to expand internationally?

2. What are the four primary benefits of an international strategy?

3. What four factors provide a basis for international business-level strategies?

4. What are the three international corporate-level strategies? How do they differ from each other? What factors lead to their development?

5. What environmental trends are affecting international strategy?

6. What five modes of international expansion are available, and what is the normal sequence of their use?

7. What is the relationship between international diversification and innovation? How does international diversification affect innovation? What is the effect of international diversification on a firm's returns?

8. What are the risks of international diversification? What are the challenges of managing multinational firms?

EXPERIENTIAL EXERCISES

EXERCISE 1: MCDONALD'S: GLOBAL, MULTICOUNTRY, OR TRANSNATIONAL STRATEGY?

McDonald's is one of the world's best-known brands: the company has approximately 31,000 restaurants located in more than 118 countries and serves 58 million customers *every day*. McDonald's opened its first international restaurant in Japan in 1971. Its Golden Arches are featured prominently in two former bastions of communism: Puskin Square in Moscow and Tiananmen Square in Beijing, China.

What strategy has McDonald's used to achieve such visibility? For this exercise, each group will be asked to conduct some background research on the firm and then make a brief presentation to identify the international strategy (i.e., global, multidomestic, or transnational) McDonald's is implementing.

Individual

Use the Internet to find examples of menu variations in different countries. How much do menu items differ for a McDonald's in the United States from other locations outside the United States?

Groups

Review the characteristics of global, multidomestic, and transnational strategies. Conduct additional research to assess what strategy best describes the one McDonald's is using. Prepare a flip chart with a single page of bullet points to explain your reasoning.

Whole Class

Each group should have five to seven minutes to explain its reasoning. Following Q&A for each group, ask class members to vote for the respective strategy choices.

EXERCISE 2: DOES THE WORLD NEED MORE BURRITOS?

Chipotle Mexican Grill (CMG) is a public company listed on the NYSE, founded in 1993. The highly recognizable brand is prolific in the United States with 837 company-operated units as of the end of 2008. There is one operating store in Toronto as of this time, which represents the only non–U.S. concern. There are plans to open about 120 new stores in 2009. Even though there are quite a few U.S. states in which the firm has no locations, the management team has been seriously considering an international expansion program.

For purposes of this exercise, assume you have been retained by the top management team of Chipotle to evaluate its international expansion options. Management has concluded that the following options are the most promising:

1. Continue expansion throughout the United States.
2. Expand into Mexico.
3. Increase expansion throughout Canada.
4. Expand to the United Kingdom.

Part One

Working in teams, select one of the four options above as approved by the instructor. Next, with Porter's determinates of national advantage as a foundation, identify the factors that work either in favor of or against your strategy.

To begin this assignment, each team must prepare a strategy for expansion. Using information gleaned from the 2008 annual report; identify Chipotle's main strategies for growth. For instance, what is their position on franchise vs. company-owned stores (this helps determine cash needs)? What are their most significant needs for expansion regarding resources? (Hint: Think through their "Food with Integrity" program.)

Conduct research on your team's selected area for expansion on the following criteria:

- Economic characteristics: Gross national product, wages, unemployment, inflation, and so on. Trend analysis of these data (e.g., are wages rising or falling, rate of change in wages, etc.) is preferable to single point-in-time snapshots.
- Social characteristics: Life expectancy, education norms, income distributions, literacy, and so on.
- Risk factors: Economic and political risk assessment.

The following Internet resources may be useful in your research:

- The Library of Congress has a collection of country studies.
- BBC News offers country profiles online.
- The Economist Intelligence Unit (http://www.eiu.com) offers country profiles.
- Both the United Nations and International Monetary Fund provide statistics and research reports.
- The CIA World Factbook has profiles of different regions.
- The Global Entrepreneurship Monitor provides reports with detailed information about economic conditions and social aspects for a number of countries.
- Links can be found at http://www.countryrisk.com to a number of resources that assess both political and economic risk for individual countries.
- For U.S. data, see http://www.census.gov.

Part Two

Based on your research, each team is to prepare a presentation (10 to 15 minutes) highlighting the strategic advantages and disadvantages of their assigned country's opportunities and threats as regards expansion potential. Each team must also decide which corporate level strategy should be utilized if their country expansion were chosen and why.

Next, as a class, be prepared to discuss what the overall consensus would be if you were making the decision at Chipotle.

VIDEO | CASE

UNDERSTAND THE DIFFERENCES WHEN DOING BUSINESS ABROAD

Andrew Sherman/Co-Founder/Grow Fast Grow Right

Andrew Sherman, cofounder of Grow Fast Grow Right, suggests that global business strategy is like the pizza business. There are four key elements: crust; cheese; sauce; and toppings. Further, he argues that only one of those four should vary by international location, the toppings.

Before you watch the video consider the following concepts and questions and be prepared to discuss them in class:

Concepts
- International expansion
- Cultural differences
- Risks
- Organizational size
- Transnational strategy

Questions

1. Given the international experience you have had or observed, do you also feel that Mr. Sherman's pizza analogy is appropriately applied to international strategy?

2. What do you consider some of the mistakes that might occur when companies go international?

3. How can a company better understand the cultures and methods of business when entering a new location?

4. Is it harder or easier for a small entrepreneurial firm to go international than a large firm?

NOTES

1. W. He & M. A. Lyles, 2009, China's outward foreign direct investment, *Business Horizons*, 51(6): 485–491.

2. B.C. Kho, R. M. Stulz, & F. E. Warnock, 2009, Financial globalization, governance, and the evolution of the home bias. *Journal of Accounting Research*, 47(2): 597–635; S. Li, 2005, Why a poor governance environment does not deter foreign direct investment: The case of China and its implications for investment protection, *Business Horizons*, 48(4): 297–302.

3. G. L. Ge & D. Z. Ding, 2009, A strategic analysis of surging Chinese manufacturers: The case of Galanz. *Asia Pacific Journal of Management*, 25(4): 667–683; A. K. Gupta & H. Wang, 2007, How to get China and India right: Western companies need to become smarter—and they need to do it quickly, *Wall Street Journal*, April 28, R4.

4. D. Kronborg & S. Thomsen, 2009, Foreign ownership and long-term survival, *Strategic Management Journal*, 30(2): 207–220; H. J. Sapienza, E. Autio, G. George, & S. A. Zahra, 2006, A capabilities perspective on the effects of early internationalization on firm survival and growth, *Academy of Management Review*, 31: 914–933; W. P. Wan, 2005, Country resource environments, firm capabilities, and corporate diversification strategies. *Journal of Management Studies*, 42: 161–182.

5. P. Enderwick, 2009, Large emerging markets (LEMs) and international strategy. *International Marketing Review*, 26(1): 7–16; F. T. Rothaermel, S. Kotha, & H. K. Steensma, 2006, International market entry by U.S. Internet firms: An empirical analysis of country risk, national culture and market size, *Journal of Management*, 32: 56–82; R. E. Hoskisson, H. Kim, R. E. White, & L. Tihanyi, 2004, A framework for understanding international diversification by business groups from emerging economies, in M. A. Hitt & J. L. C. Cheng (eds.), *Theories of the Multinational Enterprise: Diversity, Complexity, and Relevance. Advances in International Management*, Oxford, UK: Elsevier/JAI Press, 137–163.

6. M. Javidan, R. Steers, & M. A. Hitt (eds.), 2007, *The Global Mindset*. Oxford, UK: Elsevier Publishing; T. M. Begley &

D. P. Boyd, 2003, The need for a corporate global mind-set, *MIT Sloan Management Review*, 44(2): 25–32.

7. M. W. Peng & E. G. Pleggenkuhle-Miles, 2009, Current debates in global strategy, *International Journal of Management Reviews*, 11(1): 51–68; M. A. Hitt, L. Tihanyi, T. Miller, & B. Connelly, 2006, International diversification: Antecedents, outcomes and moderators, *Journal of Management*, 32: 831–867.

8. Y. Luo & R. L. Tung, 2007, International expansion of emerging market enterprises: A springboard perspective, *Journal of International Business Studies* 38: 481–498; J. E. Ricart, M. J. Enright, P. Ghemawat, S. L. Hart, & T. Khanna, 2004, New frontiers in international strategy, *Journal of International Business Studies*, 35: 175–200.

9. R. Vernon, 1996, International investment and international trade in the product cycle, *Quarterly Journal of Economics*, 80: 190–207.

10. He & Lyles, China's outward foreign direct investment; P. J. Buckley, L. J. Clegg, A. R. Cross, X. Liu, H. Voss, & P. Zheng, 2006, The determinants of Chinese outward foreign direct investment, *Journal of International Business Studies*, 38: 499–518.

11. L. Yu, 2003, The global-brand advantage, *MIT Sloan Management Review*, 44(3): 13.

12. M. E. Lloyd, 2009, IKEA sees opportunity during hard times—as expansion in U.S. continues, Swedish retailer expects its value furnishings to appeal to shoppers amid economic slump, *Wall Street Journal*, February 18, B5A.

13. X. Liu & H. Zou, 2008, The impact of greenfield FDI and mergers and acquisitions on innovation in Chinese high-tech industries, *Journal of World Business*, 43(3): 352–364.

14. F. Fortanier & R. Van Tulder, 2009, Internationalization trajectories—a cross-country comparison: Are large Chinese and Indian companies different? *Industrial and Corporate Change*, 18(2 Special Issue): 223–247.

15. K. Addae-Dapaah & W. T. Y. Hwee, 2009, The unsung impact of currency risk on the performance of international real property investment, *Review of Financial Economics*, 18(1): 56–65; C. C. Y. Kwok & D. M. Reeb,

2000, Internationalization and firm risk: An upstream-downstream hypothesis, *Journal of International Business Studies*, 31: 611–629.

16. M. Wright, I. Filatotchev, R. E. Hoskisson, & M. W. Peng, 2005, Strategy research in emerging economies: Challenging the conventional wisdom, *Journal of Management Studies*, 42: 1–30; T. London & S. Hart, 2004, Reinventing strategies for emerging markets: Beyond the transnational model, *Journal of International Business Studies*, 35: 350–370; R. E. Hoskisson, L. Eden, C. M. Lau, & M. Wright, 2000, Strategy in emerging economies, *Academy of Management Journal*, 43: 249–267.

17. P. Zheng, 2009, A comparison of FDI determinants in China and India, *Thunderbird International Business Review*, 51(3): 263–279; H. Sender, 2005, The economy; the outlook: India comes of age, as focus on returns lures foreign capital, *Wall Street Journal*, June 6, A2.

18. S. Athreye & S. Kapur, 2009, Introduction: The internationalization of Chinese and Indian firms—trends, motivations and strategy. *Industrial and Corporate Change*, 18(2 Special Issue): 209–221; M. A. Witt & A. Y. Lewin, 2007, Outward foreign direct investment as escape from home country institutional constraints, *Journal of International Business Studies*, 38: 579–594; M. W. Peng, S.-H. Lee, & D. Y. L. Wang, 2005, What determines the scope of the firm over time? A focus on institutional relatedness, *Academy of Management Review*, 30: 622–633.

19. J. W. Spencer, T. P. Murtha, & S. A. Lenway, 2005, How governments matter to new industry creation, *Academy of Management Review*, 30: 321–337; I. P. Mahmood & C. Rufin, 2005, Government's dilemma: The role of government in imitation and innovation, *Academy of Management Review*, 30: 338–360.

20. B. Elango, 2009, Minimizing effects of "liability of foreignness": Response strategies of foreign firms in the United States, *Journal of World Business*, 44(1), 51–62; L. Eden & S. Miller, 2004, Distance matters: Liability of foreignness, institutional distance and ownership strategy, in M. A. Hitt & J. L. Cheng (eds.),

Advances in International Management, Oxford, UK: Elsevier/JAI Press, 187–221.

21. S. Anand, 2008, Japan M&A, Prescription for Growth, *BusinessWeek*, http://www.businessweek.com, November 17.

22. V. Bauerlein and G. Fairclough, 2009, Beijing thwarts Coke's takeover bid, *Wall Street Journal*, http://www.wsj.com, March 19.

23. H. Barnard, 2008, Uneven domestic knowledge bases and the success of foreign firms in the USA, *Research Policy*, 37(10): 1674–1683.

24. S. Shimizutani & Y. Todo, 2008, What determines overseas R&D activities? The case of Japanese multinational firms, *Research Policy*, 37(3): 530–544; J. Cantwell, J. Dunning, & O. Janne, 2004, Towards a technology-seeking explanation of U.S. direct investment in the United Kingdom, *Journal of International Management*, 10: 5–20; W. Chung & J. Alcacer, 2002, Knowledge seeking and location choice of foreign direct investment in the United States, *Management Science*, 48(12): 1534–1554.

25. F. Jiang, 2005, Driving forces of international pharmaceutical firms' FDI into China, *Journal of Business Research*, 22(1): 21–39.

26. M. D. R. Chari, S. Devaraj, & P. David, 2007, International diversification and firm performance: Role of information technology investments, *Journal of World Business*, 42: 184–197; W. Chung, 2001, Identifying technology transfer in foreign direct investment: Influence of industry conditions and investing firm motives, *Journal of International Business Studies*, 32: 211–229.

27. M. V. S. Kumar, 2009, The relationship between product and international diversification: The effects of short-run constraints and endogeneity. *Strategic Management Journal*, 30(1): 99–116; K. J. Petersen, R. B. Handfield, & G. L. Ragatz, 2005, Supplier integration into new product development: Coordinating product process and supply chain design, *Journal of Operations Management*, 23: 371–388.

28. C. Rauwald, 2009, Porsche chooses the China road; four-door Panamera's Shanghai debut signals focus on emerging markets, *Wall Street Journal*, April 20, B2; A. Webb, 2007, China needs strong automakers—not more. *Automotive News*, http://www.autonews.com, July 20; China's SAIC says first half sales up 23 percent. 2007, *Reuters*, http://www.reuters.com, July 12; A. Taylor, 2004, Shanghai Auto wants to be the world's next great car company, *Fortune*, October 4, 103–109.

29. K. D. Brouthers, L. E., Brouthers, & S. Werner, 2008, Resource-based advantages in an international context, *Journal of Management*, 34: 189–217; N. Karra, N. Phillips, & P. Tracey, 2008, Building the born global firm developing entrepreneurial capabilities for international new venture success,

Long Range Planning, 41(4): 440–458; L. Zhou, W.-P. Wu, & X. Luo, 2007, Internationalization and the performance of born-global SMEs: The mediating role of social networks, *Journal of International Business Studies*, 38: 673–690.

30. H. Zou & P. N. Ghauri, 2009, Learning through international acquisitions: The process of knowledge acquisition in China, *Management International Review*, 48(2), 207–226; H. Berry, 2006, Leaders, laggards, and the pursuit of foreign knowledge, *Strategic Management Journal*, 27: 151–168.

31. J. Song & J. Shin, 2008, The paradox of technological capabilities: A study of knowledge sourcing from host countries of overseas R&D operations, *Journal of International Business Studies*, 39: 291–303; J. Penner-Hahn & J. M. Shaver, 2005, Does international research increase patent output? An analysis of Japanese pharmaceutical firms, *Strategic Management Journal*, 26: 121–140.

32. D. Strutton, 2009, Horseshoes, global supply chains, and an emerging Chinese threat: Creating remedies one idea at a time, *Business Horizons*, 52(1): 31–43.

33. A. M. Rugman & A. Verbeke, 2009, A new perspective on the regional and global strategies of multinational services firms, *Management International Review*, 48(4): 397–411; R. Tahir & J. Larimo, 2004, Understanding the location strategies of the European firms in Asian countries, *Journal of American Academy of Business*, 5: 102–110.

34. R. Chakrabarti, S. Gupta-Mukherjee, & N. Jayaraman, 2009, Mars-Venus marriages: Culture and cross-border M&A, *Journal of International Business Studies*, 40(2): 216–236; D. Xu & O. Shenkar, 2004, Institutional distance and the multinational enterprise, *Academy of Management Review*, 27: 608–618.

35. C. C. J. M. Millar & C. J. Choi, 2009, Worker identity, the liability of foreignness, the exclusion of local managers and unionism: A conceptual analysis, *Journal of Organizational Change Management*, 21(4): 460–470; D. Xu, Y. Pan, & P. W. Beamish, 2004, The effect of regulative and normative distances on MNE ownership and expatriate strategies, *Management International Review*, 44(3): 285–307.

36. N. Shirouzu, P. J. Ho, & K. Rapoza, 2009, Corporate news: GM plans to retain China, Brazil units, June 3, B2.

37. J. D. Stoll, 2009, Corporate news: GM pushes the throttle in China—affiliate's plan to expand into cars is seen as a key to growth in Asia, *Wall Street Journal*, April 27, B3.

38. J. Li & D. R. Yue, 2009, Market size, legal institutions, and international diversification strategies: Implications for the performance of multinational firms, *Management International Review*, 48(6): 667–688; T. D. A. Griffith & M. G. Harvey, 2001, A resource perspective of global dynamic capabilities, *Journal of*

International Business Studies, 32: 597–606; Y. Luo, 2000, Dynamic capabilities in international expansion, *Journal of World Business*, 35(4): 355–378.

39. R. Morck, B. Yeung, & M. Zhao, 2008, Perspectives on China's outward foreign direct investment, *Journal of International Business Studies*, 39: 337–350; J. Gimeno, R. E. Hoskisson, B.D. Beal, & W. P. Wan, 2005, Explaining the clustering of international expansion moves: A critical test in the U.S. telecommunications industry, *Academy of Management Journal*, 48: 297–319.

40. A. Cuervo-Cazurra & M. Gene, 2008, Transforming disadvantages into advantages: Developing-country MNEs in the least developed countries, *Journal of International Business Studies*, 39: 957–979; M. A. Hitt, L. Bierman, K. Uhlenbruck, & K. Shimizu, 2006, The importance of resources in the internationalization of professional service firms: The good, the bad and the ugly, *Academy of Management Journal*, 49: 1137–1157.

41. P. Dastidar, 2009, International corporate diversification and performance: Does firm self-selection matter?, *Journal of International Business Studies*, 40: 71–85; L. Nachum, 2001, The impact of home countries on the competitiveness of advertising TNCs, *Management International Review*, 41(1): 77–98.

42. M. E. Porter, 1990, *The Competitive Advantage of Nations*, New York: The Free Press.

43. Ibid, 84.

44. C. Storz, 2008, Dynamics in innovation systems: Evidence from Japan's game software industry. *Research Policy*, 37(9): 1480–1491; Y. Aoyama & H. Izushi, 2003, Hardware gimmick or cultural innovation? Technological, cultural, and social foundations of the Japanese video game industry, *Research Policy*, 32: 423–443.

45. B. Powell, 2009, China's new king of solar, *Fortune*, February 16, 94–97.

46. J. Ioffe, 2009, Search wars; the Russians are coming, *Fortune*, February 16, 36–38.

47. A. Tempel & P. Walgenbach, 2007, Global standardization of organizational forms and management practices? What new institutionalism and business systems approach can learn from each other, *Journal of Management Studies*, 44: 1–24.

48. Kumar, The relationship between product and international diversification; W. P. Wan & R. E. Hoskisson, 2003, Home country environments, corporate diversification strategies and firm performance, *Academy of Management Journal*, 46: 27–45; J. M. Geringer, S. Tallman, & D. M. Olsen, 2000, Product and international diversification among Japanese multinational firms, *Strategic Management Journal*, 21: 51–80.

49. Kumar, The relationship between product and international diversification; M. A. Hitt, R. E. Hoskisson, & R. D. Ireland, 1994, A mid-range theory of the interactive effects of international and product diversification on innovation and

Chapter 8: International Strategy

performance, *Journal of Management,*
20: 297–326.

50. D. A. Ralston, D. H. Holt, R. H. Terpstra, & Y. Kai-Cheng, 2008, The impact of national culture and economic ideology on managerial work values: A study of the United States, Russia, Japan, and China, *Journal of International Business Studies,* 39(1): 8–26; B. B. Alred & K. S. Swan, 2004, Global versus multidomestic: Culture's consequences on innovation, *Management International Review,* 44: 81–105.

51. D. Grewal, G. R. Iyer, W. A. Kamakura, A. Mehrotra, & A. Sharma, 2009, Evaluation of subsidiary marketing performance: Combining process and outcome performance metrics, *Academy of Marketing Science Journal,* 37(2): 117–120; A. Ferner, P. Almond, I. Clark, T. Colling, & T. Edwards, 2004, The dynamics of central control and subsidiary anatomy in the management of human resources: Case study evidence from U.S. MNCs in the U.K., *Organization Studies,* 25: 363–392.

52. N. Guimarães-Costa & M. P. E. Cunha, 2009, Foreign locals: A liminal perspective of international managers, *Organizational Dynamics,* 38(2): 158–166; B. Connelly, M. A. Hitt, A. S. DeNisi, & R. D. Ireland, 2007, Expatriates and corporate-level international strategy: Governing with the knowledge contract, *Management Decision,* 45: 564–581; L. Nachum, 2003, Does nationality of ownership make any difference and if so, under what circumstances? Professional service MNEs in global competition, *Journal of International Management,* 9: 1–32.

53. M. W. Hansen, T. Pedersen, & B. Petersen, 2009, MNC strategies and linkage effects in developing countries, *Journal of World Business,* 44(2): 121–139; Y. Luo, 2001, Determinants of local responsiveness: Perspectives from foreign subsidiaries in an emerging market, *Journal of Management,* 27: 451–477.

54. H. Kasper, M. Lehrer, J. Mühlbacher, & B. Müller, 2009, Integration-responsiveness and knowledge-management perspectives on the MNC: A typology and field study of cross-site knowledge-sharing practices, *Journal of Leadership & Organizational Studies,* 15(3): 287–303.

55. J. Neff, 2008, Unilever's CMO finally gets down to business, *Advertising Age,* July, 11; G. Jones, 2002, Control, performance, and knowledge transfers in large multinationals: Unilever in the United States, 1945–1980, *Business History Review,* 76(3): 435–478.

56. P. J. Buckley, 2009, The impact of the global factory on economic development, *Journal of World Business,* 44(2): 131–143; Tempel & Walgenbach, Global standardization of organizational forms and management practices; Li, Is regional strategy more effective than global strategy in the U.S. service industries?

57. H.C. Moon & M.-Y. Kim, 2009, A new framework for global expansion: A

dynamic diversification-coordination (DDC) model, *Management Decision,* 46(1): 131–151.

58. Connelly, Hitt, DeNisi, & Ireland, Expatriates and corporate-level international strategy; J. F. L. Hong, M. Easterby-Smith, & R. S. Snell, 2006, Transferring organizational learning systems to Japanese subsidiaries in China, *Journal of Management Studies,* 43: 1027–1058.

59. Kho, Stulz, & Warnock, Financial globalization, governance, and the evolution of the home bias; R. G. Barker, 2003, Trend: Global accounting is coming, *Harvard Business Review,* 81 (4): 24–25.

60. A. Yaprak, 2002, Globalization: Strategies to build a great global firm in the new economy, *Thunderbird International Business Review,* 44(2): 297–302; D. G. McKendrick, 2001, Global strategy and population level learning: The case of hard disk drives, *Strategic Management Journal,* 22: 307–334.

61. P. Komiak, S. Y. X. Komiak, & M. Imhof, 2008, Conducting international business at eBay: The determinants of success of e-stores, *Electronic Markets,* 18(2): 187–204; V. Shannon, 2007, eBay is preparing to re-enter the China auction business, *New York Times,* http://www.nytimes .com, June 22; B Einhorn, 2007, A break in Yahoo's China clouds? *BusinessWeek,* http://www.businessweek.com, June 20.

62. M. Demirbag & E. Tatoglu, 2009, Competitive strategy choices of Turkish manufacturing firms in European Union, *The Journal of Management Development,* 27(7): 727–743; K. E. Meyer, 2006, Globalfocusing: From domestic conglomerates to global specialists, *Journal of Management Studies,* 43: 1109–1144; A. Delios & P. W. Beamish, 2005, Regional and global strategies of Japanese firms, *Management International Review,* 45: 19–36.

63. A. Delios, D. Xu & P. W. Beamish, 2008, Within-country product diversification and foreign subsidiary performance, *Journal of International Business Studies,* 39(4): 706–724; S. Massini, A. Y. Lewin, T. Numagami, & A. Pettigrew, 2002, The evolution of organizational routines among large Western and Japanese firms, *Research Policy,* 31(8,9): 1333–1348.

64. J. Millman, 2008, The fallen: Lorenzo Zambrano: Hard times for cement man, *Wall Street Journal,* December 11, A1; K. A. Garrett, 2005, Cemex, *Business Mexico,* April 23.

65. B. Elango & C. Pattnaik, 2007, Building capabilities for international operations through networks: A study of Indian firms, *Journal of International Business Studies,* 38: 541–555; T. B. Lawrence, E. A. Morse, & S. W. Fowler, 2005, Managing your portfolio of connections, *MIT Sloan Management Review,* 46(2): 59–65; C. A. Bartlett & S. Ghoshal, 1989, *Managing across Borders: The Transnational Solution,* Boston: Harvard Business School Press.

66. A. M. Rugman & A. Verbeke, 2008, A regional solution to the strategy and structure of multinationals, *European Management Journal,* 26(5): 305–313. A. Abbott & K. Banerji, 2003, Strategic flexibility and firm performance: The case of U.S. based transnational corporations, *Global Journal of Flexible Systems Management,* 4(1/2): 1–7; J. Child & Y. Van, 2001, National and transnational effects in international business: Indications from Sino-foreign joint ventures, *Management International Review,* 41(1): 53–75.

67. Rugman & Verbeke, A regional solution to the strategy and structure of multinationals.

68. A. M. Rugman & A. Verbeke, 2003, Extending the theory of the multinational enterprise: Internalization and strategic management perspectives, *Journal of International Business Studies,* 34: 125–137.

69. H. F. Cheng, M. Gutierrez, A. Mahajan, Y. Shachmurove, & M. Shahrokhi, 2007, A future global economy to be built by BRICs, *Global Finance Journal,* 18(2): 143–156; Wright, Filatotchev, Hoskisson, & Peng, Strategy research in emerging economies: Challenging the conventional wisdom.

70. Elango, Minimizing effects of "liability of foreignness": Response strategies of foreign firms in the United States.

71. N. Y. Brannen, 2004, When Mickey loses face: Recontextualization, semantic fit and semiotics of foreignness, *Academy of Management Review,* 29: 593–616.

72. A. M. Rugman & A. Verbeke, 2007, Liabilities of foreignness and the use of firm-level versus country-level data: A response to Dunning et al. (2007), *Journal of International Business Studies,* 38: 200–205; S. Zaheer & A. Zaheer, 2001, Market microstructure in a global B2B network, *Strategic Management Journal,* 22: 859–873.

73. Rugman & Verbeke, A new perspective on the regional and global strategies of multinational services firms; S. R. Miller & L. Eden, 2006, Local density and foreign subsidiary performance, *Academy of Management Journal,* 49: 341–355.

74. Rugman & Verbeke, A new perspective on the regional and global strategies of multinational services firms; C. H. Oh & A. M. Rugman, 2007, Regional multi-nationals and the Korean cosmetics industry, *Asia Pacific Journal of Management,* 24: 27–42; A. Rugman & A. Verbeke, 2004, A perspective on regional and global strategies of multinational enterprises, *Journal of International Business Studies,* 35: 3–18.

75. A. K. Bhattacharya & D. C. Michael, 2008, How local companies keep multinationals at bay, *Harvard Business Review,* 86(3): 84–95; C. Pantzalis, 2001, Does location matter? An empirical analysis of geographic scope and MNC market valuation, *Journal of International Business Studies,* 32: 133–155.

76. A. Rugman & S. Girod, 2003, Retail multinationals and globalization: The evidence is regional, *European Management Journal*, 21(1): 24–37.

77. D. E. Westney, 2006. Review of the regional multinationals: MNEs and global strategic management (book review), *Journal of International Business Studies*, 37: 445–449.

78. R. D. Ludema, 2002, Increasing returns, multinationals and geography of preferential trade agreements, *Journal of International Economics*, 56: 329–358.

79. Meyer, Globalfocusing: From domestic conglomerates to global specialists; Delios & Beamish, Regional and global strategies of Japanese firms.

80. M. Aspinwall, 2009, NAFTA-ization: Regionalization and domestic political adjustment in the North American economic area. *Journal of Common Market Studies*, 47(1): 1–24.

81. T. L. Pett & J. A. Wolff, 2003, Firm characteristic and managerial perceptions of NAFTA: An assessment of export implications for U.S. SMEs, *Journal of Small Business Management*, 41(2): 117–132.

82. Morck, Yeung, & Zhao, Perspectives on China's outward foreign direct investment; W. Chung & J. Song, 2004, Sequential investment, firm motives, and agglomeration of Japanese electronics firms in the United States, *Journal of Economics and Management Strategy*, 13: 539–560; D. Xu & O. Shenkar, 2002, Institutional distance and the multinational enterprise, *Academy of Management Review*, 27(4): 608–618.

83. A. Ojala, 2008, Entry in a psychically distant market: Finnish small and medium-sized software firms in Japan, *European Management Journal*, 26(2): 135–144.

84. K. D. Brouthers, L. E. Brouthers, & S. Werner, 2008, Real options, international entry mode choice and performance. *Journal of Management Studies*, 45(5): 936–960.

85. C. A. Cinquetti, 2009, Multinationals and exports in a large and protected developing country, *Review of International Economics*, 16(5): 904–918.

86. Luo, Determinants of local responsiveness.

87. S. Shankar, C. Ormiston, N. Bloch, & R. Schaus, 2008, How to win in emerging markets, *MIT Sloan Management Review*, 49(3): 19–23; M. A. Raymond, J. Kim, & A. T. Shao, 2001, Export strategy and performance: A comparison of exporters in a developed market and an emerging market, *Journal of Global Marketing*, 15(2): 5–29.

88. A. Haahti, V. Madupu, U. Yavas, & E. Babakus, 2005, Cooperative strategy, knowledge intensity and export performance of small and medium-sized enterprises, *Journal of World Business*, 40(2): 124–138.

89. G. R. G. Clarke, 2008, Has the internet increased exports for firms from low and middle-income countries, *Information Economics and Policy*, 20(1): 16–37; K. A. Houghton & H. Winklhofer, 2004, The effect of Web site and ecommerce adoption on the relationship between SMEs and their export intermediaries, *International Small Business Journal*, 22: 369–385.

90. M. Bandyk, 2008, Now even small firms can go global, *U.S. News & World Report*, March 10, 52.

91. J. Slater, 2008, Weak dollar hits Europe, helps emerging markets, *Wall Street Journal (Europe)*, December 29, 1.

92. U. Lichtenthaler, 2008, Externally commercializing technology assets: An examination of different process stages, *Journal of Business Venturing*, 23(4): 445–664; D. Kline, 2003, Sharing the corporate crown jewels, *MIT Sloan Management Review*, 44(3): 83–88.

93. R. Bird & D. R. Cahoy, 2008, The impact of compulsory licensing on foreign direct investment: A collective bargaining approach, *American Business Law Journal*, 45(2): 283–330; A. Arora & A. Fosfuri, 2000, Wholly owned subsidiary versus technology licensing in the worldwide chemical industry, *Journal of International Business Studies*, 31: 555–572.

94. N. Byrnes & F. Balfour, 2009, Philip Morris unbound, *BusinessWeek*, May 4, 38–42; N. Zamiska, J. Ye, & V. O'Connell, 2008, Chinese cigarettes to go global, *Wall Street Journal*, January 30, B4; N. Zamiska & V. O'Connell, 2005, Philip Morris is in talks to make Marlboros in China, *Wall Street Journal*, April 21, B1, B2.

95. Zamiska, Ye, & O'Connell, Chinese cigarettes to go global, B4.

96. S. Nagaoka, 2009, Does strong patent protection facilitate international technology transfer? Some evidence from licensing contracts of Japanese firms, *Journal of Technology Transfer*, 34(2): 128–144.

97. M. Johnson, 2001, Learning from toys: Lessons in managing supply chain risk from the toy industry, *California Management Review*, 43(3): 106–124.

98. U. Lichtenthaler & H. Ernst, 2007, Business insight (a special report); Think strategically about technology licensing, *Wall Street Journal*, R4

99. C. A. Bartlett & S. Rangan, 1992, Komatsu limited, in C. A. Bartlett & S. Ghoshal (eds.), *Transnational Management: Text, Cases and Readings in Cross-Border Management*, Homewood, IL: Irwin, 311–326.

100. T. Audi, 2008, Last resort: Ailing Sheraton shoots for a room upgrade; Starwood to tackle biggest hotel brand; the "ugly stepchild," *Wall Street Journal*, March 25, A1.

101. T. W. Tong, J. J. Reuer, & M. W. Peng, 2008. International joint ventures and the value of growth options, *Academy of Management Journal*, 51: 1014–1029; A. A. Ziedonis, 2007, Real options in technology licensing, *Management Science*, 53(10): 1618–1633.

102. H. K. Steensma, J. Q. Barden, C. Dhanaraj, M. Lyles, & L. Tihanyi, 2008, The evolution and internalization of international joint ventures in a transitioning economy, *Journal of International Business Studies*, 39(3): 491–507; M. Nippa, S. Beechler, & A. Klossek, 2007, Success factors for managing international joint ventures: A review and an integrative framework, *Management and Organization Review*, 3: 277–310.

103. N. Rahman, 2008, Resource and risk trade-offs in Guanxi-based IJVs in China, *Asia Pacific Business Review*, 14(2): 233–251; J. S. Harrison, M. A. Hitt, R. E. Hoskisson, & R. D. Ireland, 2001, Resource complementarity in business combinations: Extending the logic to organization alliances, *Journal of Management*, 27: 679–690.

104. W. Zhan, R. Chen, M. K. Erramilli, & D. T, Nguyen, 2009, Acquisition of organizational capabilities and competitive advantage of IJVs in transition economies: The case of Vietnam. *Asia Pacific Journal of Management*, 26(2): 285–308; M. A. Hitt, D. Ahlstrom, M. T. Dacin, E. Levitas, & L. Svobodina, 2004, The institutional effects on strategic alliance partner selection in transition economies: China versus Russia, *Organization Science*, 15: 173–185.

105. E. Woyke, 2009, ZTE's smart phone ambitions; The company is betting on advanced phones to crack the U.S. market, *Forbes*, http://www.forbes.com, March 16.

106. T. Chi & A. Seth, 2009, A dynamic model of the choice of mode for exploiting complementary capabilities, *Journal of International Business Studies*, 40(3): 365–387; M. A. Lyles & J. E. Salk, 2007, Knowledge acquisition from foreign parents in international joint ventures: An empirical examination in the Hungarian context, *Journal of International Business Studies*, 38: 3–18; E. W. K. Tsang, 2002, Acquiring knowledge by foreign partners for international joint ventures in a transition economy: Learning-by-doing and learning myopia, *Strategic Management Journal*, 23(9): 835–854.

107. M. J. Robson, C. S. Katsikeas, & D. C. Bello, 2008, Drivers and performance outcomes of trust in international strategic alliances: The role of organizational complexity, *Organization Science*, 19(4): 647–668; S. Zaheer & A. Zaheer, 2007, Trust across borders, *Journal of International Business Studies*, 38: 21–29.

108. M. H. Ogasavara & Y. Hoshino, 2009, The effects of entry strategy and inter-firm trust on the survival of Japanese manufacturing subsidiaries in Brazil, *Asian Business & Management*, 7(3): 353–380; M. W. Peng & O. Shenkar, 2002, Joint venture dissolution as corporate divorce, *Academy of Management Executive*, 16(2): 92–105.

109. Y. Luo, O. Shenkar, & H. Gurnani, 2008, Control-cooperation interfaces in global strategic alliances: A situational typology and strategic responses, *Journal of International Business Studies*, 9(3): 428–453; A. Madhok, 2006, Revisiting

multinational firms' tolerance for joint ventures: A trust-based approach, *Journal of International Business Studies*, 37: 30–43; J. Child & Y. Van, 2003, Predicting the performance of international joint ventures: An investigation in China, *Journal of Management Studies*, 40(2): 283–320; J. P. Johnson, M. A. Korsgaard, & H. J. Sapienza, 2002, Perceived fairness, decision control, and commitment in international joint venture management teams, *Strategic Management Journal*, 23(12): 1141–1160.

110. X. Lin & C. L. Wang, 2008, Enforcement and performance: The role of ownership, legalism and trust in international joint ventures, *Journal of World Business*, 43(3): 340–351; L. Huff & L. Kelley, 2003, Levels of organizational trust in individualist versus collectivist societies: A seven-nation study, *Organization Science*, 14(1): 81–90.

111. D. Li, L. Eden, M. A. Hitt, & R. D. Ireland, 2008, Friends, acquaintances and strangers? Partner selection in R&D alliances, *Academy of Management Journal*, 51: 315–334; Y. Pan & D. K. Tse, 2000, The hierarchical model of market entry modes, *Journal of International Business Studies*, 31: 535–554.

112. J. Wiklund & D. A. Shepherd, 2009, The effectiveness of alliances and acquisitions: The role of resource combination activities, *Entrepreneurship Theory and Practice*, 33(1): 193–212; P. Porrini, 2004, Can a previous alliance between an acquirer and a target affect acquisition performance? *Journal of Management*, 30: 545–562.

113. C. M. Sanchez & S. R. Goldberg, 2009, Strategic M&As: Stronger in tough times, *Journal of Corporate Accounting & Finance*, 20(2): 3–7; K. Shimizu, M. A. Hitt, D. Vaidyanath, & V. Pisano, 2004, Theoretical foundations of cross-border mergers and acquisitions: A review of current research and recommendations for the future, *Journal of International Management*, 10: 307–353; M. A. Hitt, J. S. Harrison, & R. D. Ireland, 2001, *Mergers and Acquisitions: A Guide to Creating Value for Stakeholders*, New York: Oxford University Press.

114. A. Boateng, W. Qian, & Y. Tianle, 2008, Cross-border M&As by Chinese firms: An analysis of strategic motives and performance, *Thunderbird International Business Review*, 50(4): 259–270; M. A. Hitt & V. Pisano, 2003, The cross-border merger and acquisition strategy, *Management Research*, 1: 133–144.

115. International operational fact sheet, 2007, http://www.walmartfacts.com, July; J. Levine, 2004, Europe: Gold mines and quicksand, *Forbes*, April 12, 76.

116. B. Powell, 2009, Buying binge, *Time*, April 20, GB1.

117. P. X. Meschi, 2009, Government corruption and foreign stakes in international joint ventures in emerging economies, *Asia Pacific Journal of Management*, 26(2): 241–261; U. Weitzel & S. Berns, 2006, Cross-border takeovers, corruption, and related aspects of governance, *Journal of International Business Studies*, 37: 786–806.

118. Chakrabarti, Gupta-Mukherjee, & Jayaraman, Mars-Venus marriages: Culture and cross-border M&A; A. H. L. Slangen, 2006, National cultural distance and initial foreign acquisition performance: The moderating effect of integration, *Journal of World Business*, 41: 161–170.

119. S. F. S. Chen, 2008, The motives for international acquisitions: Capability procurements, strategic considerations, and the role of ownership structures, *Journal of International Business Studies*, 39(3): 454–471; I. Bjorkman, G. K. Stahl, & E. Vaara, 2007, Cultural differences and capability transfer in cross-border acquisitions: The mediating roles of capability complementarity, absorptive capacity, and social integration, *Journal of International Business Studies*, 38: 658–672.

120. J. Reed, 2008, SAIC plans U.K. comeback for MG TF roadster, *Financial Times*, April 21, 25; C. Buckley, 2005, SAIC to fund MG Rover bid, *The Times of London*, http://www.timesonline.co.uk, July 18.

121. H. Raff, M. Ryan, F. Stähler, 2009, The choice of market entry mode: Greenfield investment, M&A and joint venture, *International Review of Economics & Finance*, 18(1): 3–10; A.-W. Harzing, 2002, Acquisitions versus greenfield investments: International strategy and management of entry modes, *Strategic Management Journal*, 23: 211–227.

122. C. Bouquet, L. Hebert, & A. Delios, 2004, Foreign expansion in service industries: Separability and human capital intensity, *Journal of Business Research*, 57: 35–46.

123. K. F. Meyer, S. Estrin, S. K. Bhaumik, & M. W. Peng, 2009, Institutions, resources, and entry strategies in emerging economies, *Strategic Management Journal*, 30(1): 61–80.

124. K. F. Meyer, M. Wright, & S. Pruthi, 2009, Managing knowledge in foreign entry strategies: a resource-based analysis, *Strategic Management Journal*, 30(5): 557–574.

125. Y. Park & B. Sternquist, 2008, The global retailer's strategic proposition and choice of entry mode, *International Journal of Retail & Distribution Management*, 36(4): 281–299; S. Mani, K. D. Antia, & A. Rindfleisch, 2007, Entry mode and equity level: A multilevel examination of foreign direct investment ownership structure, *Strategic Management Journal*, 28: 857–866.

126. A. Roth, 2008, Beijing Olympics 2008: UPS markets its delivery for China only; Company transports gear for the Games; face-off with FedEx, *Wall Street Journal* (Europe), August 11, 29.

127. D. L. Paul & R. B. Wooster, 2008, Strategic investments by U.S. firms in transition economies, *Journal of International Business Studies*, 39(2): 249–266; V. Gaba, Y. Pan, & G. R. Ungson, 2002, Timing of entry in international market: An empirical study of U.S. Fortune 500 firms in China, *Journal of International Business Studies*, 33(1): 39–55; S.-J. Chang & P. Rosenzweig, 2001, The choice of entry mode in sequential foreign direct investment, *Strategic Management Journal*, 22: 747–776.

128. Meschi, Government corruption and foreign stakes in international joint ventures in emerging economies; R. Farzad, 2007, Extreme investing: Inside Colombia, *BusinessWeek*, May 28, 50–58; K. E. Myer, 2001, Institutions, transaction costs, and entry mode choice in Eastern Europe, *Journal of International Business Studies*, 32: 357–367.

129. J. Che & G. Facchini, 2009, Cultural differences, insecure property rights and the mode of entry decision, *Economic Theory*, 38(3): 465–484; S. Li, 2004, Why are property rights protections lacking in China? An institutional explanation, *California Management Review*, 46(3): 100–115.

130. A. C. Inkpen, 2008, Knowledge transfer and international joint ventures: The case of NUMMI and General Motors, *Strategic Management Journal*, 29(4): 447–453.

131. D. Hannon, 2008, Shorter is better for Toyota's supply chain, *Purchasing*, August, 46–47; M. Zimmerman, 2007, Toyota ends GM's reign as car sales leader, *Los Angeles Times*, April 25, 2007, C1; L. J. Howell & J. C. Hsu, 2002, Globalization within the auto industry, *Research Technology Management*, 45(4): 43–49.

132. J. W. Lu & X. Ma, 2008, The contingent value of local partners' business group affiliations, *Academy of Management Journal*, 51(2): 295–314; A. Chacar & B. Vissa, 2005, Are emerging economies less efficient? Performance persistence and the impact of business group affiliation, *Strategic Management Journal*, 26: 933–946; Hoskisson, Kim, Tihanyi, & White, A framework for understanding international diversification by business groups from emerging economies.

133. R. Chittoor, M. B. Sarkar, S. Ray, & P. S. Aulakh, 2009, Third-world copycats to emerging multinationals: Institutional changes and organizational transformation in the Indian pharmaceutical industry, *Organization Science*, 20(1): 187–205.

134. M. F. Wiersma & H. P. Bowen, 2008, Corporate international diversification: The impact of foreign competition, industry globalization and product diversification, *Strategic Management Journal*, 29: 115–132.

135. Dastidar, International corporate diversification and performance; L. Li, 2007, Multinationality and performance: A synthetic review and research agenda, *International Journal of Management Reviews*, 9: 117–139; J. A. Doukas & O. B. Kan, 2006, Does global diversification destroy firm value, *Journal of International Business Studies*, 37: 352–371; J. W. Lu & P. W. Beamish, 2004, International diversification and firm performance:

The S-curve hypothesis, *Academy of Management Journal*, 47: 598–609.

136. S. E. Christophe & H. Lee, 2005, What matters about internationalization: A market-based assessment, *Journal of Business Research*. 58: 536–643; J. A. Doukas & L. H. P. Lang, 2003, Foreign direct investment, diversification and firm performance, *Journal of International Business Studies*, 34: 153–172.

137. H. Zou & M. B. Adams, 2009, Corporate ownership, equity risk and returns in the People's Republic of China, *Journal of International Business Studies*, 39(7): 1149–1168; Hitt, Tihanyi, Miller, & Connelly, International diversification; Kwok & Reeb, Internationalization and firm risk.

138. A. Birnik & R. Moat, 2009, Mapping multinational operations, *Business Strategy Review*, 20(1): 30–33; T. R. Holcomb & M. A. Hitt, 2007, Toward a model of strategic outsourcing, *Journal of Operations Management*, 25: 464–481; J. P. Doh, 2005, Offshore outsourcing: Implications for international business and strategic management theory and practice, *Journal of Management Studies*, 42: 695–704.

139. Song & Shin, The paradox of technological capabilities: A study of knowledge sourcing from host countries of overseas R&D operations; J. Penner-Hahn & J. M. Shaver, 2005, Does international research and development increase patent output? An analysis of Japanese pharmaceutical firms, *Strategic Management Journal*, 26: 121–140.

140. Shimizutani & Todo, What determines overseas R&D activities? The case of Japanese multinational firms; Hitt, Bierman, Uhlenbruck, & Shimizu, The importance of resources in the internationalization of professional service firms; L. Tihanyi, R. A. Johnson, R. E. Hoskisson, & M. A. Hitt, 2003, Institutional ownership differences and international diversification: The effects of board of directors and technological opportunity, *Academy of Management Journal*, 46:195–211.

141. Zou & Ghauri, Learning through international acquisitions; B. Ambos & B. B. Schlegelmilch, 2007, Innovation and control in the multinational firm: A comparison of political and contingency approaches, *Strategic Management Journal*, 28: 473–486.

142. E. Matta & P. W. Beamish, 2008, The accentuated CEO career horizon problem: Evidence from international acquisitions, *Strategic Management Journal*, 29(7): 683; D. S. Elenkov, W. Judge, & P. Wright, 2005, Strategic leadership and executive innovation influence: An international multi-cluster comparative study, *Strategic Management Journal*, 26: 665–682; P. Herrmann, 2002, The influence of CEO characteristics on the international diversification of manufacturing firms: An empirical study in the United States, *International Journal of Management*, 19(2): 279–289.

143. H. L. Sirkin, J. W. Hemerling, & A. K. Bhattacharya, 2009, Globality: Challenger companies are radically redefining the competitive landscape, *Strategy & Leadership*, 36(6): 36–41; M. A. Hitt, R. E. Hoskisson, & H. Kim, 1997, International diversification: Effects on innovation and firm performance in product-diversified firms, *Academy of Management Journal*, 40: 767–798.

144. E. García-Canal & M. F. Guillén, 2009, Risk and the strategy of foreign location choice in regulated industries, *Strategic Management Journal*, 29(10): 1097–1115; J. Child, L. Chung, & H. Davies, 2003, The performance of cross-border units in China: A test of natural selection, strategic choice and contingency theories, *Journal of International Business Studies*, 34: 242–254.

145. C. Crossland & D. C. Hambrick, 2007, How national systems differ in their constraints on corporate executives: A study of CEO effects in three countries, *Strategic Management Journal*, 28: 767–789; M. Javidan, P. W. Dorfman, M. S. de Luque, & R. J. House, 2006, In the eye of the beholder: Cross-cultural lessons in leadership from Project GLOBE, *Academy of Management Perspectives*, 20 (1): 67–90.

146. N. Shirouzu, 2008, Corporate news: GM's car sales slide in China; Toyota, Honda zoom ahead as buyers concentrate on fuel economy, quality, *Wall Street Journal*, September 26, B1.

147. I. Alon & T. T. Herbert, 2009, A stranger in a strange land: Micro political risk and the multinational firm, *Business Horizons*, 52(2): 127–137; P. Rodriguez, K. Uhlenbruck, & L. Eden, 2005, Government corruption and the entry strategies of multinationals, *Academy of Management Review*, 30: 383–396; J. H. Zhao, S. H. Kim, & J. Du, 2003, The impact of corruption and transparency on foreign direct investment: An empirical analysis, *Management International Review*, 43(1): 41–62.

148. F. Wu, 2009, Singapore's sovereign wealth funds: The political risk of overseas investments. *World Economics*, 9(3): 97–122; P. S. Ring, G. A. Bigley, T. D'aunno, & T. Khanna, 2005, Perspectives on how governments matter, *Academy of Management Review*, 30: 308–320; A. Delios & W. J. Henisz, 2003, Policy uncertainty and the sequence of entry by Japanese firms, 1980–1998, *Journal of International Business Studies*, 34: 227–241.

149. A. Kouznetsov, 2009, Entry modes employed by multinational manufacturing enterprises and review of factors that affect entry mode choices in Russia, *The Business Review*, Cambridge, 10(2): 316–323.

150. S. Globerman & D. Shapiro, 2009, Economic and strategic considerations surrounding Chinese FDI in the United States, *Asia Pacific Journal of Management*, 26(1): 163–183.

151. I. G. Kawaller, 2009, Hedging currency exposures by multinationals: Things to consider, *Journal of Applied Finance*, 18(1): 92–98; Addae-Dapaah & Hwee, The unsung impact of currency risk on the performance of international real property investment; T. Vestring, T. Rouse, & U. Reinert, 2005, Hedging your offshoring bets, *MIT Sloan Management Review*, 46(3): 26–29.

152. T. G. Andrews & N. Chompusri, 2005, Temporal dynamics of crossvergence: Institutionalizing MNC integration strategies in post-crisis ASEAN, *Asia Pacific Journal of Management*, 22(1): 5–22; S. Mudd, R. Grosse, & J. Mathis, 2002, Dealing with financial crises in emerging markets, *Thunderbird International Business Review*, 44(3): 399–430.

153. N. Bandelj, 2009, The global economy as instituted process: The case of Central and Eastern Europe, *American Sociological Review*, 74(1): 128–149; L. Tihanyi & W. H. Hegarty, 2007, Political interests and the emergence of commercial banking in transition economies, *Journal of Management Studies*, 44: 789–813.

154. Lu & Beamish, International diversification and firm performance: The s-curve hypothesis; Wan & Hoskisson, Home country environments, corporate diversification strategies and firm performance; Hitt, Hoskisson, & Kim, International diversification.

155. A. Ojala, 2008, Entry in a psychically distant market: Finnish small and medium-sized software firms in Japan, *European Management Journal*, 26(2): 135–144; D. W. Yiu, C. M. Lau, & G. D. Bruton, 2007, International venturing by emerging economy firms: The effects of firm capabilities, home country networks, and corporate entrepreneurship, *Journal of International Business Studies*, 38: 519–540; P. S. Barr & M. A. Glynn, 2004, Cultural variations in strategic issue interpretation: Relating cultural uncertainty avoidance to controllability in discriminating threat and opportunity, *Strategic Management Journal*, 25: 59–67.

156. M. L. L. Lam, 2009, Beyond credibility of doing business in China: Strategies for improving corporate citizenship of foreign multinational enterprises in China, *Journal of Business Ethics*: Supplement, 87: 137–146; W. P. J. Henisz & B. A. Zeiner, 2005, Legitimacy, interest group pressures and change in emergent institutions, the case of foreign investors and host country governments, *Academy of Management Review*, 30: 361–382; T. P. Blumentritt & D. Nigh, 2002, The integration of subsidiary political activities in multinational corporations, *Journal of International Business Studies*, 33: 57–77.

157. D. Lavie & S. Miller, 2009, Alliance portfolio internationalization and firm performance, *Organization Science*, 19(4): 623–646.

CHAPTER 9

Cooperative Strategy

Studying this chapter should provide you with the strategic management knowledge needed to:

1. Define cooperative strategies and explain why firms use them.

2. Define and discuss three types of strategic alliances.

3. Name the business-level cooperative strategies and describe their use.

4. Discuss the use of corporate-level cooperative strategies in diversified firms.

5. Understand the importance of cross-border strategic alliances as an international cooperative strategy.

6. Explain cooperative strategies' risks.

7. Describe two approaches used to manage cooperative strategies.

USING COOPERATIVE STRATEGIES AT IBM

A company widely known throughout the world, IBM, has over 350,000 employees working in design, manufacturing, sales, and service advanced information technologies such as computer systems, storage systems, software, and microelectronics. The firm's extensive lineup of products and services is grouped into three core business units—Systems and Financing, Software, and Services.

As is true for all companies, IBM uses three means to grow—internal developments (primarily through innovation), mergers and acquisitions (such as the recent purchase of France-based ILOG, which produces software tools to automate and speed up a firm's decision-making process), and cooperative strategies. Interestingly, IBM had a ten-year partnership with ILOG before making the acquisition. By cooperating with other companies, IBM is able to leverage its core competencies to grow and improve its performance.

Through cooperative strategies (e.g., strategic alliances and joint ventures, both of which are defined and discussed in this chapter), IBM finds itself working with a variety of firms in order to deliver products and services. However, IBM has specific performance-related objectives it wants to accomplish as it engages in an array of cooperative arrangements. For example, with regard to its systems business, IBM works to develop leading-edge chip technology. In order to do this it has formed five separate alliances to develop the most advanced semiconductor research and expand its facilities by purchasing the latest chip-making equipment. These allies provide brainpower, including more than 250 scientists and engineers that work along with IBM's engineers and scientists to foster innovation. Some of these innovations come through new advances in materials and chemistry. For instance, IBM signed an agreement with Japan's JSR, a Japanese firm engaged in materials science, to develop materials and processes for circuitry necessary to advance futuristic semiconductors.

Alessandro Della Bella/Keystone/Landor

IBM works in collaboration with several companies in Europe such as CEA, a French public research and technology organization focused on semiconductor and nano-electronics technology.

Even during the economic downturn, IBM's business analytics business is growing. The ILOG acquisition, noted previously, is an example of IBM's thrust into this area. IBM has created a new unit called IBM Business Analytics and Optimization Services. This business provides software solutions to help a firm better analyze data and make smarter decisions. It has 4,000 consultants who examine IBM's research and software divisions for algorithms, applications, and other innovations to help provide solutions to companies. This is just one aspect of the services business that IBM pursues with its consulting services. Of course it needs software to produce the solutions. Many of these solutions come through partnerships with small providers that IBM manages through cooperative agreements and often these cooperative agreements lead to an acquisition (see for instance the ILOG acquisition noted earlier).

However, other firms are entering into this space through their own acquisitions or alliances. For instance, Sun Microsystems had an alliance with IBM to produce software in competition with Hewlett-Packard. IBM bid for Sun in an acquisition attempt but was bested by Oracle, which won with a $7.3 billion bid. Thus the competition for the solutions service and network business has heated up through acquisitions and especially through partnerships, which IBM has used to facilitate its change from solely producing hardware to adding solution services and software. One study concluded that IBM was able to make this significant shift by managing its alliance of networks according to three principles. First, that company alliance networks may be used not just for individual projects but to facilitate strategic change inside a company; second, that two principal mechanisms can bring about this change: (1) increasing speed of change through partners and (2) finding partners in areas outside existing competencies; and finally, that companies can shape their alliance networks by conscious actions. Other firms are observing IBM's actions and learning and seeking to catch up fast through their own partnerships, as illustrated by a recent partnership between Cisco and the Japanese firm Fujitsu. These two firms are traditionally hardware firms that build networks, such as for phone companies, but are moving to increase their service options, especially among mobile telephone providers.

As one might anticipate, a firm as large and diverse as IBM is involved with a number of cooperative relationships. Given the challenges associated with achieving and maintaining superior performance, and in light of its general success with cooperative relationships, IBM will likely continue to use cooperative strategies as a path toward growth and enhanced performance.

Sources: R. Agarwal & C. E. Helfat, 2009, Strategic renewal of organizations, *Organization Science*, 20(2): 281–293; W. M. Bulkeley, 2009, Corporate news: IBM buoyed by its balance of business, *Wall Street Journal*, April 20, B3; W. M. Bulkeley, 2009, IBM results are clouded by Oracle's deal for Sun, *Wall Street Journal*, April 21, B1; S. Hamm, 2009, Big blue goes into analysis, *BusinessWeek*, April 27, 16; J. Menn, 2009, IBM focuses on software and services to meet targets, *Financial Times*, April 21, 19; J. M. O'Brien, 2009, IBM's grand plan to save the planet, *Fortune*, May 4, 84–91; 2009, IBM completes acquisition of ILOG, *2009 Journal OR-MS Today*, 36(1): 60; W. M. Bulkeley, 2008, Business technology, A service rival looms for IBM; H-P deal for EDS to pose challenge for big blue unit, *Wall Street Journal*, May 20, B6; K. Dittrich, G. Duysters, & A.-P. de Man, 2007, Strategic repositioning by means of alliance networks: The case of IBM, *Research Policy*, 36: 1496–1511; S. Hamm, 2007, Radical collaboration: Lessons from IBM's innovation factory, *BusinessWeek*, September 10, 16.

As noted in the Opening Case, firms use three means to grow and improve their performance—internal development, mergers and acquisitions, and cooperation. In each of these cases, the firm seeks to use its resources in ways that will create the greatest amount of value for stakeholders.[1]

Recognized as a viable engine of firm growth,[2] a **cooperative strategy** is a means by which firms work together to achieve a shared objective.[3] Thus, cooperating with other firms is another strategy firms use to create value for a customer at a lower cost than it would to do it by the firm itself and thereby establish a favorable position relative to competition.[4]

As explained in the Opening Case, IBM is involved with a number of cooperative arrangements. The intention of serving customers better than its competitors serve them and of gaining an advantageous position relative to competitors drive this firm's use of cooperative strategies. IBM's corporate-level cooperative strategy in services and software finds it seeking to deliver server technologies in ways that maximize customer value while improving the firm's position relative to competitors. For example, Hewlett-Packard recently bought EDS to battle IBM for the leadership position in the global services market.[5] IBM has many business-level alliances with partner firms focusing on what they believe are better ways to improve services for customer firms, such as the cooperative agreements that IBM has through its new division in business analytics.[6] The objectives IBM and its various partners seek by working together highlight the reality that in the twenty-first century landscape, firms must develop the skills required to successfully use cooperative strategies as a complement to their abilities to grow and improve performance through internally developed strategies and mergers and acquisitions.[7]

A **cooperative strategy** is a strategy in which firms work together to achieve a shared objective.

We examine several topics in this chapter. First, we define and offer examples of different strategic alliances as primary types of cooperative strategies. Next, we discuss the extensive use of cooperative strategies in the global economy and reasons for them. In succession, we describe business-level (including collusive strategies), corporate-level, international, and network cooperative strategies. The chapter closes with discussion of the risks of using cooperative strategies as well as how effective management of them can reduce those risks.

As you will see, we focus on strategic alliances in this chapter because firms use them more frequently than other types of cooperative relationships. Although not frequently used, collusive strategies are another type of cooperative strategy discussed in this chapter. In a *collusive strategy,* two or more firms cooperate to increase prices above the fully competitive level.[8]

Strategic Alliances as a Primary Type of Cooperative Strategy

A **strategic alliance** is a cooperative strategy in which firms combine some of their resources and capabilities to create a competitive advantage.[9] Thus, strategic alliances involve firms with some degree of exchange and sharing of resources and capabilities to co-develop, sell, and service goods or services.[10] Strategic alliances allow firms to leverage their existing resources and capabilities while working with partners to develop additional resources and capabilities as the foundation for new competitive advantages.[11] To be certain, the reality today is that "strategic alliances have become a cornerstone of many firms' competitive strategy."[12]

Consider the case of Kodak. CEO Antonio Perez stated, "Kodak today is involved with partnerships that would have been unthinkable a few short years ago."[13] His comment suggests the breadth and depth of cooperative relationships with which the firm is involved. Each of the cooperative relationships is intended to lead to a new competitive advantage as a source of growth and performance improvement. Kodak has changed from a firm rooted in film and imaging into a digital technology–oriented company.[14]

A competitive advantage developed through a cooperative strategy often is called a *collaborative* or *relational* advantage.[15] As previously discussed, particularly in Chapter 4, competitive advantages enhance the firm's marketplace success. Rapid technological changes and the global economy are examples of factors challenging firms to constantly upgrade current competitive advantages while they develop new ones to maintain strategic competitiveness.[16]

Many firms, especially large global competitors, establish multiple strategic alliances. Although we discussed only a few of them in the Opening Case, the reality is that IBM has formed hundreds of partnerships through cooperative strategies. IBM is not alone in its decision to frequently use cooperative strategies as a means of competition. Focusing on developing advanced technologies, Lockheed Martin has formed more than 250 alliances with firms in more than 30 countries as it concentrates on its primary business of defense modernization and serving the needs of the air transportation industry. For instance, Lockheed Martin recently entered into an alliance with Northrop Grumman Corp. and Alliant Techsystems Inc. These three firms are contracted to develop multirole missiles which have both air-to-air and air-to-ground capabilities. This missile would give aircraft much more flexibility in pursuing either air or ground targets and thus boost the target efficiency of each flight sortie.[17] For all cooperative arrangements, including those we are describing here, success is more likely when partners behave cooperatively. Actively solving problems, being trustworthy, and consistently pursuing ways to combine partners' resources and capabilities to create value are examples of cooperative behavior known to contribute to alliance success.[18]

STRATEGY RIGHT NOW

Read about the cooperative strategy formed between Kodak and the PGA and its benefits and costs.

www.cengage.com/management/hitt

A **strategic alliance** is a cooperative strategy in which firms combine some of their resources and capabilities to create a competitive advantage.

Three Types of Strategic Alliances

The three major types of strategic alliances include joint venture, equity strategic alliance, and nonequity strategic alliance. These alliance types are classified by their ownership arrangements; later, we classify alliances by strategic categorizations.

A **joint venture** is a strategic alliance in which two or more firms create a legally independent company to share some of their resources and capabilities to develop a competitive advantage. Joint ventures, which are often formed to improve firms' abilities to compete in uncertain competitive environments,[19] are effective in establishing long-term relationships and in transferring tacit knowledge. Because it can't be codified, tacit knowledge is learned through experiences such as those taking place when people from partner firms work together in a joint venture.[20] As discussed in Chapter 3, tacit knowledge is an important source of competitive advantage for many firms.[21]

Typically, partners in a joint venture own equal percentages and contribute equally to the venture's operations. Germany's Siemens AG and Japan's Fujitsu Ltd. equally own the joint venture Fujitsu Siemens Computers. Although the joint venture has been losing money, Fujitsu has decided that it wants to increase its market share from 4 to 10 percent, so it is taking over the joint venture. The new entity will be called Fujitsu Technology Solutions.[22] Overall, evidence suggests that a joint venture may be the optimal type of cooperative arrangement when firms need to combine their resources and capabilities to create a competitive advantage that is substantially different from any they possess individually and when the partners intend to enter highly uncertain markets.[23] These conditions influenced the two independent companies' decision to form Fujitsu Siemens Computers.

An **equity strategic alliance** is an alliance in which two or more firms own different percentages of the company they have formed by combining some of their resources and capabilities to create a competitive advantage. Many foreign direct investments, such as those made by Japanese and U.S. companies in China, are completed through equity strategic alliances.[24]

Interestingly, as many banks have suffered poor results in the United States, foreign banks have been creating equity alliances to provide U.S. banks with the necessary capital to survive and expand. For instance, 21 percent of Morgan Stanley's ownership was sold to Mitsubishi UFJ Financial Group in 2008. As a result, Nobuyuki Hirano, a senior executive for Mitsubishi, took a seat on the board of directors of Morgan Stanley. This will enhance Mitsubishi's understanding of Morgan Stanley's U.S. strategy. The relationship may move towards combining Mitsubishi's and Morgan Stanley Japan's Securities Corporation into a single entity in Japan.[25]

A **nonequity strategic alliance** is an alliance in which two or more firms develop a contractual relationship to share some of their unique resources and capabilities to create a competitive advantage.[26] In this type of alliance, firms do not establish a separate independent company and therefore do not take equity positions. For this reason, nonequity strategic alliances are less formal and demand fewer partner commitments than do joint ventures and equity strategic alliances, though research evidence indicates that they create value for the firms involved.[27] The relative informality and lower commitment levels characterizing nonequity strategic alliances make them unsuitable for complex projects where success requires effective transfers of tacit knowledge between partners.[28]

Forms of nonequity strategic alliances include licensing agreements, distribution agreements, and supply contracts. Hewlett-Packard (HP), which actively "partners to create new markets … and new business models," licenses some of its intellectual property through strategic alliances.[29] Typically, outsourcing commitments are specified in the form of a nonequity strategic alliance. (Discussed in Chapter 3, *outsourcing* is the purchase of a value-creating primary or support activity from another firm.) Dell Inc. and

A **joint venture** is a strategic alliance in which two or more firms create a legally independent company to share some of their resources and capabilities to develop a competitive advantage.

An **equity strategic alliance** is an alliance in which two or more firms own different percentages of the company they have formed by combining some of their resources and capabilities to create a competitive advantage.

A **nonequity strategic alliance** is an alliance in which two or more firms develop a contractual relationship to share some of their unique resources and capabilities to create a competitive advantage.

most other computer firms outsource most or all of their production of laptop comput- ers and often form nonequity strategic alliances to detail the nature of the relationship with firms to whom they outsource. Interestingly, many of these firms that outsource introduce modularity that prevents the contracting partner or outsourcee from gaining too much knowledge or from sharing certain aspects of the business the outsourcing firm does not want revealed.[30]

Reasons Firms Develop Strategic Alliances

As our discussion to this point implies, cooperative strategies are an integral part of the competitive landscape and are quite important to many companies and even to edu- cational institutions. In fact, many firms are cooperating with educational institutions to help commercialize ideas coming from basic research at universities.[31] In for-profit organizations, many executives believe that strategic alliances are central to their firm's success.[32] One executive's position that "you have to partner today or you will miss the next wave … and that … you cannot possibly acquire the technology fast enough, so partnering is essential"[33] highlights this belief.

Among other benefits, strategic alliances allow partners to create value that they couldn't develop by acting independently and to enter markets more quickly and with greater market penetration possibilities.[34] Moreover, most (if not all) firms lack the full set of resources and capabilities needed to reach their objectives, which indicates that partnering with others will increase the probability of reaching firm-specific perfor- mance objectives.[35] Dow Jones & Co., the publisher of *Wall Street Journal* and owned by News Corp., is forming a joint venture with SBI Holdings Inc. to create a Japanese edition of the *Wall Street Journal*'s Web site. It will primarily feature Japanese translations of news articles, videos, multimedia print, and other features of online editions of the *Wall Street Journal*. In particular this venture will develop mobile products and services in conjunction with the Web site. This is the second news Web site launched by Dow Jones in Asia; the first was launched in China in 2002.[36]

The effects of the greater use of cooperative strategies—particularly in the form of strate- gic alliances—are noticeable. In large firms, for example, alliances can account for 25 percent or more of sales revenue. Many executives believe that alliances are a prime vehicle for firm growth.[37] In some industries, alliance versus alliance is becoming more prominent than firm versus firm as a point of competition. In the global airline industry, for example, competition is increasingly between large alliances rather than between airlines.[38]

In summary, we can note that firms form strategic alliances to reduce competition, enhance their competitive capabilities, gain access to resources, take advantage of oppor- tunities, build strategic flexibility, and innovate. To achieve these objectives, they must select the right partners and develop trust.[39] Thus, firms attempt to develop a network portfolio of alliances in which they create social capital that affords them flexibility.[40] Because of the social capital, they can call on their partners for help when needed. Of course, social capital means reciprocity exists: Partners can ask them for help as well (and they are expected to provide it).[41]

The individually unique competitive conditions of slow-cycle, fast-cycle, and standard-cycle markets[42] find firms using cooperative strategies to achieve slightly differ- ent objectives (see Table 9.1). We discussed these three market types in Chapter 5 while examining competitive rivalry and competitive dynamics. *Slow-cycle markets* are markets where the firm's competitive advantages are shielded from imitation for relatively long periods of time and where imitation is costly. These markets are close to monopolis- tic conditions. Railroads and, historically, telecommunications, utilities, and financial services are examples of industries characterized as slow-cycle markets. In *fast-cycle markets,* the firm's competitive advantages are not shielded from imitation, preventing their long-term sustainability. Competitive advantages are moderately shielded from imitation in *standard-cycle markets,* typically allowing them to be sustained for a longer

Table 9.1 Reasons for Strategic Alliances by Market Type

Market	Reason
Slow-Cycle	• Gain access to a restricted market • Establish a franchise in a new market • Maintain market stability (e.g., establishing standards)
Fast-Cycle	• Speed up development of new goods or services • Speed up new market entry • Maintain market leadership • Form an industry technology standard • Share risky R&D expenses • Overcome uncertainty
Standard-Cycle	• Gain market power (reduce industry overcapacity) • Gain access to complementary resources • Establish better economies of scale • Overcome trade barriers • Meet competitive challenges from other competitors • Pool resources for very large capital projects • Learn new business techniques

period of time than in fast-cycle market situations, but for a shorter period of time than in slow-cycle markets.

Slow-Cycle Markets

Firms in slow-cycle markets often use strategic alliances to enter restricted markets or to establish franchises in new markets. For example, because of consolidating acquisitions that have occurred over the last dozen or so years, the American steel industry has only two remaining major players: U.S. Steel and Nucor. To improve their ability to compete successfully in the global steel market, these companies are forming cooperative relationships. They have formed strategic alliances in Europe and Asia and are invested in ventures in South America and Australia. Most recently Nucor has established a 50/50 joint venture with Duferco Group's subsidiary Duferdofin to produce steel joists and beams in Italy and then to distribute these products in Europe and North Africa. Duferco has been seeking alliances with major players in order to continue operating on a global basis.[43] Simultaneously however, companies around the world, especially in China, are forming or expanding alliances in order to establish supply sources that are important for steelmaking, in particular coal and iron ore. In 2008 Sinosteel Corp., a Chinese state-owned steelmaker, boosted its ownership in Midwest Corp. to 44 percent. Midwest Corp. is an Australian iron ore producer. The reason for this is that the raw materials account for 50 percent of the selling price where as a decade ago iron ore accounted for about 15 percent of the selling price.[44] Although 2009 commodity prices were depressed due to the economic downturn, it is expected that commodity prices will go higher as the economy improves and the partnering and joint venturing pace will increase.

The truth of the matter is that slow-cycle markets are becoming rare in the twenty-first century competitive landscape for several reasons, including the privatization of industries and economies, the rapid expansion of the Internet's capabilities for the quick dissemination of information, and the speed with which advancing technologies make quickly imitating even complex products possible.[45] Firms competing in slow-cycle markets, including steel manufacturers, should recognize the future likelihood that they'll encounter situations in which their competitive advantages become partially sustainable (in the instance of a standard-cycle market) or unsustainable (in the case of a fast-cycle market). Cooperative strategies can be helpful to firms transitioning from relatively sheltered markets to more competitive ones.[46]

Fast-Cycle Markets

Fast-cycle markets are unstable, unpredictable, and complex; in a word, "hypercompetitive" (a concept that was discussed in Chapter 5).[47] Combined, these conditions virtually preclude establishing long-lasting competitive advantages, forcing firms to constantly seek sources of new competitive advantages while creating value by using current ones. "You are looking at the future, when U.S. companies will be competing not only with European, Japanese, South Korean and Chinese companies but also with highly competitive companies from every corner of the world: Argentina, Brazil, Chile, Egypt, Hungary, India, Indonesia, Malaysia, Mexico, Poland,

Mike Margol/PhotoEdit

The rapidly evolving media landscape lead competitors ABC, FOX, and NBC Universal to be cooperative in the development and launch of Hulu.com where many of their top rated shows can be watched online.

Russia, Thailand, Turkey, Vietnam and places you'd never expect."[48] Alliances between firms with current excess resources and capabilities and those with promising capabilities help companies compete in fast-cycle markets to effectively transition from the present to the future and to gain rapid entry into new markets. As such a "collaboration mindset" is paramount.[49]

The entertainment business is fast becoming a new digital marketplace as television content is now available on the Web. This has led the entertainment business into a fast-cycle market where collaboration is important not only to succeed but to survive. Many of the firms that have digital video content have also sought to make a profit through digital music and have had difficulties in extracting profits from their earlier ventures. In 2007 GE's NBC Universal and News Corp.'s FOX formed a new website named http://www.Hulu.com. Walt Disney Corporation in 2009 became a third partner contributing content and capital in this joint venture along with an investment stake held by private equity firm Providence Equity Partners. Thus this Web site will be co-owned by direct competitors. ABC (owned by Disney) will shift much of its content to the Hulu site and viewers will be able to stream ABC TV shows such as *Lost* and *Grey's Anatomy*. CBS will be the only major network not participating in the Hulu venture with NBC Universal, FOX, and ABC. As digital video content moves onto the Web, it will be interesting to see how the competition and cooperation between all of these firms evolve.[50]

Standard-Cycle Markets

In standard-cycle markets, alliances are more likely to be made by partners with complementary resources and capabilities. Even though airline alliances were originally set up to increase revenue,[51] airlines have realized that they can also be used to reduce costs. SkyTeam (chaired by Delta and Air France) developed an internal Web site to speed up joint purchasing and to swap tips on pricing. Managers at Oneworld (American Airlines and British Airways) say the alliance's members have already saved more than $200 million through joint purchasing, and Star Alliance (United and Lufthansa) estimates that its member airlines save up to 25 percent on joint orders.

Given the geographic areas where markets are growing, these global alliances are adding partners from Asia. In recent years, China Southern Airlines joined the SkyTeam alliance, Air China and Shanghai Airlines were added to the Star Alliance, and Dragonair joined as an affiliate of Oneworld. One of the competitive difficulties with the airline alliances is that major partners often switch between airlines. For instance, Continental

Airlines, which was part of SkyTeam, recently switched to the Star Alliance with United Airlines, Air Canada, and Lufthansa. Although this move has been approved by the U.S. Department of Transportation, it still lacks approval from the European Union regulators.[52] The fact that Oneworld, SkyTeam, and Star Alliance account for more than 60 percent of the world's airline capacity suggests that firms participating in these alliances have gained scale economies.

Business-Level Cooperative Strategy

A firm uses a **business-level cooperative strategy** to grow and improve its performance in individual product markets. As discussed in Chapter 4, business-level strategy details what the firm intends to do to gain a competitive advantage in specific product markets. Thus, the firm forms a business-level cooperative strategy when it believes that combining its resources and capabilities with those of one or more partners will create competitive advantages that it can't create by itself and will lead to success in a specific product market. The four business-level cooperative strategies are listed in Figure 9.1.

Complementary Strategic Alliances

Complementary strategic alliances are business-level alliances in which firms share some of their resources and capabilities in complementary ways to develop competitive advantages.[53] Vertical and horizontal are the two types of complementary strategic alliances (see Figure 9.1).

Vertical Complementary Strategic Alliance

In a *vertical complementary strategic alliance,* firms share their resources and capabilities from different stages of the value chain to create a competitive advantage (see Figure 9.2).[54] Oftentimes, vertical complementary alliances are formed to adapt to environmental changes;[55] sometimes the changes represent an opportunity for partnering firms to innovate while adapting.[56]

The Strategic Focus on complementary alliances discusses what is happening with vertical alliances given the downturn in the world economy. In particular, it points out that economic pressures are creating stress in the vertical alliance relationships between buyers and suppliers in the grocery and apparel retail industry supply chains. However, in other industries it is leading to new partnerships where complementary strategic alliances are more likely to increase, such as in the steelmaking industry.

Another example of a vertical complementary alliance is Nintendo and its need for additional software and games for its Wii game console. To fulfill this need Nintendo has developed a partnership with Electronic Arts. Through this partnership, it will release two sports games prior to the release of its brand new hardware: *Tiger Woods PGA Tour 10*

A firm uses a **business-level cooperative strategy** to grow and improve its performance in individual product markets.

Complementary strategic alliances are business-level alliances in which firms share some of their resources and capabilities in complementary ways to develop competitive advantages.

Figure 9.1 Business-Level Cooperative Strategies

- Complementary strategic alliances
  - Vertical
  - Horizontal
- Competition response strategy
- Uncertainty-reducing strategy
- Competition-reducing strategy

Figure 9.2 Vertical and Horizontal Complementary Strategic Alliances

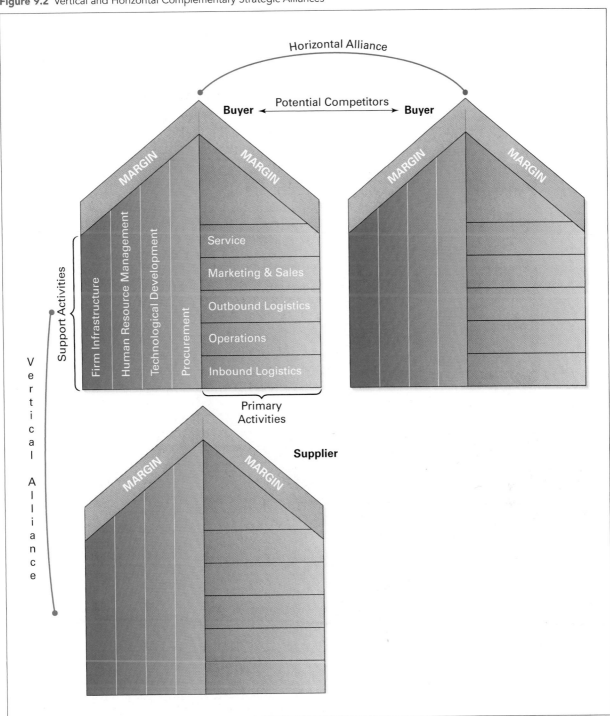

and *Grand Slam Tennis*. Nintendo is allowing these games to be sold even before it releases more of its own games. Previously, Nintendo trailed other game platforms in its production of new releases because it stressed its own games over those of other game software producers and would not release its hardware details to them in advance. It has changed its policy to encourage more vertical relationships with game software producing firms such as Electronic Arts and Activision Blizzard, Inc.[57]

STRATEGIC FOCUS

HOW COMPLEMENTARY ALLIANCES ARE AFFECTED BY THE GLOBAL ECONOMIC DOWNTURN

Supply chain management principles have changed over the last decade as suppliers have sought to work more closely with buyers. Traditionally a company's purchasing office dealt with a relatively small group of suppliers and had the overall goal of obtaining as many price cuts as possible. This changed, however, because as globalization and outsourcing increased the supply chain decision-making process involved a greater network of partners around the world. This drove companies to collaborate with suppliers and develop stronger relationships to reduce waste and develop products more quickly. As such, supply chain managers have had to shoulder a lot more responsibility, which has required much more emphasis on collaborative skills.

In the economic downturn, however, many of these collaborative relationships and partnerships—which are complementary by nature, especially in the vertical supply chain—have been strained. Large retailers have been squeezing their vendors in order to survive the requirement for heavy sales promotions and lower prices to sell their apparel products. This strategy has affected firms like Liz Claiborne, Phillips-Van Heusen, and Jones Apparel Group. Because large stores such as Macy's have many vendors to choose from, they have power to force price cuts from their suppliers. Macy's has power over Liz Claiborne because it buys in large volume. However, this has strained their relationship because both companies "require long-term, healthy partners to operate efficiently." Hartmarx Corp., a men's clothing producer whose main customers are Dillard's, Nordstrom, and Bloomingdale's (owned by Macy's), has been forced to file for Chapter 11 bankruptcy court protection due to the pressure. On the other hand, JCPenney has had long-term relationships with its vendors and its spokesperson noted, "We don't view 'squeezing' of vendors to protect our bottom line as a viable long-term strategy."

Similar events are happening in the grocery industry. For example, Unilever has been trying to stop its price margins from shrinking by forcing price increases on retailers such as the Belgian supermarket chain Delhaize Group SA. Delhaize operates the Food Lion chain and other grocery stores in the United States. In 2008, Unilever pushed worldwide price increases of more than 9 percent. Because of the price increases forced on Delhaize, it banished products by Unilever such as Dove soap and Axe deodorant from its U.S. stores. At the same time, commodity prices dropped and British retailer Tesco PLC urged suppliers to pass onto stores the recent drops in prices for commodities and oil that are used to produce food products. In response, firms like Wal-Mart (Great Value) have started to freshen up their in-house brands. As such, when large food producers such as Unilever do not respond appropriately, Wal-Mart can cut back on stocking national brands.

Shoppers at Food Lion found Axe and other Unilever products off the shelves as Delhaize, operator of the supermarket, responded to price increases passed on from the manufacturer.

AP Photo/Shoun Hill

While the downturn has put stress on some vertical alliances as previously noted, it has also created opportunities for new partnerships in other areas. For example, many private equity firms have experienced a significant decrease in the amount of funds invested in the

United States. Blackstone Group has formed global joint ventures to increase its fund supply. It has formed a joint venture with Bank Larrain Vial in Latin America and Och-Ziff Capital Management. In Latin America in particular there is a large opportunity in Chile, where private pension funds hold $82 billion in assets due to a pioneering program that places 12.3 percent of all payroll into private pension accounts. This complementary alliance would most likely not have occurred if the economy did not turn for the worse. Blackstone Group will also help diversify pension funds by investing in private equity and hedge funds. South and Central America have almost $200 billion in assets under management, which is comparable to the California Public Employees Retirement System (CalPERS). This is a significant opportunity for private equity funds such as the Blackstone Group to increase their supply of capital.

Sources: M. Arnold, 2009, Private equity boost for Latin America, *Financial Times*, May 12, 6; L. C. Gunipero, R. V. Handfield, & D. L. Johansen, 2008, Beyond buying: Supply chain managers used to have one main job: Purchasing stuff cheaply, *Wall Street Journal*, March 10, R8; P. Lattman, 2009, Schwarzman's Latin sojourn, *Wall Street Journal*, May 22, C2; S. Pignal, 2009, Delhaize shrugs off Unilever clash, *Financial Times*, March 13, 18; C. Rohwedder, A. O. Patrick, & T. W. Martin, 2009, Big grocers pulls Unilever items over pricing, *Wall Street Journal*, February 11, D1, B5l; K. Talley, 2009, Retailers, apparel firms tussle over tough deals, *Wall Street Journal*, February 11, B6.

Horizontal Complementary Strategic Alliance

A *horizontal complementary strategic alliance* is an alliance in which firms share some of their resources and capabilities from the same stage (or stages) of the value chain to create a competitive advantage (see Figure 9.2). Commonly, firms use complementary strategic alliances to focus on joint long-term product development and distribution opportunities.[58] As previously noted in the example regarding www.Hulu.com, GE's Universal Pictures, Disney's ABC, and News Corp's FOX Video Production have formed a joint Web site to distribute video content. Recently, pharmaceutical companies have been pursuing horizontal alliances as well. As healthcare reform takes place in the United States, large pharmaceutical firms are seeking relationships with generic drug producers. For example, Pfizer has reached marketing agreements with two Indian makers of generic drugs: Aurobindo Pharma Ltd. and Claris Lifesciences Ltd. These two firms produce and sell 60 and 15 off-patent drugs and injectables, respectively. Similarly, Novartis AG is acquiring Ebewe Pharma, an Austrian drugmaker, which will partner with the Novartis generic drug subsidiary, Sandoz. These moves are targeted to tap into the growing generic drug market, which was $3.5 billion in 2008 and is expected to be $9 billion by 2015.[59]

The automotive manufacturing industry is one in which many horizontal complementary strategic alliances are formed. In fact, virtually all global automobile manufacturers use cooperative strategies to form scores of cooperative relationships. The Renault-Nissan alliance, signed in March 1999, is a prominent example of a horizontal complementary strategic alliance. Thought to be successful, the challenge is to integrate the partners' operations to create value while maintaining their unique cultures.

Competition Response Strategy

As discussed in Chapter 5, competitors initiate competitive actions to attack rivals and launch competitive responses to their competitors' actions. Strategic alliances can be used at the business level to respond to competitors' attacks. Because they can be difficult to reverse and expensive to operate, strategic alliances are primarily formed to take strategic rather than tactical actions and to respond to competitors' actions in a like manner.

Many complementary horizontal alliances are created in response to heavy competition. For instance, digital music producers have been trying to extract more value from their products beyond what they can collect through middle-men such as Apple's iTunes distribution outlet. Many music producers have sought to develop their own distribution outlets through joint partnership, in response to Apple's success, such as Blue Matter Press, Jimmy and Doug's Farmclub, and eMusic, but most have failed. Now many of them are seeking online advertisements through Web sites that distribute music and video. For instance, Warner Music has invested in LaLa Media and a startup company called imeem, Inc. because MySpace Music, a joint venture among four major labels and News Corp., was not generating enough advertising revenue. In response to the focus on advertising, Universal Music, a division of Vivendi SA, through a joint venture with Google has created a new online site for music videos called VEVO. Most of these actions are attempts to bolster revenue because digital music downloads are increasing, but not quickly enough to offset the steep decline in CD sales.[60]

Uncertainty-Reducing Strategy

Some firms use business-level strategic alliances to hedge against risk and uncertainty, especially in fast-cycle markets.[61] These strategies are also used where uncertainty exists, such as in entering new product markets or emerging economies.

As large global auto firms manufacture more hybrid vehicles, there is insufficient capacity in the battery industry to meet future demand. Volkswagen AG is partnering with China's BYD Co. to produce hybrid and electric vehicles powered by lithium batteries. BYD is the one of the world's largest cell phone battery producers and is also a fledgling auto producer as it moves to launch a plug-in car before more established rival firms. Volkswagen has also made agreements with Samuel Electric and Toshiba Corp. of Japan to reduce the uncertainty about the insufficient capacity for lithium-ion batteries used in hybrid vehicles.[62]

Competition-Reducing Strategy

Used to reduce competition, collusive strategies differ from strategic alliances in that collusive strategies are often an illegal type of cooperative strategy. Two types of collusive strategies are explicit collusion and tacit collusion.

When two or more firms negotiate directly with the intention of jointly agreeing about the amount to produce and the price of the products that are produced, *explicit collusion* exists.[63] Explicit collusion strategies are illegal in the United States and most developed economies (except in regulated industries).

Firms that use explicit collusion strategies may find others challenging their competitive actions. In early 2009, for example, the U.S. Department of Justice joined forces with European officials to investigate alleged "price coordination" among three air cargo carriers. Luxembourg's Cargolux, Japan's Nippon Cargo Airlines, and Korea's Asiana Airlines plead guilty and paid criminal fines of $214 million for their role in a global conspiracy to fix prices on air freight. This investigation began in 2001 and prosecution began in 2006. Throughout the history of the investigation more than 15 air cargo airlines have been prosecuted and fined over $1.6 billion. The investigation continues in the air freight industry and is one of the world's biggest cartel probes by competition officials around the world.[64] As this example suggests, any firm that may use explicit collusion as a strategy should recognize that competitors and regulatory bodies might challenge the acceptability of their competitive actions.

Tacit collusion exists when several firms in an industry indirectly coordinate their production and pricing decisions by observing each other's competitive actions and responses.[65] Tacit collusion results in production output that is below fully competitive levels and above fully competitive prices. Unlike explicit collusion, firms engaging in tacit collusion do not directly negotiate output and pricing decisions. However, research suggests that joint ventures or cooperation between two firms can lead to less competition in other markets in which both firms operate.[66]

Tacit collusion tends to be used as a business-level, competition-reducing strategy in highly concentrated industries, such as airlines and breakfast cereals. Research in the airline industry suggests that tacit collusion reduces service quality and on-time performance.[67] Firms in these industries recognize that they are interdependent and that their competitive actions and responses significantly affect competitors' behavior toward them. Understanding this interdependence and carefully observing competitors can lead to tacit collusion.

Four firms (Kellogg's, General Mills, Post, and Quaker) have accounted for as much as 80 percent of sales volume in the ready-to-eat segment of the U.S. cereal market.[68] Some believe that this high degree of concentration results in "prices for branded cereals that are well above [the] costs of production."[69] The *Wall Street Journal* reported in 2008 that prices for breakfast cereals were among the easiest to inflate when there are commodity shortages.[70] Prices above the competitive level in this industry suggest the possibility that the dominant firms use a tacit collusion cooperative strategy.

Discussed in Chapter 6, *mutual forbearance* is a form of tacit collusion in which firms do not take competitive actions against rivals they meet in multiple markets. Rivals learn a great deal about each other when engaging in multimarket competition, including how to deter the effects of their rival's competitive attacks and responses. Given what they know about each other as a competitor, firms choose not to engage in what could be destructive competitions in multiple product markets.[71]

In general, governments in free-market economies need to determine how rivals can collaborate to increase their competitiveness without violating established regulations.[72] However, this task is challenging when evaluating collusive strategies, particularly tacit ones. For example, regulation of pharmaceutical and biotech firms who collaborate to meet global competition might lead to too much price fixing and, therefore, regulation is required to make sure that the balance is right, although sometimes the regulation gets in the way of efficient markets.[73] Individual companies must analyze the effect of a competition-reducing strategy on their performance and competitiveness.

Assessment of Business-Level Cooperative Strategies

Firms use business-level strategies to develop competitive advantages that can contribute to successful positions and performance in individual product markets. To develop a competitive advantage using an alliance, the resources and capabilities that are integrated through the alliance must be valuable, rare, imperfectly imitable, and nonsubstitutable (see Chapter 3).

Evidence suggests that complementary business-level strategic alliances, especially vertical ones, have the greatest probability of creating a sustainable competitive advantage.[74] Horizontal complementary alliances are sometimes difficult to maintain because they are often between rivalrous competitors. In this instance, firms may feel a "push" toward and a "pull" from alliances. Airline firms, for example, want to compete aggressively against others serving their markets and target customers. However, the need to develop scale economies and to share resources and capabilities (such as scheduling systems) dictates that alliances be formed so the firms can compete by using cooperative actions and responses while they simultaneously compete against one another through competitive actions and responses. As noted previously, this has led to many changes in the large airline alliances— for instance, with Continental recently aligning with United and Lufthansa rather than Delta and AirFrance-KLM.[75] The challenge in these instances is for each firm to find ways to create the greatest amount of value from both their competitive and cooperative actions. It seems that Nissan and Renault have learned how to achieve this balance.

Although strategic alliances designed to respond to competition and to reduce uncertainty can also create competitive advantages, these advantages often are more temporary than those developed through complementary (both vertical and horizontal) strategic alliances. The primary reason is that complementary alliances have a stronger focus on creating value than do competition-reducing and uncertainty-reducing alliances, which are formed to respond to competitors' actions or reduce uncertainty rather than to attack competitors.

Of the four business-level cooperative strategies, the competition-reducing strategy has the lowest probability of creating a sustainable competitive advantage. For example, research suggests that firms following a foreign direct investment strategy using alliances as a follow-the-leader imitation approach may not have strong strategic or learning goals. Thus, such investment could be attributable to tacit collusion among the participating firms rather than to forming a competitive advantage (which should be the core objective).

Corporate-Level Cooperative Strategy

A firm uses a **corporate-level cooperative strategy** to help it diversify in terms of products offered or markets served, or both. Diversifying alliances, synergistic alliances, and franchising are the most commonly used corporate-level cooperative strategies (see Figure 9.3).

Firms use diversifying alliances and synergistic alliances to grow and improve performance by diversifying their operations through a means other than a merger or an acquisition.[76] When a firm seeks to diversify into markets in which the host nation's government prevents mergers and acquisitions, alliances become an especially appropriate option. Corporate-level strategic alliances are also attractive compared with mergers and particularly acquisitions, because they require fewer resource commitments[77] and permit greater flexibility in terms of efforts to diversify partners' operations.[78] An alliance can be used as a way to determine whether the partners might benefit from a future merger or acquisition between them. This "testing" process often characterizes alliances formed to combine firms' unique technological resources and capabilities.[79]

Diversifying Strategic Alliance

A **diversifying strategic alliance** is a corporate-level cooperative strategy in which firms share some of their resources and capabilities to diversify into new product or market areas. The spread of high-speed wireless networks and devices with global positioning chips and the popularity of Web site applications running on Apple's iPhone and Research in Motion's BlackBerry (and other smartphones) shows that consumers are increasingly accessing mobile information. Equipped with this knowledge, Alcatel-Lucent is entering the market through mobile advertising, which will allow a cell phone carrier to alert customers about the location of a favorite store or the closest ATM. It is pursuing this diversification alliance with 1020 Placecast, a California-based developer of cell phone online ads associated with user locations. Hyatt, FedEx, and Avis are especially interested in using the service. The ads will also include a link to coupons or other promotions. Other mobile phone producers have started to sell mobile phone display ads in other metropolitan areas through Nokia Phones. These networks are trying to gain a share of the profits that would normally be out of their reach through revenue-sharing models with companies that are advertising as well as the ad-producing service companies.[80]

A firm uses a **corporate-level cooperative strategy** to help it diversify in terms of products offered or markets served, or both.

A **diversifying strategic alliance** is a corporate-level cooperative strategy in which firms share some of their resources and capabilities to diversify into new product or market areas.

Figure 9.3 Corporate-Level Cooperative Strategies

- Diversifying alliances
- Synergistic alliances
- Franchising

It should be noted that highly diverse networks of alliances can lead to poorer performance by partner firms.[81] However, cooperative ventures are also used to reduce diversification in firms that have overdiversified.[82] Japanese chipmakers Fujitsu, Mitsubishi Electric, Hitachi, NEC, and Toshiba have been using joint ventures to consolidate and then spin off diversified businesses that were performing poorly. For example, Fujitsu, realizing that memory chips were becoming a financial burden, dumped its flash memory business into a joint venture company controlled by Advanced Micro Devices. This alliance helped Fujitsu refocus on its core businesses.[83]

Synergistic Strategic Alliance

A **synergistic strategic alliance** is a corporate-level cooperative strategy in which firms share some of their resources and capabilities to create economies of scope. Similar to the business-level horizontal complementary strategic alliance, synergistic strategic alliances create synergy across multiple functions or multiple businesses between partner firms. The most recent development for Disney's media segment, and ABC in particular, is a partnership with Google's YouTube that will allow it to advertise its movies and products by showing short clips and selling ads.[84] This is an example of a synergistic diversification alliance.

In recent years, there has been much more competitive interaction between hardware and software firms. Cisco, traditionally a network telecommunications equipment manufacturer, is moving into computers—in particular, servers. After HP moved into selling network equipment, Cisco decided to move more fully into developing its server business. To drive its computer business Cisco needs to develop a service segment, although it is not trying to upset its historical partners, HP and IBM, which have large service businesses. Both IBM and HP have large service businesses. As such, Cisco developed partnership agreements with Accenture Ltd. and India-based Tata Consulting Services Ltd. to help market Cisco's products to businesses around the world. These were synergistic alliances to foster this diversification move by Cisco into services.[85]

AP Photo/M. Spencer Green

With apps like the Slacker personalized radio and hundreds of others available for the BlackBerry and iPhone, companies are already looking at these devices as a means of conveying personalized advertising as well.

Franchising

Franchising is a corporate-level cooperative strategy in which a firm (the franchisor) uses a franchise as a contractual relationship to describe and control the sharing of its resources and capabilities with partners (the franchisees).[86] A *franchise* is a "contractual agreement between two legally independent companies whereby the franchisor grants the right to the franchisee to sell the franchisor's product or do business under its trademarks in a given location for a specified period of time."[87] Success is often determined in these strategic alliances by how well the franchisor can replicate its success across multiple partners in a cost-effective way.[88] Research suggests that too much innovation results in difficulties for replicating this success.[89]

Franchising is a popular strategy. In the United States alone, more than 2,500 franchise systems are located in more than 75 industries; and those operating franchising outlets generate roughly one-third of all U.S. retail sales.[90] Already frequently used in developed nations, franchising is also expected to account for significant portions of growth in emerging economies in the twenty-first century.[91] As with diversifying and synergistic strategic alliances, franchising is an alternative to pursuing growth through mergers and acquisitions. McDonald's, Hilton International, Marriott International,

A **synergistic strategic alliance** is a corporate-level cooperative strategy in which firms share some of their resources and capabilities to create economies of scope.

Franchising is a corporate-level cooperative strategy in which a firm (the franchisor) uses a franchise as a contractual relationship to describe and control the sharing of its resources and capabilities with partners (the franchisees).

Mrs. Fields Cookies, Subway, and Ace Hardware are well-known examples of firms using the franchising corporate-level cooperative strategy.

Franchising is a particularly attractive strategy to use in fragmented industries, such as retailing, hotels and motels, and commercial printing. In fragmented industries, a large number of small and medium-sized firms compete as rivals; however, no firm or small set of firms has a dominant share, making it possible for a company to gain a large market share by consolidating independent companies through contractual relationships.

In the most successful franchising strategy, the partners (the franchisor and the franchisees) work closely together.[92] A primary responsibility of the franchisor is to develop programs to transfer to the franchisees the knowledge and skills that are needed to successfully compete at the local level.[93] In return, franchisees should provide feedback to the franchisor regarding how their units could become more effective and efficient.[94] Working cooperatively, the franchisor and its franchisees find ways to strengthen the core company's brand name, which is often the most important competitive advantage for franchisees operating in their local markets.[95]

Assessment of Corporate-Level Cooperative Strategies

Costs are incurred with each type of cooperative strategy.[96] Compared with those at the business level, corporate-level cooperative strategies commonly are broader in scope and more complex, making them relatively more costly. Those forming and using cooperative strategies, especially corporate-level ones, should be aware of alliance costs and carefully monitor them.

In spite of these costs, firms can create competitive advantages and value when they effectively form and use corporate-level cooperative strategies.[97] When successful alliance experiences are internalized, it is more likely that the strategy will attain the desired advantages. In other words, those involved with forming and using corporate-level cooperative strategies can also use them to develop useful knowledge about how to succeed in the future. To gain maximum value from this knowledge, firms should organize it and verify that it is always properly distributed to those involved with forming and using alliances.[98]

We explain in Chapter 6 that firms answer two questions to form a corporate-level strategy—in which businesses will the diversified firm compete and how will those businesses be managed? These questions are also answered as firms form corporate-level cooperative strategies. Thus, firms able to develop corporate-level cooperative strategies and manage them in ways that are valuable, rare, imperfectly imitable, and nonsubstitutable (see Chapter 3) develop a competitive advantage that is in addition to advantages gained through the activities of individual cooperative strategies. (Later in the chapter, we further describe alliance management as another potential competitive advantage.)

International Cooperative Strategy

A **cross-border strategic alliance** is an international cooperative strategy in which firms with headquarters in different nations decide to combine some of their resources and capabilities to create a competitive advantage. Taking place in virtually all industries, the number of cross-border alliances continues to increase.[99] These alliances too are sometimes formed instead of mergers and acquisitions (which can be riskier).[100] Even though cross-border alliances can themselves be complex and hard to manage,[101] they have the potential to help firms use their resources and capabilities to create value in locations outside their home market.

A **cross-border strategic alliance** is an international cooperative strategy in which firms with headquarters in different nations decide to combine some of their resources and capabilities to create a competitive advantage.

IMG Worldwide, Inc. is one of the largest producers and distributors of sports entertainment in the world. It pursues its strategy through international joint ventures with other broadcasting firms. The events that it currently broadcasts include two tennis "Grand Slam" events, Wimbledon and the Australian Open. In an effort to expand into emerging economies, IMG recently signed a 20-year sporting event partnership with China Central Television, the main Chinese broadcasting organization. A national broadcast of this size could have an audience of 740 million viewers daily. The first two events that will be broadcast through this venture are the China Open Tennis Tournament in Beijing and the Chengdu Open Tennis Tournament in 2009. The top 50 women players in the world are expected to play in the China Open tournament. Through this strategic alliance, IMG will substantially broaden its international reach.[102]

Several reasons explain the increasing use of cross-border strategic alliances, including the fact that in general, multinational corporations outperform domestic-only firms.[103] What takes place with a cross-border alliance is that a firm leverages core competencies that are the foundation of its domestic success in international markets.[104] Nike provides an example as it leverages its core competence with celebrity marketing to expand globally with its diverse line of athletic goods and apparel. With a $2 billion celebrity endorsement budget, Nike has formed relationships with athletes who have global appeal. Tiger Woods, Michael Phelps, and LeBron James are recent endorsers, while seven-time Tour de France winner Lance Armstrong, Michael Jordan, and Magic Johnson are historic examples of these types of individuals. In addition, Nike has endorsement relationships with star athletes and organizations outside the United States, such as Brazilian soccer star Ronaldo and Manchester United, the world's most popular soccer team.[105] Coupling these alliances with Nike's powerful global brand name helps the firm apply its marketing competencies in foreign markets. However, the downturn in the economy is causing problems such that even these relationships are not protecting sales declines.[106]

Limited domestic growth opportunities and foreign government economic policies are additional reasons firms use cross-border alliances. As discussed in Chapter 8, local ownership is an important national policy objective in some nations. In India and China, for example, governmental policies reflect a strong preference to license local companies. Thus, in some countries, the full range of entry mode choices that we described in Chapter 8 may not be available to firms seeking to diversify internationally. Indeed, investment by foreign firms in these instances may be allowed only through a partnership with a local firm, such as in a cross-border alliance. Especially important, strategic alliances with local partners can help firms overcome certain liabilities of moving into a foreign country, such as lack of knowledge of the local culture or institutional norms.[107] A cross-border strategic alliance can also be helpful to foreign partners from an operational perspective, because the local partner has significantly more information about factors contributing to competitive success such as local markets, sources of capital, legal procedures, and politics.[108] Interestingly, recent research suggests that firms with foreign operations have longer survival rates than domestic-only firms, although this is reduced if there are competition problems between foreign subsidiaries.[109]

In general, cross-border alliances are more complex and risky than domestic strategic alliances, especially in emerging economies.[110] However, the fact that firms competing internationally tend to outperform domestic-only competitors suggests the importance of learning how to diversify into international markets. Compared with mergers and acquisitions, cross-border alliances may be a better way to learn this process, especially in the early stages of the firms' geographic diversification efforts. Starbucks is a case in point.

When Starbucks sought overseas expansion, it wanted to do so quickly as a means of supporting its strong orientation to continuous growth. Thus, it agreed to a complex series of joint ventures in many countries in the interest of speed. While the company receives a percentage of the revenues and profits as well as licensing fees for supplying its coffee, controlling costs abroad is more difficult than in the United States. Starbucks is learning from the results achieved from the collaborative relationships it initially established. In light of what it has learned, the firm continues to collaborate with others in different countries including China. At Starbuck's 10-year anniversary mark in China, one analyst noted that "China, conventionally a coffee exporter, may become a net importer in 2009 with demand outpacing supply, as Starbucks Coffee Co. and other coffee chains mushroom around the country."[111] Among other actions, Starbucks is taking larger equity positions in some of the joint ventures with which it is now involved in different countries (such as China).

Network Cooperative Strategy

In addition to forming their own alliances with individual companies, a growing number of firms are joining forces in multiple networks.[112] A **network cooperative strategy** is a cooperative strategy wherein several firms agree to form multiple partnerships to achieve shared objectives. As noted, Cisco has multiple cooperative arrangements with IBM and HP, and with service providers Accenture Ltd. and Tata Consulting Services Ltd. Demonstrating the complexity of network cooperative strategies is the fact that Cisco has a set of unique collaborations with both IBM and HP, but is also competing with them as they move into servers. The fact is that the number of network cooperative strategies being formed today continues to increase as firms seek to find the best ways to create value by offering multiple goods and services in multiple geographic (domestic and international) locations.

A network cooperative strategy is particularly effective when it is formed by geographically clustered firms,[113] as in California's Silicon Valley (where "the culture of Silicon Valley encourages collaborative webs"[114]) and Singapore's Biopolis (in the bio-medical sciences) and the new fusionopolis (collaborations in "physical sciences and engineering to tackle global science and technology challenges").[115] Effective social relationships and interactions among partners while sharing their resources and capabilities make it more likely that a network cooperative strategy will be successful,[116] as does having a productive *strategic center firm* (we discuss strategic center firms in detail in Chapter 11). Firms involved in networks gain information and knowledge from multiple sources. They can use these heterogeneous knowledge sets to produce more and better innovation. As a result, firms involved in networks of alliances tend to be more innovative.[117] However, there are disadvantages to participating in networks as a firm can be locked into its partnerships, precluding the development of alliances with others. In certain types of networks, such as Japanese *keiretsus,* firms in the network are expected to help other firms in the network whenever they need aid. Such expectations can become a burden and reduce the focal firm's performance over time.[118]

Alliance Network Types

An important advantage of a network cooperative strategy is that firms gain access to their partners' other partners. Having access to multiple collaborations increases the likelihood that additional competitive advantages will be formed as the set of shared resources and capabilities expands.[119] In turn, being able to develop new capabilities further stimulates product innovations that are critical to strategic competitiveness in the global economy.[120]

A network cooperative strategy is a cooperative strategy wherein several firms agree to form multiple partnerships to achieve shared objectives.

The set of strategic alliance partnerships resulting from the use of a network cooperative strategy is commonly called an *alliance network*. The alliance networks that companies develop vary by industry conditions. A *stable alliance network* is formed in mature industries where demand is relatively constant and predictable. Through a stable alliance network, firms try to extend their competitive advantages to other settings while continuing to profit from operations in their core, relatively mature industry. Thus, stable networks are built primarily to *exploit* the economies (scale and/or scope) that exist between the partners such as in the airline industry.[121] *Dynamic alliance networks* are used in industries characterized by frequent product innovations and short product life cycles.[122] For instance, the pace of innovation in the information technology (IT) industry (as well as other industries that are characterized by fast-cycle markets) is too fast for any one company to be successful across time if it only competes independently. Another example is the movie industry, which has a lot of collaborative ventures and networked firms to produce and distribute movies.[123] In dynamic alliance networks, partners typically *explore* new ideas and possibilities with the potential to lead to product innovations, entries to new markets, and the development of new markets.[124] Often, large firms in such industries as software and pharmaceuticals create networks of relationships with smaller entrepreneurial startup firms in their search for innovation-based outcomes.[125] An important outcome for small firms successfully partnering with larger firms in an alliance network is the credibility they build by being associated with their larger collaborators.[126]

Competitive Risks with Cooperative Strategies

Stated simply, many cooperative strategies fail. In fact, evidence shows that two-thirds of cooperative strategies have serious problems in their first two years and that as many as 50 percent of them fail. This failure rate suggests that even when the partnership has potential complementarities and synergies, alliance success is elusive.[127] Although failure is undesirable, it can be a valuable learning experience, meaning that firms should carefully study a cooperative strategy's failure to gain insights with respect to how to form and manage future cooperative arrangements.[128] We show prominent cooperative strategy risks in Figure 9.4.

Figure 9.4 Managing Competitive Risks in Cooperative Strategies

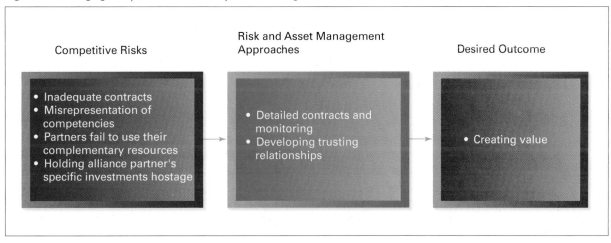

One cooperative strategy risk is that a partner may act opportunistically. Opportunistic behaviors surface either when formal contracts fail to prevent them or when an alliance is based on a false perception of partner trustworthiness. Not infrequently, the opportunistic firm wants to acquire as much of its partner's tacit knowledge as it can.[129] Full awareness of what a partner wants in a cooperative strategy reduces the likelihood that a firm will suffer from another's opportunistic actions.[130] The Strategic Focus on TNK-BP, a 50/50 joint venture between three Russian oil tycoons and British Petroleum, demonstrates potential opportunistic actions by parties involved and some of the potential risks of joint ventures, especially in an emerging economy like Russia.

Some cooperative strategies fail when it is discovered that a firm has misrepresented the competencies it can bring to the partnership. The risk of competence misrepresentation is more common when the partner's contribution is grounded in some of its intangible assets. Superior knowledge of local conditions is an example of an intangible asset that partners often fail to deliver. An effective way to deal with this risk may be to ask the partner to provide evidence that it does possess the resources and capabilities (even when they are largely intangible) it will share in the cooperative strategy.[131]

Another risk is a firm failing to make available to its partners the resources and capabilities (such as the most sophisticated technologies) that it committed to the cooperative strategy. For example, in the Strategic Focus, TNK-BP did not meet agreed-upon targets and this put them in a situation of weakness relative to both its powerful partners and the Russian government. This risk surfaces most commonly when firms form an international cooperative strategy, especially in emerging economies.[132] In these instances, different cultures and languages can cause misinterpretations of contractual terms or trust-based expectations.

A final risk is that one firm may make investments that are specific to the alliance while its partner does not. For example, the firm might commit resources and capabilities to develop manufacturing equipment that can be used only to produce items coming from the alliance. If the partner isn't also making alliance-specific investments, the firm is at a relative disadvantage in terms of returns earned from the alliance compared with investments made to earn the returns. This is certainly an issue in the TNK-BP alliance in which BP is continuing to make investments, although it is losing control in managing those investments.

Managing Cooperative Strategies

Although cooperative strategies are an important means of firm growth and enhanced performance, managing these strategies is challenging. However, learning how to effectively manage cooperative strategies is important such that it can be a source of competitive advantage.[133] Because the ability to effectively manage cooperative strategies is unevenly distributed across organizations in general, assigning managerial responsibility for a firm's cooperative strategies to a high-level executive or to a team improves the likelihood that the strategies will be well managed.

Those responsible for managing the firm's set of cooperative strategies should take the actions necessary to coordinate activities, categorize knowledge learned from previous experiences, and make certain that what the firm knows about how to effectively form and use cooperative strategies is in the hands of the right people at the right time. Firms must also learn how to manage both the tangible and intangible assets (such as knowledge) that are involved with a cooperative arrangement. Too often, partners concentrate on managing tangible assets at the expense of taking action to also manage a cooperative relationship's intangible assets.[134]

TROUBLES IN THE RUSSIAN OIL JOINT VENTURE, TNK-BP

The situation in 2009 with the joint venture that British Petroleum (BP) formed in 2003 with three Russian oil tycoons, Mikhail Fridman, Viktor Vekselberg, and Leonard Blavatnik, demonstrates opportunistic behavior as well as political risks. These three oil oligarchs own 50 percent of the venture labeled TNK-BP, and BP owns the remaining 50 percent. The venture gave a Western company unprecedented access to vital Russian oil and gas resources. However, the Kremlin is becoming increasingly involved in the nation's energy production activities and it has claimed that TNK-BP failed to fulfill all terms of its license regarding a particular oil field (the Kovykta field). This claim threatens the joint venture's viability. Part of the problem is that members of the Kremlin feel uncomfortable with the Russian tycoons having control of the state-owned assets and are even more uncomfortable with the fact that BP officials head the joint venture. It has been speculated that Gazprom, the state-run gas giant, may join the venture as a partner to improve the production deficit in the main oil field. If Gazprom does indeed become part owner, it is questionable what it will compensate BP for its ownership position. Over the years, BP has tried to develop a good relationship with the Russian government and demonstrate its commitment by investing billions of dollars. BP has also invested in other Russian ventures to drill in other oil fields, for instance, as a minority stakeholder with Rosneft.

This situation culminated with a battle over who would run TNK-BP, the third largest oil operation in Russia with 17 percent of Russia's reserves. The Russian shareholders charged that BP was running TNK-BP as a BP subsidiary and thereby depressing its values. BP officials considered the conflict as an attempt at "corporate raiding," accusing the rich Russian partners of hardball tactics. For example, Robert Dudley, the nominated chief executive of TNK-BP, was unable to get a visa and subsequently was banned by Russian courts from serving as CEO. BP officials suspected that this "paper-work problem" was orchestrated by Russian shareholders.

Fridman, one of the Russian owners, was appointed as the interim CEO, and all officials agreed to hire a new CEO that must be fluent in Russian and have business experience in Russia. New members were appointed to help keep the peace on the board, including former German Chancellor Gerhard Schroder. Not only did Dudley leave from the BP side, but the chief financial officer also felt pressure and resigned and left Russia. Thus, the bottom line appears to be that BP is conceding overall control to the Russians, but it is at least maintaining its 50 percent ownership position.

Sergei Kappukhin/Reuters/Landov

The fate of the second biggest foreign investment company in Russia and one of the world's biggest oil companies, TNK-BP, hangs in the balance amid signs of a shifting mood in the Kremlin.

Although BP has realized a positive return on its investment, it faces continued risk because of the organization's power structure and it will likely be under the control of the Russian tycoons, who are also subject to influence by government policy. As this example shows, firms that are pursuing international joint ventures need to be concerned about the opportunistic behavior of their partners as well as the political risks involved. Interestingly, other firms have had less control than BP in Russian joint ventures and in fact have lost their ownership positions through pressure by the Russian partners. In this light BP has done better than others, but risks obviously remain.

Sources: Associated Press, 2009, TNK-BP names tycoon Mikhail Fridman interim CEO, *Forbes*, http://www
.forbes.com, May 27; C. Belton & E. Krooks, 2009, Schroder a vital link with Russian TNK-BP, *Financial Times*,
January 16, 19; B. Gimbel, 2009, Russia's king of crude, *Fortune*, February 2, 88; I. Gorst, 2009, BP moves to
settle TNK clash, *Financial Times*, May 26, 15; J. Herron, 2009, Corporate news: Schroder to join TNK-BP board;
Venture makes room for ex-German leader, two other independent directors, *Wall Street Journal*, January 16,
B2; S. Reed & M. Elder, 2008, BP's dream deal hits a rough patch, *BusinessWeek*, August 11, 50; G. L. White &
G. Chazan, 2008, International business: BP retains its stake in TNK-BP; Russians gain clout, oust CEO Dudley;
IPO in 2010 likely, *Wall Street Journal*, September 5, B2; 2008, BP pays price for staying in Russia: Company
must take account of increased political risk, *Financial Times*, September 5, 8.

Two primary approaches are used to manage cooperative strategies—cost minimization and opportunity maximization[135] (see Figure 9.4). In the *cost minimization* management approach, the firm develops formal contracts with its partners. These contracts specify how the cooperative strategy is to be monitored and how partner behavior is to be controlled. The TNK-BP joint venture discussed previously is managed through contractual agreements. The goal of the cost-minimization approach is to minimize the cooperative strategy's cost and to prevent opportunistic behavior by a partner. The focus of the second managerial approach—*opportunity maximization*—is on maximizing a partnership's value-creation opportunities. In this case, partners are prepared to take advantage of unexpected opportunities to learn from each other and to explore additional marketplace possibilities. Less formal contracts, with fewer constraints on partners' behaviors, make it possible for partners to explore how their resources and capabilities can be shared in multiple value-creating ways.

Firms can successfully use both approaches to manage cooperative strategies. However, the costs to monitor the cooperative strategy are greater with cost minimization, in that writing detailed contracts and using extensive monitoring mechanisms is expensive, even though the approach is intended to reduce alliance costs. Although monitoring systems may prevent partners from acting in their own best interests, they also often preclude positive responses to new opportunities that surface to use the alliance's competitive advantages. Thus, formal contracts and extensive monitoring systems tend to stifle partners' efforts to gain maximum value from their participation in a cooperative strategy and require significant resources to be put into place and used.[136]

The relative lack of detail and formality that is a part of the contract developed by firms using the second management approach of opportunity maximization means that firms need to trust each other to act in the partnership's best interests. The psychological state of *trust* in the context of cooperative arrangements is "the expectation held by one firm that another will not exploit its vulnerabilities when faced with the opportunity to do so."[137] When partners trust each other, there is less need to write detailed formal contracts to specify each firm's alliance behaviors,[138] and the cooperative relationship tends to be more stable.[139] On a relative basis, trust tends to be more difficult to establish in international cooperative strategies compared with domestic ones. Differences in trade policies, cultures, laws, and politics that are part of cross-border alliances account for the increased difficulty. When trust exists, monitoring costs are reduced and opportunities to create value are maximized. Essentially, in these cases, the firms have built social capital.[140] According to company officials, the alliance between Renault and Nissan is built on "mutual trust between the two partners ... together with operating and confidentiality rules."[141]

Research showing that trust between partners increases the likelihood of alliance success seems to highlight the benefits of the opportunity-maximization approach to managing cooperative strategies. Trust may also be the most efficient way to influence and control alliance partners' behaviors. Research indicates that trust can be a capability that is valuable, rare, imperfectly imitable, and often nonsubstitutable.[142] Thus, firms known to be trustworthy can have a competitive advantage in terms of how they develop and use cooperative strategies.[143] One reason is that it is impossible to specify all operational details of a cooperative strategy in a formal contract. Confidence that its partner can be trusted reduces the firm's concern about the inability to contractually control all alliance details.

SUMMARY

- A cooperative strategy is one such that firms work together to achieve a shared objective. Strategic alliances, where firms combine some of their resources and capabilities to create a competitive advantage, are the primary form of cooperative strategies. Joint ventures (where firms create and own equal shares of a new venture that is intended to develop competitive advantages), equity strategic alliances (where firms own different shares of a newly created venture), and nonequity strategic alliances (where firms cooperate through a contractual relationship) are the three basic types of strategic alliances. Outsourcing, discussed in Chapter 3, commonly occurs as firms form nonequity strategic alliances.

- Collusive strategies are the second type of cooperative strategies (with strategic alliances being the other). In many economies, explicit collusive strategies are illegal unless sanctioned by government policies. Increasing globalization has led to fewer government-sanctioned situations of explicit collusion. Tacit collusion, also called mutual forbearance, is a cooperative strategy through which firms tacitly cooperate to reduce industry output below the potential competitive output level, thereby raising prices above the competitive level.

- The reasons firms use cooperative strategies vary by slow-cycle, fast-cycle, and standard-cycle market conditions. To enter restricted markets (slow cycle), to move quickly from one competitive advantage to another (fast cycle), and to gain market power (standard cycle) are among the reasons why firms choose to use cooperative strategies.

- Four business-level cooperative strategies are used to help the firm improve its performance in individual product markets. (1) Through vertical and horizontal complementary alliances, companies combine their resources and capabilities to create value in different parts (vertical) or the same parts (horizontal) of the value chain. (2) Competition-responding strategies are formed to respond to competitors' actions, especially strategic ones. (3) Competition-reducing strategies are used to avoid excessive competition while the firm marshals its resources and capabilities to improve its competitiveness. (4) Uncertainty-reducing strategies are used to hedge against the risks created by the conditions of uncertain competitive environments (such as new product markets). Complementary alliances have the highest probability of yielding a sustainable competitive advantage; competition-reducing alliances have the lowest probability.

- Firms use corporate-level cooperative strategies to engage in product and/or geographic diversification. Through diversifying strategic alliances, firms agree to share some of their resources and capabilities to enter new markets or produce new products. Synergistic alliances are ones where firms share resources and capabilities to develop economies of scope. This alliance is similar to the business-level horizontal complementary alliance where firms try to develop operational synergy, except that synergistic alliances are used to develop synergy at the corporate level. Franchising is a corporate-level cooperative strategy where the franchisor uses a franchise as a contractual relationship to specify how resources and capabilities will be shared with franchisees.

- As an international cooperative strategy, a cross-border alliance is used for several reasons, including the performance superiority of firms competing in markets outside their domestic market and governmental restrictions on growth through mergers and acquisitions. Commonly, cross-border alliances are riskier than their domestic counterparts, particularly when partners aren't fully aware of each other's purpose for participating in the partnership.

- In a network cooperative strategy, several firms agree to form multiple partnerships to achieve shared objectives. A primary benefit of a network cooperative strategy is the firm's opportunity to gain access "to its partner's other partnerships." When this happens, the probability greatly increases that partners will find unique ways to share their resources and capabilities to form competitive advantages. Network cooperative strategies are used to form either a stable alliance network or a dynamic alliance network. Used in mature industries, partners use stable networks to extend competitive advantages into new areas. In rapidly changing environments where frequent product innovations occur, dynamic networks are primarily used as a tool of innovation.

- Cooperative strategies aren't risk free. If a contract is not developed appropriately, or if a partner misrepresents its competencies or fails to make them available, failure is likely. Furthermore, a firm may be held hostage through asset-specific investments made in conjunction with a partner, which may be exploited.

- Trust is an increasingly important aspect of successful cooperative strategies. Firms recognize the value of partnering with companies known for their trustworthiness. When trust exists, a cooperative strategy is managed to maximize the pursuit of opportunities between partners. Without trust, formal contracts and extensive monitoring systems are used to manage cooperative strategies. In this case, the interest is to minimize costs rather than to maximize opportunities by participating in a cooperative strategy.

REVIEW QUESTIONS

1. What is the definition of cooperative strategy, and why is this strategy important to firms competing in the twenty-first century competitive landscape?

2. What is a strategic alliance? What are the three types of strategic alliances firms use to develop a competitive advantage?

3. What are the four business-level cooperative strategies, and what are the differences among them?

4. What are the three corporate-level cooperative strategies?

How do firms use each one to create a competitive advantage?

5. Why do firms use cross-border strategic alliances?

6. What risks are firms likely to experience as they use cooperative strategies?

7. What are the differences between the cost-minimization approach and the opportunity-maximization approach to managing cooperative strategies?

EXPERIENTIAL EXERCISES

EXERCISE 1: WHAT IS IT: TV, INTERNET, OR BOTH?

Hulu (http://www.hulu.com) is a Web site and a cooperative alliance that offers commercially supported content of TV (video on demand) shows through the Internet. The name is derived from a Chinese word which translated means "holder of precious things." The alliance has many different partners related in interesting ways. In addition, the alliance includes firms and partners from very different market types.

Working in groups, answer the following questions:

1. How would you describe the alliance partners? Characterize the market type for each (slow cycle, fast cycle, standard cycle).
2. What type of strategic alliance has Hulu become?
3. In what type of market is Hulu competing?
4. Why did this alliance form? List some competitive pressures that made this alliance a necessity for its partners.
5. What does the future hold for this alliance?

EXERCISE 2: THE SWATCHMOBILE

Swatch is well known for its line of stylish, affordable wristwatches. In the early 1990s, Swatch CEO Nicholas Hayek had a novel idea

to diversify his company's product offerings: a stylish, affordable automobile. His vision was to create a two-seat car with minimal storage space. Hayek expected these fuel-efficient cars would be highly attractive to younger European car buyers. Drawing on the company's watch designs, the Swatch car was intended to have removable body panels so that owners could change the car's look on a whim.

Swatch initially partnered with Volkswagen, but the alliance never reached production. In 1994, Swatch partnered with Mercedes-Benz. The vehicle was named SMART, which stood for "Swatch Mercedes Art."

Using Internet resources, answer the following questions:

1. What resources did each partner bring to the partnership?
2. How successful has the partnership been for each company?
3. Which company seems to be deriving the greatest benefit from the partnership and why?

VIDEO CASE

COOPERATION VS. COMPETITION

Lynda Gratton/Professor of Management Practice/London Business School

Lynda Gratton, Professor of Management Practice at the London Business School, talks about the role of cooperation coming from a profession that is really quite competitive. As you prepare for this video consider the concepts of cooperation and competition in dynamic environments. Are they complementary or contradictory?

Before you watch the video consider the following concepts and questions and be prepared to discuss them in class:

Concepts
- Trust
- Networking
- Cooperation

Questions

1. Cooperation vs. competition: Which drives performance the most? Can we have one without the other?
2. Think about what you consider to be the firm of the future. What will it look like and how will employee roles shift?
3. Is cooperation necessary in today's environment, or is it merely a nicety?

NOTES

1. D. Lavie, 2009, Capturing value from alliance portfolios, *Organizational Dynamics*, 38(1): 26–36; J. L. Morrow, Jr., D. G. Sirmon, M. A. Hitt, & T. R. Holcomb, 2007, Creating value in the face of declining performance: Firm strategies and organizational recovery, *Strategic Management Journal*, 28: 271–283.

2. T. W. Tong, J. J. Reuer, & M. W. Peng, 2008, International joint ventures and the value of growth options, *Academy of Management Journal*, 51: 1014–1029.

3. H. Ness, 2009, Governance, negotiations, and alliance dynamics: Explaining the evolution of relational practice, *Journal of Management Studies*, 46(3): 451–480; R. C. Fink, L. F. Edelman, & K. J. Hatten, 2007, Supplier performance improvements in relational exchanges, *Journal of Business & Industrial Marketing*, 22: 29–40.

4. M. J. Chen, 2008, Reconceptualizing the competition cooperation relationship: A transparadox perspective, *Journal of Management Inquiry*, 17(4): 288–304; P. E. Bierly III & S. Gallagher, 2007, Explaining alliance partner selection: Fit, trust and strategic expediency, *Long Range Planning*, 40: 134–153; K. Singh & W. Mitchell, 2005, Growth dynamics: The bidirectional relationship between interfirm collaboration and business sales in entrant and incumbent alliances, *Strategic Management Journal*, 26: 497–521.

5. W. M. Bulkeley, 2008, Business technology, A service rival looms for IBM: H-P deal for EDS to pose challenges for big blue unit, *Wall Street Journal*, May 20, B6.

6. S. Hamm, 2009, Big blue goes into analysis, *BusinessWeek*, April 27, 16.

7. R. Agarwal & C. E. Helfat, 2009, Strategic renewal of organizations, *Organization Science*, 20(2): 281–293; P. M. Senge, B. B. Lichtenstein, K. Kaeufer, H. Bradbury, & J. Carroll, 2007, Collaborating for systemic change, *MIT Sloan Management Review*, 48(2): 44–53; R. Vassolo, J. Anand, & T. B. Folta, 2004, Non-additivity in portfolios of exploration activities: A real options-based analysis of equity alliances in biotechnology, *Strategic Management Journal*, 25: 1045–1061.

8. R. C. Marshall, L. M. Marx, & M. E. Raiff, 2008, Cartel price announcement: The vitamins industry, *International Journal of Industrial Organization*, 26(3): 762–802; T. L. Sorenson, 2007, Credible collusion in multimarket oligopoly, *Managerial and Decision Economics*, 28: 115–128.

9. C. E. Ybarra & T. A. Turk, 2009, The evolution of trust in information technology alliances, *Journal of High Technology Management Research*, 20(1): 62–74; R. D. Ireland, M. A. Hitt, & D. Vaidyanath, 2002, Alliance management as a source of competitive advantage, *Journal of Management*, 28: 413–446; J. G. Coombs & D. J. Ketchen, 1999, Exploring interfirm cooperation and performance: Toward a reconciliation of predictions from the resource-based view and organizational economics, *Strategic Management Journal*, 20: 867–888.

10. M. A. Schilling, 2009, Understanding the alliance data, *Strategic Management Journal*, 30(3): 233–260; J. J. Reuer & A. Arino, 2007, Strategic alliance contracts: Dimensions and determinants of contractual complexity, *Strategic Management Journal*, 28: 313–330; M. R. Subramani & N. Venkatraman, 2003, Safeguarding investments in asymmetric interorganizational relationships: Theory and evidence, *Academy of Management Journal*, 46(1): 46–62.

11. S. Lahiri & B. L. Kedia, 2009, The effects of internal resources and partnership quality on firm performance: An examination of Indian BPO providers, *Journal of International Management*, 15(2): 209–22; R. Krishnan, X. Martin, & N. G. Noorderhaven, 2007, When does trust matter to alliance performance? *Academy of Management Journal*, 49: 894–917; P. Kale, J. H. Dyer, & H. Singh, 2002, Alliance capability, stock market response, and long-term alliance success: The role of the alliance function, *Strategic Management Journal*, 23: 747–767.

12. K. H. Heimeriks & G. Duysters, 2007, Alliance capability as a mediator between experience and alliance performance: An empirical investigation into the alliance capability development process, *Journal of Management Studies*, 44: 25–49.

13. R. E. Hoskisson, M. A. Hitt, R. D.Ireland, & J. S. Harrison, 2008, *Competing for Advantage*, 2nd ed., Thomson/Southwestern, 184.

14. B. S. Bulik, 2009, Kodak develops as modern brand with digital shift, *Advertising Age*, April 27, 26.

15. R. Lunnan & S. A. Haugland, 2008, Predicting and measuring alliance performance: A multi-dimensional analysis, *Strategic Management Journal*, 29(5): 545–556; R. Seppanen, K. Blomqvist, & S. Sundqvist, 2007, Measuring interorganizational trust—A critical review of the empirical research in 1990–2003, *Industrial Marketing Management*, 36: 249–265; T. K. Das & B.-S. Teng, 2001, A risk perception model of alliance structuring, *Journal of International Management*, 7: 1–29.

16. L. F. Mesquita, J. Anand, & T. H. Brush, 2008, Comparing the resource-based and relational views: Knowledge transfer and spillover in vertical alliances, *Strategic Management Journal*, 29: 913–941; F. F. Suarez & G. Lanzolla, 2007, The role of environmental dynamics in building a first mover advantage theory, *Academy of Management Review*, 32: 377–392; M. A. Geletkanycz & S. S. Black, 2001, Bound by the past? Experience-based effects on commitment to the strategic status quo, *Journal of Management*, 27: 3–21.

17. A. Pasztor & A. Cole, 2008, New multirole missile is planned, *Wall Street Journal*, July 16, A13.

18. K. H. Heimeriks, E. Klijn, & J. J. Reuer, 2009, Building capabilities for alliance portfolios, *Long Range Planning*, 42(1): 96–114; D. Gerwin, 2004, Coordinating new product development in strategic alliances, *Academy of Management Review*, 29: 241–257; Ireland, Hitt, & Vaidyanath, Alliance management as a source of competitive advantage.

19. X. Lin & C. L. Wang, 2008, Enforcement and performance: The role of ownership, legalism and trust in international joint ventures, *Journal of World Business*, 43(3): 340–351; Y. Luo, 2007, Are joint venture partners more opportunistic in a more volatile environment? *Strategic Management Journal*, 28: 39–60.

20. F. Evangelista & L. N. Hau, 2008, Organizational context and knowledge acquisition in IJVs: An empirical study, *Journal of World Business*, 44(1): 63–73; S. L. Berman, J. Down, & C. W. L. Hill, 2002, Tacit knowledge as a source of competitive advantage in the National Basketball Association, *Academy of Management Journal*, 45: 13–31.

21. M. Becerra, R. Lunnan, & L. Huemer, 2008, Trustworthiness, risk, and the transfer of tacit and explicit knowledge between alliance partners, *Journal of Management Studies*, 45(4): 691–713.

22. Y. Yamaguchi, 2009, Leading the news: Fujitsu targets 10% share of markets for servers, *Asian Wall Street Journal*, March 31, 3.

23. A. Tiwana, 2008, Do bridging ties complement strong ties? An empirical examination of alliance ambidexterity, *Strategic Management Journal*, 29(3): 251–272; R. E. Hoskisson & L. W. Busenitz, 2002, Market uncertainty and learning distance in corporate entrepreneurship entry mode choice, in M. A. Hitt, R. D. Ireland, S. M. Camp, & D. L. Sexton (eds.), *Strategic Entrepreneurship: Creating a New Mindset*, Oxford, UK: Blackwell Publishers, 151–172.

24. J. Xia, J. Tan, & D. Tan, 2008, Mimetic entry and bandwagon affect: The rise and decline of international equity joint venture in China, *Strategic Management Journal*, 29(2): 195–217.

25. A. Tudor & A. Lucchetti, 2009, MUFG's Hirano takes Morgan Stanley role, *Wall Street Journal*, March 12, C5.

26. Y. Wang & S. Nicholas, 2007, The formation and evolution of nonequity strategic alliances in China, *Asia Pacific Journal of Management,* 24: 131–150.

27. N. Garcia-Casarejos, N. Alcalde-Fradejas, & M. Espitia-Escuer, 2009, Staying close to the core: Lessons of studying the cost of unrelated alliances in Spanish banking, *Long Range Planning,* 42(2): 194–215; S. C. Chang, S.-S. Chen, & J. H. Lai, 2008, The wealth effect of Japanese-U.S. strategic alliances, *Financial Management,* 37(2): 271–301.

28. C. Weigelt, 2009, The impact of outsourcing new technologies on integrative capabilities and performance, *Strategic Management Journal,* 30(6): 595–616; S. Comino, P. Mariel, & J. Sandonis, 2007, Joint ventures versus contractual agreements: An empirical investigation, *Spanish Economic Journal,* 9: 159–175.

29. 2007, Intellectual property licensing, http://www.hp.com, August 30.

30. A. Tiwana, 2008, Does interfirm modularity complement ignorance? A field study of software outsourcing alliances, *Strategic Management Journal,* 29(11): 1241–1252.

31. A. L. Sherwood & J. G. Covin, 2008, Knowledge acquisition in university–industry alliances: An empirical investigation from a learning theory perspective, *Journal of Product Innovation Management,* 25: 162–179.

32. P. Beamish & N. Lupton, 2009, Managing joint ventures, *Academy of Management Perspectives,* 23(2): 75–94.

33. A. C. Inkpen & J. Ross, 2001, Why do some strategic alliances persist beyond their useful life? *California Management Review,* 44(1): 132–148.

34. A. Al-Laham, T. L. Amburgey, & K. Bates, 2008, The dynamics of research alliances: Examining the effect of alliance experience and partner characteristics on the speed of alliance entry in the biotech industry, *British Journal of Management,* 19(4): 343–364; F. Rothaermel & D. L. Deeds, 2006, Alliance type, alliance experience and alliance management capability in high-technology ventures, *Journal of Business Venturing,* 21: 429–460; L. Fuentelsaz, J. Gomez, & Y. Polo, 2002, Followers' entry timing: Evidence from the Spanish banking sector after deregulation, *Strategic Management Journal,* 23: 245–264.

35. Mesquita, Anand, Brush, Comparing the resource-based and relational views: Knowledge transfer and spillover in vertical alliances; B. L. Bourdeau, J. J. Cronink, Jr., & C. M. Voorhees, 2007, Modeling service alliances: An exploratory investigation of spillover effects in service partnerships, *Strategic Management Journal,* 28: 609–622.

36. J. Murphy, 2009, Dow Jones: Venture to launch site for newspaper in Japanese, *Wall Street Journal,* May 8, B3.

37. J. J. Reuer, P. Olk & A. Arino, 2010, *Entrepreneurial Alliances,* Prentice Hall, forthcoming.

38. R. Fores-Fillol, 2009, Allied alliances: Parallel or complementary? *Applied Economic Letters,* 16(6): 585–590; S. G. Lazzarini, 2007, The impact of membership in competing alliance constellations: Evidence on the operational performance of global airlines, *Strategic Management Journal,* 28: 345–367.

39. S. R. Holmberg & J. L. Cummings, 2009, Building successful strategic alliance: Strategic process and analytical tools for selecting partner industries and firms, *Long Range Planning,* 42(2): 164–193; M. A. Hitt, D. Ahlstrom, M. T. Dacin, E. Levitas, & L. Svobodina, 2004, The institutional effects of strategic alliance partner selection in transition economies: China versus Russia, *Organization Science,* 15: 173–185; P. A. Saparito, C. C. Chen, & H. J. Sapienza, 2004, The role of relational trust in bank-small firm relationships, *Academy of Management Journal,* 47: 400–410.

40. G. Padula, 2008, Enhancing the innovation performance of firms by balancing cohesiveness and bridging ties, *Long Range Planning,* 41(4): 395–419; A. C. Inkpen & E. W. K. Tsang, 2005, Social capital, networks and knowledge transfer, *Academy of Management Review,* 30: 146–165.

41. W. P. Wan, D. Yiu, R. E. Hoskisson, & H. Kim, 2008, The performance implications of relationship banking during macroeconomic expansion and contraction: A study of Japanese banks' social relationships and overseas expansion, *Journal of International Business Studies,* 39: 406–447; M. Hughes, R. D. Ireland, & R. E. Morgan, 2007, Stimulating dynamic value: Social capital and business incubation as a pathway to competitive success, *Long Range Planning,* 40(2): 154–177; T. G. Pollock, J. F. Porac, & J. B. Wade, 2004, Constructing deal networks: Brokers as network "architects" in the U.S. IPO market and other examples, *Academy of Management Review,* 29: 50–72.

42. J. R. Williams, 1998, *Renewable Advantage: Crafting Strategy Through Economic Time,* New York: Free Press.

43. 2008, Nucor, Duferco team up in foreign beam venture, *Metal Center News,* February, 84.

44. R. G. Matthews, 2008, World steel makers go prospecting; Industry plows profits into buying coal or mines to reduce vulnerability to rising commodity prices, *Wall Street Journal,* June 20, B1.

45. S. A. Zahra, R. D. Ireland, I. Gutierrez, & M. A. Hitt, 2000, Privatization and entrepreneurial transformation: Emerging issues and a future research agenda, *Academy of Management Review,* 25: 509–524.

46. H. K. Steensma, J. Q. Barden, C. Dhanaraj, M. Lyles, & L. Tihanyi, 2008, The evolution and internalization of international joint ventures in a transitioning economy, *Journal of International Business Studies,* 39(3): 491–507; I. Filatotchev, M. Wright, K. Uhlenbruck, L. Tihanyi, & R. E. Hoskisson, 2003, Governance, organizational capabilities, and restructuring in transition economies, *Journal of World Business,* 38(4): 331–347.

47. H. L. Sirkin, 2008, New world disorder, *Time,* October 27, GB1; J. Lash & F. Wellington, 2007, Competitive advantage on a warming planet, *Harvard Business Review,* 85(3): 94–102; K. M. Eisenhardt, 2002, Has strategy changed? *MIT Sloan Management Review,* 43(2): 88–91.

48. Ibid., GB1.

49. S. Lahiri, L. Perez-Nordtvedt, & R. W. Renn, 2008, Will the new competitive landscape cause your firm's decline? It depends on your mindset, *Business Horizons,* 51(4): 311–320.

50. S. Schechner & E. Holmes, 2009, Disney teams up with other networks online, buying stake in Hulu site, *Wall Street Journal,* May 1, B1.

51. C. Czipura & D. R. Jolly, 2007, Global airline alliances: Sparking profitability for a troubled industry, *Journal of Business Strategy,* 28(2): 57–64.

52. C. Conkey & P. Prada, 2009, Corporate news: Continental wins nod to join Star Alliance, *Wall Street Journal,* April 8, B4.

53. S. G. Lazzarini, D. P. Claro, & L. F. Mesquita, 2008, Buyer-supplier and supplier-supplier alliances: Do they reinforce or undermine one another? *Journal of Management Studies,* 45(3): 561–584; D. R. King, J. G. Covin, & H. Hegarty, 2003, Complementary resources and the exploitation of technological innovations, *Journal of Management,* 29: 589–606; J. S. Harrison, M. A. Hitt, R. E. Hoskisson, & R. D. Ireland, 2001, Resource complementarity in business combinations: Extending the logic to organizational alliances, *Journal of Management,* 27: 679–699.

54. T. E. Stuart, S. Z. Ozdemir, & W. W. Ding, 2007, Vertical alliance networks: The case of university-biotechnology-pharmaceutical alliance chains. *Research Policy,* 36(4): 477–498; F. T. Rothaermel, M. A. Hitt, & L. A. Jobe, 2006, Balancing vertical integration and strategic outsourcing: Effects on product portfolio, product success, and firm performance, *Strategic Management Journal,* 27: 1033–1056.

55. Y. Yan, D. Ding, & S. Mak, 2009, The impact of business investment on capability exploitation and organizational control in international strategic alliances, *Journal of Change Management,* 9(1): 49–65; R. Gulati, P. R. Lawrence, & P. Puranam, 2005, Adaptation in vertical relationships beyond incentive conflict, *Strategic Management Journal,* 26: 415–440.

56. J. Wiklund & D. A. Shepherd, 2009, The effectiveness of alliances and acquisitions: The role of resource combination activities, *Theory and Practice,* 31(1): 193–212; B.-S. Teng, 2007, Corporate entrepreneurship activities through strategic alliances: A resource-based

approach toward competitive advantage, *Journal of Management Studies*, 44: 119–142.

57. Y. I. Kane & D. Wakabayashi, 2009, Nintendo looks outside the box, *Wall Street Journal*, May 27, B5.

58. F. A. Ghisi, J. A.G. da Silveira, T. Kristensen, M. Hingley, & A. Lindgreen, 2008, Horizontal alliances amongst small retailers in Brazil, *British Food Journal*, 110(4/5): 514–538; Tiwana, Do bridging ties complement strong ties? An empirical examination of alliance ambidexterity; F. T. Rothaermel & M. Thursby, 2007, The nanotech versus the biotech revolution: Sources of productivity in incumbent firm research, *Research Policy*, 36: 832–849; T. H. Oum, J. H.Park, K. Kim & C. Yu, 2004, The effect of horizontal alliances on firm productivity and profitability: Evidence from the global airline industry, *Journal of Business Research*, 57: 844–853.

59. A. Johnson & A. Greil, 2009, Pfizer, Novartis disclose separate deals in generic drugs, *Wall Street Journal*, May 21, B3.

60. E. Smith, 2009, Universal takes another stab online, *Wall Street Journal*, May 15, B8.

61. Tong, Reuer, & Peng, International joint ventures and the value of growth options; J. J. Reuer & T. W. Tong, 2005, Real options in international joint ventures, *Journal of Management*, 31: 403–423; S. Chatterjee, R. M. Wiseman, A. Fiegenbaum, & C. E. Devers, 2003, Integrating behavioral and economic concepts of risk into strategic management: The twain shall meet, *Long Range Planning*, 36(1): 61–80.

62. C. Rauwald & N. Shirouzu, 2009, Volkswagen eyes China venture, *Wall Street Journal*, May 27, B4.

63. L. Tesfatsion, 2007, Agents come to bits: Toward a constructive comprehensive taxonomy of economic entities, *Journal of Economic Behavior & Organization*, 63: 333–346.

64. K. Done, 2009, Cargo airlines fined $214 for price fixing, *Financial Times*, http://www.ft.com, April 12.

65. C. d'Aspremont, R. D. S. Ferreira & L. A.Gerard-Varet, 2007, Competition for market share or for market size: Oligopolistic equilibria with varying competitive toughness, *International Economic Review*, 48: 761–784.

66. R. W. Cooper & T. W. Ross, 2009, Sustaining cooperation with joint ventures, *Journal of Law Economics and Organization*, 25(1): 31–54.

67. J. T. Prince & D. H. Simon, 2009, Multi-market contact and service quality: Evidence from on-time performance in the U.S. airline industry, *Academy of Management Journal*, 52(2): 336–354.

68. G. K. Price & J. M. Connor, 2003, Modeling coupon values for ready-to-eat breakfast cereals, *Agribusiness*, 19(2): 223–244.

69. G. K. Price, 2000, Cereal sales soggy despite price cuts and reduced couponing, *Food Review*, 23(2): 21–28.

70. S. Kilman, 2008, Food giants race to pass rising costs to shoppers, *Wall Street Journal*, August 8, A1.

71. Kilman, Food giants race to pass rising costs to shoppers; J. Hagedoorn & G. Hesen, 2007, Contract law and the governance of interfirm technology partnerships—An analysis of different modes of partnering and their contractual implications, *Journal of Management Studies*, 44: 342–366; B. R. Golden & H. Ma, 2003, Mutual forbearance: The role of intrafirm integration and rewards, *Academy of Management Review*, 28: 479–493.

72. J. Apesteguia, M. Dufwenberg, & R. Selton, 2007, Blowing the whistle, *Economic Theory*, 31: 127–142.

73. J. D. Rockoff, 2009, Drug CEOs switch tactics on reform; Pharmaceutical companies join health-care overhaul hoping to influence where costs are cut, *Wall Street Journal*, May 27, B1, B2; J. H. Johnson & G. K. Leonard, 2007, Economics and the rigorous analysis of class certification in antitrust cases, *Journal of Competition Law and Economics*, http://jcle.oxfordjournals.org, June 26.

74. Lazzarini, Claro, & Mesquita, Buyer-supplier and supplier-supplier alliances: Do they reinforce or undermine one another?; P. Dussauge, B. Garrette, & W. Mitchell, 2004, Asymmetric performances: The market share impact of scale ad link alliances in global auto industry, *Strategic Management Journal*, 25: 701–711.

75. Conkey & Prada, Corporate news: Continental wins nod to join Star Alliance.

76. Harrison, Hitt, Hoskisson, & Ireland, Resource complementarity, 684–685.

77. L. H.Lin, 2009, Mergers and acquisitions, alliances and technology development: An empirical study of the global auto industry, *International Journal of Technology Management*, 48(3): 295–307; Wiklund & Shepherd, The effectiveness of alliances and acquisitions: The role of resource combination activities; A. E. Bernardo & B. Chowdhry, 2002, Resources, real options, and corporate strategy, *Journal of Financial Economics*, 63: 211–234.

78. J. Li, C. Dhanaraj, & R. L. Shockley, 2008, Joint venture evolution: Extending the real options approach, *Managerial and Decision Economics*, 29(4): 317–336.

79. V. Moatti, 2009, Learning to expand or expanding to learn? The role of imitation and experience in the choice among several expansion modes, *European Management Journal*, 27(1): 36–46; C. C. Pegels & Y. I. Song, 2007, Market competition and cooperation: Identifying competitive/cooperative interaction groups, *International Journal of Services Technology and Management*, 2/3: 139–154

80. S. Silver & E. Steel, 2009, Alcatel gets into mobile ads; Service will target cell phone users based on location, *Wall Street Journal*, May 21, B9.

81. A. Goerzen & P. W. Beamish, 2005, The effect of alliance network diversity on multinational enterprise performance, *Strategic Management Journal*, 333–354.

82. M. V. Shyam Kumar, 2005, The value from acquiring and divesting a joint venture: A real options approach, *Strategic Management Journal*, 26: 321–331.

83. J. Yang, 2003, One step forward for Japan's chipmakers, *BusinessWeek Online*, http://www.businessweek.com, July 7.

84. J. E. Vascellaro & E. Holmes, 2009, YouTube seals deal on ABC, ESPN clips, Wall Street Journal online, http://www.wsj.com, March 31.

85. B. Worthen & J. Scheck, 2009, As growth slows, ex-allies square off in a turf war, *Wall Street Journal*, March 16, A1.

86. A. M. Doherty, 2009, Market and partner selection processes in international retail franchising, *Journal of Business Research*, 62(5): 528–534; M. Tuunanen & F. Hoy, 2007, Franchising—multifaceted form of entrepreneurship, *International Journal of Entrepreneurship and Small Business*, 4: 52–67; J. G. Combs & D. J. Ketchen Jr., 2003, Why do firms use franchising as an entrepreneurial strategy? A meta-analysis, *Journal of Management*, 29: 427–443.

87. F. Lafontaine, 1999, Myths and strengths of franchising, "Mastering Strategy" (Part Nine), *Financial Times*, November 22, 8–10.

88. A. M. Hayashi, 2008, How to replicate success, *MIT Sloan Management Review*, 49(3): 6–7.

89. G. Szulanski & R. J. Jensen, 2008, Growing through copying: The negative consequences of innovation on franchise network growth, *Research Policy*, 37(10): 1732–1741.

90. B. Barringer & R. D. Ireland, 2008, *Entrepreneurship: Successfully Launching New Ventures*, 2nd ed., Prentice Hall, 440.

91. L. Sanders, 2009, International expansion: Proven strategy during economic uncertainty, *Franchising World*, March, 16–17; B. Duckett, 2008, Business format franchising: A strategic option for business growth—at home and abroad, *Strategic Direction*, 4(2): 3–4.

92. Doherty, Market and partner selection processes in international retail franchising; R. B. DiPietro, D. H. B. Welsh, P. V. Raven, & D. Severt, 2007, A message of hope in franchises systems: Assessing franchisee, top executives, and franchisors, *Journal of Leadership & Organizational Studies*, 13(3): 59–66; S. C. Michael, 2002, Can a franchise chain coordinate? *Journal of Business Venturing*, 17: 325–342.

93. A. K. Paswan & C. M. Wittmann, 2009, Knowledge management and franchise systems, *Industrial Marketing Management*, 38(2): 173–180.

94. J. Torikka, 2007, Franchisees can be made: Empirical evidence from a follow-up study, *International Journal of Entrepreneurship and Small Business*, 4: 68–96; P. J. Kaufmann & S. Eroglu,

1999, Standardization and adaptation in business format franchising, *Journal of Business Venturing*, 14: 69–85.

95. B. Arruñada, L. Vázquez, & G. Zanarone, 2009, Institutional constraints on organizations: The case of Spanish car dealerships, *Managerial and Decision Economics*, 30(1): 15–26; J. Barthélemy, 2008, Opportunism, knowledge, and the performance of franchise chains, *Strategic Management Journal*, 29(13): 1451–1463.

96. A. Tiwana, 2008, Does technological modularity substitute for control? A study of alliance performance in software outsourcing, *Strategic Management Journal*, 29(7): 769–780; M. Zollo, J. J. Reuer, & H. Singh, 2002, Interorganizational routines and performance in strategic alliances, *Organization Science*, 13: 701–714.

97. E. Levitas & M. A. McFadyen, 2009, Managing liquidity in research-intensive firms: Signaling and cash flow effects of patents and alliance activities, *Strategic Management Journal*, 30(6): 659–678; Ireland, Hitt, & Vaidyanath, Alliance management.

98. R. Durand, O. Bruyaka, & V. Mangematin, 2008, Do science and money go together? The case of the French biotech industry, *Strategic Management Journal*, 29(12): 1281–1299; A. V. Shipilov, 2007, Network strategies and performance of Canadian investment banks, *Academy of Management Journal*, 49: 590–604; P. Almeida, G. Dokko, & L. Rosenkopf, 2003, Startup size and the mechanisms of external learning: Increasing opportunity and decreasing ability? *Research Policy*, 32(2): 301–316.

99. H. Ren, B. Gray, & K. Kim, 2009, Performance of international joint ventures: What factors really make a difference and how? *Journal of Management*, 35(3): 805–832; R. Narula & G. Duysters, 2004, Globalization and trends in international R&D alliances, *Journal of International Management*, 10: 199–218; M. A. Hitt, M. T. Dacin, E. Levitas, J.-L. Arregle, & A. Borza, 2000, Partner selection in emerging and developed market contexts: Resource-based and organizational learning perspectives, *Academy of Management Journal*, 43: 449–467.

100. W. Zhan, R. Chen, M. K. Erramilli, & D. T. Nguyen, 2009, Acquisition of organizational capabilities and competitive advantage of IJVs in transition economies: The case of Vietnam, *Asia Pacific Journal of Management*, 26(2): 285–308; Tong, Reuer, & Peng, International joint ventures and the value of growth option; J. H. Dyer, P. Kale, & H. Singh, 2004, When to ally & when to acquire, *Harvard Business Review*, 81(7/8): 109–115.

101. 1Y. Yan, D. Ding, & S. Mak, 2009, The impact of business investment on capability exploitation and organizational control in international strategic alliances, *Journal of Change Management*, 9(1): 49–65; P. Ghemawat, 2007, Managing

differences: The central challenge of global strategy, *Harvard Business Review*, 85(3): 59–68.

102. L. Chao, 2009, IMG China venture opens with tennis, *Wall Street Journal*, May 26, B10.

103. Ren, Gray, & Kim, Performance of international joint ventures: What factors really make a difference and how; L. Dong & K.W. Glaister, 2007, National and corporate culture differences in international strategic alliances: Perceptions of Chinese partners, *Asia Pacific Journal of Management*, 24: 191–205; I. M. Manev, 2003, The managerial network in a multinational enterprise and the resource profiles of subsidiaries, *Journal of International Management*, 9: 133–152.

104. P. H. Dickson, K. M. Weaver, & F. Hoy, 2006, Opportunism in the R&D alliances of SMEs: The roles of the institutional environment and SME size, *Journal of Business Venturing*, 21: 487–513; H. K. Steensma, L. Tihanyi, M. A. Lyles, & C. Dhanaraj, 2005, The evolving value of foreign partnerships in transitioning economies, *Academy of Management Journal*, 48: 213–235.

105. 2007, Branding and celebrity endorsements, *VentureRepublic*, http://venturerepublic. com, August 31.

106. 2009, Nike winded, *Financial Times*, March 20, 14.

107. B. Elango, 2009, Minimizing effects of "liability of foreignness": Response strategies of foreign firms in the United States, *Journal of World Business*, 44(1): 51–62; Y. Luo, O. Shenkar, & M.-K. Nyaw, 2002, Mitigating the liabilities of foreignness: Defensive versus offensive approaches, *Journal of International Management*, 8: 283–300.

108. T. J. Wilkinson, A. R. Thomas, & J. M. Hawes, 2009, Managing relationships with Chinese joint venture partners, *Journal of Global Marketing*, 22(2): 109–210; S. R. Miller & A. Parkhe, 2002, Is there a liability of foreignness in global banking? An empirical test of banks' x-efficiency, *Strategic Management Journal*, 23: 55–75; Y. Luo, 2001, Determinants of local responsiveness: Perspectives from foreign subsidiaries in an emerging market, *Journal of Management*, 27: 451–477.

109. D. Kronborg & S. Thomsen, 2009, Foreign ownership and long-term survival, *Strategic Management Journal*, 30(2): 207–220.

110. E. Rodríguez, 2008, Cooperative ventures in emerging economies, *Journal of Business Research*, 61(6): 640–647; D. Li, L. E. Eden, M. A. Hitt, & R. D. Ireland, 2008, Friends, acquaintances or strangers? Partner selection in R&D alliances, *Academy of Management Journal*, 51: 315–334; J. E. Oxley & R. C. Sampson, 2004, The scope and governance of international R&D alliances, *Strategic Management Journal*, 25: 723–749.

111. H. Sun, 2009, China poised to be net importer of coffee, *Wall Street Journal*,

January 20, C10; 2006, Starbucks acquires control of China joint venture, *Apostille US*, http://apostille.us/, October 25.

112. D. Lavie, 2009, Capturing value from alliance portfolios, *Organizational Dynamics*, 38(1): 26–36; D. Lavie, C. Lechner, & H. Singh, 2007, The performance implications of timing of entry and involvement in multipartner alliances, *Academy of Management Journal*, 49: 569–604.

113. K. Atkins, J. Chen, V. S. A. Kumar, M. Macauley, & A. Marathe, 2009, Locational market power in network constrained markets, *Journal of Economic Behavior & Organization*, 70(1/2): 416–430; A. Nosella & G. Petroni, 2007, Multiple network leadership as a strategic asset: The Carlo Gavazzi space case, *Long Range Planning*, 40: 178–201.

114. K. Sawyer, 2007, Strength in webs, *The Conference Board*, July/August, 9–11.

115. C. Yarbrough, 2008, Singapore to open fusionopolis, *Research Technology Management*, 51(5): 4–5; A. H. Van de Ven, H. J. Sapienza, & J. Villanueva, 2007, Entrepreneurial pursuits of self- and collective interests, *Strategic Entrepreneurship Journal*, 1(3/4): 353–370.

116. Lavie, Capturing value from alliance portfolios; D. Lavie, 2007, Alliance portfolios and firm performance: A study of value creation and appropriation in the U.S. software industry, *Strategic Management Journal*, 28(12): 1187–1212; G. K. Lee, 2007, The significance of network resources in the race to enter emerging product markets: The convergence of telephony communications and computer networking, 1989–2001, *Strategic Management Journal*, 28: 17–37.

117. R. Cowan & N. Jonard, 2009, Knowledge portfolios and the organization of innovation networks, *Academy of Management Review*, 34(2): 320–342; G. G. Bell, 2005, Clusters, networks, and firm innovativeness, *Strategic Management Journal*, 26: 287–295.

118. H. Kim, R. E. Hoskisson, & W. P. Wan, 2004, Power, dependence, diversification strategy and performance in keiretsu member firms, *Strategic Management Journal*, 25: 613–636.

119. A. V. Shipilov, 2009, Firm scope experience, historic multimarket contact with partners, centrality, and the relationship between structural holes and performance, *Organization Science*, 20(1): 85–106; M. Rudberg & J. Olhager, 2003, Manufacturing networks and supply chains: An operations strategy perspective, *Omega*, 31(1): 29–39.

120. Cowan & Jonard, Knowledge portfolios and the organization of innovation networks; E. J. Kleinschmidt, U. de Brentani, & S. Salomo, 2007, Programs: A resource-based view, *Journal of Product Innovation Management*, 24: 419–441; G. J. Young, M. P. Charns, & S. M. Shortell, 2001, Top manager and network effects on the adoption of

innovative management practices: A study of TQM in a public hospital system, *Strategic Management Journal*, 22: 935–951.

121. Prince & Simon, Multi-market contact and service quality: Evidence from on-time performance in the U.S. airline industry; E. Garcia-Canal, C. L. Duarte, J. R. Criado, & A. V. Llaneza, 2002, Accelerating international expansion through global alliances: A typology of cooperative strategies, *Journal of World Business*, 37(2): 91–107; F. T. Rothaermel, 2001, Complementary assets, strategic alliances, and the incumbent's advantage: An empirical study of industry and firm effects in the biopharmaceutical industry, *Research Policy*, 30: 1235–1251.

122. T. Kiessling & M. Harvey, 2008, Globalisation of internal venture capital opportunities in developing small and medium enterprises' relationships, *International Journal of Entrepreneurship and Innovation Management*, 8(3): 233–253; V. Shankar & B. L. Bayus, 2003, Network effects and competition: An empirical analysis of the home video game industry, *Strategic Management Journal*, 24: 375–384.

123. A. Schwab & A. S. Miner, 2008, Learning in hybrid-project systems: The effects of project performance on repeated collaboration, *Academy of Management Journal*, 51(6): 1117–1149.

124. A. E. Leiponen, 2008, Competing through cooperation: The organization of standard setting in wireless telecommunications, *Management Science*, 54(11): 1904–1919; Z. Simsek, M. H. Lubatkin, & D. Kandemir, 2003, Inter-firm networks and entrepreneurial behavior: A structural embeddedness perspective, *Journal of Management*, 29: 401–426.

125. H. W. Gottinger & C. L. Umali, 2008, The evolution of the pharmaceutical-biotechnology industry, *Business History*, 50(5): 583–601; F. T. Rothaermel & W. Boeker, 2008, Old technology meets new technology: Complementarities, similarities, and alliance formation, *Strategic Management Journal*, 29(1): 47–77; P. Puranam & K. Srikanth, 2007, What they know vs. what they do: How acquirers leverage technology acquisitions, *Strategic Management Journal*, 28: 805–825; M. Moensted, 2007, Strategic networking in small high-tech firms, *The International Entrepreneurship and Management Journal*, 3: 15–27.

126. P. Ozcan & K. M. Eisenhardt, 2009, Origin of alliance portfolios: Entrepreneurs, network strategies, and firm performance, *Academy of Management Journal*, 52(2): 246–279; C. T. Street & A.-F. Cameron, 2007, External relationships and the small business: A review of small business alliance and network research, *Journal of Small Business Management*, 45: 239–266.

127. M. Rod, 2009, A model for the effective management of joint ventures: A case study approach, *International Journal of Management*, 26(1): 3–17; T. K. Das & R. Kumar, 2007, Learning dynamics in the alliance development process, *Management Decision*, 45: 684–707.

128. A. Carmeli & Z. Sheaffer, 2008, How learning leadership and organizational learning from failures enhance perceived organizational capacity to adapt to the task environment, *Journal of Applied Behavioral Science*, 44(4): 468–489; J.-Y. Kim & A. S. Miner, 2007, Vicarious learning from the failures and near-failures of others: Evidence from the U.S. commercial banking industry, *Academy of Management Journal*, 49: 687–714.

129. Y. Li, Y. Liu, M. Li, & H. Wu, 2008, Transformational offshore outsourcing: Empirical evidence from alliances in China, *Journal of Operations Management*, 26(2): 257–274; P. M. Norman, 2002, Protecting knowledge in strategic alliances—Resource and relational characteristics, *Journal of High Technology Management Research*, 13(2): 177–202; P. M. Norman, 2001, Are your secrets safe? Knowledge protection in strategic alliances, *Business Horizons*, November–December, 51–60.

130. Heimeriks, Klijn, & Reuer, Building capabilities for alliance portfolios; Al-Laham, Amburgey, & Bates, The dynamics of research alliances: Examining the effect of alliance experience and partner characteristics on the speed of alliance entry in the biotech industry; J. Connell & R. Voola, 2007, Strategic alliances and knowledge sharing: Synergies or silos? *Journal of Knowledge Management*, 11: 52–66.

131. M. B. Sarkar, P. S. Aulakh, & A. Madhok, 2009, Process capabilities and value generation in alliance portfolios, *Organization Science*, 20(3): 583–600.

132. P.-X. Meschi, 2009, Government corruption and foreign stakes in international joint ventures in emerging economies, *Asia Pacific Journal of Management*, 26(2): 241–261.

133. M. H. Hansen, R. E. Hoskisson, & J. B. Barney, 2008, Competitive advantage in alliance governance: Resolving the opportunism minimization-gain maximization paradox, *Managerial and Decision Economics*, 29: 191–208; J. H. Dyer, P. Kale, & H. Singh, 2001, How to make strategic alliances work, *MIT Sloan Management Review*, 42(4): 37–43.

134. Connell & Voola, Strategic alliances and knowledge sharing.

135. Levitas & McFadyen, Managing liquidity in research-intensive firms: Signaling and cash flow effects of patents and alliance activities; Hansen, Hoskisson, & Barney, Competitive advantage in alliance governance: Resolving the opportunism minimization-gain maximization paradox; J. H. Dyer, 1997, Effective interfirm collaboration: How firms minimize transaction costs and maximize transaction value, *Strategic Management Journal*, 18: 535–556.

136. L. Poppo, K. Z. Zhou, & S. Ryu, 2008, Alternative origins to interorganizational trust: An interdependence perspective on the shadow of the past and the shadow of the future, *Organization Science*, 19(1): 39–56; J. H. Dyer & C. Wujin, 2003, The role of trustworthiness in reducing transaction costs and improving performance: Empirical evidence from the United States, Japan, and Korea, *Organization Science*, 14: 57–69.

137. Krishnan, Martin, & Noorderhaven, When does trust matter to alliance performance?

138. K. Langfield-Smith, 2008, The relations between transactional characteristics, trust and risk in the start-up phase of a collaborative alliance, *Management Accounting Research*, 19(4): 344–364; M. Lundin, 2007, Explaining cooperation: How resource interdependence, goal congruence, and trust affect joint actions in policy implementation, *Journal of Public Administration Research and Theory*, 17(4): 651–672.

139. T. K. Das & R. Kumar, 2009, Interpartner harmony in strategic alliances: Managing commitment and forbearance, *International Journal of Strategic Business Alliances*, 1(1): 24–52; V. Perrone, A. Zaheer, & B. McEvily, 2003, Free to be trusted? Boundary constraints on trust in boundary spanners, *Organization Science*, 14: 422–439.

140. J. W. Rottman, 2008, Successful knowledge transfer within offshore supplier networks: A case study exploring social capital in strategic alliances, *Journal of Information Technology*: Special Issue: Global Sourcing, 23(1): 31–43; R. D. Ireland & J. W. Webb, 2007, A multi-theoretic perspective on trust and power in strategic supply chains, *Journal of Operations Management*, 25: 482–497.

141. 2007, The principles of the alliance, http://www.renault.com, August 26.

142. C. E. Ybarra & T. A. Turk, 2009, The evolution of trust in information technology alliances, *Journal of High Technology Management Research*, 20(1): 62–74; F. D. Schoorman, R. C. Mayer, & J. H. Davis, 2007, An integrative model of organizational trust: Past, present, and future, *Academy of Management Review*, 344–354; J. H. Davis, F. D. Schoorman, R. C. Mayer, & H. H. Tan, 2000, The trusted general manager and business unit performance: Empirical evidence of a competitive advantage, *Strategic Management Journal*, 21: 563–576.

143. Y. Luo, 2008, Procedural fairness and interfirm cooperation in strategic alliances, *Strategic Management Journal*, 29(1): 27–46; B. Hillebrand & W. G. Biemans, 2003, The relationship between internal and external cooperation: Literature review and propositions, *Journal of Business Research*, 56: 735–744.

CHAPTER 10

Corporate Governance

Studying this chapter should provide you with the strategic management knowledge needed to:

1. Define corporate governance and explain why it is used to monitor and control managers' strategic decisions.

2. Explain why ownership has been largely separated from managerial control in the corporation.

3. Define an agency relationship and managerial opportunism and describe their strategic implications.

4. Explain how three internal governance mechanisms—ownership concentration, the board of directors, and executive compensation—are used to monitor and control managerial decisions.

5. Discuss the types of compensation executives receive and their effects on strategic decisions.

6. Describe how the external corporate governance mechanism—the market for corporate control—acts as a restraint on top-level managers' strategic decisions.

7. Discuss the use of corporate governance in international settings, especially in Germany, Japan, and China.

8. Describe how corporate governance fosters ethical strategic decisions and the importance of such behaviors on the part of top level managers.

IS CEO PAY OUTRAGEOUS, IRRESPONSIBILE, OR GREEDY?

In 2008, the ten most highly paid CEOs earned a total of $472.2 million. Furthermore, seven of these CEOs who worked at the same companies in 2007 received an increase in pay of approximately 26 percent over the previous year. Placing this in perspective, an average of $47.22 million was paid to these CEOs in a year when most large firms—including theirs—lost significant market value, and many experienced net losses. In 2008, we learned that the U.S. economy and, indeed, much of the rest of the world, was in a deep recession. In fact, it is perhaps the worst since the Great Depression in the 1930s. Many believe that this recession was largely caused by irresponsible and greedy strategies followed by top-level managers in the financial services and real estate industries. In addition, the corporate governance system failed to rein in these managers, who took extreme risks causing billions of dollars in losses. Real estate values plummeted in many parts of the country, there were a substantial number of mortgage foreclosures, unemployment increased substantially, and the stock market took a nosedive.

In this context, top executive pay came under intense criticism. In recent years, supposedly knowledgeable people argued that top-level managers were being paid for performance. If so, how could they earn such high compensation when their companies were performing poorly? Many CEOs earn more than 100 times the amount received by their firm's lowest-paid employee. Despite the average increases for the highest-paid CEOs, the median salary and bonuses for CEOs of the largest 200 U.S. firms decreased by 8.5 percent in 2008, but their total direct compensation only fell by 3.4 percent. The decline in the financial services industry was much greater, as could be expected. Still, the median value of perks provided to CEOs in 2008 increased by about 7 percent. "Perks"

Julia Hiebaum/Alamy

include many possible benefits, such as club memberships, free personal travel in company jets, bodyguards, and chauffeured cars. In fact, the CEO of Occidental Petroleum received $400,000 worth of financial planning. This was a part of his compensation in 2008, which totaled $30 million. While this benefit for financial planning is only 1.33 percent of his total pay for the year, $400,000 is greater than the total annual household income for most U.S. citizens.

In a survey conducted by the *Financial Times*, respondents from France, Germany, Italy, Spain, the United Kingdom, and the United States stated that they believed that business leaders were paid too much. The lowest percentage believing that top-level managers were overpaid was about 75 percent in France, while almost 90 percent in Germany felt they were overpaid. When the feelings of the general public are combined with the poor performance of companies in a weak economy, pundits often blame an inadequate system of corporate governance. This concern is amplified by reports of bad strategic decisions of business leaders blamed for creating the economic crisis. Thus, governments and others have begun to explore the governance mechanisms including compensation systems, boards of directors, ownership, and disciplining from the markets. It is likely that new regulations will be proposed and adopted to control what the public perceives to be irresponsibility and greed on the part of business leaders.

Sources: V. Tong, 2009, As pay falls, CEOs get more perks, YAHOO! News, http://news.yahoo.com, May 1; 2009, The pay at the top, *The New York Times*, http://www.nytimes.com, April 16; R. Milne, 2009, Sharp divide on executive pay, *Financial Times*, http://www.ft.com, April 13; J. S. Lublin, 2009, CEO pay sinks along with profits, *Wall Street Journal*, http://www.wsj.com, April 6; T. Carr, 2008, An ethical analysis of CEO compensation, *Fast Company*, http://www.fastcompany.com, November 28; A. Cohen, 2008, CEO pay; outrageous—and bad for MBA programs, *Fast Company*, http://www.fastcompany.com, April 6.

As the Opening Case illustrates, governance mechanisms designed to ensure effective leadership of firms to develop and implement strategies that create value for stakeholders is challenging. However, corporate governance is critical to firms' success and thus has become an increasingly important part of the strategic management process.[1] If the board makes the wrong decisions in selecting, governing, and compensating the firm's strategic leader (e.g., CEO), the shareholders and the firm suffer. When CEOs are motivated to act in the best interests of the firm—in particular, the shareholders—the firm's value should increase.

As suggested in the Opening Case, many people now believe that CEOs in the United States are paid too much; the hefty increases in their incentive compensation in recent years ostensibly come from trying to link pay to their firms' performance. However, research also suggests that firms with a smaller pay gap between the CEO and other top level managers perform better, especially when collaboration among top management team members is more important.[2] The performance improvement in these cases is due to better cooperation among the top management team members. Other research suggests that CEOs receive excessive compensation when corporate governance is the weakest.[3]

Corporate governance is the set of mechanisms used to manage the relationship among stakeholders and to determine and control the strategic direction and performance of organizations.[4] At its core, corporate governance is concerned with identifying ways to ensure that strategic decisions are made effectively.[5] Governance can also be thought of as a means to establish harmony between parties (the firm's owners and its top-level managers) whose interests may conflict. In modern corporations—especially those in the United States and the United Kingdom—a primary objective of corporate governance is to ensure that the interests of top-level managers are aligned with the interests of the shareholders. Corporate governance involves oversight in areas where owners, managers, and members of boards of directors may have conflicts of interest. These areas include the election of directors, the general supervision of CEO pay and more focused supervision of director pay, and the corporation's overall structure and strategic direction.[6]

Recent emphasis on corporate governance stems mainly from the failure of corporate governance mechanisms to adequately monitor and control top-level managers' decisions. This situation results in changes in governance mechanisms in corporations throughout the world, especially with respect to efforts intended to improve the performance of boards of directors. A second and more positive reason for this interest comes from evidence that a well-functioning corporate governance and control system can create a competitive advantage for an individual firm.[7] Thus, in this chapter, we describe actions designed to implement strategies that focus on monitoring and controlling mechanisms that are designed to ensure that top-level managerial actions contribute to the firm's strategic competitiveness and its ability to earn above-average returns.

Effective corporate governance is also of interest to nations.[8] Although corporate governance reflects company standards, it also collectively reflects country societal standards.[9] As with these firms and their boards, nations that effectively govern their corporations may gain a competitive advantage over rival countries. In a range of countries, but especially in the United States and the United Kingdom, the fundamental goal of business organizations is to maximize shareholder value.[10] Traditionally, shareholders are treated as the firm's key stakeholders, because they are the company's legal owners. The firm's owners expect top-level managers and others influencing the corporation's actions (e.g., the board of directors) to make decisions that will maximize the company's value and, hence, the owners' wealth.[11] Research shows that national models of corporate governance influence firms' decisions to invest and operate in different countries.[12]

In the first section of this chapter, we describe the relationship that is the foundation on which the modern corporation is built: the relationship between owners and managers. The majority of this chapter is used to explain various mechanisms owners use to govern managers and to ensure that they comply with their responsibility to maximize shareholder value.

Corporate governance is the set of mechanisms used to manage the relationship among stakeholders and to determine and control the strategic direction and performance of organizations.

Three internal governance mechanisms and a single external one are used in the modern corporation. The three internal governance mechanisms we describe in this chapter are (1) ownership concentration, represented by types of shareholders and their different incentives to monitor managers; (2) the board of directors; and (3) executive compensation. We then consider the market for corporate control, an external corporate governance mechanism. Essentially, this market is a set of potential owners seeking to acquire undervalued firms and earn above-average returns on their investments by replacing ineffective top-level management teams.[13] The chapter's focus then shifts to the issue of international corporate governance. We briefly describe governance approaches used in German, Japanese, and Chinese firms whose traditional governance structures are being affected by the realities of global competition. In part, this discussion suggests that the structures used to govern global companies in many different countries, including Germany, Japan, the United Kingdom, and the United States, as well as emerging economies such as China and India, are becoming more, rather than less, similar. Closing our analysis of corporate governance is a consideration of the need for these control mechanisms to encourage and support ethical behavior in organizations.

Importantly, the mechanisms discussed in this chapter can positively influence the governance of the modern corporation, which has placed significant responsibility and authority in the hands of top-level managers. With multiple governance mechanisms operating simultaneously, however, it is also possible for some of the governance mechanisms to be in conflict.[14] Later, we review how these conflicts can occur.

Separation of Ownership and Managerial Control

Historically, U.S. firms were managed by the founder-owners and their descendants. In these cases, corporate ownership and control resided in the same persons. As firms grew larger, "the managerial revolution led to a separation of ownership and control in most large corporations, where control of the firm shifted from entrepreneurs to professional managers while ownership became dispersed among thousands of unorganized stockholders who were removed from the day-to-day management of the firm."[15] These changes created the modern public corporation, which is based on the efficient separation of ownership and managerial control. Supporting the separation is a basic legal premise suggesting that the primary objective of a firm's activities is to increase the corporation's profit and, thereby, the financial gains of the owners (the shareholders).[16]

The separation of ownership and managerial control allows shareholders to purchase stock, which entitles them to income (residual returns) from the firm's operations after paying expenses. This right, however, requires that they also take a risk that the firm's expenses may exceed its revenues. In order to manage this investment risk, shareholders maintain a diversified portfolio by investing in several companies to reduce their overall risk.[17] The poor performance or failure of any one firm in which they invest has less overall effect on the value of the entire portfolio of investments. Thus, shareholders specialize in managing their investment risk.

In small firms, managers often are high percentage owners, which means less separation between ownership and managerial control. In fact, in a large number of family-owned firms, ownership and managerial control are not separated. In the United States, at least one-third of the S&P 500 firms have substantial family ownership, holding on average about 18 percent of the outstanding equity. And family-owned firms perform better when a member of the family is the CEO than when the CEO is an outsider.[18] In many countries outside the United States, such as in Latin America, Asia, and some European countries, family-owned firms represent the dominant form.[19] The primary purpose of most of these firms is to increase the family's wealth, which explains why a family CEO often is better than an outside CEO.

Family-controlled firms face at least two critical issues. First, as they grow, they may not have access to all of the skills needed to effectively manage the firm and maximize its returns for the family. Thus, they may need outsiders. Also, as they grow, they may need to seek outside capital and thus give up some of the ownership. In these cases, protection of the minority owners' rights becomes important.[20] To avoid these potential problems, when these firms grow and become more complex, their owner-managers may contract with managerial specialists. These managers make major decisions in the owners' firm and are compensated on the basis of their decision-making skills. As such, recent research suggests that firms in which families own enough equity to have influence without major control tend to make the best strategic decisions.[21]

Without owner (shareholder) specialization in risk bearing and management specialization in decision making, a firm may be limited by the abilities of its owners to manage and make effective strategic decisions. Thus, the separation and specialization of ownership (risk bearing) and managerial control (decision making) should produce the highest returns for the firm's owners.

Shareholder value is reflected by the price of the firm's stock. As stated earlier, corporate governance mechanisms, such as the board of directors, or compensation based on the performance of a firm is the reason that CEOs show general concern about the firm's stock price.

Agency Relationships

The separation between owners and managers creates an agency relationship. An **agency relationship** exists when one or more persons (the principal or principals) hire another person or persons (the agent or agents) as decision-making specialists to perform a service.[22] Thus, an agency relationship exists when one party delegates decision-making responsibility to a second party for compensation (see Figure 10.1).[23] In addition to shareholders and top-level managers, other examples of agency relationships are consultants and clients and insured and insurer. Moreover, within organizations, an agency relationship exists between managers and their employees, as well as between top level managers and the firm's owners.[24] However, in this chapter we focus on the agency relationship between the firm's owners (the principals) and top-level managers (the principals' agents) because these managers formulate and implement the firm's strategies, which have major effects on firm performance.[25]

The separation between ownership and managerial control can be problematic. Research evidence documents a variety of agency problems in the modern corporation.[26] Problems can surface because the principal and the agent have different interests and goals, or because shareholders lack direct control of large publicly traded corporations. Problems also arise when an agent makes decisions that result in the pursuit of goals that conflict with those of the principals. Thus, the separation of ownership and control potentially allows divergent interests (between principals and agents) to surface, which can lead to managerial opportunism.

Managerial opportunism is the seeking of self-interest with guile (i.e., cunning or deceit).[27] Opportunism is both an attitude (e.g., an inclination) and a set of behaviors (i.e., specific acts of self-interest).[28] It is not possible for principals to know beforehand which agents will or will not act opportunistically. The reputations of top level managers are an imperfect predictor, and opportunistic behavior cannot be observed until it has occurred. Thus, principals establish governance and control mechanisms to prevent agents from acting opportunistically, even though only a few are likely to do so. Interestingly, research suggests that when CEOs feel constrained by governance mechanisms, they are more likely to seek external advice that in turn helps them to make better strategic decisions.[29] Any time that principals delegate decision-making responsibilities to agents, the opportunity for conflicts of interest exists. Top-level managers, for example, may make strategic decisions that maximize their personal welfare and minimize

An **agency relationship** exists when one or more persons (the principal or principals) hire another person or persons (the agent or agents) as decision-making specialists to perform a service.

Managerial opportunism is the seeking of self-interest with guile (i.e., cunning or deceit).

Figure 10.1 An Agency Relationship

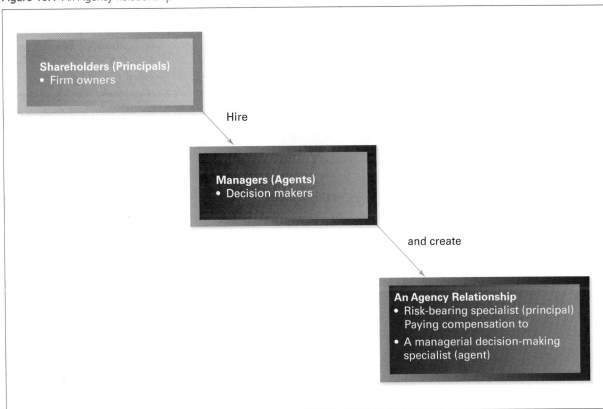

their personal risk.[30] Decisions such as these prevent the maximization of shareholder wealth. Decisions regarding product diversification demonstrate this alternative.

Product Diversification as an Example of an Agency Problem

As explained in Chapter 6, a corporate-level strategy to diversify the firm's product lines can enhance a firm's strategic competitiveness and increase its returns, both of which serve the interests of shareholders and the top-level managers. However, product diversification can result in two benefits to managers that shareholders do not enjoy, so top level managers may prefer product diversification more than shareholders do.[31]

First, diversification usually increases the size of a firm, and size is positively related to executive compensation. Also, diversification increases the complexity of managing a firm and its network of businesses, possibly requiring more pay because of this complexity.[32] Thus, increased product diversification provides an opportunity for top-level managers to increase their compensation.[33]

Second, product diversification and the resulting diversification of the firm's portfolio of businesses can reduce top-level managers' employment risk. Managerial employment risk is the risk of job loss, loss of compensation, and loss of managerial reputation.[34] These risks are reduced with increased diversification, because a firm and its upper-level managers are less vulnerable to the reduction in demand associated with a single or limited number of product lines or businesses. For example, Kellogg Co. was almost entirely focused on breakfast cereal in 2001 when it suffered its first-ever market share leadership loss to perennial number two, General Mills, Inc. Upon appointing Carlos Gutierrez, a longtime manager at Kellogg, to the CEO position, the

AP Photo/M. Spencer Green

The Kashi acquisition, one of many by Kellogg, helped drive the company's net earnings up during a recessionary economy.

company embarked on a new strategy to overcome its poor performance. A *BusinessWeek* article outlined his strategy results as follows: "To drive sales, Gutierrez unveiled such novel products as Special K snack bars, bought cookie maker Keebler Co., and ramped up Kellogg's health-foods presence by snapping up Worthington Foods Inc., a maker of soy and vegetarian products, and cereal maker Kashi. He pushed net earnings up 77 percent, to $890.6 million, from 1998 to 2004, as sales rose 42 percent, to $9.6 billion."[35] Kellogg's revenues continued to increase to approximately $13 billion a year in 2008, which was almost 8 percent higher than 2007.[36] This is a remarkable accomplishment during a recessionary economy. Kellogg's diversified scope increased, yet it was accomplished in highly related businesses that provided synergy. Through this strategy, the CEO's risk of job loss was substantially reduced. Recent research shows that this type of diversification can be profitable.[37]

Another potential agency problem is a firm's free cash flows over which top-level managers have control. Free cash flows are resources remaining after the firm has invested in all projects that have positive net present value within its current businesses.[38] In anticipation of positive returns, managers may decide to invest these funds in products that are not associated with the firm's current lines of business to increase the firm's level of diversification. The managerial decision to use free cash flows to overdiversify the firm is an example of self-serving and opportunistic managerial behavior. In contrast to managers, shareholders may prefer that free cash flows be distributed to them as dividends, so they can control how the cash is invested.[39]

Figure 10.2 Manager and Shareholder Risk and Diversification

Shareholder (business) risk profile

S

Managerial (employment) risk profile

M

Risk

A

B

Dominant business

Related-constrained

Related-linked

Unrelated businesses

Diversification

Curve *S* in Figure 10.2 depicts the shareholders' optimal level of diversification. Owners seek the level of diversification that reduces the risk of the firm's total failure while simultaneously increasing the company's value through the development of economies of scale and scope (see Chapter 6). Of the four corporate-level diversification strategies shown in Figure 10.2, shareholders likely prefer the diversified position noted by point *A* on curve *S*—a position that is located between the dominant business and related-constrained diversification strategies. Of course, the optimum level of diversification owners seek varies from firm to firm.[40] Factors that affect shareholders' preferences include the firm's primary industry, the intensity of rivalry among competitors in that industry, and the top management team's experience with implementing diversification strategies and its effects on other firm strategies, such as its entry into international markets (see Chapter 8).[41]

As do principals, top level managers—as agents—also seek an optimal level of diversification. Declining performance resulting from too much product diversification increases the probability that corporate control of the firm will be acquired in the market. After a firm is acquired, the employment risk for the firm's top-level managers increases substantially. Furthermore, a manager's employment opportunities in the external managerial labor market (discussed in Chapter 12) are affected negatively by a firm's poor performance. Therefore, top level managers prefer diversification, but not to a point that it increases their employment risk and reduces their employment opportunities.[42] Curve *M* in Figure 10.2 shows that top level managers prefer higher levels of product diversification than do shareholders. Top-level managers might prefer the level of diversification shown by point *B* on curve *M*.

In general, shareholders prefer riskier strategies and more focused diversification. They reduce their risk through holding a diversified portfolio of equity investments. Alternatively, managers cannot balance their employment risk by working for a diverse portfolio of firms, and therefore, may prefer a level of diversification that maximizes firm size and their compensation while also reducing their employment risk. Product diversification, therefore, is a potential agency problem that could result in principals incurring costs to control their agents' behaviors.

Agency Costs and Governance Mechanisms

The potential conflict illustrated by Figure 10.2, coupled with the fact that principals cannot easily predict which managers might act opportunistically, demonstrates why principals establish governance mechanisms. However, the firm incurs costs when it uses one or more governance mechanisms. **Agency costs** are the sum of incentive costs, monitoring costs, enforcement costs, and individual financial losses incurred by principals because governance mechanisms cannot guarantee total compliance by the agent. If a firm is diversified, governance costs increase because it is more difficult to monitor what is going on inside the firm.[43]

In general, managerial interests may prevail when governance mechanisms are weak; this is exemplified in situations where managers have a significant amount of autonomy to make strategic decisions. If, however, the board of directors controls managerial autonomy, or if other strong governance mechanisms are used, the firm's strategies should better reflect the interests of the shareholders. More recently, governance observers have been concerned about more egregious behavior beyond inefficient corporate strategy.

Due to fraudulent behavior such as that found at Enron and WorldCom, concerns regarding corporate governance continue to grow. In 2002, the U.S. Congress enacted the Sarbanes-Oxley (SOX) Act, which increased the intensity of corporate governance mechanisms.[44] Furthermore, the serious problems experienced in the financial services industry are likely the result of poor governance and top-level managers making very bad strategic decisions. In fact, the bonuses paid to Merrill Lynch executives after extremely poor performance (described in the Opening Case) likely reflect managerial opportunism.

Agency costs are the sum of incentive costs, monitoring costs, enforcement costs, and individual financial losses incurred by principals because governance mechanisms cannot guarantee total compliance by the agent.

While the implementation of the Sarbanes-Oxley Act in 2002 has been controversial to some, most believe that the results of it have been generally positive. Section 404 of SOX, which prescribes significant transparency improvement on internal controls associated with accounting and auditing, has arguably improved the internal auditing scrutiny and thereby trust in such financial reporting. A recent study indicated that internal controls associated with Section 404 increased shareholder value.[45] However, some argue that the Act, especially Section 404, creates excessive costs for firms. In addition, a decrease in foreign firms listing on U.S. stock exchanges occurred at the same time as listing on foreign exchanges increased. In part, this shift may be due to the costs associated with listing on U.S. exchanges associated with requirements of SOX.

More intensive application of governance mechanisms may produce significant changes in strategies. For example, because of more intense governance, firms may take on fewer risky projects and thus decrease potential shareholder wealth. Next, we explain the effects of different governance mechanisms on the decisions managers make about the choice and the use of the firm's strategies.

Ownership Concentration

Both the number of large-block shareholders and the total percentage of shares they own define **ownership concentration. Large-block shareholders** typically own at least 5 percent of a corporation's issued shares. Ownership concentration as a governance mechanism has received considerable interest because large-block shareholders are increasingly active in their demands that corporations adopt effective governance mechanisms to control managerial decisions.[46]

In general, diffuse ownership (a large number of shareholders with small holdings and few, if any, large-block shareholders) produces weak monitoring of managers' decisions. For example, diffuse ownership makes it difficult for owners to effectively coordinate their actions. Diversification of the firm's product lines beyond the shareholders' optimum level can result from ineffective monitoring of managers' decisions. Higher levels of monitoring could encourage managers to avoid strategic decisions that harm shareholder value. In fact, research evidence shows that ownership concentration is associated with lower levels of firm product diversification.[47] Thus, with high degrees of ownership concentration, the probability is greater that managers' strategic decisions will be designed to maximize shareholder value.[48]

As noted, such concentration of ownership has an influence on strategies and firm value, mostly positive but perhaps not in all cases. For example, when large shareholders have a high degree of wealth, they have power relative to minority shareholders in extracting wealth from the firm, especially when they are in managerial positions. The importance of boards of directors in mitigating expropriation of minority shareholder value has been found in firms with strong family ownership wherein family members have incentive to appropriate shareholder wealth, especially in the second generation after the founder has departed.[49] Such expropriation is often found in countries such as Korea where minority shareholder rights are not as protected as they are in the United States.[50] However, in the United States much of the ownership concentration has come from increasing equity ownership by institutional investors.

The Growing Influence of Institutional Owners

A classic work published in the 1930s argued that the "modern" corporation was characterized by a separation of ownership and control.[51] The change occurred primarily because growth prevented founders-owners from maintaining their dual positions in their increasingly complex companies. More recently, another shift has occurred: Ownership of many modern corporations is now concentrated in the hands of institutional investors rather than individual shareholders.[52]

Both the number of large-block shareholders and the total percentage of shares they own define **ownership concentration.**

Large-block shareholders typically own at least 5 percent of a corporation's issued shares.

Institutional owners are financial institutions such as stock mutual funds and pension funds that control large-block shareholder positions. Because of their prominent ownership positions, institutional owners, as large-block shareholders, are a powerful governance mechanism. Institutions of these types now own more than 60 percent of the stock in large U.S. corporations. Pension funds alone control at least one-half of corporate equity.[53]

These ownership percentages suggest that as investors, institutional owners have both the size and the incentive to discipline ineffective top-level managers and can significantly influence a firm's choice of strategies and overall strategic decisions.[54] Research evidence indicates that institutional and other large-block shareholders are becoming more active in their efforts to influence a corporation's strategic decisions, unless they have a business relationship with the firm. Initially, these shareholder activists and institutional investors concentrated on the performance and accountability of CEOs and contributed to the dismissal of a number of them. They often target the actions of boards more directly via proxy vote proposals that are intended to give shareholders more decision rights because they believe board processes have been ineffective.[55] In fact, a new rule recently proposed and approved by the U.S. Securities and Exchange Commission allows large shareholders (owning 1 to 5 percent of a company's stock) to nominate up to 25 percent of a company's board of directors.[56]

For example, CalPERS provides retirement and health coverage to more than 1.3 million current and retired public employees. At the end of 2008, it was the largest public employee pension fund in the United States, but the economic crisis caused its total assets to decrease by approximately 30 percent.[57] Still, CalPERS is respected and even feared in some companies' boardrooms. It is generally thought to act aggressively to promote governance decisions and actions that it believes will enhance shareholder value in companies in which it invests. For instance, CalPERS places five or so companies on its "Focus List" each year. This type of public acknowledgement may influence the board of directors and top-level managers to take action, which in turn often increases the firm's shareholder value. For example, the CalPERS focus list for 2009 had four firms on it led by Eli Lilly.[58] The largest institutional investor, TIAA-CREF, has taken actions similar to those of CalPERS, but with a less publicly aggressive stance. To date, research suggests that institutional activism may not have a strong effect on firm performance, but that its influence may be indirect through its effects on important strategic decisions, such as those concerned with international diversification and innovation.[59] With the increased intensity of governance associated with the passage of the SOX Act and the latest economic crisis largely created by poor strategic decisions in the financial services industry, institutional investors and other groups have been emboldened in their activism.

Board of Directors

Typically, shareholders monitor the managerial decisions and actions of a firm through the board of directors. Shareholders elect members to their firm's board. Those who are elected are expected to oversee managers and to ensure that the corporation is operated in ways that will maximize its shareholders' wealth. Even with large institutional investors having major equity ownership in U.S. firms, diffuse ownership continues to exist in most firms, which means that in large corporations, monitoring and control of managers by individual shareholders is limited. Furthermore, large financial institutions, such as banks, are prevented from directly owning stock in firms and from having representatives on companies' boards of directors, although this restriction is not the case in Europe and elsewhere.[60] These conditions highlight the importance of the board of directors for corporate governance. Unfortunately, over time, boards of directors have not been highly effective in monitoring and controlling top management's actions.[61]

Institutional owners are financial institutions such as stock mutual funds and pension funds that control large-block shareholder positions.

Given the recent problems with top-level managers making less than ethical decisions, boards are experiencing increasing pressure from shareholders, lawmakers, and regulators to become more forceful in their oversight role to prevent inappropriate actions by top-level managers. Furthermore, boards not only serve a monitoring role, but they also provide resources to firms. These resources include their personal knowledge and expertise as well as their access to resources of other firms through their external contacts and relationships.[62]

The **board of directors** is a group of elected individuals whose primary responsibility is to act in the owners' best interests by formally monitoring and controlling the corporation's top-level managers.[63] Boards have the power to direct the affairs of the organization, punish and reward managers, and protect shareholders' rights and interests. Thus, an appropriately structured and effective board of directors protects owners from managerial opportunism such as that found at Enron and WorldCom and at financial services firms including AIG and Merrill Lynch, where shareholders and employees encountered significant losses. Board members are seen as stewards of their company's resources, and the way they carry out these responsibilities affects the society in which their firm operates. For instance, research suggests that better governance produces more effective strategic decisions, which lead to higher firm performance.[64]

Generally, board members (often called directors) are classified into one of three groups (see Table 10.1). *Insiders* are active top-level managers in the corporation who are elected to the board because they are a source of information about the firm's day-to-day operations.[65] *Related outsiders* have some relationship with the firm, contractual or otherwise, that may create questions about their independence, but these individuals are not involved with the corporation's day-to-day activities. *Outsiders* provide independent counsel to the firm and may hold top-level managerial positions in other companies or may have been elected to the board prior to the beginning of the current CEO's tenure.[66]

Historically, boards of directors were primarily dominated by inside managers. A widely accepted view is that a board with a significant percentage of its membership from the firm's top-level managers provides relatively weak monitoring and control of managerial decisions.[67] Managers have sometimes used their power to select and compensate directors and exploit their personal ties with them. In response to the SEC's proposal to require audit committees to be composed of outside directors, in 1984, the New York Stock Exchange implemented a rule requiring outside directors to head the audit committee. Subsequently, other rules required important committees such as the compensation committee and the nomination committee to be headed by independent outside directors.[68] These other requirements were instituted after the Sarbanes-Oxley Act was passed, and policies of the New York Stock Exchange now require companies to maintain boards of directors that are composed of a majority of outside independent directors and to maintain full independent audit committees. Thus, corporate governance is becoming more intense especially with the oversight of the board of directors.

Table 10.1 Classifications of Board of Director Members

Insiders
• The firm's CEO and other top-level managers
Related outsiders
• Individuals not involved with the firm's day-to-day operations, but who have a relationship with the company
Outsiders
• Individuals who are independent of the firm in terms of day-to-day operations and other relationships

The **board of directors** is a group of elected individuals whose primary responsibility is to act in the owners' interests by formally monitoring and controlling the corporation's top-level managers.

Critics advocate reforms to ensure that independent outside directors represent a significant majority of the total membership of a board, which research suggests has been accomplished.[69] On the other hand, others argue that having outside directors is not enough to resolve the problems; it depends on the power of the CEO. One proposal to reduce the power of the CEO is to separate the chairperson's role and the CEO's role on the board so that the same person does not hold both positions.[70] Yet, having a board that actively monitors top executive decisions and actions does not ensure high performance. The value that the directors bring to the company also influences the outcomes. For example, boards with members having significant relevant experience and knowledge are the most likely to help the firm formulate effective strategies and to implement them successfully.[71]

Alternatively, having a large number of outside board members can also create some problems. Outsiders do not have contact with the firm's day-to-day operations and typically do not have easy access to the level of information about managers and their skills that is required to effectively evaluate managerial decisions and initiatives.[72] Outsiders can, however, obtain valuable information through frequent interactions with inside board members, during board meetings, and otherwise. Insiders possess such information by virtue of their organizational positions. Thus, boards with a critical mass of insiders typically are better informed about intended strategic initiatives, the reasons for the initiatives, and the outcomes expected from them.[73] Without this type of information, outsider-dominated boards may emphasize the use of financial, as opposed to strategic, controls to gather performance information to evaluate managers' and business units' performances. A virtually exclusive reliance on financial evaluations shifts risk to top-level managers, who, in turn, may make decisions to maximize their interests and reduce their employment risk. Reductions in R&D investments, additional diversification of the firm, and the pursuit of greater levels of compensation are some of the results of managers' actions to achieve financial goals set by outsider-dominated boards.[74] Additionally, boards can make mistakes in CEO succession decisions because of the lack of important information about candidates as well as specific needs of the firm. As you would expect, knowledgeable and balanced boards are likely to be the most effective over time.[75]

Enhancing the Effectiveness of the Board of Directors

As explained in the Strategic Focus, because of the importance of boards of directors in corporate governance and as a result of increased scrutiny from shareholders—in particular, large institutional investors—the performances of individual board members and of entire boards are being evaluated more formally and with greater intensity.[76] Given the demand for greater accountability and improved performance, many boards have initiated voluntary changes (e.g., those described at Borders and EasyJet). Among these changes are (1) increases in the diversity of the backgrounds of board members (e.g., a greater number of directors from public service, academic, and scientific settings; a greater percentage of ethnic minorities and women; and members from different countries on boards of U.S. firms), (2) the strengthening of internal management and accounting control systems, and (3) the establishment and consistent use of formal processes to evaluate the board's performance.[77] Additional changes include (4) the creation of a "lead director" role that has strong powers with regard to the board agenda and oversight of non-management board member activities, and (5) modification of the compensation of directors, especially reducing or eliminating stock options as a part of the package.

Boards are increasingly involved in the strategic decision-making process, so they must work collaboratively. Some argue that improving the processes used by boards to make decisions and monitor managers and firm outcomes is important for board effectiveness.[78] Moreover, because of the increased pressure from owners and the potential

WHERE HAVE ALL THE GOOD DIRECTORS GONE?

The global economic crisis, largely the result of extremely poor strategic decisions made by top-level managers in the financial services industry, laid bare the holes in the U.S. corporate governance system. In particular, the crisis showed that many boards of directors were very weak. In the early 2000s, boards of directors suffered significant criticism for the failures in monitoring executive actions at Enron, Tyco, WorldCom, and other companies. With more recent failures, boards are now experiencing substantial public animosity. Many people do not understand how top-level managers were allowed to take the extreme risks that have melted away corporate value when the debt became too heavy for most of the firms.

The weakness of corporate boards is exemplified by the fact that the President of the United States had to fire a highly ineffective CEO because the board of General Motors had failed to act in recent years.

As a result of the economic meltdown, the obviously poor strategic decisions leading to it, and the inability of previous boards to prevent the problems, many boards are now changing. Old board members are resigning or being replaced and many new members are joining boards. For example, in 2009, Citigroup, one of the major contributors to the problems in the financial services industry, nominated four new independent directors. Boardroom shakeups are also occurring outside of the financial services industry. For example, EasyJet announced that it had appointed a new chairman of its board to replace the current chairman, Colin Chandler. The new chairman, Michael Rake, formerly headed the BT Group.

In an industry challenged by technology developments and the recession, Borders has suffered the most. Its poor financial results are the outcome of its inability to keep pace. Thus, in 2009, Borders made major changes in the top management team and announced that seven of its ten directors were departing. Only five of them will be replaced, thereby shrinking the number of members on the board to eight. The former executive team and board tried unsuccessfully to sell the firm. The new team will focus on restructuring the firm.

Interestingly, research suggests that smaller boards are more effective in governing companies than are larger boards. Thus, Borders' decision to downsize its board may be a good one. Changes are being made in the processes used by many boards in order to improve their monitoring function. These changes extend to the balance of independent and inside members, renewed emphasis on audit and compensation committees, and ensuring that outside board members spend an adequate amount of time on board business so that they can make informed decisions. Furthermore, there are other moves afoot to change the governance practices in firms. These include new rules and a renewed scrutiny by the U.S. Securities and Exchange Commission and other governmental agencies. In addition, the chairman of the Financial Reporting Council in the United Kingdom announced a complete review of the Combined Code, a template of corporate governance used by investors and

Rick Wagoner is the former CEO of GM, who was asked to resign by President Obama.

William Thomas Cain/Getty Image News/Getty Images

listed companies. In fact, the code is commonly used by institutional investors to evaluate the boards of companies. In addition, the Institute of Company Secretaries announced plans to strengthen the norms for corporate governance practices in India.

Sources: J. A. Trachtenberg, 2009, Borders plans to install new board, *Wall Street Journal*, http://www.wsj.com, April 16; K. Shwiff, 2009, Egan-Jones urges vote against Citi directors, *Wall Street Journal*, http://www.wsj.com, April 13; J. Espinoza, 2009, EasyJet shakes up boardroom, *Forbes*, http://www.forbes.com, April 6; 2009, ICSI plans governance norms, *Business Standard*, http://www.business-standard.com, April 5; D. Serchuk, 2009, Where are Wall Street's directors? *Forbes*, http://www.forbes.com, March 31; M. Costello, 2009, New boardroom code to "draw on lessons" from bank crisis, *The Times*, http://www.business.timesonline.co.uk, March 18; 2009, Directors under fire, *Stuff*, http://www.stuff.co.nz, March 10.

conflict among board members, procedures are necessary to help boards function effectively in facilitating the strategic decision-making process.

Increasingly, outside directors are being required to own significant equity stakes as a prerequisite to holding a board seat. In fact, some research suggests that firms perform better if outside directors have such a stake; the trend is toward higher pay for directors with more stock ownership, but with fewer stock options.[79] However, other research suggests that too much ownership can lead to lower independence for board members.[80] In addition, other research suggests that diverse boards help firms make more effective strategic decisions and perform better over time.[81] Although questions remain about whether more independent and diverse boards enhance board effectiveness, the trends for greater independence and increasing diversity among board members are likely to continue. Clearly, the corporate failures in the first decade of the 21st century suggest the need for more effective boards.

Executive Compensation

As the Opening Case illustrates, the compensation of top-level managers, and especially of CEOs, generates a great deal of interest and strongly held opinions. One reason for this widespread interest can be traced to a natural curiosity about extremes and excesses. For example, the *Los Angeles Times* reported that "CEO compensation tripled from 1990 to 2004, rising at more than three times the rate of corporate earnings. CEOs at 11 of the largest U.S. companies received $865 million in a five-year period while presiding over losses in shareholder value."[82] As stated in the Opening Case, the ten highest-paid executives in 2008, during a strong recession, earned an average of $47.22 million. Some consider this excessive pay, especially for those whose firms suffered net losses during this year, because most firms lost market value in 2008. Another stems from a more substantive view that CEO pay is tied in an indirect but tangible way to the fundamental governance processes in large corporations. Some believe that while highly paid, CEOs are not overpaid.[83] Others argue that not only are they highly paid, they are overpaid. These critics are especially concerned that compensation is not as strongly related to performance as some believe.[84]

Executive compensation is a governance mechanism that seeks to align the interests of managers and owners through salaries, bonuses, and long-term incentive compensation, such as stock awards and options.[85] Long-term incentive plans have become a critical part of compensation packages in U.S. firms. The use of longer-term pay theoretically helps firms cope with or avoid potential agency problems by linking managerial wealth to the wealth of common shareholders.[86]

Sometimes the use of a long-term incentive plan prevents major stockholders (e.g., institutional investors) from pressing for changes in the composition of the board of directors, because they assume the long-term incentives will ensure that top executives will act in shareholders' best interests. Alternatively, stockholders largely assume that top-executive pay and the performance of a firm are more closely aligned when firms have boards that are dominated by outside members. However, research shows that fraudulent behavior can be associated with stock option incentives, such as earnings manipulation.[87]

STRATEGY RIGHT NOW

Read further about the GM bankruptcy and what it means for its board of directors moving forward.

www.cengage.com/management/hitt

Executive compensation is a governance mechanism that seeks to align the interests of managers and owners through salaries, bonuses, and long-term incentive compensation, such as stock awards and options.

Effectively using executive compensation as a governance mechanism is particularly challenging to firms implementing international strategies. For example, the interests of owners of multinational corporations may be best served by less uniformity among the firm's foreign subsidiaries' compensation plans.[88] Developing an array of unique compensation plans requires additional monitoring and increases the firm's potential agency costs. Importantly, levels of pay vary by regions of the world. For example, managerial pay is highest in the United States and much lower in Asia. Compensation is lower in India partly because many of the largest firms have strong family ownership and control.[89] As corporations acquire firms in other countries, the managerial compensation puzzle for boards becomes more complex and may cause additional governance problems.[90]

The Effectiveness of Executive Compensation

Executive compensation—especially long-term incentive compensation—is complicated for several reasons. First, the strategic decisions made by top-level managers are typically complex and nonroutine, so direct supervision of executives is inappropriate for judging the quality of their decisions. The result is a tendency to link the compensation of top-level managers to measurable outcomes, such as the firm's financial performance. Second, an executive's decision often affects a firm's financial outcomes over an extended period, making it difficult to assess the effect of current decisions on the corporation's performance. In fact, strategic decisions are more likely to have long-term, rather than short-term, effects on a company's strategic outcomes. Third, a number of other factors affect a firm's performance besides top-level managerial decisions and behavior. Unpredictable economic, social, or legal changes (see Chapter 2) make it difficult to identify the effects of strategic decisions. Thus, although performance-based compensation may provide incentives to top management teams to make decisions that best serve shareholders' interests, such compensation plans alone cannot fully control managers. Still, incentive compensation represents a significant portion of many executives' total pay.

Although incentive compensation plans may increase the value of a firm in line with shareholder expectations, such plans are subject to managerial manipulation.[91] Additionally, annual bonuses may provide incentives to pursue short-run objectives at the expense of the firm's long-term interests. Although long-term, performance-based incentives may reduce the temptation to under-invest in the short run, they increase executive exposure to risks associated with uncontrollable events, such as market fluctuations and industry decline. The longer term the focus of incentive compensation, the greater are the long-term risks borne by top-level managers. Also, because long-term incentives tie a manager's overall wealth to the firm in a way that is inflexible, such incentives and ownership may not be valued as highly by a manager as by outside investors who have the opportunity to diversify their wealth in a number of other financial investments.[92] Thus, firms may have to overcompensate for managers using long-term incentives.

Even though some stock option–based compensation plans are well designed with option strike prices substantially higher than current stock prices, some have been designed with the primary purpose of giving executives more compensation. Research of stock option repricing where the strike price value of the option has been lowered from its original position suggests that action is taken more frequently in high-risk situations.[93] However, repricing also happens when firm performance is poor, to restore the incentive effect for the option. Evidence also suggests that politics are often involved, which has resulted in "option backdating."[94] While this evidence shows that no internal governance mechanism is perfect, some compensation plans accomplish their purpose. For example, recent research suggests that long-term pay designed to encourage managers to be environmentally friendly has been linked to higher success in preventing pollution.[95]

Stock options became highly popular as a means of compensating top executives and linking pay with performance, but they also have become controversial of late as indicated in the Opening Case. Because all internal governance mechanisms are imperfect, external mechanisms are also needed. One such governance device is the market for corporate control.

Market for Corporate Control

The **market for corporate control** is an external governance mechanism that becomes active when a firm's internal controls fail.[96] The market for corporate control is composed of individuals and firms that buy ownership positions in or take over potentially undervalued corporations so they can form new divisions in established diversified companies or merge two previously separate firms. Because the undervalued firm's top-level managers are assumed to be responsible for formulating and implementing the strategy that led to poor performance, they are usually replaced. Thus, when the market for corporate control operates effectively, it ensures that managers who are ineffective or act opportunistically are disciplined.[97]

The takeover market as a source of external discipline is used only when internal governance mechanisms are relatively weak and have proven to be ineffective. Alternatively, other research suggests that the rationale for takeovers as a corporate governance strategy is not as strong as the rationale for takeovers as an ownership investment in target candidates where the firm is performing well and does not need discipline.[98] A study of active corporate raiders in the 1980s showed that takeover attempts often were focused on above-average performance firms in an industry.[99] Taken together, this research suggests that takeover targets are not always low performers with weak governance. As such, the market for corporate control may not be as efficient as a governance device as theory suggests.[100] At the very least, internal governance controls are much more precise relative to this external control mechanism.

Hedge funds have become a source of activist investors as noted in Chapter 7. An enormous amount of money has been invested in hedge funds, and because it is significantly more difficult to gain high returns in the market, hedge funds turned to activism. Likewise in a competitive environment characterized by a greater willingness on part of investors to hold underperforming managers accountable, hedge funds have been given license for increased activity.[101] Traditionally, hedge funds are a portfolio of stocks or bonds, or both, managed by an individual or a team on behalf of a large number of investors. Activism allows them to influence the market by taking a large position in seeking to drive the stock price up in a short period of time and then sell. Most hedge funds have been unregulated relative to the Securities and Exchange Commission because they represent a set of private investors. However, the recent economic crisis has increased the scrutiny of hedge funds' actions by government regulatory bodies.

Although the market for corporate control may be a blunt instrument for corporate governance, the takeover market continues to be active even in the economic crisis. In fact, the more intense governance environment has fostered an increasingly active takeover market. Certainly, the government has played a highly active role in the acquisitions of major U.S. financial institutions (e.g., Merrill Lynch's acquisition by Bank of America). Target firms earn a substantial premium over the acquiring firm.[102] At the same time, managers who have ownership positions or stock options are likely to gain in making a transaction with an acquiring firm. Even more evidence indicates that this type of gain may be the case, given the increasing number of firms that have golden parachutes that allow up to three years of additional compensation plus other incentives if a firm is taken over. These compensation contracts reduce the risk for managers if a firm is taken over. Private equity firms often seek to obtain a lower price in the market through initiating friendly takeover deals. The target firm's top-level managers may be amenable to such

The **market for corporate control** is an external governance mechanism that becomes active when a firm's internal controls fail.

"friendly" deals because not only do they get the payout through a golden parachute, but at their next firm they may get a "golden hello" as a signing bonus to work for the new firm.[103] Golden parachutes help them leave, but "golden hellos are increasingly needed to get them in the door" of the next firm.[104] Although the 1980s had more defenses put up against hostile takeovers, the more recent environment has been much friendlier. However, the recent economic crisis has led to significant criticism of golden parachutes, especially for executives of poorly performing firms. For example, there was significant criticism of the large bonuses paid to Merrill Lynch managers after the acquisition by Bank of America. This is because of the huge loss suffered by Merrill Lynch because of poor strategic decisions executed by these managers. Furthermore, there were issues with AIG, which received billions of dollars in government support to stay afloat yet paid huge managerial bonuses. As a result of the criticism, the firm cancelled its $10 million golden parachute for its departing CFO, Steven Bensinger.[105]

The market for corporate control governance mechanisms should be triggered by a firm's poor performance relative to industry competitors. A firm's poor performance, often demonstrated by the firm's below-average returns, is an indicator that internal governance mechanisms have failed; that is, their use did not result in managerial decisions that maximized shareholder value. Yet, although these acquisitions often involve highly underperforming firms and the changes needed may appear obvious, there are no guarantees of success. The acquired firm's assets still must be integrated effectively into the acquiring firm's operation to earn positive returns from the takeover. Also, integration is an exceedingly complex challenge.[106] Even active acquirers often fail to earn positive returns from some of their acquisitions, but some acquirers are successful and earn significant returns from the assets they acquire.[107]

Target firm managers and members of the boards of directors are commonly sensitive about hostile takeover bids. It frequently means that they have not done an effective job in managing the company. If they accept the offer, they are likely to lose their jobs; the acquiring firm will insert its own management. If they reject the offer and fend off the takeover attempt, they must improve the performance of the firm or risk losing their jobs as well.[108]

Managerial Defense Tactics

Hostile takeovers are the major activity in the market for corporate control governance mechanism. Not all hostile takeovers are prompted by poorly performing targets, and firms targeted for hostile takeovers may use multiple defense tactics to fend off the takeover attempt. Historically, the increased use of the market for corporate control has enhanced the sophistication and variety of managerial defense tactics that are used in takeovers. The market for corporate control tends to increase risk for managers. As a result, managerial pay is often augmented indirectly through golden parachutes (wherein, a CEO can receive up to three years' salary if his or her firm is taken over). Golden parachutes, similar to most other defense tactics, are controversial.

Among other outcomes, takeover defenses increase the costs of mounting a takeover, causing the incumbent management to become entrenched while reducing the chances of introducing a new management team.[109] One takeover defense is traditionally known as a "poison pill." This defense mechanism usually allows shareholders (other than the acquirer) to convert "shareholders' rights" into a large number of common shares if anyone acquires

Merrill Lynch's acquisition by Bank of America has not been without controversy, including the awarding of large bonuses to Merrill Lynch managers after the acquisition despite enormous losses.

James Leynse/Documentary Value/CORBIS

more than a set amount of the target's stock (typically 10 to 20 percent). This move dilutes the percentage of shares that the acquiring firm must purchase at a premium and in effect raises the cost of the deal for the acquiring firm.

Table 10.2 lists a number of additional takeover defense strategies. Some defense tactics necessitate only changes in the financial structure of the firm, such as repurchasing shares of the firm's outstanding stock.[110] Some tactics (e.g., reincorporation of the firm in another state) require shareholder approval, but the greenmail tactic, wherein money is used to repurchase stock from a corporate raider to avoid the takeover of the firm, does not. Some firms use rotating board member elections as a defense tactic where only one third of members are up for reelection each year. Research shows that this results in managerial entrenchment and reduced vulnerability to hostile takeovers.[111]

Most institutional investors oppose the use of defense tactics. TIAA-CREF and CalPERS have taken actions to have several firms' poison pills eliminated. Many institutional investors also oppose severance packages (golden parachutes), and the opposition is growing significantly in Europe as well.[112] However, as previously noted, an advantage to severance packages is that they may encourage top level managers to accept takeover bids that are attractive to shareholders.[113] Alternatively, recent research has shown that the use of takeover defenses reduces pressure experienced by managers for short-term performance gains. As such, managers engage in longer-term strategies and pay more

Table 10.2 Hostile Takeover Defense Strategies

Defense strategy	Category	Popularity among firms	Effectiveness as a defense	Stockholder wealth effects
Poison pill Preferred stock in the merged firm offered to shareholders at a highly attractive rate of exchange.	Preventive	High	High	Positive
Corporate charter amendment An amendment to stagger the elections of members to the board of directors of the attacked firm so that all are not elected during the same year, which prevents a bidder from installing a completely new board in the same year.	Preventive	Medium	Very low	Negative
Golden parachute Lump-sum payments of cash that are distributed to a select group of senior executives when the firm is acquired in a takeover bid.	Preventive	Medium	Low	Negligible
Litigation Lawsuits that help a target company stall hostile attacks; areas may include antitrust, fraud, inadequate disclosure.	Reactive	Medium	Low	Positive
Greenmail The repurchase of shares of stock that have been acquired by the aggressor at a premium in exchange for an agreement that the aggressor will no longer target the company for takeover.	Reactive	Very low	Medium	Negative
Standstill agreement Contract between the parties in which the pursuer agrees not to acquire any more stock of the target firm for a specified period of time in exchange for the firm paying the pursuer a fee.	Reactive	Low	Low	Negative
Capital structure change Dilution of stock, making it more costly for a bidder to acquire; may include employee stock option plans (ESOPs), recapitalization, new debt, stock selling, share buybacks.	Reactive	Medium	Medium	Inconclusive

Source: J. A. Pearce II & R. B. Robinson, Jr., 2004, Hostile takeover defenses that maximize shareholder wealth, *Business Horizons*, 47(5): 15–24.

attention to the firm's stakeholders. When they do this, the firm's market value increases, which rewards the shareholders.[114]

A potential problem with the market for corporate control is that it may not be totally efficient. A study of several of the most active corporate raiders in the 1980s showed that approximately 50 percent of their takeover attempts targeted firms with above-average performance in their industry—corporations that were neither under-valued nor poorly managed.[115] The targeting of high-performance businesses may lead to acquisitions at premium prices and to decisions by managers of the targeted firm to establish what may prove to be costly takeover defense tactics to protect their corporate positions.[116]

Although the market for corporate control lacks the precision of internal governance mechanisms, the fear of acquisition and influence by corporate raiders is an effective constraint on the managerial-growth motive. The market for corporate control has been responsible for significant changes in many firms' strategies and, when used appropriately, has served shareholders' interests. But this market and other means of corporate governance vary by region of the world and by country. Accordingly, we next address the topic of international corporate governance.

International Corporate Governance

Understanding the corporate governance structure of the United Kingdom and the United States is inadequate for a multinational firm in the current global economy.[117] The stability associated with German and Japanese governance structures has historically been viewed as an asset, but the governance systems in these countries are changing, similar to other parts of the world. The importance of these changes has been heightened by the global economic crisis.[118] These changes are partly the result of multinational firms operating in many different countries and attempting to develop a more global governance system.[119] Although the similarity among national governance systems is increasing, significant differences remain evident, and firms employing an international strategy must understand these differences in order to operate effectively in different international markets.[120]

Corporate Governance in Germany and Japan

In many private German firms, the owner and manager may still be the same individual. In these instances, agency problems are not present.[121] Even in publicly traded German corporations, a single shareholder is often dominant. Thus, the concentration of ownership is an important means of corporate governance in Germany, as it is in the United States.[122]

Historically, banks occupied the center of the German corporate governance structure, as is also the case in many other European countries, such as Italy and France. As lenders, banks become major shareholders when companies they financed earlier seek funding on the stock market or default on loans. Although the stakes are usually less than 10 percent, banks can hold a single ownership position up to but not exceeding 15 percent of the bank's capital. Shareholders can tell the banks how to vote their own-ership position, they generally do not do so. The banks monitor and control managers, both as lenders and as shareholders, by electing representatives to supervisory boards.

German firms with more than 2,000 employees are required to have a two-tiered board structure that places the responsibility for monitoring and controlling managerial (or supervisory) decisions and actions in the hands of a separate group.[123] All the functions of strategy and management are the responsibility of the management board (the Vorstand), but appointment to the Vorstand is the responsibility of the supervisory tier (the Aufsichtsrat). Employees, union members, and shareholders appoint members to the Aufsichtsrat. Proponents of the German structure suggest that it helps prevent corporate wrongdoing and rash decisions by "dictatorial CEOs." However, critics maintain that it slows decision making and often ties a CEO's hands. The corporate governance framework in Germany has made it difficult to restructure companies as quickly as can be done in the United States when performance suffers. Because of the role of local government (through the board structure) and the power of banks in Germany's corporate governance structure, private shareholders rarely have major ownership positions in German firms. Large institutional investors, such as pension funds and insurance companies, are also relatively insignificant owners of corporate stock. Thus, at least historically, German executives generally have not been dedicated to the maximization of shareholder value that occurs in many countries.[124]

However, corporate governance in Germany is changing, at least partially, because of the increasing globalization of business. Many German firms are beginning to gravitate toward the U.S. system. Recent research suggests that the traditional system produced some agency costs because of a lack of external ownership power. Interestingly, German firms with listings on the U.S. stock exchange have increasingly adopted executive stock option compensation as a long-term incentive pay policy.[125]

Attitudes toward corporate governance in Japan are affected by the concepts of obligation, family, and consensus.[126] In Japan, an obligation "may be to return a service for one rendered or it may derive from a more general relationship, for example, to one's family or old alumni, or one's company (or Ministry), or the country. This sense of particular obligation is common elsewhere but it feels stronger in Japan."[127] As part of a company family, individuals are members of a unit that envelops their lives; families command the attention and allegiance of parties throughout corporations. Moreover, a *keiretsu* (a group of firms tied together by cross-shareholdings) is more than an economic concept; it, too, is a family. Consensus, an important influence in Japanese corporate governance, calls for the expenditure of significant amounts of energy to win the hearts and minds of people whenever possible, as opposed to top executives issuing edicts.[128] Consensus is highly valued, even when it results in a slow and cumbersome decision-making process.

As in Germany, banks in Japan play an important role in financing and monitoring large public firms.[129] The bank owning the largest share of stocks and the largest amount of debt—the main bank—has the closest relationship with the company's top executives. The main bank provides financial advice to the firm and also closely monitors managers. Thus, Japan has a bank-based financial and corporate governance structure, whereas the United States has a market-based financial and governance structure.[130]

Aside from lending money, a Japanese bank can hold up to 5 percent of a firm's total stock; a group of related financial institutions can hold up to 40 percent. In many cases, main-bank relationships are part of a horizontal keiretsu. A keiretsu firm usually owns less than 2 percent of any other member firm; however, each company typically has a stake of that size in every firm in the keiretsu. As a result, somewhere between 30 and 90 percent of a firm is owned by other members of the keiretsu. Thus, a keiretsu is a system of relationship investments.

As is the case in Germany, Japan's structure of corporate governance is changing. For example, because of Japanese banks' continuing development as economic organizations, their role in the monitoring and control of managerial behavior and firm outcomes is less significant than in the past.[131] Also, deregulation in the financial sector reduced the cost of mounting hostile takeovers.[132] As such, deregulation facilitated more activity in Japan's market for corporate control, which was nonexistent in past years.[133] Interestingly, however, recent research shows that CEOs of both public and private companies in Japan receive similar levels of compensation and their compensation is tied closely to observable performance goals.[134]

Corporate Governance in China

Corporate governance in China has changed dramatically in the past decade, as has the privatization of business and the development of the equity market. The stock markets in China are young. In their early years, these markets were weak because of significant insider trading. However, research has shown that they have improved with stronger governance in recent years.[135] The Chinese institutional environment is unique. While there has been a gradual decline in the equity held in state-owned enterprises and the number and percentage of private firms have grown, the state still dominates the strategies employed by most firms through direct or indirect controls.

Recent research shows that firms with higher state ownership tend to have lower market value and more volatility in those values over time. This is because of agency conflicts in the firms and because the executives do not seek to maximize shareholder returns. They also have social goals they must meet placed on them by the government.[136] This suggests a potential conflict between the principals, particularly the state owner and the private equity owners of the state-owned enterprises.[137]

The Chinese governance system has been moving toward the Western model in recent years. For example, China YCT International recently announced that it was strengthening its corporate governance, with the establishment of an audit committee within its board of directors, and appointing three new independent directors.[138] In addition, recent research shows that the compensation of top executives of Chinese companies is closely related to prior and current financial performance of the firm.[139] While state ownership and indirect controls complicate governance in Chinese companies, research in other countries suggests that some state ownership in recently privatized firms provides some benefits. It signals support and temporarily buoys stock prices, but over time continued state ownership and involvement tend to have negative effects on the stock price.[140] Thus, the corporate governance system in China and the heavy oversight of the Chinese government will need to be observed to determine the long-term effects.

Global Corporate Governance

As noted in the Strategic Focus, corporate governance is becoming an increasingly important issue in economies around the world, even in emerging economies. The problems with Satyam in India could be repeated in other parts of the world if diligence in governance is not exercised. This concern is stronger because of the globalization in trade, investments, and equity markets. Countries and major companies based in them want to attract foreign investment. To do so, the foreign investors must be confident of adequate corporate governance. Effective corporate governance is also required to attract domestic investors. Although many times domestic shareholders will vote with management, as activist foreign investors enter a country it gives domestic institutional investors the courage to become more active in shareholder proposals, which will increase shareholder welfare.

For example, Steel Partners, LLC, focused its attention on Korean cigarette maker KT&G. Warren Lichtenstein of Steel Partners and Carl Icahn pressured KT&G to increase its market value. Lichtenstein and Icahn began their activism in February 2006, by nominating a slate of board directors as well as pushing KT&G to sell off its lucrative Ginseng unit, which manufactures popular herbal products in Korea. They also demanded that the company sell off its real estate assets, raise its dividends, and buy back common shares. Lichtenstein and Icahn threatened a hostile tender offer if their demands were not met. Shareholders showed support for Steel Partners' activism such that they elected Lichtenstein to KT&G's board. In 2008, Lichtenstein resigned from the board with the election of four new independent directors. During his service on the board, KT&G's market value increased and its corporate governance improved. [141] Steel Partners recently targeted Aderans Holdings Company Limited in Japan for major changes. Steel Partners is Aderans's largest shareholder with about 27 percent of the outstanding stock. Steel Partners is unhappy with Aderans's efforts to turnaround its performance and has proposed replacing most of its board members and undergoing

THE SATYAM TRUTH: CEO FRAUD AND CORPORATE GOVERNANCE FAILURE

In 2008, Satyam was India's fourth largest IT company with clients around the world. The firm provided IT services to more than one third of the *Fortune 500* companies. The company and its founder and CEO, Ramalinga Raju, were well known and respected. In September 2008, Raju was named the Ernst & Young Entrepreneur of the Year. On December 16, 2008, he was given the Golden Peacock Award for Corporate Governance and Compliance. But then his term as CEO started to unravel.

On December 17, 2008, Raju announced plans to acquire two companies, Maytas Infra and Maytas Properties, both owned by members of his family. The rationale was to diversify Satyam's business portfolio to avoid being so tied to the IT services market. However, the stockholders strongly protested these acquisitions. They believed that only Raju and his family would benefit from the acquisition but Satyam would not.

On December 23, 2008, the World Bank announced that Satyam was barred from doing business with the bank because of alleged malpractices in securing previous contracts (e.g., paying bribes). In turn, Satyam requested an apology from the World Bank. Shortly thereafter, the price of Satyam's stock declined to a four-year low. Then, on December 26 three major outside directors resigned from Satyam's board of directors.

Worst of all, on January 7, 2009, Raju sent a letter to the Satyam board of directors and India's Securities and Exchange Commission. In this letter, he admitted his involvement in overstating the amount of cash held by Satyam on its balance sheet. The overstatement was approximately $1 billion. Furthermore, Satyam had a liability for $253 million arranged for his personal use, and he overstated Satyam's September 2008 quarterly revenues by 76% and its quarterly profits by 97%. This announcement sent shockwaves through corporate India and through India's stock market. Not only did Satyam's stock price suffer greatly (78% decline) but the overall market decreased by 7.3% on the day of the announcement.

AP Photo/Mahesh Kumar A

Ramalinga Raju, Satyam's chairman quit after admitting the company's profits had been doctored for several years, shaking faith in the country's corporate giants as shares of the software services provider plunged nearly 80 percent.

Sadly, Satyam means "truth" in Sanskrit. While the CEO has been arrested and charged, others are working hard to save the company—and it appears that Satyam will be saved. Tech Malindra outbid two other firms to acquire an eventual 51% of Satyam and thus will have controlling interest in the company. The sale was due partly to swift government intervention to arrange a sale and save the company. Even though Satyam has been saved, corporate governance in India has taken a big hit and its reputation has been tarnished.

Sources: P. G. Thakurta, 2009, Satyam scam questions corporate governance, IPS Inter Press Service, http://www .ipsnews.net. April 21; G. Anand, 2009, How Satyam was saved, *Wall Street Journal*, http://www.wsj.com, April 14; 2009, Satyam-chronology, Trading Markets, http://www.tradingmarkets.com, April 7; H. Timmons & B. Wassener, 2009, Satyam chief admits huge fraud, *New York Times*, http://nytimes.com, January 8; H. Arakali, 2009, Satyam chairman resigns after falsifying accounts, Bloomberg, http://bloomberg.com, January 7; M. Kripalani, 2009, India's Madoff? Satyam scandal rocks outsourcing industry, *BusinessWeek*, http://www.businessweek.com, January 7; J. Riberiro, 2008, Satyam demands apology from World Bank, Network World, http://www.networkworld.com, December 26.

a major restructuring.[142] Research suggests that foreign investors are likely to focus on critical strategic decisions and their input tends to increase a firm's movement into international markets.[143] Thus, foreign investors are playing major roles in the governance of firms in many countries.

Not only has the legislation that produced the Sarbanes-Oxley Act in 2002 increased the intensity of corporate governance in the United States,[144] but other governments around the world are seeking to increase the transparency and intensity of corporate governance to prevent the types of scandals found in the United States and other places around the world. For example, the British government in 2003 implemented the findings of the Derek Higgs report, which increased governance intensity mandated by the United Kingdom's Combined Code on Corporate Governance, a template of corporate governance used by investors and listed companies. Also, as reported in the earlier Strategic Focus, in 2009 the chairman of the Financial Reporting Council in the United Kingdom announced a complete review of the Combined Code. In addition, the European Union enacted what is known as the "Transparency Directive," which is aimed at enhancing reporting and the disclosure of financial reports by firms within the European capital markets. Another European Union initiative labeled "Modernizing Company Law and Enhancing Corporate Governance" is designed to improve the responsibility and liability of executive officers, board members, and others to important stakeholders such as shareholders, creditors, and members of the public at large.[145] Thus, governance is becoming more intense around the world.

Governance Mechanisms and Ethical Behavior

The governance mechanisms described in this chapter are designed to ensure that the agents of the firm's owners—the corporation's top-level managers—make strategic decisions that best serve the interests of the entire group of stakeholders, as described in Chapter 1. In the United States, shareholders are recognized as the company's most significant stakeholders. Thus, governance mechanisms focus on the control of managerial decisions to ensure that shareholders' interests will be served, but product market stakeholders (e.g., customers, suppliers, and host communities) and organizational stakeholders (e.g., managerial and nonmanagerial employees) are important as well.[146] Therefore, at least the minimal interests or needs of all stakeholders must be satisfied through the firm's actions. Otherwise, dissatisfied stakeholders will withdraw their support from one firm and provide it to another (e.g., customers will purchase products from a supplier offering an acceptable substitute).

The firm's strategic competitiveness is enhanced when its governance mechanisms take into consideration the interests of all stakeholders. Although the idea is subject to debate, some believe that ethically responsible companies design and use governance mechanisms that serve all stakeholders' interests. The more critical relationship, however, is found between ethical behavior and corporate governance mechanisms. The Enron disaster and the sad affair at Satyam (described in the Strategic Focus) illustrate the devastating effect of poor ethical behavior not only on a firm's stakeholders, but also on other firms. This issue is being taken seriously in other countries. The trend toward increased governance scrutiny continues to spread around the world.[147]

In addition to Enron, scandals at WorldCom, HealthSouth, Tyco, and Satyam along with the questionable behavior of top-level managers in several of the major U.S. financial services firms (Merrill Lynch, AIG) show that all corporate owners are vulnerable to unethical behavior and very poor judgments exercised by their employees, including top-level managers—the agents who have been hired to make decisions that are in shareholders' best interests. The decisions and actions of a corporation's board of directors can be an effective deterrent to these behaviors. In fact, some believe that the most effective boards participate actively to set boundaries for their firms' business ethics and values.[148] Once formulated, the board's expectations related to ethical decisions and actions of all of the firm's stakeholders must be clearly communicated to its top-level managers. Moreover, as shareholders' agents, these managers must understand that the board will hold them fully accountable for the development and support of an organizational culture that allows unethical decisions and behaviors. As will be explained in Chapter 12, CEOs can be positive role models for improved ethical behavior.

Only when the proper corporate governance is exercised can strategies be formulated and implemented that will help the firm achieve strategic competitiveness and earn above-average returns. While there are many examples of poor governance, Cummins Inc. is a positive example. In 2009 it was given the highest possible rating for its corporate governance by GovernanceMetrics International. The rating is based on careful evaluation of board accountability and financial disclosure, executive compensation, shareholder rights, ownership base, takeover provisions, corporate behavior, and overall responsibility exhibited by the company.[149] As the discussion in this chapter suggests, corporate governance mechanisms are a vital, yet imperfect, part of firms' efforts to select and successfully use strategies.

SUMMARY

- Corporate governance is a relationship among stakeholders that is used to determine a firm's direction and control its performance. How firms monitor and control top-level managers' decisions and actions affects the implementation of strategies. Effective governance that aligns managers' decisions with shareholders' interests can help produce a competitive advantage.

- Three internal governance mechanisms in the modern corporation include (1) ownership concentration, (2) the board of directors, and (3) executive compensation. The market for corporate control is the single external governance mechanism influencing managers' decisions and the outcomes resulting from them.

- Ownership is separated from control in the modern corporation. Owners (principals) hire managers (agents) to make decisions that maximize the firm's value. As risk-bearing specialists, owners diversify their risk by investing in multiple corporations with different risk profiles. As decision-making specialists, owners expect their agents (the firm's top-level managers) to make decisions that will help to maximize the value of their firm. Thus, modern corporations are characterized by an agency relationship that is created when one party (the firm's owners) hires and pays another party (top-level managers) to use its decision-making skills.

- Separation of ownership and control creates an agency problem when an agent pursues goals that conflict with principals' goals. Principals establish and use governance mechanisms to control this problem.

- Ownership concentration is based on the number of large-block shareholders and the percentage of shares they own. With significant ownership percentages, such as those held by large mutual funds and pension funds, institutional investors often are able to influence top-level managers' strategic decisions and actions. Thus, unlike diffuse ownership, which tends to result in relatively weak monitoring and control of managerial decisions, concentrated ownership produces more active and effective monitoring. Institutional investors are a powerful force in corporate America and actively use their positions of concentrated ownership to force managers and boards of directors to make decisions that maximize a firm's value.

- In the United States and the United Kingdom, a firm's board of directors, composed of insiders, related outsiders, and outsiders, is a governance mechanism expected to represent shareholders' collective interests. The percentage of outside directors on many boards now exceeds the percentage of inside directors. Through the implementation of the SOX Act, outsiders are expected to be more independent of a firm's top-level managers compared with directors selected from inside the firm. New rules imposed by the U.S. Securities and Exchange Commission to allow owners with large stakes to propose new directors are likely to change the balance even more in favor of outside and independent directors.

- Executive compensation is a highly visible and often criticized governance mechanism. Salary, bonuses, and long-term incentives are used to strengthen the alignment between managers' and shareholders' interests. A firm's board of directors is responsible for determining the effectiveness of the firm's executive compensation system. An effective system elicits managerial decisions that are in shareholders' best interests.

- In general, evidence suggests that shareholders and boards of directors have become more vigilant in their control of managerial decisions. Nonetheless, these mechanisms are insufficient to govern managerial behavior in many large companies as shown in the latest economic crisis brought on by poor strategic decisions made by top-level managers in financial services firms. Therefore, the market for corporate control is an important governance mechanism. Although it, too, is imperfect, the market for corporate control has been effective in causing corporations to combat inefficient diversification and to implement more effective strategic decisions.

- Corporate governance structures used in Germany, Japan, and China differ from each other and from the structure used in the United States. Historically, the U.S. governance structure focused on maximizing shareholder value. In Germany,

employees, as a stakeholder group, take a more prominent role in governance. By contrast, until recently, Japanese shareholders played virtually no role in the monitoring and control of top-level managers. However, now Japanese firms are being challenged by "activist" shareholders. China's governance system is the youngest and has a number of characteristics that mirror those in the United States. However, the central government still plays a major role in governance in China as well. Internationally, all these systems are becoming increasingly similar, as are many governance systems both in developed countries, such as France and Spain, and in transitional economies, such as Russia and India.

- Effective governance mechanisms ensure that the interests of all stakeholders are served. Thus, long-term strategic success results when firms are governed in ways that permit at least minimal satisfaction of capital market stakeholders (e.g., shareholders), product market stakeholders (e.g., customers and suppliers), and organizational stakeholders (managerial and nonmanagerial employees; see Chapter 2). Moreover, effective governance produces ethical behavior in the formulation and implementation of strategies.

REVIEW QUESTIONS

1. What is corporate governance? What factors account for the considerable amount of attention corporate governance receives from several parties, including shareholder activists, business press writers, and academic scholars? Why is governance necessary to control managers' decisions?

2. What is meant by the statement that ownership is separated from managerial control in the corporation? Why does this separation exist?

3. What is an agency relationship? What is managerial opportunism? What assumptions do owners of corporations make about managers as agents?

4. How is each of the three internal governance mechanisms— ownership concentration, boards of directors, and executive

compensation—used to align the interests of managerial agents with those of the firm's owners?

5. What trends exist regarding executive compensation? What is the effect of the increased use of long-term incentives on executives' strategic decisions?

6. What is the market for corporate control? What conditions generally cause this external governance mechanism to become active? How does the mechanism constrain top-level managers' decisions and actions?

7. What is the nature of corporate governance in Germany, Japan, and China?

8. How can corporate governance foster ethical strategic decisions and behaviors on the part of managers as agents?

EXPERIENTIAL EXERCISES

EXERCISE 1: INTERNATIONAL GOVERNANCE CODES

As described in the chapter, passage of the Sarbanes-Oxley Act in 2002 has drawn attention to the importance of corporate governance. Similar legislation is pending in other nations as well. However, interest in improved governance predated SOX by a decade in the form of governance codes or guidelines. These codes established sets of "best practices" for both board composition and processes. The first such code was developed by the Cadbury Committee for the London Stock Exchange

in 1992. The Australian Stock Exchange developed its guidelines in the Hilmer Report, released in 1993. The Toronto Stock Exchange developed its guidelines the following year in the Dey Report. Today, most major stock exchanges have governance codes.

Working in small groups, find the governance codes of two stock exchanges. Prepare a short (two to three pages, single-spaced) bullet-point comparison of the similarities and differences between the two codes. Be sure to include the following topics in your analysis:

- How are the guidelines structured? Do they consist of rules (i.e., required) or recommendations (i.e., suggestions)? What mechanism is included to monitor or enforce the guidelines?
- What board roles are addressed in the guidelines? For example, some codes may place most or all of their emphasis on functions derived from the importance of the agency relationship illustrated in Figure 10.1 on page 289, such as monitoring, oversight, and reporting. Codes might also mention the board's role in supporting strategy, or their contribution to firm performance and shareholder wealth.
- What aspects of board composition and structure are covered in the guidelines? For instance, items included in different codes include the balance of insiders and outsiders, committees, whether the CEO also serves as board chair, director education and/or evaluation, compensation of officers and directors, and ownership by board members.

EXERCISE 2: GOVERNANCE: DOES IT MATTER COMPETITIVELY?

Governance mechanisms are considered to be effective if they meet the needs of all stakeholders, including shareholders. Governance mechanisms are also an important way to ensure that strategic decisions are made effectively. As a potential employee, how would you go about investigating a firm's governance structure and would that investigation weigh in your decision to become an employee or not? Identify a firm that you would like to join or one that you just find interesting. Working individually, complete the following research on your target firm:

- Find a copy of the company's most recent proxy statement and 10-K. Proxy statements are mailed to shareholders prior to each year's annual meeting and contain detailed information about the company's governance and present issues on which a shareholder vote might be held. Proxy statements are typically available from a firm's Web site (look for an "Investors" submenu). You can also access proxy statements and other government filings such as the 10-K from the SEC's EDGAR database (http://www.sec.gov/edgar.shtml). Alongside the proxy you should also be able to access the firm's annual 10-K. Here you will find information on performance, governance, and the firm's outlook, among other things.
- Identify one of the company's main competitors for comparison purposes. You can find this information using company analysis tools such as Datamonitor.

Some of the topics that you should examine include:

- Compensation plans (for both the CEO and board members; be sure to look for any difference between fixed and incentive compensation)
- Board composition (e.g., board size, insiders and outsiders, interlocking directorates, functional experience, how many active CEOs, how many retired CEOs, what is the demographic makeup, age diversity, etc.)
- Committees (how many, composition, compensation)
- Stock ownership by officers and directors—identify beneficial ownership from stock owned (you will need to look through the notes sections of the ownership tables to comprehend this)
- Ownership concentration. How much of the firm's outstanding stock is owned by institutions, individuals, and insiders? How many large-block shareholders are there (owners of 5 percent or more of stock)?
- Does the firm utilize a duality structure for the CEO?
- Is there a lead director who is not an officer of the company?
- Activities by activist shareholders regarding corporate governance issues of concern
- Are there any managerial defense tactics employed by the firm? For example, what does it take for a shareholder proposal to come to a vote and be adopted?
- List the firm's code of conduct.

Prepare a double-spaced memo summarizing the results of your findings with a side-by-side comparison of your target and its competitor. Your memo should include the following topics:

- Summarize what you consider to be the key aspects of the firm's governance mechanisms.
- Attach to your memo a single graph covering the last 10-year historical stock performance for both companies. If applicable, find a representative index to compare both with, such as the S&P, NASDAQ, or other applicable industry index.
- Highlight key differences between your target firm and its competitor.
- Based on your review of the firm's governance, did you change your opinion of the firm's desirability as an employer? How does the competitor stack up, governance wise? Why or why not?

VIDEO CASE

EFFECTIVE CORPORATE GOVERNANCE

Paul Skinner/Former Chairman/Rio Tinto

Paul Skinner, former chairman of Rio Tinto Corporation, discusses how the firm went through some significant governance changes. Spend some time with the Rio Tinto Web site and familiarize yourself with its governance structure and philosophy.

Before you watch the video consider the following concepts and questions and be prepared to discuss them in class:

Concepts
- CEO duality
- Board of directors
- Director demographics
- Corporate governance

Questions

1. What do you think is meant by the term *good governance*?
2. Do you think separation of the chairman and CEO positions should be mandatory for every company?
3. In designing a firm for "good governance," what do you consider important structural arrangements? For example, how should the board be organized, what roles should nonexecutive members have, how many committees should there be, what types of board members, etc.?
4. What do you think of the way that Rio Tinto views governance?

NOTES

1. B. W. Heineman, Jr., 2009, Redefining the CEO role. *BusinessWeek*, http://www.businessweek.com, April 16; C. Thomas, D. Kidd, & C. Fernández-Aráoz, 2007, Are you underutilizing your board? *MIT Sloan Management Review*, 48(2): 71–76; D. C. Carey &, M. Patsalos-Fox, 2006, Shaping strategy from the boardroom. *McKinsey Quarterly*, 3: 90–94.

2. J. B. Wade, C. A. O'Reilly, & T. G. Pollock, 2006, Overpaid CEOs and underpaid managers: Fairness and executive compensation, *Organization Science*, 17: 527–544; A. Henderson & J. Fredrickson, 2001, Top management team coordination needs and the CEO pay gap: A competitive test of economic and behavioral views, *Academy of Management Journal*, 44: 96–117.

3. A. D. F. Penalva, 2006, Governance structure and the weighting of performance measures in CEO compensation, *Review of Accounting Studies*, 11: 463–493; S. Werner, H. L. Tosi, & L. Gomez-Mejia, 2005, Organizational governance and employee pay: How ownership structure affects the firm's compensation strategy, *Strategic Management Journal*, 26: 377–384.

4. C. Crossland & D. C. Hambrick, 2007, How national systems differ in their constraints on corporate executives: A study of CEO effects in three countries, *Strategic Management Journal*, 28: 767–789; M. D. Lynall, B. R. Golden, & A. J. Hillman, 2003, Board composition from adolescence to maturity: A multitheoretic view, *Academy of Management Review*, 28: 416–431.

5. M. A. Rutherford, A. K. Buchholtz, & J. A. Brown, 2007, Examining the relationships between monitoring and incentives in corporate governance, *Journal of Management Studies* 44: 414–430; C. M. Daily, D. R. Dalton, & A. A. Cannella, 2003, Corporate governance: Decades of dialogue and data, *Academy of Management Review*, 28: 371–382; P. Stiles, 2001, The impact of the board on strategy: An empirical examination, *Journal of Management Studies*, 38: 627–650.

6. D. R. Dalton, M. A. Hitt, S. T. Certo, & C. M. Dalton, 2008, The fundamental agency problem and its mitigation: Independence, equity and the market for corporate control, in J. P. Walsh and A. P. Brief (eds.), *The Academy of Management Annals*, New York: Lawrence Erlbaum Associates, 1–64; E. F. Fama & M. C. Jensen, 1983, Separation of ownership and control, *Journal of Law and Economics*, 26: 301–325.

7. I. Le Breton-Miller & D. Miller, 2006, Why do some family businesses out-compete? Governance, long-term orientations, and sustainable capability, *Entrepreneurship Theory and Practice*, 30: 731–746; M. Carney, 2005, Corporate governance and competitive advantage in family-controlled firms, *Entrepreneurship Theory and Practice*, 29: 249–265; R. Charan, 1998, *How Corporate Boards Create Competitive Advantage*, San Francisco: Jossey-Bass.

8. X. Wu, 2005, Corporate governance and corruption: A cross-country analysis, *Governance*, 18(2): 151–170; J. McGuire & S. Dow, 2002, The Japanese keiretsu system: An empirical analysis, *Journal of Business Research*, 55: 33–40.

9. R. E. Hoskisson, D. Yiu, & H. Kim, 2004, Corporate governance systems: Effects of capital and labor market congruency on corporate innovation and global competitiveness, *Journal of High Technology Management*, 15: 293–315.

10. Crossland & Hambrick, How national systems differ in their constraints on corporate executives; R. Aguilera & G. Jackson, 2003, The cross-national diversity of corporate governance: Dimensions and determinants, *Academy of Management Review*, 28: 447–465.

11. R. P. Wright, 2004, Top managers' strategic cognitions of the strategy making process: Differences between high and low performing firms, *Journal of General Management*, 30(1): 61–78.

12. X. Luo, C. N. Chung, & M. Sobczak, 2009, How do corporate governance model differences affect foreign direct investment in emerging economies? *Journal of International Business Studies*, 40: 444–467; A. Bris & C. Cabous, 2006, In a merger, two companies come together and integrate their distribution lines, brands, work forces, management teams, strategies and cultures, *Financial Times*, October 6, 1.

13. S. Sudarsanam & A. A. Mahate, 2006, Are friendly acquisitions too bad for shareholders and managers? Long-term value creation and top management turnover in hostile and friendly acquirers, *British Journal of Management: Supplement*, 17(1): S7–S30; T. Moeller, 2005, Let's make a deal! How shareholder control impacts merger payoffs, *Journal of Financial Economics*, 76(1): 167–190; M. A. Hitt, R. E. Hoskisson, R. A. Johnson, & D. D. Moesel, 1996, The market for corporate control and firm innovation, *Academy of Management Journal*, 39: 1084–1119.

14. R. E. Hoskisson, M. A. Hitt, R. A. Johnson, & W. Grossman, 2002, Conflicting voices: The effects of ownership heterogeneity and internal governance on corporate strategy, *Academy of Management Journal*, 45: 697–716.

15. G. E. Davis & T. A. Thompson, 1994, A social movement perspective on corporate control, *Administrative Science Quarterly*, 39: 141–173.

16. R. Bricker & N. Chandar, 2000, Where Berle and Means went wrong: A reassessment of capital market agency and financial reporting, *Accounting, Organizations, and Society*, 25: 529–554; M. A. Eisenberg, 1989, The structure of corporation law, *Columbia Law Review*, 89(7): 1461, as cited in R. A. G. Monks & N. Minow, 1995, *Corporate Governance*, Cambridge, MA: Blackwell Business, 7.

17. R. M. Wiseman & L. R. Gomez-Mejia, 1999, A behavioral agency model of managerial risk taking, *Academy of Management Review*, 23: 133–153.

18. T. Zellweger, 2007, Time horizon, costs of equity capital, and generic investment strategies of firms, *Family Business Review*, 20(1): 1–15; R. C. Anderson & D. M. Reeb, 2004, Board composition: Balancing family influence in S&P 500 firms, *Administrative Science Quarterly*, 49: 209–237.

19. Carney, Corporate governance and competitive advantage in family-controlled firms; N. Anthanassiou, W. F. Crittenden, L. M. Kelly, & P. Marquez, 2002, Founder centrality effects on the Mexican family firm's top management group: Firm culture, strategic vision and goals and firm performance, *Journal of World Business*, 37: 139–150.

20. M. Santiago-Castro & C. J. Brown, 2007, Ownership structure and minority rights: A

Latin American view, *Journal of Economics and Business*, 59: 430–442; M. Carney & E. Gedajlovic, 2003, Strategic innovation and the administrative heritage of East Asian family business groups, *Asia Pacific Journal of Management*, 20: 5–26; D. Miller & I. Le Breton-Miller, 2003, Challenge versus advantage in family business, *Strategic Organization*, 1: 127–134.

21. D. G. Sirmon, J.-L. Arregle, M. A. Hitt, & J. Webb, 2008, Strategic responses to the threat of imitation, *Entrepreneurship Theory and Practice*, 32: 979–998.

22. Rutherford, Buchholtz, & Brown, Examining the relationships between monitoring and incentives in corporate governance; D. Dalton, C. Daily, T. Certo, & R. Roengpitya, 2003, Meta-analyses of financial performance and equity: Fusion or confusion? *Academy of Management Journal*, 46: 13–26; M. Jensen & W. Meckling, 1976, Theory of the firm: Managerial behavior, agency costs, and ownership structure, *Journal of Financial Economics*, 11: 305–360.

23. G. C. Rodríguez, C. A.-D. Espejo, & R. Valle Cabrera, 2007, Incentives management during privatization: An agency perspective, *Journal of Management Studies*, 44: 536–560; D. C. Hambrick, S. Finkelstein, & A. C. Mooney, 2005, Executive job demands: New insights for explaining strategic decisions and leader behaviors, *Academy of Management Review*, 30: 472–491.

24. T. G. Habbershon, 2006, Commentary: A framework for managing the familiness and agency advantages in family firms, *Entrepreneurship Theory and Practice*, 30: 879–886; M. G. Jacobides & D. C. Croson, 2001, Information policy: Shaping the value of agency relationships, *Academy of Management Review*, 26: 202–223.

25. A. Mackey, 2008, The effects of CEOs on firm performance, *Strategic Management Journal*, 29: 1357–1367; Y. Y. Kor, 2006, Direct and interaction effects of top management team and board compositions on R&D investment strategy, *Strategic Management Journal*, 27: 1081–1099.

26. Dalton, Hitt, Certo, & Dalton, 2008, The fundamental agency problem and its mitigation: Independence, equity and the market for corporate control; A. Ghosh, D. Moon, & K. Tandon, 2007, CEO ownership and discretionary investments, *Journal of Business Finance & Accounting*, 34: 819–839.

27. S. Ghoshal & P. Moran, 1996, Bad for practice: A critique of the transaction cost theory, *Academy of Management Review*, 21: 13–47; O. E. Williamson, 1996, *The Mechanisms of Governance*, New York: Oxford University Press, 6.

28. B. E. Ashforth, D. A. Gioia, S. L. Robinson, & L. K. Trevino, 2008, Reviewing organizational corruption, *Academy of Management Review*, 33: 670–684; E. Kang, 2006, Investors'

perceptions of managerial opportunism in corporate acquisitions: The moderating role of environmental condition, *Corporate Governance*, 14: 377–387; R. W. Coff & P. M. Lee, 2003, Insider trading as a vehicle to appropriate rent from R&D. *Strategic Management Journal*, 24: 183–190.

29. M. L. McDonald, P. Khanna, & J. D. Westphal, 2008, Getting them to think outside the circle: Corporate governance, CEOs' external advice networks, and firm performance, *Academy of Management Journal*, 51: 453–475.

30. Fama, Agency problems and the theory of the firm.

31. P. Jiraporn, Y. Sang Kim, W. N. Davidson, & M. Singh, 2006, Corporate governance, shareholder rights and firm diversification: An empirical analysis, *Journal of Banking & Finance*, 30: 947–963; R. C. Anderson, T. W. Bates, J. M. Bizjak, & M. L. Lemmon, 2000, Corporate governance and firm diversification, *Financial Management*, 29(1): 5–22; R. E. Hoskisson & T. A. Turk, 1990, Corporate restructuring: Governance and control limits of the internal market, *Academy of Management Review*, 15: 459–477.

32. G. P. Baker & B. J. Hall, 2004, CEO incentives and firm size, *Journal of Labor Economics*, 22: 767–798; R. Bushman, Q. Chen, E. Engel, & A. Smith, 2004, Financial accounting information, organizational complexity and corporate governance systems, *Journal of Accounting & Economics*, 7: 167–201; M. A. Geletkanycz, B. K. Boyd, & S. Finkelstein, 2001, The strategic value of CEO external directorate networks: Implications for CEO compensation, *Strategic Management Journal*, 9: 889–898.

33. S. W. Geiger & L. H. Cashen, 2007, Organizational size and CEO compensation: The moderating effect of diversification in downscoping organizations, *Journal of Managerial Issues*, 9(2): 233–252; Y. Grinstein & P. Hribar, 2004, CEO compensation and incentives: Evidence from M&A bonuses, *Journal of Financial Economics*, 73: 119–143;

34. S. Rajgopal, T. Shevlin, & V. Zamora, 2006, CEOs' outside employment opportunities and the lack of relative performance evaluation in compensation contracts, *Journal of Finance*, 61: 1813–1844.

35. J. Weber, 2007, The accidental CEO (well, not really); Kellogg needed a new boss, fast. Here's how it groomed insider David Mackay, *BusinessWeek*, April 23, 65.

36. Kellogg's Annual Report, 2008. Kellogg, Michigan.

37. M. Ganco & R. Agarwal, 2009, Performance differentials between diversifying entrants and entrepreneurial start-ups: A complexity approach, *Academy of Management Review*, 34: 228–252.

38. M. S. Jensen, 1986, Agency costs of free cash flow, corporate finance, and takeovers, *American Economic Review*, 76: 323–329.

39. A. V. Douglas, 2007, Managerial opportunism and proportional corporate payout policies, *Managerial Finance*, 33(1): 26–42; M. Jensen & E. Zajac, 2004, Corporate elites and corporate strategy: How demographic preferences and structural position shape the scope of the firm, *Strategic Management Journal*, 25: 507–524; T. H. Brush, P. Bromiley, & M. Hendrickx, 2000, The free cash flow hypothesis for sales growth and firm performance, *Strategic Management Journal*, 21: 455–472.

40. J. Lunsford & B. Steinberg, 2006, Conglomerates' conundrum, *Wall Street Journal*, September 14, B1, B7; K. Ramaswamy, M. Li, & B. S. P. Petitt, 2004, Who drives unrelated diversification? A study of Indian manufacturing firms, *Asia Pacific Journal of Management*, 21: 403–423.

41. M. V. S. Kumar, 2009, The relationship between product and international diversification: The effects of short-run constraints and endogeneity, *Strategic Management Journal*, 30: 99–116; M. F. Wiersema & H. P. Bowen, 2008, Corporate diversification: The impact of foreign competition, industry globalization and product diversification, *Strategic Management Journal*, 29: 115–132.

42. D. D. Bergh, R. A. Johnson, & R.-L. Dewitt, 2008, Restructuring through spin-off or sell-off: Transforming information asymmetries into financial gain, *Strategic Management Journal*, 29: 133–148; K. B. Lee, M. W. Peng, & K. Lee, 2008, From diversification premium to diversification discount during institutional transitions, *Journal of World Business*, 43: 47–65.

43. T. K. Berry, J. M. Bizjak, M. L. Lemmon, & L. Naveen, 2006, Organizational complexity and CEO labor markets: Evidence from diversified firms, *Journal of Corporate Finance*, 12: 797–817; R. Rajan, H. Servaes, & L. Zingales, 2001, The cost of diversity: The diversification discount and inefficient investment, *Journal of Finance*, 55: 35–79; A. Sharma, 1997, Professional as agent: Knowledge asymmetry in agency exchange, *Academy of Management Review*, 22: 758–798.

44. V. Chhaochharia & Y. Grinstein, 2007, Corporate governance and firm value: The impact of the 2002 governance rules, *Journal of Finance*, 62: 1789–1825; A. Borrus, L. Lavelle, D. Brady, M. Arndt, & J. Weber, 2005, Death, taxes and Sarbanes-Oxley? Executives may be frustrated with the law's burdens, but corporate performance is here to stay, *BusinessWeek*, January 17, 28–31.

45. D. Reilly, 2006, Checks on internal controls pay off, *Wall Street Journal*, August 10, C3.

46. F. Navissi & V. Naiker, 2006, Institutional ownership and corporate value, *Managerial Finance*, 32: 247–256; A. de Miguel, J. Pindado, & C. de la Torre, 2004, Ownership structure and

firm value: New evidence from Spain, *Strategic Management Journal*, 25: 1199–1207; J. Coles, N. Sen, & V. McWilliams, 2001, An examination of the relationship of governance mechanisms to performance, *Journal of Management*, 27: 23–50.

47. Jiraporn, Kim, Davidson, & Singh, Corporate governance, shareholder rights and firm diversification; M. Singh, I. Mathur, & K. C. Gleason, 2004, Governance and performance implications of diversification strategies: Evidence from large U.S. firms, *Financial Review*, 39: 489–526; R. E. Hoskisson, R. A. Johnson, & D. D. Moesel, 1994, Corporate divestiture intensity in restructuring firms: Effects of governance, strategy, and performance, *Academy of Management Journal*, 37: 1207–1251.

48. G. Iannotta, G. Nocera, & A. Sironi, 2007, Ownership structure, risk and performance in the European banking industry, *Journal of Banking & Finance*, 31: 2127–2149.

49. B. Villalonga & R. Amit, 2006, How do family ownership, control and management affect firm value? *Journal of Financial Economics*, 80: 385–417; R. C. Anderson & D. M. Reeb, 2004, Board composition: Balancing family influence in S&P 500 firms, *Administrative Science Quarterly*, 49: 209–237.

50. M. Fackler, 2008, South Korea faces question of corporate control, *New York Times*, http://www.nytimes.com, April 24; S. J. Chang, 2003, Ownership structure, expropriation and performance of group-affiliated companies in Korea, *Academy of Management Journal*, 46: 238–253.

51. A. Berle & G. Means, 1932, *The Modern Corporation and Private Property*, New York: Macmillan.

52. M. Gietzmann, 2006, Disclosure of timely and forward-looking statements and strategic management of major institutional ownership, *Long Range Planning*, 39(4): 409–427; B. Ajinkya, S. Bhojraj, & P. Sengupta, 2005, The association between outside directors, institutional investors and the properties of management earnings forecasts, *Journal of Accounting Research*, 43: 343–376; M. P. Smith, 1996, Shareholder activism by institutional investors: Evidence from CalPERS, *Journal of Finance*, 51: 227–252.

53. K. Schnatterly, K. W. Shaw, & W. W. Jennings, 2008, Information advantages of large institutional owners, *Strategic Management Journal*, 29: 219–227; Hoskisson, Hitt, Johnson, & Grossman, Conflicting voices.

54. S. D. Chowdhury & E. Z. Wang, 2009, Institutional activism types and CEO compensation: A time-series analysis of large Canadian corporations, *Journal of Management*, 35: 5–36; M. Musteen, D. K. Datta, & P. Herrmann, 2009, Ownership structure and CEO compensation: Implications for the choice of foreign market entry modes, *Journal*

55. T. W. Briggs, 2007, Corporate governance and the new hedge fund activism: An empirical analysis. *Journal of Corporation Law*, 32(4): 681–723, 725–738; K. Rebeiz, 2001, Corporate governance effectiveness in American corporations: A survey, *International Management Journal*, 18(1): 74–80.

56. D. Brewster, 2009, U.S. investors get to nominate boards, *Financial Times*, http://www.ft.com, May 20.

57. CalPERS, 2009, *Wikipedia*, http://en.wikipedia.org/wiki/CalPERS, May 13.

58. M. Anderson, 2009, Eli Lilly heads CalPERS' "underperforming" list, *Sacramento Business Journal*, http://www.bizjournals.com, March 19.

59. S. Thurm, When investor activism doesn't pay, *Wall Street Journal*, September 12, A2; S. M. Jacoby, 2007, Principles and agents: CalPERS and corporate governance in Japan, *Corporate Governance*, 15(1): 5–15; L. Tihanyi, R. A. Johnson, R. E. Hoskisson, & M. A. Hitt, 2003, Institutional ownership differences and international diversification: The effects of boards of directors and technological opportunity, *Academy of Management Journal*, 46: 195–211; Hoskisson, Hitt, Johnson, & Grossman, Conflicting voices; P. David, M. A. Hitt, & J. Gimeno, 2001, The role of institutional investors in influencing R&D, *Academy of Management Journal*, 44: 144–157.

60. V. Krivogorsky, 2006, Ownership, board structure, and performance in continental Europe, *International Journal of Accounting*, 41(2): 176–197; S. Thomsen & T. Pedersen, 2000, Ownership structure and economic performance in the largest European companies, *Strategic Management Journal*, 21: 689–705.

61. Dalton, Hitt, Certo, & Dalton, The fundamental agency problem and its mitigation: Independence, equity and the market for corporate control; C. M. Dalton & D. R. Dalton, 2006, Corporate governance best practices: The proof is in the process, *Journal of Business Strategy*, 27(4), 5–7; R. V. Aguilera, 2005, Corporate governance and director accountability: An institutional comparative perspective, *British Journal of Management*, 16(S1), S39–S53.

62. R. H. Lester, A. Hillman, A. Zardkoohi, & A. A. Cannella, 2008, Former government officials as outside directors: The role of human and social capital, *Academy of Management Journal*, 51: 999–1013; M. L. McDonald, J. D. Westphal, & M. E. Graebner, 2008, What do they know? The effects of outside director acquisition experience on firm acquisition performance, *Strategic Management Journal*, 29: 1155–1177; Hillman & Dalziel, Boards of directors and firm performance.

63. L. Bonazzi & S. M. N. Islam, 2007, Agency theory and corporate governance: A study of the effectiveness of board in

their monitoring of the CEO, *Journal of Modeling in Management*, 2(1): 7–23; Rebeiz, Corporate governance effectiveness in American corporations.

64. E. Kang, 2008, Director interlocks and spillover effects of reputational penalties from financial reporting fraud, *Academy of Management Journal*, 51: 537–555; N. Chipalkatti, Q. V. Le, & M. Rishi, 2007, Portfolio flows to emerging capital markets: Do corporate transparency and public governance matter? *Business and Society Review*, 112(2): 227–249.

65. Krivogorsky, Ownership, board structure, and performance in continental Europe; Hoskisson, Hitt, Johnson, & Grossman, Conflicting voices; B. D. Baysinger & R. E. Hoskisson, 1990, The composition of boards of directors and strategic control: Effects on corporate strategy, *Academy of Management Review*, 15: 72–87.

66. Y. Y. Kor & V. F. Misangyi, 2008, Outside directors' industry-specific experience and firms' liability of newness, *Strategic Management Journal*, 29: 1345–1355; E. E. Lawler III & D. Finegold, 2006, Who's in the boardroom and does it matter: The impact of having non-director executives attend board meetings, *Organizational Dynamics*, 35(1): 106–115.

67. E. M. Fich & A. Shivdasani, 2006, Are busy boards effective monitors? *Journal of Finance*, 61: 689–724; J. Westphal & L. Milton, 2000, How experience and network ties affect the influence of demographic minorities on corporate boards, *Administrative Science Quarterly*, 45(2): 366–398.

68. Fich & Shivdasani, Are busy boards effective monitors; S. T. Petra, 2005, Do outside independent directors strengthen corporate boards? *Corporate Governance*, 5(1): 55–65.

69. S. K. Lee & L. R. Carlson, 2007, The changing board of directors: Board independence in S & P 500 firms, *Journal of Organizational Culture, Communication and Conflict*, 11(1): 31–41.

70. R. C. Pozen, 2006, Before you split that CEO/chair, *Harvard Business Review*, 84(4): 26–28; J. W. Lorsch & A. Zelleke, 2005, Should the CEO be the chairman, *MIT Sloan Management Review*, 46(2): 71–74.

71. M. Kroll, B. A. Walters, & P. Wright, 2008, Board vigilance, director experience and corporate outcomes, *Strategic Management Journal*, 29: 363–382.

72. Fich & Shivdasani, Are busy boards effective monitors; J. Roberts, T. McNulty, &, P. Stiles, 2005, Beyond agency conceptions of the work of the non-executive director: Creating accountability in the boardroom, *British Journal of Management*, 16(S1): S5–S26.

73. Fich & Shivdasani, Are busy boards effective monitors; S. Zahra, 1996, Governance, ownership and corporate entrepreneurship among the *Fortune* 500: The moderating impact of industry

technological opportunity, *Academy of Management Journal*, 39: 1713–1735.

74. Baysinger, & Hoskisson, Board composition and strategic control: The effect on corporate strategy.

75. Y. Zhang, 2008, Information asymmetry and the dismissal of newly appointed CEOs: An empirical investigation, *Strategic Management Journal*, 29: 859–872.

76. Lawler & Finegold, Who's in the boardroom and does it matter?; E. E. Lawler III & D. L. Finegold, 2005, The changing face of corporate boards, *MIT Sloan Management Review*, 46(2): 67–70; A. Conger, E. E. Lawler, & D. L. Finegold, 2001, *Corporate Boards: New Strategies for Adding Value at the Top*, San Francisco: Jossey-Bass; J. A. Conger, D. Finegold, & E. E. Lawler III, 1998, Appraising boardroom performance, *Harvard Business Review*, 76(1): 136–148.

77. A. L. Boone, L. C. Field, J. M. Karpoff, & C. G. Raheja, 2007, The determinants of corporate board size and composition: An empirical analysis, *Journal of Financial Economics*, 85(1): 66–101; J. Marshall, 2001, As boards shrink, responsibilities grow, *Financial Executive*, 17(4): 36–39.

78. T. Long, 2007, The evolution of FTSE 250 boards of directors: Key factors influencing board performance and effectiveness, *Journal of General Management*, 32(3): 45–60; S. Finkelstein & A. C. Mooney, 2003, Not the usual suspects: How to use board process to make boards better, *Academy of Management Executive*, 17: 101–113.

79. J. L. Koors, 2006 Director pay: A work in progress, *The Corporate Governance Advisor*, 14(5): 25–31; W. Shen, 2005, Improve board effectiveness: The need for incentives, *British Journal of Management*, 16(S1): S81–S89; M. Gerety, C. Hoi, & A. Robin, 2001, Do shareholders benefit from the adoption of incentive pay for directors? *Financial Management*, 30: 45–61; D. C. Hambrick & E. M. Jackson, 2000, Outside directors with a stake: The linchpin in improving governance, *California Management Review*, 42(4): 108–127.

80. Y. Deutsch, T. Keil, & T. Laamanen, 2007, Decision making in acquisitions: the effect of outside directors' compensation on acquisition patterns, *Journal of Management*, 33(1): 30–56.

81. A. J. Hillman, C. Shropshire, & A. A. Cannella, Jr. 2007, Organizational predictors of women on corporate boards, *Academy of Management Journal*, 50: 941–952; I. Filatotchev & S. Toms, 2003, Corporate governance, strategy and survival in a declining industry: A study of UK cotton textile companies, *Journal of Management Studies*, 40: 895–920.

82. 2007, Wall St. roundup; pay increases for CEOs fall below 10% in 2006, *Los Angeles Times*, April 3, C4.

83. S. N. Kaplan, 2008, Are U.S. CEOs overpaid? *Academy of Management Perspectives*, 22(2): 5–20.

84. J. P. Walsh, 2009, Are U.S. CEOs overpaid? A partial response to Kaplan, *Academy of Management Perspectives*, 23(1): 73–75; J. P. Walsh, 2008, CEO compensation and the responsibilities of the business scholar to society, *Academy of Management Perspectives*, 22(3): 26–33.

85. K. Rehbein, 2007, Explaining CEO compensation: How do talent, governance, and markets fit in? *Academy of Management Perspectives*, 21(1): 75–77; J. S. Miller, R. M. Wiseman, & L. R. Gomez-Mejia, 2002, The fit between CEO compensation design and firm risk, *Academy of Management Journal*, 45: 745–756.

86. M. Larraza-Kintana, R. M. Wiseman, L. R. Gomez-Mejia, & T. M. Welbourne, 2007, Disentangling compensation and employment risks using the behavioral agency model, *Strategic Management Journal*, 28: 1001–1019; J. McGuire & E. Matta, 2003, CEO stock options: The silent dimension of ownership, *Academy of Management Journal*, 46: 255–265.

87. X. Zhang, K. M. Bartol, K. G. Smith, M. D. Pfarrer, & D. M. Khanin, 2008, CEOs on the edge: Earnings manipulations and stock-based incentive misalignment, *Academy of Management Journal*, 51: 241–258; J. P. O'Connor, R. L. Priem, J. E. Coombs, & K. M. Gilley, 2006, Do CEO stock options prevent or promote fraudulent financial reporting? *Academy of Management Journal*, 49: 483–500.

88. S. O'Donnell, 2000, Managing foreign subsidiaries: Agents of headquarters, or an interdependent network? *Strategic Management Journal*, 21: 521–548; K. Roth & S. O'Donnell, 1996, Foreign subsidiary compensation: An agency theory perspective, *Academy of Management Journal*, 39: 678–703.

89. A. Ghosh, 2006, Determination of executive compensation in an emerging economy: Evidence from India, *Emerging Markets, Finance & Trade*, 42(3): 66–90; K. Ramaswamy, R. Veliyath, & L. Gomes, 2000, A study of the determinants of CEO compensation in India, *Management International Review*, 40(2): 167–191.

90. C. L. Staples, 2007, Board globalization in the world's largest TNCs 1993–2005, *Corporate Governance*, 15(2): 311–32.

91. P. Kalyta, 2009, Compensation transparency and managerial opportunism: A study of supplemental retirement plans, *Strategic Management Journal*, 30: 405–423.

92. L. K. Meulbroek, 2001, The efficiency of equity-linked compensation: Understanding the full cost of awarding executive stock options, *Financial Management*, 30(2): 5–44.

93. C. E. Devers, R. M. Wiseman, & R. M. Holmes Jr., 2007, The effects of endowment and loss aversion in managerial stock option valuation, *Academy of Management Journal*, 50: 191–208; J. C. Bettis, J. M. Biziak, &

M. L. Lemmon, 2005, Exercise behavior, valuation and the incentive effects of employee stock options, *Journal of Financial Economics*, 76: 445–470.

94. M. Klausner, 2007, Reducing directors' legal risk, *Harvard Business Review*, 85(4), 28; T. G. Pollock, H. M. Fischer, & J. B. Wade, 2002, The role of politics in repricing executive options, *Academy of Management Journal*, 45: 1172–1182; M. E. Carter & L. J. Lynch, 2001, An examination of executive stock option repricing, *Journal of Financial Economics*, 59: 207–225; D. Chance, R. Kumar, & R. Todd, 2001, The "repricing" of executive stock options, *Journal of Financial Economics*, 59: 129–154.

95. P. Berrone & L. R. Gomez-Mejia, 2009, Environmental performance and executive compensation: An integrated agency-institutional perspective, *Academy of Management Journal*, 52: 103–126.

96. R. Sinha, 2006, Regulation: The market for corporate control and corporate governance, *Global Finance Journal*, 16(3): 264–282; R. Coff, 2002, Bidding wars over R&D intensive firms: Knowledge, opportunism and the market for corporate control, *Academy of Management Journal*, 46: 74–85; Hitt, Hoskisson, Johnson, & Moesel, The market for corporate control and firm innovation.

97. D. N. Iyer & K. D. Miller, 2008, Performance feedback, slack, and the timing of acquisitions, *Academy of Management Journal*, 51: 808–822; R. W. Masulis, C. Wang, & F. Xie, 2007, Corporate governance and acquirer returns, *Journal of Finance*, 62(4): 1851–1889; R. Sinha, 2004, The role of hostile takeovers in corporate governance, *Applied Financial Economics*, 14: 1291–1305.

98. K. Ruckman, 2009, Technology sourcing acquisitions: What they mean for innovation potential, *Journal of Strategy and Management*, 2: 56–75.

99. J. P. Walsh & R. Kosnik, 1993, Corporate raiders and their disciplinary role in the market for corporate control, *Academy of Management Journal*, 36: 671–700.

100. J. Haleblian, C. E. Devers, G. McNamara, M. A. Carpenter, & R. B. Davison, 2009, Taking stock of what we know about mergers and acquisitions: A review and research agenda, *Journal of Management*, 35: 469–502; B. Kalpic, 2008, Why bigger is not always better: The strategic logic of value creation through M&As, *Journal of Business Strategy*, 29(6): 4–13.

101. T. W. Briggs, 2007, Corporate governance and a new hedge fund activism: *Empirical Analysis*, 32(4): 681–723.

102. Thurm, When investor activism doesn't pay.

103. N. Goodway, 2009, Credit Suisse pays 25 million pounds in golden hellos, *Evening Standard*, http://www.standard.co.uk, March 24; R. B. Adams & D. Ferreira, 2007, A theory of friendly boards, *Journal of Finance*, 62: 217–250.

104. J Cresswell, 2006, Gilded paychecks: Pay packages allow executives to jump ship with less risk, *New York Times*, http://www.nyt.com, December 29.

105. C. Icahn, 2009, We're not the boss of AIG, *New York Times*, http://www.nytimes.com, March 29; G. Blain & C. Siemaszko, 2008, AIG agrees to cut golden parachute for CEO, trim spending, *New York Daily News*, http://www.nydailynews.com, October 16.

106. H. G. Barkema & M. Schjven, 2008, Toward unlocking the full potential of acquisition: The role of organizational restructuring, *Academy of Management Journal*, 51: 696–722; M. Cording, P. Chritmann, & D. R. King, 2008, Reducing causal ambiguity in acquisition integration: Intermediate goals as mediators of integration decisions and acquisition performance, *Academy of Management Journal*, 51: 744–767.

107. T. Laamanen & T. Keil, 2008, Performance of serial acquirers: Toward an acquisition program perspective, *Strategic Management Journal*, 29: 663–672; G. M. McNamara, J. Haleblian, & B. J. Dykes, 2008, The performance implications of participating in an acquisition wave: Early mover advantages, bandwagon effects, and the moderating influence of industry characteristics and acquirer tactics, *Academy of Management Journal*, 51: 113–130.

108. J. A. Krug & W. Shill, 2008, The big exit: Executive churn in the wake of M&As, *Journal of Business Strategy*, 29(4): 15–21; J. Harford, 2003, Takeover bids and target directors' incentives: The impact of a bid on directors' wealth and board seats, *Journal of Financial Economics*, 69: 51–83; S. Chatterjee, J. S. Harrison, & D. D. Bergh, 2003, Failed takeover attempts, corporate governance, and refocusing, *Strategic Management Journal*, 24: 87–96.

109. E. Webb, 2006, Relationships between board structure and takeover defenses, *Corporate Governance*, 6(3): 268–280; C. Sundaramurthy, J. M. Mahoney, & J. T. Mahoney, 1997, Board structure, antitakeover provisions, and stockholder wealth, *Strategic Management Journal*, 18: 231–246.

110. W. G. Sanders & M. A. Carpenter, 2003, Strategic satisficing? A behavioral-agency theory perspective on stock repurchase program announcements, *Academy of Management Journal*, 46: 160–178; J. Westphal & E. Zajac, 2001, Decoupling policy from practice: The case of stock repurchase programs, *Administrative Science Quarterly*, 46: 202–228.

111. O. Faleye, 2007, Classified boards, firm value, and managerial entrenchment, *Journal of Financial Economics*, 83: 501–529.

112. 2007, Leaders: Pay slips; management in Europe, *Economist*, June 23, 14: A. Cala, 2005, Carrying golden parachutes; France joins EU trend to reign in executive severance deals, *Wall Street Journal*, June 8, A13.

113. J. A. Pearce II & R. B. Robinson Jr., 2004, Hostile takeover defenses that maximize shareholder wealth, *Business Horizons*, 47(5): 15–24.

114. A. Kacperzyk, 2009, With greater power comes greater responsibility? Takeover protection and corporate attention to stakeholders, *Strategic Management Journal*, 30: 261–285.

115. Walsh & Kosnik, Corporate raiders.

116. A. Chakraborty & R. Arnott, 2001, Takeover defenses and dilution: A welfare analysis, *Journal of Financial and Quantitative Analysis*, 36: 311–334.

117. M. Wolf, 2007, The new capitalism: How unfettered finance is fast reshaping the global economy, *Financial Times*, June 19, 13: C. Millar, T. I. Eldomiaty, C. J. Choi, & B. Hilton, 2005, Corporate governance and institutional transparency in emerging markets, *Journal of Business Ethics*, 59: 163–174; D. Norburn, B. K. Boyd, M. Fox, & M. Muth, 2000, International corporate governance reform, *European Business Journal*, 12(3): 116–133.

118. China YCT International strengthens corporate governance with establishment of audit committee and appointments of three new independent directors, 2009, *Quamnet.com Stock News*, http://www.quamnet.com, April 13; P. Aldrick, 2009, RBS investors threaten to vote down pay report, *Telegraph.co.uk*, http://www.telegraph.co.uk, March 24.

119. P. Witt, 2004, The competition of international corporate governance systems—A German perspective, *Management International Review*, 44: 309–333; L. Nachum, 2003, Does nationality of ownership make any difference and if so, under what circumstances? Professional service MNEs in global competition, *Journal of International Management*, 9: 1–32.

120. Crossland & Hambrick, How national systems differ in their constraints on corporate executives; Aguilera & Jackson, The cross-national diversity of corporate governance: Dimensions and determinants.

121. Carney, Corporate governance and competitive advantage in family-controlled firms; S. Klein, 2000, Family businesses in Germany: Significance and structure, *Family Business Review*, 13: 157–181.

122. A. Tuschke & W. G. Sanders, 2003, Antecedents and consequences of corporate governance reform: The case of Germany, *Strategic Management Journal*, 24: 631–649; J. Edwards & M. Nibler, 2000, Corporate governance in Germany: The role of banks and ownership concentration, *Economic Policy*, 31: 237–268; E. R. Gedajlovic & D. M. Shapiro, 1998, Management and ownership effects: Evidence from five countries, *Strategic Management Journal*, 19: 533–553.

123. P. C. Fiss, 2006, Social influence effects and managerial compensation evidence from Germany, *Strategic Management Journal*, 27: 1013–1031; S. Douma, 1997, The two-tier system of corporate governance, *Long Range Planning*, 30(4): 612–615.

124. P. C. Fiss & E. J. Zajac, 2004, The diffusion of ideas over contested terrain: The (non) adoption of a shareholder value orientation among German firms, *Administrative Science Quarterly*, 49: 501–534.

125. W. G. Sanders & A. C. Tuschke, 2007, The adoption of the institutionally contested organizational practices: The emergence of stock option pay in Germany, *Academy of Management Journal*, 57: 33–56.

126. T. Hoshi, A. K. Kashyap, & S. Fischer, 2001, *Corporate Financing and Governance in Japan*, Boston: MIT Press.

127. J. P. Charkham, 1994. *Keeping Good Companies: A Study of Corporate Governance in Five Countries*. New York: Oxford University Press, 70.

128. M. A. Hitt, H. Lee, & E. Yucel, 2002, The importance of social capital to the management of multinational enterprises: Relational networks among Asian and Western firms, *Asia Pacific Journal of Management*, 19: 353–372.

129. W. P. Wan, D. W. Yiu, R. E. Hoskisson, & H. Kim, 2008, The performance implications of relationship banking during macroeconomic expansion and contraction: A study of Japanese banks' social relationships and overseas expansion, *Journal of International Business Studies*, 39: 406–427.

130. P. M. Lee & H. M. O'Neill, 2003, Ownership structures and R&D investments of U.S. and Japanese firms: Agency and stewardship perspectives, *Academy of Management Journal*, 46: 212–225.

131. I. S. Dinc, 2006, Monitoring the monitors: The corporate governance in Japanese banks and their real estate lending in the 1980s, *Journal of Business*, 79(6): 3057–3081; A. Kawaura, 2004, Deregulation and governance: Plight of Japanese banks in the 1990s, *Applied Economics*, 36: 479–484; B. Bremner, 2001, Cleaning up the banks—finally, *BusinessWeek*, December 17, 86; 2000, Business: Japan's corporate-governance U-turn, *The Economist*, November 18, 73.

132. N. Isagawa, 2007, A theory of unwinding of cross-shareholding under managerial entrenchment, *Journal of Financial Research*, 30: 163–179.

133. C. L. Ahmadjian & G. E. Robbins, 2005, A clash of capitalisms: Foreign shareholders and corporate restructuring in 1990s Japan, *American Sociological Review*, 70: 451–471.

134. J. M. Ramseyer, M. Nakazato, & E. B. Rasmusen, 2009, Public and private firm compensation: Evidence from Japanese tax returns, Harvard Law and Economics Discussion Paper, February 1.

135. S. R. Miller, D. Li, L. Eden, & M. A. Hitt, 2008, Insider trading and the valuation of international strategic alliances in emerging stock markets. *Journal of International Business Studies*, 39: 102–117.

136. H. Zou & M. B. Adams, 2008, Corporate ownership, equity risk and returns in the People's Republic of China, *Journal of International Business Studies*, 39: 1149–1168.

137. Y. Su, D. Xu, & P. H. Phan, 2008, Principal-principal conflict in the governance of the Chinese public corporation, *Management and Organization Review*, 4: 17–38.

138. China YCT International strengthens corporate governance with establishment of audit committee and appointments of three new independent directors, 2009.

139. T. Buck, X. Lui, & R. Skovoroda, 2008, Top executives pay and firm performance in China, *Journal of International Business Studies*, 39: 833–850.

140. P. M. Vaaler & B. N. Schrage, 2009, Residual state ownership, policy stability and financial performance following strategic decisions by privatizing telecoms, *Journal of International Business Studies*, 40: 621–641.

141. Steel Partners issues statement on changes to KT&G's board of directors, 2008, *Reuters*, http://www.reuters.com, March 13; L. Santini, 2007, Rematch: KT&G vs. Steel Partners: Korean cigarette maker again angers an activist fund, *Wall Street Journal*, June 22, C5.

142. Steel Partners LLC, 2009, *BusinessWeek*, http://investing.businessweek.com, April 16.

143. I. Filatotchev, J. Stephan, & B. Jindra, 2008, Ownership structure, strategic controls and export intensity of foreign-invested firms in transition economies, *Journal of International Business Studies*, 39: 1133–1148.

144. T. J. Healey, 2007, Sarbox was the right medicine, *Wall Street Journal*, August 9, A13.

145. J. D. Hughes & J. H. Lee, 2007, The changing landscape of D & O liability, *Risk Management Journal*, January, 18–22.

146. C. Shropshire & A. J. Hillman, 2007, A longitudinal study of significant change in stakeholder management, *Business and Society*, 46(1): 63–87; S. Sharma & I. Henriques, 2005, Stakeholder influences on sustainability practices in the Canadian Forest products industry, *Strategic Management Journal*, 26: 159–180; A. J. Hillman, G. D. Keim, & R. A. Luce, 2001, Board composition and stakeholder performance: Do stakeholder directors make a difference? *Business and Society*, 40: 295–314.

147. D. L. Gold & J. W. Dienhart, 2007, Business ethics in the corporate governance era: Domestic and international trends in transparency, regulation, and corporate governance, *Business and Society Review*, 112(2): 163–170; N. Demise, 2005, Business ethics and corporate governance in Japan, *Business and Society*, 44: 211–217.

148. R. V. Aguilera, D. E. Rupp, C. A. Williams, & J. Ganapathi, 2007, Putting the S back in corporate social responsibility: A multilevel theory of social change in organizations, *Academy of Management Review*, 32(3): 836–863; Caldwell & Karri, Organizational governance and ethical systems: A covenantal approach to building trust; A. Felo, 2001, Ethics programs, board involvement, and potential conflicts of interest in corporate governance, *Journal of Business Ethics*, 32: 205–218.

149. Cummins achieves top ranking for corporate governance, 2009, *AEDNews*, http://www.aednet.org, March 16.

CHAPTER 11

Organizational Structure and Controls

Studying this chapter should provide you with the strategic management knowledge needed to:

1. Define organizational structure and controls and discuss the difference between strategic and financial controls.

2. Describe the relationship between strategy and structure.

3. Discuss the functional structures used to implement business-level strategies.

4. Explain the use of three versions of the multidivisional (M-form) structure to implement different diversification strategies.

5. Discuss the organizational structures used to implement three international strategies.

6. Define strategic networks and discuss how strategic center firms implement such networks at the business, corporate, and international levels.

CISCO'S EVOLUTION OF STRATEGY AND STRUCTURE

Cisco's focus traditionally has been on producing network equipment that enables voice, video, and data to travel across computer networks. Accordingly, its products are at the heart of allowing the Internet and intranets to function across most corporate, public, and educational institutions around the world. Because Cisco's rapid growth was influenced by the Internet, it focused on three semiautonomous lines of business with distinct customers: Internet service providers, large enterprises, and small and medium-sized businesses. Within each of these three lines of business was a self-contained organization with separate marketing and operational groups. This allowed the firm to grow rapidly by focusing on the idiosyncratic needs of different customer segments.

This structure worked because the market was expanding quickly. However, in 2001, the explosive growth ceased when the Internet bubble burst. Thus, on August 23, 2001, Cisco announced a reorganization. The restructuring created 11 technology groups or divisions, all of which had previously been in the three separate business organizations. The sales groups, however, maintained their focus on the three particular customer segments. The integration across technologies allowed for more efficient cost reduction, which was necessary given the external environment change. Despite the many changes, Cisco emphasized its constant focus on customers because of the informal organization and previous personal interconnections between people in the reorganized engineering groups and the marketing segments.

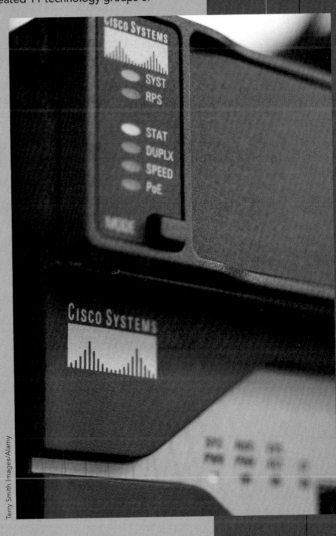

Terry Smith Images/Alamy

Over time, Cisco has also evolved its approach with the external environment. As networks matured, Cisco focused more on large-firm data centers. Therefore, Cisco has changed from a pure networking player focused on routers and switches to an overall information technology (IT) supplier. Thus it needed to build new software businesses as well as service collaborations. Furthermore it has expanded through acquisitions of software and hardware firms to create the necessary capabilities to develop a more integrated support system necessary to serve large corporate data centers. It also developed a consumer strategy by acquiring Linksys for home network systems and Scientific-Atlanta for television network boxes to facilitate cable systems. Likewise, it purchased software firms such as WebEx and IronPort to facilitate its corporate communication business and network security business, respectively. In addition, it has been collaborating with Accenture and Tata Consulting Services to provide an overall solutions business (as discussed in Chapter 9). Accordingly, not only is Cisco changing its focus on large and small customers, but it is offering software and consulting solution services.

The current downturn in the economy is forcing Cisco and other major firms to reposition and expand into nontraditional businesses in order to gain revenues lost in other areas. Most recently, it moved into "servers, which have been the traditional business of its former partners Hewlett-Packard and IBM. To manage this expansion and the integration process, Cisco needs to change its structure again. It is more likely that a corporate M-form will be necessary (this structure will be defined later in the chapter) because Cisco will need to not only have a large group of separate businesses, but it will need to integrate these businesses in a cooperative way such that all of the services are bundled and sold together to large IT centers. It will probably develop different structural approaches to manage its consumer businesses. It remains to be seen whether Cisco can make these changes effectively. Cisco does have one thing going for it—its strong culture focused on customer satisfaction. As stated earlier, customer focus is even embedded in its engineering divisions. But it will need more than a strategy—it will need a finely tuned organization to make it all work. Only time will tell whether Cisco is successful with this new strategy and the necessary structural adaptation.

Sources: R. Gulati & P. Puranam, 2009, Renewal through reorganization: The value of inconsistencies between formal and informal organization, *Organizational Science*, 20(2): 422–440; S. Lohr, 2009, In Sun, Oracle sees a software gem, *The New York Times*, http://www.nytimes.com, April 20; S. H. Wildstrom, 2009, Meet Cisco, the consumer company, *BusinessWeek*, May 4, 73; B. Worthen & J. Scheck, 2009, As growth slows, ex-allies square off in a turf war, *Wall Street Journal*, March 16, A1; J. Duffy, 2008, Cisco accelerates shift to software, data center, *Network World*, January 7, 12; J. Duffy, 2008, Cisco plans data center product overhaul, *Network World*, December 15, 1–2; B. Novak, 2008, Cisco connects the dots; aligning leaders with new organizational structure, *Global Business and Organizational Excellence*, 27(5): 22–32.

As we explain in Chapter 4, all firms use one or more business-level strategies. In Chapters 6–9, we discuss other strategies firms may choose to use (corporate-level, international, and cooperative). Once selected, strategies are not implemented in a vacuum. Organizational structure and controls, this chapter's topic, provide the framework within which strategies are used in both for-profit organizations and not-for-profit agencies.[1] However, as we explain, separate structures and controls are required to successfully implement different strategies. In all organizations, top-level managers have the final responsibility for ensuring that the firm has matched each of its strategies with the appropriate organizational structure and that both change when necessary. Thus, John Chambers, the CEO of Cisco, is responsible for changing its organizational structure if the firm decides to use a different business or corporate-level strategy. The match or degree of fit between strategy and structure influences the firm's attempts to earn above-average returns.[2] Thus, the ability to select an appropriate strategy and match it with the appropriate structure is an important characteristic of effective strategic leadership.[3]

This chapter opens with an introduction to organizational structure and controls. We then provide more details about the need for the firm's strategy and structure to be properly matched. Affecting firms' efforts to match strategy and structure is their influence on each other.[4] As we discuss, strategy has a more important influence on structure, although once in place, structure influences strategy.[5] Next, we describe the relationship between growth and structural change successful firms experience. We then discuss the different organizational structures firms use to implement the separate business-level, corporate-level, international, and cooperative strategies. A series of figures highlights the different structures firms match with strategies. Across time and based on their experiences, organizations, especially large and complex ones, customize these general structures to meet their unique needs.[6] Typically, the firm tries to form a structure that is complex enough to facilitate use of its strategies but simple enough for all parties to understand and implement.[7] When strategies become more diversified as with Cisco's in the Opening Case, a firm must adjust its structure to deal with the increased complexity.[8]

Organizational Structure and Controls

Research shows that organizational structure and the controls that are a part of the structure affect firm performance.[9] In particular, evidence suggests that performance declines when the firm's strategy is not matched with the most appropriate structure and controls.[10] Even though mismatches between strategy and structure do occur, research indicates that managers try to act rationally when forming or changing their firm's structure.[11] His record of success at General Electric (GE) suggests that CEO Jeffrey

Immelt pays close attention to the need to make certain that strategy and structure remain matched, as evidenced by restructuring alignments in GE Capital, GE's financial service group, during the economic downturn.[12]

Organizational Structure

Organizational structure specifies the firm's formal reporting relationships, procedures, controls, and authority and decision-making processes.[13] Developing an organizational structure that effectively supports the firm's strategy is difficult, especially because of the uncertainty (or unpredictable variation[14]) about cause-effect relationships in the global economy's rapidly changing and dynamic competitive environments.[15] When a structure's elements (e.g., reporting relationships, procedures, etc.) are properly aligned with one another, the structure facilitates effective use of the firm's strategies.[16] Thus, organizational structure is a critical component of effective strategy implementation processes.[17]

A firm's structure specifies the work to be done and how to do it, given the firm's strategy or strategies.[18] Thus, organizational structure influences how managers work and the decisions resulting from that work.[19] Supporting the implementation of strategies, structure is concerned with processes used to complete organizational tasks.[20] Having the right structure and process is important. For example, many product-oriented firms have been moving to develop service businesses associated with those products. This has been a strategy used by many of GE's businesses, such as medical equipment. However, research suggests that developing a separate division for such services in product-oriented companies, rather than managing the service business within the product divisions, leads to additional growth and profitability in the service business.[21]

Effective structures provide the stability a firm needs to successfully implement its strategies and maintain its current competitive advantages while simultaneously providing the flexibility to develop advantages it will need in the future.[22] *Structural stability* provides the capacity the firm requires to consistently and predictably manage its daily work routines[23] while *structural flexibility* provides the opportunity to explore competitive possibilities and then allocate resources to activities that will shape the competitive advantages the firm will need to be successful in the future.[24] An effectively flexible organizational structure allows the firm to *exploit* current competitive advantages while *developing* new ones that can potentially be used in the future.[25] For example, the management system at Cisco is said to provide "speed, skill, and flexibility."[26] Cisco is able to accomplish this by using team-based processes as an overlay to its basic structure, allowing it to exploit its current advantages while exploring for new ones.

Modifications to the firm's current strategy or selection of a new strategy call for changes to its organizational structure. However, research shows that once in place, organizational inertia often inhibits efforts to change structure, even when the firm's performance suggests that it is time to do so.[27] In his pioneering work, Alfred Chandler found that organizations change their structures when inefficiencies force them to.[28] Chandler's contributions to our understanding of organizational structure and its relationship to strategies and performance are quite significant. Indeed, some believe that Chandler's emphasis on "organizational structure so transformed the field of business history that some call the period before Dr. Chandler's publications 'B.C.,' meaning 'before Chandler.'"[29]

Firms seem to prefer the structural status quo and its familiar working relationships until the firm's performance declines to the point where change is absolutely necessary.[30] For example, necessity is obviously the case for General Motors given that it went into bankruptcy to force the required restructuring.[31]

In addition to the issues we already mentioned, it is important to note that top-level managers hesitate to conclude that the firm's structure (or its strategy, for that matter) are the problem, in that doing so suggests that their previous choices were not the best ones. Because of these inertial tendencies, structural change is often induced instead by actions

Organizational structure specifies the firm's formal reporting relationships, procedures, controls, and authority and decision-making processes.

from stakeholders (e.g., those from the capital market and customers—see Chapter 2) who are no longer willing to tolerate the firm's performance. Evidence shows that appropriate timing of structural change happens when top-level managers recognize that a current organizational structure no longer provides the coordination and direction needed for the firm to successfully implement its strategies.[32] Interestingly, many organizational changes are taking place in the current economic downturn, apparently because poor performance reveals organizational weaknesses. As we discuss next, effective organizational controls help managers recognize when it is time to adjust the firm's structure.

Organizational Controls

Organizational controls are an important aspect of structure.[33] **Organizational controls** guide the use of strategy, indicate how to compare actual results with expected results, and suggest corrective actions to take when the difference is unacceptable. When fewer differences separate actual from expected outcomes, the organization's controls are more effective.[34] It is difficult for the company to successfully exploit its competitive advantages without effective organizational controls.[35] Properly designed organizational controls provide clear insights regarding behaviors that enhance firm performance.[36] Firms use both strategic controls and financial controls to support using their strategies.

Strategic controls are largely subjective criteria intended to verify that the firm is using appropriate strategies for the conditions in the external environment and the company's competitive advantages. Thus, strategic controls are concerned with examining the fit between what the firm *might do* (as suggested by opportunities in its external environment) and what it *can do* (as indicated by its competitive advantages). Effective strategic controls help the firm understand what it takes to be successful.[37] Strategic controls demand rich communications between managers responsible for using them to judge the firm's performance and those with primary responsibility for implementing the firm's strategies (such as middle and first-level managers). These frequent exchanges are both formal and informal in nature.[38]

Strategic controls are also used to evaluate the degree to which the firm focuses on the requirements to implement its strategies. For a business-level strategy, for example, the strategic controls are used to study primary and support activities (see Tables 3.6 and 3.7, on page 87) to verify that the critical activities are being emphasized and properly executed.[39] With related corporate-level strategies, strategic controls are used by corporate strategic leaders to verify the sharing of appropriate strategic factors such as knowledge, markets, and technologies across businesses. To effectively use strategic controls when evaluating related diversification strategies, headquarter executives must have a deep understanding of each unit's business-level strategy.[40]

As we described in the Opening Case, Cisco's executives allocate a great deal of time and energy to issues related to strategic control. Constantly challenged to meet the demands of an ever-changing market, John Chambers, Cisco's CEO, was able to implement a revised strategic controls system where he "was able to surrender his role as a command-and-control CEO and institute a collaborative decision-making model that allows the company to respond speedily to emerging transitions."[41] Using this system on strategic control allowed Cisco to move to open source software development before competitors such as Microsoft. They also were one of the first companies to move to Web-based customer service centers from call centers having foreseen this change through their strategic control system.

Financial controls are largely objective criteria used to measure the firm's performance against previously established quantitative standards. Accounting-based measures such as return on investment (ROI) and return on assets (ROA) as well as market-based measures such as economic value added are examples of financial controls. Partly because strategic controls are difficult to use with extensive diversification,[42] financial controls are emphasized to evaluate the performance of the firm using the unrelated diversification strategy. The unrelated diversification strategy's focus on financial outcomes (see Chapter 6)

Organizational controls guide the use of strategy, indicate how to compare actual results with expected results, and suggest corrective actions to take when the difference is unacceptable.

Strategic controls are largely subjective criteria intended to verify that the firm is using appropriate strategies for the conditions in the external environment and the company's competitive advantages.

Financial controls are largely objective criteria used to measure the firm's performance against previously established quantitative standards.

requires using standardized financial controls to compare performances between business units and associated managers.[43]

When using financial controls, firms evaluate their current performance against previous outcomes as well as against competitors' performance and industry averages. In the global economy, technological advances are being used to develop highly sophisticated financial controls, making it possible for firms to more thoroughly analyze their performance results and to assure compliance with regulations. Companies such as Oracle and SAP sell software tools that automate processes firms use to meet the financial reporting requirements specified by the Sarbanes-Oxley Act. (As noted in Chapter 10, this act requires a firm's principal executive and financial officers to certify corporate financial and related information in quarterly and annual reports submitted to the Securities and Exchange Commission.)

Image99/Image100/Jupiter Images

The complexities of managing global companies are driving the development and implementation of sophisticated financial control applications.

Both strategic and financial controls are important aspects of each organizational structure, and as we noted previously, any structure's effectiveness is determined by using a combination of strategic and financial controls. However, the relative use of controls varies by type of strategy. For example, companies and business units of large diversified firms using the cost leadership strategy emphasize financial controls (such as quantitative cost goals), while companies and business units using the differentiation strategy emphasize strategic controls (such as subjective measures of the effectiveness of product development teams).[44] As previously explained, a corporate-wide emphasis on sharing among business units (as called for by related diversification strategies) results in an emphasis on strategic controls, while financial controls are emphasized for strategies in which activities or capabilities are not shared (e.g., in an unrelated diversification strategy).

As firms consider controls, the important point is to properly balance the use of strategic and financial controls. Indeed, overemphasizing one at the expense of the other can lead to performance declines. According to Michael Dell, an overemphasis on financial controls to produce attractive short-term results contributed to performance difficulties at Dell Inc. In addressing this issue, Dell said the following: "The company was too focused on the short term, and the balance of priorities was way too leaning toward things that deliver short-term results."[45] Executives at Dell have now achieved a more appropriate emphasis on the long term as well as the short term due a reemphasis on strategic controls, although Dell is still playing catch up to Hewlett-Packard.[46]

STRATEGY RIGHT NOW

For another example of how organizations use both strategic and financial controls, read about the FDIC's (Federal Deposit Insurance Corporation) recent passage of new rules governing deposit rates and credit reporting.

www.cengage.com/management/hitt

Relationships between Strategy and Structure

Strategy and structure have a reciprocal relationship.[47] This relationship highlights the interconnectedness between strategy formulation (Chapters 4, 6–9) and strategy implementation (Chapters 10–13). In general, this reciprocal relationship finds structure flowing from or following selection of the firm's strategy. Once in place though, structure can influence current strategic actions as well as choices about future strategies. Consider, for example, the possible influences of the Cisco's structure and control system in influencing its strategy as illustrated in the Opening Case.

The general nature of the strategy/structure relationship means that changes to the firm's strategy create the need to change how the organization completes its work. In the "structure influences strategy" direction, firms must be vigilant in their efforts to verify that how their structure calls for work to be completed remains consistent with the implementation requirements of chosen strategies. Research shows, however, that "strategy has a much more important influence on structure than the reverse."[48]

Regardless of the strength of the reciprocal relationships between strategy and structure, those choosing the firm's strategy and structure should be committed to matching each strategy with a structure that provides the stability needed to use current competitive advantages as well as the flexibility required to develop future advantages. Therefore, when changing strategies, the firm should simultaneously consider the structure that will be needed to support use of the new strategy; properly matching strategy and structure can create a competitive advantage.[49]

Evolutionary Patterns of Strategy and Organizational Structure

Research suggests that most firms experience a certain pattern of relationships between strategy and structure. Chandler[50] found that firms tend to grow in somewhat predictable

Figure 11.1 Strategy and Structure Growth Pattern

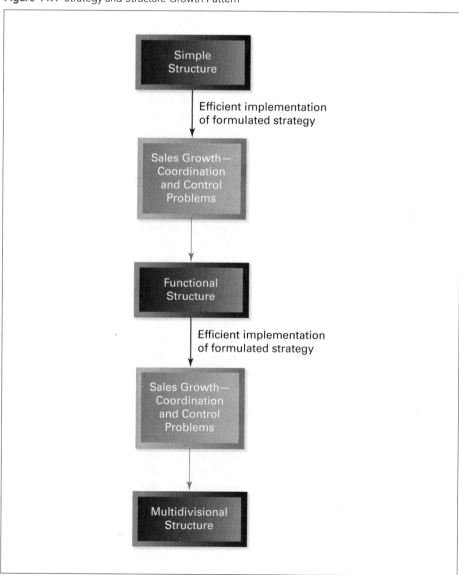

patterns: "first by volume, then by geography, then integration (vertical, horizontal), and finally through product/business diversification"[51] (see Figure 11.1). Chandler interpreted his findings as an indication that firms' growth patterns determine their structural form.

As shown in Figure 11.1, sales growth creates coordination and control problems the existing organizational structure cannot efficiently handle. Organizational growth creates the opportunity for the firm to change its strategy to try to become even more successful. However, the existing structure's formal reporting relationships, procedures, controls, and authority and decision-making processes lack the sophistication required to support using the new strategy.[52] A new structure is needed to help decision makers gain access to the knowledge and understanding required to effectively integrate and coordinate actions to implement the new strategy.[53]

Firms choose from among three major types of organizational structures—simple, functional, and multidivisional—to implement strategies. Across time, successful firms move from the simple to the functional to the multidivisional structure to support changes in their growth strategies.[54]

Simple Structure

The **simple structure** is a structure in which the owner-manager makes all major decisions and monitors all activities while the staff serves as an extension of the manager's supervisory authority.[55] Typically, the owner-manager actively works in the business on a daily basis. Informal relationships, few rules, limited task specialization, and unsophisticated information systems characterize this structure. Frequent and informal communications between the owner-manager and employees make coordinating the work to be done relatively easy. The simple structure is matched with focus strategies and business-level strategies, as firms implementing these strategies commonly compete by offering a single product line in a single geographic market. Local restaurants, repair businesses, and other specialized enterprises are examples of firms using the simple structure.

As the small firm grows larger and becomes more complex, managerial and structural challenges emerge. For example, the amount of competitively relevant information requiring analysis substantially increases, placing significant pressure on the owner-manager. Additional growth and success may cause the firm to change its strategy. Even if the strategy remains the same, the firm's larger size dictates the need for more sophisticated workflows and integrating mechanisms. At this evolutionary point, firms tend to move from the simple structure to a functional organizational structure.[56]

Functional Structure

The **functional structure** consists of a chief executive officer and a limited corporate staff, with functional line managers in dominant organizational areas such as production, accounting, marketing, R&D, engineering, and human resources.[57] This structure allows for functional specialization,[58] thereby facilitating active sharing of knowledge within each functional area. Knowledge sharing facilitates career paths as well as professional development of functional specialists. However, a functional orientation can negatively affect communication and coordination among those representing different organizational functions. For this reason, the CEO must work hard to verify that the decisions and actions of individual business functions promote the entire firm rather than a single function. The functional structure supports implementing business-level strategies and some corporate-level strategies (e.g., single or dominant business) with low levels of diversification. When changing from a simple to a functional structure, firms want to avoid introducing value-destroying bureaucratic procedures such as failing to promote innovation and creativity.[59]

Multidivisional Structure

With continuing growth and success, firms often consider greater levels of diversification. Successfully using a diversification strategy requires analyzing substantially greater

The **simple structure** is a structure in which the owner-manager makes all major decisions and monitors all activities while the staff serves as an extension of the manager's supervisory authority.

The **functional structure** consists of a chief executive officer and a limited corporate staff, with functional line managers in dominant organizational areas such as production, accounting, marketing, R&D, engineering, and human resources.

amounts of data and information when the firm offers the same products in different markets (market or geographic diversification) or offers different products in several markets (product diversification). In addition, trying to manage high levels of diversification through functional structures creates serious coordination and control problems,[60] a fact that commonly leads to a new structural form.[61]

The **multidivisional (M-form) structure** consists of a corporate office and operating divisions, each operating division representing a separate business or profit center in which the top corporate officer delegates responsibilities for day-to-day operations and business-unit strategy to division managers. Each division represents a distinct, self-contained business with its own functional hierarchy.[62] As initially designed, the M-form was thought to have three major benefits: "(1) it enabled corporate officers to more accurately monitor the performance of each business, which simplified the problem of control; (2) it facilitated comparisons between divisions, which improved the resource allocation process; and (3) it stimulated managers of poorly performing divisions to look for ways of improving performance."[63] Active monitoring of performance through the M-form increases the likelihood that decisions made by managers heading individual units will be in stakeholders' best interests. Because diversification is a dominant corporate-level strategy used in the global economy, the M-form is a widely adopted organizational structure.[64]

Used to support implementation of related and unrelated diversification strategies, the M-form helps firms successfully manage diversification's many demands.[65] Chandler viewed the M-form as an innovative response to coordination and control problems that surfaced during the 1920s in the functional structures then used by large firms such as DuPont and General Motors.[66] Research shows that the M-form is appropriate when the firm grows through diversification.[67] Partly because of its value to diversified corporations, some consider the multidivisional structure to be one of the twentieth century's most significant organizational innovations.[68]

No one organizational structure (simple, functional, or multidivisional) is inherently superior to the others.[69] Peter Drucker says the following about this matter: "There is no one right organization. ... Rather the task ... is to select the organization for the particular task and mission at hand."[70] In our context, Drucker is saying that the firm must select a structure that is "right" for successfully using the chosen strategy. Because no single structure is optimal in all instances, managers concentrate on developing proper matches between strategies and organizational structures rather than searching for an "optimal" structure. This matching of structure and strategy is taking place at Cisco. As noted in the Opening Case, John Chambers is increasing the firm's level of diversification and as such is adjusting its structure to match.

We now describe the strategy/structure matches that evidence shows positively contribute to firm performance.

Matches between Business-Level Strategies and the Functional Structure

Firms use different forms of the functional organizational structure to support implementing the cost leadership, differentiation, and integrated cost leadership/differentiation strategies. The differences in these forms are accounted for primarily by different uses of three important structural characteristics: *specialization* (concerned with the type and number of jobs required to complete work[71]), *centralization* (the degree to which decision-making authority is retained at higher managerial levels[72]), and *formalization* (the degree to which formal rules and procedures govern work[73]).

Using the Functional Structure to Implement the Cost Leadership Strategy

Firms using the cost leadership strategy sell large quantities of standardized products to an industry's typical customer. Simple reporting relationships, few layers in the decision-making and authority structure, a centralized corporate staff, and a strong focus on

---

The **multidivisional (M-form) structure** consists of a corporate office and operating divisions, each operating division representing a separate business or profit center in which the top corporate officer delegates responsibilities for day-to-day operations and business-unit strategy to division managers.

process improvements through the manufacturing function rather than the development of new products by emphasizing product R&D characterize the cost leadership form of the functional structure[74] (see Figure 11.2). This structure contributes to the emergence of a low-cost culture—a culture in which employees constantly try to find ways to reduce the costs incurred to complete their work.[75]

In terms of centralization, decision-making authority is centralized in a staff function to maintain a cost-reducing emphasis within each organizational function (engineering, marketing, etc.). While encouraging continuous cost reductions, the centralized staff also verifies that further cuts in costs in one function won't adversely affect the productivity levels in other functions.[76]

Jobs are highly specialized in the cost leadership functional structure; work is divided into homogeneous subgroups. Organizational functions are the most common subgroup, although work is sometimes batched on the basis of products produced or clients served. Specializing in their work allows employees to increase their efficiency, resulting in reduced costs. Guiding individuals' work in this structure are highly formalized rules and procedures, which often emanate from the centralized staff.

Wal-Mart Stores Inc. uses the functional structure to implement cost leadership strategies in each of its three segments (Wal-Mart Stores, Sam's Clubs, and International). In the Wal-Mart Stores segment (which generates the largest share of the firm's total sales), the cost leadership strategy is used in the firm's Supercenter, Discount, and Neighborhood Market retailing formats.[77] Long known for its "Always Low Prices" slogan (which was used for 19 years), Wal-Mart recently changed to a new slogan—"Save Money, Live Better."[78] Although the slogan is new, Wal-Mart continues using the functional organizational structure in its divisions to drive costs lower. As discussed in Chapter 4, competitors' efforts to duplicate the success of Wal-Mart's cost leadership

Figure 11.2 Functional Structure for Implementing a Cost Leadership Strategy

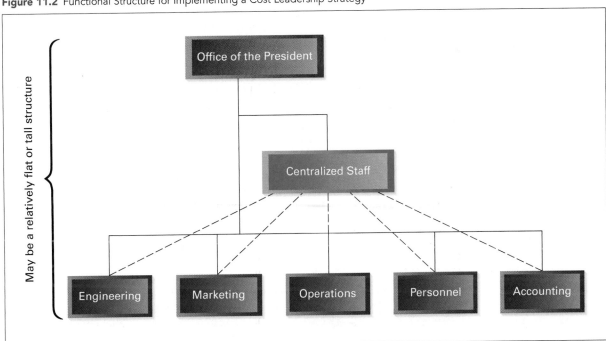

Notes:
- Operations is the main function
- Process engineering is emphasized rather than new product R&D
- Relatively large centralized staff coordinates functions
- Formalized procedures allow for emergence of a low-cost culture
- Overall structure is mechanistic; job roles are highly structured

strategies have generally failed, partly because of the effective strategy/structure matches in each of the firm's segments.

Using the Functional Structure to Implement the Differentiation Strategy

Firms using the differentiation strategy produce products customers perceive as being different in ways that create value for them. With this strategy, the firm wants to sell non-standardized products to customers with unique needs. Relatively complex and flexible reporting relationships, frequent use of cross-functional product development teams, and a strong focus on marketing and product R&D rather than manufacturing and process R&D (as with the cost leadership form of the functional structure) characterize the differentiation form of the functional structure (see Figure 11.3). From this structure emerges a development-oriented culture in which employees try to find ways to further differentiate current products and to develop new, highly differentiated products.[79]

Continuous product innovation demands that people throughout the firm interpret and take action based on information that is often ambiguous, incomplete, and uncertain. Following a strong focus on the external environment to identify new opportunities, employees often gather this information from people outside the firm (e.g., customers and suppliers). Commonly, rapid responses to the possibilities indicated by the collected information are necessary, suggesting the need for decentralized decision-making responsibility and authority. To support creativity and the continuous pursuit of new sources of differentiation and new products, jobs in this structure are not highly specialized. This lack of specialization means that workers have a relatively large number of tasks in their job descriptions. Few formal rules and procedures also characterize this structure. Low formalization, decentralization of decision-making authority and responsibility, and low specialization of work tasks combine to create a structure in which people interact frequently to exchange ideas about how to further differentiate current products while developing ideas for new products that can be crisply differentiated.

Figure 11.3 Functional Structure for Implementing a Differentiation Strategy

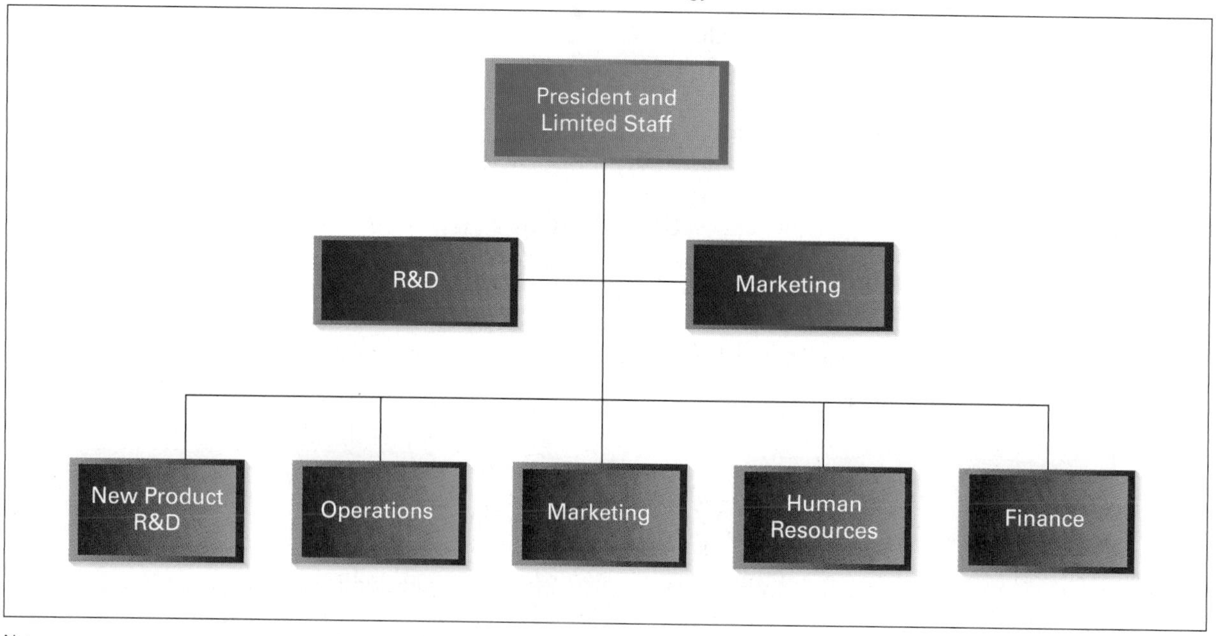

Notes:
- Marketing is the main function for keeping track of new product ideas
- New product R&D is emphasized
- Most functions are decentralized, but R&D and marketing may have centralized staffs that work closely with each other
- Formalization is limited so that new product ideas can emerge easily and change is more readily accomplished
- Overall structure is organic; job roles are less structured

Under Armour has used a differentiation strategy and matching structure to create success in the sports apparel market. Under Armour's objective was to create improved athletic performance through innovative design, testing, and marketing, especially to professional athletes and teams, and translate that perception to the broader market. With a strong match between strategy and structure, it has successfully created innovative sports performance products and challenged Nike and other sports apparel competitors.[80]

Using the Functional Structure to Implement the Integrated Cost Leadership/Differentiation Strategy

Firms using the integrated cost leadership/differentiation strategy sell products that create value because of their relatively low cost and reasonable sources of differentiation. The cost of these products is low "relative" to the cost leader's prices while their differentiation is "reasonable" when compared with the clearly unique features of the differentiator's products.

Although challenging to implement, the integrated cost leadership/differentiation strategy is used frequently in the global economy. The challenge of using this structure is due largely to the fact that different primary and support activities (see Chapter 3) are emphasized when using the cost leadership and differentiation strategies. To achieve the cost leadership position, production and process engineering are emphasized, with infrequent product changes. To achieve a differentiated position, marketing and new product R&D are emphasized while production and process engineering are not. Thus, effective use of the integrated strategy depends on the firm's successful combination of activities intended to reduce costs with activities intended to create additional differentiation features. As a result, the integrated form of the functional structure must have decision-making patterns that are partially centralized and partially decentralized. Additionally, jobs are semispecialized, and rules and procedures call for some formal and some informal job behavior.

Matches between Corporate-Level Strategies and the Multidivisional Structure

As explained earlier, Chandler's research shows that the firm's continuing success leads to product or market diversification or both.[81] The firm's level of diversification is a function of decisions about the number and type of businesses in which it will compete as well as how it will manage the businesses (see Chapter 6). Geared to managing individual organizational functions, increasing diversification eventually creates information processing, coordination, and control problems that the functional structure cannot handle. Thus, using a diversification strategy requires the firm to change from the functional structure to the multidivisional structure to develop an appropriate strategy/structure match.

As defined in Figure 6.1, corporate-level strategies have different degrees of product and market diversification. The demands created by different levels of diversification highlight the need for a unique organizational structure to effectively implement each strategy (see Figure 11.4).

Using the Cooperative Form of the Multidivisional Structure to Implement the Related Constrained Strategy

The **cooperative form** is an M-form structure in which horizontal integration is used to bring about interdivisional cooperation. Divisions in a firm using the related constrained diversification strategy commonly are formed around products, markets, or both. In Figure 11.5, we use product divisions as part of the representation of the cooperative form of the multidivisional structure, although market divisions could be used instead of or in addition to product divisions to develop the figure.

Using this structure, Hewlett-Packard (HP) has implemented the related constrained strategy as described in the Strategic Focus. HP's intent is to sell integrated solutions to corporate data centers, so it has placed an emphasis on creating more relationships

> The **cooperative form** is an M-form structure in which horizontal integration is used to bring about interdivisional cooperation.

Figure 11.4 Three Variations of the Multidivisional Structure

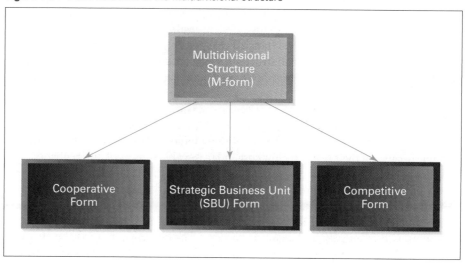

Figure 11.5 Cooperative Form of the Multidivisional Structure for Implementing a Related Constrained Strategy

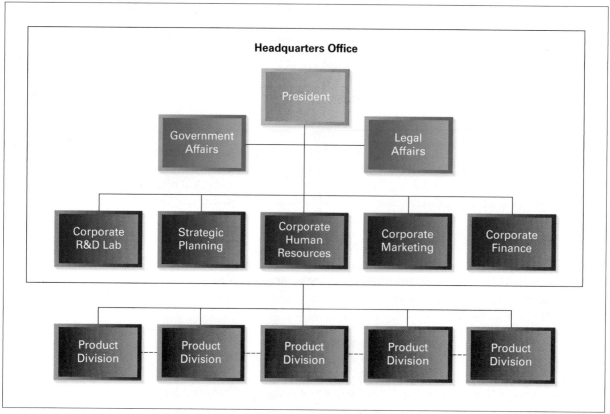

Notes:

- Structural integration devices create tight links among all divisions
- Corporate office emphasizes centralized strategic planning, human resources, and marketing to foster cooperation between divisions
- R&D is likely to be centralized
- Rewards are subjective and tend to emphasize overall corporate performance in addition to divisional performance
- Culture emphasizes cooperative sharing

HEWLETT-PACKARD IMPLEMENTS THE RELATED CONSTRAINED STRATEGY THROUGH THE COOPERATIVE M-FORM STRUCTURE

Hewlett-Packard (HP) has three main related businesses through which it pursues industry leadership and technology development. First, it has the Personal Systems Group, including business and consumer PCs, mobile computing, and workstation devices. Second, it has a complementary business with a very large market share in Imaging and Printing, which includes inkjet and laserjet printers, commercial printing, printing supplies, digital photography, and entertainment products and support. Finally, it has a Technology Service Solutions Group, which includes business products focused on servers and storage, managed services and software, and services solutions. This group has been augmented through its recent acquisition of Electronic Data Systems (EDS). HP is number nine in the 2009 *Fortune* 500 Ranking with more than $118 billion in total revenue for fiscal year 2008.

Its main focus for customers is on corporate data centers that allow connected mobile computing, printing, and imaging delivery. HP pursues a related constrained strategy (as discussed in Chapter 6) by using the cooperative M-form structure. As firms pursue diversified growth and the economy becomes more Internet based, corporate data centers are increasingly important to help firms pursue improved top-line and bottom-line growth. HP's three main businesses allow the related strategy to work well by focusing on the growing importance of corporate data centers. Firms that seek to deliver the products and services necessary to the centers are required to have interrelated services and businesses to sell integrated solutions.

This is driving firms that have a dominant focus on one product category to move into the other categories. For instance, Cisco, as noted in the Opening Case, is moving toward a corporate data center approach but coming at it from a traditional focus on network equipment. For this reason it is now moving into servers, which has been one of HP's dominant businesses (Cisco previously partnered with HP in this area). Like Cisco, HP has moved away from its formerly decentralized structure toward a related constrained strategy by seeking to implement the cooperative M-form organization structure. The cooperative M-form requires more centralization to make it function appropriately and to foster cooperation between the separate divisions within and across business unit divisions. This requires distinctive leadership and focus on improved execution to function properly.

Mark Hurd, the current CEO who succeeded Carly Fiorina in 2005, has been able to fine-tune HP's structural approach through his "get things done" mentality. One security analyst describes Hurd as someone who is, "… all about execution and has an uncanny ability to get things done." Furthermore, this same analyst suggests, "He is the most adept at taking costs out of the system than any executive I know." His no-nonsense style has led to increasing operational efficiency by realizing a strong implementation of the cooperative M-form structure. For instance, through the $13 billion acquisition of the consulting services firm

David Paul Morris/Getty Images News/Getty Images

Mark Hurd, President and CEO of Hewlett-Packard, has increased efficiency and reduced costs at HP through the implementation of the cooperative M-form structure.

EDS in 2008, Hurd cut 15,000 jobs or 10 percent of the workforce to create the synergistic effect needed across all businesses. In 2009, this led HP to project a decline of 5 percent in revenues, but to still be able to project a 6 percent growth in profits, all despite the economic downturn.

Although the cooperative structure implementation has created wealth and efficiency, there are those who speculate that Hurd's approach has an Achilles heel because it lacks an emphasis on breakthrough innovation such as Apple's iPod and iPhone. Robert Burgelman, a Stanford professor who has studied Hurd, says, "He will not tell them we should do this project or that project. He helps them think more clearly about the space in which they are operating." While these actions have made HP's R&D operations more efficient, Hurd may need to give employees more creative license if he wants breakthrough innovations that would allow HP to compete more effectively with IBM and Apple.

Sources: J. Brodkin, 2009, HP BladeSystem, Matrix takes aim at Cisco, *Network World*, April 20, 34; A. Lashinsky, 2009, Mark Hurd's moment, *Fortune*, March 16, 90–100; J. Scheck, 2009, Corporate news: HP chief sees more pain ahead, trims more jobs, *Wall Street Journal*, May 20, B3; B. Worthen & J. Scheck, 2009, H-P to step up fight in market for servers, *Wall Street Journal*, April 16, B5; C. Edwards, 2008, How HP got the wow! back, *BusinessWeek*, December 20, 60; J. Fortt, 2008, Mark Hurd, superstar, *Fortune*, June 29, 35; J. Jain, 2008, Decision sciences: A story of excellence at Hewlett-Packard, *OR-MS Today*, 35(2): 20; L. Lee, 2008, HP's Hurd is about to be tested: After a sterling three-year run, the company's CEO faces a weaker PC market and a stronger Dell, *BusinessWeek*, February 14, 59–60; 2008, Business: Now services; Hewlett-Packard, *Economist*, May, 78; D. M. Zell, A. M. Glassman, & S. A. Duron, 2007, Strategic management in turbulent times: The short and glorious history of accelerated decision making at Hewlett-Packard, *Organizational Dynamics*, 36(1): 93–104.

among its products (servers, storage, mobile computing, and high-speed printers) and coordinating these products through value-added services. This has required the implementation of the cooperative M-form and more centralization among the various business units to foster cooperation and synergy.

Sharing divisional competencies facilitates the corporation's efforts to develop economies of scope. As explained in Chapter 6, economies of scope (cost savings resulting from the sharing of competencies developed in one division with another division) are linked with successful use of the related constrained strategy. Interdivisional sharing of competencies depends on cooperation, suggesting the use of the cooperative form of the multidivisional structure.[82] HP seems to have developed the structure and processes well to accomplish this.

The cooperative structure uses different characteristics of structure (centralization, standardization, and formalization) as integrating mechanisms to facilitate interdivisional cooperation. Frequent, direct contact between division managers, another integrating mechanism, encourages and supports cooperation and the sharing of competencies or resources that could be used to create new advantages. Sometimes, liaison roles are established in each division to reduce the time division managers spend integrating and coordinating their unit's work with the work occurring in other divisions. Temporary teams or task forces may be formed around projects whose success depends on sharing competencies that are embedded within several divisions. Cisco has used these devices to develop new cooperative strategies, as illustrated in the Opening Case. Formal integration departments might be established in firms frequently using temporary teams or task forces.

Ultimately, a matrix organization may evolve in firms implementing the related constrained strategy. A *matrix organization* is an organizational structure in which there is a dual structure combining both functional specialization and business product or project specialization.[83] Although complicated, an effective matrix structure can lead to improved coordination among a firm's divisions.[84]

The success of the cooperative multidivisional structure is significantly affected by how well divisions process information. However, because cooperation among divisions implies a loss of managerial autonomy, division managers may not readily commit themselves to the type of integrative information-processing activities that this structure demands. Moreover, coordination among divisions sometimes results in an unequal flow of positive outcomes to divisional managers. In other words, when managerial rewards are based at least in part on the performance of individual divisions, the manager of the division that is able to benefit the most by the sharing of corporate competencies might be viewed as receiving relative gains at others' expense. Strategic controls are important in these instances, as divisional managers' performance can be evaluated at least partly on the basis of how well they have facilitated interdivisional cooperative efforts. In addition, using reward systems that emphasize overall company performance, besides outcomes achieved by individual divisions, helps overcome problems associated with the cooperative form.

Using the Strategic Business Unit Form of the Multidivisional Structure to Implement the Related Linked Strategy

Firms with fewer links or less constrained links among their divisions use the related linked diversification strategy. The strategic business unit form of the multidivisional structure supports implementation of this strategy. The **strategic business unit (SBU) form** is an M-form structure consisting of three levels: corporate headquarters, strategic business units (SBUs), and SBU divisions (see Figure 11.6). The SBU structure is used by large firms and can be complex, given associated organization size and product and market diversity.

The **strategic business unit (SBU) form** is an M-form consisting of three levels: corporate headquarters, strategic business units (SBUs), and SBU divisions.

Figure 11.6 SBU Form of the Multidivisional Structure for Implementing a Related Linked Strategy

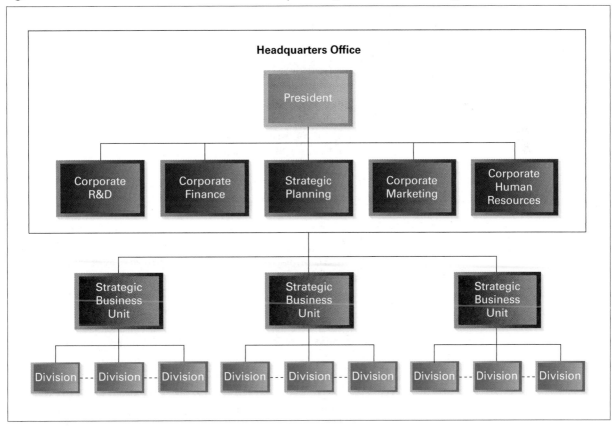

Notes:

• Structural integration among divisions within SBUs, but independence across SBUs
• Strategic planning may be the most prominent function in headquarters for managing the strategic planning approval process of SBUs for the president
• Each SBU may have its own budget for staff to foster integration
• Corporate headquarters staff members serve as consultants to SBUs and divisions, rather than having direct input to product strategy, as in the cooperative form

The divisions within each SBU are related in terms of shared products or markets or both, but the divisions of one SBU have little in common with the divisions of the other SBUs. Divisions within each SBU share product or market competencies to develop economies of scope and possibly economies of scale. The integrating mechanisms used by the divisions in this structure can be equally well used by the divisions within the individual strategic business units that are part of the SBU form of the multidivisional structure. In this structure, each SBU is a profit center that is controlled and evaluated by the headquarters office. Although both financial and strategic controls are important, on a relative basis financial controls are vital to headquarters' evaluation of each SBU; strategic controls are critical when the heads of SBUs evaluate their divisions' performances. Strategic controls are also critical to the headquarters' efforts to determine whether the company has formed an effective portfolio of businesses and whether those businesses are being successfully managed.

Sears Holdings changed to the SBU form in 2008 by dividing into five strategic business units (with multiple divisions as parts of each SBU): brands, real estate, support, online, and store operations.[85] This allowed for related businesses to work together (such as Sears and K-Mart) to focus on their distinct customer sets, but also provided for better control for headquarters in order to evaluate performance of each strategic business unit and division within the SBU.

Sharing competencies among units within an SBU is an important characteristic of the SBU form of the multidivisional structure (see the notes to Figure 11.6). A drawback to the SBU structure is that multifaceted businesses often have difficulties in communicating this complex business model to stockholders.[86] Furthermore, if coordination between SBUs is needed, problems can arise because the SBU structure, similar to the competitive form discussed next, does not readily foster cooperation across SBUs.

Using the Competitive Form of the Multidivisional Structure to Implement the Unrelated Diversification Strategy

Firms using the unrelated diversification strategy want to create value through efficient internal capital allocations or by restructuring, buying, and selling businesses.[87] The competitive form of the multidivisional structure supports implementation of this strategy.

The **competitive form** is an M-form structure characterized by complete independence among the firm's divisions which compete for corporate resources (see Figure 11.7). Unlike the divisions included in the cooperative structure, divisions that are part of the competitive structure do not share common corporate strengths. Because strengths are not shared, integrating devices are not developed for use by the divisions included in the competitive structure.

The efficient internal capital market that is the foundation for using the unrelated diversification strategy requires organizational arrangements emphasizing divisional competition rather than cooperation.[88] Three benefits are expected from the internal competition. First, internal competition creates flexibility (e.g., corporate headquarters can have divisions working on different technologies and projects to identify those with the greatest potential). Resources can then be allocated to the division appearing to have the most potential to fuel the entire firm's success. Second, internal competition challenges the status quo and inertia, because division heads know that future resource allocations are a product of excellent current performance as well as superior positioning in terms of future performance. Last, internal competition motivates effort in that the challenge of competing against internal peers can be as great as the challenge of competing against external rivals.[89] In this structure, organizational controls (primarily financial controls) are used to emphasize and support internal competition among separate divisions and as the basis for allocating corporate capital based on divisions' performances.

Textron Inc., a large "multi-industry" company seeks "to identify, research, select, acquire and integrate companies, and has developed a set of rigorous criteria to guide

The **competitive form** is an M-form structure characterized by complete independence among the firm's divisions which compete for corporate resources.

Figure 11.7 Competitive Form of the Multidivisional Structure for Implementing an Unrelated Strategy

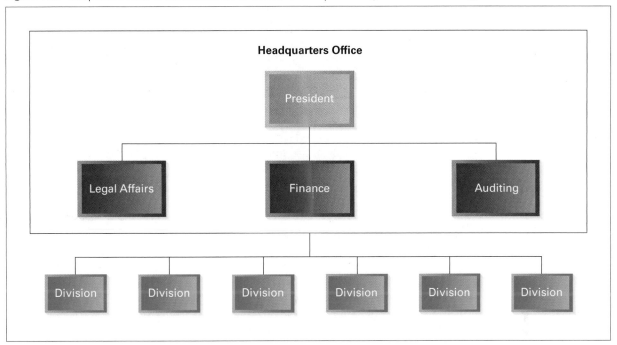

Notes:
- Corporate headquarters has a small staff
- Finance and auditing are the most prominent functions in the headquarters office to manage cash flow and assure the accuracy of performance data coming from divisions
- The legal affairs function becomes important when the firm acquires or divests assets
- Divisions are independent and separate for financial evaluation purposes
- Divisions retain strategic control, but cash is managed by the corporate office
- Divisions compete for corporate resources

decision making." Textron continuously looks "to enhance and reshape its portfolio by divesting non-core assets and acquiring branded businesses in attractive industries with substantial long-term growth potential." Textron operates four independent businesses—Bell Helicopter (20 percent of revenue), Cessna Aircraft (40 percent), Textron Systems (15 percent), Finance (5 percent), and Industrial (20 percent). The firm uses return on invested capital (ROIC) as a way to evaluate the contribution of its diversified set of businesses as they compete internally for resources.[90]

To emphasize competitiveness among divisions, the headquarters office maintains an arm's-length relationship with them, intervening

Made of up four independent businesses, including Cessna Aircraft, Textron relies on an analysis of return on invested capital to determine the allocation of internal resources.

in divisional affairs only to audit operations and discipline managers whose divisions perform poorly. In emphasizing competition between divisions, the headquarters office relies on strategic controls to set rate-of-return targets and financial controls to monitor divisional performance relative to those targets. The headquarters office then allocates cash flow on a competitive basis, rather than automatically returning cash to the division that produced it. Thus, the focus of the headquarters' work is on performance appraisal, resource allocation, and long-range planning to verify that the firm's portfolio of businesses will lead to financial success.[91]

Table 11.1 Characteristics of the Structures Necessary to Implement the Related Constrained, Related Linked, and Unrelated Diversification Strategies

Structural Characteristics	Overall Structural Form		
	Cooperative M-Form (Related Constrained Strategy)[a]	SBU M-Form (Related Linked Strategy)[a]	Competitive M-Form (Unrelated Diversification Strategy)[a]
Centralization of operations	Centralized at corporate office	Partially centralized (in SBUs)	Decentralized to divisions
Use of integration mechanisms	Extensive	Moderate	Nonexistent
Divisional performance appraisals	Emphasize subjective (strategic) criteria	Use a mixture of subjective (strategic) and objective (financial) criteria	Emphasize objective (financial) criteria
Divisional incentive compensation	Linked to overall corporate performance	Mixed linkage to corporate, SBU, and divisional performance	Linked to divisional performance

[a]Strategy implemented with structural form.

The three major forms of the multidivisional structure should each be paired with a particular corporate-level strategy. Table 11.1 shows these structures' characteristics. Differences exist in the degree of centralization, the focus of the performance appraisal, the horizontal structures (integrating mechanisms), and the incentive compensation schemes. The most centralized and most costly structural form is the cooperative structure. The least centralized, with the lowest bureaucratic costs, is the competitive structure. The SBU structure requires partial centralization and involves some of the mechanisms necessary to implement the relatedness between divisions. Also, the divisional incentive compensation awards are allocated according to both SBUs and corporate performance.

Matches between International Strategies and Worldwide Structure

As explained in Chapter 8, international strategies are becoming increasingly important for long-term competitive success[92] in what continues to become an increasingly border-less global economy.[93] Among other benefits, international strategies allow the firm to search for new markets, resources, core competencies, and technologies as part of its efforts to outperform competitors.[94]

As with business-level and corporate-level strategies, unique organizational structures are necessary to successfully implement the different international strategies.[95] Forming proper matches between international strategies and organizational structures facilitates the firm's efforts to effectively coordinate and control its global operations. More importantly, research findings confirm the validity of the international strategy/structure matches we discuss here.[96]

Using the Worldwide Geographic Area Structure to Implement the Multidomestic Strategy

The *multidomestic strategy* decentralizes the firm's strategic and operating decisions to business units in each country so that product characteristics can be tailored to local preferences. Firms using this strategy try to isolate themselves from global competitive forces by establishing protected market positions or by competing in industry segments that are most affected by differences among local countries. The worldwide geographic area structure is used to implement this strategy. The **worldwide geographic area structure** emphasizes national interests and facilitates the firm's efforts to satisfy local differences (see Figure 11.8).

The **worldwide geographic area structure** emphasizes national interests and facilitates the firm's efforts to satisfy local differences.

Figure 11.8 Worldwide Geographic Area Structure for Implementing a Multidomestic Strategy

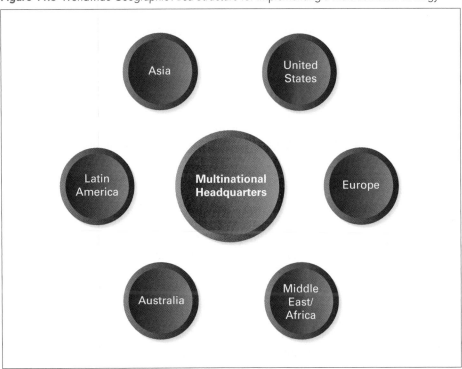

Notes:
- The perimeter circles indicate decentralization of operations
- Emphasis is on differentiation by local demand to fit an area or country culture
- Corporate headquarters coordinates financial resources among independent subsidiaries
- The organization is like a decentralized federation

Although the automobile industry is doing poorly in global markets, on a relative basis Ford of Europe is doing better than other auto firms in Europe within the same middle market segment strategy. This is due to the fact that Ford implemented the worldwide geographic area structure more than a decade ago to give local European managers more autonomy to manage their operations. One analysis called Ford "the most efficient volume carmaker in Europe."[97] Furthermore, they have an efficient set of designs matched responsively to the European market. They have kept costs down by partnering with European automakers such as Fiat and France's PSA Peugeot Citroen on chassis and engines. The timing of the release of their new models was also good to take advantage of the European "cash for clunkers" program, although the underlying market is still weak.

Using the multidomestic strategy requires little coordination between different country markets, meaning that integrating mechanisms among divisions around the world are not needed. Coordination among units in a firm's worldwide geographic area structure is often informal.

The multidomestic strategy/worldwide geographic area structure match evolved as a natural outgrowth of the multicultural European marketplace. Friends and family members of the main business who were sent as expatriates into foreign countries to develop the independent country subsidiary often used this structure for the main business. The relationship to corporate headquarters by divisions took place through informal communication among "family members."[98]

A key disadvantage of the multidomestic strategy/worldwide geographic area structure match is the inability to create strong global efficiency. With an increasing emphasis on lower-cost products in international markets, the need to pursue worldwide economies of scale has also increased. These changes foster use of the global strategy and its structural match, the worldwide product divisional structure.

Using the Worldwide Product Divisional Structure to Implement the Global Strategy

With the corporation's home office dictating competitive strategy, the *global strategy* is one through which the firm offers standardized products across country markets. The firm's success depends on its ability to develop economies of scope and economies of scale on a global level. Decisions to outsource or maintain integrated subsidiaries may in part depend on the country risk and institutional environment in which the firm is entering.[99]

The worldwide product divisional structure supports use of the global strategy. In the **worldwide product divisional structure**, decision-making authority is centralized in the worldwide division headquarters to coordinate and integrate decisions and actions among divisional business units (see Figure 11.9). This structure is often used in rapidly growing firms seeking to manage their diversified product lines effectively. Avon Products, Inc. is an example of a firm using the worldwide product divisional structure.

Avon is a global brand leader in products for women such as lipsticks, fragrances, and anti-aging skin care. Committed to "empowering women all over the world since 1886," Avon relies on product innovation to be a first-mover in its markets. For years, Avon used the multidomestic strategy. However, the firm's growth came to a screeching halt in 2006. Contributing to this decline were simultaneous stumbles in sales revenues in emerging markets (e.g., Russia and Central Europe), the United States, and Mexico. To cope with its problems, the firm changed to a global strategy and to the worldwide product divisional structure to support its use. Commenting on this change, CEO Andrea Jung noted that, "Previously, Avon managers from Poland to Mexico ran their own plants, developed new products, and created their own ads, often relying as much

Figure 11.9 Worldwide Product Divisional Structure for Implementing a Global Strategy

In the **worldwide product divisional structure**, decision-making authority is centralized in the worldwide division headquarters to coordinate and integrate decisions and actions among divisional business units.

Notes:
- The headquarters'circle indicates centralization to coordinate information flow among worldwide products
- Corporate headquarters uses many intercoordination devices to facilitate global economies of scale and scope
- Corporate headquarters also allocates financial resources in a cooperative way
- The organization is like a centralized federation

on gut as numbers."[100] Today, Avon is organized around product divisions including Avon Color, the firm's "flagship global color cosmetics brand, which offers a variety of color cosmetics products, including foundations, powders, lip, eye, and nail products," Skincare, Bath & Body, Hair Care, Wellness, and Fragrance. The analysis of these product divisions' performances is conducted by individuals in the firm's New York headquarters. One of the purposes of changing strategy and structure is for Avon to control its costs and gain additional scale economies as paths to performance improvements. Avon has announced the success of this restructuring program and vowed to cut costs even further; the original program is "expected to result in annual savings of about $430 million by 2011–12," while the new changes will result in "another $450 million expected to be saved beginning in 2010."[101]

Integrating mechanisms are important in the effective use of the worldwide product divisional structure. Direct contact between managers, liaison roles between departments, and temporary task forces as well as permanent teams are examples of these mechanisms. One researcher describes the use of these mechanisms in the worldwide structure: "There is extensive and formal use of task forces and operating committees to supplement communication and coordination of worldwide operations."[102] The disadvantages of the global strategy/worldwide structure combination are the difficulty involved with coordinating decisions and actions across country borders and the inability to quickly respond to local needs and preferences.

To deal with these types of disadvantages, Avon has a vast set of local salespeople who are committed to the organization and who help the company to become locally responsive. Another solution is to develop a regional approach in addition to the product focus, which might be similar to the combination structure discussed next.[103]

Using the Combination Structure to Implement the Transnational Strategy

The *transnational strategy* calls for the firm to combine the multidomestic strategy's local responsiveness with the global strategy's efficiency. Firms using this strategy are trying to gain the advantages of both local responsiveness and global efficiency. The combination structure is used to implement the transnational strategy. The **combination structure** is a structure drawing characteristics and mechanisms from both the worldwide geographic area structure and the worldwide product divisional structure. The transnational strategy is often implemented through two possible combination structures: a global matrix structure and a hybrid global design.[104]

The global matrix design brings together both local market and product expertise into teams that develop and respond to the global marketplace. The global matrix design (the basic matrix structure was defined earlier) promotes flexibility in designing products and responding to customer needs. However, it has severe limitations in that it places employees in a position of being accountable to more than one manager. At any given time, an employee may be a member of several functional or product group teams. Relationships that evolve from multiple memberships can make it difficult for employees to be simultaneously loyal to all of them. Although the matrix places authority in the hands of managers who are most able to use it, it creates problems in regard to corporate reporting relationships that are so complex and vague that it is difficult and time-consuming to receive approval for major decisions.

We illustrate the hybrid structure in Figure 11.10. In this design, some divisions are oriented toward products while others are oriented toward market areas. Thus, in some cases when the geographic area is more important, the division managers are area-oriented. In other divisions where worldwide product coordination and efficiencies are more important, the division manager is more product-oriented. The Strategic Focus on PepsiCo illustrates the hybrid design. Although PepsiCo is generally focused on geographic areas like most consumer product companies, as it has diversified into snacks and other foods, it also has product divisions to build better worldwide efficiencies.

> The **combination structure** is a structure drawing characteristics and mechanisms from both the worldwide geographic area structure and the worldwide product divisional structure.

Figure 11.10 Hybrid Form of the Combination Structure for Implementing a Transnational Strategy

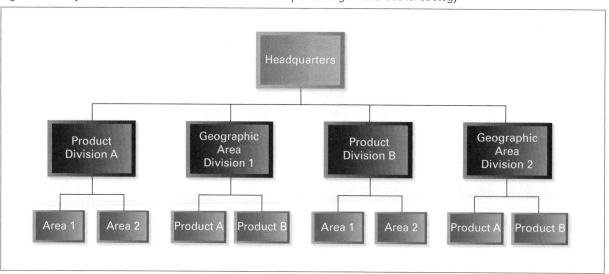

The fits between the multidomestic strategy and the worldwide geographic area structure and between the global strategy and the worldwide product divisional structure are apparent. However, when a firm wants to implement the multidomestic and global strategies simultaneously through a combination structure, the appropriate integrating mechanisms are less obvious. The structure used to implement the transnational strategy must be simultaneously centralized and decentralized; integrated and nonintegrated; formalized and nonformalized.

IKEA has done a good job of balancing these organization aspects in implementing the transnational strategy.[105] IKEA is a global furniture retailer with outlets in more than 35 countries. IKEA focuses on lowering its costs and also understanding its customers' needs, especially younger customers. It has been able to manage these seemingly opposite characteristics through its structure and management process. It has also been able to encourage its employees to understand the effects of cultural and geographic diversity on firm operations. IKEA's system also has internal network attributes, which will be discussed next in regard to external interorganizational networks.

Matches between Cooperative Strategies and Network Structures

As discussed in Chapter 9, a network strategy exists when partners form several alliances in order to improve the performance of the alliance network itself through cooperative endeavors.[106] The greater levels of environmental complexity and uncertainty facing companies in today's competitive environment are causing more firms to use cooperative strategies such as strategic alliances and joint ventures.[107]

The breadth and scope of firms' operations in the global economy create many opportunities for firms to cooperate.[108] In fact, a firm can develop cooperative relationships with many of its stakeholders, including customers, suppliers, and competitors. When a firm becomes involved with combinations of cooperative relationships, it is part of a strategic network, or what others call an alliance constellation or portfolio.[109]

A *strategic network* is a group of firms that has been formed to create value by participating in multiple cooperative arrangements. An effective strategic network facilitates discovering opportunities beyond those identified by individual network participants.[110] A strategic network can be a source of competitive advantage for its members when its operations create value that is difficult for competitors to duplicate and that network members can't create by themselves.[111] Strategic networks are used to implement business-level, corporate-level, and international cooperative strategies.

PEPSICO: MOVING FROM THE GEOGRAPHIC AREA STRUCTURE TOWARD THE COMBINED STRUCTURE IMPLEMENTING THE TRANSNATIONAL STRATEGY

PepsiCo has organized its businesses into three groups: PepsiCo North American Beverages (PNAB), PepsiCo Americas Foods (PAF), and PepsiCo International (PI). PNAB focuses on the Pepsi brand that includes carbonated soft drinks, juices and juice drinks, ready-to-drink teas and coffees, and isotonic sports drinks (Gatorade). It also has Aquafina water, Sierra Mist, Mug root beer, Tropicana juice drinks, Propel, SoBe, Slice, Dole, Tropicana Twister, and Tropicana Season's Best. Some of these drinks are through joint ventures such as with the Thomas J. Lipton Company (tea) and Starbucks coffee (Frappuccino). Gatorade became part of PepsiCo through a 2001 acquisition of Quaker Oats Company.

PAF is focused on food and snacks in North and South America including the products of Frito-Lay, Quaker Oats, Sabritas (Mexican snacks and fun food), and Gamesa (one of Mexico's top brands for cookies, pastries, oats, and cereals).

PepsiCo International includes the PepsiCo businesses in Europe, Asia, Africa, and Australia. Originally, this segment focused on distribution of beverages, but in 2003 it combined food and beverages to form PepsiCo International.

As you can see from these descriptions of its business segments, PepsiCo is primarily organized geographically—beverages in North America, food in North America, and food and beverages internationally by region. Accordingly, like most consumer product firms, it has traditionally implemented the multidomestic strategy with a regional focus, using the worldwide geographic area structure to better create a marketing approach that is adaptable to various languages, cultures, and lifestyles. However, as it has diversified into a variety of beverages and snack foods, it has consequently organized into product divisions as well to gain greater efficiencies in managing these products worldwide. Although it is still predominately area focused through the management structure, it has additional structures that allow the product divisions to be managed more efficiently. Accordingly, PepsiCo is moving toward implementing the transnational strategy through the combination structure.

Neville Elder/CORBIS

PepsiCo's geographic organization and move toward the implementation of a transnational strategy are supported by a highly diverse leadership team, headed by CEO and chairman of the board, Indra Nooyi, who is originally from India.

Interestingly, PepsiCo has one of the most diverse leadership teams. Its CEO and chairman of the board, Indra Nooyi, is originally from India. A large number of board members possess significant international experience, including the ability to speak several languages. These board members allow a broad understanding of cultures and buying habits within geographic regions outside of the United States. The diversity on the board supports the geographic focus maintained by the company and has added to the success of marketing the PepsiCo brands and products throughout the world.

Sources: 2009, The PepsiCo family, http://www.pepsico.com, June 25; H. Ehein, 2009, Internal relations, *Brand Week*, February 16, 8–9; D. Morris, 2008, The Pepsi challenge, *Fortune*, March 3, 54; M. Useem, 2008, America's best leaders: Indra Nooyi, PepsiCo CEO, *US News & World Report*, http://www.usnews.com, November 19; 2008, Global companies with global boards, *Directorship*, 34(5): 28–30; 2008, Pepsi versus Coke: An unhealthy obsession: They are global, but are they relevant? *Strategic Direction*, 24(1): 6–8.

Commonly, a strategic network is a loose federation of partners participating in the network's operations on a flexible basis. At the core or center of the strategic network, the *strategic center firm* is the one around which the network's cooperative relationships revolve (see Figure 11.11).

Because of its central position, the strategic center firm is the foundation for the strategic network's structure. Concerned with various aspects of organizational structure, such as formal reporting relationships and procedures, the strategic center firm manages what are often complex, cooperative interactions among network partners. To perform the tasks discussed next, the strategic center firm must make sure that incentives for participating in the network are aligned so that network firms continue to have a reason to remain connected.[112] The strategic center firm is engaged in four primary tasks as it manages the strategic network and controls its operations:[113]

Strategic outsourcing. The strategic center firm outsources and partners with more firms than other network members. At the same time, the strategic center firm requires network partners to be more than contractors. Members are expected to find opportunities for the network to create value through its cooperative work.

Competencies. To increase network effectiveness, the strategic center firm seeks ways to support each member's efforts to develop core competencies with the potential of benefiting the network.

Technology. The strategic center firm is responsible for managing the development and sharing of technology-based ideas among network members. The structural requirement that members submit formal reports detailing the technology-oriented outcomes of their efforts to the strategic center firm facilitates this activity.[114]

Race to learn. The strategic center firm emphasizes that the principal dimensions of competition are between value chains and between networks of value chains. Because of this interconnection, the strategic network is only as strong as its weakest value-chain link.

Figure 11.11 A Strategic Network

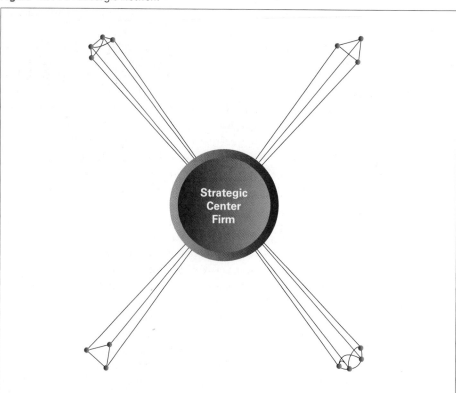

With its centralized decision-making authority and responsibility, the strategic center firm guides participants in efforts to form network-specific competitive advantages. The need for each participant to have capabilities that can be the foundation for the network's competitive advantages encourages friendly rivalry among participants seeking to develop the skills needed to quickly form new capabilities that create value for the network.[115]

Interestingly, strategic networks are being used more frequently, partly because of the ability of a strategic center firm to execute a strategy that effectively and efficiently links partner firms. Improved information systems and communication capabilities (e.g., the Internet) make such networks possible.[116]

Implementing Business-Level Cooperative Strategies

As noted in Chapter 9, the two types of business-level complementary alliances are vertical and horizontal. Firms with competencies in different stages of the value chain form a vertical alliance to cooperatively integrate their different, but complementary, skills. Firms combining their competencies to create value in the same stage of the value chain are using a horizontal alliance. Vertical complementary strategic alliances such as those developed by Toyota Motor Company are formed more frequently than horizontal alliances.[117]

A strategic network of vertical relationships such as the network in Japan between Toyota and its suppliers often involves a number of implementation issues.[118] First, the strategic center firm encourages subcontractors to modernize their facilities and provides them with technical and financial assistance to do so, if necessary. Second, the strategic center firm reduces its transaction costs by promoting longer-term contracts with subcontractors, so that supplier-partners increase their long-term productivity. This approach is diametrically opposed to that of continually negotiating short-term contracts based on unit pricing. Third, the strategic center firm enables engineers in upstream companies (suppliers) to have better communication with those companies with whom it has contracts for services. As a result, suppliers and the strategic center firm become more interdependent and less independent.[119]

The lean production system (a vertical complementary strategic alliance) pioneered by Toyota and others has been diffused throughout the global auto industry.[120] However, no auto company has learned how to duplicate the manufacturing effectiveness and efficiency Toyota derives from the cooperative arrangements in its strategic network.[121] A key factor accounting for Toyota's manufacturing-based competitive advantage is the cost other firms would incur to imitate the structural form used to support Toyota's application. In part, then, the structure of Toyota's strategic network that it created as the strategic center firm facilitates cooperative actions among network participants that competitors can't fully understand or duplicate.

In vertical complementary strategic alliances, such as the one between Toyota and its suppliers, the strategic center firm is obvious, as is the structure that firm establishes. However, the same is not always true with horizontal complementary strategic alliances where firms try to create value in the same part of the value chain, as with airline alliances that are commonly formed to create value in the marketing and sales primary activity segment of the value chain (see Table 3.6). Because air carriers commonly participate in multiple horizontal complementary alliances such as the Star Alliance between Lufthansa, United, Continental, US Airways, Thai, Air Canada, SAS, and others, it is difficult to determine the strategic center firm. Moreover, participating in several alliances can cause firms to question partners' true loyalties and intentions. Also, if rivals band together in too many collaborative activities, one or more governments may suspect the possibility of illegal collusive activities. For these reasons, horizontal complementary alliances are used less often and less successfully than their vertical counterpart, although there are examples of success, for instance, among auto and aircraft manufacturers.[122]

Implementing Corporate-Level Cooperative Strategies

Corporate-level cooperative strategies (such as franchising) are used to facilitate product and market diversification. As a cooperative strategy, franchising allows the firm to use its competencies to extend or diversify its product or market reach, but without completing a merger or an acquisition.[123] Research suggests that knowledge embedded in corporate-level cooperative strategies facilitates synergy.[124] For example, McDonald's Corporation pursues a franchising strategy, emphasizing a limited value-priced menu in more than 100 countries. The McDonald's franchising system is a strategic network. McDonald's headquarters serves as the strategic center firm for the network's franchisees. The headquarters office uses strategic and financial controls to verify that the franchisees' operations create the greatest value for the entire network.

An important strategic control issue for McDonald's is the location of its franchisee units. Because it believes that its greatest expansion opportunities are outside the United States, the firm has decided to continue expanding in countries such as China and India, where it might need to adjust its menu according to the local culture. For example, "McDonald's adapts its restaurants in India to local tastes; in a nation that is predominantly Hindu and reveres the cow, beef isn't on the menu, for instance, replaced by chicken burgers and vegetable patties."[125] It plans on expanding the number of restaurants in India by 40 in 2009 bringing the total to 200; it expanded by 25 restaurants in 2008. Accordingly, as the strategic center firm around the globe for its restaurants, McDonald's is devoting the majority of its capital expenditures to develop units in non–U.S. markets.

Implementing International Cooperative Strategies

Strategic networks formed to implement international cooperative strategies result in firms competing in several countries.[126] Differences among countries' regulatory environments increase the challenge of managing international networks and verifying that at a minimum, the network's operations comply with all legal requirements.[127]

Distributed strategic networks are the organizational structure used to manage international cooperative strategies. As shown in Figure 11.12, several regional strategic center firms are included in the distributed network to manage partner firms' multiple cooperative arrangements.[128]

Hewlett-Packard recently acquired EDS, a large information technology consulting firm. One of EDS's assets is the EDS Agility Alliance, its distributed strategic network. "The Agility Alliance is EDS' premiere partner program bringing together industry-leading technology providers to build and deliver end to end IT solutions."[129] EDS is the main strategic center firm in this alliance and has two dedicated centers that are the hubs for jointly developing initiatives with its partners. Cisco, SAP, Sun, Xerox, Oracle, EMC, and Microsoft are members of this distributed strategic network. Symantec, an Internet antivirus and security firm, was recently added as a partner to respond to clients' needs "for more innovative security products and solutions that help them better secure their mission-critical business data and address specific enterprise security issues."[130] EDS's partners each work with their own networks to complete projects that are a part of the Agility Alliance. As this example demonstrates, the structure used to implement the international cooperative strategy is complex and demands careful attention to be used successfully.

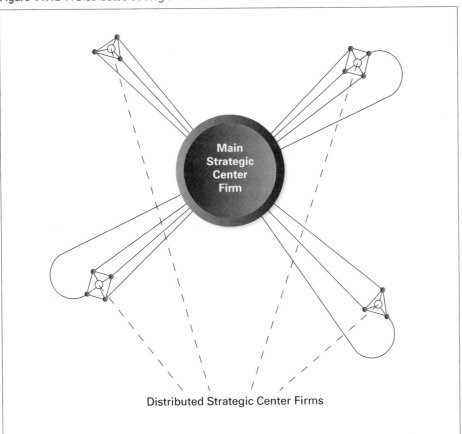

Figure 11.12 A Distributed Strategic Network

Main Strategic Center Firm

Distributed Strategic Center Firms

SUMMARY

- Organizational structure specifies the firm's formal reporting relationships, procedures, controls, and authority and decision-making processes. Essentially, organizational structure details the work to be done in a firm and how that work is to be accomplished. Organizational controls guide the use of strategy, indicate how to compare actual and expected results, and suggest actions to take to improve performance when it falls below expectations. A proper match between strategy and structure can lead to a competitive advantage.

- Strategic controls (largely subjective criteria) and financial controls (largely objective criteria) are the two types of organizational controls used to implement a strategy. Both controls are critical, although their degree of emphasis varies based on individual matches between strategy and structure.

- Strategy and structure influence each other; overall though, strategy has a stronger influence on structure. Research indicates that firms tend to change structure when declining performance forces them to do so. Effective managers anticipate the need for structural change and quickly modify structure to better accommodate the firm's strategy when evidence calls for that action.

- The functional structure is used to implement business-level strategies. The cost leadership strategy requires a centralized functional structure—one in which manufacturing efficiency and process engineering are emphasized. The differentiation strategy's functional structure decentralizes implementation-related decisions, especially those concerned with marketing, to those involved with individual organizational functions. Focus strategies, often used in small firms, require a simple structure until such time that the firm diversifies in terms of products and/or markets.

- Unique combinations of different forms of the multidivisional structure are matched with different corporate-level diversification strategies to properly implement these strategies. The cooperative M-form, used to implement the related constrained corporate-level strategy, has a centralized corporate office and extensive integrating mechanisms. Divisional incentives are linked to overall corporate performance to foster cooperation among divisions. The related linked SBU M-form structure establishes separate profit centers within the diversified firm. Each profit center or SBU may have divisions offering similar products, but the SBUs are often unrelated to each other. The competitive M-form structure, used to implement the unrelated diversification strategy, is highly decentralized, lacks integrating mechanisms, and utilizes objective financial criteria to evaluate each unit's performance.

- The multidomestic strategy, implemented through the worldwide geographic area structure, emphasizes decentralization and locates all functional activities in the host country or geographic area. The worldwide product divisional structure is used to implement the global strategy. This structure is centralized in order to coordinate and integrate different functions' activities so as to gain global economies of scope and economies of scale. Decision-making authority is centralized in the firm's worldwide division headquarters.

- The transnational strategy—a strategy through which the firm seeks the local responsiveness of the multidomestic strategy and the global efficiency of the global strategy—is implemented through the combination structure. Because it must be simultaneously centralized and decentralized, integrated and nonintegrated, and formalized and nonformalized, the combination structure is difficult to organize and successfully manage. However, two structural designs are suggested: the matrix and the hybrid structure with both geographic and product-oriented divisions.

- Increasingly important to competitive success, cooperative strategies are implemented through organizational structures framed around strategic networks. Strategic center firms play a critical role in managing strategic networks. Business-level strategies are often employed in vertical and horizontal alliance networks. Corporate-level cooperative strategies are used to pursue product and market diversification. Franchising is one type of corporate strategy that uses a strategic network to implement this strategy. This is also true for international cooperative strategies, where distributed networks are often used.

REVIEW QUESTIONS

1. What is organizational structure and what are organizational controls? What are the differences between strategic controls and financial controls? What is the importance of these differences?

2. What does it mean to say that strategy and structure have a reciprocal relationship?

3. What are the characteristics of the functional structures used to implement the cost leadership, differentiation, integrated cost leadership/differentiation, and focused business-level strategies?

4. What are the differences among the three versions of the multidivisional (M-form) organizational structures that are used to implement the related constrained, the related linked, and the unrelated corporate-level diversification strategies?

5. What organizational structures are used to implement the multidomestic, global, and transnational international strategies?

6. What is a strategic network? What is a strategic center firm? How is a strategic center used in business-level, corporate-level, and international cooperative strategies?

EXPERIENTIAL EXERCISES

EXERCISE 1: ORGANIZATIONAL STRUCTURE AND BUSINESS-LEVEL STRATEGY

The purpose of this exercise is to apply the concepts introduced in this chapter to live examples of business-level strategies and how various firms actually structure their organizations to compete. In teams, your instructor will assign a business-level strategy such as differentiation or cost leader. You are to identify a firm that exemplifies this strategy and pictorially draw out its corporate structure. You will need to present the results of your investigation by comparing your firm's organizational chart with that in your text identified for your particular business-level strategy. (See text for figures labeled "Functional Structure for Implementing a Differentiation [or Cost Leadership] Strategy.") Be prepared to address the following issues:

1. Describe your firm's business-level strategy. Why do you consider it to be a cost leader or a differentiator?

2. What is the mission statement and/or vision statement of this firm? Is this firm targeting specific strategic goals?

3. Using the text examples for a functional structure, how does your firm match those structures or differ, if it does?

4. Summarize your conclusions. Does your team believe that this firm is structured appropriately considering its current and future strategic goals?

EXERCISE 2: BURGER BUDDY AND MA MAISON

Assume that it is a few months before your college graduation. You and some classmates have decided to become entrepreneurs. The group has agreed on the restaurant industry, but your discussions thus far have gone back and forth between two different dining concepts: Burger Buddy and Ma Maison.

Burger Buddy would operate near campus in order to serve the student market. Burger Buddy would be a 1950s-themed hamburger joint, emphasizing large portions and affordable prices.

Ma Maison is the alternate concept. One of your partners has attended cooking school and has proposed the idea of a small, upscale French restaurant. The menu would have no set items, but would vary on a daily basis instead. Ma Maison would position itself as a boutique restaurant providing superb customer service and unique offerings.

Working in small groups, answer the following questions:

1. What is the underlying strategy for each restaurant concept?
2. How would the organizational structure of the two restaurant concepts differ?

3. How would the nature of work vary between the two restaurants?
4. If the business concept is successful, how might you expect the organizational structure and nature of work at each restaurant to change in the next five to seven years?

VIDEO CASE

ORGANIZATIONAL STRUCTURE AND ACCOUNTABILITY

Roger Parry/Former Chairman and CEO/Clear Channel International

Roger Parry, former chairman and CEO of Clear Channel International, discusses structure and control inside of an organization. Before you view the video, think through your concept of an organizational chart and its role in the modern corporation.

Before you watch the video consider the following concepts and questions and be prepared to discuss them in class:

Concepts

- Organizational structure
- Organizational control
- Strategy and structure
- Performance due to proper strategy and structure alignment

Questions

1. Do you think it is important for an organization to have an organizational chart?
2. How can organizations use structure to allow business units to meet their goals as well as corporate goals?
3. How important is it for everyone in the organization to know precisely their responsibility and that proper control is in place to ensure that these responsibilities are being met?

NOTES

1. P. Jarzabkowski, 2008, Shaping strategy as a structuration process, *Academy of Management Journal*, 51(4): 621–650; B. Ambos & B. B. Schlegelmilch, 2007, Innovation and control in the multinational firm: A comparison of political and contingency approaches, *Strategic Management Journal*, 28: 473–486; S. Kumar, S. Kant, & T. L. Amburgey, 2007, Public agencies and collaborative management approaches, *Administration & Society*, 39: 569–610.
2. R. Gulati & P. Puranam, 2009, Renewal through reorganization: The value of inconsistencies between formal and informal organization, *Organization Science*, 20(2): 422–440; R. E. Miles & C. C. Snow, 1978, *Organizational Strategy, Structure and Process*, New York: McGraw-Hill.
3. S. T. Hannah & P. B. Lester, 2009, A multilevel approach to building and leading learning organizations, *Leadership Quarterly*, 20(1): 34–48; E. M. Olson, S. F. Slater, & G. T. M. Hult, 2007, The importance of structure and process to strategy implementation, *Business Horizons*, 48(1): 47–54; D. N. Sull & C. Spinosa, 2007, Promise-based management, *Harvard Business Review*, 85(4):79–86.
4. R. Ireland, J. Covin, & D. Kuratko, 2009, Conceptualizing corporate entrepreneurship strategy, *Entrepreneurship Theory and*

Practice, 33(1): 19–46; T. Amburgey & T. Dacin, 1994, As the left foot follows the right? The dynamics of strategic and structural change, *Academy of Management Journal*, 37: 1427–1452.
5. L. F. Monteiro, N. Arvidsson, & J. Birkinshaw, 2008, Knowledge flows within multinational corporations: Explaining subsidiary isolation and its performance implications, *Organization Science*, 19(1): 90–107; P. Ghemawat, 2007, Managing differences: The central challenge of global strategy, *Harvard Business Review*, 85(3): 59–68; B. Keats & H. O'Neill, 2001, Organizational structure: Looking through a strategy lens, in M. A. Hitt, R. E. Freeman, & J. S. Harrison (eds.), *Handbook of Strategic Management*, Oxford, UK: Blackwell Publishers, 520–542.
6. R. E. Hoskisson, C. W. L. Hill, & H. Kim, 1993, The multidivisional structure: Organizational fossil or source of value? *Journal of Management*, 19: 269–298.
7. Jarzabkowski, Shaping strategy as a structuration process; E. M. Olson, S. F. Slater, G. Tomas, & G. T. M. Hult, 2005, The performance implications of fit among business strategy, marketing organization structure, and strategic behavior, *Journal of Marketing*, 69(3): 49–65.

8. B. Novak, 2008, Cisco connects the dots: Aligning leaders with a new organizational structure, *Global Business and Organizational Excellence*: 27(5): 22–32.
9. T. Burns & G. M. Stalker, 1961, *The Management of Innovation*, London: Tavistok; P. R. Lawrence & J. W. Lorsch, 1967, *Organization and Environment*, Homewood, IL: Richard D. Irwin; J. Woodward, 1965, *Industrial Organization: Theory and Practice*, London: Oxford University Press.
10. A. M. Rugman & A. Verbeke, 2008, A regional solution to the strategy and structure of multinationals, *European Management Journal*, 26(5): 305–313; H. Kim, R. E. Hoskisson, L. Tihanyi, & J. Hong, 2004, Evolution and restructuring of diversified business groups in emerging markets: The lessons from chaebols in Korea, *Asia Pacific Journal of Management*, 21: 25–48.
11. R. Kathuria, M. P. Joshi, & S. J. Porth, 2007, Organizational alignment and performance: Past, present and future, *Management Decision*, 45: 503–517.
12. B. Sechler, 2008, Corporate news: General Electric's reorganization resurrects GE Capital, *Wall Street Journal*, August 1, B3.
13. A. Tempel & P. Walgenbach, 2007, Global standardization of organizational forms and management practices: What new

institutionalism and the business-systems approach can learn from each other, *Journal of Management Studies*, 44: 1–24; Keats & O'Neill, Organizational structure, 533.

14. Tieying Yu, M. S. Insead, & R. H. Lester, 2008, Misery loves company: The spread of negative impacts resulting from an organizational crisis, *Academy of Management Review*, 33(2): 452–472; R. L. Priem, L. G. Love, & M. A. Shaffer, 2002, Executives' perceptions of uncertainty sources: A numerical taxonomy and underlying dimensions, *Journal of Management*, 28: 725–746.

15. A. N. Shub & P. W. Stonebraker, 2009, The human impact on supply chains: Evaluating the importance of "soft" areas on integration and performance, *Supply Chain Management*, 14(1): 31–40; S. K. Ethiraj & D. Levinthal, 2004, Bounded rationality and the search for organizational architecture: An evolutionary perspective on the design of organizations and their evolvability, *Administrative Science Quarterly*, 49: 404–437.

16. R. Khadem, 2008, Alignment and follow-up: Steps to strategy execution, *Journal of Business Strategy*, 29(6): 29–35; J. G. Covin, D. P. Slevin, & M. B. Heeley, 2001, Strategic decision making in an intuitive vs. technocratic mode: Structural and environmental consideration, *Journal of Business Research*, 52: 51–67.

17. J. R. Maxwell, 2008, Work system design to improve the economic performance of the firm, *Business Process Management Journal*, 14(3): 432–446; E. M. Olson, S. F. Slater, & G. T. M. Hult, 2005, The importance of structure and process to strategy implementation, *Business Horizons*, 48(1): 47–54.

18. L. Donaldson, 2001, *The contingency theory of organizations*, Thousand Oaks, CA: Sage; Jenster & Hussey, *Company Analysis*, 169.

19. M. A. Schilling & H. K. Steensma, 2001, The use of modular organizational forms: An industry-level analysis, *Academy of Management Journal*, 44: 1149–1168.

20. P. Legerer, T. Pfeiffer, G. Schneider, & J. Wagner, 2009, Organizational structure and managerial decisions, *International Journal of the Economics of Business*, 16(2): 147–159; C. B. Dobni & G. Luffman, 2003, Determining the scope and impact of market orientation profiles on strategy implementation and performance, *Strategic Management Journal*, 24: 577–585.

21. H. Gebauer & F. Putz, 2009, Organizational structures for the service business in product-oriented companies, *International Journal of Services Technology and Management*, 11(1): 64–81; M. Hammer, 2007, The process audit, *Harvard Business Review*, 85(4): 111–123.

22. R. D. Ireland & J. W. Webb, 2007, Strategic entrepreneurship: Creating competitive advantage through streams of innovation, *Business Horizons*, 50:

23. J. Rivkin & N. Siggelkow, 2003, Balancing search and stability: Interdependencies among elements of organizational design, *Management Science*, 49: 290–321; G. A. Bigley & K. H. Roberts, 2001, The incident command system: High-reliability organizing for complex and volatile task environments, *Academy of Management Journal*, 44: 1281–1299.

24. Monteiro, Arvidsson, & Birkinshaw, Knowledge flows within multinational corporations; S. Nadkarni & V. K. Narayanan, 2007, Strategic schemas, strategic flexibility, and firm performance: The moderating role of industry clockspeed, *Strategic Management Journal*, 28: 243–270; K. D. Miller & A. T. Arikan, 2004, Technology search investments: Evolutionary, option reasoning, and option pricing approaches, *Strategic Management Journal*, 25: 473–485.

25. S. Raisch & J. Birkinshaw, 2008, Organizational ambidexterity: Antecedents, outcomes, and moderators, *Journal of Management* 34: 375–409; C. Zook, 2007, Finding your next core business, *Harvard Business Review*, 85(4): 66–75.

26. M. Kimes, 2008, World's most admired companies: Cisco Systems layers it on, *Fortune*, December 8, 24.

27. S. K. Maheshwari & D. Ahlstrom, 2004, Turning around a state owned enterprise: The case of Scooters India Limited, *Asia Pacific Journal of Management*, 21(1–2): 75–101; B. W. Keats & M. A. Hitt, 1988, A causal model of linkages among environmental dimensions, macroorgani-zational characteristics, and performance, *Academy of Management Journal*, 31: 570–598.

28. A. Chandler, 1962, *Strategy and Structure*, Cambridge, MA: MIT Press.

29. D. Martin, 2007, Alfred D. Chandler, Jr., a business historian, dies at 88, *New York Times Online*, http://www.nytimes.com, May 12.

30. R. E. Hoskisson, R. A. Johnson, L. Tihanyi, & R. E. White, 2005, Diversified business groups and corporate refocusing in emerging economies, *Journal of Management*, 31: 941–965; J. D. Day, E. Lawson, & K. Leslie, 2003, When reorganization works, *The McKinsey Quarterly*, (2), 20–29.

31. B. Simon, 2009, Restructuring chief sees benefits in GM's maligned culture, *Financial Times*, July 4, 16.

32. S. K. Ethiraj, 2007, Allocation of inventive effort in complex product systems, *Strategic Management Journal*, 28: 563–584.

33. A. M. Kleinbaum & M. L. Tushman, 2008, Managing corporate social networks, *Harvard Business Review*, 86(7): 26–27; A. Weibel, 2007, Formal control and trustworthiness, *Group & Organization Management*, 32: 500–517; P. K. Mills & G. R. Ungson, 2003, Reassessing the

limits of structural empowerment: Organizational constitution and trust as controls, *Academy of Management Review*, 28: 143–153.

34. C. Rowe, J. G. Birnberg, & M. D. Shields, 2008, Effects of organizational process change on responsibility accounting and managers' revelations of private knowledge, *Accounting, Organizations and Society*, 33(2/3): 164–198; M. Santala & P. Parvinen, 2007, From strategic fit to customer fit, *Management Decision*, 45: 582–601; R. Reed, W. J. Donoher, & S. F. Barnes, 2004, Predicting misleading disclosures: The effects of control, pressure, and compensation, *Journal of Managerial Issues*, 16: 322–336.

35. P. Greve, S. Nielsen, & W. Ruigrok, 2009, Transcending borders with international top management teams: A study of European financial multinational corporations, *European Management Journal*, 27(3): 213–224; T. Galpin, R. Hilpirt, & B. Evans, 2007, The connected enterprise: Beyond division of labor, *Journal of Business Strategy*, 28(2): 38–47; C. Sundaramurthy & M. Lewis, 2003, Control and collaboration: Paradoxes of governance, *Academy of Management Review*, 28: 397–415.

36. M. A. Desai, 2008, The finance function in a global corporation, *Harvard Business Review*, 86(7): 108–112; Y. Li, L. Li, Y. Liu, & L. Wang, 2005, Linking management control system with product development and process decisions to cope with environment complexity, *International Journal of Production Research*, 43: 2577–2591.

37. I. Filatotchev, J. Stephan, & B. Jindra, 2008, Ownership structure, strategic controls and export intensity of foreign-invested firms in transition economies, *Journal of International Business Studies*, 39(7): 1133–1148; G. J. M. Braam & E. J. Nijssen, 2004, Performance effects of using the Balanced Scorecard: A note on the Dutch experience, *Long Range Planning*, 37: 335–349; S. D. Julian & E. Scifres, 2002, An interpretive perspective on the role of strategic control in triggering strategic change, *Journal of Business Strategies*, 19: 141–159.

38. J. Kratzer, H. G. Gemünden, C. Lettl, 2008, Balancing creativity and time efficiency in multi-team R&D projects: the alignment of formal and informal networks, *R & D Management*, 38(5): 538–549; D. F. Kuratko, R. D. Ireland, & J. S. Hornsby, 2004, Corporate entrepreneurship behavior among managers: A review of theory, research, and practice, in J. A. Katz & D. A. Shepherd (eds.), *Advances in Entrepreneurship: Firm Emergence and Growth: Corporate Entrepreneurship*, Oxford, UK: Elsevier Publishing, 7–45.

39. Y. Doz & M. Kosonen, 2008, The dynamics of strategic agility: Nokia's rollercoaster experience, *California Management Review*, 50(3): 95–118.

49–59; T. J. Andersen, 2004, Integrating decentralized strategy making and strategic planning processes in dynamic environments, *Journal of Management Studies*, 41: 1271–1299.

40. Y. Liu & T. Ravichandran, 2008, A comprehensive investigation on the relationship between information technology investments and firm diversification, *Information Technology and Management*, 9(3): 169–180; K. L. Turner & M. V. Makhija, 2006, The role of organizational controls in managing knowledge, *Academy of Management Review*, 31: 197–217; M. A. Hitt, R. E. Hoskisson, R. A. Johnson, & D. D. Moesel, 1996, The market for corporate control and firm innovation, *Academy of Management Journal*, 39: 1084–1119.

41. B. Fryer & T. A. Stewart, 2008, Cisco sees the future, *Harvard Business Review*, 86(11): 72–79.

42. Desai, The finance function in a global corporation; M. A. Hitt, L. Tihanyi, T. Miller, & B. Connelly, 2006, International diversification: Antecedents, outcomes, and moderators, *Journal of Management*, 32: 831–867; R. E. Hoskisson & M. A. Hitt, 1988, Strategic control and relative R&D investment in multiproduct firms, *Strategic Management Journal*, 9: 605–621.

43. S. Lee, K. Park, H. H. Shin, 2009, Disappearing internal capital markets: Evidence from diversified business groups in Korea, *Journal of Banking & Finance*, 33(2): 326–334; D. Collis, D. Young, & M. Goold, 2007, The size, structure, and performance of corporate headquarters, *Strategic Management Journal*, 28: 383–405.

44. X. S. Y. Spencer, T. A. Joiner, & S. Salmon, 2009, Differentiation strategy, performance measurement systems and organizational performance: Evidence from Australia, *International Journal of Business*, 14(1): 83–103; K. Chaharbaghi, 2007, The problematic of strategy: A way of seeing is also a way of not seeing, *Management Decision*, 45: 327–339; J. B. Barney, 2002, *Gaining and Sustaining Competitive Advantage*, 2nd ed., Upper Saddle River, NJ: Prentice Hall.

45. S. Lohr, 2007, Can Michael Dell refocus his namesake? *New York Times Online*, http://www.nytimes.com, September 9.

46. L. Lee, 2008, HP's Hurd is about to be tested: After a sterling three-year run, the company's CEO faces a weaker PC market and a stronger Dell, *BusinessWeek*, February 14, 59–60.

47. Gebauer & Putz, 2009, Organizational structures for the service business in product-oriented companies; X. Yin & E. J. Zajac, 2004, The strategy/governance structure fit relationship: Theory and evidence in franchising arrangements, *Strategic Management Journal*, 25: 365–383.

48. Keats & O'Neill, Organizational structure, 531.

49. K. Wakabayashi, 2008, Relationship between business definition and corporate growth: The effect of functional alignment, *Pacific Economic Review*, 13(5): 663–679; K. M. Green, J. G. Covin,

D. P. Slevin, 2008, Exploring the relationship between strategic reactiveness and entrepreneurial orientation: The role of structure-style fit. *Journal of Business Venturing*, 23(3): 356; Olson, Slater, & Hult, The importance of structure and process to strategy implementation; D. Miller & J. O. Whitney, 1999, Beyond strategy: Configuration as a pillar of competitive advantage, *Business Horizons*, 42(3): 5–17.

50. Chandler, *Strategy and Structure*.

51. Keats & O'Neill, Organizational structure, 524.

52. E. Rawley, 2009, Diversification, coordination costs and organizational rigidity: Evidence from microdata, *Strategic Management Journal*; forthcoming; M. E. Sosa, S. D. Eppinger, & C. M. Rowles, 2004, The misalignment of product architecture and organizational structure in complex product development, *Management Science*, 50: 1674–1689.

53. J. W. Yoo, R. Reed, S. J. Shin, & D. J. Lemak, 2009, Strategic choice and performance in late movers: Influence of the top management team's external ties, *Journal of Management Studies*, 46(2): 308–335; S. Karim & W. Mitchell, 2004, Innovating through acquisition and internal development: A quarter-century of boundary evolution at Johnson & Johnson, *Long Range Planning*, 37: 525–547.

54. I. Daizadeh, 2006, Using intellectual property to map the organizational evolution of firms: Tracing a biotechnology company from startup to bureaucracy to a multidivisional firm, *Journal of Commercial Biotechnology*, 13: 28–36.

55. C. Levicki, 1999, *The Interactive Strategy Workout*, 2nd ed., London: Prentice Hall.

56. E. E. Entin, F. J. Diedrich, & B. Rubineau, 2003, Adaptive communication patterns in different organizational structures, *Human Factors and Ergonomics Society Annual Meeting Proceedings*, 405–409; H. M. O'Neill, R. W. Pouder, & A. K. Buchholtz, 1998, Patterns in the diffusion of strategies across organizations: Insights from the innovation diffusion literature, *Academy of Management Review*, 23: 98–114.

57. Spencer, Joiner, & Salmon, Differentiation strategy, performance measurement systems and organizational performance; 2007, Organizational structure, *Wikipedia*, http://en.wikipedia.org; Gallbraith, *Designing Organizations*, 25.

58. Keats & O'Neill, Organizational structure, 539.

59. C. M. Christensen, S. P. Kaufman, & W. C. Shih, 2008, Innovation killers, *Harvard Business Review*: Special HBS Centennial Issue, 86(1): 98–105; J. Welch & S. Welch, 2006, Growing up but staying young, *BusinessWeek*, December 11, 112.

60. O. E. Williamson, 1975, *Markets and Hierarchies: Analysis and Anti-Trust Implications*, New York: The Free Press.

61. S. H. Mialon, 2008, Efficient horizontal mergers: The effects of internal capital reallocation and organizational form, *International Journal of Industrial Organization*, 26(4): 861–877; Chandler, *Strategy and Structure*.

62. R. Inderst, H. M. Muller, & K. Warneryd, 2007, Distributional conflict in organizations, *European Economic Review*, 51: 385–402; J. Greco, 1999, Alfred P. Sloan Jr. (1875–1966): The original organizational man, *Journal of Business Strategy*, 20(5): 30–31.

63. Hoskisson, Hill, & Kim, The multidivisional structure, 269–298.

64. Mialon, Efficient horizontal mergers: The effects of internal capital reallocation and organizational form; H. Zhou, 2005, Market structure and organizational form, *Southern Economic Journal*, 71: 705–719; W. G. Rowe & P. M. Wright, 1997, Related and unrelated diversification and their effect on human resource management controls, *Strategic Management Journal*, 18: 329–338.

65. C. E. Helfat & K. M. Eisenhardt, 2004, Inter-temporal economies of scope, organizational modularity, and the dynamics of diversification, *Strategic Management Journal*, 25: 1217–1232; A. D. Chandler, 1994, The functions of the HQ unit in the multibusiness firm, in R. P. Rumelt, D. E. Schendel, & D. J. Teece (eds.), *Fundamental Issues in Strategy*, Cambridge, MA: Harvard Business School Press, 327.

66. O. E. Williamson, 1994, Strategizing, economizing, and economic organization, in R. P. Rumelt, D. E. Schendel, & D. J. Teece (eds.), *Fundamental Issues in Strategy*, Cambridge, MA: Harvard Business School Press, 361–401.

67. Hoskisson, Hill, & Kim, The multidivisional structure: Organizational fossil or source of value?; R. M. Burton & B. Obel, 1980, A computer simulation test of the M-form hypothesis, *Administrative Science Quarterly*, 25: 457–476.

68. O. E. Williamson, 1985, *The Economic Institutions of Capitalism: Firms, Markets, and Relational Contracting*, New York: Macmillan.

69. Keats & O'Neill, Organizational structure, 532.

70. M. F. Wolff, 1999, In the organization of the future, competitive advantage will be inspired, *Research Technology Management*, 42(4): 2–4.

71. R. H. Hall, 1996, *Organizations: Structures, Processes, and Outcomes*, 6th ed., Englewood Cliffs, NJ: Prentice Hall, 13; S. Baiman, D. F. Larcker, & M. V. Rajan, 1995, Organizational design for business units, *Journal of Accounting Research*, 33: 205–229.

72. L. G. Love, R. L. Priem, & G. T. Lumpkin, 2002, Explicitly articulated strategy and firm performance under alternative levels of centralization, *Journal of Management*, 28: 611–627.

73. Hall, *Organizations*, 64–75.

74. Barney, *Gaining and Sustaining Competitive Advantage*, 257.

75. H. Karandikar & S. Nidamarthi, 2007, Implementing a platform strategy for a systems business via standardization, *Journal of Manufacturing Technology Management*, 18: 267–280.

76. Olson, Slater, Tomas, & Hult, The performance implications of fit.

77. 2007, Wal-Mart Stores, Inc, *New York Times Online*, http://www.nytimes.com, July 21.

78. 2007, Wal-Mart rolling out new company slogan, *New York Times Online*, http://www.nytimes.com, July 12.

79. Olson, Slater, Tomas, & Hult, The performance implications of fit.

80. T. Heath, 2008, In pursuit of innovation at Under Armour: Founder Kevin Plank says Super Bowl commercial has generated "buzz," *Washington Post*, February 25, D03.

81. Chandler, *Strategy and Structure*.

82. C. C. Markides & P. J. Williamson, 1996, Corporate diversification and organizational structure: A resource-based view, *Academy of Management Journal*, 39: 340–367; C. W. L. Hill, M. A. Hitt, & R. E. Hoskisson, 1992, Cooperative versus competitive structures in related and unrelated diversified firms, *Organization Science*, 3: 501–521.

83. S. H. Appelbaum, D. Nadeau, & M. Cyr, 2008, Performance evaluation in a matrix organization: A case study (part two), *Industrial and Commercial Training*, 40(6): 295–299.

84. S. H. Appelbaum, D. Nadeau, & M. Cyr, 2009, Performance evaluation in a matrix organization: A case study (part three), *Industrial and Commercial Training*, 41(1): 9–14; M. Goold & A. Campbell, 2003, Structured networks: Towards the well designed matrix, *Long Range Planning*, 36(5): 427–439.

85. P. Eavis, 2008, The pain at Sears grows, *The Wall Street Journal Online*, www.wsj.com, May 30.

86. N. M. Schmid & I. Walter, 2009, Do financial conglomerates create or destroy economic value? *Journal of Financial Intermediation*, 18(2): 193–216; P. A. Argenti, R. A. Howell, & K. A. Beck, 2005, The strategic communication imperative, *MIT Sloan Management Review*, 46(3): 84–89.

87. M. F. Wiersema & H. P. Bowen, 2008, Corporate diversification: The impact of foreign competition, industry globalization, and product diversification, *Strategic Management Journal*, 29: 115–132; R. E. Hoskisson & M. A. Hitt, 1990, Antecedents and performance outcomes of diversification: A review and critique of theoretical perspectives, *Journal of Management*, 16: 461–509.

88. Hill, Hitt, & Hoskisson, Cooperative versus competitive structures, 512.

89. Lee, Park, & Shin, Disappearing internal capital markets: Evidence from diversified business groups in Korea; J. Birkinshaw, 2001, Strategies for managing internal competition, *California Management Review*, 44(1): 21–38.

90. 2009, Vision and strategy, http://www.textron.com, July 16.

91. M. Maremont, 2004, Leadership; more can be more: Is the conglomerate a dinosaur from a bygone era? The answer is no—with a caveat, *Wall Street Journal*, October 24, R4; T. R. Eisenmann & J. L. Bower, 2000, The entrepreneurial M-form: Strategic integration in global media firms, *Organization Science*, 11: 348–355.

92. T. Yu & A. A. Cannella, Jr., 2007, Rivalry between multinational enterprises: An event history approach, *Academy of Management Journal*, 50: 665–686; S. E. Christophe & H. Lee, 2005, What matters about internationalization: A market-based assessment, *Journal of Business Research*, 58: 636–643; Y. Luo, 2002, Product diversification in international joint ventures: Performance implications in an emerging market, *Strategic Management Journal*, 23: 1–20.

93. M. Mandel, 2007, Globalization vs. immigration reform, *BusinessWeek*, June 4, 40.

94. T. M. Begley & D. P. Boyd, 2003, The need for a corporate global mind-set, *MIT Sloan Management Review*, 44(2): 25–32; Tallman, Global strategic management, 467.

95. T. Kostova & K. Roth, 2003, Social capital in multinational corporations and a micro-macro model of its formation, *Academy of Management Review*, 28: 297–317.

96. J. Jermias & L. Gani, 2005, Ownership structure, contingent-fit, and business-unit performance: A research model and evidence, *The International Journal of Accounting*, 40: 65–85; J. Wolf & W. G. Egelhoff, 2002, A reexamination and extension of international strategy-structure theory, *Strategic Management Journal*, 23: 181–189.

97. J. Ewing, 2009, A magic moment for Ford of Europe, *BusinessWeek*, July 6, 48–49.

98. C. A. Bartlett & S. Ghoshal, 1989, *Managing Across Borders: The Transnational Solution*, Boston: Harvard Business School Press.

99. S. Feinberg, & A. Gupta, 2009, MNC subsidiaries and country risk: Internalization as a safeguard against weak external institutions, *Academy of Management Journal* 52(2): 381–399; S. T. Cavusgil, S. Yeniyurt, & J. D. Townsend, 2004, The framework of a global company: A conceptualization and preliminary validation, *Industrial Marketing Management*, 33: 711–716.

100. N. Byrnes, 2007, Avon: More than cosmetic changes, *BusinessWeek*, March 12, 62–63.

101. K. Nolan, 2009, Corporate news: Avon unveils new cost cuts, *Wall Street Journal*, February 20, B2.

102. Malnight, Emerging structural patterns, 1197.

103. Rugman & Verbeke, A regional solution to the strategy and structure of multinationals.

104. B. Connelly, M. A. Hitt, A. DeNisi, & R. D. Ireland, 2007, Expatriates and corporate-level international strategy: Governing with the knowledge contract, *Management Decision*, 45: 564–581.

105. M. E. Lloyd, 2009, IKEA sees opportunity in slump, Wall Street Journal Online, http://online.wsj.com, February 17; E. Baraldi, 2008, Strategy in industrial Networks: Experiences from IKEA, *California Management Review*, 50(4): 99–126.

106. D. Lavie, 2009, Capturing value from alliance portfolios, *Organizational Dynamics*, 38(1): 26–36; S. G. Lazzarini, 2007, The impact of membership in competing alliance constellations: Evidence on the operational performance of global airlines, *Strategic Management Journal*, 28: 345–367; Y. L. Doz & G. Hamel, 1998, *Alliance Advantage: The Art of Creating Value through Partnering*, Boston: Harvard Business School Press, 222.

107. J. Li, C. Zhou, & E. J. Zajac, 2009, Control, collaboration, and productivity in international joint ventures: Theory and evidence, *Strategic Management Journal*, 30: 865–884; Y. Luo, 2007, Are joint venture partners more opportunistic in a more volatile environment? *Strategic Management Journal*, 28: 39–60; K. Moller, A. Rajala, & S. Svahn, 2005, Strategic business nets—their type and management, *Journal of Business Research*, 58: 1274–1284.

108. D. Li, L. E. Eden, M. A. Hitt, & R. D. Ireland, 2008, Friends, acquaintances, or strangers? Partner selection in R&D alliances, *Academy of Management Journal*, 51(2): 315–334.

109. Lavie, Capturing value from alliance portfolios; B. Comes-Casseres, 2003, Competitive advantage in alliance constellations, *Strategic Organization*, 1: 327–335; T. K. Das & B. S. Teng, 2002, Alliance constellations: A social exchange perspective, *Academy of Management Review*, 27: 445–456.

110. T. Vapola, P. Tossavainen, & M. Gabrielsson, 2008, The battleship strategy: The complementing role of born globals in MNC's new opportunity creation, *Journal of International Entrepreneurship*: 6(1): 1–21; S. Tallman, M. Jenkins, N. Henry, & S. Pinch, 2004, Knowledge, clusters, and competitive advantage, *Academy of Management Review*, 29: 258–271.

111. V. Moatti, 2009, Learning to expand or expanding to learn? The role of imitation and experience in the choice among several expansion modes, *European Management Journal*, 27(1): 36–46; A. Capaldo, 2007, Network structure and innovation: The leveraging of a dual network as a distinctive relational capability, *Strategic Management Journal*, 28: 585–608; A. Zaheer & G. G. Bell, 2005, Benefiting from network position: Firm capabilities, structural holes, and performance, *Strategic Management Journal*, 26: 809–825.

112. J. Wiklund & D. A. Shepherd, 2009, The effectiveness of alliances and acquisitions: The role of resource combination activities, *Theory and Practice*, 31(1): 193–212; R. D. Ireland & J. W. Webb, 2007, A multi-theoretic perspective on trust and power in strategic supply chains, *Journal of Operations Management*, 25: 482–497; V. G. Narayanan & A. Raman, 2004, Aligning incentives in supply chains, *Harvard Business Review*, 82(11): 94–102.

113. S. Harrison, 1998, *Japanese Technology and Innovation Management*, Northampton, MA: Edward Elgar.

114. M. H. Hansen, R. E. Hoskisson, & J. B. Barney, 2008, Competitive advantage in alliance governance: Resolving the opportunism minimization-gain maximization paradox, *Managerial and Decision Economics*, 29: 191–208; T. Keil, 2004, Building external corporate venturing capability, *Journal of Management Studies*, 41: 799–825.

115. Vapola, Tossavainen, & Gabrielsson, The battleship strategy: The complementing role of born globals in MNC's new opportunity creation; P. Dussauge, B. Garrette, & W. Mitchell, 2004, Learning from competing partners: Outcomes and duration of scale and link alliances in Europe, North America and Asia, *Strategic Management Journal*, 21: 99–126; G. Lorenzoni & C. Baden-Fuller, 1995, Creating a strategic center to manage a web of partners, *California Management Review*, 37(3): 146–163.

116. S. R. Holmberg & J. L. Cummings, 2009, Building successful strategic alliances: Strategic process and analytical tools for selecting partner industries and firms, *Long Range Planning*, 42(2): 164–193; B. J. Bergiel, E. B. Bergiel, & P. W. Balsmeier, 2008, Nature of virtual teams: A summary of their advantages and disadvantages, *Management Research News*, 31(2): 99–110.

117. A. C. Inkpen, 2008, Knowledge transfer and international joint ventures: The case of NUMMI and General Motors, *Strategic Management Journal*, 29(4): 447–453;

T. A. Stewart & A. P. Raman, 2007, Lessons from Toyota's long drive, *Harvard Business Review*, 85(7/8): 74–83; J. H. Dyer & K. Nobeoka, 2000, Creating and managing a high-performance knowledge-sharing network: The Toyota case, *Strategic Management Journal*, 21: 345–367.

118. L. F. Mesquita, J. Anand, & J. H. Brush, 2008, Comparing the resource-based and relational views: Knowledge transfer and spillover in vertical alliances, *Strategic Management Journal*, 29: 913–941; M. Kotabe, X. Martin, & H. Domoto, 2003, Gaining from vertical partnerships: Knowledge transfer, relationship duration and supplier performance improvement in the U.S. and Japanese automotive industries, *Strategic Management Journal*, 24: 293–316.

119. T. Nishiguchi, 1994, *Strategic Industrial Sourcing: The Japanese Advantage*, New York: Oxford University Press.

120. S. G. Lazzarini, D. P. Claro, & L. F. Mesquita, 2008, Buyer-supplier and supplier-supplier alliances: Do they reinforce or undermine one another? *Journal of Management Studies*, 45(3): 561–584; P. Dussauge, B. Garrette, & W. Mitchell, 2004, Asymmetric performance: The market share impact of scale and link alliances in the global auto industry, *Strategic Management Journal*, 25: 701–711.

121. J. Shook, 2009, Toyota's secret: The A3 report, *MIT Sloan Management Review*, 50(4): 30–33; C. Dawson & K. N. Anhalt, 2005, A "China price" for Toyota, *BusinessWeek*, February 21, 50–51; W. M. Fruin, 1992, *The Japanese Enterprise System*, New York: Oxford University Press.

122. B. Garrette, X. Castañer, & P. Dussauge, 2009, Horizontal alliances as an alternative to autonomous production: Product expansion mode choice in the worldwide aircraft industry 1945–2000, *Strategic Management Journal*, 30(8): 885–894.

123. A. M. Hayashi, 2008, How to replicate success. *MIT Sloan Management Review*, 49(3): 6–7; M. Tuunanen & F. Hoy, 2007, Franchising: Multifaceted form of

entrepreneurship, *International Journal of Entrepreneurship and Small Business*, 4: 52–67.

124. J. Li, C. Dhanaraj, & R. L. Shockley, 2008, Joint venture evolution: Extending the real options approach, *Managerial and Decision Economics*, 29(4): 317–336; B. B. Nielsen, 2005, The role of knowledge embeddedness in the creation of synergies in strategic alliances, *Journal of Business Research*, 58: 1194–1204.

125. E. Bellman, 2009, Corporate news: McDonald's plans expansion in India, *Wall Street Journal*, June 30, B4.

126. T. W. Tong, J. J. Reuer, & M. W. Peng, 2008. International joint ventures and the value of growth options, *Academy of Management Journal*, 51: 1014–1029; P. H. Andersen & P. R. Christensen, 2005, Bridges over troubled water: Suppliers as connective nodes in global supply networks, *Journal of Business Research*, 58: 1261–1273; C. Jones, W. S. Hesterly, & S. P. Borgatti, 1997, A general theory of network governance: Exchange conditions and social mechanisms, *Academy of Management Review*, 22: 911–945.

127. M. W. Hansen, T. Pedersen, & B. Petersen, 2009, MNC strategies and linkage effects in developing countries, *Journal of World Business*, 44(2): 121–139; A. Goerzen, 2005, Managing alliance networks: Emerging practices of multinational corporations, *Academy of Management Executive*, 19(2): 94–107.

128. L. H. Lin, 2009, Mergers and acquisitions, alliances and technology development: An empirical study of the global auto industry, *International Journal of Technology Management*, 48(3): 295–307; R. E. Miles, C. C. Snow, J. A. Mathews, G. Miles, & J. J. Coleman Jr., 1997, Organizing in the knowledge age: Anticipating the cellular form, *Academy of Management Executive*, 11(4): 7–20.

129. 2009, EDS Agility Alliance: Collaboration for better business outcomes, http://www.eds.com, July 16.

130. 2009, EDS Agility Alliance reaches milestone, *Wireless News*, June 3.

CHAPTER 12

Strategic Leadership

Studying this chapter should provide you with the strategic management knowledge needed to:

1. Define strategic leadership and describe top-level managers' importance.

2. Explain what top management teams are and how they affect firm performance.

3. Describe the managerial succession process using internal and external managerial labor markets.

4. Discuss the value of strategic leadership in determining the firm's strategic direction.

5. Describe the importance of strategic leaders in managing the firm's resources.

6. Define organizational culture and explain what must be done to sustain an effective culture.

7. Explain what strategic leaders can do to establish and emphasize ethical practices.

8. Discuss the importance and use of organizational controls.

SELECTING A NEW CEO: THE IMPORTANCE OF STRATEGIC LEADERS

Evidence shows that the shelf life of a CEO is not long, and it continues to get shorter. In 2005, the average CEO tenure was 7.3 years and is becoming even shorter today (about 6 years).

The brevity of CEOs and top-level managers' tenure means that planning for and selecting new leaders should be continuous processes. Furthermore, the importance of strategic leaders to a firm's overall health and success makes selecting effective leaders critical. For example, in 2008 almost 1,500 CEOs of U.S.–based firms left their jobs. Despite this high number of strategic leader departures, boards of directors are rarely effective in planning for and completing the succession. A survey of boards found that over 40 percent of the firms had no succession plan. In another survey, more than 50 percent of directors rated the boards at their firms as ineffective in succession planning. Changes in the CEO often occur without warning. For example, in 2009 the CEOs at Toyota, Lenovo, and Ranbaxy unexpectedly resigned or were replaced. In the cases of Toyota and Lenovo, poor firm performance was the reason for change. Both suffered net losses in 2008 and Lenovo's market share declined from third to fourth place in the PC industry.

The importance of CEOs and planning for succession is clearly evident with Steve Jobs at Apple. Jobs took time off from the CEO role in 2009 due to illness. Analysts expressed major concerns about his ability to continue because of his importance to the success of the firm. He is believed to be especially important to Apple's innovation capability. While he does not design new products, he reviews each new project and serves as an internal champion for those he feels are worthy. For example, Jobs supported the work on the iPod in its early stages despite the skepticism of several others in the company. Furthermore, Jobs will not accept compromises; he pushes project teams to do everything possible to make the product right.

AP Photo/Bradley C. Bower

The leadership transition at DuPont was highly successful due to the early identification of Ellen Kullman as the likely successor to CEO, Charles Holliday and his ability to then serve as her mentor.

Jobs is a co-founder of Apple but left the company for 12 years. During that time, the company foundered. He returned in 1997 and Apple has had a number of market successes since that time. This is why many wonder if Jobs can be replaced. One analyst referred to Apple without Jobs as similar to a John Wayne movie without John Wayne. Another stated that Apple without Jobs is Sony. While Jobs has trained and delegated authority over innovation at Apple, few believe that he can be adequately replaced. Thus, the selection of a new CEO for Apple whenever Jobs departs will be critical for the company.

Companies can develop effective succession plans. Usually such plans call for selecting one or more potential successors and helping them to build the capabilities necessary to be effective CEOs. For example, they may be given challenging assignments where they can build valuable knowledge of critical markets and/or establish relationships with important stakeholders. They can receive mentoring and 360-degree feedback to identify positive traits and work on negative ones. For example, Ellen Kullman was identified as a potential CEO several years before she assumed the position at DuPont. The CEO whom she replaced, Charles Holliday, mentored Kullman and gave her challenging assignments. He was especially impressed with her willingness to learn. As a result, the transition from Holliday to Kullman was seamless and successful.

Identifying potential CEOs is a difficult assignment because of the many and varied capabilities needed for the job. Recent efforts to identify potential successors for CEOs focused on people who were innovative and championed innovation, had vision and could gain others commitment to that vision, nurtured important human capital, and built relationships with critical constituencies such as customers and suppliers.

Sources: S. Tobak, 2009, What happens when Steve Jobs leaves Apple? BNET, http://www.blogs.bnet.com, May 26; L. Whipp, 2009, Ranbaxy chief to step down, *Financial Times*, http://www.ft.com, May 24; J. Soble, 2009, Toyota plans top-level overhaul, *Financial Times*, http://www.ft.com, May 14; M. Boyle, 2009, The art of succession, *BusinessWeek*, May 11, 30–37; M. Boyle, 2009, The art of CEO succession, *BusinessWeek*, http://www.businessweek.com, April 30; F. Balfour and B. Einhorn, 2009, Lenovo CEO is out; Chinese execs return, *BusinessWeek*, http://www.businessweek.com, February 5; J. Scheck & N. Wingfield, 2008, How Apple could survive without Steve Jobs, *Wall Street Journal*, http://www.wsj.com, December 19; B. Behan, 2008, Shareholder proposals on CEO succession planning, *BusinessWeek*, http://www.businessweek.com, January 24.

As the Opening Case implies, strategic leaders' work is demanding, challenging, and may last for a long period of time. Regardless of how long they remain in their positions, strategic leaders (and most prominently CEOs) can make a major difference in how a firm performs.[1] If a strategic leader can create a strategic vision for the firm using forward thinking, she may be able to energize the firm's human capital and achieve positive outcomes. However, the challenge of strategic leadership is significant. For example, replacing Steve Jobs at Apple will be difficult because of his special skills in identifying and nurturing creative new products that have significant market potential. On the other hand, the transition at DuPont was smooth because a person was identified early and groomed to take over the CEO role when change was necessary.

A major message in this chapter is that effective strategic leadership is the foundation for successfully using the strategic management process. As is implied in Figure 1.1 (on page 5), strategic leaders guide the firm in ways that result in forming a vision and mission (see Chapter 1). Often, this guidance finds leaders thinking of ways to create goals that stretch everyone in the organization to improve performance.[2] Moreover, strategic leaders facilitate the development of appropriate strategic actions and determine how to implement them. As we show in Figure 12.1, these actions are the path to strategic competitiveness and above-average returns.[3]

We begin this chapter with a definition of strategic leadership; we then discuss its importance as a potential source of competitive advantage as well as effective strategic leadership styles. Next, we examine top management teams and their effects on innovation, strategic change, and firm performance. Following this discussion, we analyze the internal and external managerial labor markets from which strategic leaders are selected. Closing the chapter are descriptions of the five key components of effective strategic leadership: determining a strategic direction, effectively managing the firm's resource portfolio (which includes exploiting and maintaining core competencies along with developing human capital and social capital), sustaining an effective organizational culture, emphasizing ethical practices, and establishing balanced organizational controls.

Strategic Leadership and Style

Strategic leadership is the ability to anticipate, envision, maintain flexibility, and empower others to create strategic change as necessary. Multifunctional in nature, strategic leadership involves managing through others, managing an entire enterprise rather than a functional subunit, and coping with change that continues to increase in the global economy. Because of the global economy's complexity, strategic leaders must learn how to effectively influence human behavior, often in uncertain environments. By word or by personal example, and through their ability to envision the future, effective strategic leaders meaningfully influence the behaviors, thoughts, and feelings of those with whom they work.[4]

Strategic leadership is the ability to anticipate, envision, maintain flexibility, and empower others to create strategic change as necessary.

Figure 12.1 Strategic Leadership and the Strategic Management Process

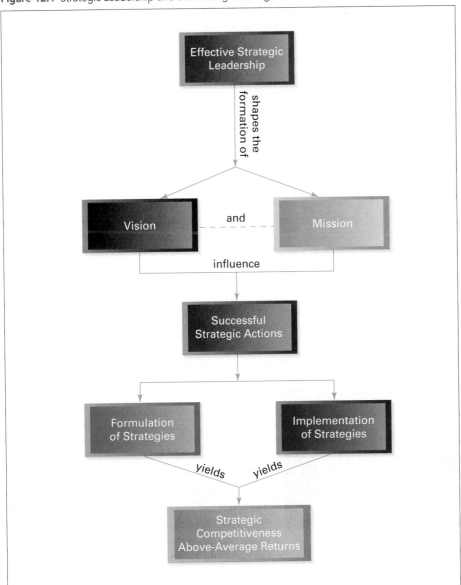

The ability to attract and then manage human capital may be the most critical of the strategic leader's skills,[5] especially because the lack of talented human capital constrains firm growth.[6] Increasingly, leaders throughout the global economy possess or are developing this skill. Some believe, for example, that leaders now surfacing in Chinese companies understand the rules of competition in market-based economies and are leading in ways that will develop their firm's human capital.[7]

In the twenty-first century, intellectual capital that the firm's human capital possesses, including the ability to manage knowledge and create and commercialize innovation, affects a strategic leader's success.[8] Effective strategic leaders also establish the context through which stakeholders (such as employees, customers, and suppliers) can perform at peak efficiency.[9] Being able to demonstrate these skills is important, given that the crux of strategic leadership is the ability to manage the firm's operations effectively and sustain high performance over time.[10]

A firm's ability to achieve a competitive advantage and earn above-average returns is compromised when strategic leaders fail to respond appropriately and quickly to changes in the complex global competitive environment. The inability to respond or to identify the need for change in the competitive environment is one of the reasons some CEOs fail, as shown by the replacement of CEOs in Toyota and Lenovo described in the Opening Case. Therefore, strategic leaders must learn how to deal with diverse and complex environmental situations. Individual judgment is an important part of learning about and analyzing the firm's competitive environment.[11] In particular, effective strategic leaders build strong ties with external stakeholders to gain access to information and advice on the events in the external environment.[12]

The primary responsibility for effective strategic leadership rests at the top, in particular with the CEO. Other commonly recognized strategic leaders include members of the board of directors, the top management team, and divisional general managers. In truth, any individual with responsibility for the performance of human capital and/or a part of the firm (e.g., a production unit) is a strategic leader. Regardless of their title and organizational function, strategic leaders have substantial decision-making responsibilities that cannot be delegated.[13] Strategic leadership is a complex but critical form of leadership. Strategies cannot be formulated and implemented for the purpose of achieving above-average returns without effective strategic leaders.[14]

Top-level management decisions influence the culture of firms as well as how organizations are structured and how goals are set and achieved.

The styles used to provide leadership often affect the productivity of those being led. Transformational leadership is the most effective strategic leadership style. This style entails motivating followers to exceed the expectations others have of them, to continuously enrich their capabilities, and to place the interests of the organization above their own.[15] Transformational leaders develop and communicate a vision for the organization and formulate a strategy to achieve the vision. They make followers aware of the need to achieve valued organizational outcomes and encourage them to continuously strive for higher levels of achievement. These types of leaders have a high degree of integrity (Roy Kroc, founder of McDonald's, was a strategic leader valued for his high degree of integrity)[16] and character. Speaking about character, one CEO said the following: "Leaders are shaped and defined by character. Leaders inspire and enable others to do excellent work and realize their potential. As a result, they build successful, enduring organizations."[17] Additionally, transformational leaders have emotional intelligence. Emotionally intelligent leaders understand themselves well, have strong motivation, are empathetic with others, and have effective interpersonal skills.[18] As a result of these characteristics, transformational leaders are especially effective in promoting and nurturing innovation in firms.[19]

The Role of Top-Level Managers

Top-level managers play a critical role in that they are charged to make certain their firm is able to effectively formulate and implement strategies.[20] Top-level managers' strategic decisions influence how the firm is designed and goals will be achieved. Thus, a critical element of organizational success is having a top management team with superior managerial skills.[21]

Managers often use their discretion (or latitude for action) when making strategic decisions, including those concerned with effectively implementing strategies.[22] Managerial discretion differs significantly across industries. The primary factors that determine the amount of decision-making discretion held by a manager (especially a top-level manager) are (1) external environmental sources such as the industry structure, the rate of market growth in the firm's primary industry, and the degree to which products can be differentiated; (2) characteristics of the organization, including its size, age, resources, and culture; and (3) characteristics of the manager, including commitment to the firm and its strategic outcomes, tolerance for ambiguity, skills in working with different people, and aspiration levels (see Figure 12.2). Because strategic leaders' decisions are intended to help the firm gain a competitive advantage, how managers exercise discretion when determining appropriate strategic actions is critical to the firm's success.[23]

In addition to determining new strategic initiatives, top-level managers develop a firm's organizational structure and reward systems. Top executives also have a major effect on a firm's culture. Evidence suggests that managers' values are critical in shaping a firm's cultural values.[24] Accordingly, top-level managers have an important effect on organizational activities and performance.[25] Because of the challenges top executives face, they often are more effective when they operate as top management teams.

Top Management Teams

In most firms, the complexity of challenges and the need for substantial amounts of information and knowledge require strategic leadership by a team of executives. Using

Figure 12.2 Factors Affecting Managerial Discretion

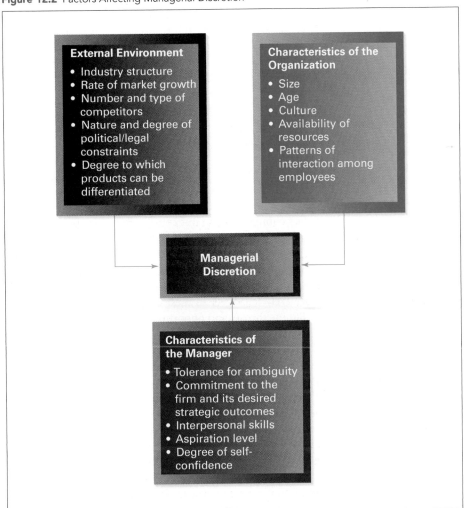

Source: Adapted from S. Finkelstein & D. C. Hambrick, 1996, *Strategic Leadership: Top Executives and Their Effects on Organizations*, St. Paul, MN: West Publishing Company.

a team to make strategic decisions also helps to avoid another potential problem when these decisions are made by the CEO alone: managerial hubris. Research evidence shows that when CEOs begin to believe glowing press accounts and to feel that they are unlikely to make errors, they are more likely to make poor strategic decisions.[26] Top executives need to have self-confidence but must guard against allowing it to become arrogance and a false belief in their own invincibility.[27] To guard against CEO overconfidence and poor strategic decisions, firms often use the top management team to consider strategic opportunities and problems and to make strategic decisions. The **top management team** is composed of the key individuals who are responsible for selecting and implementing the firm's strategies. Typically, the top management team includes the officers of the corporation, defined by the title of vice president and above or by service as a member of the board of directors.[28] The quality of the strategic decisions made by a top management team affects the firm's ability to innovate and engage in effective strategic change.[29]

Top Management Team, Firm Performance, and Strategic Change

The job of top-level executives is complex and requires a broad knowledge of the firm's operations, as well as the three key parts of the firm's external environment—the general, industry, and competitor environments, as discussed in Chapter 2. Therefore, firms try to form a top management team with knowledge and expertise needed to operate the internal organization, yet that also can deal with all the firm's stakeholders as well as its competitors.[30] To have these characteristics normally requires a heterogeneous top management team. A **heterogeneous top management team** is composed of individuals with different functional backgrounds, experience, and education.

Members of a heterogeneous top management team benefit from discussing the different perspectives advanced by team members.[31] In many cases, these discussions increase the quality of the team's decisions, especially when a synthesis emerges within the team after evaluating the diverse perspectives.[32] The net benefit of such actions by heterogeneous teams has been positive in terms of market share and above-average returns. Research shows that more heterogeneity among top management team members promotes debate, which often leads to better strategic decisions. In turn, better strategic decisions produce higher firm performance.[33]

It is also important for top management team members to function cohesively. In general, the more heterogeneous and larger the top management team is, the more difficult it is for the team to effectively implement strategies.[34] Comprehensive and long-term strategic plans can be inhibited by communication difficulties among top executives who have different backgrounds and different cognitive skills.[35] Alternatively, communication among diverse top management team members can be facilitated through electronic communications, sometimes reducing the barriers before face-to-face meetings.[36] However, a group of top executives with diverse backgrounds may inhibit the process of decision making if it is not effectively managed. In these cases, top management teams may fail to comprehensively examine threats and opportunities, leading to a suboptimal strategic decision. Thus, the CEO must attempt to achieve behavioral integration among the team members.[37]

Having members with substantive expertise in the firm's core functions and businesses is also important to a top management team's effectiveness.[38] In a high-technology industry, it may be critical for a firm's top management team members to have R&D expertise, particularly when growth strategies are being implemented. Yet their eventual effect on strategic decisions depends not only on their expertise and the way the team is managed but also on the context in which they make the decisions (the governance structure, incentive compensation, etc.).[39]

The characteristics of top management teams are related to innovation and strategic change.[40] For example, more heterogeneous top management teams are positively associated with innovation and strategic change. The heterogeneity may force the team or some of its members to "think outside of the box" and thus be more creative in making decisions.[41]

The **top management team** is composed of the key individuals who are responsible for selecting and implementing the firm's strategies.

A **heterogeneous top management team** is composed of individuals with different functional backgrounds, experience, and education.

Therefore, firms that need to change their strategies are more likely to do so if they have top management teams with diverse backgrounds and expertise. When a new CEO is hired from outside the industry, the probability of strategic change is greater than if the new CEO is from inside the firm or inside the industry.[42] Although hiring a new CEO from outside the industry adds diversity to the team, the top management team must be managed effectively to use the diversity in a positive way. Thus, to successfully create strategic change, the CEO should exercise transformational leadership.[43] A top management team with various areas of expertise is more likely to identify environmental changes (opportunities and threats) or changes within the firm, suggesting the need for a different strategic direction.

In the current competitive environment, an understanding of international markets is vital. However, recent research suggests that only about 15 percent of the top executives in *Fortune* 500 firms have global leadership expertise.[44] Executives generally gain this knowledge by working in one of the firm's international subsidiaries but can also gain some knowledge by working with international alliance partners.[45]

The CEO and Top Management Team Power

As noted in Chapter 10, the board of directors is an important governance mechanism for monitoring a firm's strategic direction and for representing stakeholders' interests, especially those of shareholders.[46] In fact, higher performance normally is achieved when the board of directors is more directly involved in shaping a firm's strategic direction.[47]

Boards of directors, however, may find it difficult to direct the strategic actions of powerful CEOs and top management teams.[48] Often, a powerful CEO appoints a number of sympathetic outside members to the board or may have inside board members who are also on the top management team and report to her or him.[49] In either case, the CEO may significantly influence the board's actions. Thus, the amount of discretion a CEO has in making strategic decisions is related to the board of directors and how it chooses to oversee the actions of the CEO and the top management team.[50]

CEOs and top management team members can achieve power in other ways. A CEO who also holds the position of chairperson of the board usually has more power than the CEO who does not.[51] Some analysts and corporate "watchdogs" criticize the practice of CEO duality (when the CEO and the chairperson of the board are the same) because it can lead to poor performance and slow response to change.[52]

Although it varies across industries, CEO duality occurs most commonly in larger firms. Increased shareholder activism, however, has brought CEO duality under scrutiny and attack in both U.S. and European firms. As reported in Chapter 10, an independent board leadership structure in which the same person did not hold the positions of CEO and chair is commonly believed to enhance a board's ability to monitor top-level managers' decisions and actions, particularly with respect to financial performance.[53] On the other hand, if a CEO acts as a steward, holding the dual roles facilitates effective decisions and actions. In these instances, the increased effectiveness gained through CEO duality accrues from the individual who wants to perform effectively and desires to be the best possible steward of the firm's assets. Because of this person's positive orientation and actions, extra governance and the coordination costs resulting from an independent board leadership structure would be unnecessary.[54]

Top management team members and CEOs who have long tenure—on the team and in the organization—have a greater influence on board decisions. CEOs with greater influence may take actions in their own best interests, the outcomes of which increase their compensation from the company.[55] As reported in Chapter 10, many people are angry about excessive top executive compensation, especially during poor economic times when others are losing their jobs because ineffective strategic decisions made by the same managers.

In general, long tenure is thought to constrain the breadth of an executive's knowledge base. Some evidence suggests that with the limited perspectives associated with a

STRATEGY RIGHT NOW

Read more about the role of the board of directors in a firm's top management dynamic.

www.cengage.com/management/hitt

restricted knowledge base, long-tenured top executives typically develop fewer alternatives to evaluate in making strategic decisions.[56] However, long-tenured managers also may be able to exercise more effective strategic control, thereby obviating the need for board members' involvement because effective strategic control generally produces higher performance.[57] Intriguingly, recent findings suggest that "the liabilities of short tenure … appear to exceed the advantages, while the advantages of long tenure—firm-specific human and social capital, knowledge, and power—seem to outweigh the disadvantages of rigidity and maintaining the status quo."[58] Overall then the relationship between CEO tenure and firm performance is complex, indicating that to strengthen the firm, boards of directors should develop an effective relationship with the top management team.

In summary, the relative degrees of power held by the board and top management team members should be examined in light of an individual firm's situation. For example, the abundance of resources in a firm's external environment and the volatility of that environment may affect the ideal balance of power between the board and the top management teams. Moreover, a volatile and uncertain environment may create a situation where a powerful CEO is needed to move quickly, but a diverse top management team may create less cohesion among team members and prevent or stall necessary strategic actions. With effective working relationships, boards, CEOs, and other top management team members have the foundation required to select arrangements with the highest probability of best serving stakeholders' interests.[59]

Managerial Succession

The choice of top executives—especially CEOs—is a critical decision with important implications for the firm's performance.[60] Many companies use leadership screening systems to identify individuals with managerial and strategic leadership potential as well as to determine the criteria individuals should satisfy to be candidates for the CEO position.[61]

The most effective of these systems assesses people within the firm and gains valuable information about the capabilities of other companies' managers, particularly their strategic leaders.[62] Based on the results of these assessments, training and development programs are provided for current individuals in an attempt to preselect and shape the skills of people who may become tomorrow's leaders. Because of the quality of its programs, General Electric "is famous for developing leaders who are dedicated to turning imaginative ideas into leading products and services."[63]

Organizations select managers and strategic leaders from two types of managerial labor markets—internal and external.[64] An **internal managerial labor market** consists of a firm's opportunities for managerial positions and the qualified employees within that firm. An **external managerial labor market** is the collection of managerial career opportunities and the qualified people who are external to the organization in which the opportunities exist.

Several benefits are thought to accrue to a firm when the internal labor market is used to select an insider as the new CEO. Because of their experience with the firm and the industry environment in which it competes, insiders are familiar with company products, markets, technologies, and operating procedures. Also, internal hiring produces lower turnover among existing personnel, many of whom possess valuable firm-specific knowledge. When the firm is performing well, internal succession is favored to sustain high performance. It is assumed that hiring from inside keeps the important knowledge necessary to sustain performance.

Results of work completed by management consultant Jim Collins support the value of using the internal labor market when selecting a CEO. Collins found that high-performing firms almost always appoint an insider to be the new CEO. He argues that bringing in a

An **internal managerial labor market** consists of a firm's opportunities for managerial positions and the qualified employees within that firm.

An **external managerial labor market** is the collection of managerial career opportunities and the qualified people who are external to the organization in which the opportunities exist.

well-known outsider, to whom he refers as a "white knight," is a recipe for mediocrity.[65] For example, given the phenomenal success of General Electric (GE) during Jack Welch's tenure as CEO and the firm's highly effective management and leadership development programs, insider Jeffrey Immelt was chosen to succeed Welch. However, shareholders have become disgruntled because GE's stock values have decreased in recent years; GE has suffered along with many other firms in the global economic crisis experienced in 2008 and 2009. Thus, GE under Immelt's leadership is not experiencing the returns achieved by his predecessor.

Employees commonly prefer the internal managerial labor market when selecting top management team members and a new CEO. In the past, companies have also had a preference for insiders to fill top-level management positions because of a desire for continuity and a continuing commitment to the firm's current vision, mission, and chosen strategies.[66] However, because of a changing competitive landscape and varying levels of performance, an increasing number of boards of directors are turning to outsiders to succeed CEOs. Although the circumstances are rather unique, Ed Whitacre, former CEO of AT&T was chosen to be the new chairman for GM. Of course, he will have to help GM come out of bankruptcy.[67] A firm often has valid reasons to select an outsider as its new CEO. In some situations, long tenure with a firm may reduce strategic leaders' level of commitment to pursue innovation. Given innovation's importance to firm success (see Chapter 13), this hesitation could be a liability for a strategic leader.

In Figure 12.3, we show how the composition of the top management team and the CEO succession (managerial labor market) interact to affect strategy. For example, when the top management team is homogeneous (its members have similar functional experiences and educational backgrounds) and a new CEO is selected from inside the firm, the firm's current strategy is unlikely to change. Alternatively, when a new CEO is selected from outside the firm and the top management team is heterogeneous, the probability is high that strategy will change. When the new CEO is from inside the firm and a heterogeneous top management team is in place, the strategy may not change, but innovation is likely to continue. An external CEO succession with a homogeneous team creates a more ambiguous situation. The selection of Sir Howard Stringer as CEO of Sony signaled major changes in that firm's future. He is not only an outsider but also a foreigner. He is making major changes in the hopes of turning around Sony's poor performance. His intent is to have Sony regain its traditional excellence in innovative products.[68]

Figure 12.3 Effects of CEO Succession and Top Management Team Composition on Strategy

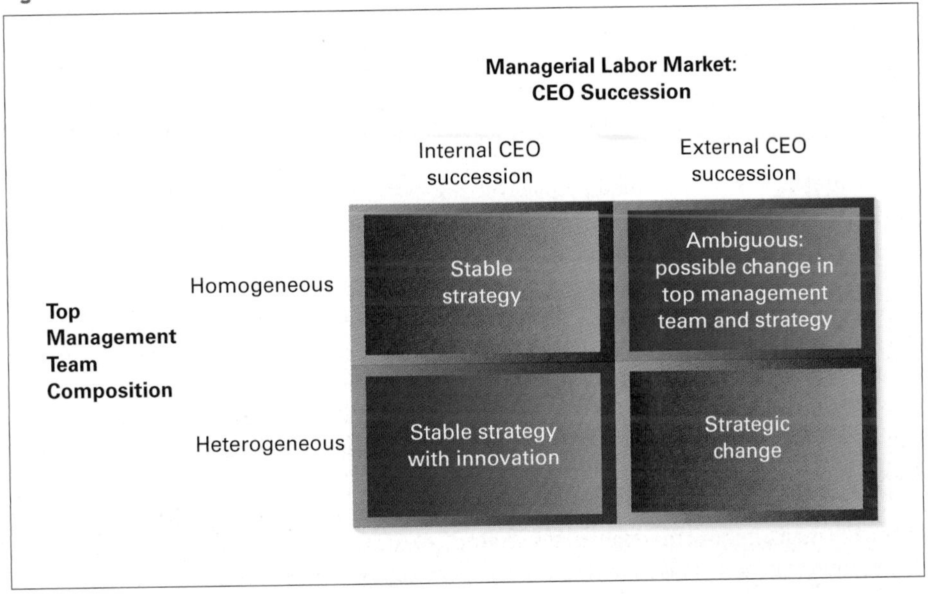

STRATEGIC FOCUS

THE MODEL SUCCESSION AT XEROX

Anne Mulcahy became CEO of Xerox in 2001 and is credited with restoring the company's profitability and market leadership during her tenure. She championed innovation and built a strong relationship with customers. In fact, the firm was close to bankruptcy when she became the CEO. She told Xerox shareholders that the company's business model at the time was not sustainable. She was advised to declare bankruptcy but refused to do so. To gain the support needed for changes, she had personal meetings with the top 100 managers at Xerox. She refused to cut R&D or sales but did reduce costs significantly in other areas. The lead independent director, N. J. Nicholas, believes she created a major turnaround that built Xerox into an innovative technology and services company. Her work as CEO has earned her recognition as one of America's best leaders.

The succession process she has used reinforces that recognition. Ursula Burns was selected as heir apparent and given the job as president to "learn the ropes" for a couple of years before Mulcahy decided to take early retirement (Mulcahy was only 56 years old in 2009). Actually, Burns played a major role in Xerox's turnaround. She served as Mulcahy's lieutenant and managed most of the day-to-day operations. She also helped to identify gaps in Xerox's product portfolio and found products to fill those gaps. With the largest product portfolio in Xerox's history, it became a major competitor in marketing products to small and medium-sized businesses. Interestingly, Burns is the first African-American woman to head a major U.S. corporation. Burns (CEO) and Mulcahy (Chairman) are planning to work as a team for a couple of years. This is probably good because Xerox faces multiple challenges given the negative economic environment. Burns receives praise from insiders and external analysts for her deep knowledge of the industry and business and her technological expertise. She is also known for her willingness to take risks. One observer called the selection of Burns and model transition between Mulcahy and Burns as a "bases-loaded home run." Xerox is a unique technology-based company because approximately one third of its almost 4,000 executives are women. Observers expect the transition from Mulcahy to Burns to be a major success.

Jeff Weiner/Courtesy of Xerox Corporation

Anne Mulcahy, Chairman of Xerox

Nik Rocklin/Courtesy of Xerox Corporation

Ursula Burns, CEO of Xerox

Sources: N. Byrnes and R. O. Crockett, 2009, An historic succession at Xerox, *BusinessWeek*, June 8, 18–22; W. M. Bulkeley, 2009, Xerox names Burns chief as Mulcahy retires early, *Wall Street Journal*, http://www.wsj.com, May 22; 2009, Chief executive is retiring at Xerox, *New York Times*, http://www.nytimes.com, May 22; 2009, Anne Mulcahy to retire as Xerox CEO; Ursula Burns named successor, FreshNews, http://www.freshnews.com, May 21; E. White, 2009, Xerox succession a 'model' case, *Wall Street Journal*, http://www.wsj.com, May 21; D. Gelles, 2009, Burns to replace Mulcahy at Xerox, *Financial Times*, http://www.ft.com, May 21; 2008, Women CEOs, Xerox, *Financial Times*, http://www.ft.com, December 31; B. George, 2008, America's best leaders: Anne Mulcahy, Xerox CEO, *US News*, http://www.usnews.com, November 19.

Including talent from all parts of both the internal and external labor markets increases the likelihood that the firm will be able to form an effective top-management team. Evidence suggests that women are a qualified source of talent as strategic leaders that have been somewhat overlooked. In light of the success of a growing number of female executives, the foundation for change may be established. Trailblazers such as Catherine Elizabeth Hughes (the first African-American woman to head a firm that was publicly traded on a U.S. stock exchange), Muriel Siebert (the first woman to purchase a seat on the New York Stock Exchange), and publisher Judith Regan have made important contributions as strategic leaders. Recent years have produced several prominent female CEOs, such as Anne Mulcahy (Xerox Corporation), Meg Whitman (eBay), and Andrea Jung (Avon Products). As noted in the Strategic Focus, Anne Mulcahy stepped out of the role of CEO and became chairman of the board for Xerox in 2009. Ursula Burns succeeded her as the CEO.

Managerial talent is critical to a firm's success as noted earlier. And, one area in which managerial talent is crucial is in the integration of an acquired firm into the acquiring business. In fact, the top management team of an acquired firm is vital to a successful integration process because they play a critical role in helping the change be implemented and accepted by the acquired firm's employees.[69] However, it is common for there to be major turnover among the top management team of acquired firms. Sometimes it occurs because the acquiring firm unwisely replaces them. In other cases, the managers depart voluntarily to seek other top management positions. Research shows that high turnover among the acquired firm's top managers often produces poor performance and perhaps even leads to a failed acquisition.[70] Therefore, acquiring firms should work hard to avoid successions during the integration process and thereafter.

Key Strategic Leadership Actions

Certain actions characterize effective strategic leadership; we present the most important ones in Figure 12.4. Many of the actions interact with each other. For example, managing the firm's resources effectively includes developing human capital and contributes to establishing a strategic direction, fostering an effective culture, exploiting core competencies, using effective organizational control systems, and establishing ethical practices. The most effective strategic leaders create viable options in making decisions regarding each of the key strategic leadership actions.[71]

Determining Strategic Direction

Determining strategic direction involves specifying the image and character the firm seeks to develop over time.[72] The strategic direction is framed within the context of the conditions (i.e., opportunities and threats) strategic leaders expect their firm to face in roughly the next three to five years.

The ideal long-term strategic direction has two parts: a core ideology and an envisioned future. The core ideology motivates employees through the company's heritage, but the envisioned future encourages employees to stretch beyond their expectations of accomplishment and requires significant change and progress to be realized.[73] The envisioned future serves as a guide to many aspects of a firm's strategy implementation process, including motivation, leadership, employee empowerment, and organizational design. The strategic direction could include such actions as entering new international markets and developing a set of new suppliers to add to the firm's value chain.[74]

Most changes in strategic direction are difficult to design and implement; however, CEO Jeffrey Immelt has an even greater challenge at GE. GE performed exceptionally well under Jack Welch's leadership. Although change is necessary because the competitive landscape has shifted significantly, stakeholders accustomed to Jack Welch and high performance are experiencing problems in accepting Immelt's changes (e.g., changes to

Determining strategic direction involves specifying the image and character the firm seeks to develop over time.

Figure 12.4 Exercise of Effective Strategic Leadership

the firm's corporate-level strategy and structure). His challenges are made even more difficult because GE is experiencing performance problems partly the result of the difficult economic climate.[75] Additionally, information regarding the firm's strategic direction must be consistently and clearly communicated to all affected parties.[76]

A charismatic CEO may foster stakeholders' commitment to a new vision and strategic direction. Nonetheless, it is important not to lose sight of the organization's strengths when making changes required by a new strategic direction. Immelt, for example, needs to use GE's strengths to ensure continued positive performance. The goal is to pursue the firm's short-term need to adjust to a new vision and strategic direction while maintaining its long-term survivability by effectively managing its portfolio of resources.

Effectively Managing the Firm's Resource Portfolio

Effectively managing the firm's portfolio of resources may be the most important strategic leadership task. The firm's resources are categorized as financial capital, human capital, social capital, and organizational capital (including organizational culture).[77]

Clearly, financial capital is critical to organizational success; strategic leaders understand this reality.[78] However, the most effective strategic leaders recognize the equivalent importance of managing each remaining type of resource as well as managing the integration of resources (e.g., using financial capital to provide training opportunities through which human capital is able to learn and maximize its performance). Most importantly, effective strategic leaders manage the firm's resource portfolio by organizing them into capabilities, structuring the firm to facilitate using those capabilities, and choosing strategies through which the capabilities are successfully leveraged to create value for customers.[79] Exploiting and maintaining core competencies and developing and retaining the firm's human and social capital are actions taken to reach these important objectives.

Exploiting and Maintaining Core Competencies

Examined in Chapters 1 and 3, *core competencies* are capabilities that serve as a source of competitive advantage for a firm over its rivals. Typically, core competencies relate to an organization's functional skills, such as manufacturing, finance, marketing, and research and development. Strategic leaders must verify that the firm's competencies are emphasized when implementing strategies. Intel, for example, has core competencies of *competitive agility* (an ability to act in a variety of competitively relevant ways) and *competitive speed* (an ability to act quickly when facing environmental and competitive pressures).[80] Capabilities are developed over time as firms learn from their actions and enhance their knowledge about specific actions needed. For example, through repeated interactions, some firms have formed a capability allowing them to fully understand customers' needs as they change.[81] Firms with capabilities in R&D that develop into core competencies are rewarded by the market because of the critical nature of innovation in many industries.[82]

In many large firms, and certainly in related diversified ones, core competencies are effectively exploited when they are developed and applied across different organizational units (see Chapter 6). For example, PepsiCo purchased Quaker Oats (now called Quaker Foods), which makes the sports drink Gatorade. PepsiCo uses its competence in distribution systems to exploit the Quaker assets. In this instance, Pepsi soft drinks (e.g., Pepsi Cola and Mountain Dew) and Gatorade share the logistics activity. Similarly, PepsiCo uses this competence to distribute Quaker's healthy snacks and Frito-Lay salty snacks through the same channels. Today, PepsiCo seeks "to be the world's premiere consumer products company focused on convenient foods and beverages."[83]

Firms must continuously develop and, when appropriate, change their core competencies to outperform rivals. If they have a competence that provides an advantage but does not change it, competitors will eventually imitate that competence and reduce or eliminate the firm's competitive advantage. Additionally, firms must guard against the competence becoming a liability, thereby preventing change.

As we discuss next, human capital is critical to a firm's success. One reason it's so critical is that human capital is the resource through which core competencies are developed and used.

Developing Human Capital and Social Capital

Human capital refers to the knowledge and skills of a firm's entire workforce. From the perspective of human capital, employees are viewed as a capital resource requiring continuous investment.[84] At PepsiCo, people are identified as the key to the firm's continuing success. Given the need to "sustain its talent," PepsiCo invests in its human capital in the form of a host of programs and development-oriented experiences.[85]

Investments such as those being made at PepsiCo are productive, in that much of the development of U.S. industry can be attributed to the effectiveness of its human capital. This fact suggests that "as the dynamics of competition accelerate, people are perhaps the only truly sustainable source of competitive advantage."[86] In all types of organizations—large and small, new and established, and so forth—human capital's increasing importance suggests a significant role for the firm's human resource management activities.[87] As a support activity (see Chapter 3), human resource management practices facilitate people's efforts to successfully select and especially to use the firm's strategies.[88]

Effective training and development programs increase the probability of individuals becoming successful strategic leaders.[89] These programs are increasingly linked to firm

Dave & Les Jacobs/Cultura/Getty Images

Training and development programs can provide the means by which new strategic leaders are cultivated within an organization.

Human capital refers to the knowledge and skills of a firm's entire workforce.

success as knowledge becomes more integral to gaining and sustaining a competitive advantage.[90] Additionally, such programs build knowledge and skills, inculcate a common set of core values, and offer a systematic view of the organization, thus promoting the firm's vision and organizational cohesion. For example, PepsiCo's development programs emphasize its "performance with purpose," which focuses on building shareholder value while simultaneously ensuring human, environmental, and talent sustainability.[91]

Effective training and development programs also contribute positively to the firm's efforts to form core competencies.[92] Furthermore, they help strategic leaders improve skills that are critical to completing other tasks associated with effective strategic leadership, such as determining the firm's strategic direction, exploiting and maintaining the firm's core competencies, and developing an organizational culture that supports ethical practices. Thus, building human capital is vital to the effective execution of strategic leadership. Indeed, some argue that the world's "best companies are realizing that no matter what business they're in, their real business is building leaders."[93]

Strategic leaders must acquire the skills necessary to help develop human capital in their areas of responsibility.[94] When human capital investments are successful, the result is a workforce capable of learning continuously. Continuous learning and leveraging the firm's expanding knowledge base are linked with strategic success.[95]

Learning also can preclude making errors. Strategic leaders tend to learn more from their failures than their successes because they sometimes make the wrong attributions for the successes.[96] For example, the effectiveness of certain approaches and knowledge can be context specific.[97] Thus, some "best practices" may not work well in all situations. We know that using teams to make decisions can be effective, but sometimes it is better for leaders to make decisions alone, especially when the decisions must be made and implemented quickly (e.g., in crisis situations).[98] Thus, effective strategic leaders recognize the importance of learning from success *and* from failure.

Learning and building knowledge are important for creating innovation in firms.[99] Innovation leads to competitive advantage. Overall, firms that create and maintain greater knowledge usually achieve and maintain competitive advantages. However, as noted with core competencies, strategic leaders must guard against allowing high levels of knowledge in one area to lead to myopia and overlooking knowledge development opportunities in other important areas of the business.[100]

When facing challenging conditions, firms sometimes decide to lay off some of their human capital. Strategic leaders must recognize though that layoffs can result in a significant loss of the knowledge possessed by the firm's human capital. Research evidence shows that moderate-sized layoffs may improve firm performance, but large layoffs produce stronger performance downturns in firms because of the loss of human capital.[101] Although it is also not uncommon for restructuring firms to reduce their expenditures on or investments in training and development programs, restructuring may actually be an important time to increase investments in these programs. The reason for increased focus on training and development is that restructuring firms have less slack and cannot absorb as many errors; moreover, the employees who remain after layoffs may find themselves in positions without all the skills or knowledge they need to perform the required tasks effectively.

Viewing employees as a resource to be maximized rather than as a cost to be minimized facilitates successful implementation of a firm's strategies as does the strategic leader's ability to approach layoffs in a manner that employees believe is fair and equitable.[102] A critical issue for employees is the fairness in the layoffs and in treatment in their jobs.[103]

Social capital involves relationships inside and outside the firm that help the firm accomplish tasks and create value for customers and shareholders.[104] Social capital is a critical asset for a firm. Inside the firm, employees and units must cooperate to get the work done. In multinational organizations, employees often must cooperate

Social capital involves relationships inside and outside the firm that help the firm accomplish tasks and create value for customers and shareholders.

across country boundaries on activities such as R&D to achieve performance objectives (e.g., developing new products).[105]

External social capital is increasingly critical to firm success. The reason for this is that few if any companies have all of the resources they need to successfully compete against their rivals. Firms can use cooperative strategies such as strategic alliances (see Chapter 9) to develop social capital. Social capital can develop in strategic alliances as firms share complementary resources. Resource sharing must be effectively managed, though, to ensure that the partner trusts the firm and is willing to share the desired resources.[106]

Research evidence suggests that the success of many types of firms may partially depend on social capital. Large multinational firms often must establish alliances in order to enter new foreign markets. Likewise, entrepreneurial firms often must establish alliances to gain access to resources, venture capital, or other types of resources (e.g., special expertise that the entrepreneurial firm cannot afford to maintain in-house).[107] Retaining quality human capital and maintaining strong internal social capital can be affected strongly by the firm's culture.

Sustaining an Effective Organizational Culture

In Chapter 1, we define **organizational culture** as a complex set of ideologies, symbols, and core values that are shared throughout the firm and influence the way business is conducted. Evidence suggests that a firm can develop core competencies in terms of both the capabilities it possesses and the way the capabilities are leveraged when implementing strategies to produce desired outcomes. In other words, because the organizational culture influences how the firm conducts its business and helps regulate and control employees' behavior, it can be a source of competitive advantage[108] and is a "critical factor in promoting innovation."[109] Given its importance, it may be that a vibrant organizational culture is the most valuable competitive differentiator for business organizations. Thus, shaping the context within which the firm formulates and implements its strategies—that is, shaping the organizational culture—is an essential strategic leadership action.[110]

Entrepreneurial Mind-Set

Especially in large organizations, an organizational culture often encourages (or discourages) strategic leaders from pursuing (or not pursuing) entrepreneurial opportunities.[111] This issue is important because entrepreneurial opportunities are a vital source of growth and innovation.[112] Therefore, a key role of strategic leaders is to encourage and promote innovation by pursuing entrepreneurial opportunities.[113]

One way to encourage innovation is to invest in opportunities as real options—that is, invest in an opportunity in order to provide the potential option of taking advantage of the opportunity at some point in the future.[114] For example, a firm might buy a piece of land to have the option to build on it at some time in the future should the company need more space and should that location increase in value to the company. Firms might enter strategic alliances for similar reasons. In this instance, a firm might form an alliance to have the option of acquiring the partner later or of building a stronger relationship with it (e.g., developing a joint new venture).[115]

In Chapter 13, we describe how large firms use strategic entrepreneurship to pursue entrepreneurial opportunities and to gain first-mover advantages. Small and medium-sized firms also rely on strategic entrepreneurship when trying to develop innovations as the foundation for profitable growth. In firms of all sizes, strategic entrepreneurship is more likely to be successful when employees have an entrepreneurial mind-set.[116]

Five dimensions characterize a firm's entrepreneurial mind-set: autonomy, innovativeness, risk taking, proactiveness, and competitive aggressiveness.[117] In combination, these dimensions influence the actions a firm takes to be innovative and launch new ventures. In sum, strategic leaders with an entrepreneurial mind-set are committed to pursuing profitable growth.[118]

An **organizational culture** consists of a complex set of ideologies, symbols, and core values that are shared throughout the firm and influence the way business is conducted.

Autonomy, the first of an entrepreneurial orientation's five dimensions, allows employees to take actions that are free of organizational constraints and permits individuals and groups to be self-directed. The second dimension, *innovativeness,* "reflects a firm's tendency to engage in and support new ideas, novelty, experimentation, and creative processes that may result in new products, services, or technological processes."[119] Cultures with a tendency toward innovativeness encourage employees to think beyond existing knowledge, technologies, and parameters to find creative ways to add value. *Risk taking* reflects a willingness by employees and their firm to accept risks when pursuing entrepreneurial opportunities. Assuming significant levels of debt and allocating large amounts of other resources (e.g., people) to projects that may not be completed are examples of these risks. The fourth dimension of an entrepreneurial orientation, *proactiveness,* describes a firm's ability to be a market leader rather than a follower. Proactive organizational cultures constantly use processes to anticipate future market needs and to satisfy them before competitors learn how to do so. Finally, *competitive aggressiveness* is a firm's propensity to take actions that allow it to consistently and substantially outperform its rivals.[120]

Changing the Organizational Culture and Restructuring

Changing a firm's organizational culture is more difficult than maintaining it; however, effective strategic leaders recognize when change is needed. Incremental changes to the firm's culture typically are used to implement strategies.[121] More significant and sometimes even radical changes to organizational culture support selecting strategies that differ from those the firm has implemented historically. Regardless of the reasons for change, shaping and reinforcing a new culture require effective communication and problem solving, along with selecting the right people (those who have the values desired for the organization), engaging in effective performance appraisals (establishing goals and measuring individual performance toward goals that fit in with the new core values), and using appropriate reward systems (rewarding the desired behaviors that reflect the new core values).[122]

Evidence suggests that cultural changes succeed only when the firm's CEO, other key top management team members, and middle-level managers actively support them.[123] To effect change, middle-level managers in particular need to be highly disciplined to energize the culture and foster alignment with the strategic vision.[124] In addition, managers must be sensitive to the effects of other major strategic changes on organizational culture. For example, major downsizings can have negative effects on an organization's culture, especially if it is not implemented in accordance with the dominant organizational values.[125]

Emphasizing Ethical Practices

The effectiveness of processes used to implement the firm's strategies increases when they are based on ethical practices. Ethical companies encourage and enable people at all organizational levels to act ethically when doing what is necessary to implement strategies. In turn, ethical practices and the judgment on which they are based create "social capital" in the organization, increasing the "goodwill available to individuals and groups" in the organization.[126] Alternatively, when unethical practices evolve in an organization, they may become acceptable to many managers and employees.[127] One study found that in these circumstances, managers were particularly likely to engage in unethical practices to meet their goals when current efforts to meet them were insufficient.[128]

To properly influence employees' judgment and behavior, ethical practices must shape the firm's decision-making process and must be an integral part of organizational culture. In fact, research evidence suggests that a value-based culture is the most effective means of ensuring that employees comply with the firm's ethical requirements.[129] As we explained in Chapter 10, managers may act opportunistically, making decisions that are in their own best interests but not in the firm's best interests when facing lax expectations regarding ethical behavior. In other words, managers acting opportunistically take advantage of their positions, making decisions that benefit themselves to the detriment of the firm's stakeholders.[130] But strategic leaders are most likely to integrate ethical values into their decisions when the company has explicit ethics codes, the code is integrated into the business through extensive ethics training, and shareholders expect ethical behavior.[131]

Firms should employ ethical strategic leaders—leaders who include ethical practices as part of their strategic direction for the firm, who desire to do the right thing, and for whom honesty, trust, and integrity are important.[132] Strategic leaders who consistently display these qualities inspire employees as they work with others to develop and support an organizational culture in which ethical practices are the expected behavioral norms.[133]

Strategic leaders can take several actions to develop an ethical organizational culture. Examples of these actions include (1) establishing and communicating specific goals to describe the firm's ethical standards (e.g., developing and disseminating a code of conduct); (2) continuously revising and updating the code of conduct, based on inputs from people throughout the firm and from other stakeholders (e.g., customers and suppliers); (3) disseminating the code of conduct to all stakeholders to inform them of the firm's ethical standards and practices; (4) developing and implementing methods and procedures to use in achieving the firm's ethical standards (e.g., using internal auditing practices that are consistent with the standards); (5) creating and using explicit reward systems that recognize acts of courage (e.g., rewarding those who use proper channels and procedures to report observed wrongdoings); and (6) creating a work environment in which all people are treated with dignity.[134] The effectiveness of these actions increases when they are taken simultaneously and thereby are mutually supportive. When strategic leaders and others throughout the firm fail to take actions such as these—perhaps because an ethical culture has not been created—problems are likely to occur. As we discuss next, formal organizational controls can help prevent further problems and reinforce better ethical practices.[135]

Establishing Balanced Organizational Controls

Organizational controls are basic to a capitalistic system and have long been viewed as an important part of strategy implementation processes.[136] Controls are necessary to help ensure that firms achieve their desired outcomes.[137] Defined as the "formal, information-based … procedures used by managers to maintain or alter patterns in organizational activities," controls help strategic leaders build credibility, demonstrate the value of strategies to the firm's stakeholders, and promote and support strategic change.[138] Most critically, controls provide the parameters for implementing strategies as well as the corrective actions to be taken when implementation-related adjustments are required.

In this chapter, we focus on two organizational controls—strategic and financial—that were introduced in Chapter 11. Our discussion of organizational controls here emphasizes strategic and financial controls because strategic leaders, especially those at the top of the organization, are responsible for their development and effective use.

As we explained in Chapter 11, financial control focuses on short-term financial outcomes. In contrast, strategic control focuses on the *content* of strategic actions rather than their *outcomes*. Some strategic actions can be correct but still result in poor financial outcomes because of external conditions such as a recession in the economy, unexpected domestic or foreign government actions, or natural disasters. Therefore, emphasizing financial controls often produces more short-term and risk-averse managerial decisions, because financial outcomes may be caused by events beyond managers' direct control. Alternatively, strategic control encourages lower-level managers to make decisions that incorporate moderate and acceptable levels of risk because outcomes are shared between the business-level executives making strategic proposals and the corporate-level executives evaluating them.

The challenge strategic leaders face is to verify that their firm is emphasizing financial and strategic controls so that firm performance improves. The Balanced Scorecard is a tool that helps strategic leaders assess the effectiveness of the controls.

The Balanced Scorecard

The **balanced scorecard** is a framework firms can use to verify that they have established both strategic and financial controls to assess their performance.[139] This technique is most appropriate for use when dealing with business-level strategies; however, it can also be used with the other strategies firms may choose to implement (e.g., corporate level, international, and cooperative).

The underlying premise of the balanced scorecard is that firms jeopardize their future performance possibilities when financial controls are emphasized at the expense of strategic controls,[140] in that financial controls provide feedback about outcomes achieved from past actions, but do not communicate the drivers of future performance.[141] Thus, an overemphasis on financial controls has the potential to promote managerial behavior that sacrifices the firm's long-term, value-creating potential for short-term performance gains.[142] An appropriate balance of strategic controls and financial controls, rather than an overemphasis on either, allows firms to effectively monitor their performance.

Four perspectives are integrated to form the balanced scorecard framework: *financial* (concerned with growth, profitability, and risk from the shareholders' perspective), *customer* (concerned with the amount of value customers perceive was created by the firm's products), *internal business processes* (with a focus on the priorities for various business processes that create customer and shareholder satisfaction), and *learning and growth* (concerned with the firm's effort to create a climate that supports change, innovation, and growth). Thus, using the balanced scorecard framework allows the firm to understand how it looks to shareholders (financial perspective), how customers view it (customer perspective), the processes it must emphasize to successfully use its competitive advantage (internal perspective), and what it can do to improve its performance in order to grow (learning and growth perspective).[143] Generally speaking, strategic controls tend to be emphasized when the firm assesses its performance relative to the learning and growth perspective, whereas financial controls are emphasized when assessing performance in terms of the financial perspective.

Firms use different criteria to measure their standing relative to the scorecard's four perspectives. We show sample criteria in Figure 12.5. The firm should select the number of criteria that will allow it to have both a strategic understanding and a financial understanding of its performance without becoming immersed in too many details.[144] For example, we know from research that a firm's innovation, quality of its goods and services, growth of its sales, and its profitability are all interrelated.[145]

Strategic leaders play an important role in determining a proper balance between strategic controls and financial controls, whether they are in single-business firms or large diversified firms. A proper balance between controls is important, in that "wealth creation for organizations where strategic leadership is exercised is possible because these leaders make appropriate investments for future viability [through strategic control], while maintaining an appropriate level of financial stability in the present [through financial control]."[146] In fact, most corporate restructuring is designed to refocus the firm on its core businesses, thereby allowing top executives to reestablish strategic control of their separate business units.[147]

Successfully using strategic control frequently is integrated with appropriate autonomy for the various subunits so that they can gain a competitive advantage in their respective markets.[148] Strategic control can be used to promote the sharing of both tangible and intangible resources among interdependent businesses within a firm's portfolio. In addition, the autonomy provided allows the flexibility necessary to take advantage of

The **balanced scorecard** is a framework firms can use to verify that they have established both strategic and financial controls to assess their performance.

Figure 12.5 Strategic Controls and Financial Controls in a Balanced Scorecard Framework

Perspectives	Criteria
Financial	• Cash flow • Return on equity • Return on assets
Customer	• Assessment of ability to anticipate customers' needs • Effectiveness of customer service practices • Percentage of repeat business • Quality of communications with customers
Internal Business Processes	• Asset utilization improvements • Improvements in employee morale • Changes in turnover rates
Learning and Growth	• Improvements in innovation ability • Number of new products compared to competitors • Increases in employees' skills

specific marketplace opportunities. As a result, strategic leadership promotes simultaneous use of strategic control and autonomy.[149]

The balanced scorecard is being used by car manufacturer Porsche. After this manufacturer of sought-after sports cars regained its market-leading position, it implemented a balanced scorecard approach in an effort to maintain this position. In particular, Porsche used the balanced scorecard to promote learning and continuously improve the business. For example, knowledge was collected from all Porsche dealerships throughout the world. The instrument used to collect the information was referred to as "Porsche Key Performance Indicators." The fact that Porsche is now the world's most profitable automaker suggests the value the firm gained and is gaining by using the balanced scorecard as a foundation for simultaneously emphasizing strategic and financial controls.[150]

As we have explained, strategic leaders are critical to a firm's ability to successfully use all parts of the strategic management process. As described in the Strategic Focus, the new CEO for Wal-Mart, Mike Duke, has the strategic leadership skills to position him and his company for future success. Certainly, the future for strategic leaders similar to Duke is likely to be challenging; but he is leading a highly successful company that is increasing its market share and is likely to grow in international markets, where he has significant experience and knowledge. He appears to emphasize balanced organizational controls and uses many of the principles of the Balanced Scorecard. With people like Mike Duke in these roles, the work of strategic leaders will remain exciting and has a strong possibility of creating positive outcomes for all of a firm's stakeholders.

STRATEGIC FOCUS

THE "GLOBAL DUKE OF RETAIL": THE NEW STRATEGIC LEADER OF WAL-MART

On February 1, 2009, Mike Duke was named the CEO of Wal-Mart. Duke had been chief of the international division and vice chairman of the board of directors prior to his new appointment. The prior CEO, Lee Scott, was in the job for almost 10 years. During his time as CEO, many changes were made in the Wal-Mart strategy. In particular, it went back to its roots with a primary focus on providing value at the lowest possible price. He also started a major public relations program to answer Wal-Mart critics and placed a major emphasis on environment and sustainability. His changes started to pay off for Wal-Mart as its stock price increased 18 percent in 2008, the best performer in the Dow Jones industrial average. Wal-Mart's profits increased during 2008, a year when most companies—especially retailers—experienced declines because of the severe economic climate.

Duke began his tenure at Wal-Mart in 1995 as vice president of logistics after 23 years with Federated Department Stores. Duke eventually ascended to the leadership of the international division and presided over its unprecedented growth. That division is larger than most multinational companies with more than 3,500 stores, 680,000 employees (or "associates" in Wal-Mart terms), and approximately $100 billion in annual sales. Duke was known for building a strong international leadership team. In fact, he is likely to emphasize global business even more for Wal-Mart as a strategy to enhance growth.

Duke is also known for emphasizing high standards of excellence for the company's resources and people. This includes the redesign of the logistics and merchandise distribution system, known as the best in the world, and in recruiting strong talent and building excellent leadership teams. He has already announced that he will increase the speed of and enlarge Wal-Mart's commitment to sustainability as a major part of the firm's organizational culture. Duke is considered to be a strategic thinker and a risk taker. He believes Wal-Mart should try to be the market share leader in every foreign market it enters. Wal-Mart pulled out of Germany and Korea for this reason. Duke is also known to have excellent interpersonal skills.

Wal-Mart is the leading retailer in the world and one of the largest corporations with more than $400 billion in sales. It has been positioned for much future growth and success and Mike Duke has the strategic leadership skills to achieve these goals.

Sources: 2009, Michael T. Duke, Wal-Mart, http://www.walmartstores.com, accessed on May 26; 2009, Wal-Mart reports first quarter financial results, New YorkTtimes, http://markets.on.nytimes.com, May 14; S. Kapner, 2009, Changing of the guard at Wal-Mart, Fortune, March 2. 68–74; S. Rosenbloom, 2009, Wal-Mart hopes to hold onto customers it gained from recession, New York Times, http://wwww.nytimes.com, February 18; 2008, Wal-Mart picks Mike Duke as new CEO, MSNBC.com, http://www.msnbc.msn.com, November 21; S. Rosenbloom, 2008, Wal-Mart taps new chief executive, New York Times, http://www.nytimes.com, October 21.

AP Photo/April L. Brown

Wal-Mart Stores Inc. President and Chief Financial Officer Mike Duke speaks during the annual Wal-Mart shareholder's meeting in Fayetteville, Arkansas. Duke has pledged to shareholders that the world's largest retailer will build on its success by keeping its customers even when the economy improves.

SUMMARY

- Effective strategic leadership is a prerequisite to successfully using the strategic management process. Strategic leadership entails the ability to anticipate events, envision possibilities, maintain flexibility, and empower others to create strategic change.

- Top-level managers are an important resource for firms to develop and exploit competitive advantages. In addition, when they and their work are valuable, rare, imperfectly imitable, and nonsubstitutable, strategic leaders are also a source of competitive advantage.

- The top management team is composed of key managers who play a critical role in selecting and implementing the firm's strategies. Generally, they are officers of the corporation and/or members of the board of directors.

- The top management team's characteristics, a firm's strategies, and its performance are all interrelated. For example, a top management team with significant marketing and R&D knowledge positively contributes to the firm's use of a growth strategy. Overall, having diverse skills increases most top management teams' effectiveness.

- Typically, performance improves when the board of directors is involved in shaping a firm's strategic direction. However, when the CEO has a great deal of power, the board may be less involved in decisions about strategy formulation and implementation. By appointing people to the board and simultaneously serving as CEO and chair of the board, CEOs increase their power.

- In managerial succession, strategic leaders are selected from either the internal or the external managerial labor market. Because of their effect on firm performance, selection of strategic leaders has implications for a firm's effectiveness. Companies use a variety of reasons for selecting the firm's strategic leaders either internally or externally. In most instances, the internal market is used to select the CEO; but the number of outsiders chosen is increasing. Outsiders often are selected to initiate major changes in strategy.

- Effective strategic leadership has five major components: determining the firm's strategic direction, effectively managing the firm's resource portfolio (including exploiting and maintaining core competencies and managing human capital and social capital), sustaining an effective organizational culture, emphasizing ethical practices, and establishing balanced organizational controls.

- Strategic leaders must develop the firm's strategic direction. The strategic direction specifies the image and character the firm wants to develop over time. To form the strategic direction, strategic leaders evaluate the conditions (e.g., opportunities and threats in the external environment) they expect their firm to face over the next three to five years.

- Strategic leaders must ensure that their firm exploits its core competencies, which are used to produce and deliver products that create value for customers, when implementing its strategies. In related diversified and large firms in particular, core competencies are exploited by sharing them across units and products.

- The ability to manage the firm's resource portfolio and manage the processes used to effectively implement the firm's strategy are critical elements of strategic leadership. Managing the resource portfolio includes integrating resources to create capabilities and leveraging those capabilities through strategies to build competitive advantages. Human capital and social capital are perhaps the most important resources.

- As a part of managing the firm's resources, strategic leaders must develop a firm's human capital. Effective strategic leaders view human capital as a resource to be maximized—not as a cost to be minimized. Such leaders develop and use programs designed to train current and future strategic leaders to build the skills needed to nurture the rest of the firm's human capital.

- Effective strategic leaders also build and maintain internal and external social capital. Internal social capital promotes cooperation and coordination within and across units in the firm. External social capital provides access to resources the firm needs to compete effectively.

- Shaping the firm's culture is a central task of effective strategic leadership. An appropriate organizational culture encourages the development of an entrepreneurial orientation among employees and an ability to change the culture as necessary.

- In ethical organizations, employees are encouraged to exercise ethical judgment and to always act ethically. Improved ethical practices foster social capital. Setting specific goals to meet the firm's ethical standards, using a code of conduct, rewarding ethical behaviors, and creating a work environment where all people are treated with dignity are actions that facilitate and support ethical behavior.

- Developing and using balanced organizational controls are the final components of effective strategic leadership. The balanced scorecard is a tool that measures the effectiveness of the firm's strategic and financial controls. An effective balance between strategic and financial controls allows for flexible use of core competencies, but within the parameters of the firm's financial position.

REVIEW QUESTIONS

1. What is strategic leadership? In what ways are top executives considered important resources for an organization?

2. What is a top management team, and how does it affect a firm's performance and its abilities to innovate and design and implement effective strategic changes?

3. How do the internal and external managerial labor markets affect the managerial succession process?

4. What is the effect of strategic leadership on determining the firm's strategic direction?

5. How do strategic leaders effectively manage their firm's resource portfolio to exploit its core competencies and leverage the human capital and social capital to achieve a competitive advantage?

6. What is organizational culture? What must strategic leaders do to develop and sustain an effective organizational culture?

7. As a strategic leader, what actions could you take to establish and emphasize ethical practices in your firm?

8. What are organizational controls? Why are strategic controls and financial controls important aspects of the strategic management process?

EXPERIENTIAL EXERCISES

EXERCISE 1: EXECUTIVE SUCCESSION

For this exercise, you will identify and analyze a case of CEO succession. Working in small groups, find a publicly held firm that has changed CEOs. The turnover event must have happened at least twelve months ago, but no more than twenty four months ago. Use a combination of company documents and news articles to answer the following questions:

1. Why did the CEO leave? Common reasons for CEO turnover include death or illness, retirement, accepting a new position, change in ownership or control, or termination. In cases of termination, there is often no official statement as to why the CEO departed. Consequently, you may have to rely on news articles that speculate why a CEO was fired, or forced to resign.

2. Did the replacement CEO come from inside the organization, or outside?

3. What are the similarities and differences between the new CEO and the CEO who was replaced? Possible comparison items could include functional experience, industry experience, etc. If your library has a subscription to *Hoover's Online*, you can find information on top managers through this resource.

4. At the time of the succession event, how did the firm's financial performance compare to industry norms? Has the firm's standing relative to the industry changed since the new CEO took over?

5. Has the firm made major strategic changes since the succession event? Has the firm made major acquisitions or divestitures? Launched or closed down product lines?

Create a PowerPoint presentation that presents answers to each of the above questions. Your presentation should be brief, consisting of no more than five to seven slides.

EXERCISE 2: STRATEGIC LEADERSHIP IS TOUGH!

Your textbook defines strategic leadership as "The ability to anticipate, envision, maintain flexibility, and empower others...." Accordingly, this exercise combines the practical elements of leadership in an experiential exercise. You are asked to replicate leaders and followers in the attainment of a defined goal.

First, the class is divided into teams of three to five individuals. Next, each team chooses a leader, which also dictates who the followers will be. It is important to choose your leader wisely. The classroom instructor will then assign the task to be completed.

Students should be prepared to debrief the assignment when completed. Your instructor will guide this discussion.

VIDEO CASE

LEADERS ARE MADE, NOT BORN

Sanjiv Ahuja/Chairman/Orange, UK

Sanjiv Ahuja, Chairman of Orange, UK talks about leadership. In particular, those who believe they have the desire and capability to be leaders and whether people are born with these traits or if they can acquire them. Much of what he talks about is having the right attitude.

Before you watch the video consider the following concepts and questions and be prepared to discuss them in class:

Concepts

- Leadership traits

- Effectively managing your personal resource portfolio

- Entrepreneurial mind-set

Questions

1. Do you believe that one's propensity to become a leader is an acquired skill or that the ability to be a leader is something that individuals are born with?

2. How well do you know yourself? Think through a top 5 list of your personal strengths and weaknesses.

3. Once you have identified personal strengths and weaknesses, think through an action plan to either leverage your strengths or work on weaknesses.

NOTES

1. A. Mackey, 2008, The effect of CEOs on firm performance, *Strategic Management Journal*, 29: 1357–1367.

2. E. F. Goldman, 2007, Strategic thinking at the top, *MIT Sloan Management Review*, 48(4): 75–81.

3. L. Bassi & D. McMurrer, 2007, Maximizing your return on people, *Harvard Business Review*, 85(3): 115–123; R. D. Ireland & M. A. Hitt, 2005, Achieving and maintaining strategic competitiveness in the 21st century: The role of strategic leadership, *Academy of Management Executive*, 19: 63–77.

4. J. P. Kotter, 2007, Leading change: Why transformation efforts fail, *Harvard Business Review*, 85(1): 96–103.

5. M. A. Hitt, C. Miller, & A. Collella, 2009, *Organizational Behavior: A Strategic Approach*, 2nd ed., New York: John Wiley & Sons; M. A. Hitt & R. D. Ireland, 2002, The essence of strategic leadership: Managing human and social capital, *Journal of Leadership and Organizational Studies*, 9: 3–14.

6. D. A. Ready & J. A. Conger, 2007, Make your company a talent factory, *Harvard Business Review*, 85(6): 69–77.

7. D. Roberts & C.-C. Tschang, 2007, China's rising leaders, *BusinessWeek*, October 1, 33–35.

8. P. A. Gloor & S. M. Cooper, 2007, The new principles of a swarm business, *MIT Sloan Management Review*, 48(3): 81–85; A. S. DeNisi, M. A. Hitt, & S. E. Jackson, 2003, The knowledge-based approach to sustainable competitive advantage, in S. E. Jackson, M. A. Hitt, & A. S. DeNisi (eds.), *Managing Knowledge for Sustained Competitive Advantage*, San Francisco: Jossey-Bass, 3–33.

9. L. Bossidy, 2007, What your leader expects of you: And what you should expect in return, *Harvard Business Review*, 85(4): 58–65; J. E. Post, L. E. Preston, & S. Sachs, 2002, Managing the extended enterprise: The new stakeholder view, *California Management Review*, 45(1): 6–28.

10. A. McKee & D. Massimilian, 2007, Resonant leadership: A new kind of leadership for the digital age, *Journal of Business Strategy*, 27(5): 45–49.

11. E. Baraldi, R. Brennan, D. Harrison, A. Tunisini, & J. Zolkiewski, 2007, Strategic thinking and the IMP approach: A comparative analysis, *Industrial Marketing Management*, 36: 879–894; C. L. Shook, R. L. Priem, & J. E. McGee, 2003, Venture creation and the enterprising individual:

A review and synthesis, *Journal of Management*, 29: 379–399.

12. M. L. McDonald, P. Khanna, & J. D. Westphal, 2008, Getting them to think outside the circle: Corporate governance, CEOs' external advice networks and firm performance, *Academy of Management Journal*, 51: 453–475.

13. R. A. Burgleman & A. S. Grove, 2007, Let chaos reign, then rein in chaos—repeatedly: Managing strategic dynamics for corporate longevity, *Strategic Management Journal*, 28: 965–979.

14. T. R. Holcomb, R. M. Holmes, & B. L. Connelly, 2009, Making the most of what you have: Managerial ability as a source of resource value creation, *Strategic Management Journal*, 30: 457–485.

15. A. E. Colbert, A. L. Kristof-Brown, B. H. Bradley, & M. R. Barrick, 2008, CEO transformational leadership: The role of goal importance congruence in top management teams, *Academy of Management Journal*, 51: 81–96; S. Borener, S. A. Eisenbeliss, & D. Griesser, 2007, Follower behavior and organizational performance: The impact of transformational leaders, *Journal of Leadership & Organizational Studies*, 13(3): 15–26.

16. T. G. Buchholz, 2007, The Kroc legacy at McDonald's, *The Conference Review Board*, July/August, 14–15.

17. H. S. Givray, 2007, When CEOs aren't leaders, *BusinessWeek*, September 3, 102.

18. D. Goleman, 2004, What makes a leader? *Harvard Business Review*, 82(1): 82–91.

19. Y. Ling, Z. Simsek, M. H. Lubatkin, & J. F. Veiga, Transformational leadership's role in promoting corporate entrepreneurship: Examining the CEO-TMT interface, *Academy of Management Journal*, 51: 557–576.

20. J. L. Morrow, Jr., D. G. Sirmon, M. A. Hitt, & T. R. Holcomb, 2007, Creating value in the face of declining performance: Firm strategies and organizational recovery, *Strategic Management Journal*, 28: 271–283; R. Castanias & C. Helfat, 2001, The managerial rents model: Theory and empirical analysis, *Journal of Management*, 27: 661–678.

21. H. G. Barkema & O. Shvyrkov, 2007, Does top management team diversity promote or hamper foreign expansion? *Strategic Management Journal*, 28: 663–680; M. Beer & R. Eisenstat, 2000, The silent killers of strategy implementation and learning, *Sloan Management Review*, 41(4): 29–40.

22. V. Santos & T. Garcia, 2007, The complexity of the organizational renewal decision: The management role, *Leadership & Organization Development Journal*, 28: 336–355; M. Wright, R. E. Hoskisson, L. W. Busenitz, & J. Dial, 2000, Entrepreneurial growth through privatization: The upside of management buyouts, *Academy of Management Review*, 25: 591–601.

23. D. G. Sirmon, J.-L. Arregle, M. A. Hitt, & J. W. Webb, 2008, The role of family influence in firms' strategic responses to threat of imitation, *Entrepreneurship Theory and Practice*, 32: 979–998; Y. L. Doz & M. Kosonen, 2007, The new deal at the top, *Harvard Business Review*, 85(6): 98–104.

24. A. S. Tsui, Z.-X. Zhang, H. Wang, K. R. Xin, & J. B. Wu, 2006, Unpacking the relationship between CEO leadership behavior and organizational culture, *The Leadership Quarterly*, 17: 113–137; J. A. Petrick & J. F. Quinn, 2001, The challenge of leadership accountability for integrity capacity as a strategic asset, *Journal of Business Ethics*, 34: 331–343.

25. D. G. Sirmon, S. Gove, & M. A. Hitt, 2008, Resource management in dyadic competitive rivalry: The effects of resource bundling and deployment, *Academy of Management Journal*, 51: 918–935; R. Martin, 2007, How successful leaders think, *Harvard Business Review*, 85(6): 60–67.

26. M. L. A. Hayward, V. P. Rindova, & T. G. Pollock, 2004, Believing one's own press: The causes and consequences of CEO celebrity, *Strategic Management Journal*, 25: 637–653.

27. K. M. Hmieleski & R. A. Baron, 2008, When does entrepreneurial self-efficacy enhance versus reduce firm performance? *Strategic Entrepreneurship Journal*, 2: 57–72; N. J. Hiller & D. C. Hambrick, 2005, Conceptualizing executive hubris: The role of (hyper-) core self-evaluations in strategic decision making, *Strategic Management Journal*, 26: 297–319.

28. A. M. L. Raes, U. Glunk, M. G. Heijitjes, & R. A. Roe, 2007, Top management team and middle managers, *Small Group Research*, 38: 360–386; I. Goll, R. Sambharya, & L. Tucci, 2001, Top management team composition, corporate ideology, and firm performance, *Management International Review*, 41(2): 109–129.

29. J. Bunderson, 2003, Team member functional background and involvement

in management teams: Direct effects and the moderating role of power and centralization, *Academy of Management Journal*, 46: 458–474; L. Markoczy, 2001, Consensus formation during strategic change, *Strategic Management Journal*, 22: 1013–1031.

30. C. Pegels, Y. Song, & B. Yang, 2000, Management heterogeneity, competitive interaction groups, and firm performance, *Strategic Management Journal*, 21: 911–923.

31. R. Rico, E. Molleman, M. Sanchez-Manzanares, & G. S. Van der Vegt, 2007, The effects of diversity faultlines and team task autonomy on decision quality and social integration, *Journal of Management*, 33: 111–132.

32. A. Srivastava, K. M. Bartol, & E. A. Locke, 2006, Empowering leadership in management teams: Effects on knowledge sharing, efficacy, and performance, *Academy of Management Journal*, 49: 1239–1251; D. Knight, C. L. Pearce, K. G. Smith, J. D. Olian, H. P. Sims, K. A. Smith, & P. Flood, 1999, Top management team diversity, group process, and strategic consensus, *Strategic Management Journal*, 20: 446–465.

33. B. J. Olson, S. Parayitam, & Y. Bao, 2007, Strategic decision making: The effects of cognitive diversity, conflict, and trust on decision outcomes, *Journal of Management*, 33: 196–222; T. Simons, L. H. Pelled, & K. A. Smith, 1999, Making use of difference, diversity, debate, and decision comprehensiveness in top management teams, *Academy of Management Journal*, 42: 662–673.

34. S. Finkelstein, D. C. Hambrick, & A. A. Cannella, Jr., 2008, *Strategic Leadership: Top Executives and Their Effects on Organizations*, New York: Oxford University Press.

35. J. J. Marcel, 2009, Why top management team characteristics matter when employing a chief operating officer: A strategic contingency perspective, *Strategic Management Journal*,30: 647–658; S. Barsade, A. Ward, J. Turner, & J. Sonnenfeld, 2000, To your heart's content: A model of affective diversity in top management teams, *Administrative Science Quarterly*, 45: 802–836.

36. B. J. Avolio & S. S. Kahai, 2002, Adding the "e" to e-leadership: How it may impact your leadership, *Organizational Dynamics*, 31: 325–338.

37. Z. Simsek, J. F. Veiga, M. L. Lubatkin, & R. H. Dino, 2005, Modeling the multilevel determinants of top management team behavioral integration, *Academy of Management Journal*, 48: 69–84.

38. A. A. Cannella, J. H. Park, & H. U. Lee, 2008, Top management team functional background diversity and firm performance: Examining the roles of team member collocation and environmental uncertainty, *Academy of Management Journal*, 51: 768–784.

39. M. Jensen & E. J. Zajac, 2004, Corporate elites and corporate strategy: How demographic preferences and structural position shape the scope of the firm, *Strategic Management Journal*, 25: 507–524.

40. R. Yokota & H. Mitsuhashi, Attributive change in top management teams as a driver of strategic change, *Asia Pacific Journal of Management*, 25: 297–315; W. B. Werther, 2003, Strategic change and leader-follower alignment, *Organizational Dynamics*, 32: 32–45.

41. H. Li & J. Li, 2009, Top management team conflict and entrepreneurial strategy making in China, *Asia Pacific Journal of Management*, 26: 263–283; S. C. Parker, 2009, Can cognitive biases explain venture team homophily? *Strategic Entrepreneurship Journal*, 3: 67–83.

42. Y. Zhang & N. Rajagopalan, 2003, Explaining the new CEO origin: Firm versus industry antecedents, *Academy of Management Journal*, 46: 327–338.

43. T. Dvir, D. Eden, B. J. Avolio, & B. Shamir, 2002, Impact of transformational leadership on follower development and performance: A field experiment, *Academy of Management Journal*, 45: 735–744.

44. J. P. Muczyk & D. T. Holt, 2008, Toward a cultural contingency model of leadership, Journal of *Leadership and Organizational Studies*, 14: 277–286.

45. C. Bouquet, A. Morrison, & J. Birkinshaw, 2009, International attention and multinational enterprise performance, *Journal of International Business Studies*, 40: 108–131; H. U. Lee & J. H. Park, 2008, The influence of top management team international exposure on international alliance formation, *Journal of Management Studies*, 45: 961–981.

46. C. Thomas, D. Kidd, & C. Fernandez-Araoz, 2007, Are you underutilizing your board? *MIT Sloan Management Review*, 48(2): 71–76.

47. F. Adjaoud, D. Zeghal & S. Andaleeb, 2007, The effect of board's quality on performance: A study of Canadian firms, *Corporate Governance: An International Review*, 15: 623–635; L. Tihanyi, R. A. Johnson, R. E. Hoskisson, & M. A. Hitt, 2003, Institutional ownership and international diversification: The effects of boards of directors and technological opportunity, *Academy of Management Journal*, 46: 195–211.

48. B. R. Golden & E. J. Zajac, 2001, When will boards influence strategy? Inclination times power equals strategic change, *Strategic Management Journal*, 22: 1087–1111.

49. M. Carpenter & J. Westphal, 2001, Strategic context of external network ties: Examining the impact of director appointments on board involvement in strategic decision making, *Academy of Management Journal*, 44: 639–660.

50. M. A. Rutherford & A. K. Buchholtz, 2007, Investigating the relationship

between board characteristics and board information, *Corporate Governance: An International Review*, 15: 576–584.

51. X. Huafang & Y. Jianguo, 2007, Ownership structure, board composition and corporate voluntary disclosure: Evidence from listed companies in China, *Managerial Auditing Journal*, 22: 604–619.

52. J. Coles, N. Sen, & V. McWilliams, 2001, An examination of the relationship of governance mechanisms to performance, *Journal of Management*, 27: 23–50; J. Coles & W. Hesterly, 2000, Independence of the chairman and board composition: Firm choices and shareholder value, *Journal of Management*, 26: 195–214.

53. C. M. Daily & D. R. Dalton, 1995, CEO and director turnover in failing firms: An illusion of change? *Strategic Management Journal*, 16: 393–400.

54. D. Miller, I. LeBreton-Miller, & B. Scholnick, 2008, Stewardship vs. stagnation: An empirical comparison of small family and non-family businesses, *Journal of Management Studies*, 51: 51–78; J. H. Davis, F. D. Schoorman, & L. Donaldson, 1997, Toward a stewardship theory of management, *Academy of Management Review*, 22: 20–47.

55. P. Kalyta, 2009, Compensation transparency and managerial opportunism: A study of supplemental retirement plans, *Strategic Management Journal*, 30: 405–423; J. G. Combs & M. S. Skill, 2003, Managerialist and human capital explanations for key executive pay premiums: A contingency perspective, *Academy of Management Journal*, 46: 63–73.

56. E. Matta & P. W. Beamish, 2008, The accentuated CEO career horizon problem: Evidence from international acquisitions, *Strategic Management Journal*, 29: 683–700; N. Rajagopalan & D. Datta, 1996, CEO characteristics: Does industry matter? *Academy of Management Journal*, 39: 197–215.

57. R. A. Johnson, R. E. Hoskisson, & M. A. Hitt, 1993, Board involvement in restructuring: The effect of board versus managerial controls and characteristics, *Strategic Management Journal*, 14 (Special Issue): 33–50.

58. Z. Simsek, 2007, CEO tenure and organizational performance: An intervening model, *Strategic Management Journal*, 28: 653–662.

59. M. Schneider, 2002, A stakeholder model of organizational leadership, *Organization Science*, 13: 209–220.

60. M. Sorcher & J. Brant, 2002, Are you picking the right leaders? *Harvard Business Review*, 80(2): 78–85; D. A. Waldman, G. G. Ramirez, R. J. House, & P. Puranam, 2001, Does leadership matter? CEO leadership attributes and profitability under conditions of perceived environmental uncertainty, *Academy of Management Journal*, 44: 134–143.

61. J. Werdigier, 2007, UBS not willing to talk about departure of chief, *New York Times Online*, http://www.nytimes.com, July 7.

62. W. Shen & A. A. Cannella, 2002, Revisiting the performance consequences of CEO succession: The impacts of successor type, postsuccession senior executive turnover, and departing CEO tenure, *Academy of Management Journal*, 45: 717–734.

63. D. Ulrich & N. Smallwood, 2007, Building a leadership brand, *Harvard Business Review*, 85(7/8): 93–100.

64. G. A. Ballinger & F. D. Schoorman, 2007, Individual reactions to leadership succession in workgroups, *Academy of Management Review*, 32: 116–136; R. E. Hoskisson, D. Yiu, & H. Kim, 2000, Capital and labor market congruence and corporate governance: Effects on corporate innovation and global competitiveness, in S. S. Cohen & G. Boyd (eds.), *Corporate Governance and Globalization*, Northampton, MA: Edward Elgar, 129–154.

65. M. Hurlbert, 2005, Lo! A white knight! So why isn't the market cheering? *New York Times Online*, http://www.nytimes.com, March 27.

66. W. Shen & A. A. Cannella, 2003, Will succession planning increase shareholder wealth? Evidence from investor reactions to relay CEO successions, *Strategic Management Journal*, 24: 191–198.

67. S. Carty and L. Cauley, 2009, AT&T's former CEO Ed Whitacre joins GM as chairman, *USA Today*, http://www.usatoday.com, June 10.

68. Y. Tanokura, 2009, Special interview: Sony chairman, CEO Howard Stringer, *Nikkei Electronics Asia*, http://www.techon.nikkeibp.co.jp, May 26.

69. T. Kiessling, M. Harvey & J. T. Heames, 2008, Operational changes to the acquired firm's top management team and subsequent organizational performance, *Journal of Leadership and Organizational Studies*, 14: 287–302.

70. J. A. Krug & W. Shill, 2008, The big exit: Executive churn in the wake of M&As, *Journal of Business Strategy*, 29(4): 15–21.

71. J. O'Toole & E. E. Lawler, Jr., 2006, The choices managers make—or don't make, *The Conference Board*, September/October, 24–29.

72. S. Nadkarni & P. S. Barr, 2008, Environmental context, managerial cognition, and strategic action: An integrated view, *Strategic Management Journal*, 29: 1395–1427; M. A. Hitt, B. W. Keats, & E. Yucel, 2003, Strategic leadership in global business organizations, in W. H. Mobley & P. W. Dorfman (eds.), *Advances in Global Leadership*, Oxford, UK: Elsevier Science, Ltd., 9–35.

73. I. M. Levin, 2000, Vision revisited, *Journal of Applied Behavioral Science*, 36: 91–107.

74. E. Verwaal, H. Commandeur, & W. Verbeke, 2009, Value creation and value claiming in strategic outsourcing decisions: A resource contingency perspective, *Journal of Management*, 35: 420–444; S. R. Miller, D. E. Thomas, L. Eden, & M. Hitt, 2008, Knee deep in the big muddy: The survival of emerging market firms in developed markets, *Management International Review*, 48: 645–666.

75. G. Hall, 2009, Today's outrage: GE's Immelt flip flops, *TheStreet.com*, http://www.thestreet.com, May 26.

76. J. Welch & S. Welch, 2007, When to talk, when to balk, *BusinessWeek*, April 30, 102.

77. J. Barney & A. M. Arikan, 2001, The resource-based view: Origins and implications, in M. A. Hitt, R. E. Freeman, & J. S. Harrison (eds.), *Handbook of Strategic Management*, Oxford, UK: Blackwell Publishers, 124–188.

78. E. T. Prince, 2005, The fiscal behavior of CEOs, *Managerial Economics*, 46(3): 23–26.

79. Holcomb, Holmes, & Connelly, Making the most of what you have; Sirmon, Gove, & Hitt, Resource management in dyadic competitive rivalry.

80. R. A. Burgelman, 2001, *Strategy Is Destiny: How Strategy-Making Shapes a Company's Future*, New York: The Free Press.

81. D. J. Ketchen, Jr., G. T. M. Hult, & S. F. Slater, 2007, Toward greater understanding of market orientation and the resource-based view, *Strategic Management Journal*, 28: 961–964; S. K. Ethiraj, P. Kale, M. S. Krishnan, & J. V. Singh, 2005, Where do capabilities come from and how do they matter? A study in the software services industry, *Strategic Management Journal*, 26: 25–45.

82. S. K. Ethiraj, 2007, Allocation of inventive effort in complex product systems, *Strategic Management Journal*, 28: 563–584; S. Dutta, O. Narasimhan, & S. Rajiv, 2005, Conceptualizing and measuring capabilities: Methodology and empirical application, *Strategic Management Journal*, 26: 277–285.

83. 2009, PepsiCo Mission and Vision, http://www.pepsico.com/Company/Our-Mission-and-Vision.aspx, June.

84. M. Larson & F. Luthans, 2006, Potential added value of psychological capital in predicting work attitudes, *Journal of Leadership & Organizational Studies*, 13: 45–62; N. W. Hatch & J. H. Dyer, 2004, Human capital and learning as a source of sustainable competitive advantage, *Strategic Management Journal*, 25: 1155–1178.

85. 2009, PepsiCo Careers: Taste the success, http://www.pepsico.com/Carers/Taste-the-Success.aspx, June.

86. M. A. Hitt, L. Bierman, K. Uhlenbruck, & K. Shimizu, 2006, The importance of resources in the internationalization of professional service firms: The good, the bad and the ugly, *Academy of Management Journal*, 49: 1137–1157; M. A. Hitt, L. Bierman, K. Shimizu, & R. Kochhar, 2001, Direct and moderating effects of human capital on strategy and performance in professional service firms: A resource-based perspective, *Academy of Management Journal*, 44: 13–28.

87. S. E. Jackson, M. A. Hitt, & A. S. DeNisi (eds.), 2003, *Managing Knowledge for Sustained Competitive Advantage: Designing Strategies for Effective Human Resource Management*, Oxford, UK: Elsevier Science, Ltd.

88. B. E. Becker & M. A. Huselid, 2007, Strategic human resources management: Where do we go from here? *Journal of Management*, 32: 898–925.

89. R. E. Ployhart, 2007, Staffing in the 21st century: New challenges and strategic opportunities, *Journal of Management*, 32: 868–897.

90. R. A. Noe, J. A. Colquitt, M. J. Simmering, & S. A. Alvarez, 2003, Knowledge management: Developing intellectual and social capital, in S. E. Jackson, M. A. Hitt, & A. S. DeNisi (eds.), 2003, *Managing Knowledge for Sustained Competitive Advantage: Designing Strategies for Effective Human Resource Management*, Oxford, UK: Elsevier Science, Ltd., 209–242.

91. PepsiCo mission and vision, http://www.pepsico.com/Company/Our-Mission-and-Vision.aspx

92. G. P. Hollenbeck & M. W. McCall Jr., 2003, Competence, not competencies: Making a global executive development work, in W. H. Mobley & P. W. Dorfman (eds.), *Advances in Global Leadership*, Oxford, UK: Elsevier Science, Ltd., 101–119; J. Sandberg, 2000, Understanding human competence at work: An interpretative approach, *Academy of Management Journal*, 43: 9–25.

93. G. Colvin, 2007, Leader machines, *Fortune*, October 1, 100–106.

94. Y. Liu, J. G. Combs, D. A. Ketchen, Jr., & R. D. Ireland, 2007, The value of human resource management for organizational performance, *Business Horizons*, 6: 503–511.

95. T. R. Holcomb, R. D. Ireland, R. M. Holmes, & M. A. Hitt, 2009, Architecture of entrepreneurial learning: Exploring the link among heuristics, Knowledge, and action, *Entrepreneurship, Theory & Practice*, 33: 173–198; J. S. Bunderson & K. M. Sutcliffe, 2003, Management team learning orientation and business unit performance, *Journal of Applied Psychology*, 88: 552–560.

96. R. J. Thomas, 2009, The leadership lessons of crucible experiences, *Journal of Business Strategy*, 30(1): 21–26; J. D. Bragger, D. A. Hantula, D. Bragger, J. Kirnan, & E. Kutcher, 2003, When success breeds failure: History, hysteresis, and delayed exit decisions, *Journal of Applied Psychology*, 88: 6–14.

97. M. R. Haas & M. T. Hansen, 2005, When using knowledge can hurt performance: The value of organizational capabilities in a management consulting company, *Strategic Management Journal*, 26: 1–24; G. Ahuja & R. Katila, 2004, Where do resources come from? The role

of idiosyncratic situations, *Strategic Management Journal*, 25: 887–907.

98. Hitt, Miller, & Colella, *Organizational Behavior*.

99. A. Carmeli & B. Azeroual, 2009, How relational capital and knowledge combination capability enhance the performance of work units in a high technology industry, *Strategic Entrepreneurship Journal*, 3: 85–103; J. W. Spencer, 2003, Firms' knowledge-sharing strategies in the global innovation system: Empirical evidence from the flat-panel display industry, *Strategic Management Journal*, 24: 217–233.

100. K. D. Miller, 2002, Knowledge inventories and managerial myopia, *Strategic Management Journal*, 23: 689–706.

101. R. D. Nixon, M. A. Hitt, H. Lee, & E. Jeong, 2004, Market reactions to corporate announcements of downsizing actions and implementation strategies, *Strategic Management Journal*, 25: 1121–1129.

102. Nixon, Hitt, Lee, & Jeong, Market reactions to corporate announcements of downsizing actions.

103. T. Simons & Q. Roberson, 2003, Why managers should care about fairness: The effects of aggregate justice perceptions on organizational outcomes, *Journal of Applied Psychology*, 88: 432–443; M. L. Ambrose & R. Cropanzano, 2003, A longitudinal analysis of organizational fairness: An examination of reactions to tenure and promotion decisions, *Journal of Applied Psychology*, 88: 266–275.

104. C.-L. Luk, O. H. M. Yau, L. Y. M. Sin, A. C. B. Tse, R. P .M. Chow, & J. S. Y. Lee, 2008, The effects of social capital and organizational innovativeness in different institutional contexts, *Journal of International Business Studies*, 39: 589–612; P. S. Adler & S. W. Kwon, 2002, Social capital: Prospects for a new concept, *Academy of Management Review*, 27: 17–40.

105. J. J. Li, L. Poppo, & K. Z. Zhou, 2008, Do managerial ties in China always produce value? Competition, uncertainty, and domestic vs. foreign firms, *Strategic Management Journal*, 29: 383–400; S. Gao, K. Xu, & J. Yang, 2008, Managerial ties, Absorptive capacity & innovation, *Asia Pacific Journal of Management*, 25: 395–412.

106. P. Ozcan & K. M. Eisenhardt, 2009, Origin of alliance portfolios: Entrepreneurs, network strategies, and firm performance, *Academy of Management Journal*, 52: 246–279; W. H. Hoffmann, 2007, Strategies for managing a portfolio of alliances, *Strategic Management Journal*, 28: 827–856.

107. H. E. Aldrich & P. H. Kim 2007, Small worlds, infinite possibilities? How social networks affect entrepreneurial team formation and search, *Strategic Entrepreneurship Journal*, 1: 147–165; P. Davidsson & B. Honig, 2003, The role of social and human capital among nascent entrepreneurs, *Journal of Business Venturing*, 18: 301–331.

108. C. M. Fiol, 1991, Managing culture as a competitive resource: An identity-based view of sustainable competitive advantage, *Journal of Management*, 17: 191–211; J. B. Barney, 1986, Organizational culture: Can it be a source of sustained competitive advantage? *Academy of Management Review*, 11: 656–665.

109. 2006, Connecting the dots between innovation and leadership, *Knowledge@Wharton*, http://www.knowledge.wharton.upenn.edu, October 4.

110. V. Govindarajan & A. K. Gupta, 2001, Building an effective global business team, *Sloan Management Review*, 42(4): 63–71; S. Ghoshal & C. A. Bartlett, 1994, Linking organizational context and managerial action: The dimensions of quality of management, *Strategic Management Journal*, 15: 91–112.

111. R. D. Ireland, J. G. Covin, & D. F. Kuratko, 2009, Conceptualizing corporate entrepreneurship strategy, *Entrepreneurship Theory and Practice*, 33(1): 19–46; D. F. Kuratko, R. D. Ireland, & J. S. Hornsby, 2001, Improving firm performance through entrepreneurial actions: Acordia's corporate entrepreneurship strategy, *Academy of Management Executive*, 15(4): 60–71.

112. J. H. Dyer, H. B. Gregersen, & C. Christensen, 2008, Entrepreneur behaviors, opportunity recognition and the origins of innovative ventures, *Strategic Entrepreneurship Journal*, 2: 317–338; R. D. Ireland & J. W. Webb, 2007, Strategic entrepreneurship: Creating competitive advantage through streams of innovation, *Business Horizons*, 50: 49–49.

113. S. A. Alvarez & J. B. Barney, 2008, Opportunities, organizations and entrepreneurship, *Strategic Entrepreneurship Journal*, 2: 171–174; D. S. Elenkov, W. Judge, & P. Wright, 2005, Strategic leadership and executive innovation influence: An international multi-cluster comparative study, *Strategic Management Journal*, 26: 665–682.

114. R. E. Hoskisson, M. A. Hitt, R. D. Ireland, & J. S. Harrison, 2008, *Competing for Advantage*, 2nd ed., Thomson Publishing; R. G. McGrath, W. J. Ferrier, & A. L. Mendelow, 2004, Real options as engines of choice and heterogeneity, *Academy of Management Review*, 29: 86–101.

115. Y. Luo, 2008, Structuring interorganizational cooperation: The role of economic integration in strategic alliances, *Strategic Management Journal*, 29: 617–637; R. S. Vassolo, J. Anand, & T. B. Folta, 2004, Non-additivity in portfolios of exploration activities: A real options analysis of equity alliances in biotechnology, *Strategic Management Journal*, 25: 1045–1061.

116. P. G. Kein, 2008, Opportunity discovery, entrepreneurial action and economic organization, *Strategic Entrepreneurship Journal*, 2: 175–190; R. D. Ireland, M. A. Hitt, & D. Sirmon, 2003, A model of strategic entrepreneurship: The construct and its dimensions, *Journal of Management*, 29: 963–989.

117. G. T. Lumpkin & G. G. Dess, 1996, Clarifying the entrepreneurial orientation construct and linking it to performance, *Academy of Management Review*, 21: 135–172; R. G. McGrath & I. MacMillan, 2000, *The Entrepreneurial Mindset*, Boston: Harvard Business School Press.

118. C. Heath & D. Heath, 2007, Leadership is a muscle, *Fast Company*, July/August, 62–63.

119. Lumpkin & Dess, Clarifying the entrepreneurial orientation construct, 142.

120. Ibid., 137.

121. D. D. Bergh, R. A. Johnson, & R. Dewitt, 2008, Restructuring through spinoff or sell-off: Transforming information asymmetries into financial gain, *Strategic Management Journal*, 29: 133–148; P. Pyoria, 2007, Informal organizational culture: The foundation of knowledge workers' performance, *Journal of Knowledge Management*, 11(3): 16–30.

122. M. Kuenzi & M. Schminke, 2009, Assembling fragments into a lens: A review, critique, and proposed research agenda for the organizational work climate literature, *Journal of Management*, 35: 634–717; C. M. Christensen & S. D. Anthony, 2007, Put investors in their place, *BusinessWeek*, May 28, 10.

123. D. D. Bergh & E. N.-K. Lim, 2008, Learning how to restructure: Absorptive capacity and improvisational views of restructuring actions and performance, *Strategic Management Journal*, 29: 593–616; J. S. Hornsby, D. F. Kuratko, & S. A. Zahra, 2002, Middle managers' perception of the internal environment for corporate entrepreneurship: Assessing a measurement scale, *Journal of Business Venturing*, 17: 253–273.

124. D. F. Kuratko, R. D. Ireland, J. G. Covin, & J. S. Hornsby, 2005, A model of middle-level managers' entrepreneurial behavior, *Entrepreneurship Theory and Practice*, 29: 699–716.

125. E. G. Love & M. Kraatz, 2009, Character, conformity, or the bottom line? How and why downsizing affected corporate reputation, *Academy of Management Journal*, 52: 314–335.

126. Adler & Kwon, Social capital.

127. J. Pinto, C. R. Leana, & F. K. Pil, 2008, Corrupt organizations or organizations of corrupt individuals? Two types of organization-level corruption, *Academy of Management Review*, 33: 685–709.

128. M. E. Scheitzer, L. Ordonez, & M. Hoegl, 2004, Goal setting as a motivator of unethical behavior, *Academy of Management Journal*, 47: 422–432.

129. D. C. Kayes, D. Stirling, & T. M. Nielsen, 2007, Building organizational integrity, *Business Horizons*, 50: 61–70; L. K. Trevino, G. R. Weaver, D. G. Toffler, & B. Ley, 1999, Managing ethics and legal compliance: What works and what hurts, *California Management Review*, 41(2): 131–151.

130. X. Zhang, K. M. Bartol, K. G. Smith, M. D. Pfaffer, & D. M. Khanin, 2008, CEOs on the edge: Earnings manipulation and stock-based incentive misalignment,

Academy of Management Journal, 51: 241–258; M. A. Hitt & J. D. Collins, 2007, Business ethics, strategic decision making, and firm performance, *Business Horizons*, 50: 353–357.

131. J. M. Stevens, H. K. Steensma, D. A. Harrison, & P. L. Cochran, 2005, Symbolic or substantive document? Influence of ethics codes on financial executives' decisions, *Strategic Management Journal*, 26: 181–195.

132. Y. Zhang & M. F. Wiersema, 2009, Stock market reaction to CEO certification: The signaling role of CEO background, *Strategic Management Journal*, 30: 693–710; C. Driscoll & M. McKee, 2007, Restorying a culture of ethical and spiritual values: A role for leader storytelling, *Journal of Business Ethics*, 73: 205–217.

133. C. Caldwell & L. A. Hayes, 2007, Leadership, trustworthiness, and the mediating lens, *Journal of Management Development*, 26: 261–281.

134. B. E. Ashforth, D. A. Gioia, S. L. Robinson, & L. K. Trevino, 2008, Re-viewing organizational corruption, *Academy of Management Review*, 33: 670–684; M. Schminke, A. Arnaud, & M. Kuenzi, 2007, The power of ethical work climates, *Organizational Dynamics*, 36: 171–186; L. B. Ncube & M. H. Wasburn, 2006, Strategic collaboration for ethical leadership: A mentoring framework for business and organizational decision making, *Journal of Leadership & Organizational Studies*, 13: 77–92.

135. J. Welch & S. Welch, 2007, Flying solo: A reality check, *BusinessWeek*, June 4, 116.

136. A. Weibel, 2007, Formal control and trustworthiness, *Group & Organization Management*, 32: 500–517; G. Redding, 2002, The capitalistic business system of China and its rationale, *Asia Pacific Journal of Management*, 19: 221–249.

137. B. D. Rostker, R. S. Leonard, O. Younassi, M. V. Arena, & J. Riposo, 2009, Cost controls: How the government can get more bag for its buck, *Rand Review*, http://www.rand.org/publications/randreview/issues/spring2009; A. C. Costa, 2007, Trust and control interrelations, *Group & Organization Management*, 32: 392–406;

138. M. D. Shields, F. J. Deng, & Y. Kato, 2000, The design and effects of control systems: Tests of direct- and indirect-effects models, *Accounting, Organizations and Society*, 25: 185–202.

139. R. S. Kaplan & D. P. Norton, 2009, The balanced scorecard: Measures that drive performance (HBR OnPoint Enhanced Edition), *Harvard Business Review*, Boston, MA, March; R. S. Kaplan & D. P. Norton, 2001, The strategy-focused organization, *Strategy & Leadership*, 29(3): 41–42; R. S. Kaplan & D. P. Norton, 2000, *The Strategy-Focused Organization: How Balanced Scorecard Companies Thrive in the New Business Environment*, Boston: Harvard Business School Press.

140. B. E. Becker, M. A. Huselid, & D. Ulrich, 2001, *The HR Scorecard: Linking People, Strategy, and Performance*, Boston: Harvard Business School Press, 21.

141. Kaplan & Norton, The strategy-focused organization.

142. R. S. Kaplan & D. P. Norton, 2001, Transforming the balanced scorecard from performance measurement to strategic management: Part I, *Accounting Horizons*, 15(1): 87–104.

143. R. S. Kaplan & D. P. Norton, 1992, The balanced scorecard—measures that drive performance, *Harvard Business Review*, 70(1): 71–79.

144. M. A. Mische, 2001, *Strategic Renewal: Becoming a High-Performance Organization*, Upper Saddle River, NJ: Prentice Hall, 181.

145. H. J. Cho & V. Pucik, 2005, Relationship between innovativeness, quality, growth, profitability and market value, *Strategic Management Journal*, 26: 555–575.

146. G. Rowe, 2001, Creating wealth in organizations: The role of strategic leadership, *Academy of Management Executive*, 15(1): 81–94.

147. R. E. Hoskisson, R. A. Johnson, D. Yiu, & W. P. Wan, 2001, Restructuring strategies of diversified business groups: Differences associated with country institutional environments, in M. A. Hitt, R. E. Freeman, & J. S. Harrison (eds.), *Handbook of Strategic Management*, Oxford, UK: Blackwell Publishers, 433–463.

148. J. Birkinshaw & N. Hood, 2001, Unleash innovation in foreign subsidiaries, *Harvard Business Review*, 79(3): 131–137.

149. Ireland & Hitt, Achieving and maintaining strategic competitiveness.

150. G. Edmondson, 2007, Pedal to the metal at Porsche, *BusinessWeek*, September 3, 68; J. D. Gunkel & G. Probst, 2003, Implementation of the balanced scorecard as a means of corporate learning: The Porsche case, European Case Clearing House, Cranfield, UK.

CHAPTER 13

Strategic Entrepreneurship

Studying this chapter should provide you with the strategic management knowledge needed to:

1. Define strategic entrepreneurship and corporate entrepreneurship.

2. Define entrepreneurship and entrepreneurial opportunities and explain their importance.

3. Define invention, innovation, and imitation, and describe the relationship among them.

4. Describe entrepreneurs and the entrepreneurial mind-set.

5. Explain international entrepreneurship and its importance.

6. Describe how firms internally develop innovations.

7. Explain how firms use cooperative strategies to innovate.

8. Describe how firms use acquisitions as a means of innovation.

9. Explain how strategic entrepreneurship helps firms create value.

THE CONTINUING INNOVATION REVOLUTION AT AMAZON: THE KINDLE AND E-BOOKS

Jeff Bezos led the Internet retailing revolution with his entry into the book retail market in 1995. Since that time, Amazon.com has significantly expanded its product lines and implemented several innovations, especially in processes and approaches to marketing their products. Recently, Bezos and Amazon are leading a potential revolution in the book market with the Kindle, which provides easy access to store and read many e-books. Let's be clear—Amazon did not create the digital book. E-books have been available for several years, but access to and use of e-books has not been necessarily easy. But, with the development of the Kindle e-reader, access to and ease of reading e-books has been simplified and it is predicted to revolutionize the book publishing business within the next five years.

The Kindle was first introduced in 2007, and two newer and improved versions were introduced in 2009. The Kindle 2 was introduced in February 2009 and according to market analysts, it literally "flew off the shelves" at a time when consumers were curtailing purchases of most other products. Then in May 2009, Amazon introduced a large-screen version of the Kindle 2, the Kindle DX, which has a 9.7-inch screen. While the DX appears to be a little cumbersome, it provides larger screen access to graphics-heavy publications common in college textbooks. The Kindle currently can be used to download any of the 285,000 e-books available in Amazon's inventory. Amazon's new Kindles are thinner than a pencil and offer a feature allowing text to be translated into voice. This means that

AP Photo/Mark Lennihan

The new Kindle 2 electronic reader "flew off the shelves" at a time when consumers were curtailing purchases of most other products.

it can read to you! Bezos demonstrated this feature at the introduction by having the computer-generated voice read the Gettysburg Address.

Amazon's success in the first quarter of 2009 (e.g., a 24 percent increase in earnings from the first quarter 2008) was largely attributed to the Kindle. It is predicted to be wildly successful. Barclays Capital has predicted that it will reach annual sales of $3.7 billion in 2012 with a profit of $840 million. This amount would account for approximately 20 percent of Amazon's predicted sales that year. Amazon also earns a return by selling content for use on the Kindle in the form of e-books and other electronic content. For example, Amazon sells subscriptions to 37 different newspapers for the Kindle at $10 per month. This set includes such respected newspapers as the *New York Times, Boston Globe,* and *Washington Post.* It also has an agreement for a pilot program at five major universities, hoping that students will soon be carrying all of their textbooks on the Kindle in their backpacks.

Clearly, Amazon's biggest potential challenge may come from competitors. The Kindle technology is likely imitable and Sony already has a competitor e-reader on the market. Thus, Amazon must entrench the Kindle quickly and continue to enrich its features (the Kindle currently only provides "black-and-white" content even though it is said to provide better resolution than can be obtained in print copies). While the Kindle may help Amazon become the Apple of the e-reader market, the Kindle is likely to revolutionize all publishing industries (e.g., book publishers, newspapers).

Sources: S. Stein, 2009, Old, real book vs. Kindle alternative: Which will win? CNET.com, http://www.cnet.com, June 12; J. M. O'Brien, 2009, Amazon's next revolution, *Fortune*, June 8, 68–76; B. Stone & M. Rich, 2009, Amazon introduces big-screen Kindle, *New York Times*, http://www.nytimes.com, May 7; D. MacMillan, 2009, Amazon's widescreen Kindle DX: Winners and losers, *BusinessWeek*, http://businessweek.com, May 7; C. Dannen, 2009, Amazon CEO Jeff Bezos unveils Kindle DX in New York, *Fast Company*, http://www.fastcompany.com, May 6; D. Darlin, 2009, First impressions of the new Kindle DX, *New York Times*, http://www.gadgetwise.blogs.nytimes.com, May 6; C. Gallo, 2009, How Amazon's Bezos sparked demand for Kindle 2, *BusinessWeek*, http://businessweek.com, February, 24.

In Chapter 1, we indicated that *organizational culture* refers to the complex set of ideologies, symbols, and core values that are shared throughout the firm and that influence how the firm conducts business. Thus, culture is the social energy that drives—or fails to drive—the organization. The Opening Case explains Amazon's new innovation, the Kindle, that is expected to revolutionize the publishing industries (any businesses which provide products printed with ink on paper). Increasingly, a firm's ability to engage in innovation makes the difference in gaining and maintaining a competitive advantage and achieving performance targets.[1]

Amazon is clearly an entrepreneurial and innovative company. Amazon is the leading Internet retailer in the world and also consistently produces innovations. Not all of them are successful, but the Kindle appears to be on the verge of being highly successful. From reading this chapter, you will understand that Amazon's ability to innovate shows that it successfully practices strategic entrepreneurship.

Strategic entrepreneurship is taking entrepreneurial actions using a strategic perspective. In this process, the firm tries to find opportunities in its external environment that it can try to exploit through innovations. Identifying opportunities to exploit through innovations is the *entrepreneurship* dimension of strategic entrepreneurship, while determining the best way to manage the firm's innovation efforts is the *strategic* dimension. Thus, firms engaging in strategic entrepreneurship integrate their actions to find opportunities and to successfully innovate in order to pursue them.[2] In the twenty-first–century competitive landscape, firm survival and success depend on a firm's ability to continuously find new opportunities and quickly produce innovations to pursue them.[3]

To examine strategic entrepreneurship, we consider several topics in this chapter. First, we examine entrepreneurship and innovation in a strategic context. Definitions of entrepreneurship, entrepreneurial opportunities, and entrepreneurs as those who engage in entrepreneurship to pursue entrepreneurial opportunities are presented. We then describe international entrepreneurship, a phenomenon reflecting the increased use of entrepreneurship in economies throughout the world. After this discussion, the chapter shifts to descriptions of the three ways firms innovate. Internally, firms innovate through either autonomous or induced strategic behavior. We then describe actions firms take to implement the innovations resulting from those two types of strategic behaviors.

In addition to innovating within the firm, firms can develop innovations by using cooperative strategies, such as strategic alliances, and by acquiring other companies to gain access to their innovations and innovative capabilities.[4] Most large, complex firms use all three methods to innovate. The chapter closes with summary comments about how firms use strategic entrepreneurship to create value and earn above-average returns.

As emphasized in this chapter, innovation and entrepreneurship are vital for young and old and for large and small firms, for service companies as well as manufacturing firms, and for high-technology ventures.[5] In the global competitive landscape, the long-term success of new ventures and established firms is a function of their ability to meld entrepreneurship with strategic management.[6]

A major portion of the material in this chapter is on innovation and entrepreneurship within established organizations. This phenomenon is called **corporate entrepreneurship**, which is the use or application of entrepreneurship within an established firm.[7] Corporate entrepreneurship has become critical to the survival and success of established organizations.[8] Indeed, established firms use entrepreneurship to strengthen their performance and to enhance growth opportunities.[9] Of course, innovation and entrepreneurship play a critical role in the degree of success achieved by startup entrepreneurial ventures as well. Much of the content examined in this chapter is equally important in entrepreneurial ventures (sometimes called "startups") and established organizations.[10]

Strategic entrepreneurship is taking entrepreneurial actions using a strategic perspective.

Corporate entrepreneurship is the use or application of entrepreneurship within an established firm.

Entrepreneurship and Entrepreneurial Opportunities

Entrepreneurship is the process by which individuals, teams, or organizations identify and pursue entrepreneurial opportunities without being immediately constrained by the resources they currently control.[11] **Entrepreneurial opportunities** are conditions in which new goods or services can satisfy a need in the market. These opportunities exist because of competitive imperfections in markets and among the factors of production used to produce them or because they were independently developed by entrepreneurs.[12] Entrepreneurial opportunities come in many forms such as the chance to develop and sell a new product and the chance to sell an existing product in a new market.[13] Firms should be receptive to pursuing entrepreneurial opportunities whenever and wherever they may surface.[14]

As these two definitions suggest, the essence of entrepreneurship is to identify and exploit entrepreneurial opportunities—that is, opportunities others do not see or for which they do not recognize the commercial potential.[15] As a process, entrepreneurship results in the "creative destruction" of existing products (goods or services) or methods of producing them and replaces them with new products and production methods.[16] Thus, firms engaging in entrepreneurship place high value on individual innovations as well as the ability to continuously innovate across time.[17]

We study entrepreneurship at the level of the individual firm. However, evidence suggests that entrepreneurship is the economic engine driving many nations' economies in the global competitive landscape.[18] Thus, entrepreneurship, and the innovation it spawns, is important for companies competing in the global economy and for countries seeking to stimulate economic climates with the potential to enhance the living standard of their citizens.[19] A recent study conducted by the Boston Consulting Group and the Small Business Division of Intuit found that 10 million people in the United States were considering starting a new business. About one-third of those who do will expand into international markets. The study suggested that by 2017 the number of entrepreneurs will increase, and the entrepreneurs will be younger and include more women and immigrants. Thus, even though the importance of entrepreneurship continues to grow, the "face" of those who start new ventures is also changing.[20]

Innovation

Peter Drucker argued that "innovation is the specific function of entrepreneurship, whether in an existing business, a public service institution, or a new venture started by a lone individual."[21] Moreover, Drucker suggested that innovation is "the means by which the entrepreneur either creates new wealth-producing resources or endows existing resources with enhanced potential for creating wealth."[22] Thus, entrepreneurship and the innovation resulting from it are critically important for all firms. The realities of competition in the competitive landscape of the twenty-first century suggest that to be market leaders, companies must regularly develop innovative products desired by customers. This means that innovation should be an intrinsic part of virtually all of a firm's activities.[23]

Innovation is a key outcome firms seek through entrepreneurship and is often the source of competitive success, especially in turbulent, highly competitive environments.[24] For example, research results show that firms competing in global industries that invest more in innovation also achieve the highest returns.[25] In fact, investors often react positively to the introduction of a new product, thereby increasing the price of a firm's stock. Furthermore, "innovation may be required to maintain or achieve competitive parity,

Entrepreneurship is the process by which individuals, teams, or organizations identify and pursue entrepreneurial opportunities without being immediately constrained by the resources they currently control.

Entrepreneurial opportunities are conditions in which new goods or services can satisfy a need in the market.

much less a competitive advantage in many global markets."[26] Investing in the development of new technologies can increase the performance of firms that operate in different but related product markets (refer to the discussion of related diversification in Chapter 6). In this way, the innovations can be used in multiple markets, and return on the investments is earned more quickly.[27]

In his classic work, Schumpeter argued that firms engage in three types of innovative activities.[28] **Invention** is the act of creating or developing a new product or process. **Innovation** is the process of creating a commercial product from an invention. Innovation begins after an invention is chosen for development.[29] Thus, an invention brings something new into being, while an innovation brings something new into use. Accordingly, technical criteria are used to determine the success of an invention, whereas commercial criteria are used to determine the success of an innovation.[30] Finally, **imitation** is the adoption of a similar innovation by different firms. Imitation usually leads to product or process standardization, and products based on imitation often are offered at lower prices, but without as many features. Entrepreneurship is critical to innovative activity in that it acts as the linchpin between invention and innovation.[31]

In the United States in particular, innovation is the most critical of the three types of innovative activities. Many companies are able to create ideas that lead to inventions, but commercializing those inventions has, at times, proved difficult.[32] This difficulty is suggested by the fact that approximately 80 percent of R&D occurs in large firms, but these same firms produce fewer than 50 percent of the patents.[33] Patents are a strategic asset and the ability to regularly produce them can be an important source of competitive advantage, especially for firms competing in knowledge-intensive industries (e.g., pharmaceuticals).[34]

Entrepreneurs

Entrepreneurs are individuals, acting independently or as part of an organization, who perceive an entrepreneurial opportunity and then take risks to develop an innovation to pursue it. Entrepreneurs can be found throughout an organization—from top-level managers to those working to produce a firm's goods or services. Entrepreneurs are found throughout Amazon, for example. Many Amazon employees must devote at least a portion of their time to develop innovations. Entrepreneurs tend to demonstrate several characteristics: They are highly motivated, willing to take responsibility for their projects, self-confident, and often optimistic.[35] In addition, entrepreneurs tend to be passionate and emotional about the value and importance of their innovation-based ideas.[36] They are able to deal with uncertainty and are more alert to opportunities than others.[37] Interestingly, recent research found that genetic factors partly influence people to engage in entrepreneurship.[38] To be successful, entrepreneurs often need to have good social skills and to plan exceptionally well (e.g., to obtain venture capital).[39] Entrepreneurship entails much hard work to be successful but it can also be highly satisfying. As noted by Mary Kay Ash, founder of Mary Kay Cosmetics, "It is far better to be exhausted from success than to be rested from failure."[40]

Evidence suggests that successful entrepreneurs have an entrepreneurial mind-set. The person with an **entrepreneurial mind-set** values uncertainty in the marketplace and seeks to continuously identify opportunities with the potential to lead to important innovations.[41] Because it has the potential to lead to continuous innovations, an individual's entrepreneurial mind-set can be a source of competitive advantage for a firm.[42] Entrepreneurial mind-sets are fostered and supported when knowledge is readily available throughout a firm. Indeed, research has shown that units within firms are more innovative when they have access to new knowledge.[43] Transferring knowledge, however, can be difficult, often because the receiving party must have adequate absorptive capacity (or the ability) to learn the knowledge.[44] Learning requires that the new knowledge be

Invention is the act of creating or developing a new product or process.

Innovation is the process of creating a commercial product from an invention.

Imitation is the adoption of a similar innovation by different firms.

Entrepreneurs are individuals, acting independently or as part of an organization, who perceive an entrepreneurial opportunity and then take risks to develop an innovation to exploit it.

The person with an **entrepreneurial mind-set** values uncertainty in the marketplace and seeks to continuously identify opportunities with the potential to lead to important innovations.

linked to the existing knowledge. Thus, managers need to develop the capabilities of their human capital to build on their current knowledge base while incrementally expanding that knowledge.[45]

Some companies are known for their entrepreneurial culture. For example, in 2008 Apple was ranked as the most innovative company for the fourth year in a row. The rest of the top 10 most innovative companies were Google, Toyota, General Electric, Microsoft, Tata Group, Nintendo, Procter & Gamble, Sony, and Nokia. Yet, there are other companies known as the antithesis of innovative. For example, GM was known for sacrificing innovation for profits. Of course, this approach eventually led to GM's demise.[46]

International Entrepreneurship

International entrepreneurship is a process in which firms creatively discover and exploit opportunities that are outside their domestic markets in order to develop a competitive advantage.[47] As the practices suggested by this definition show, entrepreneurship is a global phenomenon.[48] As noted earlier, approximately one-third of new ventures move into international markets early in their life cycle. Most large established companies have significant foreign operations and often start new ventures in domestic and international markets. Large multinational companies, for example, generate approximately 54 percent of their sales outside their domestic market, and more than 50 percent of their employees work outside of the company's home country.[49]

A key reason that entrepreneurship has become a global phenomenon is that in general, internationalization leads to improved firm performance.[50] Nonetheless, decision makers should recognize that the decision to internationalize exposes their firms to various risks, including those of unstable foreign currencies, problems with market efficiencies, insufficient infrastructures to support businesses, and limitations on market size.[51] Thus, the decision to engage in international entrepreneurship should be a product of careful analysis.

Because of its positive benefits, entrepreneurship is at the top of public policy agendas in many of the world's countries, including Finland, Ireland, Israel, and the United States. Entrepreneurship has become a particularly important public agenda item with the global economic crisis, which began in late 2007. For example, the U.S. government and the Michigan state government are emphasizing entrepreneurial activity to revitalize the Detroit area hurt seriously by the loss of jobs due to the U.S. auto companies' decline.[52]

Even though entrepreneurship is a global phenomenon, the rate of entrepreneurship differs across countries. A study of 43 countries found that the percentage of adults involved in entrepreneurial activity ranged from a high of more than 45 percent in Bolivia to a low of approximately 4.4 percent in Russia. The United States had a rate of almost 19 percent. Importantly, this study also found a strong positive relationship between the rate of entrepreneurial activity and economic development in a country.[53]

Culture is one of the reasons for the differences in rates of entrepreneurship among different countries. The research suggests that a balance between individual initiative and a spirit of cooperation and group ownership of innovation is needed to encourage entrepreneurial behavior. For firms to be entrepreneurial, they must provide appropriate autonomy and incentives for individual initiative to surface, but also promote cooperation and group ownership of an innovation if it is to be implemented successfully. Thus, international entrepreneurship often requires teams of people with unique skills and resources, especially in cultures that highly value individualism or collectivism. In addition to a balance of values for individual initiative and cooperative behaviors, firms must build the capabilities to be innovative and acquire the resources needed to support innovative activities.[54]

International entrepreneurship is a process in which firms creatively discover and exploit opportunities that are outside their domestic markets in order to develop a competitive advantage.

The level of investment outside of the home country made by young ventures is also an important dimension of international entrepreneurship. In fact, with increasing globalization, a greater number of new ventures have been "born global."[55] Research has shown that new ventures that enter international markets increase their learning of new technological knowledge and thereby enhance their performance.[56]

The probability of entering international markets increases when the firm has top executives with international experience, which increases the likelihood of the firm successfully competing in those markets.[57] Because of the learning and economies of scale and scope afforded by operating in international markets, both young and established internationally diversified firms often are stronger competitors in their domestic market as well. Additionally, as research has shown, internationally diversified firms are generally more innovative.[58]

As explained in the Strategic Focus, innovation has become highly important in the global competitive landscape. Thus, the ability of firms to gain and sustain a competitive advantage may be based partly or largely on the capability to produce innovations. Thus, we next discuss different types of innovations.

Internal Innovation

In established organizations, most innovation comes from efforts in research and development (R&D). Effective R&D often leads to firms' filing for patents to protect their innovative work. Increasingly, successful R&D results from integrating the skills available in the global workforce. Thus, the ability to have a competitive advantage based on innovation is more likely to accrue to firms capable of integrating the talent of human capital from countries around the world.[59]

Both Intel and Nokia have been innovative firms and market leaders. In 2009, they announced an agreement to jointly develop new mobile computing products that provide functions beyond the current smartphones and netbooks. The new products likely will integrate features of both phones and computers. Thus, the two companies can combine and integrate their current knowledge and capabilities of both types of products and the markets for them. While Intel has not yet "cracked" the smartphone market with its memory chips, Nokia has been successful with smartphones but was caught off guard when Apple introduced its now highly popular iPhone. Therefore, the marriage between the two should help each to overcome its weaknesses by integrating their strengths. In addition to the development of new products from their joint R&D efforts, they also plan to develop software for devices using the Linux operating system.[60]

Increasingly, it seems possible that in the twenty-first century competitive landscape, R&D may be the most critical factor in gaining and sustaining a competitive advantage in some industries, such as pharmaceuticals. Larger, established firms, certainly those competing globally, often try to use their R&D labs to create competence-destroying new technologies and products. Being able to innovate in this manner can create a competitive advantage for firms in many industries.[61] Although critical to long-term corporate success, the outcomes of R&D investments are uncertain and often not achieved in the short term, meaning that patience is required as firms evaluate the outcomes of their R&D efforts.[62]

Incremental and Radical Innovation

Firms produce two types of internal innovations—incremental and radical innovations—when using their R&D activities. Most innovations are *incremental*—that is, they build on existing knowledge bases and provide small improvements in the current product lines. Incremental innovations are evolutionary and linear in nature.[63] "The markets for incremental innovations are well-defined, product characteristics are well understood, profit margins tend to be lower, production technologies are efficient, and competition

COMPETITIVENESS AND INNOVATION: ARE WE EXPERIENCING A PARADIGM SHIFT?

In 2009, the United States continued to be ranked as the most competitive nation. This top ranking and those of some other developed countries are based on the quality of infrastructures, educational systems, and laws regarding business operations. It is also due to their advanced levels of innovation over the years. Yet, the major economic crisis beginning in late 2007 and early 2008 has shown some "cracks" in the economic leadership of these countries. In the twenty-first century, economic power has begun to shift to major emerging economies such as China and India.

However, the shift may be even more fundamental, as many believe that innovation is the most critical factor in a nation's competitiveness over time. In fact, the United States competitiveness is likely based on the significant innovative capabilities and innovative output of its businesses. While certain business leaders in the United States understand the importance of innovation (e.g., members of the U.S. Council on Competitiveness), the country is no longer ranked as the most innovative nation. In fact, the United States ranked eighth in the 2009 International Innovation Index (among the 110 countries ranked). Singapore was ranked first. In a report issued by the Information Technology and Innovation Foundation, the United States was ranked sixth among 40 countries and regions around the world. Singapore was

also ranked first in this report. Singapore developed a strategy to promote specific programs by investing heavily in attracting major technologies and recruiting top scientists to develop more innovation. That strategy is now paying substantial dividends. Firms based in the United States have focused too much on producing short-term returns, leading to an overemphasis on incremental innovations. As a result, the country is now in danger of losing its lead in science and technology. Perhaps one of the most prominent examples is Exxon-Mobil, which receives approximately $756,000 in revenue per minute. Rather than focus on developing new sources of energy, it seeks to enhance its ability to gain access to and extract with greater efficiency black gold or oil.

Corbis/PhotoLibrary

With forward-thinking investments in the recruitment of top scientists and attraction of key technologies, Singapore is the world leader in innovation.

According to a 2009 report in *BusinessWeek*, technological breakthroughs in a number of fields have been few in number since 1998 (e.g., medical science, drugs, information technology, etc.). The leadership in these fields is largely represented by firms based in the United States. However, future technological breakthroughs in these fields are likely to be produced by firms based in other countries. Regaining this lead will require a major change in mind-set, investments, and promotion of entrepreneurial endeavors. Efforts have been implemented to encourage and develop more entrepreneurial activities in a number of industries and geographic regions to stop the economic decline and facilitate economic growth in the United States. It is unclear if these efforts will be successful in the short or long term.

Sources: M. Mandel, 2009, Innovation interrupted, *BusinessWeek*, June 15, 034-040; 2009, International innovation index, Wikipedia, http://www.answers.com, June 13; B. Ott, 2009, Top companies can tame bear markets, Yahoo News, http://www .yahoo.com, June 11; A. S. Choi, 2009, Can entrepreneurs save this town? *BusinessWeek*, http://www.businessweek.com, June 5; M. Scott, 2009, Competitiveness: The U.S. and Europe are tops, *BusinessWeek*, http://www.businessweek.com, May 19; M. Richtel & J. Wortham, 2009, Weary of looking for work, some create their own, *New York Times*, http://www.nytimes .com, March 14; S. Lohr, 2009, In innovation, U.S. said to be losing competitive edge, *New York Times*, http://www.nytimes .com, February 25; J. Rae-Dupree, 2009, Innovation should mean more jobs, not less, *New York Times*, http://www.nytimes .com, January 4; R. Empson, 2008, Encouraging innovation: How can we do it better? *Fast Company*, http://www .fastcompany.com, August 1.

is primarily on the basis of price."[64] Adding a different kind of whitening agent to a soap detergent is an example of an incremental innovation, as are improvements in televisions over the last few decades. Companies launch far more incremental innovations than radical innovations because they are cheaper, easier and faster to produce, and involve less risk.[65]

In contrast to incremental innovations, *radical innovations* usually provide significant technological breakthroughs and create new knowledge.[66] Radical innovations, which are revolutionary and nonlinear in nature, typically use new technologies to serve newly created markets. The development of the original personal computer (PC) was a radical innovation at the time. Reinventing the computer by developing a "radically new computer-brain chip" (e.g., with the capability to process a trillion calculations per second) is an example of a radical innovation. Obviously, such a radical innovation would seem to have the capacity to revolutionize the tasks computers could perform. Perhaps some of the new products to be produced by the joint venture between Intel and Nokia integrating smartphones and computers will be considered to be radical innovations.

Because they establish new functionalities for users, radical innovations have strong potential to lead to significant growth in revenue and profits.[67] Developing new processes is a critical part of producing radical innovations. Both types of innovations can create value, meaning that firms should determine when it is appropriate to emphasize either incremental or radical innovation. However, radical innovations have the potential to contribute more significantly to a firm's efforts to earn above-average returns.

Radical innovations are rare because of the difficulty and risk involved in developing them. The value of the technology and the market opportunities are highly uncertain.[68] Because radical innovation creates new knowledge and uses only some or little of a firm's current product or technological knowledge, creativity is required. However, creativity does not produce something from nothing. Rather, creativity discovers, combines, or synthesizes current knowledge, often from diverse areas.[69] This knowledge is then used to develop new products that can be used in an entrepreneurial manner to move into new markets, capture new customers, and gain access to new resources.[70] Such innovations are often developed in separate business units that start internal ventures.[71]

Internally developed incremental and radical innovations result from deliberate efforts. These deliberate efforts are called *internal corporate venturing,* which is the set of activities firms use to develop internal inventions and especially innovations.[72] As shown in Figure 13.1, autonomous and induced strategic behaviors are the two types of internal corporate venturing. Each venturing type facilitates incremental and radical innovations. However, a larger number of radical innovations spring from autonomous strategic behavior while the greatest percentage of incremental innovations come from induced strategic behavior.

Autonomous Strategic Behavior

Autonomous strategic behavior is a bottom-up process in which product champions pursue new ideas, often through a political process, by means of which they develop and coordinate the commercialization of a new good or service until it achieves success in the marketplace. A *product champion* is an organizational member with an entrepreneurial vision of a new good or service who seeks to create support for its commercialization. Product champions play critical roles in moving innovations forward. Indeed, in many corporations, "Champions are widely acknowledged as pivotal to innovation speed and success."[73] Champions are vital to sell the ideas to others in the organization so that the innovations will be commercialized. Commonly, product champions use their social capital to develop informal networks within the firm. As progress is made, these networks become more formal as a means of pushing an innovation to the point of successful commercialization.[74] Internal innovations springing from autonomous strategic behavior frequently differ from the firm's current strategy, taking it into new markets and perhaps new ways of creating value for customers and other stakeholders.

Figure 13.1 Model of Internal Corporate Venturing

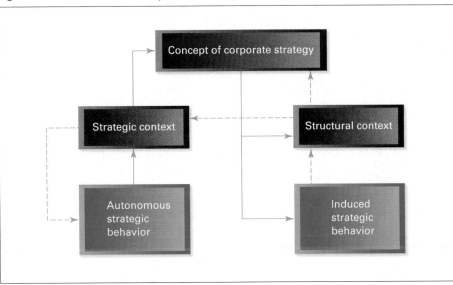

Source: Adapted from R. A. Burgelman, 1983, A model of the interactions of strategic behavior, corporate context, and the concept of strategy, *Academy of Management Review*, 8: 65.

Autonomous strategic behavior is based on a firm's wellspring of knowledge and resources that are the sources of the firm's innovation. Thus, a firm's technological capabilities and competencies are the basis for new products and processes.[75] As described in the Strategic Focus, Exxon-Mobil does not appear to use autonomous strategic behavior to identify new technologies and products that can better serve its customers. Alternatively, the iPod likely resulted from autonomous strategic behavior in Apple, though the development of the iPhone was more the result of induced strategic behavior discussed in the next section.

Changing the concept of corporate-level strategy through autonomous strategic behavior results when a product is championed within strategic and structural contexts (see Figure 13.1). Such a transformation occurred with the development of the iPod and introduction of iTunes at Apple. The strategic context is the process used to arrive at strategic decisions (often requiring political processes to gain acceptance). The best firms keep changing their strategic context and strategies because of the continuous changes in the current competitive landscape. Thus, some believe that the most competitively successful firms reinvent their industry or develop a completely new one across time as they compete with current and future rivals.[76]

To be effective, an autonomous process for developing new products requires that new knowledge be continuously diffused throughout the firm. In particular, the diffusion of tacit knowledge is important for development of more effective new products.[77] Interestingly, some of the processes important for the promotion of autonomous new product development behavior vary by the environment and country in which a firm operates. For example, the Japanese culture is high on uncertainty avoidance. As such, research has found that Japanese firms are more likely to engage in autonomous behaviors under conditions of low uncertainty.[78]

Induced Strategic Behavior

The second of the two forms of internal corporate venturing, *induced strategic behavior*, is a top-down process whereby the firm's current strategy and structure foster innovations that are closely associated with that strategy and structure.[79] In this form of venturing, the strategy in place is filtered through a matching structural hierarchy. In essence, induced strategic behavior results in internal innovations that are highly consistent with the firm's

Vivek Prakash/Reuters/Landov

Nokia is trying to overcome the iPhone's lead in the smartphone market through a joint venture with Intel.

current strategy. Thus, the top management team plays a key role in induced strategic behavior, suggesting that the composition and the effectiveness of the team are important.[80]

Nokia's joint venture with Intel is an example of induced innovation. The two firms have specific goals in the development of new products to support their strategies. Intel has had a strategic interest in the smartphone market, and Nokia is trying to overcome Apple's lead in this market with the iPhone. The strategic intent of these firms is to develop a market leading product in the smartphone market that incorporates more features of the personal computer and sophisticated software to enrich the functionality of the product. These actions and approaches are intended to ensure that both firms are number one in the global market.

Implementing Internal Innovations

An entrepreneurial mind-set is required to be innovative and to develop successful internal corporate ventures. Because of environmental and market uncertainty, individuals and firms must be willing to take risks to commercialize innovations. Although they must continuously attempt to identify opportunities, they must also select and pursue the best opportunities and do so with discipline. Employing an entrepreneurial mind-set entails not only developing new products and markets but also execution in order to do these things effectively. Often, firms provide incentives to managers to be entrepreneurial and to commercialize innovations.[81]

Having processes and structures in place through which a firm can successfully implement the outcomes of internal corporate ventures and commercialize the innovations is critical. Indeed, the successful introduction of innovations into the marketplace reflects implementation effectiveness.[82] In the context of internal corporate ventures, managers must allocate resources, coordinate activities, communicate with many different parties in the organization, and make a series of decisions to convert the innovations resulting from either autonomous or induced strategic behaviors into successful market entries.[83] As we describe in Chapter 11, organizational structures are the sets of formal relationships that support processes managers use to commercialize innovations.

Effective integration of the various functions involved in innovation processes—from engineering to manufacturing and, ultimately, market distribution—is required to implement the incremental and radical innovations resulting from internal corporate ventures.[84] Increasingly, product development teams are being used to integrate the activities associated with different organizational functions. Such integration involves coordinating and applying the knowledge and skills of different functional areas in order to maximize innovation.[85] Teams must help to make decisions as to which projects should be commercialized and which ones should end. Although ending a project is difficult, sometimes because of emotional commitments to innovation-based projects, effective teams recognize when conditions change such that the innovation cannot create value as originally anticipated.

Cross-Functional Product Development Teams

Cross-functional teams facilitate efforts to integrate activities associated with different organizational functions, such as design, manufacturing, and marketing. These teams may also include representatives from major suppliers because they can facilitate the firm's innovation processes.[86] In addition, new product development processes can be completed more quickly and the products more easily commercialized when cross-functional teams work effectively.[87] Using cross-functional teams, product development stages are grouped into parallel or overlapping processes to allow the firm to tailor its product development efforts to its unique core competencies and to the needs of the market.

Horizontal organizational structures support the use of cross-functional teams in their efforts to integrate innovation-based activities across organizational functions.[88] Therefore, instead of being designed around vertical hierarchical functions or departments, the organization is built around core horizontal processes that are used to produce and manage innovations. Some of the core horizontal processes that are critical to innovation efforts are formal; they may be defined and documented as procedures and practices. More commonly, however, these processes are informal: "They are routines or ways of working that evolve over time."[89] Often invisible, informal processes are critical to successful innovations and are supported properly through horizontal organizational structures more so than through vertical organizational structures.

Two primary barriers that may prevent the successful use of cross-functional teams as a means of integrating organizational functions are independent frames of reference of team members and organizational politics.[90] Team members working within a distinct specialization (e.g., a particular organizational function) may have an independent frame of reference typically based on common backgrounds and experiences. They are likely to use the same decision criteria to evaluate issues such as product development efforts as they do within their functional units. Research suggests that functional departments vary along four dimensions: time orientation, interpersonal orientation, goal orientation, and formality of structure.[91] Thus, individuals from different functional departments having different orientations on these dimensions can be expected to perceive product development activities in different ways. For example, a design engineer may consider the characteristics that make a product functional and workable to be the most important of the product's characteristics. Alternatively, a person from the marketing function may hold characteristics that satisfy customer needs most important. These different orientations can create barriers to effective communication across functions and even produce conflict in the team at times.[92]

Organizational politics is the second potential barrier to effective integration in cross-functional teams. In some organizations, considerable political activity may center on allocating resources to different functions. Interunit conflict may result from aggressive competition for resources among those representing different organizational functions. This dysfunctional conflict between functions creates a barrier to their integration.[93] Methods must be found to achieve cross-functional integration without excessive political conflict and without changing the basic structural characteristics necessary for task specialization and efficiency.

Facilitating Integration and Innovation

Shared values and effective leadership are important for achieving cross-functional integration and implementing innovation.[94] Highly effective shared values are framed around the firm's vision and mission and become the glue that promotes integration between functional units. Thus, the firm's culture promotes unity and internal innovation.[95]

Strategic leadership is also highly important for achieving cross-functional integration and promoting innovation. Leaders set the goals and allocate resources. The goals include integrated development and commercialization of new goods and services. Effective strategic leaders also ensure a high-quality communication system to facilitate cross-functional integration. A critical benefit of effective communication is the sharing of knowledge among team members. Effective communication thus helps create synergy and gains team members' commitment to an innovation throughout the organization. Shared values and leadership practices shape the communication systems that are formed to support the development and commercialization of new products.[96]

Creating Value from Internal Innovation

The model in Figure 13.2 shows how firms can create value from the internal corporate venturing processes they use to develop and commercialize new goods and services. An entrepreneurial mind-set is necessary so that managers and employees will consistently try to identify entrepreneurial opportunities the firm can pursue by developing new goods and services and new markets. Cross-functional teams are important for promoting integrated new product design ideas and commitment to their subsequent implementation. Effective leadership and shared values promote integration and vision for innovation and commitment to it. The end result for the firm is the creation of value for the customers and shareholders by developing and commercializing new products.[97] We should acknowledge that not all entrepreneurial efforts succeed, even with effective management. Sometimes managers must exit the market as well to avoid value decline.[98]

In the next two sections, we discuss the other ways firms innovate—by using cooperative strategies and by acquiring companies.

Innovation through Cooperative Strategies

Virtually all firms lack the breadth and depth of resources (e.g., human capital and social capital) in their R&D activities needed to internally develop a sufficient number of innovations to meet the needs of the market and remain competitive. As such, firms must be open to using external resources to help produce innovations.[99] Alliances with other firms can contribute to innovations in several ways. First, they provide information on new business opportunities and how to exploit them.[100] In other instances, firms use cooperative strategies to align what they believe are complementary assets with the potential to lead to future innovations.[101]

Figure 13.2 Creating Value through Internal Innovation Processes

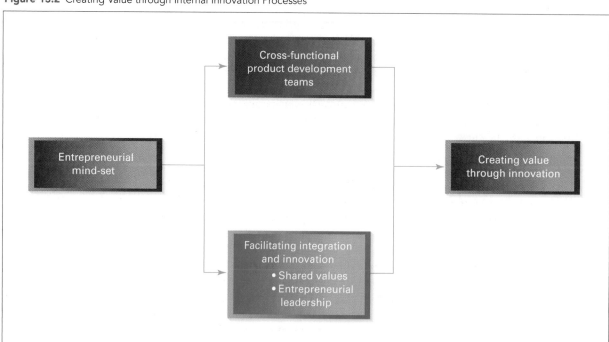

The rapidly changing technologies of the twenty-first–century competitive landscape, globalization, and the need to innovate at world-class levels are primary influences on firms' decisions to innovate by cooperating with other companies. Evidence shows that the skills and knowledge contributed by firms forming a cooperative strategy to innovate tend to be technology-based, a fact suggesting how technologies and their applications continue to influence the choices firms make while competing in the twenty-first century competitive landscape.[102] Indeed, some believe that because of these conditions, firms are becoming increasingly dependent on cooperative strategies as a path to successful competition in the global economy.[103] Even venerable old firms such as Intel and Nokia have learned that they need help to create innovations necessary to be competitive in a twenty-first–century environment. Their agreement to jointly develop products that integrate functions of the smartphones and personal computers is based on their realization that they need great capabilities to develop market-leading products in the dynamic and highly competitive markets in which they participate.

Both entrepreneurial firms and established firms use cooperative strategies (e.g., strategic alliances and joint ventures) to innovate. An entrepreneurial firm, for example, may seek investment capital as well as established firms' distribution capabilities to successfully introduce one of its innovative products to the market.[104] Alternatively, more-established companies may need new technological knowledge and can gain access to it by forming a cooperative strategy with entrepreneurial ventures.[105] Alliances between large pharmaceutical firms and biotechnology companies increasingly have been formed to integrate the knowledge and resources of both to develop new products and bring them to market.[106]

Because of the importance of strategic alliances, particularly in the development of new technology and in commercializing innovations, firms are beginning to build networks of alliances that represent a form of social capital to them.[107] Building social capital in the form of relationships with other firms provides access to the knowledge and other resources necessary to develop innovations.[108] Knowledge from these alliances helps firms develop new capabilities.[109] Some firms now even allow other companies to participate in their internal new product development processes. It is not uncommon, for example, for firms to have supplier representatives on their cross-functional innovation teams because of the importance of the suppliers' input to ensure quality materials for any new product developed.[110]

However, alliances formed for the purpose of innovation are not without risks. In addition to conflict that is natural when firms try to work together to reach a mutual goal,[111] cooperative strategy participants also take a risk that a partner will appropriate a firm's technology or knowledge and use it to enhance its own competitive abilities.[112] To prevent or at least minimize this risk, firms, particularly new ventures, need to select their partners carefully. The ideal partnership is one in which the firms have complementary skills as well as compatible strategic goals.[113] However, because companies are operating in a network of firms and thus may be participating in multiple alliances simultaneously, they encounter challenges in managing the alliances.[114] Research has shown that firms can become involved in too many alliances, which can harm rather than facilitate their innovation capabilities.[115] Thus, effectively managing a cooperative strategy to produce innovation is critical.

As explained in the Strategic Focus, the social networking Internet sites have become highly popular with the general public and with professionals as well. Furthermore, entrepreneurs have begun to use them in ways to facilitate their businesses. These sites provide many opportunities for businesses and especially for gaining access to ideas and information. Therefore, they can facilitate innovation. Firms can use them to identify unique product ideas, to do market research, and to access new markets and new customers. As a result the social networking sites are highly valuable business mechanisms.

STRATEGIC FOCUS

ALL IN A TWITTER ABOUT MY SPACE IN ORDER TO BE LINKED IN TO THE BOOK OF FACES: THE SOCIAL NETWORKING PHENOMENON

Social networks are one of the major innovations in the first decade of the twenty-first century. Perhaps the most popular and important social networking Internet sites are Facebook, MySpace, Twitter, and LinkedIn. In 2009, Facebook reached a level of approximately 1.2 million visits per month. MySpace was second with slightly more than 800,000 monthly visits, followed by Twitter in third place. LinkedIn was fifth but growing rapidly among professionals. While these are all largely used for personal social networking, their potential uses are much greater. For example, Facebook is used by approximately 150 million people globally with more than 50 million unique visitors monthly. Facebook is used in 170 different countries and territories and appears in 35 different languages. The access to people for many different reasons is substantial— perhaps larger than through any other single means other than television. In addition MySpace has 76 million members with the average user spending about 4.4 hours per month on the site, about 1.7 hours longer than users on the site of its nearest competitor. The "rage" most recently has been Twitter, which is a microblogging Web site. Its use grew by 752 percent in 2008 alone. It has attracted a more educated young adult audience.

Smart entrepreneurs are identifying ways to use these social networking sites for business purposes. For example, they may be useful to access markets. Gary Vaynerchuk used Twitter to grow his wine distribution business from $5 million (when he took over the business from his father) to $50 million within three years. He performed an experiment using a direct mail advertisement, a billboard, and a Twitter announcement to determine which would bring in more new customers (at the lowest cost). The direct mail ad brought in 200 new customers (at a cost of $75 each); the billboard brought in 300 new customers (at a cost of $25 each) and the Twitter announcement brought in 1,800 new customers (at no additional cost). He now produces short videos on wine for use on Twitter.

Social networking sites are also being used to identify potential new employees and to make all types of professional and business contacts. They provide access to new ideas and information that can be useful for solving problems and even for making strategic decisions. The access to information and ideas makes these sites excellent sources in the innovation process. For example, the use of cross-functional teams and an occasional outsider to develop new products has been valuable because of the integration of diverse ideas incorporating multiple and important perspectives. Yet, social networking sites provide access to many more and diverse perspectives and ideas. In addition, the opportunity to perform virtual market tests with a large sample from the market exists with these sites. Finally, they provide the opportunity to identify new and different markets for existing and new product ideas. Therefore, if managed properly, they could be highly valuable in the innovation process, from the identification of new product ideas, through market research to market reach (many, many potential customers).

davidbleekerphotography.com/Alamy

The demographics of social media usage are shifting quickly, with adults rapidly coming online and driving the growth of newer services such as Twitter.

Sources: L. Safko, 2009, The twitter about Twitter, *Fast Company*, http://fastcompany.com, June 13; M. Conlin & D. MacMillan, 2009, Managing the tweets, *BusinessWeek*, June 1, 20–21; A. Yee, 2009, Social network rankings: Who's hot and who's not, *ebiz*, http://www.ebizq.net, April 13; J. F. Rayport, 2009, Social networks are the new web portals, *BusinessWeek*, http://www.businessweek.com, January 21; J. Owyang, 2009, A collection of social network stats for 2009, *Web Strategist*, http://www.web-strategist.com, January 11; K. E. Klein, 2008, Are social networking sites useful for business? *BusinessWeek*, http://www.businessweek.com, August 6.

Innovation through Acquisitions

Firms sometimes acquire companies to gain access to their innovations and to their innovative capabilities. One reason companies make these acquisitions is that the capital market values growth; acquisitions provide a means to rapidly extend one or more product lines and increase the firm's revenues.[116] Acquisitions pursued for this reason should, nonetheless, have a strategic rationale. For example, several large pharmaceutical firms have made acquisitions in recent years for several reasons, such as enhancing growth. However, a primary reason for acquisitions in this industry has been to acquire innovation—new drugs that can be commercialized. In this way they strengthen their new product pipeline.[117]

Similar to internal corporate venturing and strategic alliances, acquisitions are not a risk-free approach to innovating. A key risk of acquisitions is that a firm may substitute an ability to buy innovations for an ability to produce innovations internally. In support of this contention, research shows that firms engaging in acquisitions introduce fewer new products into the market.[118] This substitution may take place because firms lose strategic control and focus instead on financial control of their original and, especially, of their acquired business units. Yet, careful selection of companies to acquire—ones with complimentary science and technology knowledge—can enhance innovation if the knowledge acquired is used effectively.[119]

We note in Chapter 7 that companies can also learn new capabilities from firms they acquire. Thus, firms may gain capabilities to produce innovation from an acquired company. Additionally, firms that emphasize innovation and carefully select companies for acquisition that also emphasize innovation are likely to remain innovative.[120] Likewise, firms must manage well the integration of the acquired firms' technical capabilities so that they remain productive and continue to produce innovation after the acquired firm is merged into the acquiring firm.[121] Cisco has been highly successful with the integration of acquired technology firms. Cisco managers take great care not to lose key personnel in the acquired firm, realizing they are the source of many innovations.

This chapter closes with an assessment of how strategic entrepreneurship helps firms create value for stakeholders through its operations.

STRATEGY RIGHT NOW

Learn more about emerging Twitter business applications, including best practices and potential pitfalls.

www.cengage.com/ management/hitt

Creating Value through Strategic Entrepreneurship

Newer entrepreneurial firms often are more effective than larger established firms in the identification of entrepreneurial opportunities.[122] As a consequence, entrepreneurial ventures often produce more radical innovations than do their larger, more established counterparts. Entrepreneurial ventures' strategic flexibility and willingness to take risks at least partially account for their ability to identify opportunities and then develop radical innovations to exploit them.

Alternatively, larger and well-established firms often have more resources and capabilities to exploit identified opportunities.[123] Younger, entrepreneurial firms generally excel in the opportunity-seeking dimension of strategic entrepreneurship while more

Spencer Platt/Getty Images

Established companies such as Williams-Sonoma are seeking to identify and capitalize on entrepreneurial opportunities by devoting top managers to the development of emerging brands.

established firms generally excel in the advantage-seeking dimension. However, to compete effectively in the twenty-first century competitive landscape, firms must not only identify and exploit opportunities but do so while achieving and sustaining a competitive advantage.[124] Thus, on a relative basis, newer entrepreneurial firms must learn how to gain a competitive advantage (advantage-seeking behaviors), and older, more established firms must relearn how to identify entrepreneurial opportunities (opportunity-seeking skills).

In some large organizations, action is being taken to deal with these matters. For example, an increasing number of widely known, large firms, including Williams-Sonoma, Inc., Wendy's International, AstraZeneca, and Choice Hotels, have created a new, top-level managerial position commonly called president or executive vice president of emerging brands. The essential responsibility for people holding these positions is to find entrepreneurial opportunities for their firms. If a decision is made to pursue one or more of the identified opportunities, this person also leads the analysis to determine whether the innovations should be internally developed, pursued through a cooperative venture, or acquired. The objective is to help firms develop successful incremental and radical innovations.

To be entrepreneurial, firms must develop an entrepreneurial mind-set among their managers and employees. Managers must emphasize the management of their resources, particularly human capital and social capital.[125] The importance of knowledge to identify and exploit opportunities as well as to gain and sustain a competitive advantage suggests that firms must have strong human capital.[126] Social capital is critical for access to complementary resources from partners in order to compete effectively in domestic and international markets.[127]

Many entrepreneurial opportunities continue to surface in international markets, a reality that is contributing to firms' willingness to engage in international entrepreneurship. By entering global markets that are new to them, firms can learn new technologies and management practices and diffuse this knowledge throughout the entire enterprise. Furthermore, the knowledge firms gain can contribute to their innovations. Research has shown that firms operating in international markets tend to be more innovative.[128] Entrepreneurial ventures and large firms now regularly enter international markets. Both types of firms must also be innovative to compete effectively. Thus, by developing resources (human and social capital), taking advantage of opportunities in domestic and international markets, and using the resources and knowledge gained in these markets to be innovative, firms achieve competitive advantages.[129] In so doing, they create value for their customers and shareholders.

Firms practicing strategic entrepreneurship contribute to a country's economic development. In fact, some countries have made dramatic economic progress by changing the institutional rules for businesses operating in the country. This approach could be construed as a form of institutional entrepreneurship. Likewise, firms that seek to establish their technology as a standard, also representing institutional entrepreneurship, are engaging in strategic entrepreneurship because creating a standard produces a competitive advantage for the firm.[130]

Research shows that because of its economic importance and individual motives, entrepreneurial activity is increasing around the globe. Furthermore, more women are becoming entrepreneurs because of the economic opportunity entrepreneurship provides and the individual independence it affords. Recent research showed that about one-third of all entrepreneurs are now women.[131] In the United States, for example, women are the nation's fastest-growing group of entrepreneurs.[132] In future years, entrepreneurial activity may increase the wealth of less-affluent countries and continue to contribute to the economic development of the more-affluent countries. Regardless, the entrepreneurial ventures and large, established firms that choose to practice strategic entrepreneurship are likely to be the winners in the twenty-first century.[133]

After identifying opportunities, entrepreneurs must develop capabilities that will become the basis of their firm's core competencies and competitive advantages. The process of identifying opportunities is entrepreneurial, but this activity alone is not sufficient to create maximum wealth or even to survive over time.[134] As we learned in Chapter 3, to successfully exploit opportunities, a firm must develop capabilities that are valuable, rare, difficult to imitate, and nonsubstitutable. When capabilities satisfy these four criteria, the firm has one or more competitive advantages to exploit the identified opportunities (as described in Chapter 3). Without a competitive advantage, the firm's success will be only temporary (as explained in Chapter 1). An innovation may be valuable and rare early in its life, if a market perspective is used in its development. However, competitive actions must be taken to introduce the new product to the market and protect its position in the market against competitors to gain a competitive advantage. [135] These actions combined represent strategic entrepreneurship.

SUMMARY

- Strategic entrepreneurship is taking entrepreneurial actions using a strategic perspective. Firms engaging in strategic entrepreneurship simultaneously engage in opportunity-seeking and advantage-seeking behaviors. The purpose is to continuously find new opportunities and quickly develop innovations to exploit them.

- Entrepreneurship is a process used by individuals, teams, and organizations to identify entrepreneurial opportunities without being immediately constrained by the resources they control. Corporate entrepreneurship is the application of entrepreneurship (including the identification of entrepreneurial opportunities) within ongoing, established organizations. Entrepreneurial opportunities are conditions in which new goods or services can satisfy a need in the market. Increasingly, entrepreneurship positively contributes to individual firms' performance and stimulates growth in countries' economies.

- Firms engage in three types of innovative activities: (1) invention, which is the act of creating a new good or process, (2) innovation, or the process of creating a commercial product from an invention, and (3) imitation, which is the adoption of similar innovations by different firms. Invention brings something new into being while innovation brings something new into use.

- Entrepreneurs see or envision entrepreneurial opportunities and then take actions to develop innovations to exploit them. The most successful entrepreneurs (whether they are establishing their own venture or are working in an ongoing

- organization) have an entrepreneurial mind-set, which is an orientation that values the potential opportunities available because of marketplace uncertainties.

- International entrepreneurship, or the process of identifying and exploiting entrepreneurial opportunities outside the firm's domestic markets, is important to firms around the globe. Evidence suggests that firms capable of effectively engaging in international entrepreneurship outperform those competing only in their domestic markets.

- Three basic approaches are used to produce innovation: (1) internal innovation, which involves R&D and forming internal corporate ventures, (2) cooperative strategies such as strategic alliances, and (3) acquisitions. Autonomous strategic behavior and induced strategic behavior are the two forms of internal corporate venturing. Autonomous strategic behavior is a bottom-up process through which a product champion facilitates the commercialization of an innovative good or service. Induced strategic behavior is a top-down process in which a firm's current strategy and structure facilitate the development and implementation of product or process innovations. Thus, induced strategic behavior is driven by the organization's current corporate strategy and structure while autonomous strategic behavior can result in a change to the firm's current strategy and structure arrangements.

- Firms create two types of innovations—incremental and radical—through internal innovation that takes place in the form of autonomous strategic behavior or induced strategic behavior. Overall, firms produce more incremental innovations but radical innovations have a higher probability of significantly increasing sales revenue and profits. Cross-functional integration is often vital to a firm's efforts to develop and implement internal corporate venturing activities and to commercialize the resulting innovation. The cross-functional teams now commonly include representatives from external organizations such as suppliers. Additionally, integration and innovation can be facilitated by developing shared values and effectively using strategic leadership.

- To gain access to the specialized knowledge commonly required to innovate in the complex global economy, firms may form a cooperative relationship such as a strategic alliance with other companies, some of which may be competitors.

- Acquisitions are another means firms use to obtain innovation. Innovation can be acquired through direct acquisition, or firms can learn new capabilities from an acquisition, thereby enriching their internal innovation abilities.

- The practice of strategic entrepreneurship by all types of firms, large and small, new and more established, creates value for all stakeholders, especially for shareholders and customers. Strategic entrepreneurship also contributes to the economic development of countries.

REVIEW QUESTIONS

1. What is strategic entrepreneurship? What is corporate entrepreneurship?

2. What is entrepreneurship, and what are entrepreneurial opportunities? Why are they important for firms competing in the twenty-first–century competitive landscape?

3. What are invention, innovation, and imitation? How are these concepts interrelated?

4. What is an entrepreneur, and what is an entrepreneurial mind-set?

5. What is international entrepreneurship? Why is it important?

6. How do firms develop innovations internally?

7. How do firms use cooperative strategies to innovate and to have access to innovative capabilities?

8. How does a firm acquire other companies to increase the number of innovations it produces and improve its capability to produce innovations?

9. How does strategic entrepreneurship help firms to create value?

EXPERIENTIAL EXERCISES

EXERCISE 1: DO YOU WANT TO BE AN ENTREPRENEUR?

Would you make a good entrepreneur? In this exercise, we will explore how individual attributes and characteristics contribute to entrepreneurial success. If you believe that you have the traits of a successful entrepreneur, would you be more effective working within a large firm or starting your own business? Complete the first stage of the exercise individually, then meet in small groups to discuss your answers.

Individual

Brainstorm a list of personal attributes or characteristics that could help (or hinder) a person's success as an entrepreneur. Next, evaluate the importance of each item on your list. Finally, compare your prioritized list against your personal characteristics. Do you think that you are a good candidate to be an entrepreneur? Why or why not?

Group

First, compare each person's list of attributes and characteristics. Combine similar items and create a composite list. Second, as a group, evaluate the importance of each item on the list. It is not important to rank order the characteristics. Rather, sort them into the categories "very important," "somewhat important," and "minimally important." Then, discuss within your group which

team member seems to be the best suited to be an entrepreneur. Create a brief profile of how to describe that person if he or she were applying for a job at an innovative company such as Google, Intel, or Motorola.

Whole Class

The instructor will ask for student volunteers to present their interview profiles.

EXERCISE 2: THE SOCIAL NATURE OF ENTREPRENEURSHIP

Entrepreneurship is said to be as much about social connections and networks as it is about the fundamentals of running a new venture. The relationships that an entrepreneur can count upon are also a key resource for financial capital, human capital, mentoring, and legal advice.

A popular blog covering social media and Web 2.0, http://mashable.com, recently identified what it considered to be the top 10 social networks for entrepreneurs (http://mashable.com, March 12, 2009):

1. Entrepreneur Connect
2. PartnerUp
3. StartupNation
4. LinkedIn

5. Biznik
6. Perfect Business
7. Go Big Network
8. Cofoundr
9. The Funded
10. Young Entrepreneur

In teams, choose one of the sites from the list; each team must select a different site. Then, spend some time reading the posts on that site to get a feel for the types of information that is presented. After your review, prepare a 10-minute presentation to the class on your network site, paying attention to address the following, at a minimum:

1. Provide an overview of the site—what it is used for, how popular is it, features, types of conversations, etc.
2. What is unique about this site? Why does it attract followers? What technologies are enabled here—RSS, Twitter, etc.?
3. Describe the target audience for this site. Who would use it and what types of information are available to entrepreneurs?
4. How do you think this site maintains it presence? Does it support itself with ad revenue, corporate sponsor, a not-for-profit sponsor, etc.?
5. Would this site be useful for corporate entrepreneurs as well as startup entrepreneurs? If so, how?

VIDEO CASE

THE DNA OF THE ENTREPRENEUR

Dame Anita Roddick/Founder/The Body Shop International

Dame Anita Roddick, founder of The Body Shop International, talks about the skill set required for an entrepreneur to grow a business. Roddick founded her firm in 1976 with no experience or training, but due to life experiences and economic necessity created a very successful firm dedicated to the pursuit of social and environmental causes.

Before you watch the video consider the following concepts and questions and be prepared to discuss them in class:

Concepts

- Entrepreneur
- Entrepreneurial mind-set
- Entrepreneurial opportunities

Questions

1. Research Dame Anita Roddick and describe her as an entrepreneur.
2. What do you think about entrepreneurs who are interested in personal wealth creation vs. those with aspirations about building a business that may not lead to personal wealth creation?
3. Can large organizations encourage entrepreneurship within their existing structures?
4. Are you a future entrepreneur? Why or why not?

NOTES

1. S. Sato, 2009, Beyond good: Great innovations through design, *Journal of Business Strategy*, 30(2/3): 40–49; D. J. Miller, M. J. Fern, & L. B. Cardinal, 2007, The use of knowledge for technological innovation within diversified firms, *Academy of Management Journal*, 50: 308–326.
2. R. D. Ireland & J. W. Webb, 2007, Strategic entrepreneurship: Creating competitive advantage through streams of innovation, *Business Horizons*, 50(4): 49–59; M. A. Hitt, R. D. Ireland, S. M. Camp, & D. L. Sexton, 2002, Strategic entrepreneurship: Integrating entrepreneurial and strategic management perspectives, in M. A. Hitt, R. D. Ireland, S. M. Camp, & D. L. Sexton (eds.), *Strategic Entrepreneurship: Creating a New Mindset*, Oxford, UK: Blackwell Publishers, 1–16; M. A. Hitt, R. D. Ireland, S. M. Camp, & D. L. Sexton, 2001, Strategic entrepreneurship:

Entrepreneurial strategies for wealth creation, *Strategic Management Journal*, 22 (Special Issue): 479–491.
3. R. Durand, O. Bruyaka & V. Mangematin, 2008, Do science and money go together? The case of the French biotech industry, *Strategic Management Journal*, 29: 1281–1299; R. K. Sinha & C. H. Noble, 2008, The adoption of radical manufacturing technologies and firm survival, *Strategic Management Journal*, 29: 943–962.
4. E. Levitas & M. A. McFadyen, 2009, Managing liquidity in research-intensive firms: Signalling and cash flow effects of patents and alliance activities, *Strategic Management Journal*, 30: 659–678.
5. J. L. Morrow, D. G. Sirmon, M. A. Hitt, & T. R. Holcomb, 2007, Creating value in the face of declining performance: Firm strategies and organizational recovery, *Strategic Management Journal*, 28: 271–283; K. G. Smith, C. J. Collins, & K. D. Clark, 2005, Existing knowledge, knowledge creation capability, and

the rate of new product introduction in high-technology firms, *Academy of Management Journal*, 48: 346–357.
6. D. F. Kuratko, 2007, Entrepreneurial leadership in the 21st century, *Journal of Leadership and Organizational Studies*, 13(4): 1–11; R. D. Ireland, M. A. Hitt, & D. G. Sirmon, 2003, A model of strategic entrepreneurship: The construct and its dimensions, *Journal of Management*, 29: 963–989.
7. B. R. Barringer & R. D. Ireland, 2008, *Entrepreneurship: Successfully Launching New Ventures*, Upper Saddle River, NJ: Pearson Prentice Hall, 5; D. T. Holt, M. W. Rutherford, & G. R. Clohessy, 2007, Corporate entrepreneurship: An empirical look at individual characteristics, context and process, *Journal of Leadership and Organizational Studies*, 13(4): 40–54.
8. M. H. Morris, S. Coombes, & M. Schindehutte, 2007, Antecedents and outcomes of entrepreneurial and market orientations in a non-profit context:

Theoretical and empirical insights, *Journal of Leadership and Organizational Studies*, 13(4): 12–39; H. A. Schildt, M. V. J. Maula, & T. Keil, 2005, Explorative and exploitative learning from external corporate ventures, *Entrepreneurship Theory and Practice*, 29: 493–515.

9. J. Uotila, M. Maula, T. Keil, & S. A. Zahra, 2009, Exploration, exploitation and financial performance: Analysis of S&P 500 corporations, *Strategic Management Journal, 30*: 221–231; G. T. Lumpkin & B. B. Lichtenstein, 2005, The role of organizational learning in the opportunity-recognition process, *Entrepreneurship Theory and Practice*, 29: 451–472.

10. B. A. Gilbert, P. P. McDougall, & D. B. Audretsch, 2006, New venture growth: A review and extension, *Journal of Management*, 32: 926–950.

11. Barringer & Ireland, *Entrepreneurship*; S. A. Zahra, H. J. Sapienza, & P. Davidsson, 2006, Entrepreneurship and dynamic capabilities: A review, model and research agenda, *Journal of Management Studies*, 43: 917–955.

12. S. A. Alvarez & J. B. Barney, 2008, Opportunities, organizations and entrepreneurship, *Strategic Entrepreneurship Journal*, 2: 265–267; S. A. Alvarez & J. B. Barney, 2005, Organizing rent generation and appropriation: Toward a theory of the entrepreneurial firm, *Journal of Business Venturing*, 19: 621–635.

13. P. G. Klein, 2008, Opportunity discovery, entrepreneurial action and economic organization, *Strategic Entrepreneurship Journal*, 2: 175–190; W. Kuemmerle, 2005, The entrepreneur's path to global expansion, *MIT Sloan Management Review*, 46(2): 42–49.

14. R. K. Mitchell, J. R. Mitchell, & J. B. Smith, 2008, Inside opportunity formation: Enterprise failure, cognition and the creation of opportunities, *Strategic Entrepreneurship Journal*, 2: 225–242; C. Marquis & M. Lounsbury, 2007, Vive la resistance: Competing logics and the consolidation of U.S. community banking, *Academy of Management Journal*, 50: 799–820.

15. S. A. Zahra, 2008, The virtuous cycle of discovery and creation of entrepreneurial opportunities, *Strategic Entrepreneurship Journal*, 2: 243–257; N. Wasserman, 2006, Stewards, agents, and the founder discount: Executive compensation in new ventures, *Academy of Management Journal*, 49: 960–976.

16. J. Schumpeter, 1934, *The Theory of Economic Development*, Cambridge, MA: Harvard University Press.

17. J. H. Dyer, H. B. Gregersen, & C. Christensen, 2008, Entrepreneur behaviors and the origins of innovative ventures, *Strategic Entrepreneurship Journal*, 2: 317–338; R. Greenwood & R. Suddaby, 2006, Institutional entrepreneurship in mature fields: The

big five accounting firms, *Academy of Management Journal*, 49: 27–48.

18. W. J. Baumol, R. E. Litan, & C. J. Schramm, 2007, *Good capitalism, bad capitalism, and the economics of growth and prosperity*, New Haven: Yale University Press; R. G. Holcombe, 2003, The origins of entrepreneurial opportunities, *Review of Austrian Economics*, 16: 25–54.

19. R. D. Ireland, J. W. Webb, & J. E. Coombs, 2005, Theory and methodology in entrepreneurship research, in D. J. Ketchen Jr. & D. D. Bergh (eds.), *Research Methodology in Strategy and Management* (Vol. 2), San Diego: Elsevier Publishers, 111–141.

20. K. E. Klein, 2007, The face of entrepreneurship in 2017, *BusinessWeek*, http://www.businessweek.com, January 31.

21. P. F. Drucker, 1998, The discipline of innovation, *Harvard Business Review*, 76(6): 149–157.

22. Ibid.

23. A. Leiponen, 2008, Control of intellectual assets in client relationships: Implications for innovation, *Strategic Management Journal*, 29: 1371–1394; M. Subramaniam & M. A. Youndt, 2005, The influence of intellectual capital on the types of innovative capabilities, *Academy of Management Journal*, 48: 450–463.

24. F. F. Suarez & G. Lanzolla, 2007, The role of environmental dynamics in building a first mover advantage theory, *Academy of Management Review*, 32: 377–392.

25. M. J. Leiblein & T. L. Madsen, 2009, Unbundling competitive heterogeneity: Incentive structures and capability influences on technological innovation, *Strategic Management Journal*, 30: 711–735; R. Price, 1996, Technology and strategic advantage, *California Management Review*, 38(3): 38–56.

26. M. A. Hitt, R. D. Nixon, R. E. Hoskisson, & R. Kochhar, 1999, Corporate entrepreneurship and cross-functional fertilization: Activation, process and disintegration of a new product design team, *Entrepreneurship: Theory and Practice*, 23(3): 145–167.

27. R. Oriani & M. Sobero, 2008, Uncertainty and the market valuation of R&D within a real options logic, *Strategic Management Journal*, 29: 343–361; D. J. Miller, 2006, Technological diversity, related diversification, and firm performance, *Strategic Management Journal*, 27: 601–619.

28. Schumpeter, *The Theory of Economic Development*.

29. R. Katila & S. Shane, 2005, When does lack of resources make new firms innovative? *Academy of Management Journal*, 48: 814–829.

30. P. Sharma & J. L. Chrisman, 1999, Toward a reconciliation of the definitional issues in the field of corporate entrepreneurship, *Entrepreneurship: Theory and Practice*, 23(3): 11–27; R. A. Burgelman & L. R. Sayles, 1986, *Inside Corporate Innovation: Strategy, Structure,*

and Managerial Skills, New York: Free Press.

31. D. G. Sirmon, J.-L. Arregle, M. A. Hitt, & J. W. Webb, 2008, The role of family influence in firms' strategic responses to the threat of imitation, *Entrepreneurship Theory and Practice*, 32: 979–998; D. K. Dutta & M. M. Crossan, 2005, The nature of entrepreneurial opportunities: Understanding the process using the 4I organizational learning framework, *Entrepreneurship Theory and Practice* 29: 425–449.

32. S. F. Latham & M. Braun, 2009, Managerial risk, innovation and organizational decline, *Journal of Management*, 35: 258–281.

33. R. E. Hoskisson & L. W. Busenitz, 2002, Market uncertainty and learning distance in corporate entrepreneurship entry mode choice, in M. A. Hitt, R. D. Ireland, S. M. Camp, & D. L. Sexton (eds.), *Strategic Entrepreneurship: Creating a New Mindset*, Oxford, UK: Blackwell Publishers, 151–172.

34. S. Thornhill, 2006, Knowledge, innovation, and firm performance in high- and low-technology regimes, *Journal of Business Venturing*, 21: 687–703; D. Somaya, 2003, Strategic determinants of decisions not to settle patent litigation, *Strategic Management Journal*, 24: 17–38.

35. K. M. Hmielski & R. A. Baron, 2009, Entrepreneurs' optimism and new venture performance: A social cognitive perspective, *Academy of Management Journal*, 52: 473–488; K. M. Hmielski & R. A. Baron, 2008, When does entrepreneurial self-efficacy enhance versus reduce firm performance? *Strategic Entrepreneurship Journal*, 2: 57–72; D. Duffy, 2004, Corporate entrepreneurship: Entrepreneurial skills for personal and corporate success, *Center for Excellence*, http://www.centerforexcellence.net, June 14.

36. M. S. Cardon, J. Wincent, J. Singh, & M. Drovsek, 2009, The nature and experience of entrepreneurial passion, *Academy of Management Review*, 34, 511–532.

37. J. O. Fiet, 2007, A prescriptive analysis of search and discovery, *Journal of Management Studies*, 44: 592–611; J. S. McMullen & D. A. Shepherd, 2006, Entrepreneurial action and the role of uncertainty in the theory of the entrepreneur, *Academy of Management Review*, 31: 132–152.

38. N. Nicolaou, S. Shane, L. Cherkas, & T. D. Spector, 2008, The influence of sensation seeking in the heritability of entrepreneurship, *Strategic Entrepreneurship Journal*, 2: 7–21.

39. X. P. Chen, X. Yao, & S. Kowtha, 2009, Entrepreneur passion and preparedness in business plan presentations: A persuasion analysis of venture capitalists' funding decisions, *Academy of Management Journal*, 52: 199–214; S. F. Matusik, J. M. George, & M. B. Heeley, 2008, Values and judgment under uncertainty:

Evidence from venture capitalist assessments of founders, *Strategic Entrepreneurship Journal,* 2: 95–115.

40. S. Allen, 2009, Entrepreneurs: Quotations from famous entrepreneurs on entrepreneurship, *About.com,* http://entrepreneurs.about.com, June 13.

41. W. Stam & T. Elfring, 2008, Entrepreneurial orientation and new venture performance: The moderating role of intra- and extraindustry social capital, *Academy of Management Journal,* 51: 97–111; R. A. Baron, 2006, Opportunity recognition as pattern recognition: How entrepreneurs "connect the dots" to identify new business opportunities, *Academy of Management Perspectives,* 20(1): 104–119; R. G. McGrath & I. MacMillan, 2000, *The Entrepreneurial Mindset,* Boston, MA: Harvard Business School Press.

42. R. D. Ireland, M. A. Hitt, & J. W. Webb, 2005, Entrepreneurial alliances and networks, in O. Shenkar and J. J. Reuer (eds.), *Handbook of Strategic Alliances,* Thousand Oaks, CA: Sage Publications, 333–352; T. M. Begley & D. P. Boyd, 2003, The need for a corporate global mind-set, *MIT Sloan Management Review,* 44(2): 25–32.

43. W. Tsai, 2001, Knowledge transfer in intraorganizational networks: Effects of network position and absorptive capacity on business unit innovation and performance, *Academy of Management Journal,* 44: 996–1004.

44. S. A. Zahra & G. George, 2002, Absorptive capacity: A review, reconceptualization, and extension, *Academy of Management Review,* 27: 185–203.

45. M. A. Hitt, L. Bierman, K. Uhlenbruck, & K. Shimizu, 2006, The importance of resources in the internationalization of professional service firms: The good, the bad and the ugly, *Academy of Management Journal,* 49: 1137–1157; M. A. Hitt, L. Bierman, K. Shimizu, & R. Kochhar, 2001, Direct and moderating effects of human capital on strategy and performance in professional service firms, *Academy of Management Journal,* 44: 13–28.

46. M. Maynard, 2008, At G.M., innovation sacrificed to profits, *New York Times,* http://www.nytimes.com, December 6; 2008, Creativity and innovation driving business—Innovation index, *BusinessWeek/Boston Consulting Group,* http://www.creativityandinnovationblogspot.com, April 22.

47. M. M. Keupp & O. Gassman, 2009, The past and future of international entrepreneurship: A review and suggestions for developing the field, *Journal of Management,* 35: 600–633.

48. H. J. Sapienza, E. Autio, G. George, & S. A. Zahra, 2006, A capabilities perspective on the effects of early internationalization on firm survival and growth, *Academy of Management Review,* 31: 914–933;

T. M. Begley, W.-L. Tan, & H. Schoch, 2005, Politico-economic factors associated with interest in starting a business: A multi-country study, *Entrepreneurship Theory and Practice,* 29: 35–52.

49. M. Javidan, R. M. Steers, & M. A. Hitt, 2007, *The Global Mindset,* Amsterdam: Elsevier Ltd.

50. S. A. Fernhaber, B. A. Gilbert, & P. P. McDougal, 2008, International entrepreneurship and geographic location: An empirical examination of new venture internationalization, *Journal of International Business Studies,* 39: 267–290; Hitt, Bierman, Uhlenbruck, & Shimizu, The importance of resources in the internationalization of professional service firm.

51. H. Ren, B. Gray, & K. Kim, 2009, Performance of international joint ventures: What factors really make a difference and how? *Journal of Management,* 35: 805–832; Q. Yang & C. X. Jiang, 2007, Location advantages and subsidiaries' R&D activities in emerging economies: Exploring the effect of employee mobility, *Asia Pacific Journal of Management,* 24: 341–358.

52. 2009, Revitalizing Detroit one business at a time, *Kauffman Foundation,* http://www.kauffman.org, June.

53. N. Bosma, Z. J. Acs, E. Autio, A. Conduras, & J. Levie, 2009, *Global Entrepreneurship Monitor: 2008 Executive Report,* Global Entrepreneurship Research Consortium, http://www.gemconsortium.org, June 23.

54. R. A. Baron & J. Tang, 2009, Entrepreneurs' social skills and new venture performance: Mediating mechanisms and cultural generality, *Journal of Management,* 35: 282–306; D. W. Yiu, C. M. Lau, & G. D. Bruton, 2007, International venturing by emerging economy firms: The effects of firm capabilities, home country networks, and corporate entrepreneurship, *Journal of International Business Studies,* 38: 519–540.

55. N. Nummeia, S. Saarenketo, & K. Puumalainen, 2005, Rapidly with a rifle or more slowly with a shotgun? Stretching the company boundaries of internationalizing ICT firms, *Journal of International Entrepreneurship,* 2: 275–288; S. A. Zahra & G. George, 2002, International entrepreneurship: The state of the field and future research agenda, in M. A. Hitt, R. D. Ireland, S. M. Camp, & D. L. Sexton (eds.), *Strategic Entrepreneurship: Creating a New Mindset,* Oxford, UK: Blackwell Publishers, 255–288.

56. S. A. Zahra, R. D. Ireland, & M. A. Hitt, 2000, International expansion by new venture firms: International diversity, mode of market entry, technological learning and performance, *Academy of Management Journal,* 43: 925–950.

57. H. U. Lee & J.H. Park, 2008, The influence of top management team international

exposure on international alliance formation, *Journal of Management Studies,* 45: 961–981; Barkema & O. Chvyrkov, 2007, Does top management team diversity promote or hamper foreign expansion? *Strategic Management Journal,* 28: 663–680.

58. T. S. Frost, 2001, The geographic sources of foreign subsidiaries' innovations, *Strategic Management Journal,* 22: 101–122.

59. J. Song & J. Shin, 2008, The paradox of technological capabilities: A study of knowledge sourcing from host countries of overseas R&D operations, *Journal of International Business Studies,* 39: 291–303.

60. A. Vance, 2009, Nokia and Intel to pair up on mobile devices, *New York Times,* http://www.nytimes.com, June 24; M. Palmer & C. Nuttall, 2009, Nokia and Intel strike research deal, *Financial Times,* http://www.ft.com, June 23.

61. W. Chung & S. Yeaple, 2008, International knowledge sourcing: Evidence from U.S. firms expanding abroad, *Strategic Management Journal,* 29: 1207–1224; J. Santos, Y. Doz, & P. Williamson, 2004, Is your innovation process global? *MIT Sloan Management Review,* 45(4): 31–37.

62. Y.-S. Su, E. W. K. Tsang, & M. W. Peng, 2009, How do internal capabilities and external partnerships affect innovativeness? *Asia Pacific Journal of Management,* 26: 309–331; J. A. Fraser, 2004, A return to basics at Kellogg, *MIT Sloan Management Review,* 45(4): 27–30.

63. F. K. Pil & S. K. Cohen, 2006, Modularity: Implications for imitation, innovation, and sustained advantage, *Academy of Management Review,* 31: 995–1011; S. Kola-Nystrom, 2003, Theory of conceptualizing the challenge of corporate renewal, Lappeenranta University of Technology, working paper.

64. 2005, Radical and incremental innovation styles, *Strategies 2 innovate,* http://www.strategies2innovate.com, July 12.

65. E. Xu & H. Zhang, 2008. The impact of state shares on corporate innovation strategy and performance in China, *Asia Pacific Journal of Management,* 25: 473–487; W. C. Kim & R. Mauborgne, 2005, Navigating toward blue oceans, *Optimize,* February, 44–52.

66. A. Phene & P. Almieda, 2008, Innovation in multinational subsidiaries: The role of knowledge assimilation and subsidiary capabilities, *Journal of International Business Studies,* 39: 901–919; G. Ahuja & M. Lampert, 2001, Entrepreneurship in the large corporation: A longitudinal study of how established firms create breakthrough inventions, *Strategic Management Journal,* 22 (Special Issue): 521–543.

67. 2005, Getting an edge on innovation, *BusinessWeek,* March 21, 124.

68. A. J. Chatterji, 2009, Spawned with a silver spoon? Entrepreneurial performance and innovation in the medical device

industry, *Strategic Management Journal,* 30: 185–206; J. Goldenberg, R. Horowitz, A. Levav, & D. Mazursky, 2003, Finding your innovation sweet spot, *Harvard Business Review,* 81(3): 120–129.

69. C. E. Shalley & J. E. Perry-Smith, 2008, The emergence of team creative cognition: The role of diverse outside ties, socio-cognitive network centrality, and team evolution, *Strategic Entrepreneurship Journal,* 2: 1, 23–41; R. I. Sutton, 2002, Weird ideas that spark innovation, *MIT Sloan Management Review,* 43(2): 83–87.

70. K. G. Smith & D. Di Gregorio, 2002, Bisociation, discovery, and the role of entrepreneurial action, in M. A. Hitt, R. D. Ireland, S. M. Camp, & D. L. Sexton (eds.), *Strategic Entrepreneurship: Creating a New Mindset,* Oxford, UK: Blackwell Publishers, 129–150.

71. S. A. Hill, M. V. J. Maula, J. M. Birkinshaw & G. C. Murray, 2009, Transferability of the venture capital model to the corporate context: Implications for the performance of corporate venture units, *Strategic Entrepreneurship Journal,* 3: 3–27; Hoskisson & Busenitz, Market uncertainty and learning distance.

72. Hill, Maula, Birkinshaw, & Murray, Transferability of the venture capital model to the corporate context; R. A. Burgelman, 1995, *Strategic Management of Technology and Innovation,* Boston: Irwin.

73. J. M. Howell, 2005, The right stuff: Identifying and developing effective champions of innovation, *Academy of Management Executive,* 19(2): 108–119.

74. M. D. Hutt & T. W. Seph, 2009, *Business Marketing Management: B@B,* 10th ed., Mason, OH: Cengage South-Western.

75. S. K. Ethiraj, 2007, Allocation of inventive effort in complex product systems, *Strategic Management Journal,* 28: 563–584; M. A. Hitt, R. D. Ireland, & H. Lee, 2000, Technological learning, knowledge management, firm growth and performance, *Journal of Engineering and Technology Management,* 17: 231–246.

76. V. Gaba & A. D. Meyer, 2008, Crossing the organizational species barrier: How venture capital practices infiltrated the information technology sector, *Academy of Management Journal,* 51: 976–998; H. W. Chesbrough, 2002, Making sense of corporate venture capital, *Harvard Business Review,* 80(3): 90–99.

77. M. Subramaniam & N. Venkatraman, 2001, Determinants of transnational new product development capability: Testing the influence of transferring and deploying tacit overseas knowledge, *Strategic Management Journal,* 22: 359–378.

78. M. Song & M. M. Montoya-Weiss, 2001, The effect of perceived technological uncertainty on Japanese new product development, *Academy of Management Journal,* 44: 61–80.

79. B. Ambos & B. B. Schegelmilch, 2007, Innovation and control in the multinational firm: A comparison of political and contingency approaches, *Strategic Management Journal,* 28: 473–486.

80. H. Li & J. Li, 2009, Top management team conflict and entrepreneurial strategy in China, *Asia Pacific Journal of Management,* 26: 263–283; S.C. Parker, 2009, Can cognitive biases explain venture team homophily, *Strategic Entrepreneurship Journal,* 3: 67–83.

81. M. Makri, P. J. Lane, & L. R. Gomez-Mejia, 2006, CEO incentives, innovation and performance in technology-intensive firms: A reconciliation of outcome and behavior-based incentive schemes, *Strategic Management Journal,* 27: 1057–1080.

82. A. Tiwana, 2008, Does technological modularity substitute for control? A study of alliance performance in software outsourcing, *Strategic Management Journal,* 29: 769–780.

83. C. Zhou & J. Li, 2008, Product innovation in emerging market-based international joint ventures: An organizational ecology perspective, *Journal of International Business Studies,* 39: 1114–1132; E. Danneels, 2007, The process of technological competence leveraging, *Strategic Management Journal,* 28: 511–533.

84. F. T. Rothaermel & W. Boeker, 2008, Old technology meets new technology: Complementarities, similarities and alliance formation, *Strategic Management Journal,* 29: 47–77; L. Yu, 2002, Marketers and engineers: Why can't we just get along? *MIT Sloan Management Review,* 43(1): 13.

85. R. Cowan & N. Jonard, 2009, Knowledge portfolios and the organization of innovation networks, *Academy of Management Review,* 34: 320–342; A. Somech, 2006, The effects of leadership style and team process on performance and innovation in functionally hetergeneous teams, *Journal of Management,* 32: 132–157.

86. A. Azadegan, K. J. Dooley, P. L. Carter & J. R. Carter, 2008, Supplier innovativeness and the role of interorganizational learning in enhancing manufacturer capabilities, *Journal of Supply Chain Management,* 44(4): 14–34; P. Evans & B. Wolf, 2005, Collaboration rules, *Harvard Business Review,* 83(7): 96–104.

87. B. Fischer & A. Boynton, 2005, Virtuoso teams, *Harvard Business Review,* 83(7): 116–123.

88. Hitt, Nixon, Hoskisson, & Kochhar, Corporate entrepreneurship.

89. Christensen & Overdorf, Meeting the challenge of disruptive change.

90. Hitt, Nixon, Hoskisson, & Kochhar, Corporate entrepreneurship.

91. A. C. Amason, 1996, Distinguishing the effects of functional and dysfunctional conflict on strategic decision making: Resolving a paradox for top management

teams, *Academy of Management Journal,* 39: 123–148; P. R. Lawrence & J. W. Lorsch, 1969, *Organization and Environment,* Homewood, IL: Richard D. Irwin.

92. M. A. Cronin & L. R. Weingart, 2007, Representational gaps, information processing, and conflict in functionally heterogeneous teams, *Academy of Management Review,* 32: 761–773; D. Dougherty, L. Borrelli, K. Muncir, & A. O'Sullivan, 2000, Systems of organizational sensemaking for sustained product innovation, *Journal of Engineering and Technology Management,* 17: 321–355.

93. Hitt, Nixon, Hoskisson, & Kochhar, Corporate entrepreneurship.

94. V. Ambrosini, N. Collier, & M. Jenkins, 2009, A configurational approach to the dynamics of firm level knowledge, *Journal of Strategy and Management,* 2: 4–30; E. C. Wenger & W. M. Snyder, 2000, Communities of practice: The organizational frontier, *Harvard Business Review,* 78(1): 139–144.

95. Gary Hamel, 2000, *Leading the Revolution,* Boston: Harvard Business School Press.

96. P. H. Kim, K. T. Dirks & C. D. Cooper, 2009, The repair of trust: A dynamic bilateral perspective and multilevel conceptualization, *Academy of Management Review,* 34: 401–422; Q. M. Roberson & J. A. Colquitt, 2005, Shared and configural justice: A social network model of justice in teams, *Academy of Management Review,* 30: 595–607.

97. N. Stieglitz & L. Heine, 2007, Innovations and the role of complementarities in a strategic theory of the firm, *Strategic Management Journal,* 28: 1–15; S. W. Fowler, A. W. King, S. J. Marsh, & B. Victor, 2000, Beyond products: New strategic imperatives for developing competencies in dynamic environments, *Journal of Engineering and Technology Management,* 17: 357–377.

98. J. C. Short, A. McKelvie, D. J. Ketchen & G. N. Chandler, 2009, Firm and industry effects on firm performance: A generalization and extension for new ventures, *Strategic Entrepreneurship Journal,* 3: 47–65; M. B. Sarkar, R. Echamabadi, R. Agarwal, & B. Sen, 2006, The effect of the innovative environment on exit of entrepreneurial firms, *Strategic Management Journal,* 27: 519–539.

99. T. Keil, M. Maula, H. Schildt, & S.A. Zahra, 2008, The effect of governance modes and relatedness of external business development activities on innovative performance, *Strategic Management Journal,* 29: 895–907; K. Larsen & A. Salter, 2006, Open for innovation: The role of openness in explaining innovation performance among U.K. manufacturing firms, *Strategic Management Journal,* 27: 131–150.

100. P. Ozcan & K. M. Eisenhardt, 2009, Origin of alliance portfolios: Entrepreneurs, network strategies, and firm performance, *Academy of Management Journal*, 52: 246–279; A. Tiwana & M. Keil, 2007, Does peripheral knowledge complement control? An empirical test in technology outsourcing alliances, *Strategic Management Journal*, 28: 623–634.

101. K. B. Whittington, J. Owen-Smith, & W. W. Powell, 2009, Networks, propinquity, and innovation in knowledge-intensive industries, *Administrative Science Quarterly*, 54: 90–122; C. Dhanaraj & A. Parkhe, 2006, Orchestrating innovation networks, *Academy of Management Review*, 31: 659–669.

102. K. Ruckman, 2009, Technology sourcing acquisitions: What they mean for innovation potential, *Journal of Strategy and Management*, 2: 56–75; F. T. Rothaermel & D. L. Deeds, 2004, Exploration and exploitation alliances in biotechnology: A system of new product development, *Strategic Management Journal*, 25: 201–221.

103. D. Li, L. Eden, M. A. Hitt, & R. D. Ireland, 2008, Friends, acquaintances, or strangers? Partner selection in R&D alliances, *Academy of Management Journal*, 51: 315–334; F. T. Rothaermel, M. A. Hitt, & L. A. Jobe, 2006, Balancing vertical integration and strategic outsourcing: Effects on product portfolio, product success and firm performance, *Strategic Management Journal*, 27: 1033–1056.

104. A. C. Cooper, 2002, Networks, alliances and entrepreneurship, in M. A. Hitt, R. D. Ireland, S. M. Camp, & D. L. Sexton (eds.), *Strategic Entrepreneurship: Creating a New Mindset*, Oxford, UK: Blackwell Publishers, 204–222.

105. B. S. Teng, 2007, Corporate entrepreneurship activities through strategic alliances: A resource-based approach toward competitive advantage, *Journal of Management Studies*, 44: 119–142; S. A. Alvarez & J. B. Barney, 2001, How entrepreneurial firms can benefit from alliances with large partners, *Academy of Management Executive*, 15(1): 139–148.

106. F. T. Rothaermel, 2001, Incumbent's advantage through exploiting complementary assets via interfirm cooperation, *Strategic Management Journal*, 22 (Special Issue): 687–699.

107. B. R. Koka & J. E. Prescott, 2008, Designing alliance networks: The influence of network position, environmental change and strategy on firm performance, *Strategic Management Journal*, 29: 639–661; A. Capaldo, 2007, Network structure and innovation: The leveraging of a dual network as a distinctive capability, *Strategic Management Journal*, 28: 585–608.

108. C. L. Luk, O. H. M. Yau, L. Y. M. Sin, A. C. B. Tse, R. P. M. Chow, & J. S. Y. Lee, 2008, The effects of social capital and organizational innovativeness in different institutional contexts, *Journal of International Business Studies*, 39: 589–612; H. Yli-Renko, E. Autio, & H. J. Sapienza, 2001, Social capital, knowledge acquisition and knowledge exploitation in young technology-based firms, *Strategic Management Journal*, 22 (Special Issue): 587–613.

109. A. Tiwana, 2008, Do bridging ties complement strong ties? An empirical examination of alliance ambidexterity, *Strategic Management Journal*, 29: 251–272; C. Lee, K. Lee, & J. M. Pennings, 2001, Internal capabilities, external networks and performance: A study of technology-based ventures, *Strategic Management Journal*, 22 (Special Issue): 615–640.

110. Azadegan, Dooley, Carter, & Carter, Supplier innovativeness and the role of interorganizational learning in enhancing manufacturer capabilities; A. Takeishi, 2001, Bridging inter- and intra-firm boundaries: Management of supplier involvement in automobile product development, *Strategic Management Journal*, 22: 403–433.

111. R. C. Sampson, 2007, R&D alliances and firm performance: The impact of technological diversity and alliance organization on innovation, *Academy of Management Journal*, 50: 364–386; J. Weiss & J. Hughes, 2005, Want collaboration? Accept—and actively manage—conflict, *Harvard Business Review*, 83(3): 92–101.

112. R. H. Shah & V. Swaminathan, 2008, Factors influencing partner selection in strategic alliances: The moderating role of alliance context, *Strategic Management Journal*, 29: 471–494; Li, Eden, Hitt, & Ireland, Friends, acquaintances, or strangers?; R. D. Ireland, M. A. Hitt, & D. Vaidyanath, 2002, Strategic alliances as a pathway to competitive success, *Journal of Management*, 28: 413–446.

113. M. A. Hitt, M. T. Dacin, E. Levitas, J. L. Arregle, & A. Borza, 2000, Partner selection in emerging and developed market contexts: Resource-based and organizational learning perspectives, *Academy of Management Journal*, 43: 449–467.

114. J. D. Westphal & M. B. Crant, 2008, Sociopolitical dynamics in relations between top managers and security analysts: Favor rendering, reciprocity, and analyst stock recommendations, *Academy of Management Journal*, 51: 873–897.

115. J. J. Reuer, M. Zollo, & H. Singh, 2002, Post-formation dynamics in strategic alliances, *Strategic Management Journal*, 23: 135–151.

116. M. A. Hitt, D. King, H. Krishnan, M. Makri, M. Schijven, K. Shimizu, & H. Zhu, 2009, Mergers and Acquisitions: Overcoming pitfalls, building synergy and creating value, *Business Horizons*, in press; H. G. Barkema & M. Schijven, 2008, Toward unlocking the full potential of acquisitions: The role of organizational restructuring, *Academy of Management Journal*, 51: 696–722.

117. 2005, Novartis announces completion of Hexal AG acquisition, http:// www .novartis.com, June 6; 2005, Pfizer sees sustained long-term growth, http://www .pfizer.com, April 5.

118. M. A. Hitt, R. E. Hoskisson, R. A. Johnson, & D. D. Moesel, 1996, The market for corporate control and firm innovation, *Academy of Management Journal*, 39: 1084–1119.

119. M. Makri, M. A. Hitt, & P. J. Lane, 2009, Complementary technologies, knowledge relatedness, and invention outcomes in high technology M&As, *Strategic Management Journal*, in press.

120. Ruckman, 2009, Technology sourcing acquisitions; P. Puranam & K. Srikanth, 2007, What they know vs. what they do: How acquirers leverage technology acquisitions, *Strategic Management Journal*, 28: 805–825; M. A. Hitt, J. S. Harrison, & R. D. Ireland, 2001, *Mergers and Acquisitions: A Guide to Creating Value for Stakeholders*, New York: Oxford University Press.

121. M. Cording, P. Christman, & D. King, 2008. Reducing causal ambiguity in acquisition integration: Intermediate goals as mediators of integration decisions and acquisition performance, *Academy of Management Journal*, 51: 744–767; P. Puranam, H. Singh, & M. Zollo, 2006, Organizing for innovation: Managing the coordination-autonomy dilemma in technology, *Academy of Management Journal*, 49: 263–280.

122. Ireland, Hitt, & Sirmon, A model of strategic entrepreneurship.

123. A. Afuah, 2009, *Strategic Innovation: New game strategies for competitive advantage*, New York: Routledge.

124. Hitt, Ireland, Camp, & Sexton, Strategic entrepreneurship.

125. D. G. Sirmon, M. A. Hitt, & R. D. Ireland, 2007, Managing firm resources in dynamic environment to create value: Looking inside the black box, *Academy of Management Review*, 32: 273–292.

126. D. G. Sirmon, S. Gove, & M. A. Hitt, 2008, Resource management in dyadic competitive rivalry: The effects of resource bundling and deployment, *Academy of Management Journal*, 51:918–935; Hitt, Bierman, Shimizu, & Kochhar, Direct and moderating effects of human capital.

127. Tiwana, Do bridging ties complement strong ties? Hitt, Bierman, Uhlenbruck, & Shimizu, The importance of resources in the internationalization of professional service firms.

128. K. Asakawa & A. Som, 2008, Internationalization of R&D in China and India: Conventional wisdom versus reality, *Asia*

Pacific Journal of Management, 25: 375–394; M. A. Hitt, R. E. Hoskisson, & H. Kim, 1997, International diversification: Effects on innovation and firm performance in product diversified firms, *Academy of Management Journal*, 40: 767–798.

129. M. A. Hitt & R. D. Ireland, 2002, The essence of strategic leadership: Managing human and social capital, *Journal of Leadership and Organization Studies*, 9(1): 3–14.

130. Baumol, Litan, & Schramm, *Good capitalism, bad capitalism*; R. Garud, S. Jain, & A. Kumaraswamy, 2002, Institutional entrepreneurship in the sponsorship of common technological standards: The case of Sun Microsystems and JAVA, *Academy of Management Journal*, 45: 196–214.

131. B. Batjargal, A. Tsui, M. A. Hitt, J. L. Arregle, T. Miller, & J. Webb, 2009, How relationships matter: Women and men entrepreneurs' social networks and new venture success across cultures, paper presented at the Academy of Management Conference, Chicago, August; I. E. Allen, N. Langowitz, & M. Minniti, 2007, Global entrepreneurship monitor: 2006 report on women in entrepreneurship, Babson College, http://www3.babson.edu/ESHIP/research-publications/gem.cfm, March 1.

132. J. D. Jardins, 2005, I am woman (I think), *Fast Company,* May, 25–26.

133. Hitt, Ireland, Camp, & Sexton, Strategic entrepreneurship.

134. C. W. L. Hill & F. T. Rothaermel, 2003, The performance of incumbent firms in the face of radical technological innovation, *Academy of Management Review*, 28: 257–274.

135. D. G. Sirmon & M. A. Hitt, 2009, Contingencies within dynamic managerial capabilities: Interdependent effects of resource investment and deployment on firm performance, *Strategic Management Journal,* in press.

Name Index

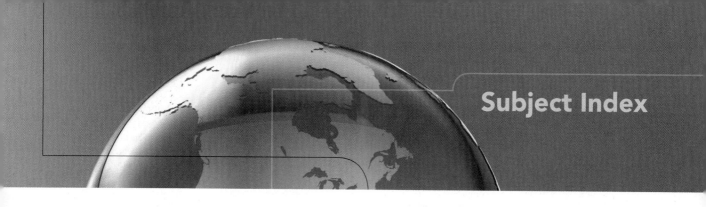